PHP 4 Bible

PHP 4 Bible

Tim Converse and Joyce Park

IDG Books Worldwide, Inc.
An International Data Group Company

Foster City, CA ✦ Chicago, IL ✦ Indianapolis, IN ✦ New York, NY

PHP 4 Bible

Published by
IDG Books Worldwide, Inc.
An International Data Group Company
919 E. Hillsdale Blvd., Suite 400
Foster City, CA 94404
www.idgbooks.com (IDG Books Worldwide Web site)

ISBN: 0-7645-4716-X

Printed in the United States of America

10 9 8 7 6 5 4 3 2

1B/ST/QY/QQ/FC

Distributed in the United States by IDG Books Worldwide, Inc.

Distributed by CDG Books Canada Inc. for Canada; by Transworld Publishers Limited in the United Kingdom; by IDG Norge Books for Norway; by IDG Sweden Books for Sweden; by IDG Books Australia Publishing Corporation Pty. Ltd. for Australia and New Zealand; by TransQuest Publishers Pte Ltd. for Singapore, Malaysia, Thailand, Indonesia, and Hong Kong; by Gotop Information Inc. for Taiwan; by ICG Muse, Inc. for Japan; by Intersoft for South Africa; by Eyrolles for France; by International Thomson Publishing for Germany, Austria, and Switzerland; by Distribuidora Cuspide for Argentina; by LR International for Brazil; by Galileo Libros for Chile; by Ediciones ZETA S.C.R. Ltda. for Peru; by WS Computer Publishing Corporation, Inc., for the Philippines; by Contemporanea de Ediciones for Venezuela; by Express Computer Distributors for the Caribbean and West Indies; by Micronesia Media Distributor, Inc. for Micronesia; by Chips Computadoras S.A. de C.V. for Mexico; by Editorial Norma de Panama S.A. for Panama; by American Bookshops for Finland.

For general information on IDG Books Worldwide's books in the U.S., please call our Consumer Customer Service department at 800-762-2974. For reseller information, including discounts and premium sales, please call our Reseller Customer Service department at 800-434-3422.

For information on where to purchase IDG Books Worldwide's books outside the U.S., please contact our International Sales department at 317-596-5530 or fax 317-572-4002.

For consumer information on foreign language translations, please contact our Customer Service department at 800-434-3422, fax 317-572-4002, or e-mail rights@idgbooks.com.

For information on licensing foreign or domestic rights, please phone +1-650-653-7098.

For sales inquiries and special prices for bulk quantities, please contact our Order Services department at 800-434-3422 or write to the address above.

For information on using IDG Books Worldwide's books in the classroom or for ordering examination copies, please contact our Educational Sales department at 800-434-2086 or fax 317-572-4005.

For press review copies, author interviews, or other publicity information, please contact our Public Relations department at 650-653-7000 or fax 650-653-7500.

For authorization to photocopy items for corporate, personal, or educational use, please contact Copyright Clearance Center, 222 Rosewood Drive, Danvers, MA 01923, or fax 978-750-4470.

Library of Congress Cataloging-in-Publication Data

Converse, Tim, 1961-
    PHP 4 bible / Tim Converse and Joyce Park.
      p. cm.
    Includes index.
    ISBN 0-7645-4716-X (alk. paper)
    1. PHP (Computer program language) I. Title: PHP four bible. II. Park, Joyce, 1969- III. Title.
QA76.73.P224 C66 2000
005.2'762--dc21   00-057549

 is a registered trademark or trademark under exclusive license to IDG Books Worldwide, Inc. from International Data Group, Inc. in the United States and/or other countries.

ABOUT IDG BOOKS WORLDWIDE

Welcome to the world of IDG Books Worldwide.

IDG Books Worldwide, Inc., is a subsidiary of International Data Group, the world's largest publisher of computer-related information and the leading global provider of information services on information technology. IDG was founded more than 30 years ago by Patrick J. McGovern and now employs more than 9,000 people worldwide. IDG publishes more than 290 computer publications in over 75 countries. More than 90 million people read one or more IDG publications each month.

Launched in 1990, IDG Books Worldwide is today the #1 publisher of best-selling computer books in the United States. We are proud to have received eight awards from the Computer Press Association in recognition of editorial excellence and three from Computer Currents' First Annual Readers' Choice Awards. Our best-selling *...For Dummies*® series has more than 50 million copies in print with translations in 31 languages. IDG Books Worldwide, through a joint venture with IDG's Hi-Tech Beijing, became the first U.S. publisher to publish a computer book in the People's Republic of China. In record time, IDG Books Worldwide has become the first choice for millions of readers around the world who want to learn how to better manage their businesses.

Our mission is simple: Every one of our books is designed to bring extra value and skill-building instructions to the reader. Our books are written by experts who understand and care about our readers. The knowledge base of our editorial staff comes from years of experience in publishing, education, and journalism — experience we use to produce books to carry us into the new millennium. In short, we care about books, so we attract the best people. We devote special attention to details such as audience, interior design, use of icons, and illustrations. And because we use an efficient process of authoring, editing, and desktop publishing our books electronically, we can spend more time ensuring superior content and less time on the technicalities of making books.

You can count on our commitment to deliver high-quality books at competitive prices on topics you want to read about. At IDG Books Worldwide, we continue in the IDG tradition of delivering quality for more than 30 years. You'll find no better book on a subject than one from IDG Books Worldwide.

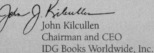

John Kilcullen
Chairman and CEO
IDG Books Worldwide, Inc.

Eighth Annual Computer Press Awards 1992

Ninth Annual Computer Press Awards 1993

Tenth Annual Computer Press Awards 1994

Eleventh Annual Computer Press Awards 1995

Credits

Acquisitions Editor
Debra Williams Cauley

Project Editors
Barbra Guerra
Neil Romanosky

Technical Editor
Richard Lynch

Copy Editor
Robert Campbell

Project Coordinators
Danette Nurse
Joe Shines

Quality Control Technician
Dina F Quan

Graphics and Production Specialists
Bob Bihlmayer
Darren Cutlip
Jude Levinson
Michael Lewis
Victor Pérez-Varela
Ramses Ramirez

Book Designer
Drew R. Moore

Illustrators
Karl Brandt
Brian Drumm
Gabriele McCann

Proofreading and Indexing
York Production Services

Cover Illustration
Peter Kowaleszyn, Murder by Design

About the Authors

Tim Converse has written software to recommend neckties, answer questions about space stations, pick value stocks, and make simulated breakfast. He has an M.S. in Computer Science from the University of Chicago, where he taught several programming classes. He is now a Senior Software Engineer at Excite@Home, where he works on the search engine.

Joyce Park has an M.A. in history from the University of Chicago and has worked on several content-rich PHP Web sites, including the award-winning MysteryGuide.com. Her writing has garnered praise from the editors and readers of Slashdot, OSOpinion, Linux.com, and many others worldwide. Joyce is now a Web Developer at Epinions.com.

This book is dedicated to our parents:
For their love,
for their sacrifices,
and for letting us read a lot when we were kids.

Preface

Welcome to the *PHP 4 Bible*! Although we're biased, we believe that the PHP Web-scripting language is the hands-down winner in its niche — by far the easiest and most flexible server-side tool for getting great Web sites up and running in a hurry. Although millions of Web programmers worldwide *could* be wrong, in this particular case they're not.

PHP 4.0, released in the spring of 2000, adds loads of cool new functionality to PHP 3 while speeding it up enormously. This book gives you a tour of the primary capabilities of this major release, with plenty of detailed examples from our combined experience building Web sites using PHP.

What Is PHP?

PHP is an open-source server-side HTML-embedded Web scripting language that is compatible with all the major Web servers (most notably Apache). PHP allows you to embed code fragments in normal HTML pages — code that is interpreted as your pages are served up to users. PHP also serves as a "glue" language, making it easy to connect your Web pages to server-side databases.

Why PHP?

We devote nearly all of Chapter 1 to this question. The super-short answer is: It's free, it's open-source, it's full-featured, it's cross-platform, it's stable, it's fast, it's clearly designed, it's easy to learn, and it plays well with others.

What's New in PHP 4?

PHP 4 offers everything that PHP 3 did, plus built-in support for sessions, more consistent parsing, a new Boolean type, and a wide array of new built-in functions. The core PHP scripting engine is now the "Zend" engine, having been rewritten from scratch for consistency and blazing speed.

PHP is a moving target. This book went to press in the spring of 2000, at approximately the same time that PHP 4 was officially released. Code in this book was tested extensively using both PHP 3 and various beta versions of PHP 4. Although we have covered the major features of PHP 4, new developments keep arriving. For the latest updates, see our Web site at `http://www.troutworks.com/phpbook`.

Who This Book Is For

This book is for anyone who wants to build Web sites that have more complex behavior than is possible with static HTML pages. Within that population, we had three particular audiences in mind:

+ Web site designers who know HTML, and want to move into creating dynamic Web sites

+ Experienced programmers (C, Java, Perl, and so on) without Web experience, who want to quickly get up to speed in server-side Web programming

+ Web programmers who have used other server-side technologies (Active Server Pages, Java Server Pages, Cold Fusion, for example) and want to sidegrade or simply add another tool to their kit.

We assume that the reader is familiar with HTML, and has a basic knowledge of the workings of the Web, but we do not assume any programming experience beyond that. To help save time for more experienced programmers, we include a number of notes and asides that compare PHP to other languages and help indicate which chapters and sections may be safely skipped. Finally, see our appendixes, which offer specific advice for C programmers, ASP coders, and pure-HTML designers.

This Book Is Not the Manual

The PHP Documentation Group has assembled a great online manual, located at `http://www.php.net`, and served up (of course) by PHP. This book is not that manual, or even a substitute for it. We see it as complementary to the manual and expect that you will want to go back and forth between them to some extent.

In general, you will find the online manual to be very comprehensive, covering all aspects and functions of the language, but inevitably without a great amount of depth in any one topic. By contrast, we have the leisure of zeroing in on aspects that are most used or least understood, and give background, explanations, and lengthy examples.

How the Book Is Organized

This book is divided into three parts:

Part I: The basics

Chapters 1 through 4 give an introduction to PHP, and tell you what you need to know to get started.

Chapters 5 through13 are a guide to the most central facets of PHP (with the exception of database interaction): the syntax, the datatypes, and the most basic built-in functions. You may want to skim here, and then use as a reference.

Chapters 14 and 15 are a guide to PHP style and the most common pitfalls of PHP programming.

Part II: PHP and databases

Chapters 16 and 17 give a general orientation to web programming with SQL databases, including advice on how to choose the database system that is right for you.

Chapter 18 is devoted to PHP functions for MySQL, the database system we focus on in the rest of Part II.

Chapters 19 through 22 are detailed, code-rich case studies of PHP/database interaction.

Chapters 23 and 24 give tips and gotchas specific to PHP/database work.

Part III: Advanced techniques

In each of Chapters 25 through 32 we cover a more advanced, self-contained topic, including: the new built-in session-handling functions, using cookies, generating Javascript code, connecting PHP to mail programs, XML support, object-oriented programming in PHP, security, and configuration options.

Conventions Used in This Book

We use a monospace font to indicate literal PHP code. Pieces of code embedded in lines of text look like this, while full code listing lines look like:

```
print("this");
```

When the visual appearance of a PHP-created Web page is crucial, we include a screen-shot figure. When it is not, we show textual output of PHP in monospace. When we want to distinguish the PHP output as seen in your browser from the actual output of PHP (which your browser renders), we call the former "browser output."

When included in a code context, *italics* indicate portions that should be filled in appropriately, as opposed to being taken literally. In normal text, an italicized *term* means a possibly unfamiliar word or phrase with a definition in the glossary.

What the Icons Mean

Icons like the following are sprinkled liberally throughout the book. Their purpose is to visually set off certain important kinds of information.

Tip icons indicate PHP tricks or techniques that may not be obvious, and that let you accomplish something more easily or efficiently

Note icons usually give additional information or clarification, but can be safely ignored if you are not already interested. Notes in this book are often audience-specific, targeted to people who already know a particular programming language or technology.

Caution icons indicate something that does not work as advertised, something that is easily misunderstood or misused, or anything else that can get programmers into trouble.

New feature icons indicate functionality that is new and importantly different in PHP 4.

We use this icon whenever there is related information in a different chapter or section.

The Web Site and Sample Code

All the sample code from the book, as well as supplementary material we develop after press time, can be found at our Web site at http://www.troutworks.com/phpbook. If you pop up one level to www.troutworks.com, you can also find links to our MysteryGuide and ScienceBookGuide sites, developed entirely in PHP.

We want to hear from you! Please send us email at phpbook@troutworks.com with comments, errata, kudos, flames, or any other communication you care to send our way.

Acknowledgments

This project began out of a conversation with Debra Williams Cauley, our acquisitions editor at IDG Books. She managed the project, found additional contributors, and maintained a sense of humor as she insulated naive first-time authors from the harsh realities of the publishing business. Susan Christopherson served for a while as our project editor, before passing the baton to Barb Guerra, who turned our collected ramblings into a manuscript. Bob Campbell did the copy editing with amazing and necessary speed.

Richard Lynch was gracious enough to serve as our technical reviewer. Richard not only stopped us from saying a number of things that weren't true, he also gave us countless good suggestions for improving the explanations and examples. Richard helped make this a much better book than it otherwise would have been. Needless to say, he is not to blame for errors or omissions that remain.

We didn't write this book by ourselves. Dustin Mitchell single-handedly wrote the chapter on security and cryptography, Patrick McCuller wrote first drafts of the XML chapter and the OOP chapter, and Ariel Garcia contributed an early draft of the chapter on PHP and JavaScript. Joyce's coworkers at Epinions (especially Lou Montulli and Jay Ashton) also deserve gratitude for contributing sample code and teaching her a great deal about using PHP in a high-traffic environment.

Our obvious thanks go to everyone who created PHP itself (Rasmus Lerdorf, Zeev Suraski, Andi Gutmans, Thies Arntzen, Stig Bakken, Sascha Schumann, Andrei Zmievski, and a host of other contributors), the people who have documented PHP (Stig Bakken, Alexander Aulbach, Egon Schmid, Lars Torben Wilson, Jim Winstead, and others), and everyone on the PHP mailing list. Special thanks to Rasmus, Sascha, and Richard Lynch for mailing-list answers to our own questions.

The authors would like to be able to acknowledge the support of their spouses ... but under the circumstances that is impossible. :)

Contents at a Glance

Contents

PHP – The Basics

Why PHP?

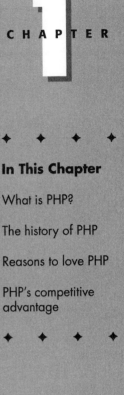

This first chapter is an introduction to PHP. In it, we'll try to address some of the most common questions about PHP, such as "What is it?" and "How does it compare to similar technologies?" Most of the chapter is taken up with an enumeration of the many, many reasons to love PHP. If you're a techie looking for some ammunition to lob at your PHB (translation: a Dilbertism meaning "Pointy-Haired Boss"), or a manager asking yourself what is this P-whatever thing your geeks keep whining to get, this chapter will provide some preliminary answers.

What Is PHP?

PHP stands for *PHP: Hypertext Preprocessor*. Actually, the product was originally named "Personal Home Page Tools"; but as it expanded in scope, a new and more appropriate (albeit GNUishly recursive) name was selected by community vote. You can use any extension you want to designate a PHP file, but the recommended ones have been `.php`, `.php3`, and `.phtml`. PHP is currently in version 4, called PHP 4 or just plain PHP.

PHP is a server-side HTML-embedded scripting language. Proprietary products in this niche are Microsoft's Active Server Pages, Allaire's ColdFusion, and Sun's Java Server Pages. PHP is sometimes called "the open source ASP" because its functionality is so similar to that of the Microsoft product/concept/whatever-it-is.

We'll explore server-side scripting more thoroughly in the next chapter, but for the moment you can think of it as a collection of super-HTML tags that let you add server-side functions to your Web pages. For example, you can use PHP to assemble a complex Web page on the fly, or to trigger a program that automatically runs a credit-card charge when a customer makes a purchase.

Strictly speaking, PHP has little to do with layout, events, or really anything about what a Web page looks and sounds like. In fact, most of what PHP does is invisible to the end user. Someone looking at a PHP page will not necessarily be able to tell that it was not written in HTML, because the end result of PHP *is* HTML.

PHP is an official module of Apache HTTP Server, the market-leading free Web server that runs about 55 percent of the World Wide Web. This means that the PHP scripting engine can be built into the Web server itself, leading to faster data manipulation. Like Apache Server, PHP is cross-platform, meaning it runs native on several flavors of UNIX, as well as Windows. All projects under the aegis of the Apache Software Foundation—including PHP—are open source software.

The various versions of PHP have garnered much acclaim and many awards over the years. PHP3 was a finalist in the 1999 *LinuxWorld* Editor's Choice Awards (programming library/tools category) and the runner-up to ColdFusion in the 1998 CNet Builder.com Product Awards (best server-side scripting tool category—they gave a lot of weight to the IDE), whereas the PHP3/MySQL combination won the Database of the Year award at Web98. Not bad for a piece of software with no PR, no advertising, and no perceptible major media agenda.

The History of PHP

Rasmus Lerdorf—software engineer, Apache team member, and international man of mystery—is the creator and original driving force behind PHP. The first part of PHP was developed for his personal use in late 1994. This was a Perl CGI wrapper that helped him keep track of people who looked at his personal site. The next year, he put together a package called the Personal Home Page Tools (a.k.a. the PHP Construction Kit) in response to demand from users who had stumbled into his work by chance or word of mouth. Version 2 was soon released under the title PHP/FI, and included the Form Interpreter, a tool for parsing SQL queries.

By the middle of 1997, PHP was being used on approximately 50,000 sites worldwide. It was clearly becoming too big for any single person to handle, even someone as focused and energetic as Rasmus. A small core development team now runs the project on the open source "benevolent junta" model, with contributions from developers and users around the world. Zeev Suraski and Andi Gutmans, the two Israeli programmers who developed the PHP 3 and PHP 4 parsers, have also generalized and extended their work under the rubric of Zend.com (Zeev, Andi, Zend, get it?).

The fourth quarter of 1998 initiated a period of explosive growth for PHP, as all open source technologies enjoyed massive publicity. In October 1998, according to the best guess, just over 100,000 unique domains used PHP in some way. Just over a year later, PHP broke the one million domain mark. As we write this book, the number has exploded to about two million domains.

Reasons to Love PHP

There are ever so many reasons to love PHP. Let us acquaint you with a few.

PHP is free

PHP costs you nothing. Zip, zilch, nada, not one red cent. Nothing up front, nothing over the lifetime of the application, nothing when it's over. Did we mention that the Apache/PHP/MySQL combo runs great on cheap low-end hardware that you couldn't even *think* about for IIS/ASP/SQL Server?

For purposes of comparison, Table 1-1 shows some approximate retail figures for similar products.

Table 1-1 Comparative Out-of-Pocket Costs				
Item	*ASP*	*ColdFusion*	*JSP*	*PHP*
Development	$0–480	$395	$0	$0
Server	$620	$1,295	$0–595	$0
RDBMS	$1,220–4,220	$0– ~10,000	$0– ~10,000	$0
Support incident	$0–245	$0–75	$0–75	$0

Open source software: don't fear the cheaper

But as the bard so pithily observed, we are living in a material world — where we've internalized maxims like, "You get what you pay for," "There's no such thing as a free lunch," and "Things that sound too good to be true usually are." Therefore, you (or your boss) may have some lingering doubts about the quality and viability of no-cost software. It probably doesn't help that until recently software that didn't cost money — formerly called freeware, shareware, or Free Software — was generally thought to fall into one of three categories:

✦ Programs filling small, uncommercial niches

✦ Programs performing grungy, low-level jobs

✦ Programs for people with bizarre socio-political "issues"

It's time to update some stereotypes once and for all. We are clearly in the middle of a sea change in the business of software. Much (if not most) major consumer software is distributed without cost today: e-mail clients, Web browsers, games, and even full-service office suites are all being given away as fast as their makers can whip up Web versions or set up FTP servers. Consumer software is increasingly seen as a loss-leader, the flower that attracts the pollinating honeybee — in other words, a way to sell more server hardware, operating systems, connectivity, advertising, optional widgets, or stock shares. Therefore, the full retail price of a piece of software is no longer a reliable gauge of its quality or the eccentricity-level of its user.

On the server side, open source products have come on even stronger; not only do they compete with the best commercial stuff, in many cases there's a feeling that they far exceed the competition. Don't take our word for it! Ask IBM, any hardware manufacturer, NASA, France Telecom, Siemens, Kinko's, the Queen of England, or the Mexican school system. If you still need to be convinced, you can learn a lot more at:

```
http://www.opensource.org
http://www.fsf.org
```

The PHP license

The freeness of open source and Free Software is guaranteed by a gaggle of licensing schemes, most famously the GPL (Gnu General Public License) or "copyleft." PHP used to be released under both the GPL and its own license, with each user free to choose between them. However, this has recently changed: the program as a whole is now released under its own extremely laissez-faire PHP 4 license; whereas Zend as a stand-alone product is released under the Q Public License (this clause applies *only* if you unbundle Zend from PHP and try to sell it).

You can read the fine print about the relevant licenses at these Web sites:

```
http://www.php.net/license.html
http://www.troll.no/qpl/annotated.html
```

Most people get PHP via free download, but you may have paid for it as part of a Linux distribution, a technical book, or some other product. In that case, you may now be mentally disputing our assertion that PHP costs nothing. Here's the twist: although you can't require a fee for most open source software, you *can* charge for delivering that software in a more convenient format — as by putting it on a disk and shipping the disk to the customer. You can also charge anything the market will bear for being willing to perform certain services or accept certain risks that the development team may not wish to undertake. For instance, you are allowed to charge money for guaranteeing that every copy of the software you distribute will be virus-free or of reasonable quality, taking on the risk of being sued if a bunch of customers get bad CD-ROMs with hard-drive-erasing viruses on them.

Usually, open source software users can freely choose the precisely optimal cost-benefit equation for each particular situation: no cost and no warranties, or expensive but well supported, or something in between. However, no organized attempt has been made yet to sell service and support for PHP (although presumably that will be one of the value-adds of Zend). Other open source products, such as Linux, have companies like Red Hat standing by to answer your questions; but the commercialization process has just begun for PHP.

PHP is easy

PHP is easy to learn, compared to the other ways to achieve similar functionality. Unlike Java Server Pages or C-based CGI, PHP doesn't require you to gain a deep understanding of a major programming language before you can make a trivial database call. Unlike Perl, which has been semi-jokingly called a "write-only language," PHP has a syntax that is quite easy to parse and human-friendly. And unlike Active Server Pages, PHP doesn't make you learn two different programming languages for different occasions!

Also, many of the most useful specific functions (such as those for opening a connection to an Oracle database, or fetching e-mail from an IMAP server) are predefined for you. There are also a lot of complete scripts waiting out there for you to look at as you're learning PHP. In fact, it's entirely possible to use PHP just by modifying freely available scripts rather than starting from scratch—you'll still need to understand the basic principles, but you can avoid many frustrating and time-consuming minor mistakes.

However, we must mention one caveat: "easy" means different things to different people, and for some Web developers it has come to connote a graphical, drag-and-drop, What You See Is What You Get development environment. To become truly proficient at PHP, you need to be comfortable editing HTML by hand. You can use WYSIWYG editors to design sites, format pages, and insert client-side features before you add PHP functionality to the source code. There are even ways, which we'll detail in Chapter 3, to add PHP functions to your favorite editing environment. However, it's not realistic to think you can take full advantage of PHP's capabilities without ever looking at source code.

Most advanced PHP users (including most of the development team members) are diehard hand-coders. They tend to share certain gut-level subcultural assumptions— for instance, that hand-written code is beautiful and clean and maximally browser-compatible, and therefore the only way to go—that they do not hesitate to express in vigorous terms. The PHP community offers help and trades tips mostly by e-mail, and if you want to participate, you have to be able to parse plain-text source code with facility. Some WYSIWYG users occasionally ask list members to diagnose their problems by looking at their Web pages instead of their source code, but this rarely ends well.

That said, let us reiterate that PHP really is easy. It's just a little more involved than HTML but probably simpler than JavaScript or ASP, and definitely less conceptually complex than JSP.

PHP is embedded

PHP is embedded within HTML. In other words, PHP pages are ordinary HTML pages that "escape" into PHP mode only when necessary. Here is an example:

```
<HTML>
<HEAD>
<TITLE>A greeting</TITLE>
```

```
</HEAD>
<BODY>
<P>Hi,
<?php
/*  We have now escaped into PHP mode.
Instead of static variables, the next three lines
could easily be database calls. */
$firstname = "Mata";
$lastname = "Hari";
$title = "Ms.";
PRINT("$title $lastname");
// We're about to go back to HTML now.
?>.
May I call you <?php PRINT("$firstname"); ?>?</P>
</BODY>
</HTML>
```

When a client requests this page, the Web server preprocesses it. This means it goes through the page from top to bottom, looking for sections of PHP, which it will try to resolve. For one thing, the parser will suck up all assigned variables (marked by dollar signs) and try to plug them into later PHP commands (in this case, the print() function). If everything goes smoothly, the preprocessor will eventually return a normal HTML page to the client's browser, as shown in Figure 1-1.

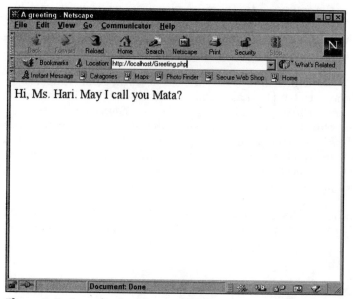

Figure 1-1: A result of preprocessed PHP

If you peek at the source code from the client browser (select "Source" or "Page Source" from the View menu, or right-click on AOL), it will look like this:

```
<HTML>
<HEAD>
<TITLE>A greeting</TITLE>
</HEAD>
<BODY>
<P>Hi, Ms. Hari. May I call you Mata?</P>
</BODY>
</HTML>
```

This is exactly the same as if you wrote the HTML by hand. So simple!

The HTML-embeddedness of PHP has many helpful consequences:

✦ PHP can quickly be added to code produced by WYSIWYG editors.

✦ PHP lends itself to a division of labor between designers and scripters.

✦ Every line of HTML does not need to be rewritten in a programming language.

✦ PHP can reduce labor costs and increase efficiency.

No compilation

Perhaps the sweetest thing of all about embedded scripting languages is that they don't need to be compiled into binary code before they can be tested or used — just write and run. PHP is interpreted (as are almost all newish computer languages), although Zend does some behind-the-scenes precompiling into an intermediate form for greater speed with complex scripts.

But what if you happen to *want* compilation? This can be desirable if you wish to distribute nonreversible binaries so others can use the code without being able to look at the source. The Zend team is working on an optimizing compiler that will make this possible, as well as substantially speeding up large complex PHP scripts.

PHP is cross-platform

PHP runs native on every popular flavor of UNIX and Windows. A huge percentage of the world's HTTP servers run on one of these two classes of operating system.

PHP is compatible with the three leading Web servers: Apache HTTP Server for UNIX and Windows, Microsoft Internet Information Server, and Netscape Enterprise Server (a.k.a. iPlanet Server). It also works with several lesser-known servers, including Alex Belits's fhttpd, Microsoft's Personal Web Server, AOLServer, and Omnicentrix's Omniserver application server. PHP is *not* supported on the Macintosh platform.

Table 1-2 shows a brief matrix of the possible OS/Webserver combinations.

Table 1-2 Operating Systems and Web Servers for PHP		
Variables	**UNIX**	**Windows**
Flavors	AIX, A/UX, BSDI, Digital UNIX/Tru64, FreeBSD, HP-UX, IRIX, Linux, NetBSD, OpenBSD, SCO UnixWare, Solaris, SunOS, Ultrix, Xenix, and more	Windows 95 Windows 98 Windows NT Windows 2000
Web servers	Apache, fhttpd, Netscape	IIS, PWS, Netscape, Apache, Omni

Although PHP does not currently run on Macintosh, BeOS, or some other well-loved platforms, you can develop on these (or any) client using your favorite tools and then upload your PHP scripts to a UNIX or Windows server. We'll discuss this process in more detail in Chapter 3.

PHP isn't tag-based

PHP is a real programming language. ColdFusion, by contrast, is a bunch of predefined tags, like HTML. In PHP, you can define functions to your heart's content just by typing a name and a definition. In ColdFusion, you have to use tags developed by other people, or go through the Custom Tag Extension development process.

As a witty PHP community member once said, "ColdFusion makes easy things easy, and medium-hard things impossible." And as every programmer will agree: once you experience the power of curly brackets and loops, you never go back to tags.

PHP is stable

The word "stable" means two different things in this context:

1. That the server doesn't need to be rebooted often.
2. That the software doesn't change radically and incompatibly from release to release.

Happily, both of these connotations apply to PHP.

Apache Server is generally considered to be the most stable of major Web servers, with a reputation for enviable uptime percentages. Although it is not the fastest nor the easiest to administer, once you get it set up, Apache HTTP Server seemingly never crashes. It also doesn't require server reboots every time a setting is changed (at least on the UNIX side). PHP inherits this reliability; plus, its own implementation is solid yet lightweight. In a two-and-a-half-month head-to-head test conducted by the Network Computing labs in October 1999, Apache Server with PHP handily beat both IIS/Visual Studio and Netscape Enterprise Server/Java for stability of environment.

PHP is also stable in the sense of feature stability. The development team has thus far enjoyed a clear vision of their project and refused to be distracted by every new fad and ill-thought-out user demand that comes along. Much of their effort goes into incremental improvements, such as getting the parser to run faster, communicating with more major databases, or adding better session support. Historically, very few functions have had to be dropped between versions of PHP.

PHP is fast

PHP is pleasingly zippy in its execution, especially when compiled as an Apache module on the UNIX side.

PHP 4 is now much faster for almost every use than CGI scripts. There is an unfortunate grain of truth to the joke that CGI stands for "Can't Go Instantly." Although many CGI scripts are written in C, one of the lowest-level and therefore speediest of the major programming languages, they are hindered by the fact that each request must spawn an entirely new process after being handed off from the http daemon. The time and resources necessary for this handoff and spawning are considerable, and there can be limits to the number of concurrent processes that can be running at any one time. Other CGI scripting languages such as Perl and Tcl can be quite slow. Most Web sites are moving away from use of CGI for performance and security reasons.

Although it takes a slight performance hit by being interpreted rather than compiled, this is far outweighed by the benefits PHP derives from its status as a Web server module. When compiled this way, PHP becomes part of the http daemon itself. Because there is no transfer to and from a separate application server (as there is with ColdFusion, for instance) requests can be filled more efficiently.

Although no extensive formal benchmarks have compared the two, much anecdotal evidence and many small benchmarks suggest that PHP is at least as fast as ASP in most applications (see the Zend.com site, for instance).

PHP is open

We've already dealt with the cost advantages of open source software. The other major consequence of these licenses is that the complete source code for the software must be included in any distribution.

In fact, the UNIX version of PHP is only released as source code; so far, the development team has staunchly resisted countless pleas to distribute official binaries for any of the UNIXes. At first, new users (particularly those who are also new to UNIX) tend to feel that source code is about as useful as a third leg, and most would vastly prefer a nice convenient rpm. But there are both pragmatic and idealistic reasons for including folders full of pesky .c and .h files.

The most immediate pragmatic advantage is that you can compile your PHP installation with only the stuff you really need for any given situation. This approach has speed and security advantages. For instance, you can put in hooks to the database(s) of your choice. You can recompile as often as you want: maybe if an Apache security release comes out, or when you come to the conclusion you need XML support.

What sets open source software apart from its competitors is not just price but control. Plenty of consumer software is now given away under various conditions. However, careful scrutiny of the relevant licenses will generally reveal limits as to how the software can be used. Maybe you can run it at home, but not at the office. Perhaps you can load it on your laptop, but you're in violation if you use it for business purposes. Or, most commonly, you can use it for anything you want, but forget about looking at the code much less changing it. There are even "community licenses" that force you to donate your improvements to the codebase but charge you for use of the product at the end!

Caution   Don't even *think* about coming back with a riposte that involves violating a software license—we're covering our ears, we're not listening! Especially with the explosion in no-cost software, there's just no good reason to break the law. Besides, it's bad karma for software developers: what goes around, comes around, don't ya know.

Table 1-3 shows examples of the various source and fee positions in today's software marketplace:

		Table 1-3 Source/Fee Spectrum	
Fee Structure	*Closed Source*	*Controlled Source*	*Open Source*
Fee for all uses	Allaire ColdFusion	—	—
Fee for some uses	Corel WordPerfect	Sun Java	MySQL
No fee for any use	Microsoft IE	Sun StarOffice	GPLed software

Genuinely open source software like PHP cannot seek to limit the purposes for which it is used, the people who are allowed to use it, or a host of other factors. The most critical of these rights is the one allowing users to make and distribute any modifications along with the original software. In the most extreme case, this is referred to as "code forking."

This means that if somewhere down the road you develop irreconcilable differences with the PHP development team, you can take every bit of code they've labored over for all these years and use it as the basis of your own product. You couldn't call it PHP, and you'd have to include stuff in your documentation that gave due credit to the authors, and in most circumstances it's just a stupid idea— but you always have the right to fork, and it has been exercised many times for reasons good, bad, and ugly. The rationale is that source code distributions make it next to impossible for any single person or group to hijack a program to the detriment of the community as a whole, because every user always has the power to take all the source and walk.

Users new to the open source model should be aware that this right is also enjoyed by the developers. At any time, Rasmus and company can choose to defect from the community and put all their future efforts into a commercial or competing product based on PHP. Of course, the codebase up to this point would still be available to anyone who wanted to pick up the baton, and for a product as large as PHP that could be a considerable number of volunteer developers.

This leads to one other oft-forgotten advantage of open source software: you can be pretty sure the software will be around in a few years, no matter what. In these days of products with the life spans of morning glories, it's hard to pick a tool with staying power. Fans of OS/2, Amiga, NeXT, Newton, Firefly, Netscape, and a host of other once-hot technologies know the pain of abandonment when a company goes belly-up, decides to stop supporting a technology, or is sold to a buyer with a new agenda. We were ourselves seduced and tossed aside by another (now-defunct) server-side scripting tool before we discovered PHP; and although we've gotten past the denial and anger, there's still a hollow feeling when we think of the years we gave to our ex-scripting language. The open source model reduces the chances of an ugly emergency port in a couple of years and thus makes long-term planning more realistic.

PHP plays well with others

PHP makes it easy to communicate with other programs and protocols. The PHP development team seems committed to providing maximum flexibility to the largest number of users.

Database connectivity is especially strong, with native-driver support for about 15 of the most popular databases plus ODBC. In addition, PHP supports a large number of major protocols such as POP3, IMAP, and LDAP. PHP 4 also has new support for Java and distributed object architectures (COM and CORBA), making n-tier development a possibility for the first time.

Most things that PHP does not support are ultimately attributable to closed-source shops on the other end. For instance, Apple Computer and Microsoft have not thus far been eager to cooperate with open source projects like PHP. Potential users who complain about lack of native Mac or SQL Server support on the PHP mailing list are simply misinformed about where the fault lies.

PHP is popular and growing

PHP is fast becoming one of the most popular choices for so-called two-tier development (Web plus data). Figure 1-2 charts growth since mid-1998.

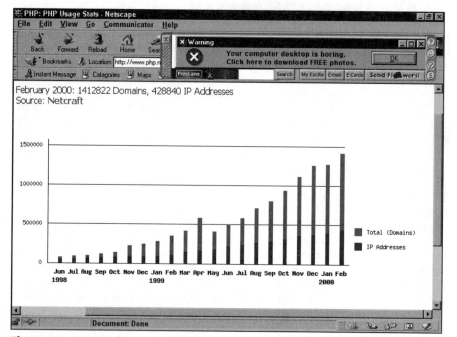

Figure 1-2: A Netcraft survey of PHP use

As you can see, the period October 1998 through October 1999 showed 800 percent growth in the number of domains. As Web sites become even more ubiquitous, and as more of them go beyond simple static HTML pages, PHP is expected to gain ground quickly in absolute numbers of users.

Although it's somewhat more difficult to get firm figures, it seems that PHP is also in a strong position relative to similar products. Microsoft Active Server Pages technology appears to be utilized on 12 percent of Web servers, whereas ColdFusion is implemented on approximately 4 percent of surveyed domains. PHP is used on 12 percent of all Web servers, as measured by a larger and more accurate sample.

Active Server Pages and ColdFusion are highly visible because they tend to be disproportionately selected by large e-commerce sites. However, the vast majority of Web sites are informational rather than direct revenue centers and therefore do not repay high development expenses in a visible way. PHP enjoys substantial advantages over its competitors in this development category.

PHP is not proprietary

The history of the personal computer industry to date has largely been a chronicle of proprietary standards: attempts to establish them, clashes between them, their benefits and drawbacks for the consumer, and how they are eventually replaced with new standards.

But in the past few years the Internet has demonstrated the great convenience of voluntary, standards-based, platform-independent compatibility. For example, e-mail works so well because it enjoys a clear, firm standard to which every program on every platform must conform. New developments that break with the standard (for example, HTML-based e-mail "stationery") are generally regarded as deviations, and their users find themselves having to bear the burdens of early adoption.

Right now, software developers are in a period of experimentation and flux concerning proprietary versus open standards. Companies want to be sure they can maintain profitability while adopting open standards. There have been some major legal conflicts related to proprietary standards, which are still being resolved. These could eventually result in mandated changes to the codebase itself, or even affect the future existence of the companies involved. In the face of all this uncertainty, a growing number of businesses are attracted to solutions that they know will not have these problems in the foreseeable future.

PHP is in a position of maximum flexibility because it is, so to speak, antiproprietary. It is not tied to any one server operating system, unlike Active Server Pages. It is not tied to any proprietary cross-platform standard or middleware, as Java Server Pages or ColdFusion are. It is not tied to any one browser or implementation of a programming language or database. PHP isn't even doctrinaire about working only with other open source software. This independent but cooperative pragmatism should help PHP ride out the stormy seas that seem to lie ahead.

The PHP community

PHP is developed and supported in a collaborative fashion by a worldwide community of users. It's true that some animals (such as the core developers) are more equal than others — but that's hard to argue with, because they put in the most work, had the best ideas, and have managed to maintain civil relationships with the greatest number of other users.

The main advantage for most new users is technical support without charge, without boundaries, and without the runaround. People on the mailing list are available 24-and-7 to answer your questions, help debug your code, and listen to your gripes. The support is human and real. PHP community members might tell you to read the manual, take your question over to the appropriate database mailing list, or just stop your whining — but they'll never tell you to wipe your C drive and then charge you for the privilege. Often they'll look at your code and tell you what you're doing wrong, or even help you design an application from the ground up.

As you become more comfortable with PHP, you may wish to contribute. Bug tracking, offering advice to others on the mailing lists, posting scripts to public repositories, editing documentation, and of course writing C or C++ code are all ways you can give back to the community.

Summary

PHP isn't the panacea for every Web development problem, but it has a lot of advantages. It's built by Web developers for Web developers and supported by a large and enthusiastic community. It sits on a sweet-spot of lightness, power, reliability, and ease of use. It offers best-of-breed connectivity to backend servers of all types. And did we mention it's free? To know PHP is to love it for many of the most common Web development tasks have been selected.

✦   ✦   ✦

Server-Side Web Scripting

In This Chapter

Understanding
static and dynamic
Web pages

Client-side versus
server-side scripting

An introduction to
server-side scripting

This chapter is about server-side scripting and its
relationship to both static HTML and common client-
side technologies. By the end, you can expect to have a clear
understanding of what kinds of things PHP can and cannot do
for you, along with a general understanding of how it can
interact with client-side code.

Static HTML

The most basic type of Web page is a completely static, text-
based one written entirely in HTML. Take the simple HTML-
only page that Figure 2-1 shows as an example.

This is the source code for Figure 2-1:

```
<HTML>
<HEAD>
<TITLE>Books about hardware</TITLE>
<META NAME=KEYWORDS CONTENT="computer,
hardware, chip, business, book">
</HEAD>
<BODY>
<CENTER><H3>Books about the computer hardware
business</H3></CENTER>
<H5>Apple Computer</H5>
<UL>
<LI><A HREF="book1.html">Apple</A> by Carlton,
Jim (1997)
<LI><A HREF="book2.html">Insanely Great</A> by
Levy, Steven (1993)
<LI><A HREF="book3.html">Odyssey:  Pepsi to
Apple</A> by Sculley, John (1997)
<LI><A HREF="book4.html">Steve Jobs and the
NeXT Big Thing</A> by Stross, Randall (1993)
</UL>
<H5>Dell Computer</H5>
<UL>
<LI><A HREF="book5.html">Direct from Dell</A>
```

```
by Dell, Michael (1999)
</UL>
<H5>Intel</H5>
<UL>
<LI><A HREF="book6.html">Only the Paranoid Survive</A> by
Grove, Andrew S. (1996)
<LI><A HREF="book7.html">Inside Intel</A> by Jackson, Tim
(1997)
</UL>
<H5>Sun Microsystems</H5>
<UL>
<LI><A HREF="book8.html">High Noon</A> by Southwick, Karen
(1999)
</UL>
</BODY>
</HTML>
```

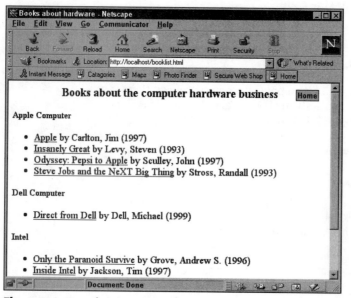

Figure 2-1: A static HTML example

When the client computer makes an HTTP request for this page from the server machine over the Web or an intranet as shown in Figure 2-2, the server simply passes along whatever text it finds in the file.

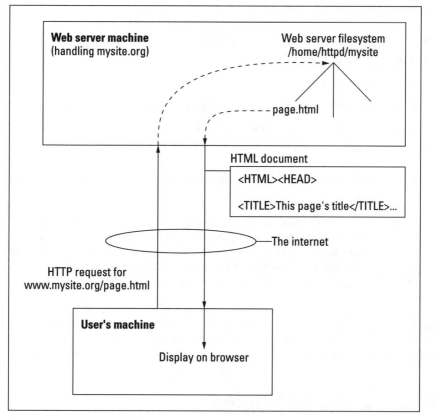

Figure 2-2: A simple HTTP request

When this data gets back to the client machine, the browser does its best to render the page according to its understanding of precisely what kind of code it is, user preferences, monitor size, and other factors. The contents of the HTML file on the server will be exactly the same as the source code of the page on the client.

Very plain, static HTML such as this has certain advantages:

✦ Any browser can display it adequately.

✦ Many kinds of devices can display it adequately.

✦ Each request is fulfilled quickly and uses minimal resources.

✦ HTML is easy to learn or produce automatically.

✦ Small changes to individual pages can be made quickly.

Of course, static HTML has its downsides, including these:

✦ It makes control of design and layout difficult.

✦ It doesn't scale up well.

✦ It's not very interactive.

✦ It makes including meaningful metadata about the page difficult.

✦ It can't cope with rapidly changing content or personalization.

✦ It's not very attractive.

For all these reasons, static HTML has quickly become a mark of amateurishness or ideological rigor.

Numerous additional technologies have been developed in response to these limitations. These include JavaScript, Cascading Style Sheets, and Java applets on the client side, and server-side scripting with database connectivity on the server side. Upcoming technologies include XML and XSL, both of which appear as part of various other specifications (XHTML, XSLT, Xpath, ICE, and so on).

You'll save yourself a lot of headaches if you take the time to understand exactly what functionality each of these technologies can and can't be expected to add to your Web site. The basic question to ask yourself about any given Web site task is: Where is the computation happening, on the client or on the server?

Client-Side Technologies

The most common additions to plain HTML are on the client side. These include the following: formatting extensions such as Cascading Style Sheets and Dynamic HTML; client-side scripting languages; and Java applets. Support for all these technologies is (or is not, as the case may be) built into the Web browser. They perform the tasks described in Table 2-1, with some overlap.

What does "dynamic" mean?

There's a basic and often-repeated distinction between "static" and "dynamic" Web pages — but "dynamic" can mean almost anything beyond plain vanilla HTML. It is used to describe both client- and server-side functions. On the client, it can mean multimedia presentations, scrolling headlines, pages that update themselves automatically, or elements that appear and disappear. On the server, the term is generally taken to denote content that is assembled on the fly.

Table 2-1
Client-Side HTML Extensions

Client-Side Technology	Main Use	Example Effects
Cascading Style Sheets, Dynamic HTML	Formatting pages: controlling size, color, placement, layout, timing of elements	Overlapping,different colored/sized, fonts Layers
Client-side scripting (JavaScript, VBScript)	Event handling: controlling consequences of defined events	Link that changes color when cursor passes over Mortgage calculator
Java applets	Delivering small stand-alone applications	Spinning logo Crossword puzzle

The page shown in Figure 2-3 is based on the same content as that in Figure 2-1.

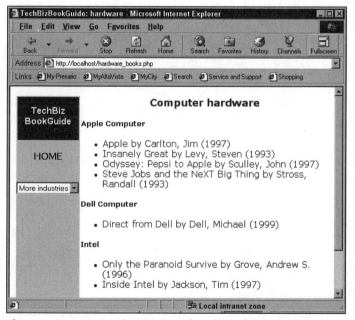

Figure 2-3: An example of HTML plus client-side scripting

As you can see from the source, though, this example adds style sheets and client-side scripting as well as somewhat more sophisticated HTML

```html
<HTML>
<HEAD>
<TITLE>TechBizBookGuide: hardware</TITLE>
<STYLE TYPE="text/css">
<!--
BODY        {color: black; font-family: verdana; font-size: 10
pt}
H1          {margin-top: 10; color: white; font-family: arial;
font-size: 12 pt}
H2          {margin-bottom: -10; color: black; font-family:
verdana; font-size: 18 pt}
A:link      {color: #000080; text-decoration: none}
.roll       {   }
A.roll:hover  {color: #008080}
-->
</STYLE>

<SCRIPT LANGUAGE="JavaScript">
<!--
    function ListVisit(form, i) {
        // get the URL from options
        var site = form.elements[i].selectedIndex;
        // if it's not the first (null) option, go there
        if( site >= 1 ) {
            top.location = form.elements[i].options[ site].value;
        }
        // and then reselect the null (it functions as a label)
        form.elements[i].selectedIndex = 0;
    }

//-->
</SCRIPT>
</HEAD>

<BODY>
<TABLE BORDER=0 CELLPADDING=0 WIDTH=100%>
<TR>
<TD BGCOLOR="#F0F8FF" ALIGN=CENTER VALIGN=TOP WIDTH=17%>
    <TABLE CELLPADDING=5 WIDTH=100%>
    <TR ALIGN=CENTER>
    <TD BGCOLOR="#000080">
    <H1>TechBiz<BR>BookGuide</H1>
    </TD></TR></TABLE>
    <BR>
    <A HREF="index.php"><B>HOME</B></A><BR><BR>
    <BR>
    <FORM action="">
```

```
    <SELECT NAME="industries" onChange="ListVisit(this.form,
0)">
    <OPTION>More industries
    <OPTION VALUE="software.html">Software
    <OPTION VALUE="biotech.html">Biotech
    <OPTION VALUE="aerospace.html">Aerospace
    <OPTION VALUE="telephone.html">Telephony
    </SELECT></FORM><BR>
</TD>
<TD BGCOLOR="#FFFFFF" ALIGN=LEFT VALIGN=TOP WIDTH=83%>
<CENTER><H3>Computer hardware</H3></CENTER>
<H5>Apple Computer</H5>
<UL>
<LI><A HREF="book1.html" class="roll">Apple</A> by Carlton, Jim
(1997)
<LI><A HREF="book2.html" class="roll">Insanely Great</A> by
Levy, Steven (1993)
<LI><A HREF="book3.html" class="roll">Odyssey:  Pepsi to
Apple</A> by Sculley, John (1997)
<LI><A HREF="book4.html" class="roll">Steve Jobs and the NeXT
Big Thing</A> by Stross, Randall (1993)
</UL>
<H5>Dell Computer</H5>
<UL>
<LI><A HREF="book5.html" class="roll">Direct from Dell</A> by
Dell, Michael (1999)
</UL>
<H5>Intel</H5>
<UL>
<LI><A HREF="book6.html" class="roll">Only the Paranoid
Survive</A> by Grove, Andrew S. (1996)
<LI><A HREF="book7.html" class="roll">Inside Intel</A> by
Jackson, Tim (1997)
</UL>
<H5>Sun Microsystems</H5>
<UL>
<LI><A HREF="book8.html" class="roll">High Noon</A> by
Southwick, Karen (1999)
</UL>
</TD>
</TR></TABLE>
</BODY>
</HTML>
```

Unfortunately, the best thing about client-side technologies is also the worst thing about them: they depend entirely on the browser. There are wide variations in the capabilities of each browser and even between versions of the same brand of browser. So-called Dynamic HTML amounts to two different scripting concepts that just happen to have the same name. Individuals can also choose to configure their own browsers in awkward ways: for instance, some people disable JavaScript for security reasons, which makes it impossible for them to view sites that overuse JavaScript for navigation (as we've deliberately done in the preceding page).

Furthermore, many consumers are very slow to upgrade their browsers for reasons of cost or technical anxiety or both. The savvy Web developer should also be giving thought to device-based browsing, universal accessibility, and a global audience. It's no accident that the huge mass-market sites trying to reach the widest audiences, such as Yahoo! and Amazon, continue to resist using style sheets and JavaScript more than three years after these standards were adopted. Against the urging of the World Wide Web Consortium, many sites continue to stubbornly cling to their FONT tags and BGCOLOR attributes as the only way to survive in the face of customers who insist on using AOL 3.0 on five-year-old Macintoshes with 13-inch monitors. The stubborn unwillingness of the public to upgrade is the bane of client-side developers, causing them to frequently suffer screaming nightmares and/or existential meltdowns in the dark, vulnerable hours before dawn. The bottom-line irony is this: even after five years of explosive Web progress, the only thing a developer can be absolutely positive the client will see is plain text-based HTML (or rather, the subset of HTML which has been widely supported and stood the tests of time and usefulness).

Finally, client-side technologies cannot do anything that requires connecting to a back-end server. JavaScript cannot assemble a customized pull-down list on the fly from user preferences stored in a database — when a change is needed in the list, the Web developer has to go in and change it by hand. (There is server-side Java-Script, but at the moment it is not much used.) This is the gap that server-side scripting can fill.

Java applets

Java applets, also known as "client-side Java," are considerably less dependent on the browser than other client-side technologies. As the name suggests, these are complete little Java applications that are delivered over the Internet. But instead of interacting directly with the client's operating system like applications written in other programming languages, Java applets run on a piece of middleware called a Java Virtual Machine. The JVM can be thought of as an operating system living on top of your real operating system, like the aliens taking over human bodies in a gazillion cheesy sci-fi movies. Most recent browsers incorporate a JVM, and you can also download one separately. This division of labor lets applets use the rendering capabilities of a browser without being limited to the browser's relatively puny functionality.

Applets have suffered under an early reputation for picayune pointlessness because they were initially used for a category of thing we might term "dancing Chihuahuas": logos that look like they're made out of gelatin, scrolling headlines, bouncing links, and other headache-inducing frivolities. Luckily, applets have since been redeemed by useful, humanistic purposes such as crossword puzzles, Tower of Hanoi simulations, and virtual ways to "try on" ensembles of clothing and accessories.

In sum: anything to do with layout or browser events happens on the client. Generally speaking, anything that looks cool or depends on the movements of your mouse is client-side. The faster you see some event happening, the more likely that it is being handled by the client, because high speed indicates that no download from the server is necessary.

Server-Side Scripting

Figure 2-4 is a schematic representation of server-side scripting data flow.

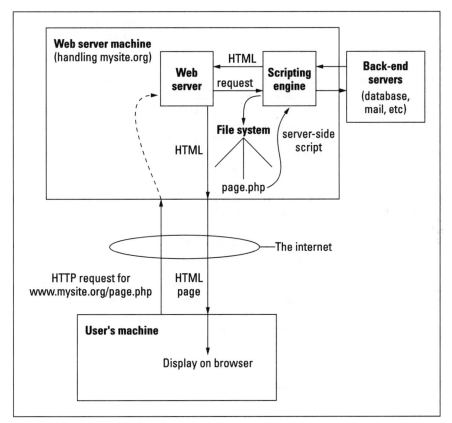

Figure 2-4: Server-side tasks

Client-side scripting is the glamorous, eye-catching part of Web development. In contrast, server-side scripting is invisible to the user. Pity the poor server-side scripters, toiling away in utter obscurity, trapped in the no-man's land between the Web server and the database while their arty brethren brazenly flash their wares before the public gaze.

Server-side Web scripting is mostly about connecting Web sites to back-end servers, such as databases. This enables two-way communication:

✦ Server to client: Web pages can be assembled from backend-server output.

✦ Client to server: Customer-entered information can be acted upon.

Common examples of client-to-server interaction are online forms and some pull-down lists (usually the ones that require you to click a button) that are assembled dynamically on the server.

Server-side scripting products have two main parts: the scripting language and the scripting engine (which may or may not be built into the Web server). The engine parses and interprets pages written in the language. Often, both parts are developed by the same company or team for use only with each other—PHP 3 and ColdFusion are both examples of this practice. However, there are exceptions to this rule. For instance, Java Server Pages is written in a standard programming language rather than a special-purpose scripting language; but several interchangeable engines have been developed by third parties (for example, Allaire JRun, Apache JServ). In theory, Active Server Pages allows you to use almost any scripting language and one of several matching ActiveX scripting engines (although in practice, it's highly problematic to use anything but the NT/IIS/VBScript/JScript combination). PHP 4 is also a "bikini" scripting technology now, since the scripting engine (Zend) is now theoretically separable from the PHP programming language.

Figure 2-5 shows a simple example of server-side scripting, a page assembled on the fly from a database, followed by the server-side source and the client-side source. We've included database calls (which we won't get around to explaining for a while yet) and left out some of the included files, since this example is intended to show the final product of PHP rather than serve as a piece of working code.

This is the source on the server:

```
<HTML>
<HEAD>
<TITLE>TechBizBookGuide example from server</TITLE>
<?php include("tbbg-style.css"); ?>
```

```
<?php include("javascript.inc"); ?>
</HEAD>
<BODY>
<?php include("tbbg-navbar.txt"); ?>
<TD BGCOLOR="#FFFFFF" ALIGN=LEFT VALIGN=TOP WIDTH=83%>
    <TABLE CELLPADDING=5 WIDTH=100%><TR><TD ALIGN=LEFT
VALIGN=MIDDLE>
    <H2>Books about <?php print("$co"); //passed in from URL
?></H2><BR></TD></TR>
    <TR><TD WIDTH=50% ALIGN=LEFT>
    <?php
    $dbh = mysql_connect('localhost', 'joyce') or die("Unable to
open database");

    mysql_select_db("techbizbookguide") or die("Unable to access
database");
    $query = "SELECT Blurb FROM Company WHERE CompanyName =
'$co'";
    $qresult = mysql_query($query) or die(mysql_error());
    $blurb = mysql_fetch_array($qresult) or die(mysql_error());
    print("$blurb[0]");
    ?>
    </TD></TR>
    <TR><TD ALIGN=LEFT>
       <TABLE BORDER=1 CELLPADDING=3>
       <?php
       $query2 = "SELECT ID, Title, AuthorFirst, AuthorLast FROM
bookinfo WHERE CompanyName='$co' ORDER BY AuthorLast";
       $qresult2 = mysql_query($query2) or die(mysql_error());
       while($titlelist = mysql_fetch_array($qresult2))
       {
           $bookID = $titlelist[0];
           $title = $titlelist[1];
           $authorfirst = $titlelist[2];
           $authorlast = $titlelist[3];
           print("<TR><TD><A HREF=\"book.php?bn=$bookID\"
class=\"roll\"> $title</A></TD><TD>$authorfirst
$authorlast</TD>");
       }
       ?>
       </TR></TABLE>
    </TD></TR></TABLE>
</TD></TR></TABLE>
</BODY></HTML>
```

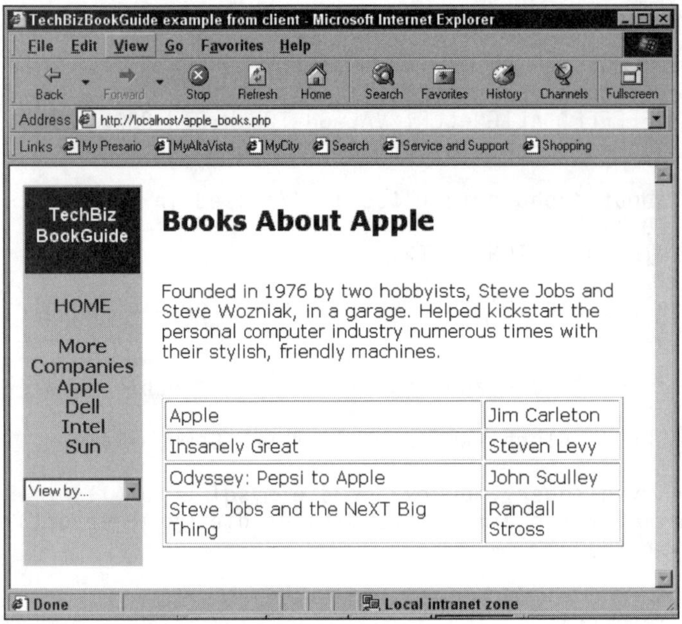

Figure 2-5: Server-side scripting example

This is what the source for the same page looks like by the time it reaches the client:

```
<HTML>
<HEAD>
<TITLE>TechBizBookGuide example from client</TITLE>
<STYLE TYPE="text/css">
<!--
BODY        {color: black; font-family: verdana; font-size: 10
pt}
H1          {margin-top: 10; color: white; font-family: arial;
font-size: 12 pt}
H2          {margin-bottom: -10; color: black; font-family:
verdana; font-size: 18 pt}
A:link      {color: #000080; text-decoration: none}
.roll       {    }
A.roll:hover   {color: #008080}
-->
</STYLE>
<SCRIPT LANGUAGE="JavaScript">
<!--
    function ListVisit(form, i) {
        // get the URL from options
        var site = form.elements[i].selectedIndex;
        // if it's not the first (null) option, go there
```

```
        if( site >= 1 ) {
        top.location = form.elements[i].options[site].value;
        }
        // and then reselect the null (it functions as a label)
        form.elements[i].selectedIndex = 0;
    }
    //-->
</SCRIPT>
</HEAD>

<BODY>
<TABLE BORDER=0 CELLPADDING=0 WIDTH=100%>
<TR>
<TD BGCOLOR="#F0F8FF" ALIGN=CENTER VALIGN=TOP WIDTH=17%>
    <TABLE CELLPADDING=5 WIDTH=100%>
    <TR ALIGN=CENTER>
    <TD BGCOLOR="#000080">
    <H1>TechBiz<BR>BookGuide</H1>
    </TD></TR></TABLE>
    <BR>
    <A HREF="index.php"><B>HOME</B></A><BR><BR>
    <B>More</B><BR>
    <B>Companies</B><BR>
    <A HREF="company.php?co=apple" class="roll"><B>Apple</B></A>
    <BR>
    <A HREF="company.php?co=dell" class="roll"><B>Dell</B></A>
    <BR>
    <A HREF="company.php?co=intel" class="roll"><B>Intel</B></A>
    <BR>
    <A HREF="company.php?co=sun" class="roll"><B>Sun</B></A>
    <BR><BR>
    <FORM action="">
    <Select onChange="ListVisit(this.form, 0)">
    <OPTION>View by...
    <OPTION VALUE="author.php">Author
    <OPTION VALUE="people.php">People
    <OPTION VALUE="themes.php">Themes
    <OPTION VALUE="role.php">Roles
    <OPTION VALUE="size.php">Company size
    </SELECT></FORM><BR>
</TD>
<TD BGCOLOR="#FFFFFF" ALIGN=LEFT VALIGN=TOP WIDTH=83%>
    <TABLE WIDTH=100% CELLPADDING=15><TR><TD ALIGN=LEFT
VALIGN=MIDDLE>
    <H2>Books About Apple</H2><BR></TD></TR>
    <TR><TD WIDTH=50% ALIGN=LEFT>Founded in 1976 by two
hobbyists, Steve Jobs and Steve Wozniak, in a garage.  Helped
kickstart the personal computer industry numerous times with
their stylish, friendly machines.</TD></TR>
    <TR><TD ALIGN=LEFT>
        <TABLE BORDER=1 CELLPADDING=3>
```

```
      <TR><TD><A HREF="book.php?book=1"
class="roll">Apple</A></TD><TD>Jim Carleton</TD>
      <TR><TD><A HREF="book.php?book=2" class="roll">Insanely
Great</A></TD><TD>Steven Levy</TD>
      <TR><TD><A HREF="book.php?book=3" class="roll">Odyssey:
Pepsi to Apple</A></TD><TD>John Sculley</TD>
      <TR><TD><A HREF="book.php?book=4" class="roll">Steve Jobs
and the NeXT Big Thing</A></TD><TD>Randall Stross</TD>
      </TR></TABLE>
    </TD></TR></TABLE>
  </TD></TR></TABLE>
  </BODY></HTML>
```

This particular page isn't significantly more impressive to look at than the plain HTML version at the beginning of the chapter. However, one different variable being passed will result in the automatic generation of any number of unique pages — in this case, pages listing the books by criteria other than author's last name — without any further work. If we added some new books about another company to the database, these lists would be automatically updated to reflect the new data.

As you can see from these two different source code listings, you cannot view server-side scripts from the client. All the heavy lifting happens before the code gets shoved down the pipe to the client. After emerging from Web server, the code appears on the other end as normal HTML. This also means that you can't tell which server-side scripting language was used unless something in the header gives it away. These scripts happen to have been written in PHP and the MySQL database; you can learn all about these techniques in Part II of this book.

Two tickets to paradise

There are client-side ways and server-side ways to accomplish many tasks. Sending e-mail, for example: the client-side way is to open up the mail client software with a preaddressed blank e-mail message when the user clicks a MAILTO link; the server-side method is to make the user fill out a form, the contents of which are formatted as e-mail and sent via an SMTP server. You can also choose between client methods and server methods of browser-sniffing, form-validation, pull-down lists, and arithmetic calculation. Sometimes there are subtle but meaningful differences in functionality (server-side pull-downs can be assembled dynamically, client-side cannot), but not always.

How to choose? Know your audience. Server-side methods are generally a bit slower at run time due to the extra transits but don't assume anything about your visitor's browser capabilities and take less developer time to maintain. This makes them good for mass-market and educational sites. If you're one of the lucky few who's absolutely positive your visitors all have up-to-date browsers and good throughput, you can feel free to go wild with the scripting and graphics. Finally, remember that you can use PHP to generate static HTML and JavaScript — thus enjoying the best of both worlds, as we will explain later.

What Is Server-Side Scripting Good For?

The client looks good, but the server cooks good. What server-side scripting lacks in eye-candy sex appeal, it more than makes up for in sheer usefulness. Most Web users probably interact with the products of server-side scripting on a daily if not an hourly basis.

There's one category of thing that the server just absolutely can't help you with: real-time 3-D shoot-'em-ups. The more immediately responsive and graphics-intensive a project needs to be, the less suitable PHP will be for it. At the moment, the Web is simply too slow a channel for these purposes (although broadband pioneers are eager to change that).

On the other hand, most of the truly useful aspects of the Web are perfectly served by server-side scripting languages like PHP:

- ✦ Content sites (both production and display)
- ✦ Community features (forums, bulletin boards, and so on)
- ✦ E-mail (Webmail, mail forwarding)
- ✦ Customer-support and technical-support systems
- ✦ Advertising networks
- ✦ Web-delivered business applications
- ✦ Directories and membership rolls
- ✦ Surveys, polls, and tests
- ✦ Filling out and submitting forms online
- ✦ Personalization technologies
- ✦ Groupware
- ✦ Catalog, brochure, and informational sites
- ✦ Basically any other application that needs to connect a back-end server (database, mail, LDAP, and so on) to a Web server

PHP can handle all these essential tasks, and then some.

But enough rhetoric! Now that you have a firm grasp of the differences between client-side and server-side technologies, it's on to the practical stuff. Next, we show you how to get, install, and configure PHP for yourself (or find someone to do it for you).

Programming versus scripting

The difference between programming and scripting is being increasingly blurred by recent developments in programming languages. For instance, PHP definitely uses most of the same control structures as other programming languages. However, fully-interpreted HTML-embedded languages such as ASP are still considered to be on the scripting side of the line, whereas separately compiled binaries are a definite mark of programming. But since PHP 4 is now dynamically compiled (the compiled binary is stored and reused until the source code changes), it's officially a "real" programming language—and don't let anyone tell you otherwise. This change accounts for much of the screaming speed of PHP 4, which moves into the same class as Perl.

Summary

To understand what PHP (or any server-side scripting technology) can do for you, it's crucial to have a firm grasp on the division of labor between client and server. In this chapter, we worked through examples of plain static HTML; HTML with client-side additions like JavaScript and Cascading Style Sheets; and PHP-generated Web pages viewed from both the server and the client.

Client-side scripting can be visually attractive and quickly responsive to user inputs, but anything beyond the most basic HTML is subject to browser variation. Static client-side scripts also require more developer time to maintain and update, since pages cannot be dynamically generated from a constantly changing data store. Server-side programming and scripting languages, such as PHP, are able to connect databases and other servers to Web pages.

PHP 4 differs architecturally from some other server-side tools, and even from PHP 3. It is dynamically compiled, which makes it faster at run time. PHP 4 also separates the scripting engine, Zend, from the scripting language.

✦   ✦   ✦

Getting Started with PHP

In this chapter, we'll discuss the pros and cons of the various Web hosting options: outsourcing, self-hosting, and various compromises. Then we'll give detailed directions for installing PHP and finish with a few tips on finding the right development tool. By the end of the chapter, you should be ready to write your first script.

Hosting versus DIY

The first major decision you need to make is: who will host your PHP-enabled Web site, you or a Web hosting service? Also, will you need a separate development setup; and if so, who will host it? If you've already made these decisions, feel free to skip right to the installation section of this chapter.

The ISP option

Remote hosting is becoming a more popular option as a range of companies begin to offer PHP-enabled Web sites. These are some basic pros and cons to keep in mind.

The good

Outsourced hosting has a lot of advantages. The ISP will (in theory) handle many of the crucial technical and administrative details necessary to keep a site running, such as:

- ✦ Hardware
- ✦ Software upgrades
- ✦ InterNIC registration, IP addressing, DNS
- ✦ Mail servers (POP/IMAP and SMTP)

✦ Bandwidth

✦ Power supply

✦ Backups

✦ Security

There's no cozier feeling than the one you get just before you fall asleep, knowing that some poor schmo at your ISP will be getting the pager message in the middle of the night if something goes wrong with your site. Lurking crackers, downed power lines, munged backup tapes — all that is your host's headache now.

Web hosting is also extremely cost effective in most situations. PHP on Linux or one of the BSDs is almost ridiculously inexpensive and widely available. Currently, only a few companies offer PHP on an NT server platform, and some of them can be pricey. As the Miracles so eloquently urge: you better shop around (shop, shop ooh).

The bad

Of course, there can be some serious disadvantages to ISP hosting too.

Most of these have to do with control. When you go ISP, you're basically a guest in someone else's house and have to play by their rules. Maybe you're a welcome paying guest, a veritable parlor boarder — but the fact remains that when you live in someone else's establishment, you can't just strip down to your undies and lipsync your way through a high-volume version of "Proud Mary" on the dining room table whenever you feel like it. People are trying to eat, pal.

The most central issue for PHP is module versus CGI. PHP runs best and fastest as a — module, in other words built into the Web server itself rather than running as a separate process. Almost everyone prefers to use the module version if they can. However, many ISPs prefer to run the CGI version because it's much simpler to administer safely. There are Web hosting services now that offer the module version, but they tend to be the smaller ones with less bandwidth to offer. There are many other issues like this, where the desires of the individual PHP user conflict with the convenience of the hosting service.

A good rule of thumb is: the more common your needs are, the more possible and appropriate it is to outsource your hosting. The more oddball and/or bleeding edge your needs are, the more you're going to be pushed to host your own whether you want to or not. Of course the unspoken realpolitik addendum to this is: the bigger you are and the more money you have to spend, the more weight you have available to throw around.

There are a few factors that will make it considerably more difficult for you to find a hosting service:

✦ Generally objectionable content (hate, porn)

✦ Unsolicited mailings, a.k.a spam

✦ Content that attracts crackers (security info)

✦ Potentially legally actionable content

✦ Need for unusual server-side hardware, OS, or software

✦ Need for super-high bandwidth, especially if unpredictable

If you're in one of these situations, you need to mention it up front — you'll just get the boot anyway once they find out. Chances are good that you won't get to do much shopping around — if you can find any hosting situation, grab it before they change their minds, and look for a better deal later.

Finally, we must mention the most important negative factor of all: the frustration and anxiety caused by a bad hosting experience. Words cannot describe the tooth grinding, stomach churning, scream suppressing state of existence caused by your site crashing just when you've been featured on Slashdot, thereby making you look like a total technoposer as well as losing all the good pub you so richly deserve. That's not even mentioning more common problems like lost e-mail, disappearing DNS, suffering through an hour-long telephone wait just to talk to some tech supportie who's never been within ten feet of a server, never getting a response to your polite e-mails, and being overbilled for the privilege (not that we're bitter, and anyway our lawyer says we can't name any names).

Bottom line: if you choose hosting, you do so at your own peril. Always be ready to make a quick getaway, which might entail eschewing the cheapest or most fully-featured deal in favor of one without long-term contracts and/or prepayments. Conversely, don't be an utter jerk when you deal with them. If you've never out-sourced hosting before, take the time to understand the difference between things you can legitimately blame on the Web host (bad tech support), and things that are basically Acts of Fate (Internet traffic in your entire metro area goes out).

The details

If you've decided on the hosting option, you will enjoy a plethora of choices in today's marketplace. However, novice shoppers should be aware that the word "ISP" (or even "Web host") can mean almost anything these days. Table 3-1 provides a guide to the specializations and their most appropriate uses (the companies mentioned are intended as examples only; this does not constitute an endorsement or recommendation of their services).

Table 3-1
Varieties of ISPs

Type of ISP	Keywords	PHP Users
Consumer ISP (AOL, RoadRunner)	Dialup, ISDN, home DSL, ADSL, cable modem	Tiny sites (such as résumé of a Linux/BSD wiz)
Free Web hosting (Linuxbox.com)	Free under certain conditions	Nonprofit or open source sites
Commercial Web hosting	Web hosting, virtual hosting, colocation, dedicated server	Most outsourced sites
Site development	Design, promotion, custom development, consulting	Sites that want to outsource Web development as well as hosting
Access provider (@Work, UUNet)	T-1, DS-3, DSL, Frame Relay	Self-hosters

Although finding a good Web hosting service sometimes seems as difficult as finding a lifelong mate, there are now listing resources to make it easier:

```
http://hosts.php.net
http://www.od-site.com/php
http://www.ispcheck.com
```

Pay special attention to the user comments, good and bad. Ask your friends and colleagues about their experiences. Search the PHP user list archives — people occasionally make recommendations and comment on bad experiences they've had.

Probably the single most contentious post-signup issue is throughput. Be wary of the phrase "unlimited traffic/bandwidth/hits." Recall the query of the wise middle-aged baseball manager when the elderly team owner offered him the job for life: "Whose life are we talking about?" Analogously, a level of bandwidth that would never be tested by Joe's Epic Poetry Appreciation Site is probably not going to feel quite so roomy to a Web site featuring free streaming video of scantily clad supermodels. Before you sign up for any deal, you need to assess where you're going to fall on this continuum.

Tip   How to guesstimate your bandwidth needs: 1GB of traffic per month is equal to 100,000 views of files averaging 10K (including graphics, text, ads unless they're being third-party served, everything — measure from a client, not the server).

Be extra careful of the amount of disk space that comes with your service plan, especially if you have a large or graphics-heavy site. If you exceed the limit, you will generally be charged exorbitant rates for every fraction of a megabyte of extra space per month. One thing that contributes to this problem is log files; delete them or download them to some cheaper form of storage on a regular basis.

The self-hosting option: pros and cons

Self-hosting is becoming a realistic option for more sites as the price of connectivity goes down. It's the ultimate in command and control, and it offers substantial security advantages — if you have the expertise to take advantage of them. Running your own setup means problems get solved faster because you don't have to waste time hanging on a tech support line, and many just feel it's more fun: there's just no substitute for being able to put your hands on the actual server machine whenever you want. Finally, if you have unusual, objectionable, or cutting-edge needs, you may be forced to serve your own site whether you want to or not.

On the flip side, self-hosting requires tons more work and can be quite a bit more expensive, especially for the smallish-to-midsize site. Plus, a self-hosted site is only going to be as good as your available skill set. So if no one on your team knows much about security, you can expect to have security problems (although at least you'll be aware of your weaknesses, unlike the false comfort that comes when your hosting service fails to inform you their security expert quit three months ago).

More existentially, you have no one to blame but yourself if things go wrong. If you can look yourself in the mirror every morning and think "It's all on me and I feel great," you have the necessary self-confidence for self-hosting.

Compromise solutions

Of course, outsourcing and self-hosting are actually poles on a continuum. There are several "compromise" solutions that attempt to offer the best of both worlds.

Colocation

Colocation means you crate up your server machine and ship it to the hosting company, who will hook it up to their network and monitor it for you. You are responsible for purchasing, licensing, insuring, installing, configuring, and maintaining all software and hardware, except the uninterruptible power supply. The host does not mess with your box at all, beyond the occasional reboot — for which they generally charge you extra. If you want any technical support whatsoever, you must either go to the location yourself or pay hundreds of dollars an hour for the staff's gentle ministrations — and if you're in a colocation situation, chances are good you're using products for which they have no training.

Dedicated server

A dedicated server is just what it sounds like: the hosting service will buy a server, fit it out to your tastes (on your dime, of course), and hook it up to their network; then all the processor cycles belong to you. Generally you get technical support with your service. This is much more secure than a shared server environment, and relatively cost-effective for a midsize or larger site.

Outsource production, self-host development

This option involves two complete setups: an outsourced production site and an identical in-house development server or servers. Dividing things up this way can offer the best of both worlds, letting someone else take the emergency pager messages in the middle of the night while still enjoying the intimacy of playing on your very own server. If you're located in an area with limited connectivity choices, this option can be a lifesaver. It is also one of the best choices for larger sites with more developers.

Installing PHP

If you've decided to completely outsource PHP hosting, feel free to skip the rest of this chapter. These installation instructions apply only to self-hosters.

Before you can begin

Before you can install PHP on any platform, you need:

✦ A server machine with enough RAM for your OS

✦ A UNIX or Windows 95/98/NT/2000 operating system installed

✦ A working dedicated Internet connection if this is a production site; and/or installation on an intranet for a development site; or neither if this is a totally stand-alone setup (although without an Internet connection, you must find another source for the necessary software packages)

Help for these prerequisites is beyond the scope of this book. You might want to look at the following sources for networking information:

```
http://164.109.153.102/idgsearchresult.asp?searchtype=2&keyword
=networking
```

```
http://www.linuxdoc.org/HOWTO/HOWTO-INDEX/howtos.html
```

If you plan to install PHP on Windows, you'll also need:

✦ A working PHP-supported Web server. Under PHP 3, IIS/PWS was the easiest choice because a module version of PHP was available for it; but PHP 4 offers a much wider selection of modules for Windows.

✦ An installed PHP-supported database (if you plan to use one)

✦ The path to your Windows directory (usually `C:\Windows` for Windows 95/98; you'll be prompted when installing on NT or Windows 2000)

✦ For Windows 95 only, the DCOM update, which you can download for free from `http://download.microsoft.com/msdownload/dcom/95/x86/en/dcom95.exe`

✦ The PHP Windows binary distribution (download it at `www.php.net/downloads.php`)

✦ A utility to unzip files (search `http://download.cnet.com` for PC file compression utilities)

If you plan to install PHP on UNIX, you'll need:

✦ The PHP source distribution (`www.php.net/downloads.php`)

✦ The latest Apache source distribution (`www.apache.org/dist/` — look for the highest number that ends with the ".tar.gz" suffix)

✦ A working PHP-supported database if you plan to use one

✦ Any other supported software to which PHP must connect (mail server, BC math package, JDK, and so forth)

✦ An ANSI C compiler

✦ Gnu make (starting with PHP 4, it can't be any other make version — you can freely download it at `www.gnu.org/software/make`)

✦ Bison and flex (Enter **"find . -name bison –print"** and **"find . -name flex –print"** from the /usr directory to check if you have them already or just let gcc check for them during the make process. If not, you can download Bison from `www.gnu.org/software/bison` and flex from `ftp://ftp.ee.lbl.gov`)

✦ The path to your HTTP configuration file(s). Until recently these were `access.conf`, `httpd.conf`, and `srm.conf` for Apache; but now they have been combined into a single file called `httpd.conf`. This will vary depending on the specific OS, distribution, Web server, and version you're running; you can use `find` to pin down the location.

✦ The path to your Apache source files (usually `/usr/local/apache_1.3.x`)

✦ The path to your Apache daemon a.k.a. httpd (usually `/usr/local/bin`)

Now you're ready to actually install PHP.

Tip   Remember that any extra servers or software libraries to which PHP will connect need to be installed *before* you build. A database is the most common type of external server. Other examples are the BCmath package, an IMAP server, the mcrypt library, and the Expat XML parser (unless you use Apache, with which it is bundled).

The difference between building as an Apache module and building as a CGI executable is very small. In fact, it comes down to leaving off the `-with-apache` or `-with-apxs` flags when configuring. Many users compile both the module and the CGI versions at the same time for convenience.

Installation procedures

Due to PHP's strong commitment to cross-platform operability, there are far too many specific installation methods to fully list here. We have tried to cover what we believe to be the most popular platforms for PHP, but trying to write out the installation instructions for every possible operating system and Web server would have resulted in a prohibitively long chapter.

Windows NT/2000 and IIS

The Windows NT/2000 installation of PHP 4 running IIS 4.0 is very simple. The main thing to remember is that the directions for Windows NT/2000 *are not applicable* to Windows 95/98 and vice versa. Later in the chapter there are notes on a 95/98 installation; this set applies to Windows NT/2000 only.

1. Extract the binary archive using your unzip utility. Place the whole thing in a `C:\PHP` folder.

2. Copy the `php.ini-dist` file in the PHP folder, paste it into your Windows directory, and rename it `php.ini`. This file must exist first, or the rest of the installation will not succeed!

3. Go to your System32 directory, which is under the Windows directory. You should see a large number of DLL files there. Look for `msvcrt.dll`; if it doesn't exist, you will need to copy and paste it from the PHP file. Also copy and paste the `php4ts.dll` into the System32 directory.

4. Start the Microsoft Management Console, a.k.a. Internet Service Manager. You should see a graphical representation of all the Web sites you're running on this server (usually as little globes).

5. Right-click the icon representing the Web site you want to PHP-enable (creating a new one first if necessary), and select Properties. Click the ISAPI filters tab. Click Add to add a new filter. Give the filter name as **PHP**, and the location as **C:\PHP\php4isapi.dll**. You must do this entire step separately for each site you want to run PHP.

6. Click the Home directory tab. Check to make sure that the Execute permissions radio button has been selected. Click Configuration. Click Add under Application Mappings. Type **C:\PHP\php4isapi.dll** into the Executable box, type **.php** into the Extension box, leave Method exclusions blank, and check the Script Engine check box.

7. Stop and restart the WWW service. Go to the Start menu, Settings, Control Panel, Services. Scroll down the list to IIS Admin Service. Select it and click Stop. After it stops (the status message will inform you), select World Wide Web Publishing Service and click Start. Stopping and restarting the service from within Internet Service Manager (by right-clicking the globe icon) will not suffice. Since this is Windows, you may now wish to reboot.

8. Start Notepad. Type: **<?php phpinfo(); ?>**. Save into your Web server's document root as `info.txt`, then rename as `info.php`. Start any Web browser and browse the file—you must always use a URL (`www.testdomain.com/info.php`) or HTTP request (`http://hostname/info.php`) rather than a filename (`C:\inetpub\wwwroot\info.php`). You should see a long table of information about your new PHP4 installation. Congratulations!

> **Tip**   Some Windows users have reported they must put their `php.ini` file in the same directory as their `php.exe` executable. This is not ideal for security reasons, since it would be better to keep this file out of the Web tree entirely—but since the OS is closed source, the reason for the problem is not yet understood well enough to fix it.

UNIX and Apache

The first time you build your own HTTP daemon from source, you might be a little apprehensive. But the process is fairly straightforward, and it's worth the effort to compile your Web server yourself instead of being dependent on other people's RPMs, which are often weeks or months out of date. And hey, it's a genuine rush when it works!

For those who have already done this with an earlier version of PHP, the procedure is exactly the same—only it takes longer than before.

> **Caution**   Your Red Hat or Mandrake Linux installation may have come with RPM versions of Apache and PHP. You *must* remove these packages before compiling your new PHP! In addition, you may have RPM versions of third-party servers, such as MySQL or PostgreSQL, which are installed differently than their source counterparts. If you encounter problems, blow away the RPM and reinstall from source.

In the following directions, the code fragments are what you will type into each shell prompt.

> **Tip**   Remember to log in as the root user first.

1. If you haven't already done so, unzip and untar your Apache source distribution. Unless you have a reason to do otherwise, /usr/local is the standard place.

```
gunzip -c apache_1.3.x.tar.gz
tar -xf apache_1.3.x.tar
cd apache_1.3.x
./configure
```

2. Unzip and untar your PHP source distribution. Unless you have a reason to do otherwise, /usr/local is the standard place. If Apache and PHP are not under the same directory, you must replace every ".." below with the full pathname to the relevant package.

```
cd ..
gunzip -c php-4.x.tar.gz
tar -xvf php-4.x.tar
cd php-4.x
```

3. Configure your build. (Configuring PHP is a topic so large and important that it would not fit into this chapter, so please flip over to Chapter 31 for more information.) The most common are the options to build as an Apache module, which you almost certainly want, and with specific database support. Java and XML support are also increasingly popular. The example build here is an Apache module with MySQL and XML support, but your flags may be completely different.

```
./configure --with-apache=../apache_1.3.x --with-mysql --with-
xml --enable-track-vars
```

4. Make and install the PHP module.

```
make
make install
```

5. Configure and make the Apache daemon. In the sample that follows, /etc/httpd is the path to our HTTP configuration file (e.g. /conf/httpd.conf) — if yours are located elsewhere, substitute the correct path for your system. If you're using a recent version of Apache with configuration files in apache_1.3.x/conf and you have no conflicting pre-existing configuration files, you can leave off the -prefix flag.

```
cd ../apache_1.3.x
./configure --prefix=/etc/httpd --activate-module=src/
modules/php4/libphp4.a
make
```

6. Stop and replace the httpd executable. There are several different ways to stop and start the httpd; if you already use a different method that's known to be good, by all means continue to use it. If necessary, replace the /usr/local/bin here with the correct path for your HTTP daemon. If you are absolutely positive you have no pre-existing httpd, you may run make install in lieu of the directions below. In a high-availability environment, you might wish to postpone this step until after you've configured PHP and Apache (7. and 8. below) so Web service will be interrupted as briefly as possible.

```
cd src/support
./apachectl stop
cd ..
cp httpd /usr/local/bin
```

7. Set the php.ini file. Edit this file; see the options listed in Chapter 31. We highly recommend new users set error reporting to E_ALL (15) at this point.

```
cd ../../php-4.x
cp php.ini-dist /usr/local/lib/php.ini
```

8. Tell your Web server what extension(s) you want to identify PHP files (.php is the standard, but you can use .html, .phtml, or whatever you want). Go to your HTTP configuration files (/etc/httpd/conf or whatever your path is), and open httpd.conf (or srm.conf if you use the older system of Apache configuration files) with a text editor. Add at least one PHP extension directive as shown in the first line below; in the second line, we've added another handler to have all HTML files parsed as PHP:

```
AddType application/x-httpd-php .php
AddType application/x-httpd-php .html
```

9. Restart your server. Every time you change your HTTP configuration or php.ini files, you must stop and start your server again. An HUP signal will not suffice.

```
cd ../apache_1.3.x/src/support
./apachectl start
```

10. Set the document rootdirectory permissions to world-executable. PHP files need only be world-readable (644). If necessary, replace /home/httpd/html/php with your document root below.

```
chmod 755 /home/httpd/html/php
```

11. Open a text editor. Type: **<?php phpinfo(); ?>**. Save in your Web server's document root as info.php. Start any Web browser and browse the file — you must always use a URL (www.testdomain.com/info.php) or HTTP request (http://localhost/info.php) rather than a filename (/home/httpd/html/info.php). You should see a long table of information about your new PHP 4 installation. Congratulations!

Windows 95/98 and PWS

It's unfortunate but common that newbie Windows users want to check out PHP at the lowest cost and risk (or so they think) and decide to do so by installing it on a Windows 95/98 box with Personal Web Server. This is not at all a good idea!

The problem is that Windows 95/98 wasn't intended to be used as a server platform, and it isn't going to go along quietly. Therefore, to install a Web server and third-party scripting engine, you're going to have to perform fairly major surgery by delving into the Registry. If something goes wrong here, your whole system could be damaged. Furthermore, if you decide you don't want to keep PHP on that computer, it's not at all a trivial matter to cleanly uninstall—you have to go back into the Registry and exactly reverse your actions from the first time. There's a script you can use to install PHP, but none to uninstall.

If you're determined to go through with this despite our warnings, here are the directions:

1. For Windows 95, install the DCOM update.

2. Extract the binary archive using your unzip utility. Place the whole thing in a C:\PHP folder.

3. Copy the php.ini-dist file from the PHP folder, paste it into your Windows directory, and rename it php.ini. This file must exist first, or the rest of the installation will not succeed!

4. Go to your System directory, which is under the Windows directory. You should see a large number of DLL files there. Look for msvcrt.dll; if it doesn't exist, you will need to copy and paste it from the PHP file. Also copy and paste the php4ts.dll into the System directory.

5. Open your php.ini file. Change the extension_dir setting to point to C:\PHP (or whatever you named the PHP directory). Set the doc_root variable to point to your Web server's document root directory (C:\Webroot). Uncomment the extension=php_*.dll lines of your choice to load the indicated modules at run time.

6. Tell PWS where to find the PHP 4 ISAPI module. To do this, add the ISAPI path to the PWS-php4.reg file that came with your PHP installation (the double backslashes are escaped backslashes). If you've installed somewhere other than C:\PHP, you will need to alter that portion of the path:

   ".php"="C:\\PHP\\php4isapi.dll"

7. Open the PWS Manager. Right-click on your document root folder (for example, C:\Webroot) and select Properties. Check the "Execute" checkbox and confirm. Reboot.

8. Start Notepad. Type: **<?php phpinfo(); ?>**. Save into your Web server's document root as info.txt, then rename as info.php. Start any Web browser and browse info.php—you must always use a URL (www.testdomain.com/info.php) or HTTP request (http://hostname/info.php) rather than a filename (C:\inetpub\wwwroot\info.php). You should see a long table of information about your new PHP 4 installation. Congratulations!

Tip   Even though it's possible to use folder names with spaces in them under Windows, we recommend you do not do so for PHP-enabled directories because it can cause installer problems.

Other Web servers

PHP 4 has been successfully built and run with many other Web servers, such as Netscape Enterprise Server, Xitami, Zeus, and thttpd. The development team has also announced forthcoming NSAPI (and possibly other) module support. Unfortunately, at press time installation procedures for all of these were undocumented or severely underdocumented. Please see the following references for more installation information.

Apache for Windows (CGI version):

```
http://www.apache.org/docs/windows.html
```

fhttpd:

```
http://www.fhttpd.org/www/install.html
```

Omni

```
http://www.umcsd.k12.or.us/php/win32install.html
```

Development tools

PHP does not have a plush graphical development environment with wizards and check boxes and drag-and-drop icons. If that sort of thing is important to you, you can use a WYSIWIG editor to format the page and then add PHP functionality by hand later. The downside of this strategy is, of course, that machine-written code is often not very human-readable — but one must suffer to be pretty.

Caution

Be particularly careful with Microsoft FrontPage, which seems to cause problems for many users. At a minimum, you will need to enable (by choosing the option in your php.ini file) and use ASP-style tags; or use JavaScript-style tags consistently, which can be a pain.

Most PHP users seem to prefer text editors. Generally, these products will afford you a modest amount of help, such as syntax highlighting, brace matching, or tag closing — most of which is about helping you avoid stupid mistakes and/or functioning as a handy reference (what's the HTML code for a lowercase e-accent-grave again?) rather than actually writing the script for you.

Remember that your development client doesn't have to be on the same operating system as the server. This is particularly valuable if you're using a UNIX server, where (to paraphrase *The Blues Brothers*) "We have both kinds of editor: emacs and vi." It must be admitted that Macintosh, Be, and Windows all have a wider selection of slicker, more user-friendly text editors. UNIX, on the other hand, makes it easy to support multiple client OSes. Many development shops take advantage of this "best of all worlds" situation.

Table 3-2
Popular PHP Editors by Platform

Platform	Product	Description
Macintosh	BBEdit (`www.barebones.com`)	Many Mac developers can't imagine life without it. Included in the Mac version of WYSIWYG package Macromedia Dreamweaver.
UNIX	emacs (`www.emacs.org`) and xemacs (`www.xemacs.org`)	Not for the faint of heart. PHP syntax highlighting for xemacs (might work for emacs) is available at `http://www.cs.huji.ac.il/~baryudin/php3_mode.html`. vim (`www.vim.org`): An improved variant of vi. This is the kinder, gentler UNIX hacker's editor, with a notably friendly community and beautiful PHP syntax highlighting. Available on almost every OS.
Windows	HomeSite (`www.allaire.com/homesite`)	Perennially popular Windows commercial text editor. Included in the Windows version of WYSIWYG package Macromedia Dreamweaver. Notepad (included with all Windows systems): Believe it or not, many people build fine sites using the crudest of tools.

Keith Edmunds maintains a longer running list of PHP-suitable text editors, many available at no or low cost:

`http://www.itworks.demon.co.uk/phpeditors.htm`

Tip   We have heard rumors that Zend is working on a full-featured IDE for PHP development — but at press time these remain nothing but rumors.

Take a deep breath — after all that installing and configuring, you should now be ready to write your first PHP script.

Summary

Before you can use PHP, you need to decide whether you will self-host, outsource, or adopt a compromise solution, such as colocation. Some important factors in the decision are cost, size and traffic of site, unusual hardware or software needs, type of content, and desire for control. The best candidate for external Web hosting is a small site without unusual requirements.

If you decide to self-host or maintain a development server, detailed installation instructions are provided above for the most common platforms. PHP 4 supports many other Web servers, but installation directions for most of them are undocumented at press time.

Finally, you may be wondering which development tools are best adapted to PHP. At the moment there is no PHP-specific IDE; most PHP developers simply use their favorite text editor. It is possible to add PHP to the product of a WYSIWYG editor, but it can be messy.

✦   ✦   ✦

Adding PHP to HTML

◆ ◆ ◆ ◆

In This Chapter

Escaping into
PHP mode

Choosing PHP
tag styles

Writing a Hello
World program
in PHP

Including and
requiring files

◆ ◆ ◆ ◆

After all those preliminary exertions, we finally get to the point of writing our first PHP scripts. Here you'll learn about PHP mode, PHP tags, and how to include and require other files. You'll also write your very first PHP script.

Your HTML Is Already PHP-Compliant!

PHP is already perfectly at home with HTML—in fact, it must generally be embedded within HTML. As you'll see later, PHP can use some of the cleverer parts of the HTML standard, such as forms, to do all kinds of useful things.

Anything that is compatible with HTML on the client side is also compatible with PHP. PHP could not care less about chunks of JavaScript, calls to music and animation, applets, or anything else on the client side. PHP will simply ignore those parts, and the Web server will happily pass them on to the client.

It should thus be clear that you can use any method of developing Web pages, and simply add PHP to that. If you're comfortable having teams work on each page using huge multi-media graphics suites, you can keep on doing that. The general point is, you don't need to change tools or workflow order—just do what you've been doing, and add the server-side functionality at the end.

Escaping from HTML

So how do you indicate the PHP sections of your HTML document? By using special PHP tags at the beginning and end of each PHP section. This process is called "escaping from HTML."

Everything within these tags is understood by the module or CGI to be PHP. Everything outside of these tags does not concern the server and will simply be passed along and left for the client to sort out whether it's HTML or JavaScript or something else.

There are four styles of PHP tags, and different rationales for using them. However, some of it is simply personal preference and what the individual programmer is comfortable with.

Canonical PHP tags

The PHP tag style that is most universally effective is

```
<?php   ?>
```

If you use this style, you can be positive that your tags will always be correctly interpreted. Unless you have a good reason to prefer one of the other styles, it's best to use this one.

You *must* choose this style to write XML in PHP. The reason is that XML uses the short-open tag style for its own purposes.

Short-open (SGML-style) tags

Short or short-open tags look like this:

```
<?   ?>
```

They are, as one might expect, the shortest option. Those who escape into and out of HTML frequently in each script will be attracted by the prospect of fewer keystrokes. However, the price of shorter tags is pretty high. You must do one of three things to enable PHP to recognize the tags:

1. Choose the -enable-short-tags configuration option when you're building PHP.

2. Enable the short_open_tag setting in your php.ini file. This option must be disabled to use XML with PHP.

3. Use the short_tags() function.

Additionally, support for short-open tags was not enabled in the beta versions of PHP 4. This gap forced many developers to convert over to the canonical style, at least temporarily, and pointed to a possible shaky future for the short-open tag. Beginners should be encouraged to start off with the canonical style tag if possible.

ASP-style tags

ASP-style tags look like this:

```
<%     %>
```

People who use FrontPage as a development tool often choose this style. To use ASP-style tags, you will need to set the configuration option in your `php.ini` file. Obviously, if you use ASP-style tags and the `.asp` suffix (which you may wish to do if you're converting from an ASP site), you will need to disable ASP on your IIS server.

HTML script tags

This means

```
<SCRIPT LANGUAGE="PHP">   </SCRIPT>
```

Although this is effective and also gets around the FrontPage problems, it can be cumbersome in certain situations, such as quick pop-in variable replacement. In particular, be careful if you use lots of JavaScript on your site since the close-script tags are fatally ambiguous. The HTML script tag is best used for fairly sizable blocks of PHP code.

Hello World

Now we're ready to write our first PHP program. Open up a new file in your preferred editor. Type:

```
<HTML>
<HEAD>
<TITLE>My first PHP program</TITLE>
</HEAD>

<BODY>
<?php print("Hello, cruel world"); ?>
</BODY>
</HTML>
```

In most browsers, nothing but the PHP section is strictly necessary. However, it's a good idea to get in the habit of always using a normal HTML structure in which to embed your PHP.

If you don't see something pretty close to the output shown in Figure 4-1, we have a problem—most likely some kind of installation or configuration glitch.

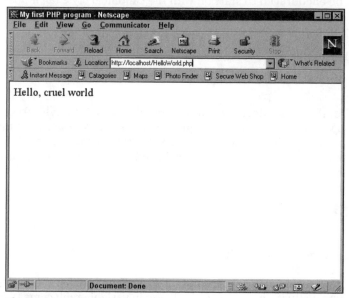

Figure 4-1: A first PHP script

Refer back to Chapter 3 for installation instructions and forward to Chapter 31 for configuration options. Chapter 15 diagnoses some common early problems and gives debugging hints.

Tip   Anyone who's programmed for any length of time is bored stiff with the obligatory Hello World script. If you're in this category, you can try adding a line to the file above with the phpinfo() function. We will explain the contents of phpinfo() in more detail in Chapter 31, but for the moment it's an impressive way to test out your installation.

In and out of PHP mode

At any given moment in a PHP script, you are either in PHP mode or you're out of it in HTML. There's no middle ground. Anything within the PHP tags is PHP; everything outside is plain HTML as far as the server is concerned.

You can escape into PHP mode with giddy abandon, as often and as briefly or lengthily as necessary. For example:

```
<?php $id = 1; ?>
<FORM METHOD="POST" ACTION="registration.php">
```

```
<P>First name:
<INPUT TYPE="TEXT" NAME="firstname" SIZE=20>
<P>Last name:
<INPUT TYPE="TEXT" NAME="lastname" SIZE=20>
<P>Rank:
<INPUT TYPE="TEXT" NAME="rank" SIZE=10>
<INPUT TYPE="HIDDEN" NAME="serial number" VALUE="<?php
print("$id"); ?>">
<INPUT TYPE="SUBMIT" VALUE="INPUT">
</FORM>
```

Notice that things that happened in the first PHP mode instance — in this case, a variable being assigned — are still valid in the second. In the next chapter, you'll learn more about what happens to variables when you skip in and out of PHP mode. In Chapter 14, you'll also learn about different styles of using PHP mode.

Including files

Another way you can add PHP to your HTML is by putting it in a separate file and calling it by using PHP's `include` function. For example, a file named `girlfriend.inc` contains nothing but the following content:

```
<?php $girlfriend = "Jane";
print("$girlfriend"); ?>
```

which can be called from a Web page this way:

```
<HTML>
<HEAD>
<TITLE>A sincere letter</TITLE>
</HEAD>

<BODY>
<P>I implore you to believe me when I tell you I cannot live
without you, my darling <?php include("girlfriend.inc"); ?>.
The name "<?php include("girlfriend.inc"); ?>" resounds in my
ears like the memory of distant temple bells.
</BODY>
</HTML>
```

Not only will you get the nice result shown in Figure 4-2, but when your affections change, you can reuse the Web page by simply altering one variable in `girlfriend.inc`! (Okay, so maybe that's a silly example — but later you'll learn a lot of uses for this technique that are less silly.)

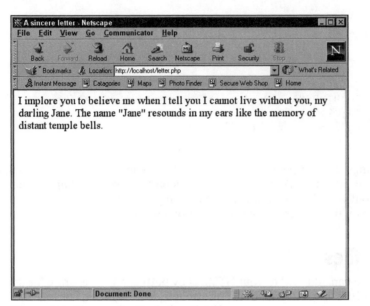

Figure 4-2: The result of including the file

However, a big warning: `include` simply passes along the contents of the included file *as text*. Many people think that because the `include` function occurs inside PHP mode, the included file will also be in PHP mode. This is not true! Actually, the server escapes back into HTML mode at the beginning of each included file and silently returns to PHP mode at the end, just in time to catch the semicolon.

If you leave off the PHP tags in `girlfriend.inc`, like so,

```
$girlfriend = "Jane";
print("$girlfriend");
```

you will be in a lot of trouble (especially if Jane knows PHP), because now the full text of `girlfriend.inc` will appear as plain HTML within your Web page!

To make sure this doesn't happen, you need to always say when you intend something to be PHP. Any part of the included file that needs to be executed as PHP should be enclosed in valid PHP tags.

Some people use the `require` construct instead of the `include` function in this situation, but `include` is more forgiving in most cases On the other hand, `require` is faster. This is explained further in the chapter on Functions.

Because the `include` function simply passes text rather than PHP, it can also be used to include chunks of plain HTML. For example, you can put a copyright date in a text file, and then `include` it on every page of your Web site. This makes updating the copyright notice much quicker and less repetitive.

Summary

PHP is easy to embed in HTML. You can use whatever HTML-production method you're already comfortable with, and simply add the PHP sections later. PHP additions can range from simply echoing a single-digit integer, to writing long chunks of code.

Every PHP block, short or long, is set off by PHP tags. There are several styles of PHP tag, but beginners should be encouraged to use the canonical style. You can also include PHP in files by using the `include()` or `require()` functions — but the contents of the included files will not be recognized as PHP unless surrounded by PHP tags.

✦   ✦   ✦

Syntax, Variables, and Output

In this chapter, we cover the basic syntax of PHP — the rules
that all well-formed PHP code must follow. We also explain
how to use variables to store and retrieve information as your
PHP code executes. Finally, we look at the simplest ways to
display text that will show up in your user's browser window.

PHP Is Forgiving

The first and most important thing to say about the PHP language is that it tries to be as forgiving as possible. Programming
languages vary quite a bit in terms of how stringent a syntax
they enforce. Pickiness can be a *good* thing because it helps
make sure that the code you're writing is really what you mean.
If you are writing a program to control a nuclear reactor and you
forget to assign a variable, it is far better to have the program be
rejected than to have the behavior be different from what you
intended. PHP's design philosophy, however, is at the other end
of the spectrum. Because PHP started life as a handy utility for
making quick-and-dirty Web pages, it emphasizes convenience
for the programmer over correctness; rather than have a programmer do the extra work of redundantly specifying what is
meant by a piece of code, PHP requires the minimum and then
tries its best to figure out what was meant. Among other things,
this means that certain syntactical features that show up in
other languages, such as variable declarations and function
prototypes, are simply not necessary.

With that said, though, PHP can't read your mind; it has a
minimum set of syntactical rules that your code must follow.
Whenever you see the words "parse error" in your browser
window instead of the cool Web page you thought you had just
written, it means that you've broken these rules to the point
that PHP has had to give up on your page.

HTML Is Not PHP

The second most important thing to understand about PHP syntax is that it applies only within PHP. Because PHP is embedded in HTML documents, every part of such a document will be interpreted as either PHP or HTML, depending on whether that section of the document is enclosed in PHP tags.

PHP syntax is relevant only within PHP, so we assume for the rest of the chapter that PHP mode is in force—that is, most code fragments will be assumed to be embedded in an HTML page and surrounded with the appropriate tags.

PHP's Syntax Is C-Like

The third most important thing to know about PHP syntax is that, broadly speaking, it is like the C programming language. If you happen to be one of the lucky people who already know C, then this is very helpful; if you are uncertain about how a statement should be written, try it first the way you would do it in C, and if that doesn't work . . . look it up in the manual. The rest of this section is for the other people, the ones who don't already know C. (C programmers might want to skim the headers of this section and also should see our appendix that is specifically for C programmers.)

PHP is whitespace-insensitive

Whitespace is the stuff you type that is typically invisible on the screen, including spaces, tabs, and carriage returns (end-of-line characters). PHP's whitespace insensitivity does not mean that spaces and such never matter (in fact, they are crucial for separating the "words" in the PHP language). Instead, it means that it never matters how many whitespace characters you have in a row—one whitespace character is the same as many such characters.

For example, each of the following PHP statements that assigns the sum of 2 + 2 to the variable $four is equivalent:

```
$four = 2 + 2;     // single spaces
$four <tab>=<tab>2<tab>+<tab>2  ;     // spaces and tabs
$four            =
2
+
2;  // multiple lines
```

The fact that end-of-line characters count as whitespace is handy, because it means you never have to strain to make sure that a statement fits on a single line.

PHP is sometimes case sensitive

Having read that PHP isn't picky, you may be surprised to learn that it is sometimes case sensitive (that is, it cares about the distinction between lowercase and capital letters). In particular, all variables are case sensitive. If you embed the following code in an HTML page:

```
<?php
  $capital = 67;
  print("Variable capital is $capital<BR>");
  print("Variable CaPiTaL is $CaPiTaL<BR>");
?>
```

the output you will see is

```
Variable capital is 67
Variable CaPiTaL is
```

because the different capitalization schemes make for different variables. (Surprisingly, under the default settings for error reporting, code like this fragment will not produce a PHP error — see the section "Unassigned variables" later in the chapter.)

On the other hand, unlike in C, function names are *not* case sensitive, and neither are the basic language constructs (if, then, else, while, and the like).

Statements are expressions terminated by semicolons

Here is a typical statement in PHP, which in this case assigns a string of characters to a variable called $greeting:

```
$greeting = "Welcome to PHP!";
```

The rest of this subsection is about how such statements are built from smaller components and how the PHP interpreter handles the evaluation of statements. (If you already feel comfortable with statements and expressions, feel free to skip ahead.)

The smallest building blocks of PHP are the indivisible tokens, such as numbers (3.14159), strings ("two"), variables ($two), constants (TRUE), and the special words that make up the syntax of PHP itself (if, else, and so forth). These are separated from each other by whitespace and by other special characters such as parentheses and braces.

The next most complex building block in PHP is the expression, which is any combination of tokens that has a value. A single number is an expression, as is a single variable. Simple expressions can also be combined to make more complicated expressions, usually either by putting an *operator* in between (for example, 2 + (2 + 2)), or by using them as input to a *function* call (for example, power_of(2 * 3, 3 * 2)). Operators that take two inputs go in between their inputs, whereas functions take their inputs in parentheses immediately after their names, with the inputs (known as *arguments*) separated by commas.

Expressions are evaluated

Whenever the PHP interpreter encounters an expression in code, that expression is immediately *evaluated*. This means that PHP calculates values for the smallest elements of the expression, and then successively combines those values that are connected by operators or functions, until it has produced an entire value for the expression. For example, successive steps in an imaginary evaluation process might look like:

```
$result = 2 * 2 + 3 * 3 + 5;
        (= 4 + 3 * 3 + 5)   //imaginary evaluation steps
        (= 4 + 9 + 5)
        (= 13 + 5)
        (= 18)
```

with the result that the number 18 is stored in the variable $result.

Precedence, associativity, and evaluation order

There are two kinds of freedom PHP might have in expression evaluation: how it groups or associates subexpressions, and the order in which it evaluates them. For example, in the evaluation process just shown, multiplications were associated more tightly than additions, which affects the end result.

The particular ways that operators group expressions are called *precedence* rules — operators that have higher precedence win in "grabbing" the expressions around them. If you want, you can memorize the rules, such as the fact that '*' always has higher precedence than '+' (we will cover the rules more fully in later chapters). Or, you can just use the following cardinal rule: When in doubt, use parentheses to group expressions.

For example:

```
$result1 = 2 + 3 * 4 + 5 // is equal to 19
$result2 = (2 + 3) * (4 + 5) // is equal to 45
```

Operator precedence rules remove much of the ambiguity about how subexpressions are associated, but what about when two operators have the same precedence? Consider this expression:

```
$how_much = 3.0 / 4.0 / 5.0;
```

Whether this is equal to 0.15 or 3.75 will depend on which division operator gets to "grab" the number 4.0 first. There is an exhaustive list of rules of associativity in the online manual, but the rule to remember is that associativity is usually left-before-right — that is, the preceding expression would evaluate to 0.15, because the leftmost of the two division operators wins the dispute over precedence.

The final wrinkle is order of evaluation, which is not quite the same thing as associativity. For example, look at the arithmetic expression

```
3 * 4 + 5 * 6
```

We know that the multiplications will happen before the additions, but that is not the same as knowing which multiplication PHP will perform first. In general, you need not worry about evaluation order, because in almost all cases it will not affect the result. You can construct weird examples where the result does depend on order of evaluation, usually by making assignments in subexpressions that are used in other parts of the expression. For example,

```
$huh = ($this = $that + 5) + ($that = $this + 3);   // BAD
```

But don't do this, okay? PHP may or may not have a predictable order of evaluation of expressions, but you shouldn't depend on it — so we're not going to tell you! (The one legitimate use of relying on left-to-right evaluation order is in "short-circuiting" Boolean expressions, which we will cover in Chapter 7.)

Expressions and types

Usually, the programmer is careful to match the types of expressions with the operators and functions that combine them. Common expressions are mathematical (with mathematical operators combining numbers), or Boolean (combining true-or-false statements with "and"s and "or"s), or string expressions (with operators and functions constructing strings of characters). As with the rest of PHP, though, the treatment of types is surprisingly forgiving. For example, consider the following expression, which deliberately mixes the type of subexpressions in an inappropriate way:

```
2 + 2 * "nonsense" + TRUE
```

Rather than produce an error, this evaluates to the number 3. (You can take this as a puzzle for now, but we will explain how such a thing could happen in the next chapter.)

Assignment expressions

A very common kind of expression is the assignment, where a variable is set to equal the result of evaluating some expression. These have the form of a variable name (which always starts with a '$'), followed by a single equal sign, followed by the expression to be evaluated. For example,

```
$eight = 2 * (2 * 2)
```

would assign the variable $eight the value you would expect.

An important thing to remember is that even assignment expressions are expressions and so have values themselves! The value of an expression that assigns a variable is the same as the value that is assigned. This means that you can use assignment expressions in the middle of more complicated expressions. If you evaluated the statement

```
$ten = ($two = 2) + ($eight = 2 * (2 * 2))
```

each variable would be assigned a numerical value equal to its name.

Finally, a *statement* in PHP is any expression that is followed by a semicolon (;). If expressions correspond to phrases, then statements correspond to entire sentences, and the semicolon is the full stop at the end. Any sequence of valid PHP statements that is enclosed by the PHP tags is a valid PHP program.

Reasons for Expressions and Statements

There are usually only two reasons to write an expression in PHP: for its *value*, or for a *side effect*. The value of an expression is what is passed on to any more complicated expression that includes it; side effects are anything else that happens as a result of the evaluation. The most typical side effects involve assigning or changing a variable, printing something to the user's screen, or making some other persistent change to the program's environment (such as interacting with a database).

Although statements are expressions, they are not themselves included in more complicated expressions. This means that the only good reason for a statement is a side effect! It also means that it is possible to write legal yet totally useless statements such as the second of these:

```
print("Hello");  // side effect is printing to screen
2 * 3 + 4;  // useless - no side effect
$value_num = 3 * 4 + 5;  // side effect is assignment
store_in_database(49.5);  // side effect to DB
```

Braces make blocks

Although statements cannot be combined like expressions, you can always put a sequence of statements anywhere a statement can go, by enclosing them in a set of curly braces.

For example, the if construct in PHP has a test (in parentheses) followed by the statement that should be executed if the test is true. If you want more than one statement to be executed when the test is true, you can use a brace-enclosed sequence instead. The following pieces of code (which simply print a reassuring statement that it is still true that 1 + 2 is equal to 3) are equivalent:

```
if (3 == 2 + 1)
  print("Good - I haven't totally lost my mind.<BR>");
```

```
if (3 == 2 + 1)
  {
    print("Good - I haven't totally ");
    print("lost my mind.<BR>");
  }
```

You can put any kind of statement in a brace-enclosed block, including, say, an if statement that itself has a brace-enclosed block. This means that if statements can have other if statements inside them, and in fact this kind of nesting can be done to an arbitrary number of levels.

Comments

A *comment* is the portion of a program that only exists for the human reader. The very first thing that a program executor does with program code is to strip out the comments, so they cannot have any effect on what the program does. Comments are invaluable in helping the next person who reads your code figure out what you were thinking when you wrote it, even when that person is yourself a week from now.

PHP drew its inspiration from several different programming languages, most notably C, Perl, and UNIX shell scripts. As a result, PHP supports styles of comments from all of those languages, and those styles can be intermixed freely in PHP code.

C-style multiline comments

The multiline style of commenting is the same as in C: a comment starts with the character pair /* and terminates with the character pair */. For example,

```
/*  This is
    a comment in
    PHP */
```

The most important thing to remember about multiline comments is that they cannot be nested. You cannot put one comment inside another. If you try, the comment will be closed off by the first instance of the */ character pair, and the rest of what was intended to be an enclosing comment will instead be interpreted as code, probably failing horribly. For example:

```
/* This comment will /* fail horribly on the
    last word of this */ sentence
*/
```

This is an easy thing to do unintentionally, usually when you try to deactivate a block of commented code by "commenting it out."

Single-line comments: # and //

In addition to the /* ... */ multiple-line comments, PHP supports two different ways of commenting to the end of a given line, one inherited from C++ and Java and the other from Perl and shell scripts. The shell-script-style comment starts with a pound sign, whereas the C++ style comment starts with two forward slashes. Both of them cause the rest of the current line to be treated as a comment, as in,

```
#  This is a comment, and
#  this is the second line of the comment
// This is a comment too.  Each style comments only
// one line so the last word of this sentence will fail
horribly.
```

The very alert reader might argue that single-line comments are incompatible with what we said earlier about blank-insensitivity. That would be correct—you will get a very different result if you take a single-line comment and replace one of the spaces with an end-of-line character. A more accurate way of putting it is that, after the comments have been stripped out of the code, PHP code is blank insensitive.

Variables

The main way to store information in the middle of a PHP program is by using a *variable*—a way to name and hang on to any value that you want to use later.

Here are the most important things to know about variables in PHP (more detailed explanations will follow):

✦ All variables in PHP are denoted with a leading dollar sign ($).

✦ The value of a variable is the value of its most recent assignment.

✦ Variables are assigned with the '=' operator, with the variable on the left-hand side and the expression to be evaluated on the right.

✦ Variables do not need to be declared before assignment.

✦ Variables have no intrinsic type other than the type of their current value.

✦ Variables that are used before they are assigned have default values.

PHP variables are Perl-like

All variables in PHP start with a leading '$' sign just like scalar variables in the Perl scripting language, and in other ways they have similar behavior (need no type declarations, may be referred to before they are assigned, and so on). Perl hackers may need to do no more than skim the headings of this section, which is really for the rest of us.

After the initial '$', variable names must be composed of letters (uppercase or lowercase), digits (0-9), and underscore characters ('_'). Furthermore, the first character after the '$' may not be a number.

Declaring variables

This subheading is here simply because programmers from some other languages might be looking for it — in languages such as C, C++, and Java, the programmer must declare the name and type of any variable before making use of it. However, because in PHP types are associated with values rather than variables, no such declaration is necessary — the first step in using a variable is to assign it a value.

Assigning variables

Variable assignment is simple — just write the variable name, then a single equal sign ('='), and then the expression that you want to assign to that variable.

```
$pi = 3 + 0.14159; // approximately
```

Note that what is assigned is the result of evaluating the expression, not the expression itself. Once the preceding statement is evaluated, there is no way to tell that the value of $pi was created by adding two numbers together.

Reassigning variables

There is no interesting distinction in PHP between assigning a variable for the first time, and changing its value later. This is true even if the assigned values are of different types. For example, the following is perfectly legal:

```
$my_num_var = "This should be a number - hope it's reassigned";
$my_num_var = 5;
```

If the second statement immediately follows the first one, the first statement has essentially no effect.

Unassigned variables

Many programming languages will object if you try to use a variable before it is assigned; others will let you, but if you do you may find yourself reading the random contents of some area of memory. In PHP, the default error-reporting setting allows you to use unassigned variables without errors, and PHP ensures that they have reasonable default values.

Note   If you would like to be warned about variables that have not been assigned, you should change the error-reporting level to 15 from the default level of 7. You can do this either by including the statement `error_reporting(15);` at the top of a script, or by changing your php.ini file to set the default level (see Chapter 32).

Default values

Variables in PHP do not have intrinsic types—a variable does not know in advance whether it will be used to store a number or a string of characters. So how does it know what type of default value to have when it hasn't yet been assigned?

The answer is that, just as with assigned variables, the type of a variable is interpreted depending on the context in which it is used. In a situation where a number is expected, a number will be produced, and similarly with character strings. In any context that treats a variable as a number, an unassigned variable will be evaluated as 0; in any context that expects a string value, an unassigned variable will be the empty string (the string that is zero characters long).

Checking assignment with IsSet

Because variables do not have to be assigned before use, in some situations you can actually convey information by selectively setting or not setting a variable! PHP provides a function, called IsSet, which tests a variable to see whether it has been assigned a value.

As the following code illustrates, an unassigned variable is distinguishable even from a variable that has been given the default value:

```
$set_var = 0; //set_var has a value
               //never_set does not
print("set_var print value: $set_var<BR>");
print("never_set print value: $never_set<BR>");
if ($set_var == $never_set)
  print("set_var is equal to never_set!<BR>");
if (IsSet($set_var))
  print("set_var is set.<BR>");
else
  print("set_var is not set.<BR>");
if (IsSet($never_set))
  print("never_set is set.<BR>");
else
  print("never_set is not set.");
```

Oddly enough, this code will produce the following output:

```
set_var print value: 0
never_set print value:
set_var is equal to never_set!
set_var is set.
never_set is not set.
```

The variable $never_set has never been assigned, so it produces an empty string when a string is expected (as in the print statement), and a zero value when a number is expected (as in the comparison test that concludes that the two variables are the same). Still, IsSet can tell the difference between $set_var and $never_set.

The act of assigning a variable is not irrevocable—the function unset() will restore a variable to an unassigned state (for example, unset($set_var); will make $set_var into an unbound variable, regardless of its previous assignments).

Variable scope

Scope is the technical term for the rules about when a name (for, say, a variable or function) has the same meaning in two different places, and in what situations two names that are spelled exactly the same way can actually refer to different things.

Any PHP variable that is not inside a function has *global* scope and extends throughout a given "thread" of execution. In other words, if you assign a variable near the top of a PHP file, the variable name has the same meaning for the rest of the file, and if it is not reassigned, it will have the same value as the rest of your code executes (except inside the body of functions).

The assignment of a variable will not affect the value of variables with the same name in other PHP files, or even in repeated uses of the same file. For example, let's say that you have two files: startup.php, and next_thing.php, which are typically visited in that order by a user. Let's also say that near the top of startup.php we have the line

```
$username = "Jane Q. User";
```

which is only executed in certain situations. Now, you might hope that, after setting that variable in startup.php, it would also be preset automatically when the user visited next_thing.php, but no such luck. Each time a PHP page executes, it assigns and reassigns variables as it goes, and those variables "disappear" at the end of a page's production. Assignments of variables in one file do not affect variables of the same name in a different file, or even in other requests for the same file.

Obviously, there are many situations in which you would like to hold onto information for longer than it takes to generate a particular Web page. There are a variety of ways you can accomplish this, and the different techniques are a lot of what the rest of this book is about. For example, you can pass information from page to page using GET and POST variables (Chapter 12), store information persistently in a database (all of Part II of this book), associate it with a user's session using PHP's new session mechanism (Chapter 25), or store it on a user's hard disk via a cookie (Chapter 26).

Functions and variable scope

Except inside the body of a function, variable scope in PHP is quite simple: within any given execution of a PHP file, just assign a variable and its value will be there for you later. We haven't yet covered how to define your own functions, but it's worth a look-ahead note: variables assigned within a function are *local* to that function, and unless you make a special declaration in a function, that function won't have access to the global variables that are defined outside the function, even when they are defined in the same file. (We will discuss the scope of variables in functions in depth when we cover function definitions in Chapter 11.)

You can switch modes if you want

One scoping question that we had the first time we saw PHP code was does variable scope persist across tags? That is, if we have a single file that looks like

```
<HTML>
<HEAD>
<?php
  $username = "Jane Q. User";
?>
</HEAD>
<BODY>
<?php
  print("$username<BR>");
?>
</BODY>
</HTML>
```

should we expect our assignment to $username to survive through the second of the two PHP-tagged areas? The answer is yes — variables persist throughout a thread of PHP execution (in other words, through the whole process of producing a Web page in response to a user's request). This is a single manifestation of a general PHP rule, which is that the *only* effect of the tags is to let the PHP engine know whether you want your code to be interpreted as PHP or passed through untouched as HTML. You should feel free to use the tags to switch back and forth between modes whenever it is convenient.

Output

Most of the constructs in the PHP language execute *silently* — they don't print anything to output. The only way that your embedded PHP code will display anything in a user's browser program is either by means of statements that print something to output, or by calling functions that in turn call `print` statements.

Echo and print

The two most basic constructs for printing to output are echo and print. Their language status is somewhat confusing, because they are basic constructs of the PHP language, rather than being functions. As a result, they can be used either with parentheses or without them. (Function calls always have the name of the function first, followed by a parenthesized list of the arguments to the function.)

Echo

The simplest use of echo is to print out a string as argument, for example:

```
echo "This will print in the user's browser window.";
```

or, equivalently,

```
echo("This will print in the user's browser window.");
```

Both of these statements will cause the given sentence to be displayed, without displaying the quote signs. (Note for C programmers: think of the HTTP connection to the user as the "standard output stream" for these functions.)

You can also give multiple arguments to the unparenthesized version of echo, separated by commas, as in:

```
echo "This will print in the ", "user's browser window.";
```

but the parenthesized version will not accept multiple arguments:

```
echo ("This will produce a ", "PARSE ERROR!");
```

Print

The command print is very similar to echo, with two important differences:

> Unlike echo, print can accept only one argument.

> Unlike echo, print returns a value, which represents whether the print statement succeeded.

The value returned by print will be 1 if the printing was successful, and 0 if unsuccessful. (It is rare that a syntactically correct print statement will fail, but in theory this provides a means to test, for example, if the user's browser has closed the connection.)

Both echo and print are usually used with string arguments, but PHP's type flexibility means that you can throw pretty much any type of argument at them without causing an error. For example, the following two lines will print exactly the same thing:

```
print("3.14159");  // print a string
print(3.14159);    // print a number
```

Technically, what is happening in the second line is that, because `print` expects a string argument, the floating-point version of the number is converted to a string value before `print` gets hold of it. However, the effect is that both `print` and `echo` will reliably print out numbers as well as string arguments.

For the sake of simplicity and uniformity, we will typically use the parenthesized version of `print` in our examples, rather than using `echo`.

Variables and strings

C programmers are accustomed to using a function called `printf`, which allows you to splice values and expressions into a specially formatted printing string. PHP has analogous functions (which we will cover in Chapter 9), but as it turns out we can get much of the same functionality just by using `print` (or `echo`) with quoted strings.

For example, the code fragment

```
$animal = "antelope";
$animal_heads = 1;
$animal_legs = 4;
print("The $animal has $animal_heads head(s).<BR>");
print("The $animal has $animal_legs leg(s).<BR>");
```

will produce the following output in the browser:

```
The antelope has 1 head(s).
The antelope has 4 leg(s).
```

The values for the variables we included in the string have been neatly spliced into the printed output. This is a very cool and useful feature that makes it very easy to quickly produce Web pages with content that varies depending on how variables have been set. It is not due to any magical properties of `print`, however—the magic is really happening in the interpretation of the quoted string itself.

Single versus double quotation marks

PHP does some preprocessing of doubly quoted strings (strings with quotes like "this") before constructing the string value itself. For one thing, variables are replaced by their values (as in the preceding example). To see that this is really about the quoted string rather than the `print` construct, consider the following code:

```
$animal = "antelope"; // first assignment
$saved_string = "The animal is $animal<BR>";
$animal = "zebra"; // reassignment
print("The animal is $animal<BR>"); //first display line
print($saved_string); //second display line
```

What output would you expect here? As it turns out, your browser would display

```
The animal is zebra
The animal is antelope
```

in that order. This is because "antelope" is spliced into the string $saved_string, before the $animal variable is reassigned.

In addition to splicing variable values into doubly quoted strings, PHP also replaces some special multiple-character "escape sequences" with their single-character values. The most commonly used is the end-of-line sequence ("\n")—in reading a string like

```
"The first line \n\n\nThe fourth line"
```

PHP would first replace each "\n" with the single end-of-line character. If you viewed the HTML source produced by this line, you would see a couple of blank lines in the middle of the output. (In a browser window, however, everything would probably be on the same line—see "HTML and line breaks" later in this chapter.)

Singly quoted strings (like 'this') behave differently—PHP does not perform any variable interpolation on them, and it pays attention to only two escape sequences. (You can include a literal ' in the middle of your string by escaping it as \', and a literal \ by escaping it as \\.) With these two exceptions, PHP interprets singly quoted strings as the literal string of characters that were typed. If you type a '$' character into such a string and send it to output with print, you will see a '$' in your browser window. This literal-mindedness can be useful, as in the example of printing a Windows-style pathname. The statement

```
print('C:\newcode\php\myphp.php');
```

will print out the literal path as desired, where the double-quoted version would interpret the backslashes as starting escape sequences, inserting a line break immediately after 'C:'.

HTML and linebreaks

One mistake often made by new PHP programmers (especially those from a C background) is to try to break lines of text in their browsers by putting end-of-line characters ("\n") in the strings they print. To understand why this doesn't work, you have to distinguish the *output* of PHP (which is usually HTML code, ready to be sent over the Internet to a browser program) from the way that output is *rendered* by the user's browser. Most browser programs will make their own choices about how to split up lines in HTML text, unless you force a line break with the <BR> tag. End-of-line characters in strings will put line breaks in the HTML source that PHP sends to your user's browser, but they will usually have no effect on the way that text looks in a Web page.

Summary

PHP code follows a basic set of syntactical rules, mostly borrowed from programming languages such as C and Perl. The syntactical requirements of PHP are minimal, and in general PHP tries to display results when it can rather than generating an error.

PHP code is blank insensitive, and although variable names are case sensitive, basic language constructs and function names are not. Simple PHP expressions are combined into larger expressions by operators and function calls, and statements are expressions with a terminating semicolon. Variables are denoted by a leading '$' character, are assigned using the '=' operator, need no type declarations, and have reasonable default values if used before they are assigned. Variable scope is global except inside the body of functions, where it is local to the function unless explicitly declared otherwise.

The simplest way to send output to the user is by using either `echo` or `print`, which output their string arguments. They are particularly useful in combination with doubly quoted strings, which automatically replace embedded variables with their values.

✦ ✦ ✦

Types in PHP

◆ ◆ ◆ ◆

In This Chapter

Understanding
the six PHP types:
integer, double,
Boolean, string,
array, and object

Creating, reading,
printing, and
manipulating
objects of
different types

Converting from
one type to another

◆ ◆ ◆ ◆

All programming languages have some kind of type system, which specifies the different kinds of values that can appear in programs. These different types often correspond to different bit-level representations in computer memory, although in many cases programmers are insulated from having to think about (or being able to mess with) representations in terms of bits. PHP's type system is simple, streamlined, and flexible, and it insulates the programmer from low-level details.

In this chapter we cover the fundamental types of PHP (integers, doubles, Booleans, strings, arrays, and objects) and show how they are read in, printed out, assigned to variables, converted, and combined. The chapter is both as overview and a reference—those familiar with programming can skim it, those less familiar can read only the early parts of sections, and both can check back later for those details that didn't seem to matter the first time around.

The First Rule: Don't Worry, Be Happy

PHP makes it easy not to worry too much about typing of variables and values, both because it does not require variables to be typed, and because it handles a lot of type conversions for you.

No variable type declarations

As we saw in the last chapter, the type of a variable does not need to be declared in advance. Instead, the programmer can jump right ahead to assignment and let PHP take care of figuring out the type of the expression that is assigned:

```
$first_number = 55.5;
$second_number = "Not a number at all";
```

Automatic type conversion

PHP does a good job of automatically converting types when necessary. Like most other modern programming languages, PHP will "do the right thing" when, for example, doing math with mixed numerical types. The result of the expression

```
$pi = 3 + 0.14159
```

will be a floating-point (double) number, with the integer 3 implicitly converted into floating point before the addition is performed.

Types assigned by context

PHP goes further than most languages in performing automatic type conversions. Consider this example:

```
$sub = substr(12345, 2, 2);
print("sub is $sub<BR>");
```

The `substr` function is designed to take a string of characters as its first input and return a substring of that string, with the start point and length determined by the next two inputs to the function. Instead of handing it a character string, though, we gave it the integer 12345. What happens? As it turns out, there is no error, and we get the browser output

```
sub is 34
```

Because `substr` expects a character string rather than an integer, PHP does us the favor of converting the number 12345 to the character string `'12345'`, which `substr` then slices and dices.

Because of this automatic type conversion it is very difficult to persuade PHP to give a type error—in fact, PHP programmers need to exercise a little care sometimes to make sure that type confusions do not lead to error-free but unintended results.

Type Summary

PHP only has six types: integers, doubles, Booleans, strings, arrays, and objects.

- ✦ *Integers* are whole numbers, without a decimal point, like 495.
- ✦ *Doubles* are floating-point numbers, like 3.14159, or 49.0.
- ✦ *Booleans* have only two possible values: TRUE and FALSE.
- ✦ *Strings* are sequences of characters, like `'PHP 4.0 supports string operations.'`
- ✦ *Arrays* are named and indexed collections of other values.

✦ *Objects* are instances of programmer-defined classes, which can package up both other kinds of values and functions that are specific to the class.

Of these, the first four are simple types, and the last two are compound — the compound types can package up other arbitrary values of arbitrary type, whereas the simple types cannot. We will treat the compound types (arrays and objects) lightly in this chapter, because they really deserve chapters of their own.

The Simple Types

The simple types in PHP (integers, doubles, Booleans, and strings) should be familiar to those with programming experience (although we will not assume that experience and will explain them in detail). The only thing likely to surprise C programmers is how few types there are.

Many programming languages have several different sizes of numerical types, with the larger ones allowing a greater range of values, but also taking up more room in memory. For example, the C language has a `short` type (for relatively small integers), a `long` type (for possibly larger integers), and an `int` type (which might be intermediate, but in practice is often identical either to the `short` or `long` type). This kind of typing choice made sense in an era when tradeoffs between memory use and functionality were often agonizing. The PHP designers made what we think is a good decision to simplify this by having only two numerical types, corresponding to the largest of the integral and floating-point types in C.

Integers

Integers are the simplest type — they correspond to simple whole numbers, both positive and negative. Integers can be assigned to variables, or they can be used in expressions, like so:

```
$int_var = 12345;
$another_int = -12345 + 12345; // will equal zero
```

Read formats

Integers can actually be read in three formats, which correspond to bases: decimal (base 10), octal (base 8), and hexadecimal (base 16). Decimal format is the default, octal integers are specified with a leading '0', and hexadecimals have a leading '0x'. Any of the formats can be preceded by a '-' sign to make the integer negative. For example:

```
$integer_10 = 1000;
$integer_8 = -01000;
```

```
$integer_16 = 0x1000;
print("integer_10: $integer_10<BR>");
print("integer_8: $integer_8<BR>");
print("integer_16: $integer_16<BR>");
```

will yield the browser output:

```
integer_10: 1000
integer_8: -512
integer_16: 4096
```

(Note that the read format only affects how the integer is converted as it is read—the value stored in $integer_8 does not remember that it was originally written in base 8. Internally, of course, these numbers are represented in binary format, and we see them in their base 10 conversion in the preceding output, because that is the default for printing and incorporating int variables into strings.)

Range

How big (or small) can integers get? Because PHP integers correspond to the C long type, which in turn depends on the word size of your machine, this is difficult to answer definitively. For most common platforms, though, the largest integer is $2^{31} - 1$ (or 2,147,483,647), and the smallest (most negative) integer is $-(2^{31} - 1)$ (or −2,147,483,647).

As far as we know, there is no PHP constant (like MAXINT in C) that will tell you the largest integer on your implementation—if in doubt, though, see the addendum at the very end of this chapter. If you really need very large integers, PHP does have some arbitrary-precision functions—see the BC section Chapter 10.

Doubles

Doubles are floating-point numbers, such as

```
$first_double = 123.456;
$second_double = 0.456
$even_double = 2.0;
```

Note that the fact that $even_double is a "round" number does not make it an integer. Integers and doubles are stored in different underlying formats, and the result of the expression

```
$five = $even_double + 3;
```

will be a double, not an integer, even if it prints as '5'. In almost all situations, though, you should feel free to mix doubles and integers in mathematical expressions, and let PHP sort out the typing.

By default, doubles print with the minimum number of decimal places needed—
for example, the code

```
$many = 2.2888800;
$many_2 = 2.2111200;
$few = $many + $many_2;
print("$many + $many_2 = $few<BR>");
```

produces the browser output

```
2.28888 + 2.21112 = 4.5
```

Cross-Reference   If you need finer control of printing, see the `printf` function in Chapter 9.

Read formats

The typical read format for doubles is -X.Y where the - optionally specifies a negative number, and both X and Y are sequences of digits between 0 and 9. The X part
may be omitted (if the number is between −1.0 and 1.0), and the Y part can also
(pointlessly) be omitted. Leading or trailing zeros have no effect. All of the following are legal doubles:

```
$small_positive = 0.12345;
$small_negative = -.12345
$even_double = 2.00000;
$still_double = 2.;
```

In addition, doubles can be specified in scientific notation, by adding the letter e
and a desired integral power of 10 to the end of the previous format—for example,
2.2e-3 would correspond to $2.2 \_ 10^{-3}$. The floating-point part of the number need
not be restricted to a range between 1.0 and 10.0. All of the following are legal:

```
$small_positive = 5.5e-3;
print("small_positive is $small_positive<BR>");
$large_positive = 2.8e+16;
print("large_positive is $large_positive<BR>");
$small_negative = -2222e-10;
print("small_negative is $small_negative<BR>");
$large_negative = -0.00189e6;
print("large_negative is $large_negative<BR>");
```

They produce the browser output:

```
small_positive is 0.0055
large_positive is 2.8E+16
small_negative is -2.222E-07
large_negative is -1890
```

Notice that, just as with octal and hexadecimal integers, the read format is irrelevant once PHP has finished reading in the numbers—the preceding variables retain no memory of whether they were originally specified in scientific notation. In printing out the values, PHP is making its own decisions to print the more extreme values in scientific notation, but this has nothing to do with the original read format.

Booleans

Booleans are true-or-false values, which are used in control constructs like the "testing" portion of an `if` statement. As we will see in the next chapter, Boolean truth values can be combined using logical operators to make more complicated Boolean expressions.

A genuine Boolean type is a new addition to PHP 4—PHP 3 had no distinct Boolean type but instead simply treated certain values of other types as being true and false. (This approach should be familiar to Perl hackers.) This difference doesn't make as much difference as you might think, because you can still use other types in a Boolean context—PHP 4 will just do an automatic type conversion first. (See the very end of this section for a couple of cases in which the PHP 3 and PHP 4 behavior will be different.)

Boolean constants

PHP provides a couple of constants especially for use as Booleans: `TRUE` and `FALSE`, which can be used like so:

```
if (TRUE)
  print("This will always print<BR>");
else
  print("This will never print<BR>");
```

Interpreting other types as Booleans

Here are the rules for determine the "truth" of any value that is not already of the Boolean type:

1. If the value is a number, it is false if exactly equal to zero, and true otherwise.

2. If the value is a string, it is false if the string is empty (has zero characters) *or* is the string `"0"`, and is true otherwise.

3. If the value is a compound type (an array or an object), it is false if it contains no other values, and is true otherwise.

Examples

Each of the following variables will have the truth value that is embedded in its name when it is used in a Boolean context.

```
$true_num = 3 + 0.14159;
$true_str = "Tried and true"
$true_array[49] = "An array element"; // see next section
$false_num = 999 - 999;
$false_str = ""; // a string zero characters long
```

Don't use doubles as Booleans

Note that, although rule 1 implies that the double 0.0 converts to a false Boolean value, it is dangerous to use floating-point expressions as Boolean expressions, due to possible rounding errors. For example,

```
$floatbool = sqrt(2.0) * sqrt(2.0) - 2.0;
if ($floatbool)
   print("Floating-point Booleans are dangerous!<BR>");
else
   print("It worked ... this time.<BR>");
print("The actual value is $floatbool<BR>");
```

The variable $floatbool is set to the result of subtracting two from the square of the square root of two—this should be equal to zero, which should mean that $floatbool is false. Instead, the browser output we get is

```
Floating-point Booleans are dangerous!
The actual value is 4.4408920985006E-16
```

The value of $floatbool is very close to 0.0, but it is nonzero and therefore unexpectedly true. Integers are much safer in a Boolean role—as long as their arithmetic happens only with other integers and stays within integral sizes, they should not be subject to rounding errors.

PHP 3 Booleans versus PHP 4 Booleans

Because PHP 3 has no independent Boolean type, the real values of the constants TRUE and FALSE are of other types, and some experimentation can reveal what those values are. Remember, though, that using these constants in a non-Boolean context is in the poorest possible taste and also likely to lead to PHP 4 incompatibilities. The general rule to follow is: do not do explicit equality comparisons with Booleans—just incorporate them into tests directly.

For example, imagine that as a result of some cool function you wrote, you now have a value assigned to the variable $truth_value. This variable might be a number or a string, but it should have the right truth value when interpreted according to the conversion rules stated earlier. What is the right way to use this variable? The right way, which will work in either PHP 3 or PHP 4, is

```
if ($truth_value) // good PHP! Safe in PHP 3 or PHP 4
    print("truth_value is true!<BR>");
```

and the wrong way looks like

```
if ($truth_value == TRUE) // bad PHP! compares to Boolean
    print("truth_value is true!<BR>");
```

The behavior of PHP 3 and PHP 4 might be different in the bad example, in the case where $truth_value is, say, the number 3. PHP 4 may convert 3 to the Boolean value TRUE before doing the equality comparison, where PHP 3 will test the number 3 to see if it is equal to whatever the actual value of TRUE is, and the test will probably fail.

Strings

Strings are character sequences, as in the following:

```
$string_1 = "This is a string in double quotes.";
$string_2 = 'This is a somewhat longer, singly quoted string';
$string_39 = "This string has thirty-nine characters.";
$string_0 = ""; // a string with zero characters
```

Strings can be enclosed in either single or double quotation marks, with different behavior at read time. Singly quoted strings are treated almost literally, whereas doubly quoted strings replace variables with their values as well as specially interpreting certain character sequences.

Singly quoted strings

Except for a couple of specially interpreted character sequences, singly quoted strings read in and store their characters literally. The following code

```
$literally = 'My $variable will not print!\n';
print($literally);
```

will produce the browser output

```
My $variable will not print!\n
```

Singly quoted strings also respect the general rule that quotes of a different type will not break a quoted string. This is legal:

```
$singly_quoted = 'This quote mark: " is no big deal';
```

To embed a single quote (such as an apostrophe) in a singly quoted string, escape it with a backslash, as in

```
$singly_quoted = 'This quote mark\'s no big deal either';
```

Although in most contexts backslashes are interpreted literally in singly quoted strings, you may also use two backslashes (\\) as an escape sequence for a single (nonescaping) backslash. This is useful when you want a backslash as the final character in a string, as in

```
$win_path = 'C:\\InetPub\\PHP\\';
print("A Windows-style pathname: $win_path<BR>");
```

which will display as

```
A Windows-style pathname: C:\InetPub\PHP\
```

Note   We could have used single backslashes to produce the first two backslashes in the output, but the escaping is necessary at the end of the string so that the closing quote will *not* be escaped.

These two escape sequences (\\ and \') are the *only* exceptions to the literal-mindedness of singly quoted strings.

Doubly quoted strings

Strings that are delimited by double quotes (as in "this") are preprocessed in two ways by PHP:

1. Certain character sequences beginning with backslash ('\') are replaced with special characters.
2. Variable names (starting with $) are replaced with string representations of their values.

The escape-sequence replacements are:

\n is replaced by the newline character

\r is replaced by the carriage-return character

\t is replaced by the tab character

\$ is replaced by the dollar sign itself ($)

\" is replaced by a single double-quote (")

\\ is replaced by a single backslash (\)

The first three of these replacements make it easy to visibly include certain white-space characters in your strings. The \$ sequence lets you include the $ symbol when you want it, without it being interpreted as the start of a variable. The \" sequence is there so that you can include a double-quote symbol without terminating your doubly quoted string. Finally, because the \ character starts all these sequences, you need a way to include that character literally, without it starting an escape sequence—to do this, you preface it with itself.

Just as with singly quoted strings, quotes of the opposite type can be freely included without an escape character:

```
$has_apostrophe = "There's no problem here";
```

Variable interpolation

Whenever an unescaped $ symbol appears in a doubly quoted string, PHP tries to interpret what follows as a variable name and splices the current value of that variable into the string. Exactly what this means depends on how the variable is set:

✦ If the variable is currently set to a string value, that string is interpolated (or spliced) into the doubly quoted string.

✦ If the variable is currently set to a nonstring value, the value is converted to a string, and then that string value is interpolated.

✦ If the variable is not currently set, PHP interpolates nothing (or, equivalently, PHP splices in the empty string).

An example:

```
$this = "this";
$that = "that";
$the_other = 2.2000000000;
print("$this,$not_set,$that+$the_other<BR>");
```

produces the PHP output

```
this,,that+2.2<BR>
```

which in turn, when seen in a browser, will look like

```
this,,that+2.2
```

If you find any part of this example puzzling, it is worth working through exactly what PHP does to parse the string in the print statement. First, notice that the string has four $ signs, each of which is interpreted as starting a variable name. These variable names terminate at the first occurrence of a character that is not legal in a variable name. Legal characters are letters, numbers, and underscores; the "illegal" terminating characters in the preceding print string are (in order) a comma, another comma, the plus symbol (+), and a left angle bracket (<). The first two variables are bound to strings (this and that), so those strings are spliced in literally. The next variable ($not_set) has never been assigned, so it is omitted entirely from the string under construction. Finally, the last variable ($the_other) is discovered to be bound to a double — that value is converted to a string (2.2), which is then spliced into our constructed string.

 Cross-Reference For more about converting numbers to strings, see the "Assignment and coercion" section that follows in this chapter.

As we said in the previous chapter, all of this interpretation of doubly quoted strings happens when the string is *read,* not when it is printed. If we saved the example string in a variable and printed it out later, it would reflect the variable values in the preceding code even if the variables had been changed in the meantime.

Newlines in strings

Although PHP offers an escape sequence (\n) for newline characters, it is good to know that you can literally include new lines in the middle of strings, which PHP treats the same way. This turns out to be convenient when creating HTML strings, because browsers will ignore the line breaks anyway, and so we can format our strings with line breaks to make our PHP code lines short:

```
print("<HTML><HEAD></HEAD><BODY>My HTML page is too big
to fit on a single line, but that doesn't mean that I
need multiple print statements!</BODY></HTML>");
```

We produced this statement in our text editor by literally hitting the Enter key at the end of the first two lines — these newlines are preserved in the string, so the single print statement will produce three distinct lines of PHP output. (Your mileage may vary depending on your text editor — if your editor automatically wraps lines in displaying them, you may see three lines of code that are actually one long line.) Of course, the browser program will ignore these newlines and will make its own decisions about whether and where to break the lines in display.

Limits

There are no artificial limits on string length — within the bounds of available memory, you ought to be able to make strings that are arbitrarily long.

Arrays

The PHP array type gives the programmer a way to group a bunch of different values together and index them by number (and also, as we'll see later, by name). If you ever find yourself using variables with names like $thing1, $thing2, $thing3..., it might be time to use an array instead ($things[1], $things[2], $things[3],...). Array elements are referred to via indices in brackets (the [1], [2], [3]... in this example), and elements of different type can be assigned into the same array.

The best way to learn about PHP arrays is by example. Here is some simple code that inspects an array variable both before and after the very first value is assigned into it:

```
print("my_array is $my_array<BR>");
print("my_array[0] is $my_array[0]<BR>");
print("my_array[5] is $my_array[5]<BR>");
$my_array[5] = "Slot #6";
print("my_array is $my_array<BR>");
print("my_array[0] is $my_array[0]<BR>");
print("my_array[5] is $my_array[5]<BR>");
```

The browser output this yields is:

```
my_array is
my_array[0] is
my_array[5] is
my_array is Array
my_array[0] is
my_array[5] is Slot #6
```

Let's explain this in terms of what is true before and after that first assignment is made. Before the assignment, despite the name, PHP doesn't know that the variable $my_array is destined to become an array—it is simply an unassigned variable like any other. This means that it is interpreted as the empty string when included in a doubly quoted string. As it turns out, an array index reference ([5]) into an unassigned variable is treated as an unassigned variable also. The result is that the first three print statements end inconclusively in is.

After the assignment, $my_array is now officially an array, and as a result it prints with the generic Array string when it is included in a doubly quoted string. The array slot indexed by the number 5 has been filled with the string Slot #6 (in recognition of the fact that, in most languages, array elements are numbered beginning with zero) and can be recovered with the index 5. This is really the only thing that has changed—the zeroth slot of $my_array is still unbound, just as it was before.

Array implementation

Arrays are one of the coolest and most useful features of PHP, and although they look deceptively like arrays in other languages, they are really implemented quite differently.

In most programming languages, you would declare an array with a statement like

```
int int_array[10]; // NOT PHP!
```

which amounts to setting up a block of 10 contiguous integer variables in memory, which can be accessed by indexes of int_array ranging from 0 to 9.

By contrast, PHP arrays are *associative* — when you make an array assignment, you are really adding a new array slot, associated with a new index that can be used to recover the value. (This may make sense to programmers who are familiar with hash tables — PHP arrays are more like hash tables than like arrays in other languages.)

One implication of this is that you don't need to be afraid to assign a very high array slot, like

```
my_array[100000000] = "not scary" // this is OK
```

because it won't result in a sudden allocation of 100 million array slots. The slots indexed by lower numbers probably do not yet exist, and so they do not use up any memory.

Strings as array indices

Our array examples so far have used only integers as indices, but string values may also be used, such as:

```
$tasty['Spanish'] = "paella";
$tasty['Japanese'] = "sashimi";
$tasty['Scottish'] = "haggis?";
```

These indices are used in the same way as numerical indices, and numerical and string indices may be used in the same array without conflicting with each other.

Note: Where is the structure type?

Some programming languages (C, Pascal) offer a "structure" or "record" type that allows variables of different types to be packaged together. The rule of thumb in such languages for choosing a compound type is: if all of the contained values will be of the same type, use an array, and otherwise use a structure.

Now, PHP does have an object type that, in addition to its more exotic properties, can act much like a record or structure type. Even before this was introduced, however, PHP did not really need a structure type, because its arrays are not restricted to only one type of value. If you are porting code to PHP from a language with a structure type, for example, one possibility is to use an associative array with string indices corresponding to the original field names.

Other array features

We have only scratched the surface of arrays in this chapter — in addition, arrays can be multidimensional; can have their values assigned using a variety of methods; and have a wealth of associated functions that make them easy to inspect, iterate over, and manipulate. We will return to arrays in Chapter 11.

Objects

The last of PHP's five datatypes is the object—PHP's entry into the glamorous world of object-oriented programming (OOP). We will give only the briefest of introductions to the OOP concept and the syntax of the PHP implementation here—a fuller treatment awaits in Chapter 33.

OOP overview

In object-oriented programming, programmers can define new entities called *classes*. Each programmer-defined class is essentially a new datatype, with specified data members. Once a class is defined, an arbitrary number of objects can be created, each of which is an *instance* of the class.

So far, this is much like defining a structure or record type in a language like C or Pascal. OOP languages go further, though, by including one or more of the following features:

✦ *Member functions:* In addition to having data members, objects can have function implementations that are particular to that class.

✦ *Inheritance:* A class can inherit from another class, which means that it starts off with all the data members and functions belonging to its parent. These inherited attributes can be extended (by adding new members and member functions) or overridden (by redefining selected inherited member functions).

✦ *Encapsulation:* A class definition can limit the extent to which its members can be viewed or modified by code that is not part of the class.

✦ *Polymorphism:* Function (or method) behavior can vary according to the number and type of the arguments in the call.

How OOP is PHP?

PHP provides a limited implementation of object-oriented programming—the short version is that PHP supports class definitions, member functions, and inheritance, but it does not support multiple inheritance or true encapsulation, and it is only now beginning to support polymorphism. Programmers familiar with C++, Java, Smalltalk, or Common Lisp will miss some of the subtleties and advanced features of those object systems, but the PHP object system can still be extremely useful.

Defining classes in PHP

See Listing 6-1 for a sample PHP class definition. This class acts like a "stack," supporting push() (which puts a new thing onto the stack) and pop() (which removes and returns the thing at the top of the stack). In addition, this stack restricts itself to stacking integers and refuses to push any nonintegral value.

Cross-Reference In addition to using the OOP constructs, this example uses some PHP features not yet covered, including function definitions. If you find this confusing, please feel free to skip OOP until its treatment in Chapter 30.

Listing 6-1: A simple PHP class definition

```
class IntStack
{   /* a stack with type restricted to int */
    var $the_stack;  //
    var $count = 0;

    function push ($intvar)
      {
        if (is_integer($intvar))
          {
            $this->the_stack[$this->count]
              = $intvar; // put on stack
            $this->count++; // increment count
            print("Push of $intvar succeeded.<BR>");
          }
        else
          print("Hey, IntStack is for ints only!<BR>");
      }
    function pop ()
      {
        if ($this->count > 0)
          {
            $this->count--; // decrement count
            $top = $this->the_stack[$this->count];
            return($top);
          }
        else
          print("Hey, the stack is empty!<BR>");
      }
  }
```

This IntStack class has two member variables ($the_stack and $count), and two member functions (push() and pop()). The variables are declared with the var keyword, while the function definitions are (as we will see later) much like regular PHP functions except that they are inside the body of the class definition. Member functions can access member variables by using the special $this variable, which refers to the object itself.

Creating objects

Once a class is defined, new instances can be created by using the new keyword in front of the name of the class, and then member functions can be accessed by using the -> operator on the resulting object. Here is an example of using the IntStack class that we created in Listing 6-1:

```
$my_stack = new IntStack;
$my_stack->push(1);
$my_stack->push(49);
$my_stack->push("It's a no-go!");
$pop_result = $my_stack->pop();
print("Top of the stack was $pop_result<BR>");
$pop_result = $my_stack->pop();
print("Top of the stack was $pop_result<BR>");
$pop_result = $my_stack->pop();
```

The output we would see looks like:

```
Push of 1 succeeded.
Push of 49 succeeded.
Hey, IntStack is for ints only!
Top of the stack was 49
Top of the stack was 1
Hey, the stack is empty!
```

Type Testing

Especially because variables can change types due to reassignment, it is sometimes necessary to find out the type of a value at program execution time. PHP offers both a general type-testing function (gettype()) and individual Boolean functions for each of the five types. These functions, some of which have alternate names, are summarized in Table 6-1.

<table>
<tr><td colspan="2" align="center">Table 6-1
Functions for Type Testing</td></tr>
<tr><td>*Function*</td><td>*Behavior*</td></tr>
<tr><td>gettype(arg)</td><td>Returns a string representing the type of arg: either integer, double, string, array, object, or unknown type</td></tr>
<tr><td>is_int(arg)
is_integer(arg)
is_long(arg)</td><td>Returns a true value if arg is an integer, and false if not</td></tr>
<tr><td>is_double(arg)
is_float(arg)
is_real(arg)</td><td>Returns a true value if arg is a double, and false if not</td></tr>
</table>

Function	Behavior
is_bool(arg)	Returns a true value if arg is a Boolean value (TRUE or FALSE), and false if not
is_string(arg)	Returns a true value if arg is a string, and false if not
is_array(arg)	Returns a true value if arg is an array, and false if not
is_object(arg)	Returns a true value if arg is an object, and false if not

Assignment and Coercion

As we have said, PHP often automatically converts from one type to another when the context demands it, and as it turns out the PHP programmer can also force some of these conversions to happen. In either situation, the programmer should know what to expect.

Type conversion behavior

Here are some general rules for PHP's conversion from one type to another (we have left objects out entirely, largely because there are no really useful conversions):

✦ *Integer to double:* The exact corresponding double is created (for example, the int 4 becomes the double 4.0).

✦ *Double to integer:* The fractional part is dropped, truncating the number toward zero.

✦ *Number to Boolean:* FALSE if exactly equal to 0, TRUE otherwise.

✦ *Number to string:* A string is created that looks exactly the way the number would print. Integers are printed as a sequence of digits, and doubles are printed with the minimum precision needed. Extreme double values will be converted to scientific notation.

✦ *Boolean to number:* 1 if TRUE, 0 if FALSE.

✦ *Boolean to string:* '1' if TRUE, the empty string if FALSE.

✦ *String to number:* Equivalent to "reading" a number from the string, then making a conversion to the given type. If a number cannot be read, the value is zero. Not all of the string needs to be read for the reading to be considered a success.

✦ *String to Boolean:* FALSE if the empty string or the string '0', TRUE otherwise.

✦ *Simple type (number or string) to array:* Equivalent to creating a new array with the simple value assigned to index zero.

✦ *Array to number:* The number 1 if the array contains any values, and 0 otherwise.

✦ *Array to Boolean:* FALSE if the array has no elements, TRUE otherwise.

✦ *Array to string:* 'Array'.

Explicit conversions

PHP offers three different ways for the programmer to manipulate types: conversion functions, type casts (as in the C language), and calling settype() on variables:

1. The functions intval(), doubleval(), and strval() will convert their respective arguments to an integer, a double, or a string, respectively. (At this writing, there does not seem to be a boolval() function.)

2. Any expression can be preceded by a type cast (the name of the type in parentheses), which converts the expression result to the desired type.

3. Any variable can be given as a first argument to settype(), which will change the type of that variable to the type named in the second string argument.

For example, each of the following approaches will put the correct count of canines (101) into the integer variable $dog_count:

Approach 1:

```
$dog_count = intval (strval (doubleval("101 Dalmatians")));
```

Approach 2:

```
$dog_count = (int) (string) (double) "101 Dalmatians";
```

Approach 3:

```
$dog_count = "101 Dalmatians"
settype($dog_count, "double");
settype($dog_count, "string");
settype($dog_count, "int");
```

Tip

Of course, each approach in the example takes an indirect route, converting needlessly to string and double types — it would suffice to convert immediately to the integer type.

Each of the six type names (integer, double, Boolean, string, array, and object) is valid in a cast and is valid as a string argument to settype(). In addition, certain alternate names are valid in casts (but not in settype()): (int) instead of (integer), (float) or (real) instead of (double), and (bool) instead of (boolean).

Conversion examples

Just for fun, Listing 6-2 shows some PHP code that displays various type conversions in an HTML table, with the resulting table shown in Figure 6-1. (This code is not intended as a style example, and it uses several constructs that have not yet been covered — feel free to just look at the output).

Listing 6-2: **Type conversions**

```
$type_examples[0] = 123; // an integer
$type_examples[1] = 3.14159; // a double
$type_examples[2] = "a non-numeric string";
$type_examples[3] = "49.990 (begins with number)";
$type_examples[4] = array(90,80,70);

print("<TABLE BORDER=1><TR>");
print("<TH>Original</<TH>");
print("<TH>(int)</<TH>");
print("<TH>(double)</<TH>");
print("<TH>(string)</<TH>");
print("<TH>(array)</<TH></TR>");

for ($index = 0; $index < 5; $index++)
  {
    print("<TR><TD>$type_examples[$index]</TD>");
    $converted_var =
       (int) $type_examples[$index];
    print("<TD>$converted_var</TD>");
    $converted_var =
       (double) $type_examples[$index];
    print("<TD>$converted_var</TD>");
    $converted_var =
       (string) $type_examples[$index];
    print("<TD>$converted_var</TD>");
    $converted_var =
       (array) $type_examples[$index];
    print("<TD>$converted_var</TD></TR>");
  }
 print("</TABLE>");
```

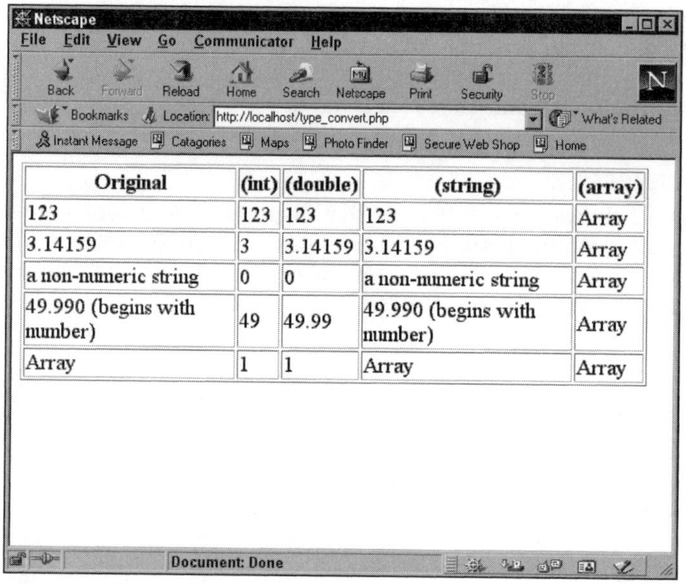

Original	(int)	(double)	(string)	(array)
123	123	123	123	Array
3.14159	3	3.14159	3.14159	Array
a non-numeric string	0	0	a non-numeric string	Array
49.990 (begins with number)	49	49.99	49.990 (begins with number)	Array
Array	1	1	Array	Array

Figure 6-1: Type conversion examples

Other useful type conversions

The functions listed in Table 6-2 do not exactly convert types, but they return a different type than their main argument in a useful way.

Table 6-2
Other Type-Conversion Functions

From\To	*Integer*	*String*	*Array*
Integer		`ord()`	
Double	`ceil()`, `floor()`, `round()`		
String	`chr()`		`explode()`
Array		`implode()`	

The function `ceil()` takes a double and returns the integer greater than or equal to that double. For example,

```
$my_double = 4.7;
$my_int = ceil($my_double); // $my_int is equal to 5
$my_double = -4.7;
$my_int = floor($my_double) // $my_int is equal to -4
```

The floor() function is the opposite of ceil() (we'll drop the intermediate assignment to $my_double now):

```
$my_int = floor(4.7); // $my_int is equal to 4
$my_int = floor(-4.7); // $my_int is equal to -5
```

The round() function takes a double and returns the nearest integer. If the fractional part of the double is exactly one half, the rounding is to the nearest even number.

```
$my_int = round(4.7); // $my_int is equal to 5
$my_int = round(-4.7); // $my_int is equal to -5
$my_int = round(-4.5); // $my_int is equal to -4
```

Tip   If you're looking for a truncate function (simply dropping the fractional part and therefore rounding toward zero), notice that this is the behavior you get simply from typecasting from double to int.

The function chr() takes an integer and returns a one-character string with that ASCII value, while ord() reverses this, returning the ASCII value of the first character in a string.

Finally, implode() and explode() allow a certain kind of conversion between strings and arrays. Implode() creates a string out of the array it is given as second argument, separating the elements with the string that is its first argument. For example:

```
$words[0] = "My";
$words[1] = "short";
$words[2] = "sentence.";
$sentence = implode(" ", $words);
print("$sentence<BR>");
```

will produce the browser output

```
My short sentence.
```

Explode() reverses the process, creating an array from, for example,

```
$words = explode(" ", "My short sentence.");
```

Integer overflow

One clever automatic type conversion built into PHP relatively recently is that when integer values "overflow" (that is, they are assigned a value larger than they can hold), they become doubles—this makes some sense, because doubles can accommodate larger magnitudes than integers can. For example:

```
$too_big = 111;
for ($count = 0; $count < 5; $count++)
```

```
   {
     $too_big = 1000 * $too_big;
     print("Is $too_big still an integer?<BR>");
   }
```

produces the following browser output:

```
Is 111000 still an integer?
Is 111000000 still an integer?
Is 111000000000 still an integer?
Is 1.11E+14 still an integer?
Is 1.11E+17 still an integer?
```

The shift you see in the this example from literal integers to scientific notation reflects a change of $too_big's type from integer to double. Of course, this may lose some information, because the precision of doubles is limited, but it is in keeping with the PHP philosophy of doing the best it can in preference to causing an error.

Addendum: finding the largest integer

If you need to know the largest integer your PHP will support, and for some reason believe that it is not the usual $2^{31} - 1$, here's a handy function (which uses concepts not yet covered):

```
function maxint()
{ /* quick-and-dirty function for PHP int size --
     assumes largest integer is of form 2^n - 1 */
  $to_test = 2;
  while(1)
    {
      $last = $to_test;
      $to_test = 2 * $to_test;
      if (($to_test < $last) || (!is_int($to_test)))
          return($last + ($last - 1));
    }
}
/* sample use */
$maxint = maxint();
print("Maxint is $maxint<BR>");
```

Summary

PHP 4 has six types: integer, double, Boolean, string, array, and object. Four of these are simple types: integers are whole numbers, doubles are floating-point numbers, Booleans are true-or-false values, and strings are sequences of characters. (The Boolean type is a new addition in PHP 4.) Arrays are a compound type that hold other PHP values, indexed either by integers or by strings. Objects are instances of programmer-defined classes, which can contain both member variables and member functions, and which can inherit functions and data types from other classes.

Only values are typed in PHP — variables have no inherent type other than the value of their most recent assignment. PHP automatically converts value types as demanded by the context in which the value is used. The programmer can also explicitly control types by means of both conversion functions and type casts.

✦   ✦   ✦

Control

I t's difficult to write interesting programs if you can't make the course of program execution depend on anything. In a weak sense, the behavior of code that prints out variables depends on the variable values, but that is as exciting as filling out a template — as programmers, we want programs that react to something (the world, the time of day, user input, or the contents of a database) by doing something different.

This kind of program reaction requires a *control structure,* which indicates how different situations should lead to the execution of different code. In the last chapter, we informally used the if control structure without really explaining it; in this chapter we lay out every kind of control structure offered by PHP and study their workings in detail.

Note Experienced C programmers: Of all the features in PHP, control is probably the most reliably C-like — all the structures you are used to are here, and they work the same way. You might want to jump to the Summary section at the end of the chapter.

The two broad types of control structures we will talk about are *branches* and *loops.* A branch is a fork in the road for a program's execution — depending on some test or other the program goes either left or right, possibly following a different path for the rest of the way, and possibly rejoining. A loop is a special kind of branch where one of the execution paths jumps back to the beginning of the branch, repeating the test and possibly the body of the loop.

Before we can make interesting use of control structures, though, we have to be able to construct interesting tests. We'll start from the very simplest of tests, working our way up from the constants TRUE and FALSE, and then move on to using these tests in more complicated code.

Boolean Expressions

Every control structure in this chapter has two distinct parts: the test (which determines which part of the rest of the structure executes), and the dependent code itself (whether separate branches or the body of a loop). Tests work by evaluating a Boolean expression, an expression with a result that is treated as either true or false.

Boolean constants

The simplest kind of expression is a simple value, and the simplest Boolean values are the constants TRUE and FALSE. We can use these constants anywhere we would use a more complicated Boolean expression, and vice versa. For example, we can embed them in the test part of an if-else statement:

```
if (TRUE)
  print("This will always print<BR>");
else
  print("This will never print<BR>");
```

or, equivalently,

```
if (FALSE)
  print("This will never print<BR>");
else
  print("This will always print<BR>");
```

Logical operators

Logical operators combine other logical (a.k.a. Boolean) values to produce new Boolean values. The standard logical operations (and, or, not, and exclusive-or) are supported by PHP, which has alternate versions of the first two, as shown in Table 7-1.

| | Table 7-1 |
| | **Logical Operators** |
Operator	*Behavior*
and	Is true if and only if both of its arguments are true
or	Is true if either (or both) of its arguments are true
!	Is true if its single argument (to the right) is false, and false if its argument is true

Operator	Behavior
xor	Is true if either (but not both) of its arguments are true
&&	Same as 'and', but binds to its arguments more tightly (see the discussion of precedence later in the chapter)
||	Same as 'or', but binds to its arguments more tightly

The && and || operators will be familiar to C programmers. The '!' operator is usually called "not," for obvious reasons.

As an example of using logical operators, consider the following expression:

```
(($statement_1 && $statement_2) ||
 ($statement_1 && !$statement_2) ||
 (!$statement_1 && $statement_2) ||
 (!$statement_1 && !$statement_2))
```

This is a "tautology," meaning that it is always true regardless of the values of the "statement" variables. There are four possible combinations of truth values for the two variables, each of which is represented by one of the && expressions. One of these four must be true, and because they are linked by the || operator, the entire expression must be true.

Here's another, slightly trickier tautology, using xor:

```
(($statement_1 and $statement_2 and
  $statement_3) xor
 ((!($statement_1 and $statement_2)) or
  (!($statement_1 and $statement_3)) or
  (!($statement_2 and $statement_3))))
```

In English, this expression says, "Given three statements, one and only one of the following two things hold—either 1) all three statements are true, or 2) there is a pair of statements that are not both true."

Precedence of logical operators

Just as with any operators, some logical operators have higher precedence than others, although precedence can always be overridden with parentheses. The logical operators listed in declining order of precedence are: !, &&, ||, and, xor, or. Actually, and, xor, and or have much lower precedence than the others, so that the assignment operator ('=') binds more tightly than and, but less tightly than &&.

Cross-Reference A complete table of operator precedence and associativity can be found in the online manual at http://www.php.net.

Logical operators short-circuit

One very handy feature of Boolean operators is that they associate left-to-right, and they "short-circuit," meaning that they do not even evaluate their second argument if their truth value is unambiguous from their first argument. For example, imagine that you wanted to determine a very approximate ratio of two numbers, but also wanted to avoid a possible division-by-zero error. You can first test to make sure that the denominator is not zero, by using the "!=" (not-equal-to) operator:

```
if ($denom != 0 && $numer / $denom > 2)
    print("More than twice as much!");
```

In the case where $denom is zero, the && operator should return false regardless of whether the second expression is true or false. Because of short-circuiting, the second expression is not evaluated, and so an error is avoided. In the case where $denom is not zero, the && operator does not have enough information to reach a conclusion about its truth value, and so the second expression is evaluated.

So far, all we've formally covered are the TRUE and FALSE constants, and how to combine them to make other true-or-false values. Now we'll move on to operators that actually let you make meaningful Boolean tests.

Comparison operators

Table 7-2 shows the comparison operators, which can be used for either numbers or strings (although see the cautionary sidebar).

Table 7-2 Comparison Operators		
Operator	**Name**	**Behavior**
==	Equal	True if its arguments are equal to each other, false otherwise
!=	Not equal	False if its arguments are equal to each other, true otherwise
<	Less than	True if the left-hand argument is less than its right-hand argument, false otherwise
>	Greater than	True if the left-hand argument is greater than its right-hand argument, false otherwise
<=	Less than or equal to	True if the left-hand argument is less than its right-hand argument, *or* equal to it, and false otherwise

Operator	Name	Behavior
>=	Greater than or equal to	True if the left-hand argument is greater than its right-hand argument, *or* equal to it, and false otherwise
===	Identical	True if its arguments are equal to each other and of the same type, and false otherwise (This is a new addition in PHP 4.)

As an example, here are some variable assignments, followed by a compound test that will always be true:

```
$three = 3;
$four = 4;
$my_pi = 3.14159;
if (($three == $three) and
    ($four === $four) and
    ($three != $four) and
    ($three < $four) and
    ($three <= $four) and
    ($four >= $three) and
    ($three <= $three) and
    ($my_pi > $three) and
    ($my_pi <= $four))
  print("My faith in mathematics is restored!<BR>");
else
  print("Sure you typed that right?<BR>");
```

Caution   Watch out for a very common mistake: confusing the assignment operator ('=') with the comparison operator ('==='). The statement if ($three = $four) .. will (probably unexpectedly) set the variable $three to be the same as $four, and what's more the test will be true if $four is a true value!

Operator precedence

Although over-reliance on precedence rules can be confusing for the person who reads your code next, it's useful to note that comparison operators have higher precedence than Boolean operators. This means that a test like

```
if ($small_num > 2 && $small_num < 5) ...
```

doesn't need any parentheses other than those shown.

Careful with nonintegral comparisons

Although comparison operators work with numbers or strings, a couple of gotchas lurk here.

First of all, although it is always safe to do less-than or greater-than comparisons on doubles (or even between doubles and integers), it can be dangerous to rely on equality comparisons on doubles, especially if they are the result of a numerical computation. The problem is that rounding error may make two values that are theoretically equal differ slightly.

Second, although comparison operators work for strings as well as numbers, PHP's automatic type conversions can lead to counterintuitive results when the strings are interpretable as numbers. For example, the code

```
$string_1 = "00008";
$string_2 = "007";
$string_3 = "00008-OK";
if ($string_2 < $string_1)
  print("$string_2 is less than $string_1<BR>");
if ($string_3 < $string_2)
  print("$string_3 is less than $string_2<BR>");
if ($string_1 < $string_3)
  print("$string_1 is less than $string_3<BR>");
```

gives this output (with comments added):

```
007 is less than 00008  // numerical comparison
00008-OK is less than 007 // string comparison
00008 is less than 00008-OK // string comp. - contradiction!
```

When it can, PHP will convert string arguments to numbers, and when both sides can be treated that way, the comparison ends up being numerical, not alphabetic. The PHP 4 designers view this as a feature, not a bug. Our view is that if you are comparing strings that have any chance of being interpreted as numbers, you're better off using the `strcmp()` function (see Chapter 9).

String comparison

The comparison operators may be used to compare strings as well as numbers (but see the cautionary sidebar). We would expect the following code to print its associated sentence (with apologies to Billy Bragg):

```
if (("Marx" < "Mary") and
    ("Mary" < "Marzipan"))
{
  print("Between Marx and Marzipan in the ");
  print("dictionary, there was Mary.<BR>");
}
```

The comparisons are case-sensitive, and the only reason that this example will print anything is that we have inappropriately capitalized *marzipan*. Due to capitalization, the following will not print anything:

```
if (("deep blue sea" < "Dennis") and
    ("Dennis" < "devil"))
{
   print("Between the deep blue sea and ");
   print("the devil, that was me.<BR>");
}
```

The trinary operator

One especially useful construct is the trinary conditional operator, which plays a role somewhere between a Boolean operator and a true branching construct. Its job is to take three expressions and use the truth value of the first expression to decide which of the other two expressions to evaluate and return. The syntax looks like

```
test-expression ? yes-expression : no-expression
```

and the value of this expression is the result of `yes-expression` if `test-expression` is true; otherwise, it is the same as `no-expression`.

For example, the following expression assigns to `$max_num` either `$first_num` or `$second_num`, whichever is larger:

```
$max_num = $first_num > $second_num ? $first_num : $second_num;
```

As we will see, this is equivalent to

```
if ($first_num > $second_num)
   $max_num = $first_num;
else
   $max_num = $second_num;
```

but is somewhat more concise.

Branching

The two main structures for branching are `if` and `switch`. If is a workhorse and is usually the first conditional structure anyone learns. Switch is a useful alternative for certain situations where you want multiple possible branches based on a single value, and where a series of `if` statements would be cumbersome.

If-else

The syntax for if is

```
if (test)
   statement-1
```

or, with an optional else branch

```
if (test)
   statement-1
else
   statement-2
```

When an if statement is processed, the test expression is evaluated, and the result is interpreted as a Boolean value. If test is true, statement-1 is executed. If test is not true, and there is an else clause, then statement-2 is executed. If test is false, and there is no else clause, then execution simply proceeds with the next statement after the if construct.

Note that a "statement" in this syntax can either be a single statement that ends with a semicolon, or a brace-enclosed block of statements, or another conditional construct (which itself counts as a single statement). Conditionals can be nested inside each other to arbitrary depth. Also, the Boolean expression can be a genuine Boolean (that is, TRUE, FALSE, or the result of a Boolean operator or function), or it can be a value of another type that is interpreted as a Boolean.

Cross-Reference   For the full story on this, see Chapter 6. The short version is that the number 0, the string "0", and the empty string, " ", are false, and almost every other value is true.

The following example, which prints a statement about the absolute difference between two numbers, shows both the nesting of conditionals and the interpretation of the test as a Boolean:

```
if ($first - $second)
   if ($first > $second)
     {
       $difference = $first - $second;
       print("The difference is $difference<BR>");
     }
   else
     {
       $difference = $second - $first;
       print("The difference is $difference<BR>");
     }
else
   print("There is no difference<BR>");
```

This code relies on the fact that the number 0 is interpreted as a false value—if the difference is zero, then the test fails, and the "no difference" message is printed.

If there is a difference, then a further test is performed. (This example is artificial, because a test like $first != $second would accomplish the same thing more comprehensibly.)

Else attachment

At this point, former Pascal programmers may be warily wondering about else attachment — that is, how does an else clause know which if it belongs to? The rules are simple and are the same as in most languages other than Pascal. Each else is matched with the nearest unmatched if that can be found, while respecting the boundaries of braces. If you want to make sure that an if statement stays solo and does not get matched to an else, wrap it up in braces like so:

```
if ($num % 2 == 0) // $num is even?
  {
    if ($num > 2)
      print("num is not prime<BR>");
  }
else
  print("num is odd<BR>");
```

This code will print "num is not prime" if $num happens to be an even number greater than 2, "num is odd" if $num is odd, and nothing if $num happens to be 2. If we had omitted the curly braces, then the else would attach to the inner if, and so the code would buggily print "num is odd" if $num were equal to 2, and would print nothing if $num were actually odd.

Note
In this chapter's examples, we often use the modulus operator ('%'), which is explained in Chapter 10. For the purposes of these examples, all you need to know is that $x % $y is zero means that $x is evenly divisible by $y.

Elseif

It's very common to want to do a cascading sequence of tests, as in the following nested if statements:

```
if ($day == 5)
  print("Five golden rings<BR>");
else
  if ($day == 4)
    print("Four calling birds<BR>");
  else
    if ($day == 3)
      print("Three French hens<BR>");
    else
      if ($day == 2)
        print("Two turtledoves<BR>");
      else
        if ($day == 1)
          print("A partridge in a pear tree<BR>");
```

Note   We have indented this code in to show the real syntactic structure of inclusions—although this is always a good idea, you will often see code that does not bother with this, and where each else line starts in the first column.

This pattern is common enough that there is a special elseif construct to handle it. We can rewrite the preceding example as

```
if ($day == 5)
   print("Five golden rings<BR>");
elseif ($day == 4)
   print("Four calling birds<BR>");
elseif ($day == 3)
   print("Three French hens<BR>");
elseif ($day == 2)
   print("Two turtledoves<BR>");
elseif ($day == 1)
   print("A partridge in a pear tree<BR>");
```

The if, elseif, elseif, ... construct allows for a sequence of tests that executes only the first branch that has a successful test. In theory, this is syntactically different from the previous example (we have a single construct with five branches, rather than a nesting of five two-branch constructs), but the behavior is identical. Use whichever syntax you find more appealing.

Branching and HTML mode

As you may have learned from earlier chapters, you should feel free to use the PHP tags to switch back and forth between HTML mode and PHP mode, whenever it seems convenient. If you need to include a large chunk of HTML in your page that has no dynamic code or interpolated variables, it can be simpler and more efficient to escape back into HTML mode and include it literally than it is to send it using print or echo.

What may not be as obvious is that this strategy works even inside conditional structures. That is, you can use PHP to decide what HTML to send, and then "send" that HTML by temporarily escaping back to HTML mode.

For example, the following cumbersome code uses print statements to construct a complete HTML page based on the supposed gender of the viewer. (We're assuming a nonexistent Boolean function called female() that tests for this.)

```
<HTML><HEAD>
<?php
if (female())
   {
      print("<TITLE>The women-only site</TITLE><BR>");
      print("</HEAD><BODY>");
```

```
         print("This site has been specially constructed ");
         print("for women only.<BR>  No men allowed here!");
      }
   else
      {
         print("<TITLE>The men-only site</TITLE><BR>");
         print("</HEAD><BODY>");
         print("This site has been specially constructed ");
         print("for men only.<BR>  No women allowed here!");
      }
?>
</BODY></HTML>
```

Instead of all these `print` statements, we can duck back into HTML mode within each of the two branches:

```
<HTML><HEAD>
<?php
if (female())
   {
?>
<TITLE>The women-only site</TITLE>
</HEAD><BODY>
This site has been specially constructed
for women only.<BR>  No men allowed here!
<?php
   }
else
   {
?>
<TITLE>The men-only site</TITLE><BR>
</HEAD><BODY>
This site has been specially constructed
for men only.<BR>  No women allowed here!
<?php
   }
?>
</BODY></HTML>
```

This version is somewhat more difficult to read, but the only difference is that we have replaced each set of `print` statements with a block of literal HTML that starts with a closing PHP tag (`?>`) and ends with a starting PHP tag (`<?php`).

In this book's examples, we mostly avoid this kind of conditional inclusion, simply because we feel that it may be harder for the novice PHP programmer to decipher. But that shouldn't stop you—literal inclusion has advantages, including fast execution. (When in HTML mode, all the PHP engine has to do is pass on characters and watch for the next PHP start tag. This is inevitably faster than parsing and executing `print` statements, especially when they include doubly quoted strings.)

Switch

For a specific kind of multiway branching, the switch construct can be useful. Rather than branch on arbitrary logical expressions, switch takes different paths according to the value of a single expression. The syntax is as follows, with the optional parts enclosed in square brackets ([ ]):

```
switch(expression)
{
    case value-1:
        statement-1
        statement-2
        ...
        [break;]
    case value-2:
        statement-3
        statement-4
        ...
        [break;]
    ...
    [default:
        default-statement]
}
```

The expression can be a variable or any other kind of expression, as long as it evaluates to a simple value (that is, an integer, a double, or a string). The construct executes by evaluating the expression and then testing the result for equality against each case value. As soon as a matching value is found, subsequent statements are executed in sequence until the special statement 'break;', or until the end of the switch construct. (As we'll see later, break can also be used to break out of looping constructs.) A special default tag can be used at the end, which will "match" the expression if no other case has matched it so far.

For example, we can rewrite our if-else example as follows:

```
switch($day)
{
  case 5:
    print("Five golden rings<BR>");
    break;
  case 4:
    print("Four calling birds<BR>");
    break;
  case 3:
    print("Three French hens<BR>");
    break;
  case 2:
    print("Two turtledoves<BR>");
    break;
  default:
    print("A partridge in a pear tree<BR>");
}
```

This will print a single appropriate line for days 2–5; for any day other than those it will print "A partridge in a pear tree."

Caution   The single most confusing aspect of switch is that all cases after a matching case will execute, unless there are break statements to stop the execution. In the "partridge" example, the break statements ensure that we see only one line from the song at a time. If we remove the break statements, then we will see a sequence of lines counting down to the final line, just as in the song.

Looping

Congratulations! You just passed the boundary from scripting into "real programming." The branching structures we have looked at so far are useful, but there are limits to what can be computed with them alone. On the other hand, it's well established in theoretical computer science that any language with tests plus unbounded looping can do pretty much anything that any other language can do. You may not actually want to write a C compiler in PHP, for example, but it's nice to know that no inherent language limits are going to stop you.

Bounded loops versus unbounded loops

A *bounded loop* is a loop that will execute a fixed number of times—you can tell by looking at the code how many times the loop will iterate, and the language guarantees that it won't loop more times than that. An *unbounded loop* is one that repeats until some condition becomes true (or false), and that condition is dependent on the action of the code within the loop. Bounded loops are predictable, whereas unbounded loops can be as tricky as you like.

Unlike some languages, PHP doesn't actually have any constructs specifically for bounded loops—while, do-while, and for are all unbounded constructs—but as we will see, an unbounded loop can do anything a bounded loop can do.

Cross-Reference   In addition to the looping constructs in this chapter, PHP provides functions for iterating over the contents of arrays, which will be covered in Chapter 11.

While

The simplest PHP looping construct is while, which has the following syntax:

```
while (condition)
    statement
```

The while loop evaluates the *condition* expression as a Boolean—if it is true, it executes *statement* and then starts again by evaluating *condition*. If the condition is false, the while loop terminates. Of course, just as with if, *statement* may be a single statement, or it may be a brace-enclosed block.

The body of a while loop may not execute even once, as in

```
while (FALSE)
   print("This will never print.<BR>");
```

or it may execute "forever," as in

```
while (TRUE)
   print("All work and no play makes
         Jack a dull boy.<BR>");
```

or it may execute a predictable number of times, as in

```
$count = 1;
while ($count <= 10)
   {
      print("count is $count<BR>");
      $count = $count + 1;
   }
```

which will print exactly ten lines. (For more interesting examples, see the "Looping examples" section later in this chapter.)

Do-while

The do-while construct is similar to while, except that the test happens at the end of the loop. The syntax is

```
do statement
   while (expression);
```

The statement is executed once, and then the expression is evaluated. If the expression is true, the statement is repeated until the expression becomes false.

The only practical difference between while and do-while is that the latter will always execute its statement at least once. For example,

```
$count = 45;
do
   {
      print("count is $count<BR>");
      $count = $count + 1;
   }
   while ($count <= 10)
```

will print the single line

```
count is 45
```

For

The most complicated looping construct is for, which has the following syntax

```
for (initial-expression;
     termination-check;
     loop-end-expression)
  statement
```

In executing a for statement, first the *initial-expression* is evaluated just once, usually to initialize variables. Then the *termination-check* is evaluated — if it is false, the for statement concludes, and if it is true, the statement executes. Finally, the *loop-end-expression* is executed and the cycle begins again with the termination check. As always, by *statement* we mean either a single (semicolon-terminated) statement, a brace-enclosed block, or a conditional construct.

If we rewrote the preceding for loop as a while loop, it would look like this:

```
initial-expression;
while (termination-check)
  {
     statement
     loop-end-expression;
  }
```

Actually, although the typical use of for has exactly one initial expression, one termination check, and one loop-end expression, it is legal to omit any of them. The termination check is taken to be always true if omitted, so

```
for (;;)
  statement
```

is equivalent to

```
while (TRUE)
  statement
```

It is also legal to include more than one of each kind of for clause, separated by commas. The termination check will be considered to be true if any of its subclauses are true; it is like an "or" test. For example, the following statement:

```
for ($x = 1, $y = 1, $z = 1;    //initial expressions
     $y < 10, $z < 10;          // termination checks
     $x = $x + 1, $y = $y + 2,  // loop-end expressions
     $z = $z + 3)
  print("$x, $y, $z<BR>");
```

would give the browser output

```
1, 1, 1
2, 3, 4
3, 5, 7
```

Although the for syntax is the most complex of the looping constructs, it is often used for simple bounded loops, using the following idiom:

```
for ($count = 0; $count < $limit; $count = $count + 1)
    statement
```

Looping examples

Now let's look at some examples.

A bounded for loop

Listing 7-1 shows a typical use of bounded for loops. Because most readers already know the multiplication table, we made this a division table instead. The page produced by Listing 7-1 is shown in Figure 7-1.

Listing 7-1: **A division table**

```php
<?php
  $start_num = 1;
  $end_num = 10;
?>
<HTML>
<HEAD>
<TITLE>A division table</TITLE>
</HEAD>
<BODY>
<H2>A division table</H2>
<TABLE BORDER=1>
<?php
  print("<TR>");
  print("<TH> </TH>");
  for ($count_1 = $start_num;
       $count_1 <= $end_num;
       $count_1++)
    print("<TH>$count_1</TH>");
  print("</TR>");

  for ($count_1 = $start_num;
       $count_1 <= $end_num;
       $count_1++)
  {
    print("<TR><TH>$count_1</TH>");
```

```
      for ($count_2 = $start_num;
           $count_2 <= $end_num;
           $count_2++)
        {
          $result = $count_1 / $count_2;
          printf("<TD>%.3f</TD>",
                 $result);  // see Chapter 9
        }
      print("</TR>\n");
    }
?>
</TABLE>
</BODY>
</HTML>
```

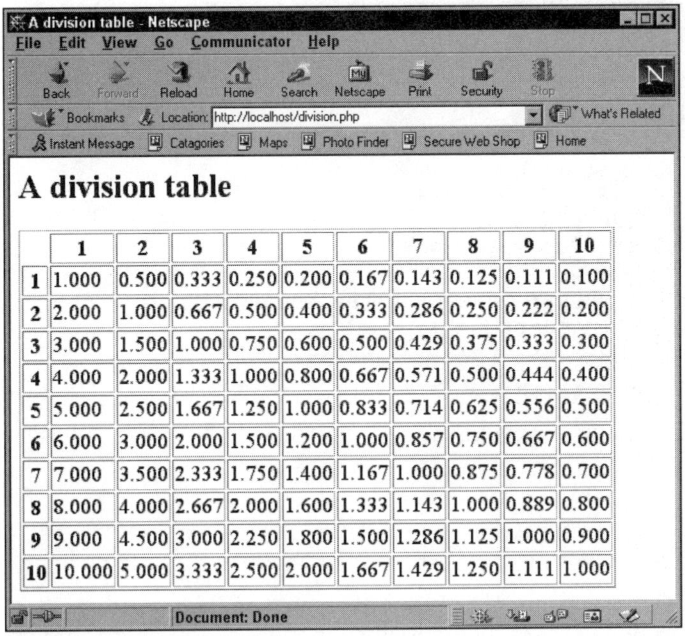

	1	2	3	4	5	6	7	8	9	10
1	1.000	0.500	0.333	0.250	0.200	0.167	0.143	0.125	0.111	0.100
2	2.000	1.000	0.667	0.500	0.400	0.333	0.286	0.250	0.222	0.200
3	3.000	1.500	1.000	0.750	0.600	0.500	0.429	0.375	0.333	0.300
4	4.000	2.000	1.333	1.000	0.800	0.667	0.571	0.500	0.444	0.400
5	5.000	2.500	1.667	1.250	1.000	0.833	0.714	0.625	0.556	0.500
6	6.000	3.000	2.000	1.500	1.200	1.000	0.857	0.750	0.667	0.600
7	7.000	3.500	2.333	1.750	1.400	1.167	1.000	0.875	0.778	0.700
8	8.000	4.000	2.667	2.000	1.600	1.333	1.143	1.000	0.889	0.800
9	9.000	4.500	3.000	2.250	1.800	1.500	1.286	1.125	1.000	0.900
10	10.000	5.000	3.333	2.500	2.000	1.667	1.429	1.250	1.111	1.000

Figure 7-1: A division table

The main body of this code simply has one for loop nested inside another, with each loop executing ten times, resulting in a 10 × 10 table. Each iteration of the outer loop prints a row, while each inner iteration prints a cell. The only novel feature is the way we chose to print out the numbers — we used `printf` (covered in Chapter 9), which allows us to control the number of decimal places that are printed.

An unbounded while loop

Now let's look at a loop that is not so obviously bounded. The sole purpose of the code in Listing 7-2 is to approximate the square root of 81 (using Newton's method). The approximation starts with a guess of 1 and then "zeros in" on the actual square root of 9 by improving the guesses. A trace of this approximation is shown in Figure 7-2.

Listing 7-2: **Approximating a square root**

```
<HTML>
<HEAD>
<TITLE>Approximating a square root</TITLE>
</HEAD>
<BODY>
<H3>Approximating a square root</H3>

<?php
$target = 81;
$guess = 1.0;
$precision = 0.0000001;

$guess_squared = $guess * $guess;
while (($guess_squared - $target > $precision) or
       ($guess_squared - $target < - $precision))
{
  print("Current guess: $guess is the square
        root of $target<BR>");
  $guess = ($guess + ($target / $guess)) / 2;
  $guess_squared = $guess * $guess;
}
print("$guess squared = $guess_squared<BR>");
?>
</BODY>
</HTML>
```

Now, although it nicely illustrates a potentially unbounded loop, this approximation example is very artificial—first, because PHP already has a perfectly good square-root function (sqrt), and second because the number 81 is hard-coded into the page. We can't use this page to find the square root of any other number.

Cross-Reference   In the next chapter we'll show how to wrap code like this into a function that can take the number as a parameter, and in Chapter 12 we'll look at how you could pass that parameter from one page to another.

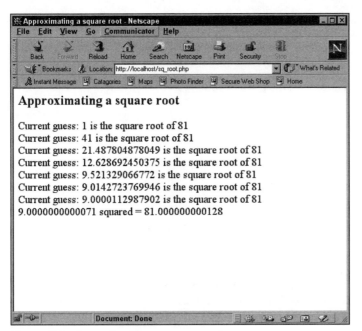

Figure 7-2: Approximating a square root

Break and continue

The standard way to get out of a looping structure is for the main test condition to become false. The special commands break and continue offer an optional side exit from all the looping constructs, including while, do-while, and for:

✦ The break command exits the innermost loop construct that contains it.

✦ The continue command skips to the end of the current iteration of the innermost loop that contains it.

For example, the following code

```
for ($x = 1; $x < 10; $x++)
{
  // if $x is odd, break out
  if ($x % 2 != 0)
    break;
  print("$x ");
}
```

will print nothing because 1 is odd, which terminates the `for` loop immediately. On the other hand, the code

```
for ($x = 1; $x < 10; $x++)
{
  // if $x is odd, skip this loop
  if ($x % 2 != 0)
    continue;
  print("$x ");
}
```

will print

```
2 4 6 8
```

because the effect of the `continue` statement is to skip the printing of any odd numbers.

Using the `break` command, the programmer can choose to dispense with the main termination test altogether. Consider the following code, which prints out a list of prime numbers (that is, numbers that are not divisible by something other than one or the number itself).

```
$limit = 500;
$to_test = 2;
while(TRUE)
{
  $testdiv = 2;
  if ($to_test > $limit)
    break;
  while (TRUE)
  {
    if ($testdiv > sqrt($to_test))
      {
        print "$to_test ";
        break;
      }
    // test if $to_test is divisible by $testdiv
    if ($to_test % $testdiv == 0)
      break;
    $testdiv = $testdiv + 1;
  }
  $to_test = $to_test + 1;
}
```

In the preceding code, we have two `while` loops—the outer loop works through all the numbers between 1 and 500, and the inner loop actually does the testing with each possible divisor. If the inner loop finds a divisor, the number is not prime, so it breaks out without printing anything. If, on the other hand, the testing gets as high as the square root of the number, then we can safely assume that the number must be prime, and the inner loop is broken without printing. Finally, the outer loop is broken when we have reached the limit of numbers to test. The result in this case is a list of primes less than 500:

```
  2   3   5   7  11  13  17  19  23  29  31  37  41  43  47  53  59  61  67  71  73  79
 83  89  97 101 103 107 109 113 127 131 137 139 149 151 157 163
167 173 179 181 191 193 197 199 211 223 227 229 233 239 241 251
257 263 269 271 277 281 283 293 307 311 313 317 331 337 347 349
353 359 367 373 379 383 389 397 401 409 419 421 431 433 439 443
449 457 461 463 467 479 487 491 499
```

Notice that it is crucial to this code that break only interrupts the inner while loop.

A note on infinite loops

If you've ever programmed in another language, you've probably had the experience of accidentally creating an infinite loop (a looping construct whose exit test never becomes true, and so never returns) The first thing to do when you realize this has happened is to interrupt the program, which will otherwise continue "forever" and use up a lot of CPU time. But what does it mean to interrupt a PHP script? Is it sufficient to press the Stop button on your browser?

As it turns out, the answer is dependent on some PHP configuration settings — you can set the PHP engine to ignore interruptions from the browser (like the result of pressing Stop) and also to impose a time limit on script execution (so that "forever" will only be a short time). The default configuration for PHP 4 is to ignore interruptions, but with a script time limit of 30 seconds — the time limitation means that you can afford to forget about infinite loops that you may have started. (This may not be true in some versions of PHP 3 though, and was buggy in PHP 4 beta 3.)

Cross-Reference   For more on the configuration of PHP, see Chapter 31.

Alternate Control Syntaxes

PHP offers another way to start and end the bodies of the if, switch, for, and while constructs. It amounts to replacing the initial brace of the enclosed block with a colon, and the closing brace with a special ending statement for that construct (endif, endswitch, endfor, and endwhile).

For example, the if syntax becomes

```
if (expression):
   statement1
   statement2
   ..
endif;
```

or

```
if (expression):
  statement1
  statement2
  ..
elseif (expression2):
  statement3
  ..
else:
  statement4
  ..
endif;
```

Note that the `else` and `elseif` bodies also begin with colons. The corresponding `while` syntax is

```
while (expression):
  statement
endwhile;
```

Which syntax you use is a matter of taste. The non-standard syntax is in PHP largely for historical reasons, and for the comfort of people who are familiar with it from the early versions of PHP. We will consistently use the standard syntax in the rest of this book.

Terminating Execution

Sometimes you just have to give up, and PHP offers two constructs that help you do just that:

1. The `exit()` construct takes no arguments, and terminates parsing of the script wherever it is encountered.

2. The `die()` construct takes a string as argument and terminates parsing of the script immediately after sending the string as output.

Everything that PHP produces up to the point of invoking `exit()` or `die()` will be sent to the client browser as usual, and nothing in your script after that point will even be parsed — execution of the script stops immediately.

So what's the point of `exit()` and `die()`? One possible use is to cut off production of a Web page when your script has determined that there is no more interesting information to send, without bothering to wrap up the different branches in a conditional construct. This usage can make long scripts somewhat difficult to read and debug, however.

A better use for die() is to make your crashes informative. It's good to get into the habit of testing for unexpected conditions that would crash your script if they were true, and throw in a die() statement with an informative message. If you're correct in your expectations, then the die() will never be invoked; if you're wrong, then you will have an error message of your own, rather than a possibly obscure PHP error.

For example, consider the following pseudocode, which assumes that we have functions to make a database connection, and we then use that database connection:

```
$connection = make_database_connection();
if (!$connection)
  die("No database connection!");
use_database_connection($connection);
```

This example assumes that our imaginary function make_database_connection(), like many PHP functions, returns a useful value if it succeeds, and a false value if it fails. An even more compact version of the preceding code takes advantage of the fact that or has lower precedence than the = assignment operator.

```
$connection = make_database_connection()
    or die("No database connection!");
use_database_connection($connection);
```

This works because the or operator short-circuits, and therefore the die() construct will only be evaluated if the expression $connection = make_database_connection() has a false value. Because the value of an assignment expression is the value assigned, this ends up being equivalent to the earlier version.

Summary

PHP has a C-like set of control structures, which branch or loop depending on the value of Boolean expressions, which in turn can be combined using Boolean operators (and, or, xor, !, &&, ||). The structures if and switch are used for simple branching; while, do-while, and for are used for looping; and exit and die terminate script execution.

Table 7-3 summarizes all the control structures from this chapter, with the exception of the alternative : .. endif syntax.

Table 7-3
PHP Control Structures

Name	Syntax	Behavior

If
(or if-else)
	```if (test)```
	   ```statement-1```
	-or-
	```if (test)```
	   ```statement-1```
	```else```
	   ```statement-2```
	-or-
	```if (test)```
	   ```statement-1```
	```elseif (test2)```
	   ```statement-2```
	```else```
	   ```statement-3```
		Evaluate *test* and if it is true, execute *statement-1*. If *test* is false and there is an ```else``` clause, execute *statement-2*. The ```elseif``` construct is a syntactic shortcut for ```else``` clauses where the included statement is itself an ```if``` construct. Statements may be single statements terminated with a semicolon, or brace-enclosed blocks.

Trinary operator	```expression-1 ?```
	```expression-2 :```
	```expression-3```
		Evaluate *expression-1* and interpret it as a Boolean. If it is true, evaluate *expression-2* and return it as the value of the entire expression. Otherwise, evaluate and return *expression-3*.

Switch	```switch(expression)```
	```{```
	   ```case value-1:```
	     ```statement-1```
	     ```statement-2```
	     ```...```
	     ```[break;]```
	   ```case value-2:```
	     ```statement-3```
	     ```statement-4```
	     ```...```
	     ```[break;]```
	   ```...```
	   ```[default:```
	    ```default-statement]```
	```}```
		Evaluate *expression,* and compare its value to the value in each case clause. When a matching case is found, begin executing statements in sequence (including those from later cases), until the end of the switch statement or until a break statement is encountered. The optional default case will execute no other case has matched the if expression.

Name	Syntax	Behavior
While	`while (condition)` `statement`	Evaluate *condition* and interpret it as Boolean. If condition is false, the `while` construct terminates. If it is true, execute *statement*, and keep executing it until *condition* becomes false. Terminate the `while` loop if the special `break` command is encountered, and skip the rest of the current iteration if `continue` is encountered.
Do-while	`do statement` `while (condition);`	Perform *statement* once unconditionally, then keep repeating statement until *condition* becomes false. (The break and continue commands are handled as in while.)

For	`for (initial-expression;`
	    `termination-check;`
	    `loop-end-expression)`
	    `statement`
		Evaluate *initial-expression* once unconditionally. Then if *termination-check* is true, evaluate *statement*, and then *loop-end-expression*, and repeat that loop until *termination-check* becomes false. Clauses may be omitted, or multiple clauses of the same kind can be separated with commas — a missing termination check is treated as true. (The `break` and `continue` commands are handled as in `while`.)

Exit	`exit()`	Terminate script immediately, without further parsing.
Die	`die(message-string)`	Send the *message-string* to output, and then terminate script.

✦　　✦　　✦

Using and Defining Functions

CHAPTER

8

◆ ◆ ◆ ◆

In This Chapter

Using built-in
PHP functions

Exploring the
online function
documentation

Defining your
own functions

Advanced tricks:
variable arguments,
call-by-reference,
variable functions

◆ ◆ ◆ ◆

Any real programming language has some kind of capability for *procedural abstraction* — a way to name pieces of code so that you can use them as building blocks in writing other pieces of code. Some scripting languages lack this capability, and we can tell you from our own sorrowful experience that complex server-side code can quickly become unmanageable without it.

PHP's mechanism for this kind of abstraction is the *function*. There are really two kinds of functions in PHP — those that have been built into the language by the PHP developers, and those that are defined by individual PHP programmers.

In this chapter, we look at how to use the large body of functions already provided in PHP and then, a bit later, how to define your own functions. Luckily, there is no real difference between using a built-in function and using your own functions.

Using Functions

The basic syntax for using (or *calling*) a function is:

```
function_name(expression_1, expression_2, ...,
expression_n)
```

That is, the name of the function followed by a parenthesized and comma-separated list of input expressions (which are called the *arguments* to the function). Functions can be called with zero or more arguments, depending on their definitions.

When PHP encounters a function call, it first evaluates each argument expression and then uses these values as inputs to the function. After the function executes, the returned value (if any) is the result of the entire function expression.

All of the following are valid calls to built-in PHP functions:

```
sqrt(9) // square root function, evaluates to 3
rand(10, 10 + 10) // random number between 10 and 20
strlen("This has 22 characters") // returns the number 22
pi() // returns the approximate value of pi
```

These functions are called with 1, 2, 1, and 0 arguments, respectively.

Return values versus side effects

Every function call is a PHP expression, and (just as with other expressions) there are only two reasons why you might want to include one in your code: for the return value or for the side effects.

The return value of a function is the value of the function expression itself. You can do exactly the same things with this value as with the results of evaluating any other expression. For example, you can assign it to a variable, as in

```
$my_pi = pi();
```

Or you can embed it in more complicated expressions, as in

```
$approx = sqrt($approx) * sqrt($approx)
```

Functions are also used for a wide variety of side effects, including writing to files, manipulating databases, and printing things to the browser window. It's okay to make use of both return values and side-effects at the same time—for example, it is very common to have a side-effecting function return a value that indicates whether or not the function succeeded.

The result of a function may be of any type, and it is common to use the array type as a way for functions to return multiple values.

Function Documentation

The architecture of PHP has been cleverly designed to make it easy for other developers to extend. The basic PHP language itself is very clean and flexible, but there is not a lot there—most of PHP's power resides in the large number of built-in functions. This means that developers can contribute simply by adding new built-in functions, which is nice especially because it does not change anything that PHP users may be relying on.

Although this book covers many of these built-in functions, explaining some of them in greater detail than the online manual can, the manual at `http://www.php.net` is the authoritative source for function information. In this book, we get to choose our topics to some extent, whereas the PHP documentation group has the awesome responsibility of covering every aspect of PHP in the manual. Also, although we hope to keep updating this book in future editions, the manual will have the freshest information on new additions to the ever-growing PHP functionality. It's worth looking at some of the different resources that the PHP site and manual offer.

Note   Although the following information is correct at this writing, some details may date or become inapplicable if the online manual is reorganized.

To find the manual, head to `http://www.php.net` and look for the "Documentation" tab on the left-hand navigation bar. The page that this tab leads to has links to manual information in a wide variety of formats. Our favorite is the online annotated manual, which allows users to post their own clarifying comments to each page. (Please note: the manual annotation system is not the right place to post questions! For that, see the section on mailing lists under the "Support" tab on `www.php.net`, or see our appendix on PHP resources. But it *is* the right place to explain something in your own words once you understand it. If you offer a better explanation, it might well show up in a later version of the documentation, which is a cool way to contribute.)

The largest section of the manual is the function reference, where each built-in function gets its own page of documentation. Each page starts off with a the name of the function and a one-line description, then a C-style header declaration of the function (explained in the next section), followed by a slightly longer description and possibly an example or two, and then (in the annotated manual) clarifications and gotcha reports from users.

Headers in documentation

For those unfamiliar with C function headers, the very beginning of a function documentation page might be confusing. The format is

```
return-type function-name(type1 arg1, type2 arg2, . . .);
```

This specifies the type of value the function is expected to return, the name of the function, and the number and expected types of its arguments.

Here is a typical header description:

```
string substr(string string, int start[, int length]);
```

This says that the function `substr` will return a string and expects to be given a string and two integers as its arguments. Actually, the square brackets around `length` indicate that this argument is optional—so `substr` should be called either with a string and an int, or a string and two ints.

Unlike in C, the argument types in these documentary headers are not absolute requirements. If you call `substr` with a number as its first argument, you will not get an error. Instead, PHP will convert the first argument to a string as it begins to execute the function. However, the argument types do document the intent of the function's author, and it is a good idea either to use the function as documented or to understand the type conversion issues well enough that you are sure the result will be what you expect.

In general, the type names used in function documentation will be those of the six basic types, or their aliases: integer (or int), double (or float, real), Boolean, string, array, and object. In addition, you may see the types `void` and `mixed`. The "void" return type means that the function does not return a value at all, whereas the "mixed" argument type means that the argument might be of any type.

Finding function documentation

What's the best way to find information about a function in the manual? That is likely to depend on what kind of curiosity you have. The most common questions about functions are:

> I want to use function X. Now, how does X work again?

> I'd really like to do task Y. Is there a function that handles that for me?

For the first type of curiosity, the full version of the online manual offers an automatic lookup by function name. The "quick ref" button in the left-hand navigation bar pops up on mouseover a box that prompts you to type in a function name, and then takes you to that function's manual page. Actually clicking the "quick ref" button will lead you to a complete list of all functions, sorted alphabetically.

For the second type of curiosity, your best bet is probably to use the hierarchical organization of the function reference, which is split (at press time) into about sixty-two "chapters." For example, the `substr` function shown previously is found in the "String functions" section. You can browse the chapter list of the function reference for the best fit to the task you want to do. Alternatively, if you happen to know the name of a function that seems to be in the same general area as your task, you can use the "quick ref" button to jump to that chapter.

Defining Your Own Functions

User-defined functions are not a requirement in PHP. You can produce interesting and useful Web sites simply with the basic language constructs and the large body of built-in functions. However, if you find that your code files are getting longer, harder to understand, and more difficult to manage, it may be an indication that you should start wrapping some of your code up into functions.

What is a function?

A function is a way of wrapping up a chunk of code and giving that chunk a name, so that you can use that chunk later in just one line of code. Functions are most useful when you will be using the code in more than one place, but they can be helpful even in one-use situations, because they can make your code much more readable.

Function definition syntax

Function definitions have the following form:

```
function function-name ($argument1, $argument2, ..)
{
   statement1;
   statement2;
   ...
}
```

That is, function definitions have four parts:

1. The special word `function`

2. The name that you want to give your function

3. The function's parameter list — dollar-sign variables separated by commas

4. The function body — a brace-enclosed set of statements

Just as with variable names, the name of the function must be made up of letters, numbers, and underscores, and it must not start with a number. Unlike variable names, function names are converted to lowercase before they are stored, so a function is the same regardless of capitalization.

The short version of what happens when a user-defined function is called is:

1. PHP looks up the function by its name (you will get an error if the function has not yet been defined).

2. PHP substitutes the values of the calling arguments (or the "actual parameters") into the variables in the definition's parameter list (or the "formal parameters").

3. The statements in the body of the function are executed. If any of the executed statements are "return" statements the function stops and returns the given value. Otherwise, the function completes after the last statement is executed, without returning a value.

Note   The alert and experienced programmer will have noticed that the preceding description implies call-by-value, rather than call-by-reference. In the last section of this chapter we explain the difference and show how to get call-by-reference behavior.

Function definition example

As a contrived example, imagine that we have the following code that helps decide which size of bottled soft drink to buy. (This is sometime next year, when supermarket shoppers routinely use their wearable wireless Web browsers to get to your handy price comparison site.)

```
$liters_1 = 1.0;
$price_1 = 1.59;
$liters_2 = 1.5;
$price_2 = 2.09;

$per_liter_1 = $price_1 / $liters_1;
$per_liter_2 = $price_2 / $liters_2;
if ($per_liter1 < $per_liter2)
  print("The first deal is better!<BR>");
else
  print("The second deal is better!<BR>");
```

Because this kind of comparison happens in our Web site code all the time, we would like to make part of this a reusable function. One way to do this would be the following rewrite:

```
function better_deal ($amount_1, $price_1,
                      $amount_2, $price_2)
{
  $per_amount_1 = $price_1 / $amount_1;
  $per_amount_2 = $price_2 / $amount_2;
  return($per_amount_1 < $per_amount_2);
}

$liters_1 = 1.0;
$price_1 = 1.59;
$liters_2 = 1.5;
$price_2 = 2.09;

if (better_deal($liters_1, $price_1,
                $liters_2, $price_2))
  print("The first deal is better!<BR>");
else
  print("The second deal is better!<BR>");
```

Our `better_deal` function abstracts out the three lines in the previous code that did the arithmetic and comparison. It takes four numbers as arguments and returns the value of a Boolean expression. As with any Boolean value, we can embed it in the test portion of an `if` statement. Although this function is longer than the original code, there are two benefits to this rewrite: we can use the function in multiple places (saving lines overall), and if we decide to change the calculation, we only have to make the change in one place.

Alternatively, if the only way we ever use these price comparisons is to print out which deal is preferred, we can include the printing in the function, like this:

```
function print_better_deal ($amount_1, $price_1,
                            $amount_2, $price_2)
{
  $per_amount_1 = $price_1 / $amount_1;
  $per_amount_2 = $price_2 / $amount_2;
  if ($per_amount_1 < $per_amount_2)
    print("The first deal is better!<BR>");
  else
    print("The second deal is better!<BR>");
}

$liters_1 = 1.0;
$price_1 = 1.59;
$liters_2 = 1.5;
$price_2 = 2.09;

print_better_deal($liters_1, $price_1,
                  $liters_2, $price_2);
```

Our first function used the `return` statement to send back a Boolean result, which was used in an `if` test. The second function has no `return` statement, because it is used for the side effect of printing text to the user's browser. When the last statement of this function is executed, PHP simply moves on to executing the next statement after a function call.

Formal parameters versus actual parameters

In the preceding examples, the arguments we passed to our functions happened to be variables, but this is not a requirement. The actual parameters (that is, the arguments that are in the function call) may be any expression that evaluates to a value. In our examples, we could have passed numbers to our function calls rather than variables, as in:

```
print_better_deal(1.0, 1.59, 1.5, 2.09);
```

Also, notice that in the examples we had a couple of cases where the actual parameter variable had the same name as the formal parameter (for example, $price_1), and we also had cases where the actual and formal names were different ($liters_1 is not the same as $amount_1). As we will see in the next section, this doesn't matter either way—the names of a function's formal parameters are completely independent of the world outside the function, including the function call itself.

Argument number mismatches

What happens if you call a function with fewer arguments than appear in the definition, or with more? As you might have come to expect by now, PHP forgives this, at least under the default settings for error and warning reporting. If you supply fewer actual parameters than formal parameters, PHP will treat the unfilled formal parameters as if they were unbound variables. If you hand too many arguments to a function, the "excess" arguments will simply be ignored. As we will see near the end of this chapter, this tolerance turns out to be helpful in defining functions that can take a variable number of arguments.

Functions and Variable Scope

As we said in Chapter 5, outside of functions the rules about variable scope are simple: assign a variable anywhere in the execution of a PHP code file and the value will be there for you later in that file's execution. The rules become somewhat more complicated in the bodies of function definitions, but not much.

The basic principle governing variables in function bodies is: each function is its own little world. That is, barring some special declarations, the meaning of a variable name inside a function has nothing to do with the meaning of that name elsewhere. (This is a feature, not a bug—you want functions to be reusable in different contexts, and so having the behavior be independent of the context is a good thing. If not for this kind of scoping, you would waste a lot of time chasing down bugs caused by using the same variable name in different parts of your code.)

The only variable values that a function has access to are the formal parameter variables (which have the values copied from the actual parameters), plus any variables that are assigned inside the function. This means that you can use local variables inside a function, without worrying about their effect on the outside world. For example, consider this function and its subsequent use:

```
function SayMyABCs ()
{
  $count = 0;
  while ($count < 10)
    {
```

```
        print(chr(ord('A') + $count));
        $count = $count + 1;
    }
    print("<BR>Now I know $count letters<BR>");
}
$count = 0;
SayMyABCs();
$count = $count + 1;
print("Now I've made $count function call(s).<BR>");
SayMyABCs();
$count = $count + 1;
print("Now I've made $count function call(s).<BR>");
```

The intent of SayMyABCs() is to print out a sequence of letters. (The functions chr() and ord() translate between letters and their numeric ASCII codes — we use them here just as a trick to generate letters in sequence.) The output of this code is:

```
ABCDEFGHIJ
Now I know 10 letters
Now I've made 1 function call(s).
ABCDEFGHIJ
Now I know 10 letters
Now I've made 2 function call(s).
```

Both the function definition and the code outside the function make use of variables called $count, but they refer to different variables and do not clash.

The default behavior of variables assigned inside functions is that they do not interact with the outside world, and they act as though they are newly created each time the function is called. Both of these behaviors, however, can be overridden with special declarations.

Global versus local

The scope of a variable defined inside a function is local by default. Using the global declaration, you can inform PHP that you want a variable name to mean the same thing as it does in the context outside the function. The syntax of this declaration is simply the word global, followed by a comma-delimited list of the variables that should be treated that way, with a terminating semicolon. To see the effect, consider a new version of the previous example. The only difference is that we have declared $count to be global, and we have removed its initial assignment to zero inside the function:

```
function SayMyABCs2 ()
{
    global $count;
    while ($count < 10)
```

```
    {
      print(chr(ord('A') + $count));
      $count = $count + 1;
    }
  print("<BR>Now I know $count letters<BR>");
}
$count = 0;
SayMyABCs2();
$count = $count + 1;
print("Now I've made $count function call(s).<BR>");
SayMyABCs2();
$count = $count + 1;
print("Now I've made $count function call(s).<BR>");
```

Our revised version prints the following browser output:

```
ABCDEFGHIJ
Now I know 10 letters
Now I've made 11 function call(s).

Now I know 11 letters
Now I've made 12 function call(s).
```

This is buggy behavior, and the global declaration is to blame. There is now only one $count variable, and it is being increased both inside and outside the function. When the second call to SayMyABCs() happens, $count is already 11, and so the loop that prints letters is never entered.

Although this example shows global to bad advantage, it can be quite useful, especially because (as we'll see in Chapter 12) PHP provides some variable bindings to every page even before any of your own code is executed. It can be helpful to have a way for functions to see these variables without the bother of passing them in as arguments with each call.

Static variables

By default, functions retain no memory of their own execution, and with each function call local variables act as though they have been newly created. The static declaration overrides this behavior for particular variables, causing them to retain their values in between calls to the same function. Using this, we can modify our earlier function to give it some memory:

```
function SayMyABCs3 ()
{
  static $count = 0; //assignment only if first time called
  $limit = $count + 10;
  while ($count < $limit)
    {
```

```
        print(chr(ord('A') + $count));
        $count = $count + 1;
    }
  print("<BR>Now I know $count letters<BR>");
}
$count = 0;
SayMyABCs3();
$count = $count + 1;
print("Now I've made $count function call(s).<BR>");
SayMyABCs3();
$count = $count + 1;
print("Now I've made $count function call(s).<BR>");
```

This memory-enhanced version gives us the following output:

```
ABCDEFGHIJ
Now I know 10 letters
Now I've made 1 function call(s).
KLMNOPQRST
Now I know 20 letters
Now I've made 2 function call(s).
```

The static keyword allows for an initial assignment, which has an effect only if the function has not been called before. The first time SayMyABCs executes, the local version of $count is set to zero. The second time the function is called, it has the value it had at the end of the last execution, so we are able to pick up our studies where we left off. Notice that changes to $count outside the function still have no effect on the local value.

Function Scope

Although the rules about the scope of variable names are fairly simple, the scoping rules for function names are even simpler. There is just one rule in PHP 4: functions must be defined once (and only once) somewhere in the script that uses them. (See the "New Feature" note about differences between this behavior and PHP 3.) The scope of function names is implicitly global, and so a function that is defined in a script is available everywhere in that script. For clarity's sake, though, it is often a good idea to define all your functions first before any code that uses those functions.

New Feature

In PHP 3, functions could be used only after they were defined. This meant that the safest practice was to define (or include the definitions of) all functions early in a given script, before actually using any of them. PHP 4 actually pre-compiles scripts before running them, and one effect of this is that it discovers all function definitions before actually running the code. This means that functions and code can appear in any order in a script, as long as all functions are defined once (and only once).

Include and require

It's very common to want to use the same set of functions across a set of Web site pages, and the usual way to handle this is with either `include` or `require`, both of which import the contents of some other file into the file being executed. Using either one of these forms is vastly preferable to *cloning* your function definitions (that is, repeating them at the beginning of each page that uses them) because when you want to modify your functions, you will only have to do it once.

For example, at the top of a PHP code file we might have lines like

```
include "basic-functions.inc"
include "advanced-function.inc";
(.. code that uses basic and advanced functions ..)
```

which import two different files of function definitions. (Note that parentheses are optional with both `include()` and `require()`.) As long as the only things in these files are function definitions, the order of their inclusion will not matter.

Both `include` and `require` have the effect of splicing in the contents of their file at the point that they are called. Unlike `include`, a given `require` statement will not execute more than once, even if the same `require` statement would apparently be called more than once (as when embedded in a loop)—PHP actually substitutes the file's contents for the `require` statement the first time it is encountered.

Unfortunately, `require` is not a magic solution to the problem of making sure no function file is loaded twice—it is not smart enough to keep track of previous calls to `require` or `include`. If you repeat exactly the same `require` statement twice in a row, the file will load twice, double-loading any functions in that file. Similarly, let's say that both the basic and advanced function files cited here have the same `require` statement in them, intended to pull in a file of even more basic utility functions. In this case, you will get a double-definition error, because the utility file will be loaded twice.

One quick-and-dirty technique for avoiding double-loading files is to embed `include` statements in an `if` statement, like so:

```
if (!IsSet($myfuncs_loaded))
    include("myfuncs.inc");
```

where `$myfuncs_loaded` is a variable set in the file `myfuncs.inc`.

Recursion

Some compiled languages like C and C++ impose somewhat complex ordering constraints on how functions are defined. To know how to compile a function, the compiler must know about all the functions that the function calls, which means the called functions must be defined first. So what do you do if two functions each call the other, or one function calls itself? Issues like this led the designers of C to a separation of function declarations (or prototypes) from function definitions (or implementations). The idea is that you use declarations to inform the compiler in advance about the types of arguments and return types of the functions you plan to use, which is enough information for the compiler to handle the actual definitions in any order.

In PHP, this problem goes away, and so there is no need for separate function prototypes. In PHP 3, functions need to be defined before they are used, but defining one function to call another does not yet count as use of either function. When PHP 3 encounters the definition of function A, it does not object if the body of A includes calls to function B, which has not yet been defined. Function B just needs to be defined by the time function A is actually called. In PHP 4, even the ordering issue is not an issue.

This means that recursive functions (functions that call themselves) are no problem. For example, we can define a recursive function and then immediately call it:

```
function countdown ($num_arg)
   {
     if ($num_arg > 0)
        {
          print("Counting down from $num_arg<BR>");
          countdown($num_arg - 1);
        }
   }
countdown(10);
```

This produces the browser output

```
Counting down from 10
Counting down from 9
Counting down from 8
Counting down from 7
Counting down from 6
Counting down from 5
Counting down from 4
Counting down from 3
Counting down from 2
Counting down from 1
```

As with all recursive functions, it's important to be sure that the function has a base case (a nonrecursive branch) in addition to the recursive case, and that the base case is certain to eventually occur. If the base case is never invoked, the situation is much like a `while` loop where the test is always true — we will have an infinite loop of function calling. In the case of the preceding function, we know that the base case will happen, because every invocation of the recursive case reduces the countdown number, which must eventually become zero. Of course this assumes that the input is a positive integer, rather than a negative number or a double. Notice that our "greater than zero" test guards against infinite recursion even in these cases, whereas a "not equal to zero" test would not.

Similarly, mutually recursive functions (functions that each call each other) work without a hitch. For example, the following definitions plus function call:

```
function countdown_first ($num_arg)
  {
    if ($num_arg > 0)
      {
        print("Counting down (first) from $num_arg<BR>");
        countdown_second($num_arg - 1);
      }
  }
function countdown_second ($num_arg)
  {
    if ($num_arg > 0)
      {
        print("Counting down (second) from $num_arg<BR>");
        countdown_first($num_arg - 1);
      }
  }

countdown_first(5);
```

would produce the browser output:

```
Counting down (first) from 5
Counting down (second) from 4
Counting down (first) from 3
Counting down (second) from 2
Counting down (first) from 1
```

Advanced Function Tricks

Now we move on to some more exotic properties of functions, including ways to use variable numbers of arguments, ways to have functions actually modify the variables they are passed, and (cooler still) using functions as data.

Note This final section is more challenging than the rest of the chapter, and it may be of interest only to the adventurous, the curious, or more experienced programmers.

Variable numbers of arguments

It's often useful to have the number of actual arguments that are passed to a function depend on the situation in which it is called. There are three possible ways to handle this in PHP, one of which is only available in PHP 4:

1. Define the function with default arguments—any that are missing in the function call will have the default value, and no warning will be printed.

2. Use an array argument to hold the values — it is the responsibility of the calling code to package up the array, and the function body must appropriately take it apart.

3. Use the variable-argument functions (`func_num_args()`, `func_get_arg()`, and `func_get_args()`) introduced in PHP 4.

Default arguments

To define a function with default arguments, simply turn the formal parameter name into an assignment expression. If the actual call has fewer parameters than the definition has formal parameters, PHP will match actual with formal until it runs out, and then will use the default assignments to fill in the rest.

For example, the following function has all of its variables defined with defaults:

```
function tour_guide($city = "Gotham City",
                    $desc = "vast metropolis",
                    $how_many = "dozens",
                    $of_what = "costumed villains")
{
  print("$city is a $desc filled with
         $how_many of $of_what.<BR>");
}
tour_guide();
tour_guide("Chicago");
tour_guide("Chicago", "wonderful city");
tour_guide("Chicago", "wonderful city",
           "teeming millions");
tour_guide("Chicago", "wonderful city",
           "teeming millions",
           "gruff people with hearts of
            gold and hard-luck stories to tell");
```

The browser output is something like this, with the intra-sentence line breaks, of course, determined by your browser:

```
Gotham City is a great metropolis filled with dozens of
costumed villains.
Chicago is a great metropolis filled with dozens of costumed
villains.
Chicago is a wonderful city filled with dozens of costumed
villains.
Chicago is a wonderful city filled with teeming millions of
costumed villains.
Chicago is a wonderful city filled with teeming millions of
gruff people with hearts of gold and hard-luck stories to tell.
```

The main limitation of default arguments is that the matching of actual to formal parameters is determined by the ordering of both — it's first-come, first-served. This means that there is absolutely no way to use the default-argument mechanism to tell someone about hard-luck stories in Gotham City.

Arrays as multiple-argument substitutes

If you are dissatisfied with the flexibility of multiple arguments, you can bypass the whole argument-counting issue by using an array as your communication channel.

The following example uses this strategy and in addition uses a few tricks like the ternary operator (introduced in Chapter 7) and the associative array (touched on in Chapter 6 and covered completely in Chapter 11):

```
function tour_brochure($info_array)
{
$city =
 IsSet($info_array['city']) ?
  $info_array['city'] : "Gotham City";
$desc =
 IsSet($info_array['desc']) ?
  $info_array['desc'] : "great metropolis";
$how_many =
 IsSet($info_array['how_many']) ?
  $info_array['how_many'] : "dozens";
$of_what =
 IsSet($info_array['of_what']) ?
  $info_array['of_what'] : "costumed villains";

print("$city is a $desc filled with
       $how_many of $of_what.<BR>");
}
```

This function checks the single incoming array argument for four different values associated with particular strings. Using the ternary conditional operator ?, local variables are assigned to either the incoming value (if it has been stored in the array) or to our comic-book defaults. Now, let's try calling this function with a couple of different arrays:

```
tour_brochure(array()); // empty array
$tour_info =
 array('city' => 'Cozumel',
       'desc' => 'destination getaway',
       'of_what' => 'sandy beaches');
tour_brochure($tour_info);
```

In this example, we call `tour_brochure` first with an empty array (corresponding to no arguments), and then with an array that has three of the four possible associative values stored in it. The browser output we get is:

```
Gotham City is a great metropolis filled with dozens of
costumed villains.
Cozumel is a destination getaway filled with dozens of sandy
beaches.
```

In both cases, the `"dozens"` amount is defaulted, because neither array had anything stored under the `"how_many"` association.

Multiple arguments in PHP 4

Finally, PHP 4 offers some functions that can be used inside function bodies to recover the number and values of arguments. They are:

`func_num_args()`	Takes no arguments and returns the number of arguments that were passed to the function it is called from.
`func_get_arg()`	Takes an integer argument *n*, and returns the *n*th argument to the function it is called from. Arguments are numbered starting from zero.
`func_get_args()`	Takes no arguments and returns an array containing all the arguments in the function it is called from, with array indices starting from zero.

All three of these functions will produce a warning if called outside a function body, and `func_get_arg()` will give a warning if it is called with an index higher than the index of the final argument that was passed.

If your function is going to handle the decoding of arguments using these functions, then you can take advantage of the fact that PHP doesn't complain about function calls that have more arguments than formal parameters in the definition — simply define your function to take no arguments, and then use the functions to catch any that are actually passed.

As an example, consider the following two functions, both of which return an array of the arguments they are given:

```
function args_as_array_1 ()
{
$arg_count = func_num_args();
$counter = 0;
$local_array = array();
while ($counter < $arg_count)
   {
    $local_array[$counter] =
       func_get_arg($counter);
    $counter = $counter + 1;
   }
return($local_array);
}

function args_as_array_2 ()
{
    return(func_get_args());
}
```

The first cumbersome function uses `func_get_arg()` to retrieve the individual arguments and bounds the loop using the result of `func_num_args()`, so that no attempt is made to retrieve more arguments than were actually passed. Each argument is individually stored in an array, which is then returned. Packaging up the arguments like this is already done for free by `func_get_args()`, so the second version of the function is extremely short.

As another example, let's rewrite our earlier `tour_guide()` function to use the multiple-argument functions instead of default arguments:

```
function tour_guide_2()
{
$num_args = func_num_args();
$city = $num_args > 0 ?
  func_get_arg(0) : "Gotham City";
$desc = $num_args > 1 ?
  func_get_arg(1) : "great metropolis";
$how_many = $num_args > 2 ?
  func_get_arg(2) : "dozens";
$of_what = $num_args > 3 ?
  func_get_arg(3) : "costumed villains";

print("$city is a $desc filled with
      $how_many of $of_what.<BR>");
}
tour_guide2();
```

This has exactly the same behavior as the default-argument version and is subject to the same limitation. The arguments are passed in by position, and so there is no way to replace "costumed villains" with something else while leaving "Gotham City" as the default.

Call-by-value versus call-by-reference

The default behavior for user-defined functions in PHP is "call-by-value." This means that when you pass variables to a function call, PHP makes copies of the variable values to pass on to the function. So, whatever the function does, it is not able to change the actual variables that appear in the function call. This behavior can be good or bad. It's a nice reassurance if you only want to use a function for its returned value, but it can also be a source of confusion and frustration if changing the passed variable is actually your goal.

Let's demonstrate call-by-value with a fragile and extremely inefficient implementation of subtraction:

```
function lame_subtract ($num1, $num2)
{
  if ($num1 < $num2)
    die("Negative numbers are imaginary");
```

```
   $return_result = 0;
   while($num1 > $num2)
     {
        $num1 = $num1 - 1;
        $return_result = $return_result + 1;
     }
   return($return_result);
}
$first_op = 493;
$second_op = 355;
$result1 = lame_subtract($first_op, $second_op);
print("result1 is $result1<BR>");
$result2 = lame_subtract($first_op, $second_op);
print("result2 is $result2<BR>");
```

Reassuringly, we find that our result is the same both times we perform the same subtraction:

```
result1 is 138
result2 is 138
```

This is true even though `lame_subtract` changes the value of its formal parameter `$num1` — that variable only holds a copy of the value that was in the actual parameter `$first_op`, and so `$first_op` cannot be affected.

Call by reference

PHP offers two different ways to have functions actually modify their arguments: in the function definition and in the function call.

If you want to define a function to operate directly on a passed variable, simply put an ampersand in front of the formal parameter in the definition, like so:

```
function lame_subtract_ref (&$num1, &$num2)
{
  if ($num1 < $num2)
    die("Negative numbers are imaginary");
  $return_result = 0;
  while($num1 > $num2)
    {
       $num1 = $num1 - 1;
       $return_result = $return_result + 1;
    }
  return($return_result);
}
$first_op = 493;
$second_op = 355;
$result1 = lame_subtract_ref($first_op, $second_op);
print("result1 is $result1<BR>");
$result2 = lame_subtract_ref($first_op, $second_op);
print("result2 is $result2<BR>");
```

Now, if we perform exactly the same subtraction calls as we did the first time, we get the output:

```
result1 is 138
result1 is 0
```

This is because the formal parameter $num1 refers to the same thing as the actual parameter $first_op—changing one means changing the other.

You can also force a function to take arguments by reference by prepending the actual parameters with ampersands. That is, we can use our original call-by-value function and get the by-reference behavior, like so:

```
$first_op = 493;
$second_op = 355;
$result1 = lame_subtract(&$first_op, &$second_op);
print("result1 is $result1<BR>");
$result2 = lame_subtract(&$first_op, &$second_op);
print("result2 is $result2<BR>");
```

producing, once again

```
result1 is 138
result1 is 0
```

As of PHP 4, variable references can now be used outside of function calls as well. In general, assigning a variable reference (&$varname) to a variable will make the two variables aliases of each other rather than distinct variables with the same value. For example,

```
$name_1 = "Manfred von Richtofen";
$name_2 = "Percy Blakeney";
$alias_1 = $name_1;  // vars have same value
$alias_2 = &$name_2; // vars are the same

$alias_1 = "The Red Baron"; // doesn't change real name
$alias_2 = "The Scarlet Pimpernel"; // anonymous forever

print("$alias_1 is $name_1<BR>");
print("$alias_2 is $name_2<BR>");
```

will give the browser output:

```
The Red Baron is Manfred von Richtofen
The Scarlet Pimpernel is The Scarlet Pimpernel
```

Variable function names

One of the neater tricks you can do in PHP is to use variables in place of the names of user-defined functions. That is, rather than typing a literal function name into your code, you type a dollar-sign variable—the function that is actually called at run time will depend on the string that that variable has been assigned to. In some sense, this allows us to use functions as data. This kind of trick will be familiar to advanced C programmers, and to even beginning users of any kind of Lisp language (for example, Scheme or Common Lisp).

For example, the following two function calls are exactly equivalent:

```
function customized_greeting ()
{
   print("You are being greeted in a customized way!<BR>");
}
customized_greeting();
$my_greeting = 'customized_greeting';
$my_greeting();
```

and produce the same output:

```
You are being greeted in a customized way!
You are being greeted in a customized way!
```

Because function names are just strings, they can also be used as arguments to functions, or be returned as a function's result.

An extended example

Just for fun, let's see what kinds of trouble we can get into by using some of the more advanced features of functions, including using function names as function arguments.

Listing 8-1 shows an extended example of functions that implement a substitution cipher—a rudimentary kind of cryptography that scrambles messages by substituting one letter of the alphabet for another.

 Note   This code is both longer and more advanced than anything in the book so far. It is both skippable and skimmable for those who don't want to work through the details.

Listing 8-1: **A substitution cipher**

```
/* Part 1 - cipher algorithm and utility functions */
function add_1 ($num)
{
  return(($num + 1) % 26);
}

function sub_1 ($num)
{
  return(($num + 25) % 26);
}

function swap_2 ($num)
{
  if ($num % 2 == 0)
    return($num + 1);
  else
    return($num - 1);
}

function swap_26 ($num)
{
  return(25 - $num);
}

function lower_letter($char_string)
{
 return ((ord($char_string) >= ord('a')) &&
         (ord($char_string) <= ord('z')));
}

function upper_letter($char_string)
{
 return ((ord($char_string) >= ord('A')) &&
         (ord($char_string) <= ord('Z')));
}

/* Part 2 - the letter_cipher function */
function letter_cipher ($char_string, $code_func)
{
  if (!(upper_letter($char_string) ||
        lower_letter($char_string)))
    return($char_string);
  if (upper_letter($char_string))
    $base_num = ord('A');
  else
    $base_num = ord('a');
  $char_num = ord($char_string) -
                    $base_num;
```

```
    return(chr($base_num +
            ($code_func($char_num)
            % 26)));
}

/* Part 3 - the main string_cipher function */
function string_cipher($message, $cipher_func)
{
  $coded_message = "";
  $message_length = strlen($message);
  for ($index = 0;
       $index < $message_length;
       $index++)
    $coded_message .=
       letter_cipher($message[$index], $cipher_func);
  return($coded_message);
}
```

Listing 8-1 is in three parts. In the first part, we define a few functions that do simple math on the numbers from 0 through 25, which will represent the letters A–Z in our cipher codes. Function add_1 simply adds 1 to the number it is given, modulo 26 (which just means that numbers that are 26 and larger "wrap around" to start from zero again). 0 becomes 1, 1 becomes 2, . . . , and 25 becomes 0. Sub_1 shifts numbers in the other direction, by adding 25 (which in this modular arithmetic is equivalent to subtracting 1) — 25 becomes 24, 24 becomes 23 . . . , and 0 becomes 25. Swap_2 trades the places of pairs of numbers — 0 to 1, 1 to 0, 2 to 3, 3 to 2 . . . . Swap_26 trades high numbers for low numbers (25 to 0, 0 to 25, 24 to 1, 1 to 24 . . .). Each one of these functions will be the basis of a simple cipher code. Finally, we have a couple of utility functions that test whether a character is an uppercase or lowercase letter.

Part 2 is a single function called letter_cipher(), whose job it is to take a math function like the ones in Part 1, and apply it to encode a single letter. First it tests whether the string it is handed (which should be a single character) is an alphabetic letter; if not, it returns it as is. If the character is a letter, it is transformed into a number using ord(), and the appropriate letter ('a' or 'A') is subtracted from it to bring the number into the 0–25 range. Once it is in that range, we apply the cipher function whose name was passed in as a string, and then we convert the number back into a letter and return it.

Finally, part 3 is the single string_cipher() function, which takes a string message and a cipher function and returns a new string that is the message encoded via the function. This uses a couple of features we haven't seen before (including the string concatenation operator '.=', which we will cover in Chapter 9). For now, though, it's enough to know that this function builds a new string, letter by letter, from the message string, and that each new letter is the result of applying $cipher_func to the numerical representation of the old letter.

Now let's write some code to try out `string_cipher()`:

```
$original = "My secret message is ABCDEFG";
print("Original message is: $original<BR>");

$coding_array = array('add_1',
                      'sub_1',
                      'swap_2',
                      'swap_26');
for ($count = 0;
     $count < sizeof($coding_array);
     $count++)
{
  $code = $coding_array[$count];
  $coded_message =
    string_cipher($original, $code);
  print("$code encoding is: $coded_message<BR>");
}
```

This testing code takes our four predefined letter-encoding functions, stashes them in an array, and then loops through the array, encoding the `$original` message, and printing out the encoded version. The browser output looks like:

```
Original message is: My secret message is ABCDEFG
add_1 encoding is: Nz tfdsfu nfttbhf jt BCDEFGH
sub_1 encoding is: Lx rdbqds ldrrzfd hr ZABCDEF
swap_2 encoding is: Nz tfdqfs nfttbhf jt BADCFEH
swap_26 encoding is: Nb hvxivg nvhhztv rh ZYXWVUT
```

We can take this function-as-data approach one step further and write a function that applies more than one cipher to a message in sequence. This function also uses the variable-argument functions of PHP 4:

```
function chained_code ($message)
{
  /* takes a message, then an arbitrary number of
     cipher-code function names. Returns
     result of applying each code to the previous
     result. */
  $argc = func_num_args();
  $coded = $message;
  for ($count = 1; $count < $argc; $count++)
    {
      $function_name = func_get_arg($count);
      $coded =
        string_cipher($coded,
                      $function_name);
    }
  return($coded);
}
```

The first argument to `chained_code()` should be a message string, followed by any number of names corresponding to cipher functions. The coded message is the result of applying the first coding function to the message, then applying the second coding function to the result, and so on. We can test it with various combinations of our predefined letter-coding functions.

```
$tricky =
   chained_code($original,
                'add_1', 'swap_26',
                'add_1', 'swap_2');
print("Tricky encoded version is $tricky<BR>");

$easy =
   chained_code($original,
                'add_1', 'swap_26',
                'swap_2', 'sub_1',
                'add_1', 'swap_2',
                'swap_26', 'sub_1');
print("Easy encoded version is $easy<BR>");
```

with these results:

```
Tricky encoded version is Ma guwjuh muggysu qg YZWXUVS
Easy encoded version is My secret message is ABCDEFG
```

As you can see, the "tricky" encoding of our message is a combination of our previous codes that doesn't correspond exactly to any of those single coding functions. And the "easy" coding is an even more complicated combination of those functions that produces . . . our original message unchanged! (No, it's not that our cipher code doesn't work—we'll leave it to you to figure out why that particular sequence of coding functions brings us around to our starting message again.)

The moral of our little cryptographic scripting story is that, although the cipher code was mildly complicated, it was made considerably simpler by PHP's support for using function names as function arguments.

Summary

Most of the power of PHP resides in the large number of built-in functions provided by PHP's benevolent army of open-source developers. Each of these functions should be documented (albeit briefly) in the online manual at `http://www.php.net`.

You can also write your own functions, which are then used in exactly the same way as the built-in functions. Functions are written in a simple C-style syntax, as in

```
function my_function ($arg1, $arg2, ..)
{
statement1;
statement2;
..
return($value);
}
```

User-defined functions can use arguments of any PHP type and can also return values of any type. The types of arguments and return value do not need to be declared.

In PHP 4, the ordering of function definitions and function calls makes no difference, as long as every function that is called is defined exactly once. There is no need for separate function declarations or prototypes. Variables assigned inside a function are local to that function, unless specified otherwise with the global declaration. Local variables may be declared to be *static,* which means that they hold onto their values in between function calls.

The default behavior for user-defined functions is "call-by-value," meaning that functions work on copies of their arguments and so cannot modify the original variables in the function call. You can force call-by-reference behavior by preceding parameters with '&', on either the definition side or the calling side. PHP offers more than one way to let functions take a variable number of arguments. Finally, the functions to be called can be determined at run time, by substituting a string variable for the literal name of the user-defined function — this allows functions to be treated as data and passed back and forth between other functions.

✦   ✦   ✦

Strings and String Functions

◆ ◆ ◆ ◆

In This Chapter

How to create and manipulate strings

Inspecting, comparing, and searching strings

Advanced string manipulation using regular expressions

HTML-specific string functions

◆ ◆ ◆ ◆

Although images, sound files, videos, animations, and applets make up an increasingly important portion of the World Wide Web, much of the Web is still text — one character's worth after another, like this sentence. The basic PHP datatype for representing text is the *string*.

Strings in PHP

Strings are sequences of characters that can be treated as a unit — assigned to variables, given as input to functions, returned from functions, or sent as output to appear on your user's Web page.

The simplest way to specify a string in PHP code is to enclose it in quotes, whether single quotes (') or double quotes ("), like this:

```
$my_string = 'A literal string';
$another_string = "Another string";
```

The difference between single and double quotes lies in how much interpretation PHP does of the characters between the quote signs, before creating the string itself. If you enclose a string in single quotes, almost no interpretation will be performed; if you enclose it in double quotes, then PHP will splice in the values of any variables you include, as well as make substitutions for certain special character sequences that begin with the backslash (\) character. For example, if you evaluate the following code in the middle of a Web page:

```
$statement = 'everything I say';
$question_1 =
  "Do you have to take $statement so literally?\n<BR>";
$question_2 =
  'Do you have to take $statement so literally?\n<BR>';
echo $question_1;
echo $question_2;
```

you should expect to see the browser output

```
Do you have to take everything I say so literally?
Do you have to take $statement so literally?\n
```

For the details on exactly how PHP interprets both singly and doubly quoted strings, see the "Strings" section of Chapter 6.

Characters and string indexes

Unlike some programming languages, PHP has no distinct character type that is different from the string type. In general, functions that would take character arguments in other languages expect strings of length 1 in PHP.

You can retrieve the characters in a string simply by treating it as an integer-indexed array of characters, with indices starting at 0. These "characters" will actually be one-character strings. For example, the code

```
$my_string = "Doubled";
for ($index = 0; $index < 7; $index++)
  print("$my_string[$index]$my_string[$index]");
```

would give the browser output

```
DDoouubblleedd
```

with each character of the string being printed twice per loop. (The number 7 is hard-coded in this example only because we haven't yet covered how to find out the length of a string—see the function `strlen()` in the later section "Inspecting strings.")

String Operators

PHP offers only one real operator on strings: the dot (.) or concatenation operator. This operator, when placed between two string arguments, produces a new string that is the result of putting the two strings together in sequence. For example,

```
$my_two_cents = "I want to give you a piece of my mind";
$third_cent = "And another thing ...";
print($my_two_cents . "..." . $third_cent);
```

would give the browser output:

```
I want to give you a piece of my mind ... And another thing
```

Note that we are not passing multiple string arguments to the print statement—we are handing it one string argument, which was created by concatenating three strings together. The first and third strings are variables, but the middle one is a literal string enclosed in double quotes.

Note Note that the concatenation operator is not + as in Java, and it does not overload anything else. If you forget this and add strings using +, they will be interpreted as numbers, with the result that one + two equals 0 (because no successful string-to-number conversion can be made).

Concatenation and assignment

Just as with arithmetic operators, PHP has a shorthand operator (.=) that combines concatenation with assignment. The following statement

```
$my_string_var .= $new_addition;
```

is exactly equivalent to

```
$my_string_var = $my_string_var . $new_addition;
```

Note that, unlike commutative addition and multiplication, with this shorthand operator it matters that the new string is added on to the right. If you want the new string tacked on to the left, there's no alternative shorter than

```
$my_string_var = $new_addition . $my_string_var;
```

String Functions

PHP gives you a huge variety of functions for the munching and crunching of strings. If you're ever tempted to roll your own function that reads strings character-by-character to produce a new string, pause for a moment to think whether the task might be common. If so, there is probably a built-in function that handles it. In this section, we present the basic functions for inspecting, comparing, modifying, and printing strings.

Note A note for C programmers. Many of the PHP string function names should be familiar to you. Just keep in mind that, because PHP takes care of memory management for you, the functions that return strings are allocating the string storage on their own and do not need to be given a preallocated string to write into.

Inspecting strings

What kinds of questions can you ask strings? First on the list is how long the string is, using the strlen() function.

```
$short_string = "This string has 29 characters";
print("It does have . strlen($short_string) .
        characters");
```

would give the output

```
It does have 29 characters
```

Knowing the string's length is particularly useful for situations in which we'd like to loop through a string character by character. A useless but illustrative example, using the preceding example string, is

```
for ($index = 0; $index < strlen($short_string); $index++)
   print("$short_string[$index]");
```

This simply prints

```
This string has 29 characters
```

which is the string we started with.

Finding characters and substrings

The next category of question you can ask your strings is what they contain. For example, the strpos() function finds the numerical position of a particular character in a string, if it exists.

```
$twister = "Peter Piper picked a peck of pickled peppers";
print("Location of 'p' is " . strpos($twister, 'p') .'<BR>');
print("Location of 'q' is "  . strpos($twister, 'q') .'<BR>');
```

gives us the browser output

```
Location of 'p' is 8
Location of 'q' is
```

The reason that the 'q' location is apparently blank is that strpos() returns false when the character in question cannot be found, and a false value prints as the empty string.

Caution   The strpos() function is one of those cases where PHP's type-looseness can be problematic. If no match can be found, the function returns a false value; if the very first character is a match, the function returns 0 (because the indexing count starts with 0 rather than 1). Both of these values look false if used in a Boolean test. One way to distinguish them is to use the identity comparison operator (===, introduced as of PHP 4), which is only true if its arguments are the same and of the same type—you can use it to test if the returned value is 0 (or is FALSE) without risk of confusion with other values that might be the same after type coercion. If you are using PHP 3 you need to do explicit type testing with, for example, is_integer().

The `strpos()` function can also be used to search for a substring rather than a single character, simply by giving it a multicharacter string rather than a single-character string. You can also supply an extra integer argument specifying the position to begin searching forward from.

Searching in reverse is also possible, using the `strrpos()` function (note the extra 'r', which you can think of as standing for "reverse"). This function takes a string to search and a single-character string to locate, and it returns the last position of occurrence of the second argument in the first argument. (Unlike with `strpos()`, the string that is searched for must only have one character.) If we use this function on our example sentence, we find a different position:

```
$twister = "Peter Piper picked a peck of pickled peppers";
printf("Location of 'p' is " . strrpos($twister, 'p') .'<BR>');
```

Specifically, we find the third 'p' in "peppers":

```
Location of 'p' is 40
```

Are strings immutable?

In some programming languages (like C) it is common to manipulate strings by directly changing them — that is, storing new characters into the middle of an existing string, replacing old characters. Other languages (like Java) try to keep the programmer out of certain kinds of trouble by making string classes that are *immutable* (or unchangeable) — you can make new strings by creating modified copies of old ones, but once you have made a string, you are not allowed to change it by directly changing the characters that make it up.

Where does PHP fit in? As it turns out, PHP strings can be changed, but the most common practice seems to be to treat strings as immutable.

Strings can be changed by treating them as character arrays and assigning directly into them, like this:

```
$my_string = "abcdefg";
$my_string[5] = "X";
print($my_string . "<BR>");
```

which will give the browser output:

```
abcdeXg
```

However, this modification method seems to be undocumented and shows up nowhere in the online manual, even though the corresponding extraction method is highlighted. Also, almost all PHP string manipulation functions return modified copies of their string arguments rather than making direct changes, which seems to indicate that this is the style that the PHP designers prefer. Our advice is not to use this direct-modification method to change strings, unless you know what you are doing and there is some large benefit in terms of memory savings.

Comparison and searching

Is this string the same as that string? It's a question that your code is likely to have to answer frequently, especially when dealing with input typed by the end user.

The simplest method to find an answer is to use the basic comparison operator ('=='), which does equality testing on strings as well as numbers.

Note
For the '==' operator, two strings are the same if they contain exactly the same sequence of characters. It does not test any stricter notion of being the same, such as being stored at the same memory address.

Caution
Comparing two strings using '==' (or the corresponding '<' and '>' operators) is trustworthy if both the arguments are in fact strings and you know that no type conversion is being performed. (See Chapter 6 for more on this.) Using strcmp() (described next) is always trustworthy.

The most basic workhorse string-comparison function is strcmp(). It takes two strings as arguments and compares them byte by byte until it finds a difference. It returns a negative number if the first string is "less than" the second, a positive number if the second string is less, and 0 if they are identical.

The strcasecmp() function works the same way, except that the equality comparison is case-insensitive. The function call strcasecmp("hey!", "HEY!") should return 0.

Searching

The comparison functions just described tell you whether one string is equal to another. To find out if one string is contained within another, use the strpos() function (covered earlier) or the strstr() function (or one of its relatives).

The strstr() function takes a string to search in and a string to look for (in that order). If it succeeds, it returns the portion of the string that starts with (and includes) the first instance of the string it is looking for. If the string is not found, then a false value is returned. For example, here is a successful search followed by an unsuccessful search:

```php
$string_to_search = "showsuponceshowsuptwice";
$string_to_find = "up";
print("Result of looking for $string_to_find" .
        strstr($string_to_search, $string_to_find));
$string_to_find = "down";
print("Result of looking for $string_to_find" .
        strstr($string_to_search, $string_to_find));
```

which gives us:

```
Result of looking for up: uponceshowsuptwice
Result of looking for down:
```

The blank space after the colon in the second line is the result of trying to print a false value, which prints as the empty string.

The `strstr()` function also has an alias by the name of `strchr()`. Other than the name, the two functions are identical.

Just as with `strcmp()`, `strstr()` has a case-insensitive version, by the name of `stristr()`. (That i in the middle stands for "insensitive"). It is identical to `strstr()` in every way, except that the comparison treats lowercase letters as indistinguishable from their uppercase counterparts.

The string functions we have covered so far are summarized in Table 9-1.

Table 9-1 Simple Inspection, Comparison, and Searching Functions	
Function	**Behavior**
`strlen()`	Takes a single string argument and returns its length as an integer.
`strpos()`	Takes two string arguments: a string to search, and the string being searched for. Returns the (0-based) position of the beginning of the first instance of the string if found, and a false value otherwise. Also takes a third optional integer argument, specifying the position at which the search should begin.
`strrpos()`	Like `strpos()`, except that it searches backward from the end of the string, rather than forward from the beginning. The search string must only be one character long, and there is no optional position argument.
`strcmp()`	Takes two strings as arguments and returns 0 if the strings are exactly equivalent. If `strcmp()` encounters a difference, it returns a negative number if the first different byte is a smaller ASCII value in the first string, and a positive number if the smaller byte is found in the second string.
`strcasecmp()`	Identical to `strcmp()`, except that lowercase and uppercase versions of the same letter compare as equal.
`strstr()`	Searches its first string argument to see if its second string argument is contained in it. Returns the substring of the first string that starts with the first instance of the second argument, if any is found — otherwise, returns false.
`strchr()`	Identical to `strstr()`.
`stristr()`	Identical to `strstr()` except that the comparison is case-independent.

Substring selection

Many of PHP's string functions have to do with slicing and dicing your strings. By *slicing*, we mean choosing a portion of a string, and by *dicing*, we mean selectively modifying a string. Keep in mind that (most of the time) even dicing functions do not change the string you started out with. Usually such functions return a modified copy, leaving the original argument intact.

The most basic way to choose a portion of a string is the substr() function, which returns a new string that is a subsequence of the old one. As arguments, it takes a string (that the substring will be selected from), an integer (the position at which the desired substring starts), and an optional third integer argument that is the length of the desired substring. If no third argument is given, the substring is assumed to continue until the end. (Remember that, as with all PHP arguments that deal with numerical string positions, the numbering starts with 0 rather than 1.)

For example, the statement

```
echo(substr("Take what you need, and leave the rest behind",
    23));
```

will print out the string "leave the rest behind"; whereas the statement

```
echo(substr("Take what you need, and leave the rest behind",
    5, 13));
```

will print out "what you need" — a 13-character string starting at (0-based) position 5.

Both the start-position argument and the length argument can be negative, and in each case the negativity has a different meaning. If the start-position is negative, it means that the starting character is determined by counting backward from the end of the string, rather than forward from the beginning. (A start position of –1 means start with the last character, –2 means second-to-last, and so on.)

Now, you might expect that a negative length would similarly imply that the substring should be determined by counting backward from the start character, rather than forward. This is not the case — it is always true that the character at the start-position is the first character in the returned string (not the last). Instead, a negative length argument means that the final character is determined by counting backward from the end, rather than forward from the start position.

Some examples, with positive and negative arguments:

```
$alphabet_test = "abcdefghijklmnop";
print("3: " . substr($alphabet_test, 3) . "<BR>");
print("-3: " . substr($alphabet_test, -3) . "<BR>");
print("3, 5: " . substr($alphabet_test, 3, 5) . "<BR>");
print("3, -5: " . substr($alphabet_test, 3, -5) . "<BR>");
```

```
print("-3, -5: " . substr($alphabet_test, -3, -5) . <BR>");
print("-3, 5: " . substr($alphabet_test, -3, 5) . <BR>");
```

This gives us the output

```
3: defghijklmnop
-3: nop
3, 5: defgh
3, -5: defghijk
-3, -5:
-3, 5: nop
```

Caution

In the `substr()` example with a start position of –3 and a length of –5, the ending position is before the starting position, which in a sense specifies a string with "negative length." The manual at `http://www.php.net/manual` currently says that such "negative length" calls to `substr()` will result in returning a string containing the single character at the start position. Instead, as in the preceding example, PHP 4.0.0 seems to return empty strings in such cases. Caveat coder.

Notice that there is an intimate relationship between the functions `substr()`, `strstr()`, and `strpos()`. The `substr()` function selects a substring by numerical position, `strstr()` selects a substring by its content, and `strpos()` finds the numerical position of a given substring. In the case where we're sure in advance that the string `$containing` has the string `$contained` as a substring, then the expression

```
strstr($containing, $contained)
```

should be equivalent to the code

```
substr($containing, strpos($containing, $contained))
```

String cleanup functions

Although technically substring functions just like the others in this chapter, the functions `chop()`, `ltrim()`, and `trim()` are really used for cleaning up untidy strings. They trim "whitespace" off of the end, beginning, and beginning-and-end, respectively, of their single string argument. Some examples:

```
$original = "  More than meets the eye    ";
$chopped = chop($original);
$ltrimmed = ltrim($original);
$trimmed = trim($original);
print("The original is '$original'<BR>");
print("Its length is " . strlen($original) . "<BR>");
print("The chopped version is '$chopped'<BR>");
print("Its length is " . strlen($chopped) . "<BR>");
print("The ltrimmed version is '$ltrimmed'<BR>");
print("Its length is " . strlen($ltrimmed) . "<BR>");
```

```
print("The trimmed version is '$ltrimmed'<BR>");
print("Its length is " . strlen($trimmed) . "<BR>");
```

The result as viewed by a browser is:

```
The original is ' More than meets the eye '
Its length is 28
The chopped version is ' More than meets the eye'
Its length is 25
The ltrimmed version is 'More than meets the eye '
Its length is 26
The trimmed version is 'More than meets the eye'
Its length is 23
```

The original string had three spaces at the end (subject to removal by `chop()` or `trim()`), and two at the beginning (removed by `ltrim()` and `trim()`). (If the naming of these functions were consistent, then `chop()` would be known as `rtrim()`). We were careful to describe our result "as viewed by a browser" because the multiple spaces have apparently been collapsed to one in the output, as browsers will do. If we viewed the HTML source produced by PHP originally, we would still see sequences of two and three spaces.

In addition to spaces, these functions remove "whitespace" like that denoted by the escape sequences \n, \r, \t, and \0 (end-of-line characters, tabs, and the null character used to terminate strings in C programs).

Finally, notice that although `chop()` sounds extremely destructive, it does not harm the `$original` argument, which retains the same value.

String replacement

The substring functions we've seen so far are all about choosing a portion of the argument, rather than building a genuinely new string. Enter the functions `str_replace()` and `substr_replace()`.

The `str_replace()` function enables you to replace all instances of a particular substring with an alternate string. It takes three arguments: the string to be searched for, the string to replace it with when it is found, and the string to perform the replacement on. For example,

```
$first_edition =
    "Burma is similar to Rhodesia in at least one way.";
$second_edition = str_replace("Rhodesia", "Zimbabwe",
                              $first_edition);
$third_edition = str_replace("Burma", "Myanmar",
                             $second_edition);
print($third_edition);
```

gives us

```
Myanmar is similar to Zimbabwe in at least one way.
```

This replacement will happen for all instances of the search string that are found. If our outdated encyclopedia could be snarfed into a single PHP string, then we could update it in one pass.

One subtlety to be aware of: What happens when multiple instances of the search string overlap? For example, with code like

```
$tricky_string = "ABA is part of ABABA";
$maybe_tricked = str_replace("ABA", "DEF", $tricky_string);
print("Substitution result is '$maybe_tricked'<BR>");
```

the behavior we see is

```
Substitution result is 'DEF is part of DEFBA'
```

which is probably as reasonable as any other alternative.

As we've seen, `str_replace()` picks out portions to replace by matching to a target string; by contrast, `substr_replace()` chooses a portion to replace by its absolute position. The function takes up to four arguments: the string to perform the replacement on, the string to replace with, the starting position for the replacement, and (optionally) the length of the section to be replaced. For example,

```
print(substr_replace("ABCDEFG", "-", 2, 3));
```

gives us

```
AB-FG
```

The `CDE` portion of the string has been replaced with the single `-`. Notice that we are allowed to replace a substring with a string of different length. If the length argument is omitted, it is assumed that you want to replace the entire portion of the string after the start position.

The `substr_replace()` function also takes negative arguments for starting position and length, which are treated exactly the same way as in the `substr()` function (described in the earlier section "Substring selection").

Finally, we have a couple more whimsical functions that produce new strings from old. The `strrev()` function simply returns a new string with the characters of its input in reverse order. The `str_repeat()` function takes a string argument and an integer argument and returns a string that is the appropriate number of copies of the string argument tacked together. For example,

```
print(str_repeat("cheers ", 3));
```

gives us

```
cheers cheers cheers
```

for the end of this section at long last.

The substring search and replacement functions are summarized in Table 9-2.

Table 9-2
Substring and String Replacement Functions

Function	Behavior
substr()	Returns a subsequence of its initial string argument, as specified by the second (position) argument and optional third (length) argument. The substring starts at the indicated position and continues for as many characters as specified by the length argument, or until the end of the string if there is no length argument. A negative position argument means that the start character is located by counting backward from the end, whereas a negative length argument means that the end of the substring is found by counting back from the end, rather than forward from the start position.
chop()	Returns its string argument with trailing (right-hand side) whitespace removed. Whitespace is " ", \n, \r, \t, and \0.
ltrim()	Returns its string argument with leading (left-hand side) whitespace removed.
trim()	Returns its string argument with both leading and trailing whitespace removed.
str_replace()	Used to replace target substrings with another string. Takes three string arguments: a substring to search for, a string to replace it with, and the containing string. Returns a copy of the containing string with *all* instances of the first argument replaced by the second argument.
substr_replace()	Puts a string argument in place of a position-specified substring. Takes up to four arguments: the string to operate on, the string to replace with, the start position of the substring to replace, and the length of the string segment to be replaced. Returns a copy of the first argument with the replacement string put in place of the specified substring. If the length argument is omitted, the entire tail of the first string argument is replaced. Negative position and length arguments are treated as in substr().

Strings and character collections

Moving beyond substring searching, PHP offers some pretty specialized functions that treat strings more as collections of characters than as sequences.

The first is strspn(), which you can use to see what portion of a string is composed only of a given set of characters. For example,

```
$twister = "Peter Piper picked a peck of pickled peppers";
$charset = "Peter picked a";
print("The segment matching '$charset' is " .
      strspn($twister, $charset) . " characters long");
```

gives us

```
The segment matching 'Peter picked a' is 26 characters long
```

because the first character not found in $charset is the o in of, and there are 26 characters that precede it.

The strcspn() function (where that internal c stands for "complement") does the same thing, except that it accepts characters that are *not* in the character set argument. For example, the statement

```
echo(strcspn($twister, "abcd"));
```

would print the number 14, because it would accept a 14-character sequence with the last character being the c in "picked."

Finally, although it uses some properties of arrays that we have not yet studied, check out the following for an acute analysis of alliteration:

```
$twister = "Peter Piper picked a peck of pickled peppers";
print("$twister<BR>");
$letter_array = count_chars($twister, 1);
while ($cell = each($letter_array)){
  $letter = chr($cell['key']);
  $frequency = $cell['value'];
  print("Character: '$letter'; frequency:  $frequency<BR>");
}
```

This gives the browser output

```
Peter Piper picked a peck of pickled peppers
Character: ' '; frequency: 7
Character: 'P'; frequency: 2
Character: 'a'; frequency: 1
Character: 'c'; frequency: 3
```

```
Character: 'd'; frequency: 2
Character: 'e'; frequency: 8
Character: 'f'; frequency: 1
Character: 'i'; frequency: 3
Character: 'k'; frequency: 3
Character: 'l'; frequency: 1
Character: 'o'; frequency: 1
Character: 'p'; frequency: 7
Character: 'r'; frequency: 3
Character: 's'; frequency: 1
Character: 't'; frequency: 1
```

The count_chars() function returns a report on the occurrences of characters in its string argument, packaged up as an array where the keys are the ASCII values of characters, and the values are the frequencies of those characters in the string. The second argument to count_chars() is an integer that determines which of several modes the results should be returned in. In mode 0, an array of key/value pairs is returned, where the keys are every ASCII value from 0 to 255, and the corresponding values are the frequencies of each character in the string. Modes 1 and 2 are variants that include only ASCII values that occurred in the string (mode 1) or that did not occur (mode 2). Finally, modes 3 and 4 return a string instead of an array, where the string contains all characters that occur (mode 3) or do not occur (mode 4).

Cross-Reference For an explanation of how to take apart array formats like that returned by count_chars(), see Chapter 11. The chr() function used in the preceding example, which maps from ASCII numbers to the corresponding characters, is covered in Chapter 6.

Table 9-3
Functions for Examining Character Contents

Function	Behavior
count_chars()	Takes a single string argument and an integer mode argument from 0 to 4. Returns a report about frequencies of characters in the string argument, as either an array or a string. (See the accompanying text for more detail.)
strspn()	Takes two string arguments and returns the length of the initial substring of the first argument that is composed entirely of characters found in its second argument.
strcspn()	Takes two string arguments and returns the length of the initial substring of the first argument that is composed entirely of characters that are *not* found in its second argument.

Parsing functions

Sometimes you need to take strings apart at the seams, and you have your own notions of what should count as a seam. The process of breaking up a long string into "words" is called *tokenizing,* and among other things it is part of the internals of interpreting or compiling any computer program, including PHP. PHP offers a special function for this purpose, by the name of strtok().

The strtok() function takes two arguments: the string to be broken up into tokens, and a string containing all the delimiters (characters that count as boundaries between tokens). On the first call, both arguments are used, and the string value returned is the first token. To retrieve subsequent tokens, make the same call, but omit the source string argument. It will be remembered as the current string, and the function will remember where it left off. For example,

```
$token = strtok(
    "open-source HTML-embedded server-side Web scripting",
    " ");
while($token){
  print($token . "<BR>");
  $token = strtok(" ");
}
```

would give the browser output

```
open-source
HTML-embedded
server-side
Web
scripting
```

The original string would be "broken" at each space. At our discretion, we could change the delimiter set, like so:

```
$token = strtok(
    "open-source HTML-embedded server-side Web scripting",
    "-");
while($token){
  print($token . "<BR>");
  $token = strtok("-");
}
```

This gives us (less sensibly)

```
open
source HTML
embedded server
side Web scripting
```

Finally, we can break the string at all these places at once, by giving it a delimiter string like " -", containing both a space and a dash. The code

```
token = strtok(
     "open-source HTML-embedded server-side Web scripting",
     " -");
while($token){
  print($token . "<BR>");
  $token = strtok("-");
}
```

will print

```
open
source
HTML
embedded
server
side
Web
scripting
```

Notice that in every case the delimiter characters do not show up anywhere in the retrieved tokens.

The strtok() function doles out its tokens one by one. You can also use the explode() function to do something similar but store the tokens all at once into an array. Once the tokens are in the array, you can do anything you like with them, including sort them.

The explode() function takes two arguments: a separator string and the string to be separated. It returns an array where each element is a substring between instances of the separator in the string to be separated. For example,

```
$explode_result = explode("AND", "one AND a two AND a three");
```

would result in the array $explode_result having three elements, each of which is a string: "one ", " a two ", and " a three". In this particular example, there would be no capital letters anywhere in the strings contained in the array, because the 'AND' separator does not show up in the result.

The separator string in explode() is significantly different from the delimiter string used in strtok(). The separator is a full-fledged string, and all of its characters must be found in the right order for an instance of the separator to be detected. The delimiter string of strtok() specifies a set of single characters, any one of which will count as a delimiter. This makes explode() both more precise and more brittle—if you leave out a space or a newline character from a long string, the entire function will be broken.

Because the entire separator string will disappear into the ether when `explode()` is used, this function can be the basis for many useful effects. The examples given in most PHP documentation use short strings for convenience, but remember that a string can be almost any length — and `explode()` is especially useful with longer strings that might be tedious to parse some other way. For instance, you can use it to count how many times a particular string appears within a text file by turning the file into a string and using `explode()` on it, as in this example (which uses some functions we haven't explained yet, but hopefully makes sense in context).

```php
<?php
//First, turn a text file into a string called $filestring.
$filename = "complex_layout.html";
$fd = fopen($filename, "r");
$filestring = fread($fd, filesize($filename));
fclose ($fd);

//Explode on the beginning of the <TABLE> HTML tag
$pieces = explode("<TABLE", $filestring);
//Count the number of pieces
$num_pieces = count($tables);

//Subtract one to get the number of <TABLE> tags, and echo
echo ($num_pieces - 1);
?>
```

The `explode()` function has an inverse function, `implode()`, which takes two arguments: a "glue" string (analogous to the separator string in `explode()`), and an array of strings like that returned by `explode()`. It returns a string created by inserting the glue string between each string element in the array.

You can use the two functions together to replace every instance of a particular string within a text file. Remember that the separator string will vanish into the ether when you perform an `explode()` — if you want it to appear in the final file, you have to replace it by hand. In this example, we're changing the font tags on a Web page.

```php
<?php
//Turn text file into string
$filename = "someoldpage.html";
$fd = fopen($filename, "r");
$filestring = fread($fd, filesize($filename));
fclose ($fd);

$parts = explode("arial, sans-serif", $filestring);

$whole = implode("arial, verdana, sans-serif", $parts);

//Overwrite the original file
$fd = fopen($filename, "w");
fwrite($fd, $whole);
fclose ($fd);
?>
```

Case functions

These functions change lowercase to upper and vice versa. The first two (de)capitalize entire strings, whereas the second two operate only on first letters of words.

strtolower()

The strtolower() function returns an all-lowercase string. It doesn't matter if the original is all-uppercase or mixed. This fragment:

```php
<?php
$original = "They DON'T KnoW they're SHOUTING";
$lower = strtolower($original);
echo $lower;
?>
```

returns the string "they don't know they're shouting".

strtoupper()

The strtoupper() function returns an all-uppercase string, regardless of whether the original was all-lowercase or mixed.

```php
<?php
$original = "make this link stand out";
echo("<B>strtoupper($original)</B>");
?>
```

ucfirst()

The ucfirst() function capitalizes only the first letter of a string.

```php
<?php
$original = "polish is a word for which pronunciation depends
on capitalization";
echo(ucfirst($original));
?>
```

ucwords()

The ucwords() function capitalizes the first letter of each word in a string.

```php
<?php
$original = "truth or consequences";
$capitalized = ucwords($original);
echo "While $original is a parlor game, $capitalized is a town
in New Mexico.";
?>
```

Note Neither `ucwords()` nor `ucfirst()` convert anything into lowercase. They only make the appropriate leading letters into uppercase. If there are inappropriate capital letters in the middle of words, they will not be corrected.

Escaping functions

One of the virtues of PHP is that it is willing to talk to almost anybody. In its role as a "glue" language, PHP talks to database servers, to LDAP servers, over sockets, and over the HTTP connection itself. Frequently it accomplishes this communication by first constructing a message string (like a database query) and then shipping it off to the receiving program. Often, however, the program attaches special meanings to certain characters, which therefore have to be *escaped,* meaning that the receiving program is told to take them as a literal part of the string rather than treating them specially.

Many users deal with this issue by enabling magic-quotes. However, if that's not feasible or desirable, there's good old-fashioned strip-slashing and add-slashing by hand.

Strip-slashing and add-slashing can come in handy in the other direction too: echoing HTML forms with PHP variables, for instance, may involve a lot of quotes that are part of the HTML and shouldn't be evaluated by PHP. If you have a bunch of these, it can save time to add slashes instead of escaping each quote by hand.

The `addslashes()` function escapes quotes, double quotes, backslashes, and NULLs with backslashes, because these are the characters that typically need to be escaped for database queries.

```php
<?php
$escapedstring = addslashes("He said, 'I'm a dog.'");
$query = "INSERT INTO test (quote) values ('$escapedstring')";
$result = mysql_query($query) or die(mysql_error());
?>
```

This will prevent the SQL statement from thinking it's finished right before the letter "I." When you pull the data back out, you'll need to use `stripslashes()` to get rid of the slashes.

```php
<?php
$query = "SELECT quote FROM test WHERE ID=1";
$result = mysql_query($query) or die(mysql_error());
$new_row = mysql_fetch_array($result);
$quote = stripslashes($new_row[0]);

echo $quote;
```

The quotemeta() function escapes a wider variety of characters, all of which usually have a special meaning in the UNIX command line: . \ + * ? [^] ($). For example, the code

```
$literal_string =
  'These characters ($, *) are very special to me\n<BR>';
$qm_string = quotemeta($literal_string);
echo $qm_string;
```

will print

```
These characters \(\$, \*\) are very special to me;
```

Cross-Reference   For escaping functions that are specific to HTML, see the very end of this chapter.

Printing and output

The workhorse constructs for printing and output are print and echo, which we covered in detail in Chapter 5. The standard way to print the value of variables to output is to include them in a doubly-quoted string (which will interpolate their values), and then give that string to print or echo.

If you need even more tightly formatted output, PHP also offers printf() and sprintf(), which are modeled on C functions of the same name. The two functions take identical arguments: A special format string (described later in this section), and then any number of other arguments which will be spliced into the right places in the format string to make the result.

The only difference between printf() and sprintf() is that printf() sends the resulting string directly to output, while sprintf() returns the result string as its value.

Note   To C programmers: This sprintf() function is slightly different from C's version in that you need not supply an allocated string for sprintf() to write into — PHP allocates the result string for you.

The complicated bit about these functions is the format string. Every character that you put in the string will show up literally in the result, except the % character and characters that immediately follow it. The % character signals the beginning of a "conversion specification," which indicates how to print one of the arguments that follow the format string.

After the %, there are five elements that make up the conversion specification, some of which are optional: padding, alignment, minimum width, precision, and type.

1. The single (optional) padding character is either a 0 or a space ( ). This character is used to fill any space that would otherwise be unused, but that you have insisted (with the minimum width argument) be filled with something. If this padding character is not given, the default is to pad with spaces.

2. The optional alignment character - indicates whether the printed value should be left- or right-justified. If present, the value will be left-justified; if absent, it will be right-justified.

3. An optional width number that indicates how many spaces this value should take up, at a minimum. (If more spaces are needed to print the value, it will overflow beyond its bounds.)

4. An optional width specifier, which is a dot (.) followed by a number. It indicates how many decimal points of precision a double should print with. (This has no effect on printing things other than doubles.

5. A single character indicating how the type of the value should be interpreted. The f character indicates printing as a double, the s character indicates printing as a string, and then the rest of the possible characters (b, c, d, o, x, X) mean that the value should be interpreted as an integer, and printed various formats. Those formats are b for binary, c for printing the character with the corresponding ASCII values, o for octal, x for hexadecimal (with lowercase letters) and X for hexadecimal with uppercase letters.

An example, printing the same double in several different ways:

```
<pre>
<?php
$value = 3.14159;
printf("%f,%10f,%-010f,%2.2f\n",
        $value, $value, $value, $value);
?>
</pre>
```

gives us

```
3.141590, 3.141590,3.141590000000000, 3.14
```

The <pre></pre> construct is HTML that tells the browser to format the enclosed block literally, without collapsing many spaces into one, and so on.

Advanced String Features

We have now covered the most basic things to do with strings: making them, breaking them, comparing them, finding substrings, and printing them out. On to a quick tour of more ambitious functions.

Regular expressions

A full treatment of regular expressions is well beyond our scope in this chapter. Instead, we will explain what regular expressions are good for and give some examples of their use.

Why regexps?

The string-comparison and substring-finding functions we saw earlier are fine as far as they go, but they are on the literal-minded side. As an example of their weakness, let's say that you wanted to test strings to see if they were a particular kind of Web address: addresses that started with `www.` and ended with `.com`, and had one lowercase alphabetic word in the middle. For example, these would be strings we wanted:

```
'www.ibm.com'
'www.zend.com'
```

and these would not:

```
'java.sun.com'
'www.java.sun.com'
'www.php.net'
'www.IBM.com'
'www.Web addresses can't have spaces.com'
```

With a little thought, it's obvious that there is no convenient way to simply use string and substring comparison to build the test that we want. We can test for the presence of `www.` and `.com`, but it is difficult to enforce what should be happening in between them. This is what regular expressions are good for.

Regexps in PHP

A regular expression (or "regexp") is a pattern for string matching, with special wildcards that can match entire portions of the target string. There are two broad classes of regular expression that PHP works with: POSIX regexps and Perl-compatible regexps. The differences mostly have to do with syntax. (We do not cover Perl-compatible regexps in this book.)

Here are a few of the rules for POSIX-style regular expressions, simplified:

✦ Characters that are not "special" get matched literally. For example, the letter a in a pattern will match the same letter in a target string.

✦ The special character ^ matches the beginning of a string only, and the special character $ matches the end of a string only.

✦ The special character . matches any character. The special character *
matches 0 or more instances of the previous regular expression, and +
matches one or more instances of the previous expression.

✦ A set of characters enclosed in square brackets matches any of those characters—the pattern [ab] matches either a or b. You can also specify a range of
characters in brackets by using a dash—the pattern [a-c] matches a, b, or c.

✦ Special characters that are escaped with a backslash \ lose their special
meaning, and are matched literally.

Now we can use the above rules to construct an expression that matches the kind
of Web address we wanted earlier in this section. Our chosen expression is:

```
^www\.[a-z]+\.com$
```

In this expression we have the ^' symbol, which says that the www portion must
start at the beginning of the string. Then comes a dot (.), preceded by a backslash
that says we really want a dot, not the special . wildcard character. Then we have a
bracket-enclosed range of all the lowercase alphabetic letters. The following + indicates that we are willing to match any number of these lowercase letters in a row,
as long as we have at least one of them. Then another literal ., the .com, and the
special $ that says that "com" is the end of it.

Now let's use that expression as an argument to the function ereg(), which takes
as arguments a pattern string and a string to match against. We can use an ereg()
call to build a test function for our kind of Web address.

```
function simple_dot_com ($url)
{
   return(ereg('^www\.[a-z]+\.com$', $url));
}
```

This function will return true or false, depending on whether it succesfully matched
our pattern. Now we can use our function to test some of the addresses listed earlier. (This code loops through an array, which we will formally cover in the next
chapter.)

```
$urls_to_test =
   array('www.ibm.com', 'www.java.sun.com',
         'www.zend.com', 'java.sun.com',
         'www.java.sun.com', 'www.php.net',
         'www.IBM.com',
         'www.Web addresses can\'t have spaces.com');
while($test = array_pop($urls_to_test)){
   if (simple_dot_com($test))
     print("\"$test\" is a simple dot-com<BR>");
   else
```

```
        print("\"$test\" is NOT a simple dot-com<BR>");

    }
```

The results of our tests are as follows.

```
"www.Web addresses can't have spaces.com" is NOT a simple dot-
com
"www.IBM.com" is NOT a simple dot-com
"www.php.net" is NOT a simple dot-com
"www.java.sun.com" is NOT a simple dot-com
"java.sun.com" is NOT a simple dot-com
"www.zend.com" is a simple dot-com
"www.java.sun.com" is NOT a simple dot-com
"www.ibm.com" is a simple dot-com
```

This is the kind of discriminating behavior we were looking for.

Tip   On many UNIX systems, typing "man 7 regex" will lead you to a guide to POSIX regular expressions. If that does not work, try "man regex" and follow any pointers to related pages.

Regular expression functions

The regular expression functions in PHP are summarized in Table 9-4.

Tip   If you find yourself using a regular expression function with a "pattern" that has no special characters, you are probably using an expensive tool where a cheap one would do. If you are trying to match a simple string to a simple string, then you only need one of the more basic (and faster) functions covered earlier in this chapter.

Table 9-4
Regular expression functions

Function	Behavior
ereg()	Takes two string arguments and an optional third array argument. The first string is the POSIX-style regular expression pattern, and the second string is the target string that is being matched. The function returns true if the match was successful, and false otherwise. In addition, if an array argument is supplied and portions of the pattern are enclosed in parentheses, the parts of the target string that match successive parenthesized portions will be copied into successive elements of the array.

Function	Behavior
ereg_replace()	Takes three arguments: a POSIX regular expression pattern, a string to do replacement with, and a string to replace into. The function scans the third argument for portions that match the pattern and replaces them with the second argument. The modified string is returned. If there are parenthesized portions of the pattern (as with ereg()), then the replacement string may contain special substrings of the form '\\digit' (that is, two backslashes followed by a single-digit number), which will themselves be replaced with the corresponding piece of the target string.
eregi()	Identical to ereg(), except that letters in regular expressions are matched in a case-independent way.
eregi_replace()	Identical to ereg_replace(), except that letters in regular expressions are matched in a case-independent way.
split()	Takes a pattern, a target string, and an optional limit on the number of portions to split the string into. Returns an array of strings created by splitting the target string into chunks delimited by substrings that match the regular expression. (Note that this is analogous to the explode() function, except that it splits on regexps rather than literal strings.)

HTML functions

Finally, PHP offers a number of Web-specific functions for string manipulation, which are summarized in Table 9-5.

Table 9-5
HTML-specific string functions

Function	Behavior
htmlspecialchars()	Takes a string as argument and returns the string with replacements for four characters that have special meaning in HTML. Each of these characters is replaced with the corresponding HTML entity, so that it will look like the original when rendered by a browser. The '&' character is replaced by '&amp'; '"' (the double-quote character) is replaced by '&quot'; '<' is replaced by '&lt'; '>' is replaced by '&gt'.

Continued

Table 9-5 *(continued)*	
Function	**Behavior**
`htmlentities()`	Goes further than `htmlspecialchars()`, in that it replaces all characters that have a corresponding HTML entity with that HTML entity.
`get_html_translation_table()`	Takes one of two special constants (HTML_SPECIAL_CHARS HTML_ENTITIES), and returns the translation table used and by htmlspecialchars() and htmlentities(), respectively. The translation table is an array where keys are the character strings and the corresponding values are their replacements.
`nl2br()`	Takes a string as argument and returns that string with ' ' inserted before all newlines ('\n'). This is helpful, for example, in maintaining the apparent line length of text paragraphs when they are displayed in a browser.
`strip_tags()`	Takes a string as argument and does its best to return that string stripped of all HTML tags and all PHP tags.

Summary

Strings are sequences of characters, and the string is one of the six basic datatypes in PHP. Unlike in some other languages, there is no distinct character type, since single characters behave as strings of length 1. Literal strings are specified in code by either single (') or double (") quotes. Singly-quoted strings are interpreted nearly literally, while doubly-quoted strings interpret a number of escape sequences and automatically interpolate variable values.

The main string operator is '.', which concatenates two strings together. In addition, there is a dizzying array of string functions, which help you inspect, compare, search, extract, chop, replace, slice, and dice strings to your heart's content. For the most sophisticated string manipulation needs, PHP supports both POSIX and Perl-compatible regular expressions.

✦   ✦   ✦

Math

◆ ◆ ◆ ◆

In This Chapter

Understanding the
basic numerical
types and arithmetic
operations

Exponential,
trigonometric, and
base-conversion
functions

Generating random
numbers

Arbitrary-precision
arithmetic

◆ ◆ ◆ ◆

If you need to do serious numerical, scientific, or statistical
computation, then a Web-scripting language is probably
not where you want to be doing it. With that said, though,
PHP does offer a generous array of functions that nicely cover
most of the mathematical tasks that arise in Web scripting.
It also offers some more advanced capabilities such as arbitrary-precision arithmetic and access to hashing and cryptographic libraries.

The PHP designers have, quite sensibly, not tried to reinvent
any wheels in this department. Instead, they found about
eighteen perfectly good wheels by the side of the road and
built a lightweight fiberglass chassis to connect them all
together. Many of the more basic math functions in PHP are
simple wrappers around their C counterparts (for more on
this, see the sidebar "A glimpse behind the curtain" in the
middle of this chapter).

Numerical Types

PHP has only two numerical types: integer (also known
as long), and double (a.k.a. float), which correspond to the
largest numerical types in C. PHP does automatic conversion
of numerical types, so they can be freely intermixed in numerical expressions and the Right Thing will typically happen.
PHP also converts strings to numbers where necessary.

In situations where you want a value to be interpreted as
a particular numerical type, you can force a typecast by
prepending the type in parentheses, like

```
(double) $my_var
(integer) $my_var
```

Or you can use the functions intval() and doubleval(),
which convert their arguments to integers and doubles,
respectively.

For more detail on the integer and double types, see Chapter 6.

Mathematical Operators

Most of the mathematical action in PHP is in the form of built-in functions, rather than in operators. In addition to the comparison operators covered in Chapter 7, PHP offers five operators for simple arithmetic, as well as some "shorthand" operators that make incrementing and assigning statements more concise.

Arithmetic operators

The five basic arithmetic operators are those you would find on a four-function calculator, plus the modulus operator (%). (If you are unfamiliar with modulus, see the discussion following.) They are summarized in Table 10-1.

	Table 10-1 Arithmetic Operators	
Operator	**Behavior**	**Examples**
+	Sum of its two arguments.	4 + 9.5 evaluates to 13.5
–	If there are two arguments, the right-hand argument is subtracted from the left-hand argument. If there is just a right-hand argument, then the negative of that argument is returned.	50 - 75 evaluates to -25 - 3.9 evaluates to -3.9
*	Product of its two arguments.	3.14 * 2 evaluates to 6.28
/	Floating-point division of the left-hand argument by the right-hand argument.	5 / 2 evaluates to 2.5
%	Integer remainder from division of left-hand argument by the absolute value of the right-hand argument. (See discussion following.)	101 % 50 evaluates to 1 999 % 3 evaluates to 0 43 % 94 evaluates to 43 -12 % 10 evaluates to -2 -12 % -10 evaluates to -2

Arithmetic operators and types

With the first three arithmetic operators — +, -, * — you should expect "type contagion" from doubles to integers; that is, if both arguments are integers, the result will be an integer, but if either argument is a double, then the result will be a double. With the division operator, there is the same sort of contagion, and in addition the result will be a double if the division is not even.

> **Tip**
>
> If you want integer division rather than floating-point division, simply coerce or convert the division result to an integer. For example, intval(5 / 2) evaluates to the integer 2.

The modulus operator

Modular arithmetic is sometimes taught in school as "clock arithmetic." The process of taking one number modulo to another amounts to "wrapping" the first number around the second, or (equivalently) taking the remainder of the first number after dividing by the second. The result of such an operation is always less than the second number.

Roughly speaking, a conventional civilian analog clock displays hours elapsed modulo 12, while "military time" is modulo 24. (The "roughly" in the previous sentence is because the real modulus function converts numbers to the range 0 to n-1, rather than the range 1 to n. If bell-tower clocks respected this, noontime would be marked by silence, rather than twelve chimes.)

The modulus operator in PHP (%) expects integer arguments — if it is given doubles, they will simply be converted to integers (by truncation) first. The result is always an integer.

Most programming languages have some form of the modulus operator, but they differ in how they handle negative arguments. In some languages, the result of the operator is always positive, and -2 % 26 would equal 24. In PHP, though, -2 % 26 is -2, and in general, the statement $mod = $first_num % $second_num is exactly equivalent to the expression

```
if ($first_num >= 0)
    $mod = $first_num % abs($second_num)
else
    $mod = - (abs($first_num) % abs($second_num));
```

where abs() is the absolute value function.

Incrementing operators

PHP inherits a lot of its syntax from C, and C programmers are famously proud of their own conciseness. The incrementing/decrementing operators taken from C make it possible to more concisely represent statements like $count = $count + 1, which tend to be typed frequently.

The increment operator (++) adds one to the variable it is attached to, and the decrement operator (--) subtracts one from the variable. Each one comes in two flavors, "postincrement" (which is placed immediately after the affected variable), and "preincrement" (which comes immediately before). Both flavors have the same side effect of changing the variable's value, but they have different values as expressions. The "postincrement" operator acts as if it changes the variable's value after the expression's value is returned, whereas the "preincrement" operator acts as though it makes the change first and then returns the variable's new value. You can see the difference by using the operators in assignment statements, like this:

```
$count = 0;
$result = $count++;
print("Post ++: count is $count, result is $result<BR>");
$count = 0;
$result = ++$count;
print("Pre ++: count is $count, result is $result<BR>");
$count = 0;
$result = $count--;
print("Post --: count is $count, result is $result<BR>");
$count = 0;
$result = --$count;
print("Pre --: count is $count, result is $result<BR>");
```

which gives the browser output:

```
Post ++: count is 1, result is 0
Pre ++: count is 1, result is 1
Post --: count is -1, result is 0
Pre --: count is -1, result is -1
```

In this example, the statement $result = $count++; is exactly equivalent to

```
$result = $count;
$count = $count + 1;
```

while $result = ++$count; is equivalent to

```
$count = $count + 1;
$result = $count;
```

Assignment operators

Incrementing operators like ++ save keystrokes when adding one to a variable, but they don't help when adding another number or performing another kind of arithmetic. Luckily, all five arithmetic operators have corresponding assignment operators (+= , -= , *= , /= , and %=) that assign to a variable the result of an arithmetic operation on that variable, in one fell swoop. The statement

```
$count = $count * 3;
```

can be shortened to

```
$count *= 3;
```

and the statement

```
$count = $count + 17;
```

becomes

```
$count += 17;
```

Comparison operators

PHP includes the standard arithmetic comparison operators, which take simple values (numbers or strings) as arguments and evaluate to either TRUE or FALSE:

- ✦ The < ("less than") operator is true if its left-hand argument is strictly less than its right-hand argument, and false otherwise.

- ✦ The > ("greater than") operator is true if its left-hand argument is strictly greater than its right-hand argument, and false otherwise.

- ✦ The <= ("less than or equal") operator is true if its left-hand argument is less than or equal to its right-hand argument, and false otherwise.

- ✦ The >= ("greater than or equal") operator is true if its left-hand argument is greater than or equal to its right-hand argument, and false otherwise.

- ✦ The == ("equal to") operator is true if its arguments are exactly equal, and false otherwise.

- ✦ The != ("not equal") operator is false if its arguments are exactly equal, and true otherwise.

- ✦ The === operator ("identical to") is true if its two arguments are exactly equal, and of the same type.

Cross-Reference   For examples of using the comparison operators, and some gotcha issues with comparing doubles and strings, see Chapter 7.

New Feature   The "identical to" operator (===) is new to PHP 4 and at times can be a necessary antidote to PHP's automatic type conversions. None of the following expressions will have a true value:

```
2 === 2.0
2 === "2"
"2.0" === 2.0
0 === FALSE
```

This behavior can be invaluable, for example, if you have a function that returns a string when it succeeds (which might be the empty string), and a FALSE value when it fails. Testing the truth of the return value would confuse FALSE with the empty string, whereas the "identical" operator can distinguish them.

Precedence and parentheses

Operator *precedence* rules govern the relative "stickiness" of operators, deciding which operators in an expression get first claim on the arguments that surround them. You can find a complete table of all operator precedences in the manual at http://www.php.net, but the important precedence rules for arithmetic are:

✦ Arithmetic operators have higher precedence (that is, bind more tightly) than comparison operators.

✦ Comparison operators have higher precedence than assignment operators.

✦ The *, /, and % arithmetic operators have the same precedence.

✦ The + and - arithmetic operators have the same precedence.

✦ The *, /, and % operators have higher precedence than + and -.

✦ When arithmetic operators are of the same precedence, associativity is left to right (that is, a number will associate with an operator to its left in preference to the operator on its right).

If you find the precedence rules difficult to remember, then the next person who reads your code may have the same problem, so feel free to parenthesize when in doubt. For example, can you easily figure out the value of this expression?

```
1 + 2 * 3 - 4 - 5 / 4 % 3
```

As it turns out, the value is 2, as we can see more easily when we add parentheses that are not, strictly speaking, necessary:

```
((1 + (2 * 3)) - 4) - ((5 / 4) % 3)
```

Simple Mathematical Functions

The next step up in sophistication from the arithmetic operators consists of miscellaneous functions that perform tasks like converting between the two numerical types (which we discussed in Chapter 6) and finding the minimum and maximum of a set of numbers (see Table 10-2).

Table 10-2 **Simple Math Functions**	
Function	*Behavior*
floor()	Takes a single argument (typically a double) and returns the largest integer that is less than or equal to that argument.
ceil()	Takes a single argument (typically a double) and returns the smallest integer that is greater than or equal to that argument.
round()	Takes a single argument (typically a double) and returns the nearest integer. If the fractional part is exactly 0.5, it returns the nearest even number.
abs()	Absolute value—if the single numerical argument is negative, the corresponding positive number is returned; if the argument is positive, the argument itself is returned.
min()	Takes any number of numerical arguments (but at least one) and returns the smallest of the arguments.
max()	Takes any number of numerical arguments (but at least one) and returns the largest of the arguments.

For example, the result of the following expression

```
min(3, abs(-3), max(round(2.7), ceil(2.3), floor(3.9)))
```

is 3, because the value of every function call is also 3.

A glimpse behind the curtain

How are built-in PHP functions really implemented? This is likely to be of interest only to C programmers and/or those who care about the inner workings of PHP, but we thought that it might be revealing to see why so many PHP functions work just like their C counterparts.

What follows is the actual implementation for the PHP function `ceil`, which is intended to convert a double to the smallest integer that is greater than or equal to it.

```
PHP_FUNCTION(ceil)
{
  zval **value;

  if (ARG_COUNT(ht)!=1||getParametersEx(1,&value)==FAILURE) {
              WRONG_PARAM_COUNT;
  }
    convert_scalar_to_number_ex(value);

    if ((*value)->type == IS_DOUBLE) {
      RETURN_LONG((long)ceil((*value)->value.dval));
        } else if ((*value)->type == IS_LONG) {
          RETURN_LONG((*value)->value.lval);
        }
    RETURN_FALSE;
}
```

While the capitalized portions (including the `PHP_FUNCTION` declaration) are macros specific to the PHP framework, much of the body of this code is straight C. The code might look dense and confusing at first, but most of the action has to do with PHP's special treatment of types. Here is roughly what is happening, in order:

1. The arguments that `ceil()` was called with are retrieved and counted—if the count is anything other than 1, the function call returns with an error.

2. The single argument is converted to a number if it is a scalar type other than a number—this handles the possibility of string arguments, as in `ceil("5.4")`.

3. Now the numerical argument is tested to see whether it is a PHP long (a.k.a. integer) or a PHP double. If it turns out to be a long, the value as a long is returned.

4. The interesting case is if the value is a PHP double. If so, the C double value is extracted, it is run through the C function `ceil`, the result is converted to a C long, and then that value is wrapped up and returned as a PHP long.

In other words, the PHP implementation of `ceil` is simply the C function `ceil`, wrapped up in a lot of type conversion and argument checking. This is the case with many of PHP's functions that have exact analogues in C.

Base Conversion

The default base in PHP for reading in or printing out numbers is 10. In addition, you can instruct PHP to read octal numbers in base 8 (by starting the number with a leading 0) or hexadecimal numbers in base 16 (by starting the number with a 0x).

Cross-Reference For more on read formats of numbers, including octal and hexadecimal notation, see Chapter 6.

Once numbers are read in, of course, they are represented in binary format in memory, and all the basic arithmetic and mathematical calculations are carried out internally in base 2. PHP also has a number of functions for translating between different bases, which are summarized in Table 10-3.

Table 10-3
Base Conversion Functions

Function	Behavior
BinDec()	Takes a single string argument representing a binary (base 2) integer, and returns a string representation of that number in base 10.
DecBin()	Like BinDec(), but converts from base 10 to base 2.
OctDec()	Like BinDec(), but converts from base 8 to base 10.
DecOct()	Like BinDec(), but converts from base 10 to base 8.
HexDec()	Like BinDec(), but converts from base 16 to base 10.
DecHex()	Like BinDec(), but converts from base 10 to base 16.
baseconvert()	Takes a string argument (the integer to be converted) and two integer arguments (the original base, and the desired base). Returns a string representing the converted number — digits higher than 9 (from 10 to 35) are represented by the letters a–z. Both the original and desired bases must be in the range 2–36.

All of the base conversion functions are special-purpose, converting from one particular base to another, except for base_convert(), which accepts an arbitrary start base and destination base. Here's an example of base_convert() in action:

```
function display_bases($start_string, $start_base)
{
  for ($new_base = 2; $new_base <= 36; $new_base++)
    {
      $converted =
```

```
        base_convert($start_string, $start_base, $new_base);
        print("$start_string in base $start_base
            is $converted in base $new_base<BR>");
    }
}

display_bases("1jj", 20);
```

which yields the browser output

```
1jj in base 20 is 1100011111 in base 2
1jj in base 20 is 1002121 in base 3
1jj in base 20 is 30133 in base 4
1jj in base 20 is 11144 in base 5
1jj in base 20 is 3411 in base 6
1jj in base 20 is 2221 in base 7
1jj in base 20 is 1437 in base 8
1jj in base 20 is 1077 in base 9
1jj in base 20 is 799 in base 10
1jj in base 20 is 667 in base 11
1jj in base 20 is 567 in base 12
1jj in base 20 is 496 in base 13
1jj in base 20 is 411 in base 14
1jj in base 20 is 384 in base 15
1jj in base 20 is 31f in base 16
1jj in base 20 is 2d0 in base 17
1jj in base 20 is 287 in base 18
1jj in base 20 is 241 in base 19
1jj in base 20 is 1jj in base 20
1jj in base 20 is 1h1 in base 21
1jj in base 20 is 1e7 in base 22
1jj in base 20 is 1bh in base 23
1jj in base 20 is 197 in base 24
1jj in base 20 is 16o in base 25
1jj in base 20 is 14j in base 26
1jj in base 20 is 12g in base 27
1jj in base 20 is 10f in base 28
1jj in base 20 is rg in base 29
1jj in base 20 is qj in base 30
1jj in base 20 is po in base 31
1jj in base 20 is ov in base 32
1jj in base 20 is o7 in base 33
1jj in base 20 is nh in base 34
1jj in base 20 is mt in base 35
1jj in base 20 is m7 in base 36
```

Note   The base conversion functions expect their string arguments to be integers, not floating-point numbers. That is, you can't use these functions to convert a binary "10.1" to a decimal "2.5." In fact, in PHP 4.0 beta 3 the `base_convert()` function gives nonsensical answers when handed a string containing a decimal point (it apparently interprets "." as "0").

Notice that although all of the base-conversion functions take string arguments and return string values, you can use decimal numerical arguments and rely on PHP's type conversion (but see the cautionary note that follows). In other words, both DecBin("1234") and DecBin(1234) will yield the same result.

 Caution Don't confuse the read formats of numbers with their representations as strings for the purposes of base conversion. For example, although "10" in base 16 is the number 16 in base 10, the expression HexDec(0x10) evaluates to the string "22." Why? There are really three conversions happening: when 0x10 is read (converts from hex to internal binary), when the argument is auto-converted (from internal binary number to the decimal string "16"), and in the operation of the function (from assumed base-16 "16" to decimal "22"). If you want just one conversion, then the desired expression is HexDec("10").

Exponents and Logarithms

PHP includes the standard exponential and logarithmic functions, in both base 10 and base e varieties (shown in Table 10-4).

	Table 10-4
	Exponential Functions

Function	*Behavior*
pow()	Takes two numerical arguments and returns the first argument raised to the power of the second. The value of pow($x, $y) is x^y.
exp()	Takes a single argument and raises e to that power. The value of exp($x) is e^x.
log()	The "natural log" function. Takes a single argument and returns its base e logarithm. If $e^y = x$, then the value of log($x) is y.
log10()	Takes a single argument and returns its base-10 logarithm. If $10^y = x$, then the value of log10($x) is y.

Note The special mathematical constant 'e' (approximately equal to 2.718) is not a PHP constant, but its approximation as a double can be recovered at will by evaluating log(1).

Unlike with exp() and the base e, there is no single-argument function to raise 10 to a given power, but in its place you can use the two-argument function pow() with 10 as the first argument.

You can verify for yourself that exponential and power functions of the same base are inverses of each other, by testing an "identity" like this:

```
$test_449 = 449.0;
$test_449 = pow(10, exp(log(log10($test_449)))));
print("test_449 is $test_449<BR>");
```

which gives the browser output

```
test_449 is 449
```

Trigonometry

Although explaining the math behind the PHP functions in this chapter is beyond the scope of this book, we've made an exception just this once (see the sidebar "Trigonometry in one paragraph"). Anyone who doesn't already know trigonometry will, of course, find it completely impenetrable, but we hope that those who know trig will at least be amused by how short it is.

PHP offers the standard set of basic trigonometric functions as well as the constant M_PI, an approximation of pi as a double, that prints as 3.1415926535898. (To our knowledge, this is the only mathematical constant in PHP.) This constant can be used anywhere you would use the literal number itself, and it is also interchangeable with the pi() function. Both of the following statements have the same result:

```
$my_pi = M_PI;
$my_pi = pi();
```

The basic trig functions are summarized in Table 10-5.

<table>
<tr><th colspan="2">Table 10-5
Trigonometric Functions</th></tr>
<tr><th>*Function*</th><th>*Behavior*</th></tr>
<tr><td>pi()</td><td>Takes no arguments and returns an approximation of pi (3.1415926535898). Can be used interchangeably with the constant M_PI.</td></tr>
<tr><td>sin()</td><td>Takes a numerical argument in radians and returns the sine of the argument as a double.</td></tr>
<tr><td>cos()</td><td>Takes a numerical argument in radians and returns the cosine of the argument as a double.</td></tr>
</table>

Function	Behavior
tan()	Takes a numerical argument in radians and returns the tangent of the argument as a double.
asin()	Takes a numerical argument and returns the arcsine of the argument in radians. Inputs must be between –1.0 and 1.0 [inputs outside that range will return a result of NaN (for "not a number")]. Results are in the range –pi / 2 to pi / 2.
acos()	Takes a numerical argument and returns the arccosine of the argument in radians. Inputs must be between –1.0 and 1.0 [inputs outside that range will return a result of NaN (for "not a number")]. Results are in the range 0 to pi.
atan()	Takes a numerical argument and returns the arctangent of the argument in radians. Results are in the range –pi / 2 to pi / 2.
atan2()	A variant of atan() that takes 2 arguments. atan($y, $x) is identical to atan($y/$x) when $x is positive, but the quadrant of atan2's result depends on the signs of both $y and $x. Range of the result is from – pi to pi.

Rather than writing down a table of sample function results, let's resort to our usual trick of writing code that will automatically display examples as an HTML table. Listing 10-1 shows both a generalized function for displaying a set of one-argument functions applied to a set of numerical arguments, and then the result of using this display function to make trigonometric and inverse trigonometric example tables. The results are displayed in Figure 10-1.

Trigonometry in one paragraph

Imagine a circle with a radius of 1, centered at 0,0 in the coordinate plane. Start at the right-hand edge (at position (1,0)), and trace a certain distance along the circle counter-clockwise. For example, a distance of 2 pi would take you once around the circle and back to your starting point. Clockwise travel counts as a negative distance. For any such distance, the sine function tells you the y-value of the coordinate you arrive at, the cosine function tells you the x-value of that coordinate, and the tangent function is a ratio of the two, from which you can infer the slope of the line tangent to the circle at that point. The functions arccosine, arcsine, and arctangent are in some sense inverses of their corresponding functions—they map back from an x, y, or y/x ratio to the distance of a circular trip that would arrive at that x-coordinate, y-coordinate, or ratio thereof. Because adding a multiple of 2 pi to any distance brings you around to the same point again, these inverse functions might have an infinite number of answers per input, making them ill-defined—instead, though, they are restricted to a range corresponding to one particular trip around half of the circle and so have well-defined results.

Listing 10-1: **Displaying trigonometric function results**

```php
<?php

function display_func_results($func_array, $input_array)
{
/* print a function header */
print("<TABLE BORDER=1><TR><TH>INPUT\\FUNCTION</TH>");
for($y = 0;
        $y < count($func_array);
        $y++)
    print("<TH>$func_array[$y]</TH>");
print("</TR><TR>");
/* print the rest of the table */
for($x = 0;
    $x < count($input_array);
    $x++)
  {
    /* print column entries for inputs */
    print("<TH>".
          sprintf("%.4f", $input_array[$x])
          ."</TH>");
    for($y = 0;
        $y < count($func_array);
        $y++)
    {
      $func_name = $func_array[$y];
      $input = $input_array[$x];
      print("<TD>");
      printf("%4.4f", $func_name($input));
      print("</TD>");
    }
    print("</TR><TR>");
  }
print("</TR></TABLE>");
}
?>

<HTML>
<HEAD>
<TITLE>Figure 10-1</TITLE>
</HEAD>
<BODY>

<?php
/* using the function displayer */
print("<H3>Trigonometric function examples</H3>");
display_func_results(array("sin", "cos", "tan"),
                     array(-1.25 * pi(),
                           -1.0 * pi(),
```

```
                                    -0.75 * pi(),
                                    -0.5 * pi(),
                                    -0.25 * pi(),
                                     0,
                                     0.25 * pi(),
                                     0.5 * pi(),
                                     0.75 * pi(),
                                     pi(),
                                     1.25 * pi()));
print("<H3>Inverse trigonometric function examples</H3>");
display_func_results(array("asin", "acos", "atan"),
                     array(-1.0, -0.5, 0.0, 0.5, 1.0));
?>
</BODY>
</HTML>
```

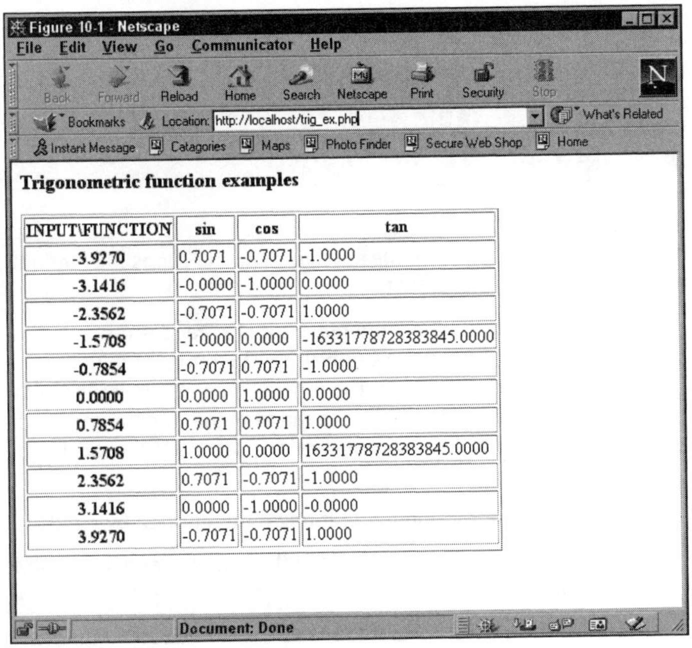

INPUT\FUNCTION	sin	cos	tan
-3.9270	0.7071	-0.7071	-1.0000
-3.1416	-0.0000	-1.0000	0.0000
-2.3562	-0.7071	-0.7071	1.0000
-1.5708	-1.0000	0.0000	-16331778728383845.0000
-0.7854	-0.7071	0.7071	-1.0000
0.0000	0.0000	1.0000	0.0000
0.7854	0.7071	0.7071	1.0000
1.5708	1.0000	0.0000	16331778728383845.0000
2.3562	0.7071	-0.7071	-1.0000
3.1416	0.0000	-1.0000	-0.0000
3.9270	-0.7071	-0.7071	1.0000

Figure 10-1: Trigonometric function examples

Figure 10-1 shows the basic trigonometric functions over an input range of –5/4 pi to 5/4 pi, and the basic inverse trigonometric function over inputs from –1.0 to 1.0. The very large tangent values are due to denominators that should theoretically be zero but instead differ slightly from zero due to rounding error.

Cross-Reference   The `display_func_results()` function of Listing 10-1 uses several tricks we've seen in previous chapters: using a string variable as the name of a function to call (covered near the end of Chapter 8), and using the string concatenation operator ('.') to pull together a print string in the middle of a print statement (covered in Chapter 9).

New Feature   In Listing 10-1 we take advantage of the "variable function" feature in PHP, which enables us to retrieve and call trigonometric functions by their stored names. Although previous versions of PHP permitted user-defined functions to be called this way, the capability to do the same with built-in functions is new in PHP 4.

Randomness

PHP's functions for generating pseudo-random numbers are summarized in Table 10-6. (If you are new to random number generation and are wondering what the "pseudo" is all about, please see the accompanying sidebar.)

Table 10-6	
Random Number Functions	
Function	**Behavior**
srand()	Takes a single positive integer argument and seeds the random number generator with it.
rand()	When called with no arguments, returns a "random" number between 0 and RAND_MAX (which can be retrieved with the function getrandmax()). The function can also be called with two integer arguments to restrict the range of the number returned—the first argument is the minimum and the second is the maximum (inclusive).
getrandmax()	Returns the largest number that might be returned by rand().
mt_srand()	Like srand(), except that it seeds the "better" random number generator.
mt_rand()	Like rand(), except that it uses the "better" random number generator.
mt_getrandmax()	Returns the largest number that might be returned by mt_rand().

There are two random number generators, each with the same three associated functions: a seeding function, the random-number function itself, and a function that retrieves the largest integer that might be returned by the generator.

The particular pseudo-random function that is used by rand() may depend on the particular libraries that PHP was compiled with. By contrast, the mt_rand() generator always uses the same random function (the "Mersenne Twister") and the author of mt_rand()'s online documentation argues that it is also faster and "more random" (in a cryptographic sense) than rand(). We have no reason to believe that this is not correct, and so we prefer mt_rand() to rand().

Note   On some PHP versions and some platforms, you can apparently get seemingly random numbers from rand() and mt_rand() without seeding first—this should not be relied upon, however, both for reasons of portability and because the unseeded behavior is not guaranteed.

Pseudo-random number generators

As with all programming languages, the "random" number functions offered by PHP are really implemented by pseudo-random number generators. This is because conventional computer architectures are deterministic machines that will always produce the same results given the same starting conditions and inputs and have no good source of randomness. (Here we're talking about the ideal computer as it is supposed to work, not the actual physically embodied, power-interruptible, cosmic-ray flippable, seemingly very random machines we all struggle with daily!) You could imagine connecting a conventional computer to a source of random bits such as a mechanical coin-flip reader, or a device that observed quantum-level events, but such peripherals don't seem to be widely available at this time.

So we must make do with pseudo-random generators, which produce a deterministic sequence of numbers that looks random enough for most purposes. They typically work by running their initial input number (the *seed*) through a particular mathematical function to produce the first number in the sequence; each subsequent number in the sequence is the result of applying that same function to the previous number in the sequence. The sequence will repeat at some point (once it generates a particular number for the second time, it is doomed to follow the same sequence as it did the first time around), but a good iteration function will generate a very long sequence of numbers that have little apparent pattern before the loop occurs.

How do you choose a seed to start off with? Because of the generator's determinism, if you hard-code a PHP page to have a particular seed, then that page will always see the same sequence from the generator. (Although this is not usually what you want, it can be an invaluable trick when you are trying to debug behavior that depends on the particular numbers that are generated.) The typical seeding technique is to use a fast-changing digit from the system clock as the initial seed—although those numbers are not exactly random, they are likely to vary quickly enough that subsequent page executions will start with a different seed every time.

Seeding the generator

The typical way to seed either of the PHP random-number generators (using `mt_srand()` or `srand()`) looks like this:

```
mt_srand((double)microtime()*1000000);
```

This sets the seed of the generator to be the number of microseconds that have elapsed since the last "whole" second. (Yes, the typecast to "double" is necessary here, because `microtime()` returns a string, which would treated as an integer in the multiplication but for the cast.) Feel free to use this seeding statement even if you don't understand it—just place it in any PHP page, once only, before you use the corresponding `mt_rand()` or `rand()` functions, and it will ensure that you have a varying starting point, and therefore random sequences that are different every time.

Here is some representative code that uses the pseudo-random functions:

```
print("Seeding the generator<BR>");
mt_srand((double)microtime() * 1000000);
print("With no arguments: " . mt_rand() . "<BR>");
print("With no arguments: " . mt_rand() . "<BR>");
print("With no arguments: " . mt_rand() . "<BR>");
print("With two arguments: " .
        mt_rand(27, 31) . "<BR>");
print("With two arguments: " .
        mt_rand(27, 31) . "<BR>");
print("With two arguments: " .
        mt_rand(27, 31) . "<BR>");
```

with the browser output:

```
Seeding the generator
With no arguments: 992873415
With no arguments: 656237128
With no arguments: 1239053221
With two arguments: 28
With two arguments: 31
With two arguments: 29
```

Obviously, if you run exactly this code, you will get numbers that differ from those above, since the point of seeding the generator this way is to ensure that different executions produce different sequences of numbers.

Caution In some old versions of PHP 3, the `rand()` function buggily ignored its arguments, returning numbers between 0 and `getrandmax()` regardless of restrictions. We have also heard some reports of that behavior under more recent Windows implementations. If you suspect that you are suffering from such a bug, you can define your own restricted version of `rand()` like so:

```
function my_rand ($min, $max)
{
```

```
        return(rand() % (($max - $min) + 1)
                + $min);
    }
```

Unlike rand(), this version requires the min and max arguments.

 Tip

Although the random-number functions only return integers, it is easy to convert a random integer in a given range to a corresponding floating-point number (say, one between 0.0 and 1.0 inclusive) with an expression like rand() / getrandmax(). You can then scale and shift the range as desired (to, say, a number between 100.0 and 120.0) with an expression like 100.0 + 20.0 * (rand() / getrandmax()).

Example: making a random selection

Now let's use the random functions for something useful (or, at least, something that could be used for something useful). The following two functions let you construct a random string of letters, which could in turn be used as a random login or password string:

```
function random_char($string)
{
  $length = strlen($string);
  $position = mt_rand(0, $length - 1);
  return($string[$position]);
}
function random_string ($charset_string, $length)
{
    $return_string = ""; // the empty string
  for ($x = 0; $x < $length; $x++)
    $return_string .= random_char($charset_string);
  return($return_string);
}
```

The random_char() function chooses a character (or, actually, a substring of length 1) from its input string. It does this by restricting the mt_rand() function to positions within the length of the string (with chars numbered starting at zero), and then returning the character that is at that random position. The random_string() function calls random_char() a number of times on a string representing the universe of characters to be chosen from and concatenates together a string of the desired length.

Now, to demonstrate this code, we first seed the generator, define our universe of allowable characters, and then call random_string() a few times in a row:

```
mt_srand((double)microtime() * 1000000);
$charset = "abcdefghijklmnopqrstuvwxyz";

$random_string = random_string($charset, 8);
print("random_string: $random_string<BR>");
```

```
$random_string = random_string($charset, 8);
print("random_string: $random_string<BR>");
$random_string = random_string($charset, 8);
print("random_string: $random_string<BR>");
```

with the result:

```
random_string: eisexkio
random_string: mkvflwfy
random_string: gpulbwth
```

In this example, we only seed the generator once, and we draw that seed value from the system clock. Notice what happens if we make the mistake of repeatedly seeding the generator with the same value:

```
mt_srand(43);
$random_string = random_string($charset, 8);
print("random_string: $random_string<BR>");

mt_srand(43);
$random_string = random_string($charset, 8);
print("random_string: $random_string<BR>");

mt_srand(43);
$random_string = random_string($charset, 8);
print("random_string: $random_string<BR>");
```

Because the sequence that is generated depends deterministically on the seed, we get the same behavior each time:

```
random_string: qgkxvurw
random_string: qgkxvurw
random_string: qgkxvurw
```

In these examples, we chose to draw random characters from strings, but this kind of selection process is generalizable to drawing items from arrays, or any situation in which you need to choose random members from a set. All you need is the universe of items, a way to put them in numerical order, and a way to retrieve them by order number, and you can then use the rand() or mt_rand() function to choose a random order number for the retrieval.

Arbitrary Precision (BC)

The integer and double types are fine for most of the mathematical tasks that arise in Web scripting, but each instance of these types is stored in a fixed amount of computer memory, and so the size and precision of the numbers they can represent is inherently limited. Although the exact range of these types may depend on the architecture of your server machine, integers typically range from $-2^{31} - 1$ to $2^{31} - 1$, and doubles can represent about 13 to 14 decimal digits of precision. For tasks that require greater range or precision, PHP offers the arbitrary-precision math functions (also known as "BC" functions, from the name of the UNIX-based arbitrary-precision calculating utility).

Note

Especially if you compiled PHP yourself, the arbitrary-precision functions may not have been included in the compilation — you need to have included the flag `--enable-bcmath` at configuration time. To check whether the functions are present, try evaluating `bcadd("1", "1")` — if you get an unbound function error, you will have to reconfigure and recompile PHP.

Instead of using the fixed-length numerical types, the BC functions have strings as arguments and return values. Because strings in PHP are limited only by available memory, this means that numbers can be as long as you like. The underlying computations are performed in decimal and are much like you would do them with pen and paper if you were very fast and very patient. When operating with "integers," the BC functions are exact and use as many digits as needed; when operating with "floating-point" numbers, computations are done to as many decimal places as you specify. The BC functions are summarized in Table 10-7.

Table 10-7	
Arbitrary-Precision (BC) Math Functions	
Function	***Behavior***
bcadd()	Takes two string arguments representing numbers, and an optional integer scale parameter. Returns the sum of the first two arguments as a string, with the number of decimal places in the result determined by the scale parameter. If no scale parameter is supplied, the default scale is used (which is settable by bcscale()).
bcsub()	Similar to bcadd(), except that it returns the subtraction of the second argument from the first.
bcmul()	Similar to bcadd() but returns the product of its arguments.
bcdiv()	Similar to bcadd() but returns the result of dividing the first argument by the second.
bcmod()	Returns the modulus (remainder) of the first argument as divided by the second. Because the return type is "integral," no scale argument is taken.
bcpow()	Raises the first argument to the power of the second argument. The number of decimal places in the result is set by the scale factor if supplied.
bcsqrt()	Returns the square root of its argument, with number of decimal places set by the optional scale factor.
bcscale()	Sets the default scale factor for subsequent BC function calls.

Most of the functions take an optional scale factor (an integer) as a final argument, which determines how many decimal places will be in the result. If such an argument is not supplied, the scale is the default scale, which in turn can be set by calling bcscale(). The default for the default value (that is, if bcscale() has never been called) can also be set in the initialization file php.ini.

An arbitrary-precision example

Here's an example of using the arbitrary-precision functions for exact integer arithmetic. The following code

```
for ($x = 1; $x < 25; $x++) {
    print("$x to the $x power is " . bcpow($x, $x) . "<BR>");
}
```

will print like this:

```
1 raised to the power of 1 is 1
2 raised to the power of 2 is 4
3 raised to the power of 3 is 27
4 raised to the power of 4 is 256
5 raised to the power of 5 is 3125
6 raised to the power of 6 is 46656
7 raised to the power of 7 is 823543
8 raised to the power of 8 is 16777216
9 raised to the power of 9 is 387420489
10 raised to the power of 10 is 10000000000
11 raised to the power of 11 is 285311670611
12 raised to the power of 12 is 8916100448256
13 raised to the power of 13 is 302875106592253
14 raised to the power of 14 is 11112006825558016
15 raised to the power of 15 is 437893890380859375
16 raised to the power of 16 is 18446744073709551616
17 raised to the power of 17 is 827240261886336764177
18 raised to the power of 18 is 39346408075296537575424
19 raised to the power of 19 is 1978419655660313589123979
20 raised to the power of 20 is 104857600000000000000000000
21 raised to the power of 21 is 5842587018385982521381124421
22 raised to the power of 22 is 341427877364219557396646723584
23 raised to the power of 23 is
2088046799984791203435503291056
24 raised to the power of 24 is
1333735776850284124449081472843776
25 raised to the power of 25 is
88817841970012523233890533447265625
```

If we had used the regular PHP integer type for this computation, the integers would have "overflowed" well before the end, and the rest of the loop would have been calculated in approximate floating point.

Converting code to arbitrary-precision

Let's see what it's like to take an existing piece of mathematical code and retrofit it to use the arbitrary-precision functions.

The following function approximates pi, using the series approximation

$$\text{sqrt} (\ 12\ -\ (12/2^2)\ +\ (12/3^2)\ -\ (12/4^2)\ +\ (12/5^2)\ -\ \dots\ )$$

(As we'll see, this series does not converge fast enough for our purposes, but it has the virtue of being a simple formula.)

```
function pi_approx($iterations, $print_frequency)
{
  $squared_approx = 12;
  $next_sign = -1;
  $denom = 2;

  for ($iter = 0; $iter < $iterations; $iter++)
    {
      $squared_approx += $next_sign * 12/(pow($denom,2));
      $denom++;
      $next_sign = - $next_sign;
      if ($denom % $print_frequency == 0)
        {
          $estimate = sqrt($squared_approx);
          print("$denom iterations: $estimate<BR>");
        }
    }
}
```

In addition to performing the calculation itself, this code periodically prints out its current estimate of pi, so we can see how we are doing. We can call it as follows, and then print out PHP's value for comparison:

```
pi_approx(10000, 1000);
print("PHP value: " . pi() . "<BR>");
```

The result looks like:

```
1000 iterations: 3.1415936094742
2000 iterations: 3.1415928924416
3000 iterations: 3.1415927597285
4000 iterations: 3.1415927132878
5000 iterations: 3.1415926917946
6000 iterations: 3.14159268012
7000 iterations: 3.141592673081
8000 iterations: 3.1415926685124
9000 iterations: 3.1415926653804
10000 iterations: 3.1415926631401
PHP value: 3.1415926535898
```

Now, not only are we not that close, but we can't hope to be more accurate than PHP's value for pi, because that already uses all the precision available in the double type.

To convert this to an arbitrary-precision version, we must replace all the math functions and operators that need precision with their BC counterparts, like so:

```
function pi_approx_bc($iterations, $print_frequency, $scale)
{
  $squared_approx = "12";
  $next_sign = -1;
  $denom = 2;
  for ($iter = 0; $iter < $iterations; $iter++)
    {
      $squared_approx
        = bcadd(
            $squared_approx,
            bcmul($next_sign,
                bcdiv(12,
                    bcpow($denom,
                        2,
                        $scale),
                    $scale),
                $scale),
            $scale);
      $denom++;
      $next_sign = - $next_sign;
      if ($denom % $print_frequency == 0)
        {
          $estimate = bcsqrt($squared_approx,$scale);
          print("$denom iterations: $estimate<BR>");
        }
    }
}
```

Notice that although the BC functions want string arguments, we can as always use regular numbers in their place and rely on PHP to convert the arguments to strings for us. Also notice that we did not bother making the numerical computations that do not require great precision into BC computations (for instance, we still have $denom++ rather than bcadd($denom, 1). Finally, we added a scale argument to the entire function, which turns the decimal precision of each BC function it calls.

Unfortunately, both your authors and our browsers ran out of patience with this series before it got even got to the level of precision of PHP's value. Here are some late results of calling (pi_approx_bc(1250000, 50000, 50):

```
50000 iterations:
3.14159265397177274129723551068347726371297686926596
100000 iterations:
3.14159265368528715924598769254390594927146205337113
```

```
150000 iterations:
3.14159265363223483956231649503922042729332175382O2
[..]
1150000 iterations:
3.14159265359051530310455255409602580003265549955003
1200000 iterations:
3.14159265359045638461148087403458918944405547147211
1250000 iterations:
3.14159265359040439393304018710072157703501022388304
```

The correct digits in the preceding output are about one digit shy of the PHP value. This is the fault of the series we chose, rather than the arbitrary-precision libraries — with a more sophisticated and speedier approximation series, you too can serve up millions of digits of pi to your eager audience.

Somewhat more satisfyingly, evaluating

```
print("The square root of two is " . bcsqrt(2, 40));
```

gives us many more digits of precision than we could get using doubles:

```
The square root of two is
1.41421356237309504880168872420969807856960
```

Summary

The highlights of PHP math are summarized in Table 10-8.

Table 10-8
Summary of PHP Math Operators and Functions

Category	Description
Arithmetic operators	Operators +, -, *, /, % perform basic arithmetic on integers and doubles.
Incrementing operators	The ++ and -- operators change the values of numerical variables, increasing them by one, or decreasing them by one (respectively). The value of the postincrement form ($var++) is the same as the variable's value before the change; the value of the preincrement form (++$var) is the variable's value after the change.
Assignment operators	Each arithmetic operator (like '+') has a corresponding assignment operator ('+='). The expression $count += 5 is equivalent to $count = $count + 5.

Continued

Table 10-8 *(continued)*

Category	Description
Comparison operators	`<`, `<=`, `>`, `>=`, `==`, `!=`. The `===` operator is true if its arguments are equal and of the same type.
Basic math functions	`floor()`, `ceil()`, and `round()` convert doubles to integers, `min()` and `max()` take the minimum and maximum of their numerical arguments, and `abs()` is the absolute value function.
Base conversion functions	Special-purpose functions (`OctDec()`, `DecOct()`, `BinDec()`, `DecBin()`, `HexDec()`, `DecHex()`) convert between particular pairs of bases, while `base_convert()` translates between arbitrary bases.
Exponential functions	`log()` (natural log), `log10()` (base-10 log), `exp()` (e raised to the power of the argument), and `pow()` (first argument to the power of the second).
Trigonometric functions	`pi()` (and the equivalent constant M_PI), `sin()`, `cos()`, `tan()`, `acos()`, `asin()`, `atan()`, and `atan2()` (a two-argument version of `atan()`).
Arbitrary-precision (BC) functions	Functions that do arithmetic on arbitrary-length strings representing decimal integers and floating-point numbers: `bdadd()`, `bcsub()`, `bcmult()`, `bcdiv()`, `bcmod`, `bcpow()`, `bcsqrt()`. Most of these functions take an optional scale parameter specifying the number of decimal points of precision desired—the default for that parameter is settable using `bcscale()`.

✦   ✦   ✦

Arrays and Array Functions

◆ ◆ ◆ ◆

In This Chapter

How arrays
work in PHP

Using multi-
dimensional arrays

Imitating other data
structures with arrays

Sorting and other
transformations

◆ ◆ ◆ ◆

Arrays are definitely one of the coolest and most flexible features of PHP. Unlike vector arrays from other languages (C, C++, Pascal), PHP arrays can store data of varied types and automatically organize it for you in a large variety of ways.

Cross-Reference   This chapter treats arrays and array functions in some depth. For a very quick introduction to the syntax and use of arrays, see Chapter 6.

New Feature   Warning—although arrays have been a feature of PHP for some time and work substantially the same way in PHP 3 and PHP 4, many of the specific functions documented in this chapter are new as of PHP 4.

The Uses of Arrays

Throughout much of this chapter, we will be looking at the inner workings of arrays and exploring all the built-in PHP functions that manipulate them. Before we get too deep into that, though, it's worth listing the common ways that arrays are used in real PHP Web site code:

◆ Many built-in PHP environment variables are in the form of arrays (for example, `$HTTP_COOKIE_VARS`, which contains all the variables and values stored in a client-side cookie). If you want access to them, you need to understand at a minimum how to reference arrays.

◆ Most database functions transport their info via arrays, making a compact package of an arbitrary chunk of data.

✦ It's easy to pass entire sets of HTML form arguments from one page to another in a single array (see the next chapter).

✦ Arrays make a nice container for doing manipulations (sorting, counting, and so on) of any data you develop while executing a single page's script.

Almost any situation that calls for a number of pieces of data to be packaged and handled as one is appropriate for a PHP array.

What Are PHP Arrays?

PHP arrays are *associative* arrays, with a little extra machinery thrown in. The "associative" part means that arrays store element values in association with key values, rather than in a strict linear index order. (If you have seen arrays in other programming languages, they are likely to have been *vector* arrays rather than associative arrays — see the sidebar for an explanation of the difference.) If you store an element in an array, in association with a key, all you need to retrieve it later from that array is the key value. For example, storage is as simple as this:

```
$state_location['San Mateo'] = 'California';
```

which stores the element 'California' in the array variable $state_location, in association with the lookup key 'San Mateo'. Once this has been stored, you can look up the stored value by using the key, like so:

```
$state = $state_location['San Mateo'];   // equals 'California'
```

Simple, no?

If all you want arrays for is to store key/value pairs, then the preceding information is all you need to know. Similarly, if you want to associate a numerical ordering with a bunch of values, then all you have to do is use integers as your key values, as in:

```
$my_array[1] = "The first thing";
$my_array[2] = "The second thing"; // and so on ...
```

In addition to the machinery that makes this kind of key/value association possible, arrays track some other things behind the scenes, which enable treating them as other kinds of data structures. As we will see in a later section, arrays can be multi-dimensional. They can store values in association with a sequence of key values rather than a single key. Also, arrays automatically maintain an ordered list of the elements that have been inserted in them, independent of what the key values happen to be. This makes it possible to treat arrays as linked lists. In general, we will reveal the workings of this extra machinery as we explore the functions that use it.

Associative arrays versus vector arrays

If you have programmed in languages like C, C++, and Pascal, you are probably used to a particular usage of the word "array," one that doesn't match the PHP usage very well at all. A more specific term for a C-style array is a "vector array," whereas a PHP-style array is an "associative array."

In a vector array, the contained elements all need to be of the same type, and usually the language compiler needs to know in advance how many such elements there are likely to be. For example, in C you might declare an array of 100 double-precision floating-point numbers with a statement like

```
double my_array[100]; // This is C, not PHP!
```

The restriction on types and the advance declaration of size have an associated benefit: vector arrays are very fast, both for storage and lookup. The reason is that the compiler will usually lay out the array in a contiguous block of computer memory, as large as the size of the element type multiplied by the number of elements. This makes it very easy for the programming language to locate a particular array slot — all it needs to know is the starting memory address of the array, the size of the element type, and the index of the element it wants to look up, and it can directly compute the memory address of that slot.

By contrast, PHP arrays are associative (and so some would call them *hashes,* rather than arrays). Rather than having a fixed number of slots, PHP creates array slots as new elements are added to the array. Rather than requiring elements to be of the same type, PHP arrays have the same type-looseness that PHP variables have — you can assign arbitrary PHP values to be array elements. Finally, because vector arrays are all about laying out their elements in numerical order, the "keys" that are used for lookup and storage must be integer numbers. PHP arrays can have keys of arbitrary type, instead, including string keys. So, you could have successive array assignments like

```
$my_array[1] = 1;
$my_array['orange'] = 2;
$my_array[3] = 3;
```

without any paradox. The result is that your array has three values (1, 2, 3), each of which is stored in association with a key (1, `'orange'`, and 3, respectively).

The extra flexibility of associative arrays comes at a price, because there is a little bit more going on between your code and the actual computation of a memory address than is true with vector arrays. For most Web programming purposes, however, this extra access time is not a significant cost.

The fact that integers are legal keys for PHP arrays means that you can easily imitate the behavior of a vector array, simply by restricting your code to use only integers as keys.

Note For Perl programmers: Arrays in PHP are much like hashes in Perl, with some syntactic differences. For one thing, all variables in PHP are denoted with a leading '$', not just scalar variables. Secondly, even though the array is associative, the indices are grouped by square brackets ('[]') rather than curly braces ('{}'). Finally, there is no array type that is indexed only by integers. The convention is to use integers as associative indices, and the array itself maintains an internal ordering for iteration purposes.

Note A note for C++ programmers: You should be aware that arrays can handle some of the same tasks that require the use of template libraries in C++. This is because much of the reason for having templates in the first place is to get around restrictions having to do with strict typing of data. PHP's looser typing system makes it possible, for example, to write general algorithms that iterate over the contents of arrays without committing as to the type of the array elements themselves.

Note A general note for programmers familiar with other languages: PHP does not need very many different kinds of data structures, in part because of the great flexibility offered by PHP arrays. By careful choice of a subset of array functions, you can make arrays "pretend" to act like vector arrays, structure/record types, linked lists, hash tables, or stacks and queues—data structures that in other languages either require their own data types or more abstruse language features such as pointers and explicit memory management.

Creating Arrays

There are three main ways to create an array in a PHP script: by assigning a value into one (and thereby implicitly creating it), by using the array() construct, and by calling a function that happens to return an array as its value.

Direct assignment

The simplest way to create an array is to act as though a variable is already an array and assign a value into it, like this:

```
$my_array[1] = "The first thing in my array that I just made";
```

If $my_array was an unbound variable (or bound to a nonarray variable) before this statement, it will now be a variable bound to an array with one element. If instead $my_array was already an array, the string will be stored in association with the integer key 1. If no value was associated with that number before, then a new array slot will be created to hold it; if a value was associated with 1, then the previous value will be overwritten. (You can also assign into an array by omitting the index entirely as in $my_array[], described later in this chapter.)

The array() construct

The other way to create an array is via the `array()` construct, which creates a new array from the specification of its elements and associated keys. In its simplest version, `array()` takes a comma-separated list of elements to be stored, without any specification of keys. The result is that the elements are stored in the array, in the order specified, and are assigned integer keys beginning with zero. For example, the statement

```
$fruit_basket = array('apple', 'orange', 'banana', 'pear');
```

would cause the variable `$fruit_basket` to be assigned to an array with four string elements ('apple', 'banana', 'orange', 'pear'), with the indices 0, 1, 2, and 3 respectively. In addition (as we'll see in the section on iteration) the array will remember the order in which the elements were stored.

The assignment to `$fruit_basket`, then, has exactly the same effect as the following:

```
$fruit_basket[0] = 'apple';
$fruit_basket[1] = 'orange';
$fruit_basket[2] = 'banana';
$fruit_basket[3] = 'pear';
```

assuming that the `$fruit_basket` variable was unbound at the first assignment. The same effect could also have been accomplished by omitting the indices in the assignment, like so:

```
$fruit_basket[] = 'apple';
$fruit_basket[] = 'orange';
$fruit_basket[] = 'banana';
$fruit_basket[] = 'pear';
```

In this case, PHP again assumes that you are adding sequential elements that should have numerical indices counting upward from zero.

Note
A digression: Yes, the default numbering for array indices starts at zero, not one. This is the convention for arrays in most programming languages. We're not sure why computer scientists start counting at zero (mathematicians, like everyone else in the world, start with one), but it may have its origin in the kind of pointer arithmetic that calculates memory addresses for vector arrays. Addresses for successive elements of such arrays are found by adding successively larger offsets to the array's address, but the offset for the first element is zero (because the first element's address is the same as the array's).

Specifying indices using array()

The simple example of `array()` in the preceding section assigns indices to our elements, but those indices will be the integers, counting upward from zero—we're not getting a lot of choice in the matter. As it turns out, `array()` offers us a special syntax for specifying what the indices should be. Instead of element values separated by commas, you supply key-value pairs separated by commas, where the key and value are separated by the special symbol =>.

Consider the following statement:

```
$fruit_basket = array(0 => 'apple', 1 => 'orange',
                      2 => 'banana', 3 => 'pear');
```

Evaluating it will have exactly the same effect as our earlier version—each string will be stored in the array in succession, with the indices 0, 1, 2, 3 in order. Instead, though, we can use exactly the same syntax to store these elements with different indices:

```
$fruit_basket = array('red' => 'apple', 'orange' => 'orange',
                      'yellow' => 'banana', 'green' => 'pear');
```

This gives us the same four elements, added to our new array in the same order, but indexed by color names rather than numbers. To recover the name of the yellow fruit, for example, we just evaluate the expression

```
$fruit_basket['yellow'] // will be equal to 'banana'
```

Finally, you can create an empty array by calling the array function with no arguments. For example,

```
$my_empty_array = array();
```

creates an array with no elements. This can be handy for passing to a function that expects an array as argument.

Note   Although we've only used `array()` for simple arrays so far, it can also be used to create multidimensional arrays—see the section that follows.

Functions returning arrays

The final way to create an array in a script is to call a function that returns an array. This may be a user-defined function (in which case it may in turn construct the returned array by using one of the methods we've already talked about), or it may be a built-in function that makes an array via methods internal to PHP.

Many database-interaction functions, for example, return their results in arrays that the functions create on the fly. Other functions exist simply to create arrays that are handy to have as grist for later array-manipulating functions. One such is `range()`, which takes two integers as arguments and returns an array filled with all the integers (inclusive) that are between the arguments. In other words,

```
$my_array = range(1,5);
```

is equivalent to

```
$my_array = array(1, 2, 3, 4, 5);
```

Retrieving Values

Once we have stored some values in an array, how do we get them out again?

Retrieving by index

The most direct way to retrieve a value is to use its index. If we have stored a value in `$my_array` at index 5, then `$my_array[5]` should evaluate to the stored value. If `$my_array` has never been assigned, or if nothing has been stored in it with an index of 5, then `$my_array[5]` will behave like an unbound variable.

The list() construct

There are a number of other ways to recover values from arrays without using keys, most of which exploit the fact that arrays are silently recording the order in which elements are stored. We cover this in more detail in the "Iteration" section, but one such example is `list()`, which is used to assign several array elements to variables in succession. Suppose, for example, the following two statements are executed:

```
$fruit_basket = array('apple', 'orange', 'banana');
list($red_fruit, $orange_fruit) = $fruit_basket;
```

This will have the result of assigning the string `'apple'` to the variable `$red_fruit`, and the string `'orange'` to the variable $orange_fruit (with no assignment of `'banana'`, because we didn't supply enough variables). The variables in `list()` will be assigned to elements of the array, in the order they were originally stored in the array. Notice the unusual behavior here—the `list()` construct is on the left-hand side of the assignment operator (=), where we normally only find variables.

In some sense, `list()` is the opposite or inverse of `array()`, since `array()` packages its arguments into an array, and `list()` takes the array apart again into individual variable assignments. If we evaluate

```
list($first, $second) = array($first, second);
```

then the original values of $first and $second will be assigned to those variables again, after having been briefly stored in an array.

> **Note**
>
> We have been careful to refer to both array() and list() as constructs, rather than functions. This is because they are not in fact functions—like certain other specialized PHP language features (if, while, function, and so on) they are interpreted specially by the language itself and are not run through the usual routine of function-call interpretation. Remember that the arguments to a function call are evaluated before the function is really invoked on those arguments, so constructs that need to do other kinds of interpretation on what they are given cannot be implemented as function calls. It's a useful exercise to look hard at the example uses of both array() and list() to figure out why treating them as function calls could not result in the behavior advertised.

Multidimensional Arrays

So far the array examples we have looked at have all been one-dimensional, with only one level of bracketed keys. However, PHP can easily support multiple dimensional arrays, with arbitrary numbers of keys. And just as with one-dimensional arrays, there is no need to declare our intentions in advance—your first reference to an array variable can be an assignment like:

```
$multi_array[1][2][3][4][5] = "deeply buried treasure";
```

That is a five-dimensional array with successive keys that happen, in this case, to be five successive integers.

Actually, in our opinion, thinking of arrays as multidimensional makes matters more confusing than they need to be. Instead, just remember that the values that are stored in arrays can themselves be arrays, just as legitimately as they can be strings or numbers. The multiple-index syntax in the preceding example is simply a concise way to refer to a (four-dimensional) array that is stored with a key of 1 in $multi_array, which in turn has a (three-dimensional) array stored in it, and so on. Note also that you can have different "depths" of reference in different parts of the array, like so:

```
$multi_level_array[0] = "a simple string";
$multi_level_array[1]['contains'] = "a string stored deeper";
```

The integer key of 0 stores a string, and the key of 1 stores an array that in turn has a string in it. However, you cannot continue on with this assignment:

```
$multi_level_array[0]['contains'] = "another deep string";
```

without the result of losing the first assignment to "a simple string". The key of 0 can be used to store a string, or another array, but not both at once.

If we remember that multidimensional arrays are simply arrays that have other arrays stored in them, it's easier to see how the array() creation construct generalizes. In fact, even this seemingly complicated assignment is not that complicated:

```
$cornucopia = array('fruit' =>
                    array('red' => 'apple',
                          'orange' => 'orange',
                          'yellow' => 'banana',
                          'green' => 'pear'),
                    'flower' =>
                    array('red' => 'rose',
                          'yellow' => 'sunflower',
                          'purple' => 'iris'));
```

It is simply an array with two values stored in association with keys, each of which values is an array itself. Once we have made the array, we can reference it like this:

```
$kind_wanted = 'flower';
$color_wanted = 'purple';
print("The $color_wanted $kind_wanted is " .
      $cornucopia[$kind_wanted][$color_wanted]);
```

See the browser output:

```
The purple flower is iris
```

Note
There's a reason that we used the string concatenation operator "." in the preceding print statement, rather than simply embedding the $cornucopia[$kind_wanted][$color_wanted] in our print string as we do with other variables. PHP3 string parsing can be confused by multiple array indices within a double-quoted string, so it needs to be concatenated separately. PHP4 handles this in a better way—you are safe embedding array references in a string as long as you enclose the reference in curly braces, like this:

```
print( "The thing we want is
{$cornucopia[$kind_wanted][$color_wanted]}");
```

Finally, notice that there is no great penalty for misindexing into a multidimensional array when we are trying to retrieve something; if no such key is found, the expression is treated like an unbound variable. So, if we tried the following instead:

```
$kind_wanted = 'fruit';
$color_wanted = 'purple'; //uh-oh, we didn't store any plums
print("The $color_wanted $kind_wanted is " .
      $cornucopia[$kind_wanted][$color_wanted]);
```

the worst that happens is the unsatisfying

```
The purple fruit is
```

Inspecting Arrays

Now we can make arrays, store values in arrays, and then pull the values out again when we want them. Table 11-1 summarizes a few other functions we can use to ask questions of our arrays.

Table 11-1 Simple Functions for Inspecting Arrays	
Function	*Behavior*
is_array()	Takes a single argument of any type and returns a true value if the argument is an array, and false otherwise.
()count()	Takes an array as argument and returns the number of nonempty elements in the array. (This will be 1 for strings and numbers.)
sizeof()	Identical to count().
in_array()	Takes two arguments: an element (that might be in an array), and an array (that might contain the element). Returns true if the element is contained in the array, false otherwise.

Deleting from Arrays

Deleting an element from an array is simple, exactly analogous to getting rid of an assigned variable. Just call unset(), as in the following:

```
$my_array[0] = 'wanted';
$my_array[1] = 'unwanted';
$my_array[2] = 'wanted again';
unset($my_array[1]);
```

Assuming that $my_array was unbound when we started, at the end it has two values ('wanted', 'wanted again'), in association with two keys (0 and 2, respectively). It is as though we had skipped the original 'unwanted' assignment.

Note that this is *not* the same as setting the contents to an empty value. If, instead of calling unset(), we had the following statement:

```
$my_array[1] = '';
```

at the end we would have three stored values ('wanted', '', 'wanted again') in association with three keys (0, 1, and 2, respectively).

Iteration

In addition to storing values in association with their keys, PHP arrays silently build an ordered list of the key/value pairs that are stored, in the order that they are stored. The reason for this is to support operations that iterate over the entire contents of an array. (Notice that this is difficult to do simply by building a loop that increments an index, because array indices are not necessarily numerical.)

There is, in fact, sort of a hidden pointer system built into arrays. Each stored key/value pair points to the next one, and one side-effect of adding the first element to an array is that a "current" pointer points to the very first element, where it will stay unless disturbed by one of the iteration functions.

This linked-list pointer system is an alternative way to inspect and manipulate arrays, which exists alongside the system that allows key-based lookup and storage. Figure 11-1 shows an abstract view (not necessarily reflecting the real implementation) of how these systems locate elements in an array.

Internal structure of an array

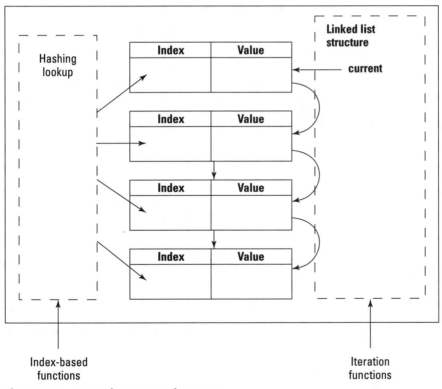

Figure 11-1: Internal structure of an array

Note   Each array remembers a particular stored key/value pair as being the "current" one, and array iteration functions work in part by shifting that current marker through the internal list of keys and values. Although we will call this marker the "current pointer," PHP does not support full pointers in the sense that C and C++ programmers may be used to, and this usage of the word will only turn up in the context of iterating through arrays.

Using iteration functions

To explore the iteration functions, let's construct a sample array that we can iterate over.

```
$major_city_info = array();
$major_city_info[0] = 'Caracas';
$major_city_info['Caracas'] = 'Venezuela';
$major_city_info[1] = 'Paris';
$major_city_info['Paris'] = 'France';
$major_city_info[2] = 'Tokyo';
$major_city_info['Tokyo'] = 'Japan';
```

In this example, we created an array and stored some names of cities into it, in association with numerical indices. We also stored the names of the relevant countries into the array, indexed by the city names. (We could have accomplished all this with one big call to array(), but the separate statements make the structure of the array somewhat clearer.)

Now, we can use the array key system to pull out the data we have stored. If we want to rely on the convention in the preceding example (cities stored with numerical indices, countries stored with city-name indices), we can write a function that prints out the city and the associated country, like so:

```
function city_by_number ($number_index, $city_array)
{
  if (IsSet($city_array[$number_index]))
    {
      $the_city = $city_array[$number_index];
      $the_country = $city_array[$the_city];
      print("$the_city is in $the_country<BR>");
    }
}
city_by_number(0, $major_city_info);
city_by_number(1, $major_city_info);
city_by_number(2, $major_city_info);
```

If we have set $major_city as in the previous block of code, the browser output we should expect is:

```
Caracas is in Venezuela
Paris is in France
Tokyo is in Japan
```

Now, this method of retrieval is fine when we know how the array is structured, and we know what all the keys are. But what if you would simply like to print everything that an array contains? There is no good way to test for all possible keys, and such a method would be horribly inefficient even if it existed.

Iterating with current() and next()

Instead, we can print out an array's contents with the iteration functions `current()` and `next()`, as in the following example. (Notice that the final function call is repeated.)

```
function print_all_array($city_array)
{  // warning—doesn't quite work. See the function each()
  $current_item = current($city_array);
  if ($current_item)
    print("$current_item<BR>");
  else
    print("There's nothing to print");
  while($current_item = next($city_array))
    print("$current_item<BR>");
}
print_all_array($major_city_info);
print_all_array($major_city_info);// again, to see what happens
```

The `current()` function returns the stored value that the "current" pointer points to. (See Figure 11-1 earlier in the chapter for a diagram of the array internals.) When an array is newly created with elements, this will always be the first element. The `next()` function first advances that pointer and then returns the current value pointed to. If the `next()` function is called when the current pointer is already pointing to the last stored value and therefore "runs off the end" of the array, the function will return a false value.

Caution   There is a gotcha lurking in the preceding code example, which doesn't bite us in this particular example but makes this function untrustworthy as a general method for finding everything in an array. That is that we may have stored a "false" value in the array, which our `while` loop won't be able to distinguish from the false value that `next()` returns when it has run out of array elements. See the discussion of the `each()` function later in this chapter under "Empty values and the each() function" for a solution.

When we execute this array-printing code, we get the following:

```
Caracas
Venezuela
Paris
France
Tokyo
Japan
Caracas
```

```
Venezuela
Paris
France
Tokyo
Japan
```

That is, all the elements that we stored in the array, in the order we stored them, and then another repetition because we called the function twice.

Now, how is it that we are seeing the same thing from the second call to print_all_array()? How did the "current" pointer get back to the beginning to start all over again the second time? The answer lies in the fact that PHP function calls are "call-by-value," meaning that they copy their arguments rather than operating directly on them. Both of the function calls, then, are getting a fresh copy of their array argument, which has never itself been disturbed by a call to next().

Cross-Reference   For more on what circumstances functions copy their arguments rather than operating on them directly, see Chapter 8.

We can test this explanation by passing the arrays by reference rather than by value. If we define the same function but call it with ampersands (&) like this:

```
print_all_array(&$major_city_info);
print_all_array(&$major_city_info);// again
```

we get the following printing behavior:

```
Caracas
Venezuela
Paris
France
Tokyo
Japan
There's nothing to print
```

The reason is that this time the "current" pointer of the global version of the array was moved by the first function call.

Note   Most of the iteration functions have both a returned value and a side-effect. In the case of the functions next(), prev(), reset(), and end(), the side-effect is to change the position of the internal pointer, and what is returned is the value from the key/value pair pointed to *after* the pointer's position is changed.

Starting over with reset()

In the preceding section, we wrote a function intended to print out all of the values in an array, and we saw how it could fail if the array's internal pointer did not start off at the beginning of the list of key/value pairs. The reset() function gives us a way to "rewind" that pointer to the beginning—it sets the pointer to the first key/value pair and then returns the stored value. We can use it to make our printing function more robust, by replacing the call to current() with a call to reset().

```
function print_all_array_reset($city_array)
{  // warning—still not reliable. See the function each()
  $current_item = reset($city_array); //rewind, return value
  if ($current_item)
    print("$current_item<BR>");
  else
    print("There's nothing to print");
  while($current_item = next($city_array))
    print("$current_item<BR>");
}
```

This function is somewhat more predictable, in that it will always start with the first element, regardless of the pointer's location in the array it is handed. (Whether this is a good idea depends, of course, on what the function is used for, and whether its arguments are passed by value or by reference.)

Possibly confusingly, we use our call to reset() in the preceding example both for its side-effect (rewinding the pointer) and for its return value (the first value stored). Alternatively, we could replace the first real line of the function body with these two lines:

```
reset($city_array);  // rewind to the first element
$current_item = current($city_array); // the first value
```

Reverse order with end() and prev()

We have seen the functions next() (which moves the current pointer ahead by one) and reset() (which rewinds the pointer to the beginning). Analogously, there are also the functions prev() (which moves the pointer back by one), and end() (which jumps the pointer to the last entry in the list). We can use these, for example, to print our array entries in reverse order.

```
function print_all_array_backwards($city_array)
{  // warning—still not reliable. See the function each()
  $current_item = end($city_array); //fast-forward to last
  if ($current_item)
    print("$current_item<BR>");
  else
    print("There's nothing to print");
  while($current_item = prev($city_array))
    print("$current_item<BR>");
}
print_all_array_backwards($major_city_info);
```

If we call this on the same $major_city_info data as in previous examples, we get the same printout in reverse order:

```
Japan
Tokyo
France
Paris
Venezuela
Caracas
```

Extracting keys with key()

So far we have only printed out the values stored in arrays, even though we are storing keys as well. The keys are also retrievable from the internal linked list of an array, by using the key() function—this acts just like current() except that it returns the key of a key/value pair, rather than the value. (See Figure 11-1 from a few pages back.) Using the key() function, we can modify one of our earlier printing functions to print out keys as well as values.

```
function print_keys_and_values($city_array)
{  // warning—See the discussion of each() below
  reset($city_array);
  $current_value = current($city_array);
  $current_key = key($city_array);
  if ($current_value)
    print("Key: $current_key; Value: $current_value<BR>");
  else
    print("There's nothing to print");
  while($current_value = next($city_array))
  {
      $current_key = key($city_array);
      print("Key: $current_key; Value: $current_value<BR>");
  }
}
print_keys_and_values($major_city_info);
```

With the same data as before, this gives us the browser output:

```
Key: 0; Value: Caracas
Key: Caracas; Value: Venezuela
Key: 1; Value: Paris
Key: Paris; Value: France
Key: 2; Value: Tokyo
Key: Tokyo; Value: Japan
```

Empty values and the each() function

We have written several functions that print out the contents of arrays by iterating through them, and as we have pointed out, they all have the same weakness. Each one of them tests for doneness by seeing whether `next()` returns a false value. This will reliably happen when the array runs out of values, but it will also happen if and when we encounter a "false" value that we have actually stored. False values include the empty string (`""`), the number 0, and the Boolean value `FALSE`, any or all of which we might reasonably store as a data value for some task or other.

To our rescue comes `each()`, which is somewhat similar to `next()` but has the virtue of returning false only when it has run out of array to traverse. Oddly enough, when it has not run out, `each()` returns an array itself, which holds both keys and values for the key/value pair it is pointing at. This makes `each()` confusing to talk about, because we have to keep two arrays straight: the array we are traversing, and the array that `each()` returns each time it is called. The array that `each()` *returns* has four key/value pairs:

- ✦ Key: 0, Value: *current-key*

- ✦ Key: 1, Value: *current-value*

- ✦ Key: 'key', Value: *current-key*

- ✦ Key: 'value', Value: *current-value*

The *current-key* and *current-value* are the key and value from the array being traversed. In other words, the returned array packages up the current key/value pair from the traversed array and offers both numerical and string indices to specify whether you are interested in the key or the value.

Note

In addition to having a different type of return value, `each()` differs from `next()` in that `each()` returns the value that was pointed to *before* moving the current pointer ahead, whereas `next()` returns the value *after* the pointer is moved. This means if you start with a current pointer pointing to the first element of an array, successive calls to `each()` will cover each array cell, whereas successive calls to `next()` will skip the first value.

We can use `each()` to write a more robust version of a function to print out all keys and values in an array:

```
function print_keys_and_values_each($city_array)
{   // reliably prints everything in array
  reset($city_array);
  while ($array_cell = each($city_array))
  {
    $current_value = $array_cell['value'];
    $current_key = $array_cell['key'];
    print("Key: $current_key; Value: $current_value<BR>");
  }
}
print_keys_and_values_each($major_city_info);
```

Applying this function to our standard sample array gives the following browser output:

```
Key: 0; Value: Caracas
Key: Caracas; Value: Venezuela
Key: 1; Value: Paris
Key: Paris; Value: France
Key: 2; Value: Tokyo
Key: Tokyo; Value: Japan
```

This is exactly the same as was produced by our earlier function `print_keys_and_values()`. The difference is that our new function will not stop prematurely if one of the values is 'false,' or empty.

Walking with array_walk()

Our last iteration function lets you pass an arbitrary function of your own design over an array, doing whatever your function pleases with each key/value pair. The `array_walk()` function takes two arguments: an array to be traversed, and the name of a function to apply to each key/value pair. (It also takes an optional third argument, discussed later in this section.)

The function that is passed in to `array_walk()` should take two (or three) arguments. The first argument will be the value of the array cell that is visited, and the second argument will be the key of that cell. For example, here is a function that prints out a descriptive statement about the string length of an array value:

```
function print_value_length($array_value, $array_key_ignored)
{
  $the_length = strlen($array_value);
  print("The length of $array_value is $the_length<BR>");
}
```

(Notice that this function intentionally does nothing with the second argument.) Now let's pass this function over our standard sample array using `array_walk()`:

```
array_walk($major_city_info, 'print_value_length');
```

which gives the browser output

```
The length of Caracas is 7
The length of Venezuela is 9
The length of Paris is 5
The length of France is 6
The length of Tokyo is 5
The length of Japan is 5
```

The final flexibility that `array_walk()` offers is accepting an optional third argument that, if present, will be passed on in turn as a third argument to the function that is applied. This argument will be the same throughout the array's traversal, but it offers an extra source of run-time control for the passed function's behavior.

Table 11-2 shows a summary of the behavior of the array iteration functions that have been covered in this section.

<table>
<tr><td colspan="4" align="center">Table 11-2
Functions for Iterating over Arrays</td></tr>
<tr><td>*Function*</td><td>*Arguments*</td><td>*Side Effect*</td><td>*Return Value*</td></tr>
<tr><td>`current()`</td><td>One array argument</td><td>None.</td><td>The value from the key/value pair currently pointed to by the internal "current" pointer (or false if no such value).</td></tr>
<tr><td>`next()`</td><td>One array argument</td><td>Advances the pointer by one. If already at the last element, it will move the pointer "past the end," and subsequent calls to `current()` will return false.</td><td>The value pointed to after the pointer has been advanced (or false if no such value).</td></tr>
<tr><td>`prev()`</td><td>One array argument</td><td>Moves the pointer back by one. If already at the first element, will move the pointer "before the beginning."</td><td>The value pointed to after the pointer has been moved back (or false if no such value).</td></tr>
<tr><td>`reset()`</td><td>One array argument</td><td>Moves the pointer back to point to the first key/value pair, or "before the beginning" if the array is empty.</td><td>The first value stored in the array, or false for an empty array</td></tr>
<tr><td>`end()`</td><td>One array argument</td><td>Moves the pointer ahead to the last key/value pair.</td><td>The last value that is currently in the list of key/value pairs.</td></tr>
</table>

Continued

		Table 11-2 *(continued)*	
Function	*Arguments*	*Side Effect*	*Return Value*
pos()	One array argument	None. (This function is an alias for current().)	The value of the key/value pair that is currently pointed to.
each()	One array argument	Moves the pointer ahead to the next key/value pair.	An array that packages the keys and values of the key/value pair that was current before the pointer was moved (or false if no such pair). The returned array stores the key and value under its own keys 0 and 1, respectively, and also under its own keys 'key' and 'value.'
array_walk()	1) An array argument, 2) the name of a two- (or three-) argument function to call on each key/value, and 3) an optional third argument.	This function invokes the function named by its second argument on each key/value pair. Side-effects depend on the side-effects of the passed function.	(Returns 1.)

Stacks and Queues

Stacks and queues are abstract data structures, frequently used in computer science, that enforce a certain kind of access discipline on the objects they contain, without necessarily committing to what those objects are. As we've said before, PHP arrays are well suited to imitating other kinds of data structures, and the loose typing of PHP array elements makes it easy for them to imitate stacks and queues. PHP provides some array functions specifically for this purpose—if you use them exclusively, you can forget that arrays are involved at all.

A *stack* is a container that stores values and supports last-in-first-out (LIFO) behavior. This means that the stack maintains an order on the values you store, and the only way you can get a value back is by retrieving (and removing) the most recently stored value. The usual analogy is a stack of cafeteria trays, in one of those dispensers that keeps the top tray at a constant level. You can push new trays down on top of the old ones, and you can take trays off the top, but you can't grab an older tray without taking the newer ones first. The act of adding into the stack is called "pushing" a value onto the stack, whereas the act of taking off the top is called "popping" the stack. Another analogy is the way some Web browsers store the pages you have visited for use by the Back button; visiting a new page pushes a new URL onto that stack, and using the Back button pops the stack.

A *queue* is similar to a stack, but its behavior is first-in-first-out (FIFO). The usual analogy here is what the British call a "queue" and what Americans call a "line," where people line up to wait for something in order. The rule is that whoever has been in the queue the longest is the next to be "served."

The stack functions are `array_push()` and `array_pop()`. The `array_push()` function takes an initial array argument and then any number of elements to push onto the stack. The elements will be inserted at the end of the array, in order from left to right. The `array_pop()` function takes such an array and removes the element at the end, returning it. Take the following fragment:

```
$my_stack = array();  // needed—array_push() will not create
array_push($my_stack, "the first", "the middle");
array_push($my_stack, "the last");
while ($popped = array_pop($my_stack))
  print("Popped the stack and got: $popped<BR>");
```

This will produce the browser output

```
Popped the stack and got: the last
Popped the stack and got: the middle
Popped the stack and got: the first
```

PHP4 also offers functions that behave exactly the same way as `array_push()` and `array_pop()`, except that they work at the other end, adding to and removing from the beginning of the array. The `array_unshift()` function is analogous to `array_push()`, and `array_shift()` is like `array_pop()`. If you choose one function from column A and one from column B, you can get the behavior of a queue. For example, we can rewrite our previous example to push into the beginning of the array (using `unshift()`) and pop from the end (using `array_pop()`, as before):

```
$my_queue = array();// needed—array_unshift() will not create
array_unshift($my_queue, "the first", "the middle");
array_unshift($my_queue, "the last");
while ($popped = array_pop($my_queue))
  print("Popped the queue and got: $popped<BR>");
```

It produces the output

```
Popped the stack and got: the first
Popped the stack and got: the middle
Popped the stack and got: the last
```

Caution

The array_unshift() and array_shift() functions are somewhat different from array_push() and array_pop(), in that the former do some renumbering of the array indices if the indices are integers. The idea is that some people may be relying on the numerical indices to order the array contents, so using array_unshift() to insert a new element at the beginning should assign an index of 0 to the new element, and renumber those above. Similarly, popping an element from the beginning with array_shift() causes integral indices of other elements to be reduced. (This is not an issue with array_push and array_pop, because changes are at the end and no renumbering is needed.) If you are using string indices exclusively, this has no effect. This is a general pattern with PHP array functions: some of them treat integer indices like any other associative index, whereas others assume that integers imply order, and redo them if the order has changed.

The stack and queue functions are summarized in Table 11-3.

Table 11-3 Stack and Queue Functions			
Function	**Arguments**	**Side-Effect**	**Returns**
array_push()	An initial array argument, then any number of values to be pushed onto the stack	Modifies the array by adding the elements in order to the end of the array.	The number of elements in the array after the push.
array_pop()	A single array argument	Removes the element at the end of the array.	Returns the last (removed) value, or a false value if the array is empty.
array_unshift()	An initial array argument, then any number of values to be pushed onto the front of the array	Modifies the array by adding the successive elements to the beginning. (The last argument will be at the beginning of the array.)	The number of elements in the array after the new elements are added.
array_shift()	A single array argument	Removes the element at the beginning of the array.	Returns the first (removed) value, or a false value if the array is empty.

Transformations of Arrays

PHP4 offers a host of functions for manipulating your data once you have it nicely stored in an array. What the functions in this section have in common is that they take your array, do something with it, and return the results in another array. (We will defer the array-sorting functions to the next section.)

Earlier in the chapter we incrementally developed a function to print out the entire contents of an array, and in this section will use the last of these (`print_keys_and_values_each()`) to show the arrays that are being returned in examples.

Retrieving keys and values

The `array_keys()` function returns the keys of its input array, in the form of a new array where the keys are the stored values. The keys of the new array are the usual automatically incremented integers, starting from 0. The `array_values()` function does exactly the same thing, except the stored values are the values from the original array.

If we start with an array like the following:

```
$pizza_requests = array('Alice' => 'pepperoni',
                        'Bob' => 'mushrooms',
                        'Carl' => 'sausage',
                        'Dennis' => 'mushrooms');
```

and then we print the arrays resulting from calls to the these two functions:

```
print("Array keys:<BR>");
print_keys_and_values_each(array_keys($pizza_requests));
print("Array values:<BR>");
print_keys_and_values_each(array_values($pizza_requests));
```

we get output like this:

```
Array keys:
Key: 0; Value: Alice
Key: 1; Value: Bob
Key: 2; Value: Carl
Key: 3; Value: Dennis
Array values:
Key: 0; Value: pepperoni
Key: 1; Value: mushrooms
Key: 2; Value: sausage
Key: 3; Value: mushrooms
```

The second of these (`array_values()`) may seem uninteresting, because we have essentially taken our old array and produced a new one with the keys renamed to successive numbers.

We can do something slightly more useful (and more helpful for ordering) with the function `array_count_values()`. This takes an array and returns a new array where the old values are now the new keys and the new values are the number of times each old value occurs in the original array.

```
print_keys_and_values_each(
    array_count_values($pizza_requests));
```

gives us

```
Key: pepperoni; Value: 1
Key: mushrooms; Value: 2
Key: sausage; Value: 1
```

Flipping, reversing, shuffling

A even odder function is `array_flip()`, which changes the keys of an array into the values, and vice versa. For example

```
print_keys_and_values_each(array_flip($pizza_requests));
```

gives us

```
Key: pepperoni; Value: Alice
Key: mushrooms; Value: Dennis // what happened to Bob?
Key: sausage; Value Carl
```

Notice that, although array keys are guaranteed to be unique, array values are not—because of this, any duplicate values in the original array will become the same key in the new array. Only one of the original keys will survive to become the corresponding new value.

Reversing an array is simpler: `array_reverse()` returns a new array with the key/value pairs in reverse order. So, with the usual printing test,

```
print_keys_and_values_each(array_reverse($pizza_requests));
```

we get the result

```
Key: Dennis; Value: mushrooms
Key: Carl; Value: sausage
Key: Bob; Value: mushrooms
Key: Alice; Value: pepperoni
```

In this case, although the internal order has been reversed, all the key/value pairs end up being the same. However, this function (like several other PHP array functions) treats integer keys somewhat specially. It assumes that the ordering of integer keys on those key/value pairs should also be reversed, for the use of code that is taking the keys as the ordering, rather than using the internal linked-list ordering. So, `array_reverse()` swaps integer keys to make the new key ordering match the internal list.

If you need some extra randomness in your life, the `shuffle()` function can give it to you — `shuffle()` takes an array argument and randomizes the order of the elements in the array. It uses `rand()` (a function that generates successive random numbers), and so before you use `shuffle()` you need to have seeded the random-number generator with a call to `srand()`. A reasonable calling sequence looks like this:

```
srand((double)microtime() * 1000000);  // for random # gen
shuffle($pizza_requests);
print_keys_and_values_each(array_flip($pizza_requests));
```

which *might* give us output like

```
Key: Carl; Value: sausage
Key: Bob; Value: mushrooms
Key: Dennis; Value: mushrooms
Key: Alice; Value: pepperoni
```

(Of course, we emphasize *might* because the point is that the order is not predictable.)

Cross-Reference

For more on random-number generation, see Chapter 10. If you want to use the `shuffle()` function without having to consult Chapter 10, simply make sure that any page that uses `shuffle()` has the call to `srand()` once (and only once) in the script, before any calls to `shuffle()`, as in the preceding example.

Caution

Unlike many of the array functions in this chapter, `shuffle()` is *destructive*, meaning that it operates directly on its array argument and changes it, rather than returning a newly created array. (Functions that return a new thing without disturbing their arguments might be called "constructive," or just "nondestructive.") Among other things, this means that the correct way to call the shuffle function is not

```
$my_new_array = shuffle($my_old_array); WRONG!
```

especially because the `shuffle()` function does not return a value. Instead, the right call is

```
shuffle($my_array);   // change the array itself
```

These array-manipulating functions, and a few extra besides, are summarized in Table 11-4.

Table 11-4 Array Transformation Functions	
Function	*Behavior*
array_keys()	Takes a single array argument and returns a new array where the new values are the keys of the input array, and the new keys are the integers incremented from zero.
array_values()	Takes a single array argument and returns a new array where the new values are the original values of the input array, and the new keys are the integers incremented from zero.
array_count_values()	Takes a single array argument and returns a new array where the new keys are the old array's values, and the new values are a count of how many times that original value occurred in the input array.
array_flip()	Takes a single array argument and changes that array so that the keys are now the values and vice versa.
array_reverse()	Takes a single array argument and changes the internal ordering of the key/value pairs to reverse order. Numerical keys will also be renumbered.
shuffle()	Takes a single array argument and randomizes the internal ordering of key/value pairs. Also renumbers integer keys to match the new ordering. This function itself uses the random-number generator rand(), so srand() must be called to seed the generator before the call to shuffle().
array_merge()	Takes two array arguments, merges them, and returns the new array, which has (in order) the first array's elements and then the second array's elements. (Note: This is most useful for arrays that are being used for simple linked lists, rather than for their associative keys, because keys that appear in both arrays will have one of the values overwritten. Also, numerical keys will be renumbered from 0 to reflect the new ordering.)

Function	Behavior
array_pad()	Takes three arguments: an input array, a pad size, and a value to pad with. Returns a new array that is "padded" by the following rules: if the pad size is greater than the length of the input array, then the array is lengthened with the pad value to the pad size, as though by successive assignments like $my_array[] = $pad_value. A negative pad size will act the same way as with the absolute value of that pad size, except that the padding will occur at the beginning of the array rather than the end. If the array is already longer than the (absolute value of) the pad size, then the function has no effect.
array_slice()	Takes three arguments: an input array, an integer offset, and an (optional) integer length. Returns a new array that is a "slice" of the old one—a subsequence of its list of key/value pairs. The starting and stopping point of the slice are determined by the offset and length. A positive offset means that the starting point is that number of elements after the beginning; a negative offset means that it is that many elements before the end. The optional length argument specifies how long the resulting slice is (if positive) or how many elements before the end it should stop (if negative). If the length argument is not present, the slice continues to the end of the array.
array_splice()	Removes a chunk (or a slice) of an array and replaces it with the contents of another array. Takes four arguments: an input array, an offset, an optional integer length, and an optional replacement array. Returns a new array containing the slice that was removed from the input array. The rules for using the offset and length arguments to determine the slice that is removed are the same as in the previous array_slice() function. If no replacement array is supplied, this function simply (destructively) removes a slice of the input array and returns it. If there is a replacement array, the elements of that array are inserted in place of the removed slice.

Translating between Variables and Arrays

PHP4 offers a couple of unusual functions for mapping between the name/value pairs of regular variable bindings and the key/value pairs of an array. The compact() function translates from variable bindings to an array, and the extract() function goes in the opposite direction. These are summarized briefly in Table 11-5.

Table 11-5 Array/Variable-Binding Functions	
Function	**Behavior**
compact()	Takes a specified set of strings, looks up bound variables (if any) in the current environment that are named by those strings, and returns an array where the keys are the variable names, and the values are the corresponding values of those variables. This function takes any number of arguments, each of which is either a string or an array that contains strings at some level of index depth. The entire set of strings that are included in the argument(s) is used as the candidate set of variable names. Strings that do not correspond to bound variables are ignored.
extract()	Takes an array (plus two optional arguments explained in the next paragraph) and imports the key/value pairs into the current variable-binding context. The array keys become the variable names, and the corresponding array values become the values of the variables. Any keys that do not correspond to a legal variable name will not produce an assignment. The optional arguments are an integer (intended to receive one of a small set of constants) and a prefix string. The point of these arguments is to specify what should happen in the case of a collision between the name of an existing variable and one that would be created from an array key. The intended possible constants for the optional integer arguments are 1) EXTR_OVERWRITE, 2) EXTR_SKIP, 3) EXTR_PREFIX_SAME, and 4) EXTR_PREFIX_ALL. The corresponding behaviors are 1) go ahead and overwrite existing variables, 2) skip any new assignments that would require overwriting, 3) use the optional prefix string to distinguish the new variable from the old one, or 4) prefix all the new variables with the string. For example, extract(array('my_var' => 4), EXTR_PREFIX_SAME, 'diff_'); would cause $my_var to be 4 if $my_var were not already bound; otherwise, it would assign the value 4 to $diff_my_var.

Sorting

Finally, PHP 4 offers a host of functions for sorting arrays. As we saw earlier, a tension sometimes arises between respecting the key/value associations in an array and treating numerical keys as ordering info that should be changed when the order changes. Luckily, PHP offers variants of the sorting functions for each of these behaviors and also allows sorting in ascending or descending order and by user-supplied ordering functions.

The function names are terse, but each letter (other than the 'sort' part) has its meaning. The decoder ring is something like:

✦ An initial a means that the function sorts by value but maintains the association between key/value pairs the way it was.

✦ An initial k means that it sorts by key but maintains the key/value associations.

✦ A lack of that initial a or k means that it sorts by value but doesn't maintain the key/value association. In particular, numerical keys will be renumbered to reflect the new ordering.

✦ An r before the sort means that the sorting order will be reversed.

✦ An initial u means that a second argument is expected: the name of a user-defined function that specifies the ordering of any two elements that are being sorted. (See the description in Table 11-6.)

Table 11-6 Array Sorting Functions	
Function	**Behavior**
asort()	Takes a single array argument. Sorts the key/value pairs by value but keeps the key/value mapping the same. Good for associative arrays.
arsort()	Same as asort(), but sorts in descending order.
ksort()	Takes a single array argument. Sorts the key/value pairs by key but maintain the key/value associations the same.
krsort()	Same as ksort(), but sorts in descending order.
sort()	Takes a single array argument. Sorts the key/value pairs of an array by their values. Keys may be renumbered to reflect the new ordering of the values.

Continued

	Table 11-6 *(continued)*
Function	***Behavior***
rsort()	Same as sort(), but sorts in descending order.
uasort()	Sorts key/value pairs by value using a comparison function. Similar to asort(), except the actual ordering of the values is determined by the second argument, which is the name of a user-defined ordering function. That function should return a negative number if its first argument is "before" the second, a positive number if the first argument comes "after" the second, and zero if the elements are "the same."
uksort()	Sorts key/value pairs by key, using a comparison function. Similar to uasort(), except that the ordering is by key, rather than by value.
usort()	Sorts an array by value using a supplied comparison function. Similar to uasort(), except that (as in sort()), the key/value associations are not maintained.

Summary

The array is a basic PHP datatype, and plays the role of both record types and vector array types in other languages. PHP arrays are associative, meaning that they store their values in association with unique "keys" or "indices." Indices can be either strings or numbers, and are denoted as indices by square brackets. (The expression $my_array[4] refers to the value stored in $my_array in association with the integer index 4, and not necessarily to the 4th element of $my_array.)

The loose typing of PHP means that any PHP value can be stored as an array. In turn, this means that arrays can be stored as array elements. "Multidimensional arrays" are simply arrays that contain other arrays as elements, with a reference syntax of successive brackets. (The expression $my_array[3][4] refers to the element (indexed by 4) of an array which is an element (indexed by 3) of $my_array.)

The array is the standard vehicle for PHP functions that returned structured data, and so PHP programmers should learn to unpack arrays, even if they are not interested in constructing them. PHP also offers a huge variety of functions for manipulating data once you have it stored in an array, including functions for counting, summarizing, and sorting.

✦   ✦   ✦

Passing Information Between Pages

In this chapter, we'll briefly discuss some things you need
to know about passing data, such as variables, between
Web pages. Some of this information is not specific to PHP but
is a consequence of the PHP/HTML interaction or of the HTTP
protocol itself.

HTTP Is Stateless

The most important thing to recall about Web service is that
the HTTP protocol itself is stateless. If you were a poetic soul,
you might say that each HTTP request is on its own with no
direction home, like a complete unknown . . . you know how
the rest goes.

For the less lyrical among us, this means that each HTTP
request—each page being asked for and delivered—is independent of all the others, knows nothing substantive about
the identity of the client, and has no memory. Each request
spawns a discrete process, which goes about its humble but
worthy task of serving up one single solitary file and then is
automatically killed off (although that sounds so harsh;
maybe we can say "flits back to the pool of available processes" instead?).

Even if you design your site with very strict one-way navigation (Page 1 leads only to Page 2, which leads only to Page 3,
and so on), the HTTP protocol will never know or care that
someone browsing Page 2 must have come from Page 1.
Therefore, you can't set the value of a variable on Page 1 and
expect it to be imported to Page 2 by the exigencies of HTML

itself. You can use HTML to display a form, and someone can enter some information using it—but unless you employ some extra means to pass the information to another page or program, the variable will simply vanish into the ether as soon as you move to another page.

This is where a form processing technology like PHP comes in. PHP will catch the variable tossed from one page to the next and make it available for further use. PHP happens to be unusually good at this type of data-passing function, which makes it fast and easy to employ for a wide variety of Web site tasks.

There are more advanced ways to construct a memory of a client's interaction with a site, such as cookies and sessions. However, this chapter will focus on the most basic techniques of information-passing between Web pages, which utilize the GET and POST methods in HTML.

Note   This is where ASP developers invariably say "PHP sucks!" because they think ASP session variables are magic. Not to burst anyone's bubble, but Microsoft is just using cookies to store session variables—thereby opening the door to all kinds of potential problems. See Appendix B for more.

GET Arguments

The GET method passes arguments from one page to the next as part of the Uniform Resource Indicator (you may be more familiar with the term Uniform Resource Locator or URL) query string. When used for form handling, GET appends the indicated variable name(s) and value(s) to the URL designated in the ACTION attribute with a question-mark separator and submits the whole thing to the processing agent (in this case PHP).

This is an example HTML form using the GET method (save the file under a name other than baseball.php):

```
<HTML>
<HEAD>
<TITLE>A GET example, part 1</TITLE>
</HEAD>

<BODY>
<FORM ACTION="http://localhost/baseball.php" METHOD="GET">
<P>Root, root, root for the:<BR>
<SELECT NAME="Team" SIZE=2>
<!-- It's a good idea to use the VALUE attribute even though it
is not mandatory with the SELECT element. In this example, it's
extremely necessary. -->
<OPTION VALUE="Cubbies">Chicago Cubs (National League)
```

```
<OPTION VALUE="Pale Hose">Chicago White Sox (American League)
</SELECT>
<P><INPUT TYPE="submit">
</FORM>
</BODY>
</HTML>
```

When the user makes a selection and clicks the Submit button, the browser agglutinates these elements in this order, with no spaces:

✦ The URL in quotes after the word ACTION (http://localhost/ baseball.php)

✦ A question mark (?)

✦ A variable NAME, an equal sign, and the matching VALUE (Team=2)

✦ An ampersand (&) and the next NAME=VALUE pair (Submit=Submit); this can be repeated as many times as the server query string length limit allows

It thereby constructs the URL string

```
http://localhost/baseball.php?Team=Cubbies&Submit=Submit
```

which it then forwards into the browser's address space as a new request. The PHP script to which the preceding form is submitted (baseball.php) will grab the GET variables from the end of the request string, and do something useful with them — in this case, plug one of two values into a text string.

```
<HTML>
<HEAD>
<TITLE>A GET example, part 2</TITLE>
<STYLE TYPE="text/css">
<!--
BODY   {font-size: 24pt;}
-->
</STYLE>
</HEAD>

<BODY>
<P>Go,
<?php print("$Team"); ?>
!
</BODY>
</HTML>
```

The final result looks like Figure 12-1.

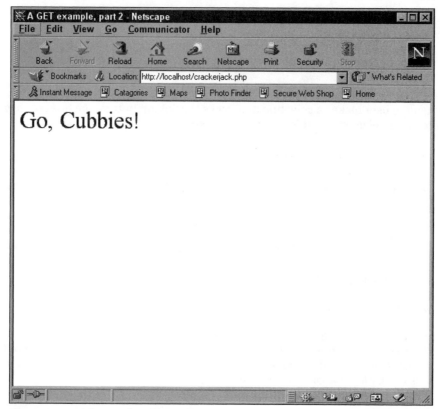

Figure 12-1: A form using METHOD=GET

The GET method of form handling has one big advantage over the POST method: it constructs an actual new and differentiable URL query string. Therefore, users can now bookmark this page (and thus find the oh-so-necessary encouraging word when their team starts to fade in the doldrums of August). The result of forms using the POST method are not bookmarkable.

The disadvantages of GET for most types of form handling are so substantial that the original HTML 4.0 specification deprecated its use. These flaws include:

✦ GET is not suitable for logins, since the username and password are fully visible onscreen as well as potentially stored in the client browser's memory as a visited page.

✦ Every GET submission is recorded in the Web server log, data set included.

✦ Because GET assigns data to a server environment variable, the length of the URL is limited. You may have seen what seem like very long URLs using GET — but you really wouldn't want to try passing a 300-word chunk of HTML-formatted prose using this method.

Caution The original HTML spec called for query strings to be limited to 255 characters. Although this stricture was later loosened to mere "encouragement" of a 255-character limit, using a longer string is asking for trouble.

The GET method of form handling had to be reinstated by the W3 after much outcry, largely because of the bookmarkability factor. However, despite the fact that it's still the default choice for form handling, GET now comes with a strong recommendation to deploy it only in idempotent usages — in other words, those that have no permanent side-effects. Putting two and two together, the single most appropriate form-handling use of GET is the search box. Unless you have a compelling reason to use GET for non–search box form handling, use POST instead.

A Better Use for GET-Style URLs

Although the actual GET method of form handling is semideprecated, the style of URL associated with it turns out to be very useful for site navigation. This is especially true for dynamically generated sites such as those often constructed with PHP, because the appended-variable style of URL works particularly smoothly with a template-based content-development system.

As an illustration, let's pretend you are the proud proprietor of an informational Web site about fiber-producing animals. You've toiled long and hard over informative and attractive pages such as these:

```
alpaca.html
guanaco.html
llama.html
vicuna.html
```

But as your site grows, a flat-file site structure like this can take a lot of time to administer, as even the most trivial changes must be repeated on every page. If the structure of these pages is very similar, you might want to move to a template-based system with PHP.

You might decide to utilize a single template with separate text files for each animal (containing information, photos, poems, and so on):

```
fleecee.php
  alpaca.inc
  guanaco.inc
  llama.inc
  vicuna.inc
```

Or you might decide you needed a larger, more specialized choice of templates:

```
goat.php
   cashmere.inc
insect.php
   silkworm.inc
llamoid.php
   alpaca.inc
rabbit.php
   angora.inc
sheep.php
   merino.inc
```

Either way, a template file might look something like this (since we haven't included all the necessary text files, this example will not actually work):

```
<HTML>
<HEAD>
<TITLE>Fiber-producing animals</TITLE>
<STYLE TYPE="text/css">
<!--
BODY  {font: verdana; font-size: 14pt}
-->
</STYLE>
</HEAD>

<BODY>
<TABLE BORDER=0 CELLPADDING=0 WIDTH=100%>
<TR>
<!-- Navbar, with Get-style URLs. -->
<TD BGCOLOR="#4282B4" ALIGN=CENTER VALIGN=TOP WIDTH=25%>
  <P>
  <A HREF="fleecee.php?Name=alpaca"><B>Alpaca</B></A>
  <BR>
  <A HREF="fleecee.php?Name=guanaco"><B>Guanaco</B></A>
  <BR>
  <A HREF="fleecee.php?Name=llama"><B>Llama</B></A>
  <BR>
  <A HREF="fleecee.php?Name=vicuna"><B>Vicu&#241a</B></A>
  <BR><BR>
</TD>
<TD BGCOLOR="#FFFFFF" ALIGN=LEFT VALIGN=TOP WIDTH=75%>
<? include("$Name.inc"); ?>
</TD></TR></TABLE>
</BODY>
</HTML>
```

Notice that the links on the navbar will be handled by the browser when clicked as if they were the product of a GET submission.

But even with this solution, you would still have to tend part of your garden by hand: making sure each include file is properly formatted in HTML, adding a new link to the navbar each time you add a new page to the site, and other such chores. Following the general rule to separate form and content as much as possible, you might choose to go to another level of abstraction with a database. In that case, a URL such as:

```
fleecee.php?animalID=2
```

would point to a PHP template that makes database calls (using a number variable rather than a word makes for faster database interaction). This system could automatically add a link to the navbar whenever you added new animals to the database, and so it could produce Web pages entirely without ongoing human intervention (all right, maybe "entirely" is an exaggeration).

POST Arguments

POST is the preferred method of form handling today, particularly in non-idempotent usages (those which will result in permanent side-effects), such as adding information to a database. The form data set is included in the body of the form when it is forwarded to the processing agent (in this case PHP). There is no visible change to the URL according to the different data submitted.

The POST method has these advantages:

✦ It is more secure than GET because user-entered information is never visible in the URL query string, in the server logs, or (if precautions are taken) onscreen.

✦ There is a much larger limit on the amount of data that can be passed (a couple of kilobytes rather than a couple of hundred characters).

However, POST has these disadvantages:

✦ The results cannot be bookmarked.

✦ This method can be incompatible with certain firewall setups, which strip the form data as a security measure.

We use POST consistently in this book for form handling—in other words, for putting data into a system. We use GET for site navigation and search boxes—in other words, for pulling it back out and displaying it.

Although many if not most POST submissions involve back-end connectivity, Listing 12-1 shows an example that does not (in the interest of focusing on the POST method, we have omitted validation, so this form is admittedly not very robust)

Listing 12-1: **A retirement savings worksheet**

```
<HTML>
<HEAD>
<TITLE>A POST example, part 1</TITLE>
<STYLE TYPE="text/css">
<!--
BODY     {font-size: 14pt}
.heading     {font-size: 18pt; color: red}
-->
</STYLE>
</HEAD>

<?php
/* This test, along with the hidden value in the form below,
will check to see if the form is being rendered for the first
time (in which case it will display with only the default
annual gain filled in) or if it has already been submitted with
values entered. */
if (!IsSet($stage))
  {
  $AnnGain = 7;
  }
else
  {
  $Years = $RetireAge - $CurrentAge;
  $YearCount = 0;
  $Total = $Contrib;
  while($YearCount <= $Years)
    {
    $Total = round($Total * (1.0 + $AnnGain/100) + $Contrib);
    $YearCount = $YearCount + 1;
    }
  }
?>
<BODY>
<DIV ALIGN=CENTER ID=Div1 class=heading>
A retirement-savings calculator
</DIV>
<P class=blurb>Fill in all the values (except "Nest Egg") and
see how much money you'll have for your retirement under
different scenarios!  You can change the values and resubmit
the form as many times as you like.  You must fill in the two
"Age" variables.  The "Annual return" variable has a default
inflation-adjusted value (7% = 8% growth minus 1% inflation)
which you can change to reflect your greater optimism or
pessimism.</P>

<FORM ACTION="<?php print("$PHP_SELF"); ?>" METHOD="POST">
<P>Your age now:  <INPUT TYPE="text" SIZE=5 NAME="CurrentAge"
VALUE="<?php print("$CurrentAge"); ?>">
```

```
<P>The age at which you plan to retire:  <INPUT TYPE="text"
SIZE=6 NAME="RetireAge" VALUE="<?php print("$RetireAge"); ?>">
<P>Annual contribution:  <INPUT TYPE="text" SIZE=15
NAME="Contrib" VALUE="<?php print("$Contrib"); ?>">
<P>Annual return:  <INPUT TYPE="text" SIZE=5 NAME="AnnGain"
VALUE="<?php print("$AnnGain"); ?>"> %
<BR><BR>
<P><B>NEST EGG</B>:  <?php print("$Total"); ?>
<P><INPUT TYPE="hidden" NAME="stage" VALUE=1>
<P><INPUT TYPE="submit">
</FORM>
</BODY>
</HTML>
```

Figure 12-2 shows the result of Listing 12-1.

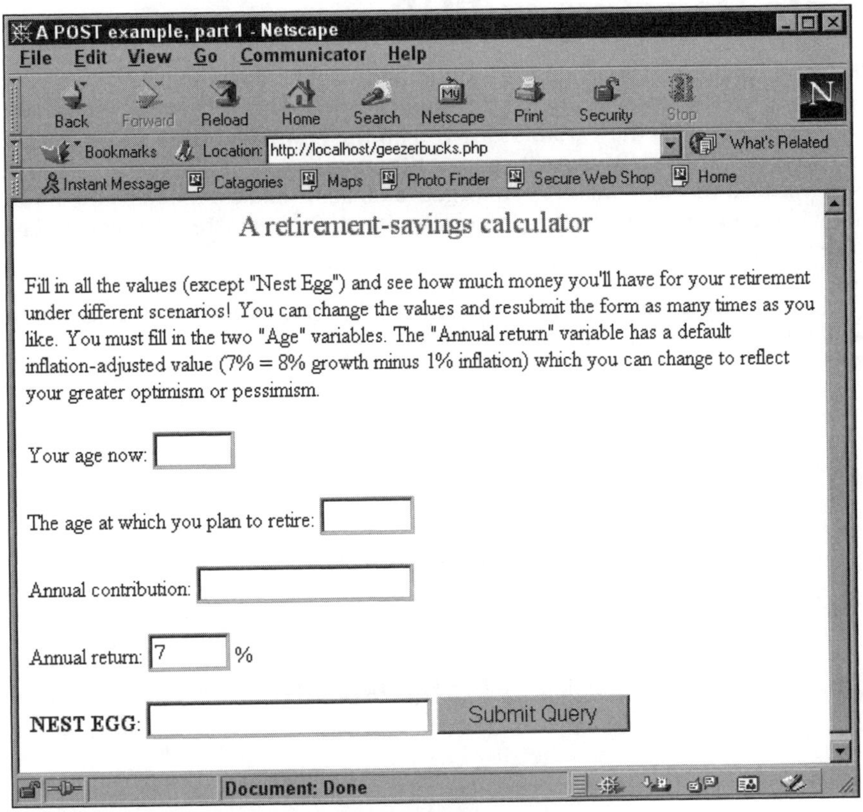

Figure 12-2: A form using METHOD=POST

GET and POST both

Did you know that with PHP you can use both GET and POST variables on the same page? So feel free to go wild with the dynamically generated forms!

But a burning question immediately arises: what if you (deliberately or otherwise) use the same variable name in both the GET and the POST arrays? PHP keeps GET, POST, and COOKIE variables in arrays called $HTTP_GET_VARS, $HTTP_POST_VARS, and $HTTP_COOKIE_VARS, as well as in the $GLOBALS array. If there is a conflict, it is resolved by overwriting the variable values in the order you set using the "gpc_order" option in your php.ini file (you must also set the track_vars option also). Later trumps earlier, so if you use the default "GPC" value, cookies will triumph over posts that will themselves obliterate gets. You can control the order of overwriting by simply changing the order of the three letters on the appropriate line of this file.

Variable Handling in PHP

PHP is so efficient at passing data around because the developers made a very handy but (in theory) slightly risky design decision. This is that PHP automatically but invisibly assigns the variables for you on the new page when you submit a data set using GET or POST. Most of its competitors make you explicitly do this assignment yourself on each page; if you forget to do so or make a mistake, the information will not be available to the processing agent. PHP is faster, simpler, and mostly more goof-proof.

The easiest way to illustrate this is to show different methods of processing the same form submission. Here's the form:

```
<HTML>
<HEAD>
<TITLE>Candy preference form</TITLE>
</HEAD>

<BODY>
<FORM ACTION="candy.php" METHOD="POST">
What's your most favorite kind of candy?<BR>
<INPUT TYPE="radio" NAME="Candy" VALUE="peanut butter
cups">Peanut butter cups<BR>
<INPUT TYPE="radio" NAME="Candy" VALUE="Snickers">Snickers<BR>
<INPUT TYPE="radio" NAME="Candy" VALUE="Turtles">Turtles<BR>
<INPUT TYPE="submit">
</FORM>
</BODY>
</HTML>
```

This is a PHP script to handle the form:

```
<HTML>
<HEAD>
<TITLE>Candy preference reply</TITLE>
</HEAD>

<BODY>
Yum, <?php print("$Candy!  ");
if($Candy == "peanut butter cups")
  print("There are several excellent brands of ice cream which
contain small or broken-up $Candy.");
else
  {
  print("I don't think there's an ice-cream with $Candy in it
yet, ");
  if($Candy == "Snickers")
    print("but have you tried the $Candy ice cream bar?");
  elseif($Candy == "Turtles")
    print("but the world definitely needs an ice cream with
$Candy in it.");
  }
?>
</BODY>
</HTML>
```

Here is an ASP script that performs the same function (to use it, remember to reset the form's ACTION argument to "candy.asp"):

```
<HTML>
<HEAD>
<TITLE>Candy preference reply</TITLE>
</HEAD>

<BODY>
Yum,
<% Candy = Request.Form("Candy") %>
<%= Response.Write (Candy)%>
!
<% If Candy = "peanut butter cups" Then %>
There are several excellent brands of ice cream which contain
small or broken-up <%= Response.Write(Candy) %>.
<% Else %>
I don't think there's an ice-cream with <%
Response.Write(Candy) %> in it yet,
<% End If %>

<% If Candy = "Snickers" Then %>
but have you tried the <% Response.Write(Candy) %> ice cream
bar?
```

```
<% Else If Candy = "Turtles" Then %>
but the world definitely needs an ice cream with <%
Response.Write(Candy) %> in it.
<% End If %>
<% End If %>
</BODY>
</HTML>
```

The results either way are exactly the same, as seen in Figure 12-3.

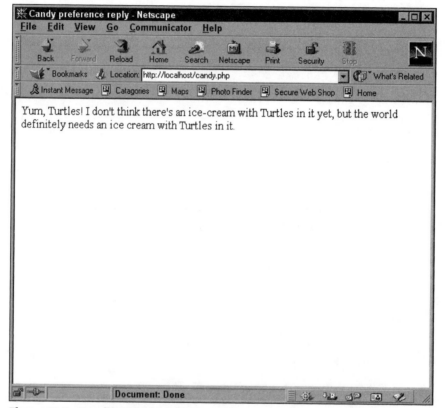

Figure 12-3: Results with either PHP or ASP

But the PHP script is faster to write because of the automatic variable assignment feature. The PHP script enables you to simply use the variable without requesting or redefining it. This is a trivial example with only one variable, but in more complex situations—forms with many variables or long series of forms that need to share many variables—PHP can save you considerable time and frustration.

Note that the ASP script must identify each variable as having come from a `POST`, whereas the PHP script does not: with Active Server Pages, you are supposed to use `Request.Form` for a `POST` argument, and `Request.QueryString` for a `GET` argument. If for whatever reason you change the method, you must change the collection name in every single instance, which increases potential maintenance problems.

However, PHP's automatic variable-assigning can lead to a conflict between variables with the same name. PHP will resolve any such conflict the way it normally does, which is to supersede the earlier assignment with one or more later ones. You can use the `GPC` option in `php.ini` to set the order in which conflicting variables should overwrite each other, and of course you should always choose good and differentiable variable names. In most real-world uses, PHP users find that the benefits of automatic variable-assignment far, far outweigh the potential pitfall of conflicting variable names.

Summary

The HTTP protocol is, strictly speaking, stateless. This means HTML itself is incapable of exchanging values between the pages of a Web site. It can be used to pass values, but a separate program called a form-handler must step in to perform actions with the passed values. PHP is perhaps the easiest and most natural of form-handlers.

Information is passed using one of three main methods: GET, POST, or a cookie. (We deal with cookies in Chapter 26.) GET is mainly used to construct complex URL strings for use with templates on dynamic sites. It is deprecated for use with forms. POST is the method recommended for forms.

✦   ✦   ✦

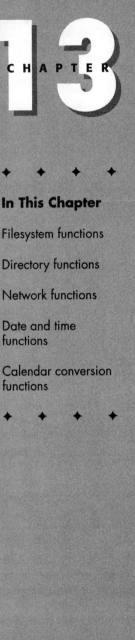
Filesystem and System Functions

This chapter contains information on the multiplicity of system functions built into PHP. Many of these functions duplicate system functions from HTTP. Among the most useful are file reading and writing functions, and those that return dates or times.

Caution   Many of the functions in this chapter have serious security implications. You are inviting bad news if you use them without thinking pretty hard about the consequences! We'll try to point out the most scary ones as we go, but nothing that allows the system to be altered via HTTP should be undertaken lightly.

Caution   Some of these functions are UNIX-only. The Windows system is deliberately made less available to users, especially to non-Administrator users, and lacks many utilities that UNIX-heads take for granted. If you're having problems and you run on Windows, make sure the function is enabled on your platform.

File Reading and Writing Functions

This is a supremely useful set of functions, particularly for data sets too small or scattered to merit the use of a database. File reading is pretty safe unless you keep unencrypted passwords lying around; but file writing can be quite unsafe.

A file manipulation session might have the following steps:

1. Open the file for read/write.
2. Read in the file.
3. Close the file (may happen later).
4. Perform operations on the file.
5. Write results out.

Each step has a corresponding PHP filesystem function.

This archetypal example illustrates some subtleties of the syntax:

```
$fd = fopen($filename, "r+") or die("Can't open file $filename");
$fstring = fread($fd, filesize($filename));
$fout = fwrite($fd, $fstring);
fclose($fd);
```

The effect of this particular example will be to "double" the file—in other words, the end result will be a file with the original contents of the file written out twice. This function will not overwrite the file, as some might expect.

File open

It's essentially mandatory to assign the result of fopen() to a variable (traditionally $fd for file descriptor, or $fp for file pointer—but a better new tradition would be to employ more descriptive variable names). If successful, PHP will assign the result an integer value, which it requires for further operations such as fread or fwrite. Otherwise, the value will be false.

Caution   The system only makes a certain number of file descriptors available, which is a good argument for closing files as soon as you can. If you anticipate a large demand and have access to system settings, you may increase the number.

Files may be opened in any of six modes (similar to permissions levels). If you try to do mode-inappropriate things, you will be denied:

✦ Read-only ("r").

✦ Read and write if the file exists already ("r+"): will write to the beginning of the file, "doubling" original contents of file.

✦ Write-only ("w"): will create a file of this name if one doesn't already exist; and will erase the contents of any file of this name before writing!

✦ Write and read even if the file doesn't exist already ("w+"): will create a file of this name if one doesn't already exist; and will erase the contents of any file of this name before writing!

✦ Write-only to the end of a file whether it exists or not ("a").

✦ Read and write to the end of a file whether it exists or not ("a+").

You need to be very sure you have read in the contents of any preexisting file before using "w" or "w+" on it. Your chances of losing data with the other modes is much less.

Caution Some users have reported problems with the "+" modes. Many of these problems actually appear to be caused by slightly faulty understanding of the six modes. When in doubt, try opening in separate read and write modes. Also see the section on file-writing below.

Varieties of file-open

There are four main types of connections that can be opened: HTTP, FTP, standard IO, and filesystem.

HTTP fopen

An `fopen` tries to open an HTTP 1.0 connection to a file of a type which would normally be served by a Web server (such as, HTML, PHP, ASP, and so on). PHP actually "fakes out" the Web server into thinking the request is coming from a normal web browser surfin' the net rather than a file-open operation.

You should be able to use forward slashes like this on either UNIX or Windows:

```
$fd = fopen("http://www.somedomain.org/openfile.html/", "r");
```

However, you *must* remember to use the trailing slash, because this function does not support redirects.

Remember that you need not necessarily use an HTTP connection to open an HTML file. You can open from the filesystem instead and treat the file as a text file. This alternative is mostly useful for remote Web servers. The effect will be much like viewing an HTML page and saving the source code.

FTP fopen

An FTP `fopen` attempts to establish an FTP connection to a remote server, by pretending to be an FTP client. This is the trickiest of the four options, because you need to use an FTP username and password in addition to the hostname and path.

```
$fd =
fopen("ftp://username:password@somedomain.org/openfile.txt/",
"r");
```

The FTP server must support passive mode for this method to work correctly. Also, FTP file opens can only be read or write, not both at once.

Standard I/O fopen

Standard I/O read/writes are indicated by `php://stdin`, `php://stdout`, or `php://stderr` (depending on the desired stream). Standard I/O fopens come into play mostly when PHP is used on the command line or as a system scripting language à la Perl, since standard IO is usually associated with terminal windows. This usage is so rare in PHP that we have never seen a real-life example of any length.

Filesystem fopen

But the most common and useful way to use `fopen` is from the filesystem. Unless specifically directed otherwise, PHP will attempt to open from the filesystem.

On Windows systems, you can choose to use the Windows format with backslashes if desired—but remember to escape them:

```
$fp = fopen("c:\\php\\phpdocs\\navbar.inc", "r");
```

> **Tip**
>
> Remember that your files and potentially your directories need to be readable or writable by the PHP process UID rather than by you as a system user or by your username. If you share a server, this means any of the other legitimate PHP users will be able to read and/or write to your files. Yes, we know this is not particularly safe.

File read

The `fread()` function takes a file pointer identifier and a file size in bytes as its arguments. If the file size given is not sufficient to read in the whole file, you will have mysterious problems (unless you're passing in a smaller file size on purpose, which is useful when reading huge files in chunks). Unless you have a reason to do otherwise (such as, a huge unwieldy file), it's best just to let PHP fill in the file size itself, by using the `filesize()` function with the name of the file (or a variable) as the argument:

```
$fstring = fread($fd, filesize($filename));
```

A common error is to type `filesize($fd)` rather than `filesize($filename)`.

This is an extremely useful function because it allows you to turn any file into a string, which can then be manipulated with PHP's large variety of useful string functions. Any string can also be broken up into an array through use of a function like `file()` or `explode()`, which gives you access to the large arsenal of PHP array-manipulation functions. PHP gives you more slicing and dicing functions than a whole set of Ginsu knives.

If you wish to read a file to standard output (meaning, for most PHP installations, echoing it to the Web browser window), use `readfile()` instead. This function has file opening built in, so you need not use a separate function to open the file first.

If you wish to read in and perform operations on a file line by line, you can use fgets() instead of fread().

```
$fd = fopen("samplefile.inc", "r");
while(!feof($fd))
   {
   $line = fgets($fd, 4096);
   if(strcmp($line,$targetline) == 0)
     {echo "A match was found!";}
   }
fclose($fd);
```

If you would rather read the file in as an array, you can use the function file() instead. This creates an array, each element of which is a line from the original file including an ending newline character. The function file() does not require a separate file open or file close step. A single operation using file(), such as:

```
$line_array = file(samplefile.inc);
```

is the equivalent of this:

```
$fd = fopen($filename, "r+") or die("Can't open file
$filename");
$fstring = fread($fd, filesize($filename));
$line_array = explode("\n", $fstring);
```

Finally, if you'd like to read in a file character by character, you can use the fgetc() function. This will return a character from the file pointer, until the end-of-file.

File write

File writing is pretty straightforward if you've successfully opened in the correct mode for your intended purpose. The function fwrite() takes arguments of a file pointer and a string, with an optional length in bytes, which should not be used unless you have a specific reason to do so. It returns the number of characters written.

```
$fout = fwrite($fp, $fstring);
```

echo "I just wrote $fout characters to a file." The function fputs() is identical to fwrite() in every way. They are simply aliases for one another, but fputs() is the C-style function name.

Keep in mind that file writing in "w" or "w+" modes will result in the complete and utter obliteration of any file contents. These modes are meant for clean overwrites only. If you want to write to the beginning or end of a file, use "r+" or "a+."

Probably the most common error with PHP file-writing modes involves using a web interface (in other words, an HTML form) to edit a text file. If you want to open a file, read in and view the contents, then write an edited version to the same file-name, you cannot depend on "w+" mode. The "w" modes erase the contents of the file immediately upon opening it—you can only read from a "w+" file after writing to it. To get around this issue, you need to open once in read mode and once in write mode, as in the example below (where $filename denotes any text file):

```php
<?php
if(IsSet($submitted))
{
   $fd = fopen($filename, "w+") or die("Can't open file
$filename");
   $fout = fwrite($fd, $newstring);
   fclose($fd);
}
$fd = fopen($filename, "r") or die("Can't open file
$filename");
$initstring = fread($fd, filesize($filename));
fclose($fd);
echo "<HTML>";
echo "<FORM METHOD='POST' ACTION=\"$PHP_SELF\">";
echo "<INPUT TYPE='text' SIZE=50 NAME='newstring'
VALUE=\"$initstring\">";
echo "<INPUT TYPE='HIDDEN' NAME='submitted' VALUE=1>";
echo "<INPUT TYPE='SUBMIT'>";
echo "</FORM>";
echo "</HTML>";
?>
```

Let us reiterate that file writing is not at all a good idea unless you can control your environment very tightly! In other words, a well-hardened intranet server might be appropriate, but file writing on a production Web site can be a security risk. For more information, see Chapter 31, "Security and Cryptography."

If you compile your own PHP and know a little bit of C, you can choose to disable the capability to file-write (actually, you're disabling the capability to open a file in writing mode—but the effect is the same). This is a great idea especially if your site is entirely database-driven, because you don't have any legitimate need to write to the filesystem with PHP anyway.

To disable file writing, you need to look for a file named fopen-wrappers.c in the main PHP directory. Open it in a text editor, and search for the function php_fopen_with_path(). You want to add these lines in an appropriate spot (there's a good one about 10 lines down):

```c
// Only allow "r" mode
if(!strcmp(mode, "r"))
  return NULL;
```

If you're really brave, there's some stuff you might want to take out too — but we leave that to you on the theory that you should only attempt this if you know what you're doing with the C code.

 Tip   If you disable file writing, attempts to write will appear as parse errors or "variable passed to file is not an array or object" errors.

File close

File closing is straightforward:

```
fclose($fd);
```

Unlike fopen(), the result of fclose() does not need to be assigned to a variable. File closing may seem like a waste of time; but your system has only so many file descriptors available, and you may run out if you do not close your files. You know your own setup best, and you can make the call.

Filesystem and Directory Functions

Most of these functions will be quite familiar to UNIX users, as they closely replicate common system commands.

Many of the functions in this section are dangerous. Because they duplicate functions that can and should be performed from the local system, they can be a cracker's bonanza without providing much value to legitimate users.

The one piece of good news is that some of these functions will only work if the PHP process is running as the superuser. Because this is not the default case, presumably only those sysadmins who know what they're doing are even in a position to shoot themselves in the foot this way.

The most common and safe functions are listed first; the less common and less safe are in Table 13-1.

feof

The feof function tests for end-of-file on a file pointer and takes a filename as argument.

file_exists

The file_exists function is a simple function you will use again and again if you use filesystem functions at all. It simply checks the local filesystem for a file of the specified name.

```
if(!file_exists("testfile.php"))
  {
  $fd = fopen("testfile.php", "w+");
  }
```

The function returns true if the file exists, false if not found. The results of this test are stored in a cache, which may be cleared by use of the function `clearstatcache()`.

filesize

Another simple but useful function is `filesize`, which returns and caches the size of a file in bytes. We use it in all the `fread()` examples earlier in this chapter. Never pass in a filesize as an integer if you can possibly do it by using `filesize()` instead.

Table 13-1	
Filesystem Functions	

Function	Description
basename (*filepath*)	Returns the filename portion of a stated path.
chgrp(*file, group*)	Change file to any group to which the PHP process belongs. Inoperative on Windows systems.
chmod(*file, mode*)	Changes to the stated octal mode. Inoperative on Windows systems.
chown(*file, user*)	If executed by the superuser, changes file owner to stated owner. Inoperative but returns true on Windows systems.
clearstatcache	Clears cache of file status info.
copy(*file, destination*)	Copies file to stated destination.
delete(*file*)	See "unlink."
dirname(*path*)	Returns the directory portion of a stated path.
diskfreespace("*/dir*")	Returns the number of free bytes in a given directory.
fgetcsv(*fp, length, delimiter*)	Reads in a line and parses for CSV format.
fgetss(*fp, length [, allowable_tags]*)	Gets a file line (delimited by a newline character) and strips all HTML and PHP tags except those specifically allowed.
fileatime(*file*)	Returns (and caches) last time of access.
filectime(*file*)	Returns (and caches) last time of inode change.

Function	Description
filegroup(*file*)	Returns (and caches) file group ID number. Names can be determined by using posix_getgrgid().
fileinode(*file*)	Returns (and caches) file inode.
filemtime(*file*)	Returns (and caches) last time of modification.
fileowner(*file*)	Returns (and caches) owner ID number. Names can be determined by using posix_getpwuid().
fileperms(*file*)	Returns (and caches) file permissions level.
filetype(*file*)	Returns (and caches) one of: fifo, char, dir, block, link, file, unknown.
flock(*file*, *operation*)	Advisory file locking. Operation value must be 1 (shared), 2 (exclusive), 3 (release), or +4 (don't block while locking).
fpassthru(*fp*)	Standard output of all data from file pointer to EOF.
fseek(*fp*, *offset*, *whence*)	Moves file pointer offset number of bytes into file stream from the position indicated by whence.
ftell(*fp*)	Returns offset position into file stream.
set_file_buffer(*fp* [, *buffersize*])	Sets a buffer for file writing; 8K is the default.
is_dir(*directory*)	Returns (and caches) true if named directory exists.
is_executable(*file*)	Returns (and caches) true if named file is executable.
is_file(*file*)	Returns (and caches) true if named file is a regular file.
is_link(*file*)	Returns (and caches) true if named file is a symlink.
is_readable(*file*)	Returns (and caches) true if named file is readable by PHP.
is_writeable (*file/directory*)	Returns (and caches) true if named file or directory is writable by PHP.
link(*target*, *link*)	Creates hard link. Inoperative on Windows systems.
linkinfo(*path*)	Confirms existence of link. Inoperative on Windows systems.
mkdir(*path*, *mode*)	Makes directory at location *path* with the given permissions in octal mode.
pclose(*fp*)	Closes process file pointer opened by popen().
popen(*command*, *mode*)	Opens process file pointer.
readlink(*link*)	Returns target of a symlink. Inoperative on Windows systems.

Continued

Table 13-1 *(continued)*

Function	Description
rename(*oldname*, *newname*)	Renames file.
rewind(*fp*)	Resets file pointer to beginning of file stream.
rmdir(*directory*)	Removes an empty directory.
stat(*file*)	Returns a selection of info about file.
lstat(*file*)	Returns a selection of info about file or symlink.
symlink(*target*, *link*)	Creates a symlink from target to link. Inoperative on Windows systems.
touch(*file*, [*time*])	Sets modification time; creates file if it does not exist.
umask(*mask*)	Returns umask, and sets to mask & 0777. With no argument passed, it simply returns the umask.
unlink(*file*)	Deletes file.

Network Functions

The network functions are a bunch of relatively little-used functions that provide network information or connections. Many of these may be more useful from the command line than the Web page, unless you're writing some kind of monitoring tool.

Syslog functions

The syslog functions allow you to open the system log for a program, generate a message, and close it again.

✦ openlog([*ident*], *option*, *facility*) is entirely optional when used with syslog(). The ident value is generated automatically.

✦ syslog(*priority*, *message*)

✦ closelog() is entirely optional when used with syslog(). It takes no arguments.

DNS functions

PHP offers some very slick DNS-querying functions, outlined in the Table 13-2 below.

Table 13-2
DNS Functions

Function	Description
checkdnsrr($host, [$type])	Checks for existence of DNS records. Default is MX; other types are A, ANY, CNAME, NS, SOA.
gethostbyaddr($Ipaddress)	Gets host name corresponding to address.
gethostbyname($hostname)	Gets address corresponding to hostname.
gethostbyname1($hostname)	Gets list of addresses corresponding to hostname.
getmxrr($hostname, [mxhosts array], [weight])	Checks for existence of MX records corresponding to hostname, places in mxhosts array, fills in weight info.

Socket functions

A socket is a kind of dedicated connection that allows different programs (which may be on different machines) to communicate by sending text back and forth. PHP socket functions allow scripts to establish such connections to socket-based servers. The connection can then be read from or written to with the standard file-writing functions (fputs(), fgets(), and so on).

The standard socket-opening function is fsockopen(). The pfsockopen() function is identical except that sockets are not destroyed when your script exits; instead, the connection is pooled for later use. The blocking behavior of socket connections can be toggled with set_socket_blocking(). When blocking is enabled, functions that read from sockets will hang until there is some input to return; when it is disabled, such functions will return immediately if there is no input. These functions are summarized in Table 13-3.

Table 13-3
Socket Functions

Function	Description
fsockopen($hostname, $port, [error number], [error string], [timeout in seconds])	Opens the socket connection to specified port on the host, and returns a file pointer suitable for use by functions like fgets().
getservbyname($service, $protocol)	Returns the port number of the specified service.

Continued

Table 13-3 *(continued)*	
Function	**Description**
`getservbyport($port, $protocol)`	Returns service name on port.
`pfsockopen($hostname, $port, [error number], [error string], [timeout in seconds])`	Opens the specified persistent socket connection.
`set_socket_blocking($socket descriptor, $mode)`	TRUE for blocking mode, FALSE for nonblocking. Default is nonblocking.

Date and Time Functions

These functions are basic tools used in many self-defined functions. You may use them simply to output the date or time, to keep track of microtime for a PHP performance-tracking utility, or to initiate a function over a particular date range (such as putting a "Happy Holidays" message on your site during holiday seasons).

These are pretty straightforward to use if you understand the UNIX timestamp. They fall into three main categories: returns date or time, formats date or time, and validates date.

Tip   The UNIX timestamp measures time as a number of seconds since the beginning of the UNIX Epoch (midnight Greenwich Mean Time on January 1, 1970). Despite the name, these functions mostly work on Windows also.

If you don't know either date or time

The fastest way to get a time is to use the function `time()`. This will return the UNIX timestamp for your locale, which will look something like "961906652." If you plan to pass this timestamp to another function or program, this is the best format. Alternatively, you can then use one of the functions in the next section to format the timestamp into something a bit more human-readable.

You could also use `microtime()` to return the current time in seconds and microseconds since the UNIX epoch. This can be supremely helpful for utilities that are designed to measure performance. The format is "0.74321900 961906846," where the first part is microseconds and the second is the UNIX timestamp. If you're trying to (for instance) measure the performance of different parts of your Web page, you really just want the microseconds part, which can be cut out like so:

```php
<?php
$stampmebaby = microtime();
$chunks = explode(" ", $stampmebaby);
```

```
$microseconds = $chunks[0];
echo $microseconds;
?>
```

The main function used to return a date is `getdate($timestamp)`. When used with the argument `time()`, as in `getdate(time())`, it returns an associative array with the following numeric elements derived from the UNIX timestamp:

> seconds
>
> minutes
>
> hours
>
> mday: day of the month, for example, 1–31
>
> wday: day of the week, for example, 1–7
>
> mon: month, for example, 1–12
>
> year
>
> yday: day of the year, for example, 1–356
>
> weekday: day of the week, for example, Sunday–Saturday
>
> month: January–December

You can also use the `getdate()` function with another UNIX timestamp than that representing the current time.

If you want to get the time and format it in one step, you can use `date()` instead of `getdate()`. In the absence of a UNIX timestamp argument, `date()` will default to the current local date. This has the advantage of allowing nicer formatting, as we will explain in the next subsection. The function `strftime()` will also format the current UNIX timestamp for you (as we explain in the next subsection) unless another is specified.

If you've already determined the date/time/timestamp

The functions in this section come into play if you already have a timestamp and merely wish to format the information more finely. For instance, you may like to express your dates European style (2000.20.04) rather than American (4/20/2000).

The main method to format a timestamp is using `date($format...$formatn[, $timestamp])`. You pass a series of codes indicating your formatting preferences, plus an optional timestamp. You can choose a date with two-zero day identifiers or strictly numeric date identifiers, 12 or 24 hour format, or abbreviated month name. (See the PHP manual for all the options.) An analogous function is `gmdate ($format...$formatn [, $timestamp])`, which will return a Greenwich Mean Date.

The function `strftime($format...$formatn[, $timestamp])` is similar but specializes in formatting the time rather than the date; `gmstrftime($format... $formatn [, $timestamp])` returns the time in formatted Greenwich Mean Time

The function `mktime()` allows you to convert any date into a timestamp. It's subtly different in the order of arguments from the UNIX command of the same name, so pay attention. The function `gmmktime()` gives the Greenwich alternative.

Finally, `checkdate($month, $day, $year)` allows you to quickly ensure that a particular date is a valid one. This is great for leap-year questions.

Calendar Conversion Functions

Finally, we have some optional calendar conversion routines, available to those who are in a position to compile with the calendar dynamic library.

Tip
Many new users have made the mistake of thinking "Calendar Functions" means date functions. Not so. These functions strictly convert between different (largely historical) calendar systems. See "Date and time functions" earlier in this chapter if you feel you have entered this section in error.

If you happen to be a French historian, you'll be happy to know PHP can automatically convert between the French Revolutionary calendar and the Gregorian calendar with but a couple of commands. What can we say to that but: Bon Thermidor, Citoyens et Citoyennes!

Seriously, these functions have real uses—particularly on the global Internet. (And not to be ungrateful or anti-Judeo-Christian-centric . . . but Joyce is patiently and lazily waiting for someone to add the Chinese lunar calendar to PHP, so she can always know when Chinese New Year celebrations will occur.)

To use calendar functions, you need to compile your own PHP from source. These functions are provided in the not-yet-stable dynamic library format, which is sketchily documented in `dl/README`. Calendar functions are not available in the precompiled Windows binaries at press time.

Conversion between systems is made possible because all the calendar functions share a universal referent, the so-called "Julian Day Number" (a.k.a. "Julian Day Count"). This is an integer that represents the days since noon on the first of January, 4713 BC by the Julian calendar (which wasn't in use at the time, but why niggle?). This date would be the 14th of January in the Gregorian calendar, which is commonly used in secular societies today. The so-called "Julian Date" is a double that represents the days and hours since Julian Day Zero—but PHP does not allow this level of specificity; we're just mentioning it here in case anyone is looking for this information.

> **Tip** Remember that the Julian Day changes at noon, rather than midnight, which is the convention today.

PHP's calendar conversion functions translate a date in some calendar into or out of Julian Day Count. To convert between two calendars, you will need to use two separate functions: one to give the date from one calendar as a Julian Day Number, and the other to convert JD into another calendar's date. In this example, we are converting a Gregorian date into its equivalent in the Jewish calendar.

```
$jd_no = gregoriantojd(8, 11, 1945);
$hebrew = jdtojewish($jd_no);
echo $hebrew;
```

This will return a date of 2, 6 [Elul], 5705.

The calendars offered at the moment are:

- ✦ French Republican
- ✦ Gregorian
- ✦ Jewish
- ✦ Julian
- ✦ Unixian

Each of these calendars has associated "JDToX" and an "XToJD" functions.

Finally, there are two other pairs of miscellaneous calendar functions. JDMonthName() and JDDayofWeek() return the month and day of week of any Julian Day Number in any of the supported calendars; whereas easter_date() and easter_days() will tell you when (Western or Catholic, as opposed to Eastern or Orthodox) Easter falls/fell/will fall in any given year. Easter_date() is the more straightforward method but can only be used within a UNIX date range (1970–2037). It returns the UNIX timestamp of Easter midnight in the specified year.

Summary

PHP has numerous filesystem and system functions built in, which can be extremely handy if sometimes potentially insecure. For instance, there are a large number of PHP functions that duplicate UNIX systems utilities, such as chmod() and copy(). PHP can also boast some extra-clever functions such as DNS-querying. Although we might wish it were easier to turn off some of these functions, they can be useful in trusted hands and a well-planned environment.

PHP's file opening, reading, and writing functions are extremely powerful tools. Most problems with these functions result from a slightly incorrect understanding of the file-opening modes. In addition to filesystem fopens, PHP also supports very slick http, ftp, and standard I/O file-opening.

Finally, PHP offers a plethora of time, date, and calendar functions so you always know what time it is.

✦   ✦   ✦

PHP Style

This chapter is about the major points of PHP style, and how it can enhance the functionality, maintainability, and attractiveness of your code. This discussion is intended to help new PHP developers make the main stylistic decisions, most of which are common to all programming languages.

We also hope this chapter may help new PHPers decipher other people's code. It can be very alarming to someone just learning scripting to read three different tutorials, which appear totally incongruent but lack any explanation of the discrepancies. The information in this chapter will help you tease out the functionally important bits of code from the mere stylistic quirks and thus gain a better understanding of what you're seeing.

The Uses of Style

The primary goal of a program is, of course, functionality. After all, if your PHP script chokes, who's even going to care how good it looks? Error messages are never all that stylin'. But there is a vast difference between simply whipping up something that will work, and writing well-formed code that can be clearly understood by others.

PHP programmers confront all the same style issues that other programmers do, including:

✦ *Readability:* Sure, you understood it when you wrote it, but what about the next person who reads it? What about if the next person is you?

✦ *Maintainability:* What happens when your health-advice site finally makes that conversion from Fahrenheit to Celsius? (A wrong answer: replacing 790 occurrences of the string "98.6" in your source code.)

✦ *Robustness:* Your Web site works fine when it's getting the inputs you expect. What about when it gets the inputs you don't expect?

✦ *Conciseness and efficiency:* Fast code is better than slow code, and (others things equal) code using fewer keystrokes is better than code with more keystrokes (but other things are almost never equal).

This chapter will give a quick overview of some strategies for achieving these goals in PHP, before moving on to some code organization issues that are unique to PHP.

Readability

Before a PHP script can aspire to be maintainable or elegant, it has to be human-readable. The human eye likes clear patterns, logical organization, and meaningful repetition. It also helps to have the most significant word or character at the beginning of a line, instead of buried in the middle.

If you develop HTML mostly through use of a WYSIWYG tool, your notions of legibility may be very odd indeed. These programs are notorious for writing badly structured graphics-oriented HTML, filled with invisible GIFs and absolute sizing and other little horrors. All these errors and more are demonstrated in this example, developed with a well-known IDE that must remain nameless (we have done nothing to this code to make it look worse than it is).

```
<HTML><HEAD><TITLE>Recipe: poached peaches</title><meta http-
equiv="Content-Type"content"text/html;
charset=iso-8859-1"></HEAD><body bgcolor="#FFFFFF"
text="#666666" link="#CC3300" vlink="#CC3300" alink="#CC3300">
          <table width="401" align="center" border="0"
CELLSPACING="1" CELLPADDING="1">
                <tr>
                    <td width="50"><img src="spacer.gif"
width="50" height="1"></td></tr>
                    <td width="300" height="30"
colspan="5"><b><font face="sans-serif" size="2"
color="#DDA0DD">Poached Peaches</font></b></td>
                    <td width="51"><img src="spacer.gif"
width="51" height="1"></td></tr>
                </tr>

            <tr>
        <td width="401" colspan="7"><img src="spacer.gif"
width="300" height="5"></td>
                </tr>

            <tr>
```

```
                          <td width="50"><img src="spacer.gif"
width="50" height="1"></td></tr>
                      <td width="300" colspan="5"><font face="sans-
serif" size="2"><b><i>Ingredients</i></b></font></td>
                              <td width="51"><img src="spacer.gif"
width="51" height="1"></td></tr>
               </tr>

               <tr>
                <td width="300" colspan="7"><font face="sans-
serif" size="1"><img src="line.gif" width="300" height="1"
border="0" align="top"></font></td>
               </tr>

                    <tr>
                        <td width="50" align="left"><font
size="1" face="sans-serif"> </td>


                       <td width="100" align="left"><font
size="1" face="sans-serif">Large peaches</font></td>

                         <td width="50" align="left"
colspan="2"><font size="1" face="sans-
serif">6 </font></td>

                       <td align="left" width="100">

                         <font size="1" face="sans-
serif"><NULL> </font>

                       </td>


                       <td width="51"><img src="spacer.gif"
width="51" height="1"></td></tr>

                    </tr>

                    <tr>
                       <td width="50" align="left"><font
size="1" face="sans-serif"> </td>


                       <td width="100" align="left"><font
size="1" face="sans-serif">White wine</font></td>

                       <td width="50" align="left"
colspan="2"><font size="1" face="sans-serif">2 </font></td>
```

```
                            <td align="left" width="100">

                    <font size="1" face="sans-
serif">cups</font>

                    </td>


                    <td width="51"><img
src="spacer.gif" width="51" height="1"></td></tr>

                    </tr>


                    <tr>
                    <td width="50" align="left"><font
size="1" face="sans-serif"> </td>



                    <td width="100"
align="left"><font size="1" face="sans-serif">Granulated
sugar</font></td>

                    <td width="50" align="left"
colspan="2"><font size="1" face="sans-
serif">1 </font></td>

                    <td align="left" width="100">

                    <font size="1" face="sans-
serif">cup</font>

            </td>


                    <td width="51"><img src="spacer.gif"
width="51" height="1"></td></tr>

                    </tr>


                    <tr>
                    <td width="50" align="left"><font
size="1" face="sans-serif"> </td>


                    <td width="100"
align="left"><font size="1" face="sans-serif">Fresh
ginger</font></td>
```

```
                                    <td width="50" align="left"
colspan="2"><font size="1" face="sans-
serif">2 </font></td>

                          <td align="left" width="100">

                <font size="1" face="sans-
serif">slices  </font>

                          </td>


                          <td width="51"><img src="spacer.gif"
width="51" height="1"></td></tr>

                          </tr>

            </table>


        <table border="0" width="300" align="center">
            <tr height="30"></tr>

            <tr>
             <td width="29" align="center"> </td>

            <td colspan="2"><font face="sans-serif"
size="2"><b><i>Procedures</i></b></font></td>
            </tr>

            <tr>
            <td colspan="2"><font face="sans-serif"
size="1"><img src="line.gif" width="300" height="1" border="0"
align="top"></font></td>
                </tr>


            <tr>
                <td valign="top"><font size="1"
face="sans-serif" valign="top">1. </font></td>
                <td><font size="1" face="sans-
serif">Drop the peaches into boiling water for 15 seconds; the
skins will peel off easily. Carefully slice in half and remove
pit. </font></td>
                </tr>


                <tr>
                <td valign="top"><font size="1" face="sans-
serif" valign="top">2. </font></td>
```

```
                    <td><font size="1" face="sans-
serif">Combine all ingredients except peaches in a large
saucepan. Simmer until sugar is dissolved. </font></td>
                      </tr>


                      <tr>
                        <td valign="top"><font size="1"
face="sans-serif" valign="top">3. </font></td>
                        <td><font size="1" face="sans-
serif">Poach peaches in liquid over low heat for 15 minutes.
Turn every 5 minutes. Serve lukewarm with poaching liquid in
the hollow. </font></td>
                      </tr>

                  </table>

</table>
</body></html>
```

Trying to add PHP directly to HTML files like this is an exercise in frustration, like trying to dance with someone who has no rhythm. If you insist on doing so, remember: it's not PHP's fault, so please direct your abuse to the other vendor.

However, in lieu of yet another moralistic UNIX-centric anti-WYSIWYG lecture, we'll now try to make a concrete suggestion or two for those who can't totally avoid graphics.

Probably the single most effective step you can take to increase legibility is to run all machine-produced HTML through a utility that will make it more human-readable. It doesn't take very long at all, and will improve matters substantially. A good one for UNIX is HTML Tidy, freely available from:

```
http://www.w3.org/People/Raggett/tidy/
```

This utility will also clean up common errors in your HTML source, such as missing end tags. Furthermore, it has some (admittedly limited at this point) capability to cope with PHP, if you've used the standard <?php ... ?> tags — so you can also try cleaning up those "I'm in such a hurry so just this once I'll save a Microsoft Office document in HTML format and then stick in a couple of PHP tags" situations. It will read Microsoft Office documents saved as HTML, although HTML Tidy is not available on the Windows platform (at press time).

A somewhat more labor-intensive approach that gives you finer control is to run the code through an HTML validator. This is a utility (many are Web-delivered) that lists all the specific points at which a page is not in compliance with HTML standards. However, unlike HTML Tidy, it does not actually rewrite the source code; you can choose to make changes on a point-by-point basis.

The next most effective way to increase code legibility involves lobbying your boss to move the whole shop over to a development environment that supports both a good WYSIWYG editor and a good text editor. Although this is not an endorsement, a well-known product of this description is Macromedia Dreamweaver, which is available in both Mac and Windows versions, has some PHP support, and can interoperate with a variety of image manipulation packages.

Even PHP developers who code entirely by hand can help themselves in the long run by selecting a congenial text editor (as discussed in Chapter 3). Why waste time closing HTML tags or chasing down a missing parenthesis if you don't have to? Most text editors today have the capability to automatically close tags and brackets appropriately, and otherwise help you avoid trivial but time-consuming mistakes.

You want something that is available on your preferred development platform and can be configured to closely match your personal style. Some people love syntax highlighting in many colors on black, others think it's too much like programming a Lite-Brite; some people use tab indentations, others prefer spaces; some people like the program to do everything but make coffee for them, others want a dumb but obedient terminal. It's all good, and you can find almost any combination of features you want — if you're willing to put the time into customizing your editor. Because a programmer's text editor is like a desperado's horse — you have to ride that nag until one of you drops — this is definitely time well spent. All text editors today have Web sites with lots and lots of screenshots; look around until you see the configuration of your dreams.

Caution Make sure your chosen editor is compatible with whatever your coworkers are using. Some editors strip out tab-indenting, cause documents to be formatted oddly, use strange quote marks, and so forth. Your codevelopers won't elect you Employee of the Month if they have to reformat every page after you look at it.

One of our pet peeves is about programmers who haven't yet accepted that computer memory is no longer worth any kind of premium, and thus it's counterproductive to spend time trying to squeeze a program into the smallest space possible. This practice is unfortunately recapitulated by some misguided technical book and magazine publishers, who still ask their authors to use various dodges to reduce the length of printed code samples, like so:

```
<?php if($UserID && strlen($Horse)>0) {
  if($Horse=="Man O'War") print("Chestnut, white snip");
  elseif($Horse=="Native Dancer") print("Light grey");
  elseif($Horse=="Seattle Slew") print("Black");
} else {
  print("Please try again."); }?>
```

This example features Kernighan and Ritchie braces, indentations consisting of a single space per level, absence of repetitive but meaningful file elements such as HTML headers, and an overall lack of breathing room. None of this is at all incorrect, but neither does it particularly aid readability. Compare that format to this (and try to imagine both being embedded in a much longer, more complex script that you've been assigned to change ASAP):

```
<HTML><BODY>
<?php
if($UserID && strlen($Horse)>0)
{
    if($Horse == "Man O'War")
        print("Chestnut, white snip");
    elseif($Horse == "Native Dancer")
        print("Light grey");
    elseif($Horse == "Seattle Slew")
        print("Black");
}
else
{
    print("Please try again.");
}
?>
</BODY></HTML>
```

New programmers might do well to keep in mind that the code in books or even on the Internet (where space literally costs *nothing*) does not necessarily represent the pinnacle of human legibility.

And finally, not to belabor the obvious, but neatness does count. This becomes more true as the number of codevelopers rises and issues of maintainability come to the fore.

Comments

Putting comments in code is just like flossing your teeth: important for health and hygiene, the object of many good intentions, all too often skipped "just this once," and long regretted later if undone.

The problem is that there's no immediate glory to be had from commenting—all the benefits are longer term and diffuse. Let's face it: you rarely hear hackers oohing and aahing over the beautiful commenting of the guy in the next cubicle, and few Web sites' go-live dates are allowed to slip so that the programmers can put the finishing touches on their comments. Commenting comes into its own later, when your team leader quits to join a neo-Luddite community in the middle of a major site redesign, and the rest of you are sitting around scratching your heads and thinking "Huh?" in unison as you desperately try to write up some documentation in time for the scheduled release.

So what kinds of things should you comment? We feel you *must* explain:

✦ Anything with future "what the heck was I thinking?" potential (usually due to extreme cleverness or extreme ugliness)

✦ Anything you suspect might be a temporary expedient (yeah, right—like you've never once used a magic number?)

✦ Anything that will lead to dire consequences if tampered with by ignorant people

Things that ideally should be noted include:

✦ The date the file was originally created, and the name of the creator

✦ The date the file was most recently altered, and the name of the alterer, and possibly an explanation of the rationale behind the alteration

✦ Any other files or programs that depend on the existence of this file

✦ The intended purpose of the file, and of its constituent parts

✦ Things you might want to mention in documentation you're planning to write later

✦ The reason why you want to save something that isn't being used (alternate versions, archive copies, and so on), conditions under which it might become okay to throw it away, or your plans for what to do with it

Obviously, you're in a better position than we to decide whether these items are strictly necessary. If you're using PHP for a very small, purely personal site, maybe commenting would be superfluous; but the bigger and more complex the site, the more you need to annotate your own work. In theory it's possible to overcomment, but in practice few programmers are guilty of the practice.

Tip   As we detailed in Chapter 5, there are several styles of PHP comments. Remember that none of these will be visible from the client machine. If you want client-readable hidden text, you must use HTML comments.

File and variable names

Some people act like thinking up variable names is equivalent to being forced to write an epic poem—they go into a kind of writer's block and become creatively incapacitated. For instance, we once had an intern who was apparently unable to think up a single name, or even a halfway decent scheme for doing so. This person's habit was to name every new file according to simple sequential order: `file16.html`, `file17.html`, `file18.html`, and so forth. Each variable on a Web page was called `var1`, `var2`, and so on. This story would be a lot funnier if it had happened to someone else.

Because PHP generally requires lot more variables than HTML, you need a robust naming scheme for all occasions. The following sections include a few tips.

Long versus Short

Longer is generally better because it's more informative. You can break up long names with underscores or capitalization if necessary.

Even though most filesystems technically allow for long filenames, the results are not pretty when viewed as icons — so GUI users may be consciously or unconsciously averse to using long filenames. Icon labels are usually quite short and thus naturally lend themselves to very concise filenames. Try giving a file a long, complex name (like PoachedPeachesRecipe.php) and putting it on your desktop — the result is just viscerally displeasing.

Caution Most GUI-oriented filesystems allow and even encourage filenames with spaces in them (for example, My Document.doc). UNIX systems do in theory, but in practice it's not such a good idea. However, PHP will try to cope gracefully with such filenames, but it may not be able to do so in all situations.

One benefit of using PHP for dynamic content generation is that you can use shorter filenames that will be expanded and differentiated by GET-style query strings. For example, a static site might use this style of filename to uniquely identify each page:

```
FeatureHitchcockBirds.html
MiniseriesIrvinSpy.html
```

A dynamic site, on the other hand might identify the same pages like this:

```
feature.php?ID=1
miniseries.php?ID=2
```

In this situation, you can have the best of both worlds: short filename plus unique identifier.

PHP sets no particular limit on the length of variable names. So feel free to invent lengthy but informative variables like $AddressOfClientCompanyIn Saskatchewan. Hey, it's your script — we're just living in it. You only need to be careful if you plan to use a lot of long-name variables as part of a GET-method form.

Underscores versus camelcaps

There are two typical ways to break up long variable and file names in Unix. Underscores look like this:

```
$name_of_favorite_beer
```

while "camelcaps" look like this, with the internal capital letters giving the name a humped profile:

```
$NameOfFavoriteBeer
```

It's a purely personal preference which you use. PHP itself uses underscores ($PHP_SELF), but this could be construed as an argument in favor of either scheme. Just remember you can't use dashes and should be careful with dots.

 Caution UNIX filenames are case sensitive all the time. Filenames in other OSs, such as Windows, are not case-sensitive. If you might be in a position to move PHP files between OSes, be careful.

The main thing to strive for here is consistency. It's frustrating to spend a lot of time trying to figure out why $My_Number was never assigned, only to find out that it's because you called it $MyNumber when you assigned it.

Reassigning variables

Situations arise in which you deliberately want to keep using the same variable name over and over rather than coming up with new names. This happens when you need to be certain only one variable of a particular type will be valid at any given time. For instance, you might want to be sure there can be no confusion about which of two database queries will be used for an operation, which you can ensure by using the same name for both (for example, $query). PHP will overwrite the former with the latter, and your variable will always be minty fresh.

Maintainability

Many seasoned programming veterans, especially those who are also managers, tout the importance of maintainability above that of any other virtue.

The problem is, of course, that maintainability is in direct conflict with all the other goals — especially speed. When Internet Time gets into the ring with Hypothetical Future Code Maintenance By Someone Probably Not Myself, everyone knows how the story is going to end.

Still, the main mental mantras of maintainability are worth keeping in mind:

✦ The things that are most likely to be changed should be the easiest to find.

✦ Changing those things should not have unpredictable effects.

✦ Each change should have to be made in only one place.

Avoid magic numbers

A "magic number" is a numerical value that might someday have to be changed but is buried deep in code, often in multiple places. Imagine, for example, these lines of code found in your bank's hypothetical PHP-based Web site:

```
print("The interest rate on your CD can be as high as
      5.5%!<BR>");
$sample_gains = 5000 * 1.055;
print("After a year, a \$5000 investment could grow to
      \$$sample_gains!<BR>");
```

Now, when times get tighter and the rate goes down to 5.0%, someone has to find and change every instance of the rate. So, someone does a text search for "5.5", which misses the 1.055 in the second line here, and now your bank is engaging in false advertising.

For simple sites, a better alternative can be as easy using an $interest\_rate$ variable, which is assigned very visibly at the top of a script — a change in rate means a change only to that assignment statement. More complex sites might produce their pages as function calls, with variables like $interest\_rate$ being passed in as an actual parameter. Finally, some sites will go so far as to have all of their content imported from a database, so that no piece of information has to ever be changed directly in code.

Functions

Having tried to maintain a complex site using a Web-scripting language that did not support functions, we can say from our own experience that functions are crucial to maintenance. The art of procedural abstraction via functions needs a book in itself, but here's some brief advice:

✦ Always look for opportunities to bundle naked PHP code into a function, especially in cases where it might be reused.

✦ Try to keep function definitions short — if a definition gets too long, break it up into multiple functions.

✦ Always load all of your function definitions before any code that calls any functions. (The order of function definitions doesn't matter, and this will ensure that you don't use any before they are defined.)

Include files

One of the great benefits of dynamic Web page generation over static HTML is the opportunity to fight redundancy. Anyone who has ever managed a static site of any size knows how much of each file is boilerplate — and even editing a single character on each page isn't a picnic if your site has 200 pages.

PHP makes it incredibly easy to drop in anything from one character to a whole separate program into your scripts, by using the built-in `include` or `require` functions. The syntax is simply:

```
<?php include("filename.ext"); ?>
```

You can also use a variable filename, like this:

```
<?php
$LastName = "Park";
include("$LastName.inc");
?>
```

which will result in the contents of the file `Park.inc` being included. See Figure 14-1 for an example of a PHP file with included files.

You can use any extension you want for the included file. Popular choices include .txt, .inc, and even .html to remind yourself that the file will show up in HTML mode.

A few things to remember:

✦ PHP will drop the entire text of the file into your PHP script *in HTML mode* (as explained in Chapter 4). If the included file is itself meant to be parsed as PHP, you must use valid PHP tags at the beginning and end. If any part of the file is meant to be parsed as PHP, you must use valid PHP tags around that section.

✦ Recall the difference (explained in detail in Chapter 5) between the `include` function and the `require` construct. Require is said to be much the faster in PHP4. PHP4 also supports a new `include_once()` function which can reduce load time in circumstances where files might be included multiple times.

✦ `Include` can also be used to assemble complex Web pages from text files instead of from a database. In some cases, this can even be faster — usually when the included data is just a sizable text file(s). However, once you go to the trouble to make a database connection for any reason, it's probably just as fast to store your big chunks of text there too.

This is an example of multiple `include` functions on a single page:

```
<HTML>
<HEAD>
<!-- If you wanted, you could choose to put this header in an
include file. -->
<TITLE>Menu of the day</TITLE>
<STYLE TYPE="text/css">
<!--
```

```
BODY        {color: #000000; font-family: verdana; font-size: 10
pt}
H1          {margin-top: 10; color: #FFA500; font-family:
verdana; font-size: 16 pt; font-weight: bold}
H2          {color: #FFA500; font-family: verdana; font-size: 10
pt}
A:link      {color: #FFEFD5; text-decoration: none}
-->
</STYLE>
</HEAD>

<BODY>
<TABLE BORDER=0 CELLPADDING=0 WIDTH=100%>
<TR>
<?php include("navbar.inc"); ?>
</TD>
<TD BGCOLOR="#FFFFFF" ALIGN=LEFT VALIGN=TOP WIDTH=80%>
     <TABLE CELLPADDING=15><TR><TD ALIGN=LEFT VALIGN=MIDDLE>
     <H1>Today's menu</H1></TD></TR>
     <TR><TD ALIGN=LEFT>
     <?

     $today = date("Ymd");
     include("$today.inc");
     ?>
     </TD></TR></TABLE>
</TD></TR></TABLE><BR><BR>
<!-- There's no particular reason to put this footer in an
include file; we're doing it out of pure whimsy. -->
<?php include("footer.inc"); ?>


navbar.inc
     <TD BGCOLOR="#FFA500" ALIGN=CENTER VALIGN=TOP WIDTH=20%>
     <H2>Corporate<BR>Cafe</H2>
     <BR><BR>
     Make a <BR>
     <A HREF="suggestion.php">suggestion</A><BR><BR>
     Tell us your <BR>
     <A HREF="preferences.php">preferences</A><BR><BR>
     Sign up for special <BR>
     <A HREF="holidays.php">holiday menus</A><BR><BR>


20000110.inc
<P><B>January 10, 2000</B></P>
<P>Soup: Tomato Bisque<P>
<P>Sandwich: Chicken Salad</P>
<P>Veggie: Macaroni and Cheese</P>
<P>Dessert: Chocolate Pudding</P>
<P><?php
```

```
//You can include within an included file
include("always.inc");
?></P>


always.inc
<P>Rolls, crackers, breadsticks</P>
<P>Water, coffee, tea, milk, soft drinks</P>
<P>Soft-serve vanilla ice cream</P>


footer.inc
<P>Copyright <?php print("$today"); ?>, Chef</P>
</BODY></HTML>
```

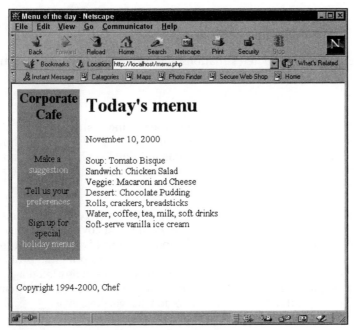

Figure 14-1: A PHP file with included files

As with any modular design concept, the whole trick with including files is deciding when to do it and when it's not worth the effort. Only you can decide when the value of having flexible components outweighs the potential confusion of having multiple parts.

Object wrappers

While we haven't covered PHP's object system in detail yet, it's worth noting that consistent use of objects can make code more maintainable, much as functions do. For example, some developers of database-enabled PHP sites are disciplined enough to wrap up all of their database-specific functionality in the methods of an object, so that the rest of their code doesn't even know what kind of database is supporting the site. In theory, then, if they decide to move from a mySQL database to an Oracle database, only the object-level code will have to be changed.

Cross-Reference   For detail on PHP's support for object-oriented programming, see Chapter 29.

Robustness

The two commandments of robustness are:

1. Code should detect unexpected situations and respond gracefully rather than dying.

2. If code must die, better that it die informatively.

Fancy languages like Java have elaborate exception-handling systems that require code to specify in advance the ways that it might die, and what significance should be attached to such deaths. Unfortunately PHP has nothing like this—the humble PHP programmer must make do with conditional tests and branches, and (like a spy's cyanide tooth) the die() function.

Writing robust code is at first a difficult task of imagination, where the programmer tries to think ahead to all the things that might go wrong, and covers those cases. The ideal situation is for that habit of mind to become a habit of code, so that the coder has a standard set of tests that wrap around the standard potential problems. Although most of the robustness issues in PHP are the same as in any language, there are two kinds of situations to cover that are more specific to PHP: problems with an external service, and problems having to do with variable type.

Unavailability of service

PHP is in part a "glue" language, offering a single environment where a variety of different code libraries and external services can be invoked. Any given PHP page might open a file, connect to a database, query an LDAP server, send an HTTP header, or send mail via an SMTP server. The important habit to develop is covering cases where for some external reason a service is unavailable, or times out, or behaves oddly, or gets interrupted in the middle.

Often such services have error states that can be retrieved and printed if the only option left is to informatively die. For example, a reasonable construct for making a connection to a mySQL database is

```
$connection = mysql_connect([arguments]) or
               die("Connection failed:  $php_errormsg<BR>");
```

This is preferable to the weird and unexpected errors you would see if your code went happily ahead assuming that it had a live database connection.

Unexpected variable types

Although the type-looseness of PHP is for the most part a good thing, it leaves a little bit of uncertainty for the programmer about exactly what type a variable or value will turn out to be. Unless you come to know all the type-conversion rules very well, it can be surprising to have code that is accustomed to strings suddenly run across a value that is a number, all because some PHP construct decided that any string composed only of numerical digits must really be a number at heart. One interesting robustness check is to use a text editor to search your code for '$' (thereby finding every variable) and ask yourself for each one what would happen if the type turned out to be surprisingly different.

Conciseness and Efficiency

Conciseness and efficiency are not the same thing. Concise code accomplishes a given task in a small number of lines or keystrokes, and efficient code runs using a small amount of execution time or computer memory. In this section we give some quick tips toward writing concise and efficient PHP code, along with our extremely opinionated commentary about in what senses these goals are worth striving for.

Efficiency: Only the algorithm matters

There was a time when computer memory and computer cycles were so precious that it was worth a lot of effort to boil down your code to the smallest number of resulting machine instructions possible. This is still true in certain areas of software development (kernel programming, graphics libraries), but for most development tasks saving a few instructions or a few K is not worth backing off on any other goal. This is especially true for Web scripting, where there is always going to be some overhead of purely Internet-related execution delay. If it takes half a second for a user to fetch your page, regardless of how your page is produced, then an extra five milliseconds on the server side will be lost in the noise.

With that said, there's one variety of efficiency that matters, and will probably always matter: the broad algorithm or approach that your code uses for a task. For example, if your code locates a name in a database by querying the database for all names and then doing a string comparison for each name to see if it's the one you want, then you'll soon find out how much efficiency can matter.

Efficiency optimization tips

Here are some quick mantras to repeat to yourself as you code.

Don't reinvent the wheel

It's usually a bad idea to write code that duplicates a language-level facility, unless it's for purposes of fun or education. For example, any programmer worth his or her salt should write sorting routines at some point in their education, but no programmer should have to keep writing them (unless it is actually in their job description). Most high-level programming languages offer some kind of sorting capability (either as part of the language or in a library), and it's very likely that the programmer who wrote them did a better job than you will. PHP is no exception here—the array type supports several types of sorting, and most of the databases supported by PHP have sorting options built into the query language. Either of these options will be faster and more reliable than what you get by rolling your own.

Discover the bottleneck

Although it's good to try to use efficient algorithms from the beginning, it's often not worth doing other kinds of optimization until you find out that too much of some resource is being used. At that point, you want to tighten things up, and you'll get the most reward for your effort if you focus on the piggiest parts of your code. Most code follows the 90/10 rule: 90 percent of the time is spent in 10 percent of the code, and you want to locate that 10 percent.

One technique that programmers often use to locate that 10 percent is called *profiling*. A profiler is a utility that tracks code as it runs, noting the time spent in every function call, and producing a neat summary of the results. Unfortunately, at this writing, there is no good general profiling utility for PHP (although one may be on the way for later versions of PHP4). So the best bet for now is the poor man's profiling technique: printing the value of the function call `microtime()` in various places in your script to see where the time is going. If the 90/10 rule is in effect, the time sink will usually be glaringly obvious.

Focus on database queries

Although it involves a bit of look-ahead to the next part of the book, you should be aware that database queries are usually the biggest time sink for PHP sites that have database back ends. Especially if your database-enabled site doesn't do a lot of other computationally intensive work, your first suspicious glance should be at the queries, and your next task should be to try to identify a query that is particular time-consuming. Once you've identified a guilty query, there are a host of techniques available to speed that query up, many of which don't have anything to do with PHP.

Cross-Reference

For detail on optimizing database-enabled PHP sites, see Chapter 23.

Focus on the innermost loop

Let's say that you have a page with embedded looping constructs, like the following:

```
for ($x = 0; $x < 100; $x++)
{
  do_X();
  for ($y = 0; $y < 100; $y++)
    {
      do_XY();
      for ($z = 0; $z < 100; $z++)
        {
          do_XYZ();
        }
    }

}
```

Unless you have a really good reason to think otherwise, your optimization focus should be on the function do_XYZ() (which will execute 1,000,000 times) rather than on the other two functions (10,000 times and 100 times).

Conciseness: the downside

Before we get into how to write more concise code, let us say that we think conciseness is an overrated virtue, for the following reasons.

Conciseness rarely implies efficiency

Although it's true that somewhere in the guts of the PHP engine the characters of the code you write are being consumed one by one, and so in theory more code takes more time, in practice the Zend-based parsing engine of PHP4 is so zippy that it just doesn't matter. Ditto for the time or space consumed in extra variable assignments, or the overhead of extra function calls.

Conciseness trades off with readability

Remember that every keystroke you omit might be the keystroke that would have let someone figure out what the heck you were thinking when you wrote the code. For example, take a look at the following admirably concise function:

```
function sieve($n) {
  for ($i = 2; $i <= sqrt($n); $i++)
    for ($j = $i, $ind = $i * $j; $ind <= $n;
          $j++, $ind = $i * $j)
      $carray[$ind] = TRUE;
  for ($i = $n, $plist = array(); $i > 1; $i--)
    if (!IsSet($carray[$i]))

      $plist = $i;
  return($plist);
}
```

Obviously, this implements the Sieve of Erasthones, and $plist is a list of all the prime numbers less than $n. Obviously.

So why do programmers strive for conciseness? The first reason is that it saves them time (but only at the time of actual code writing). The second reason (and we're only half-joking) is that they're afraid some other programmer (probably one trained in C) will come along later, laugh at them, and point out that their code could have been written in only half the space.

Conciseness tips

If you must write code that fits in less space, try some of the following techniques.

Use return values and side-effects at the same time

It's a very common trick to exploit the fact that the value of an assignment is the value assigned, as in the following pseudocode:

```
while ($next = GetNextOne())
    DoSomethingWith($next);
```

where GetNextOne() is some function that returns useful values in sequence and then returns a false value when it runs out of them. When a false value is returned, $next is false, and the while loop terminates.

Use incrementing and assignment operators

The incrementing operators (++ and --) shorten up statements that involve adding or subtracting one from a variable, and the combined assignment operators (+=, *=, .=, and so on) make certain kinds of assignments more concise.

The incrementing operators and the arithmetic assignment operators are covered
in Chapter 10, and the combined string assignment operator ('.=') is covered in
Chapter 9.

Often these operators are used in combination with the previous trick, as in

```
while ($count--)
    DoSomethingWith($count);
```

which (assuming that $count starts as a positive integer) would call its function
for the very last time on the value 1.

Reuse functions

This is one case where conciseness is good, because functions are good. If you can
identify any stretches of code that get duplicated in your pages, try to replace each
one with a call to a single function that packages up that code. Your code will be
shorter by the amount of the duplication and also probably easier to maintain.

There's nothing wrong with Boolean

Beginning programmers often have an odd distrust of Boolean values, not realizing
that they can be passed around as freely as any other kind of value. This leads to
code that wastes a lot of space, like the following:

```
function DivisibleByBad($num1, $num2)
{
    if ($num1 % $num2 == 0)
        return(TRUE);
    else
        return(FALSE);
}
/* using the function */
if (DivisibleByBad(9, 3))
    $divisible_result = TRUE;
else
    $divisible_result = FALSE;
if ($divisible_result == TRUE)
    print("It's divisible!<BR>");
else
    if ($divisible_result == FALSE)
        print("It's not divisible!<BR>");
```

A more concise version would look like:

```
function DivisibleByBetter($num1, $num2)
{
    return ($num1 % $num2 == 0);
```

```
  }
  /* using the function */
  if (DivisibleByBetter(9,3))
    print("It's divisible!<BR>");
  else
    print("It's not divisible!<BR>");
```

You could obviously take this one step further and get rid of the function itself, like so:

```
  if (9 % 3 == 0)
    print("It's divisible!<BR>");
  else
    print("It's not divisible!<BR>");
```

But (once again) Functions Are Good — an explanatory function name is a little piece of documentation in itself, and any function you write gives you a chance to reuse it later, which it turn makes your code more maintainable.

Use short-circuiting Boolean expressions

Certain kinds of Boolean tests aren't safe to apply until you've done other tests. It's tempting to deal with this by insulating the problematic tests with if constructs. For example, imagine that you want to print the ratio of two variables that are bound to integers, but only if they are bound to integers, and only if the ratio is greater than two. Also, you want to avoid a division-by-zero warning. You might overcautiously write:

```
  if (IsSet($x))
    {
      if (IsSet($y))
      {
        if (Is_Integer($x))
        {
          if (Is_Integer($y))
          {
            if ($y != 0)
              {
                if ($x / $y > 2)
                  print("Ratio is " . ($x / $y));
              }
          }
        }
      }
    }
```

You can be equally overcautious and still type a little less, as in

```
  if (IsSet($x) && IsSet($y) && Is_Integer($x) &&
      Is_Integer($y) && $y != 0 && $x / $y > 2)
    print("Ratio is " . ($x / $y));
```

The tests will be applied in left-to-right order, and if any test fails, the tests to the right of it will not be evaluated.

HTML Mode or PHP Mode?

There's a spectrum of ways to combine PHP and HTML, functionally all pretty much the same. Your choice will depend on extrinsic factors such as your particular team's workflow.

The easiest way to demonstrate all this is to simply write the same script in "minimal PHP," "maximal PHP," and "medium PHP" styles. Remember, these are equally correct and return much the same result. The stylistic decision is just a matter of preference and consistency, and sometimes slight differences in functionality.

In the examples below, the e-mail address is a dummy value—please change it if you want to test this code on a PHP server which has Sendmail capability.

Minimal PHP (see Figures 14-2 and 14-3):

```
<HTML>
<HEAD>
<TITLE>MorningService.html</TITLE>
<STYLE TYPE="text/css">
<!--
BODY       {color: #000000; font-family: times; font-size: 12
pt}
H1         {margin-top: 10; margin-bottom: 10; color: red; font-
family: cursive; font-size: 16 pt; font-weight: bold}
A:link     {color: red}
-->
</STYLE>
</HEAD>

<BODY>
<CENTER><H1>Hotel California</H1></CENTER>
<P>Thank you for staying at the Hotel California!<BR>
Please indicate what we can do to make your morning sun shine a
little more brightly.
<FORM METHOD="POST" ACTION="MorningService.php">
<P>Room number  <INPUT TYPE="TEXT" NAME="Room" SIZE=10>
<P>Do you want a wake-up call?<BR>
If so, please input a time <B>in 24-hour format (HH:MM)</B>
<INPUT TYPE="TEXT" NAME="WakeupTime" SIZE=10><BR>
<P>Select a newspaper:<SELECT NAME="Newspaper" SIZE=1>
<!-- Because we're cleanly separating HTML from PHP, we won't
be able to make this a dynamic pulldown list. If the list of
newspapers changes, the only option is to edit this form by
hand. -->
```

```
<OPTION VALUE=0>Please deliver the...
<OPTION VALUE=1>USA Today
<OPTION VALUE=2>New York Times
<OPTION VALUE=3>Wall Street Journal
</SELECT>
<P><INPUT TYPE="Submit">
</FORM>
</BODY></HTML>
```

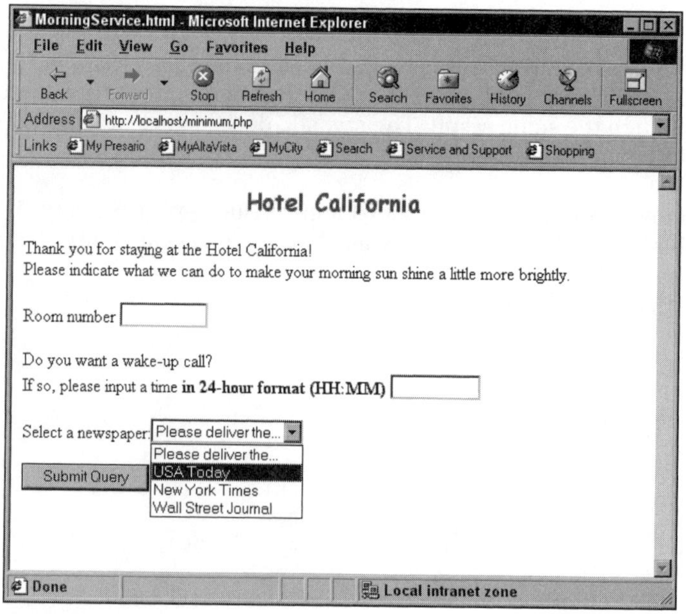

Figure 14-2: Minimal PHP, part 1

```
<HTML>
<HEAD>
<TITLE>MorningService.php</TITLE>
</HEAD>

<BODY>
<?php if($Newspaper == 0 && $WakeupTime == "") {?>
<P>I'm sorry, but you haven't told us to do anything!
<?php } elseif($Newspaper == 0 && $WakeupTime != "")
   {
   mail("deskclerk@hotelcali.com", "$Room", "Wakeup at
$WakeupTime"); ?>
   <P>Your wakeup call has been recorded. Sleep tight!
<?php } elseif($Newspaper > 0) {
```

```
    mail("deskclerk@hotelcali.com", "$Room", "Wakeup at
$WakeupTime and delivery $Newspaper"); ?>
    <P>Your wakeup call and newspaper preference have been
recorded. Sleep tight!
<?php }; ?>
</BODY></HTML>
```

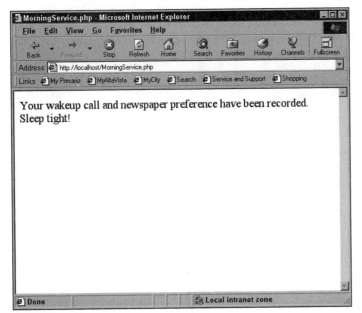

Figure 14-3: Minimal PHP, screen two

This minimal style separates HTML and PHP completely with two discrete files, `MorningService.html` (a form) and `MorningService.php` (a form processing script). It is particularly useful for workgroups large enough to have both client-side and server-side developers, because this format allows them to work in parallel and make design changes more quickly. However, this style generally makes it harder to do self-referential tricks, such as showing a slightly different HTML page under certain conditions.

Maximal PHP (see Figure 14-4):

```
<?php
print("<HTML>\n");
print("<HEAD>\n");
print("<TITLE>MorningService.html</TITLE>\n");
print("<STYLE TYPE=\"text/css\">\n");
print("<!--\n");
```

```
print("BODY          {color: #000000; font-family: times; font-
size: 12 pt}\n");
print("H1            {margin-top: 10; margin-bottom: 10; color:
red; font-family: cursive; font-size: 16 pt; font-weight:
bold}\n");
print("A:link        {color: red}\n");
print("-->\n");
print("</STYLE>\n");

print("</HEAD>\n");
print("<BODY>\n");
print("<CENTER><H1>Hotel California</H1></CENTER>\n");
print("<P>Thank you for staying at the Hotel
California!<BR>\n");
/* The following test uses the value of the form's SUBMIT
button to check if the user is viewing the page for the first
time (in which case we won't send a message to the desk clerk)
or submitting/editing a previous request. */
    if(!IsSet($Submit))
{
/* These empty variables will cause the form below to print
without visible values. */
    $Room = "";
    $WakeupTime = "";
    $Newspaper = "";
    print("Please indicate what we can do to make your morning
sun shine a little more brightly.\n");
}
else
{
    if($Newspaper == 0 && $WakeupTime == "")
        print("<P>You have just cancelled all instructions for
morning service.\n");
    elseif($Newspaper == 0 && $WakeupTime != "")
        {
        mail("deskclerk@hotelcali.com", "$Room", "Wakeup at
$WakeupTime");
        print("<P>Your wakeup call has been recorded. Sleep
tight!\n");
        }
    elseif($Newspaper > 0)
        {
        mail("deskclerk@hotelcali.com", "$Room", "Wakeup at
$WakeupTime and deliver $Newspaper");
        print("<P>Your wakeup call and newspaper preference have
been recorded. Sleep tight!\n");
        }
print("You may change the values in the form below and resubmit
it.\n");
}
```

```
/* Note that we're displaying this form with pre-set values
(which can be empty strings). */
print("<FORM METHOD=\"POST\" ACTION=\"$PHP_SELF\">\n");
print("<P>Room number  <INPUT TYPE=\"TEXT\" NAME=\"Room\"
SIZE=10 VALUE=\"$Room\">\n");
print("<P>Do you want a wake-up call/?<BR>\n");
print("If so, please input a time <B>in 24-hour format
(HH:MM)</B>  <INPUT TYPE=\"TEXT\" NAME=\"WakeupTime\" SIZE=10
VALUE=\"$WakeupTime\"><BR>\n");
print("<P>Select a newspaper:<SELECT NAME=\"Newspaper\" SIZE=1
VALUE=\"$Newspaper\">\n");
/* This pulldown list could be dynamically generated from a
database. */
print("<OPTION VALUE=0>Please deliver the...\n");
print("<OPTION VALUE=1>USA Today\n");
print("<OPTION VALUE=2>New York Times\n");
print("<OPTION VALUE=3>Wall Street Journal\n");
print("</SELECT>\n");
print("<P><INPUT TYPE=\"Submit\" NAME=\"Submit\"
VALUE=\"Send\">\n");
print("</BODY></HTML>\n");
?>
```

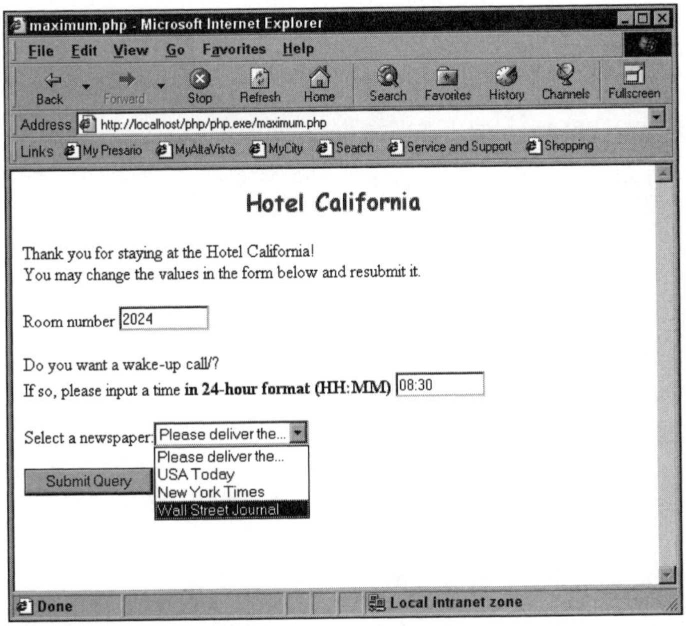

Figure 14-4: Maximal PHP after submission

This maximal style is favored by C programmers because it's very similar to the way you'd perform the task in that programming language. Unless you have considerable practice writing code that will produce HTML rather than writing HTML directly, this mode can seem awkward and error-prone. Because the HTML and PHP are integrated so closely, you can make every line of HTML dependent on as many conditions as you can stuff into your PHP. On the other hand, look and feel changes aren't as easy with this style.

> **Caution**
>
> Remember to escape double-quotes and dollar signs in this style. If you want your HTML source to be human-legible, remember to use appropriate line breaks (\n), returns (\r), and tabs (\t) within functions that return HTML.

Medium PHP:

```php
<?php
function display_form()
{
?>
<CENTER><H1>Hotel California</H1></CENTER>
<P>Thank you for staying at the Hotel California!<BR>
Please indicate what we can do to make your morning sun shine a
little more brightly.
<FORM METHOD="POST" ACTION="<?php echo($PHP_SELF); ?>">
<P>Room number  <INPUT TYPE="TEXT" NAME="Room" SIZE=10>
<P>Do you want a wake-up call?<BR>
If so, please input a time <B>in 24-hour format (HH:MM)</B>
<INPUT TYPE="TEXT" NAME="WakeupTime" SIZE=10><BR>
<P>Select a newspaper:<SELECT NAME="Newspaper" SIZE=1>
<OPTION VALUE=0>Please deliver the...
<OPTION VALUE=1>USA Today
<OPTION VALUE=2>New York Times
<OPTION VALUE=3>Wall Street Journal
</SELECT>
<P><INPUT TYPE="Submit" Name="Submit" Value="Send">
<?php
}

function process_form()
{
global $Newspaper, $WakeupTime, $Room;
if($Newspaper == 0 && $WakeupTime == "")
    print("<P>I'm sorry, but you haven't told us to do
anything!");

elseif($Newspaper == 0 && $WakeupTime != "")
    {
    mail("deskclerk@hotelcali.com", "$Room", "Wakeup at
$WakeupTime");
```

```
    print("<P>Your wakeup call has been recorded. Sleep
tight!");
    }

elseif($Newspaper > 0)
    {
    mail("deskclerk@hotelcali.com", "$Room", "Wakeup at
$WakeupTime and delivery $Newspaper");
    print("<P>Your wakeup call and newspaper preference have
been recorded. Sleep tight!");
    }
}
?>

<HTML>
<HEAD>
<TITLE>MorningService.php</TITLE>
<STYLE TYPE="text/css">
<!--
BODY      {color: #000000; font-family: times; font-size: 12
pt}
H1          {margin-top: 10; margin-bottom: 10; color: red; font-
family: cursive; font-size: 16 pt; font-weight: bold}
A:link     {color: red}
-->
</STYLE>
</HEAD>

<BODY>
<?php
if(!IsSet($Submit))
{
    $room = "";
    $WakeupTime = "";
    $Newspaper = "";
    display_form();
}
else
{
    process_form();
    print("<P>You may change the values in the form below and
resubmit it.\n");
    display_form();
}
?>
</BODY></HTML>
```

This is, as one might expect, a compromise style. Basically, the HTML part (minus the header) is defined as a function, whereas the PHP form-handling part is defined as a second function. A simple control (wrapped in the HTML header and footer) tests whether to run just the first function or both functions.

This mode is perhaps not as aesthetically pellucid as the others and may even appear scruffily muttly, but in a sense it makes the fullest use of PHP's unique capabilities. PHP is rather a hybrid product—not C or Perl or HTML, but influenced by them—and perhaps the best style is a hybrid style.

Separating Code from Design

The WYSIWYG code at the beginning of this chapter is ugly in part because it violates the principle of separating Web page function from design. These editors, evidently never having heard that beauty is on the inside, focus on what the page looks like rather than its logical structure. As HTML evolves, divorcing function and design will become mandatory instead of just advisable, because important advances in functionality (such as XML) demand better-formed code.

Many of the topics in this chapter have obvious implications for the separation of code and design. Here are a few additional techniques we should mention.

Functions

As you can see from our "Medium PHP" example, self-defined functions can be a very flexible and powerful formatting tool as well as one of the things that make PHP better than a tag-based scripting language.

Cascading style sheets in PHP

As you doubtless already know, there are four generally accepted ways to apply styles to your Web pages:

   ✦ Applying CSS formatting to individual tags
   ✦ Using <STYLE> tags (optionally inside a pair of HTML comment tags)
   ✦ <LINK> tags
   ✦ @import

Caution   In this book, we've consistently used the <STYLE> tag in each code sample rather than an external style sheet. This is solely so you, Dear Reader, can see the style declarations we used to get the results we display in the figures. There is absolutely no PHP-intrinsic reason for this usage.

In PHP, you could also use the `include` function to apply styles in a nonstandard way, although it's not clear how much of a gain this would be. For instance, you could `include` a text file containing everything between the `<STYLE>` tags, instead of linking to an external style sheet.

We should also mention the anti-style-sheet, a practice almost as long-deprecated as it is common: using outdated HTML tags such as `FONT`, `BGCOLOR`, and `ALINK`. Although you shouldn't do it at all, PHP can help you do it more efficiently if for some reason you must. This usage, for instance,

```
<FONT FACE="<?php include("fontlist.txt"); ?>" SIZE=+2>
```

would at least allow the poor overworked Web developer to change the fonts throughout the whole site with a single edit of the text file. Not that we can condone this kind of thing! Only slightly less kludgy would be this alternative:

```
<P STYLE="font-family: <?php include("fontlist.txt"); ?>">Text
here</P>
```

Templates and page consistency

As you can now imagine, PHP allows a wide variety of approaches to site design, which you can fit to your particular style and the organization of the people who work on the site. If your techies can't talk to your artists, you may want to set things up so that they never touch the same files; if you're a tech artist, you may express yourself by the very intermingling of code and graphics. However, if your site has a large number of pages or is very content-rich, you may find (as we have) that it's helpful to choose a particular kind of file organization or template, and stick to it across the site. One simplified example follows, which is similar to templates we have used on www.mysteryguide.com and www.sciencebookguide.com.

```
<?
/* load general functions */
include("general-functions.inc");
/* load functions specific to this page */
include("renaissance-functions.inc");
/* page-wide variables */
$PageTitle = "Painters of the Renaissance";
$db_connection = make_database_connection();
?>

<HTML>
<HEAD>
<TITLE>
    <?php print("$PageTitle"); ?>
</TITLE>
</HEAD>
```

```
<BODY>
<H3>
   <?php print("$PageTitle"); ?>
</H3>
<TABLE>
<TR><TD>
   <?php print-left-side($db_connection); ?>
</TD><TD>
   <?php print-right-side($db_connection); ?>
</TD></TR>
</TABLE>
   <?php print-footer($db_connection); ?>
</BODY><HTML>
```

In this example, every page loads the same file of site-wide utility functions, then loads a file of functions specific to that page, then defines variables that will be global for the page, and finally intersperses PHP commands in some boilerplate HTML. The content is in columns, and the actual content displayed depends on the particular page's functions, which always have the same names, but with definitions varying for each page. Changing what's displayed in the columns means either changing the per-page functions or (more likely) modifying the database contents. It would be possible for a nonprogrammer to do some limited design on this page by operating directly on the HTML and being careful to leave the PHP alone.

The preceding example is just one simplified possibility from a range of ways to divide up the labor of displaying a PHP page—your particular strategy will depend on the type of site, the size of the site, and the styles of the people contributing.

Summary

Most of the elements of PHP style are desirable in any programming language. You want to write readable code, with appropriately abstracted functions, consistent indentation, and explanatory comments. You want to stay away from magic numbers, "cloned" code repetition, overuse of global variables, and cryptically clever tricks. Your program should work on the inputs you expect, do something reasonable with inputs you didn't expect, and have the grace to die informatively in situations you really didn't expect.

Some of the PHP-specific style issues have to do with organizing file inclusions, how intimately you mix your PHP with your HTML, and more generally the separation of code from design. A wide range of styles are okay here, but you should strive for page-level and site-wide consistency.

In the next chapter we move from such stylistic questions to a much more basic one: what do you do if your PHP code isn't working?

✦   ✦   ✦

Basic PHP Gotchas

Even though we've tried to give clear instructions, and you've no doubt followed them to the letter, there are still many potential glitches that can arise. This chapter will lay out some of the most common ones by symptom and suggest some frequent causes.

 There is a whole other universe of "gotchas" involving database connectivity. This chapter deals with PHP-only problems. You may want to also skip ahead to Chapter 24 if you're experiencing problems with PHP and a database. Also, problems specific to certain more advanced features (including sessions, cookies, building graphics, e-mail, and XML) are dealt with in their individual chapters in Part III.

Installation-Related Problems

Instead of getting moralistic about people who rush through their installs without understanding the documentation, we'll point out a few common symptoms that characteristically appear when you've just installed PHP for the first time.

 If you are seeing similar errors but are confident that your installation is stable, follow the cross-references to later parts of this chapter.

Symptom: text of file displayed in browser window

If you are seeing the text of the your PHP script instead of the resulting HTML, the PHP engine is clearly not being invoked. Check that you are accessing the site by invoking the httpd, not via the filesystem. Do this:

```
http://localhost/mysite/mypage.php
```

rather than this:

```
file:/home/httpd/html/mysite/mypage.php
```

Symptom: PHP blocks showing up as text under HTTP, or browser prompts you to save file or visit an external file repository

The PHP engine is not being invoked properly. If you're properly requesting the file via HTTP as explained previously, the most common reason for this error is that you haven't specified all the filename extensions you want PHP to recognize, at least not for this directory. The second most common reason is that your php.ini file is in the wrong place or has a bad configuration directive.

Cross-Reference

If you see PHP code in your Web browser and you have a stable installation, your problem is probably due to missing PHP tags. See the "Rendering Problems" section later in this chapter.

Symptom: server or host not found/page cannot be displayed

If your server is not being found, you may have a DNS (Domain Name Service) or Web server configuration issue.

If you can get to the site via IP address rather than domain name, your problem is probably DNS-related. Maybe your DNS alias hasn't propagated throughout the Internet yet. This problem does occur occasionally even after the site has been up for awhile, either because your DNS server goes down without a valid secondary server or because of local Internet conditions.

If you cannot get to the site via IP address, it's likely you haven't successfully bound the IP address to your network interface or configured httpd to handle requests for a particular domain (see Chapter 4).

Rendering Problems

This section covers problems where PHP does not report an error per se, but what you see is not what you thought you would get.

Totally blank page

A blank page is very frequently an HTML problem rather than PHP per se (except insofar as you use PHP to produce HTML). If you *do not* use the maximal style of PHP (in other words, if there is any part of your script that should be renderable without first being preprocessed), the problem is almost sure to be in the HTML. So you should first try doing whatever you usually do to debug HTML.

> **Note**
>
> In general, one of your best debugging tools when faced with puzzling browser output is simply to view the HTML source that the browser is trying to render. All browsers have some command for viewing such source. For example, in Internet Explorer it is 'Source' under the 'View' menu.

If you wrote the file using a plain text editor, quickly check to make sure you haven't left out something crucial, such as a closing </TABLE> or </FORM> tag. If you used a WYSIWYG editor at some stage, the problem is more likely to be an extra element of some kind. The WYSIWYG file at the beginning of Chapter 14, for instance, had way more </TR> tags than table rows — a fact that different browsers will cope with differently. HTML produced with a programmer's text editor is less likely to have these issues.

You may get edifying results by viewing the HTML source from a client (especially if you use a maximal PHP style), or from a different browser. Internet Explorer is supposedly the most forgiving of mistakes, whereas Opera and Amaya are the strictest at enforcing HTML style.

If you just can't find anything wrong with your HTML — and especially if you are using the maximal style of PHP — the PHP module may not be working at all. Test by browsing a different page in the same directory that you've previously verified is being correctly handled by PHP. If you are a developer who does not maintain your own site, you may need to talk to your sysadmin.

Symptom: incomplete or unintended page

These problems are also usually in the HTML parts of the script and should be debugged as described previously. Figure 15-1 shows an interesting example (which is highly browser dependent; this is the IE5 product).

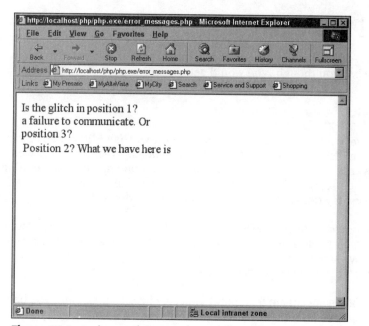

Figure 15-1: An incomplete or unintended HTML result

View the HTML source from a client. Sometimes the source will break off at the problematic point. If the source doesn't conveniently break off, try putting temporary error messages (in HTML mode) in different parts of the script to narrow down the location of the breakdown point, like this:

```
<HTML>
<HEAD></HEAD>
<BODY>Is the glitch in position 1?
<TABLE><TR><TD>Position 2? What we have here is </TD></TR>
<?php
$Problem = "a failure to communicate";
print("$Problem"); ?>. Or position 3?
</BODY>
</HTML>
```

This test would show the result seen in Figure 15-2, indicating that the temporary error messages in positions one and three are showing up in the right places relative to the other elements. It's position two that's out of place, indicating a likely problem (lack of a </TABLE> tag) with this line.

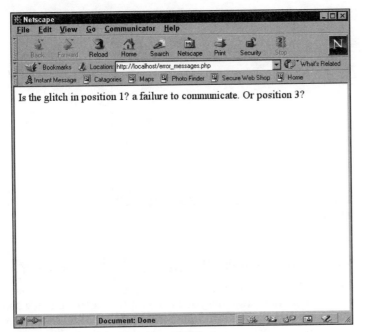

Figure 15-2: Using temporary HTML error messages

Your page may be incomplete due to a complete lack of PHP preprocessing, as in a script like this:

```
<HTML>
<HEAD></HEAD>
<BODY>
<P>What we have here is
<?php
$Problem = "a failure to communicate";
print("$Problem"); ?>.
</BODY>
</HTML>
```

This script will show up as seen in Figure 15-3.

In other words, all HTML-mode stuff will show up, but no PHP-mode stuff or error messages will appear. This is diagnostic of the PHP module not working at all or of the page residing on a computer without a PHP-enabled Web server (don't laugh, it happens a lot when you forget that you've been working on a particular version of a page on your client).

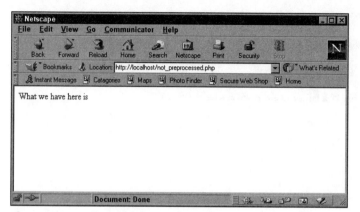

Figure 15-3: Failure to be preprocessed

Symptom: PHP code showing up in Web browser

If you are seeing literal PHP code in your browser, rather than a rendering of the HTML it should be producing, then probably you have omitted a PHP start tag somewhere. (This assumes that you have had PHP running successfully, and that you are using the correct tags for your installation. If not, see the first section of this chapter.)

It's easy to forget that PHP treats included files as HTML, not PHP, unless you tell it otherwise with a start tag at the beginning of the file. For example, assume that we load the following PHP file:

```
<HTML><HEAD></HEAD><BODY>
<?php include("secret.php");
secret_function(); ?>
</BODY></HTML>
```

which includes the file `secret.php`, which in turn looks like this:

```
function secret_function ()
{
  print("Open sesame!");
}
```

The result is shown in Figure 15-4.

This can be fixed by adding PHP tags to the included file like so:

```
<?php
function secret_function ()
{
  print("Open sesame!");
}
?>
```

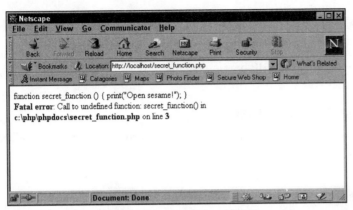

Figure 15-4: A PHP include appearing as HTML

Failures to Load Page

A couple of different kinds of errors are seen when PHP is unable to find a file that you have asked it to load.

Symptom: page cannot be found

If your browser can't find a PHP page you've created, and you have recently installed PHP, please see the first section of this chapter. If you get this message when you have been loading other PHP files without incident, then it's quite likely you are just misspelling the filename or path.

Symptom: failed opening [file] for inclusion

Under the Windows NT/IIS version of PHP, we sometimes see errors like this:

```
Warning Failed opening 'C:\InetPub\wwwroot\asdf.php' for
inclusion (include_path='') in [no active file] on line 0
```

It turns out that this is the NT version of "Page cannot be found" — that is, PHP hasn't even gotten to loading the first line of the active file, because there is no active file, and there is no active file because no file by that name could be found.

It's also possible that you will see this message under NT as a result of incorrect permissions on the file you are trying to load.

Parse Errors

The most common category of error arises from mistyped or syntactically incorrect PHP code, which confuses the PHP parsing engine.

Symptom: parse error message

Although the causes of parsing problems are many, the symptom is almost always the same: a parse error message like that in Figure 15-5.

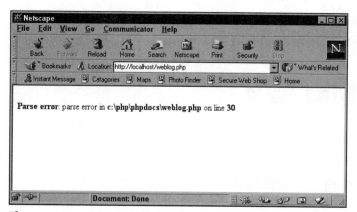

Figure 15-5: A parse error message

These errors occur in PHP mode by definition. This is actually good, because PHP returns more informative error messages than HTML—notably the line number of the problematic parsable.

The most common causes of parse errors, detailed in the subsections that follow, are all quite minor and easy to fix, especially with PHP lighting the way for you. However, every parse error returns the identical message (except for filenames and line numbers) regardless of cause. Any HTML that may be in the file, even if it appears before the error-causing PHP fragment, will not be displayed or appear in the source code.

The missing semicolon

If each PHP instruction is not duly finished off with a semicolon, a parse error will result. For instance, in this example fragment the first line lacks a semicolon and therefore the variable assignment is never completed.

```
What we have here is
<?php
$Problem = "a silly misunderstanding"
print("$Problem"); ?>.
```

Tip
If you spend any significant portion of your time debugging PHP code, an editor that can jump to specific line numbers can be invaluable. Note that the actual mistake that caused the error may be on the line that PHP complains about, or before it, but never after it. For example, because there's nothing wrong with commands that span several lines, a missed semicolon won't cause a parse error until PHP tries to interpret subsequent lines as being part of the same statement.

No dollar signs

Another very common problem is that a dollar sign prepending a variable name is missing. If the dollar sign is missing during the initial variable assignment, like so,

```
What we have here is
<?php
Problem = "a big ball of earwax";
print("$Problem"); ?>.
```

a parse error message will result. However, if instead the dollar sign is missing from a later output of the variable, like this,

```
What we have here is
<?php
$Problem = "a big ball of earwax";
print("Problem"); ?>.
```

PHP will not indicate a parse error. Instead, you will get the screen shown in Figure 15-6.

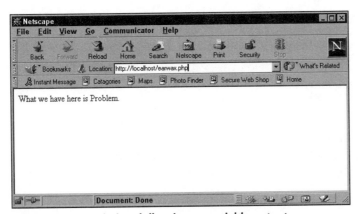

Figure 15-6: A missing dollar sign on variable output

Mode issues

Another family of glitches arises from faulty transitions in and out of PHP mode.

A parse error will result if you fail to close off a PHP block properly, as in:

```
What we have here is
<?php
$Problem = "an awful kerfuffle";
print("$Problem"); .
```

This particular mode issue is very common with short PHP blocks. Conversely, if you fail to begin the PHP block properly, the rest of the intended block will simply appear as HTML.

A slightly more tricky issue is engendered by the use of the "minimal" PHP style, which entails weaving in and out of HTML mode frequently. For instance, this fragment (which omits the ?> after the first curly brace, when we intend to return to HTML mode) will return a parse error:

```
<?php if(!IsSet($stage))
{
What we have here is
<?php
$Problem = "an awful kerfuffle ";
print("$Problem"); ?>.
<?php
} else {
print("$Stage"); }
?>
```

Another instance of a very common problem is this one, which combines the short block and weaving-in-and-out-of-HTML issues neatly:

```
<FORM>
<INPUT TYPE="TEXT" SIZE=15 NAME="FirstName" VALUE="<?php
print("$FirstName"); ?>">
<INPUT TYPE="TEXT" SIZE=15 NAME="LastName" VALUE="<?php
print("$LastName"); ?>">
<INPUT TYPE="TEXT" SIZE=10 NAME="PhoneNumber" VALUE="<?php
print($PhoneNumber); ?>"
<INPUT TYPE="SUBMIT" NAME="Submit">
</FORM>
```

A PHP double-quote and the HTML closing bracket have been forgotten on the PhoneNumber input line here. This will both cause a parse error and prevent the Submit button from displaying on a client browser.

The sample code is meant to demonstrate how easy it can be to forget an element on a crowded page with lots of small but important symbols. You can reduce this type of error by either using a good programmer's text editor; or completing and testing the HTML first and adding the PHP later; or both.

Unescaped quotes

Another type of parse error is characteristic of "maximal" PHP: the unescaped quote.

```
<?php
print("She said, /"What we have here is ");
$Problem = "a difference of opinion\"";
print("$Problem"); ?>.
```

In this case, the double-quote just before the word "What" is falsely escaped by a forward slash rather than a backslash. If you simply forgot the backslash, the effect would be the same.

Other parse error causes

The problems we have named are not an exhaustive list of the sources of parse errors. Anything that makes a PHP statement malformed will confuse the parser, including unclosed parentheses, unclosed brackets, unclosed strings, operators without arguments, control structure tests without parentheses, and so on. Sometimes the parse error will include a statement about what it was expecting and didn't find, which can be a helpful clue. If the line of the parse error is the very last line of the file, it usually means that some kind of enclosure (quotes, parentheses, braces) was opened and never closed, and PHP kept on hoping until the very end.

File Permissions

Most operating systems have some scheme of file and directory permissions that specifies which users have what kind of access to which files. The Web server runs as some user under this system, and so must have read permission for any files it looks at, including HTML and PHP source files.

Symptom: HTTP error 403

When a browser page presents you with error 403, it means that your file permissions are incorrect. Some browsers will not mention the error number but will complain that you do not have access to the given Web page.

The most common reason for this is that you haven't made this directory world-executable (UNIX) or enabled script execution (Windows). Remember that PHP scripts may run under a user ID different than your own. Under UNIX, PHP usually inherits the "nobody" UID, which (hopefully) is pretty much restricted to the HTTP service. Under Windows, each HTTP request is logged as the anonymous guest user.

Missing Includes

In addition to loading top-level source files, PHP also needs to be able to load in any files you bring in via include() or require().

Symptom: include warning

This kind of error is shown in Figure 15-7.

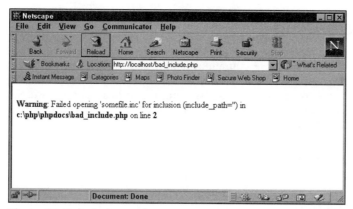

Figure 15-7: Include warning

The problem is that you call somewhere in the script for a file to be included but PHP can't find it. Check to see that the path is correct. You might also have a case sensitivity or other typographic issue.

You will also get this message if your script tries to include a file that is in another directory with incorrect permissions for the PHP user. Generally the directory must be specifically readable and executable by the Web-server user (often "nobody" under UNIX), or generally world-read/ executable (for example, 755under UNIX systems) for this usage, and of course the file must be world-readable (often 744).

Unbound Variables

PHP is different from many programming languages in that variables do not have to be declared before being assigned, and (under its default settings) PHP will not complain if they are used before being assigned (or "bound") either. As a result, forgetting to assign a variable will not result in direct errors — either you will see puzzling but error-free output or you will see a downstream error that is a result of variables not having the values you expected. (If you would rather be warned, you can set the error reporting level to 15 by evaluating either error_reporting(15) or error_reporting(E_ALL)). Some symptoms of this kind of problem follow.

Symptom: variable not showing up in print string

If you embed a variable in a double-quoted string ("like $this"), and then print out the string using print or echo, the variable's value should show up in the string. If it seems to not be there at all in the output ("like "), then the variable has probably never been assigned.

Symptom: numerical variable unexpectedly zero

Although it's possible to have a math error or misunderstanding result in this symptom, it's much more likely that you believe that the variable has been assigned when it actually hasn't been.

How unbound variables behave

PHP automatically converts the types of variables depending on the context in which they are used, and this is also true of unbound variables. In general, unbound variables are interpreted as 0 in a numerical context, "" in a string context, FALSE in a Boolean context, and as an empty array in an array context. The following piece of code shows the effect of forgetting to bind two variables ($two_string and $three); the resulting display appears in Figure 15-8:

```php
<?php
$one_string = "one";
$three_string = "three";
$one = 1;
$two = 2;
print("This math is as easy as $one_string, $two_string,
$three_string!<BR>");
print("$one_string is equal to $one<BR>");
print("$two_string is equal to $two<BR>");
print("$three_string is equal to $three<BR>");
print("$one_string divided by $two_string is " .
      ($one / $two) . "<BR>");
```

```
print("$one_string divided by $three_string is " .
      ($one / $three) . "<BR>");
?>
```

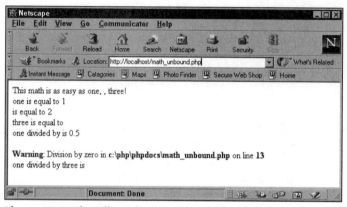

Figure 15-8: The effect of unbound variables

Case problems

Variables in PHP are case sensitive, and so the same name with different capitalization results in a different variable. Even after a value is assigned to the variable `$Mississippi`, the variable `$mississippi` will still be unbound. (Capitalization aside, variables that are this difficult to spell are probably to be avoided for the same reason.)

Scoping problems

As long as no function definitions are involved, PHP variable scoping is simple: assign a variable, and its value will be there for you from that point on in that script's execution (until the variable is reassigned). However, the only variables that are available inside a function body are the function's formal parameters and variables that have been declared to be global—if you have a puzzling unbound variable inside a function, this is probably something you've forgotten. In the following code, for example, the variable `$serial_no` is neither passed in to the function nor declared to be global:

```
$name = "Bond, James Bond";
$rank = "Spy";
$serial_no = "007";

function Answer($name)
{
```

```
global $rank;
print("Name: $name; Rank: $rank;
    serial no: $serial_no<BR>");
}
Answer($name);
```

The resulting browser output looks like:

```
Name: Bond, James Bond, Rank: Spy, serial no:
```

because the variable is unbound inside the function.

 Tip Under its default setting for error reporting, PHP will not warn about use of unbound variables. However, this setting can be changed, and doing so temporarily is often the fastest way to get to the bottom of unbound-variable problems. Simply put the line

```
error-reporting(15);
```

early in your script, and PHP will warn you about all such uses. You can delete the statement when done debugging, or return it to the default value explicitly with

```
error-reporting(7);
```

Alternatively, if you always want to be warned, you change the default error-reporting level to 15 in the php.ini file. The error-reporting levels and configuration issues are explained in more detail in Chapter 32.

Function Problems

Many problems having to do with function calls result in "fatal errors," which means that PHP gives up on processing the rest of the script.

Symptom: call to undefined function my_function()

PHP is trying to call the function my_function(), which has not been defined. This could be because you misspelled the name of a function (built-in or user-defined), or because you have simply omitted the function definition. If you use include/require files to load user-defined functions, make sure that you are loading the appropriate files.

If the problem involves a fairly specialized built-in function (for instance, it is related to XML or arbitrary-precision math), it may be that you did not enable the relevant function family when you included PHP. If, for example, all of the BC functions seem to be undefined, this is the problem — to fix it (under UNIX systems), you would need to reconfigure PHP and recompile.

Symptom: call to undefined function ()

In this case, PHP is trying to call a function and doesn't even know the function's name. This is invariably because you have code of the form `$my_function()`, where the name of the function is itself a variable. Unless you are intentionally trying to exploit the variable-function-name feature of PHP, then you probably accidentally put a '$' in front of a sensible call to `my_function()`. Because `$my_function` is an unbound variable, PHP interprets it as the empty string—which is not the name of a defined function—and so gives this uninformative error message.

Symptom: cannot redeclare my_function()

This is a simple one—somewhere in your code you have two definitions of `my_function()`, which PHP will not stand for. Make sure that you are not using `include` to pull in the same file of function definitions more than once.

Symptom: wrong parameter count

The function named in the error message is being called with either fewer or more arguments than it is supposed to handle. The function in question is usually a built-in function, because user-defined functions do not warn about number of arguments by default.

Math Problems

The problems that follow are specific to math and the numerical data types.

Symptom: division-by-zero warning

Somewhere in your code you have a division operator where the denominator is zero. The most common cause of this is an unbound variable, as in

```
$numerator = 5;
$ratio = $numerator / $denominator;
```

where `$denominator` is unbound. It's also possible, of course, that the legitimate result of a computation is producing a zero denominator. In this case, the only thing to do is catch it with a test, and do something reasonable if the test applies. As in

```
$numerator = 5;
if ($denominator != 0)
    $ratio = $numerator / $denominator;
else
    print("I'm sorry, Dave, I cannot do that<BR>");
```

Symptom: unexpected arithmetic result

Sometimes things just don't add up (or multiply up, or subtract up). If you are having this experience, check any complex arithmetic expressions for unbound variables (which would act as zeros) and for precedence confusions. If you have any doubt about the precedence of operators, add (possibly redundant) parentheses to make sure.

Symptom: NaN (or NAN)

If you ever see this dreaded acronym, it means that some mathematical function you used has gone out of range or given up on its inputs. The value "NAN" stands for "Not a Number," and it has some special properties. Here's what happens if we try to take the arccosine of 45, even though arccosine is only defined when applied to numbers between –1.0 and 1.0:

```
$value = acos(45);
print("acos result is $value<BR>");
print("The type is " . gettype($value) . "<BR>");
$value_2 = $value + 5;
print("Derived result is $value<BR>");
print("The type is " . gettype($value_2) . "<BR>");
if ($value == $value)
  print("At least that much makes sense<BR>");
else
  print("Hey, value isn't even equal to itself!<BR>");
```

The browser output looks like:

```
acos result is NAN
The type is double
Derived result is NAN
The type is double
Hey, value isn't even equal to itself!
```

Oddly enough, "NAN" is a number, at least in the sense that its PHP type in this example turns out to be "double" rather than "string." It also "infects" other values with not-a-numberness when used in math expressions. (This behavior is a feature, not a bug, when used in very complex calculations that must be correct. It's better to have the whole value be tagged as untrustworthy than have one subexpression be silently bogus.) Finally, any equality comparison that involves NAN will be false—NAN is neither less than, nor greater than, nor equal to any other number, including itself. It is always unequal (!=) to all numbers, including itself. (The NAN value is not a PHP-specific feature—it is part of the IEEE standard for floating-point arithmetic, which is implemented by the C functions that underlie PHP.)

Because of the contagion of NAN values, this kind of problem can be difficult to debug. The best way to try to find the original offending NAN is with diagnostic print statements, especially because comparison tests will give counterintuitive results. If you need to explicitly test for NANs, one hack is this function:

```
function is_nan($value)
{
   return($value != $value);
}
```

It uses the weird comparison properties of NAN as a type checker.

Time-Outs

Of course any download can occasionally time out before a complete page can be delivered. However, this shouldn't be happening frequently on your local development server! If it does, you may have an issue that has nothing to do with slow Internet channels or server overload.

The most interesting reason for a time-out is an infinite loop. These can be difficult to track down quickly, as in this example:

```
//compute the factorial of 10
$Fact = 1;
for ($Index = 1; $Index <= 10; $index++)
   $Fact *= $Index;
```

This code shows a nasty little collaboration between a loop and an case confusion — the lowercase "$index" that is incremented has nothing to do with the "$Index" that is being tested, and so the test will never become false.

Summary

In Table 15-1 we summarize the gotchas in this chapter by mapping symptoms to possible causes. We also offer some suggestions on how to fix the most common problems.

Table 15-1
From symptoms to causes

Symptom	Possible Causes	Advice
(New installation) Text of file displayed in browser window	The PHP engine is not being invoked, possibly because you are opening it via the local file-system rather than as a request to your server.	Make sure that your request is to the Web server, either via localhost (`http://localhost/[path]`) if testing on the server machine, or by the full URL (`http://www.site.com/[path]`).
(New installation) PHP blocks showing up as text under HTTP, or browser prompts you to save file or visit an external file repository	PHP is not being invoked properly. Your Web server may not be set up to map the right suffixes (e.g., `.php`) to the PHP engine, or there may be a problem with the location or contents of `php.ini`.	Check your Web server configuration, and the PHP init file (`php.ini`).
(New installation) Server or host not found/page cannot be displayed	Often due to Internet/DNS/Web-server configuration problems, rather than PHP.	Try loading a pure HTML file with a suffix you have not set up for PHP (e.g., `.html`) to rule out PHP problems. Try getting to the same file using an IP address rather than a domain name—if that works, the problem is DNS-related.
Totally blank page	Usually due to malformed HTML(whether produced by PHP or not).	View the HTML source from a browser. Look especially for unclosed `<TABLE>`, `<FORM>`, or `<SELECT>` forms.
Incomplete or unintended page	Usually due to malformed HTML (whether produced by PHP or not).	View the HTML source from a browser. Try to narrow down the source of the problem with diagnostic printing statements (in either HTML or PHP).

Continued

Table 15-1 *(continued)*

Symptom	Possible Causes	Advice
PHP code showing up in browser window	If the PHP engine is installed and functioning properly, this is usually due to a missing PHP start tag.	Check start and end tags, and make sure that any include files of PHP code have correct tags at beginning and end.
Page cannot be found	Usually means that the file-name or path of the PHP file is incorrect.	Double-check the name and directory path.
Failed opening [file] for inclusion	Same as the preceding error, as reported under some NT configurations.	Double-check the name and directory path.
Parse error message	A variety of causes, including missing semicolons, variables without a '$', unescaped quotes, unclosed quotes, brackets, or parentheses, and HTML being interpreted as PHP.	Locate the line of the parse error in the PHP file, and look for one of the causes in that line or the lines immediately preceding. If the "error" is on the final line of the file, look for an unclosed quote, paren, or bracket, possibly much earlier in the file.
HTTP error 403	The file permissions are incorrect.	Check the permissions of the file itself and the directories (or folders) in the path to that file.
Include warning	For one reason or another, PHP was not able to load a file named in an include statement.	Check that the file actually exists, the spelling of the filename, the pathname, and (on UNIX systems) the case of the name. Also make sure that the file permissions allow the file to be read.

Symptom	Possible Causes	Advice
Variable value not showing up in print string	The variable has not been assigned, and so its value in a printed string is the empty string.	Check that you are assigning the variable before the print statement, and compare spelling and case (capitalization). Make sure that you are not embedding any objects or multi-dimensional arrays in quoted strings. You can also use the statement `error-reporting(15)` to tell PHP to warn about any unbound variables.
Numerical variable unexpectedly zero	Often due to the variable never having been assigned.	(See preceding.)
Call to undefined function `my_function()`	Function `my_function()` is being called without having been defined first.	If you are trying to call a function of your own, check that the definition (or inclusion of the file containing the definition) is before the use. If you are trying to call a built-in function, check the spelling. If it is correct, investigate whether that "family" of functions was included when you configured PHP (for example, either all the XML functions will work, or none will).
Call to undefined function ()	An expression of the form `$my_function()` is being evaluated, and `$my_function` is not bound to the name of a defined function.	If you intend to be using the variable-function feature, then add (or correct) the assignment of `$my_function`. If you are just trying to call `my_function()`, remove the '$'.

Continued

Table 15-1 *(continued)*

Symptom	Possible Causes	Advice
Cannot redeclare `my_function()`	The function `my_function()` is being defined twice in a page's execution.	Look for double definitions of `my_function` in the PHP file, or double-inclusions of the file that defines it.
Wrong parameter count	The named function (usually a built-in function) is being called with an incorrect number of arguments.	Compare the function call to the definition in the online PHP manual (`http://www.php.net`)
Division-by-zero warning	A '/' operator has a right-hand argument of zero. Can be due to an unbound variable in the denominator.	Assign the unbound variable if that's the cause. If the desired logic could actually result in zero denominators, install a test to catch that case.
Unexpected arithmetic result	Frequently due to an unbound variable in an arithmetic expression.	Check for unbound variables (see preceding), and make sure that arithmetic expressions are parenthesized appropriately.
NAN value	A built-in math function is being given inputs outside its acceptable range. If that function's results are used in arithmetic, the results are also NAN.	Trace backward from the NAN value to function calls that contribute to its computation. Test with print statements, or test for values that fail to be self-equal (a diagnostic for NAN).
Page takes forever to load, or browser times out	Internet congestion, heavy load on your server machine, computationally intensive PHP code, or an infinite loop.	Check if Web sites other than your own are giving you the same trouble. Check all looping constructs in your code for errors that could cause them to never terminate.

✦   ✦   ✦

PHP and Databases

Choosing a Database for PHP

◆ ◆ ◆ ◆

In This Chapter

Why a database?

Choosing a database

Supported databases

Database design

◆ ◆ ◆ ◆

Databases and PHP go together like cake and ice cream, Trinidad and Tobago, green eggs and ham—you get the picture.

After all, what's the Web about? Making vast stores of information available to a more or less wide public, that's what. Not that there aren't small "brochureware" sites galore; but the bigger and more frequently updated the data source, the more comparative value is provided by the Web over other media.

Perhaps the single greatest advantage of PHP over similar products is the unsurpassed choice and ease of database connectivity it offers. As detailed later in this chapter, PHP supports native connections to a number of the most popular databases, Open Source and commercial alike. Almost any database that will open its API to the public seems to be included eventually. For any unsupported databases, there's generic ODBC support.

Why a Database?

If you're going to the trouble to use PHP at all, you're likely to need a database sooner or later—probably sooner. Even for something small, like a personal Web log, you want to think hard about the advantages of using a database instead of static pages or included text files.

Avoiding redundancy

Having PHP assemble your pages on the fly from a template and a database is an addictive experience. Once you enjoy it, you'll never go back to managing a static HTML site of any size. For the effort of programming one page, you can produce an infinite number of uniform pages. Change one, and you've changed them all.

Until recently, databases were too expensive to use for most nonprofit projects. However, a number of excellent low-cost databases are now widely available; and some commercial products are altering their licenses in the face of this healthy competition.

You may be concerned about performance. It's true that some databases are faster than others. However, once you need to go into the database for even *one piece* of information, it's almost always cost-effective to put everything in the database. Most of the overhead of a database query is front-loaded in establishing a connection. If you have to do that to get a name or title, downloading a couple thousand words of text is almost free.

Avoiding awkward programming

There are certain things that can be done with PHP but probably shouldn't because they entail ugly or risky programming moves.

For example, let's say you're writing a serial hypertext novel. Each episode is contained in a numbered text file, which is plugged into a template by PHP. You want to put automatically generated "Next" and "Previous" links on each page for those who wish to read in straight chronological order. It's pretty easy to use PHP to find the previously numbered entry; but any attempt to locate the next entry can quickly become an infinite loop—because it's easier to prove something does exist than that it doesn't. On the other hand, if you put your novel chapters in a database, the whole job becomes trivial.

The moral is that although databases lack general-purpose programmability, they are very highly optimized for a few tasks—so take advantage of their specialized capabilities where you can.

Searching

Although it's possible to search multiple text files for strings (especially on UNIX platforms) it's not something most Web developers will want to do all the time. After a few hundred files, the task becomes slow and hard to manage. Databases exist to make searching easy. With a single command, you can find anything from one ID number to a large text block to a JPEG-format image.

In some cases, information attains value only when put into a searchable database. For instance, relatively few people would want to read a long text list of movie directors and their films; but many might occasionally want to search a database of that information. You could argue that it's the searchability that creates the value here, not the information itself.

Security

A database adds another layer of security if used with its own password or passwords.

Let's say you use PHP to keep a diary, filled with the most personal secrets and observations. Because you don't host your own site, you want to be able to browse and edit your diary via HTTP with password authentication. However, if you have PHP write each new entry to a text file for inclusion in a template, you must give the HTTP daemon user (usually Nobody or Everybody) write access to your directory. This is not a good idea. By having PHP write to a database instead, you can maintain read-only directory permissions and also ask for a second password before the database can be altered.

Or take the case of a content site with a large number of visitors, a smaller number of writers, and handful of editors. You can easily set database permission levels for each group so that visitors can just look at the database content (as formatted in Web pages), writers can browse and change only their own entries, and editors can browse/change/delete anything in the site.

N-tier architecture

So far, we've only been considering so-called two-tier sites: PHP takes raw data from some kind of storage system and turns it into HTML. However, one of the intentions of PHP is to become the "glue" in three-tier or n-tier development. If you have anything more complex than the simplest two-tier architecture, you *really* need a database.

An n-tier architecture is an arbitrary number of software subsystems linked by a Web site on the front end and one or more databases on the back end. One fairly common n-tier architecture is that of a big e-commerce site, which has shopping carts linking up to order-taking systems linking up to supply-chain management routines; plus product databases, customer databases, credit-card debiting, FAQ-o-matics, recommendation engines, Web log analysis tools, caching proxies, phone center knowledge bases, and who knows what else lurking behind the scenes. Under these conditions, you need advanced database capabilities that we'll describe later.

Choosing a Database

Although databases (even relational ones) have been around for a long time, they were quite expensive or limited in functionality until very recently. Therefore, even a lot of experienced programmers never had to learn much about choosing a database for a particular need. For that reason, we feel it's worthwhile to review the basic factors that go into making such a decision.

You may not have a choice

Realistically, you may not have much of a choice. Many people are specifically looking for the fastest way to put their legacy database online, rather than enjoying the luxury of deciding on a scripting language first and choosing a database later.

Furthermore, decisions about OS, Web server, and programming languages can make some of your decision for you. A custom Java application on a "Big Iron" UNIX platform is just not going to mesh very smoothly with Microsoft SQL Server (in theory it's possible, but in practice you'd have to be a glutton for punishment — although the other way around isn't so bad). The bigger the system gets, the more constrained one's choices are likely to be by previous decisions.

The good news is that PHP is committed to supporting many databases and other back-end servers. It can help you knit up the loose ends of an architecture that has grown organically over time, as so many have. For instance, some functions in PHP exist solely to aid in porting your data over to a more modern database.

Flat-file, relational, object-relational

Databases are kind of like kitchen equipment: the simpler the tool, the more skilled the operator needs to be to achieve a great result. Expert chefs can produce gourmet fare using nothing but a very sharp knife and a few old pots and pans; whereas amateurs must whip out the Cuisinart and the Calphalon to produce similar results.

So it is with databases. It can get almost laughable to read people's arguments about the purported failings of this or that database, knowing that the skill of the individual user is reflected back by this piece of software more than almost any other. Suffice it to say that many technical masterpieces live in the simplest hash tables, while untold botched messes are simmering along on the latest and greatest object-oriented Java-enabled DBMS.

You can use three main types of databases with PHP: flat-file, relational, and object-relational.

Flat-file or hashing databases, such as Gnu DBM and Berkeley DB (a.k.a. Sleepycat DB2), are mostly used by or within other programs such as e-mail servers. They provide the lightest-weight and fastest means of storing and searching for data such as username/password pairs or dated e-mail messages.

These databases do not themselves create a representation of more complex relationships between data points. Instead, this is done by the accessing client program. Although the results can be extremely impressive, it all depends on your skill as a programmer.

The relational variety is now the most common type of database. People have different ideas of what constitutes a relational database, and we don't want to get pulled down into that particular definitional tar pit. Therefore, we're going to arbitrarily say that databases that speak fluent SQL are relational. Most of the popular databases commonly used with PHP are relational.

But there's relational and relational. Certain very popular commercial databases, such as Filemaker Pro and Microsoft Access, were not designed to be used on the back end of a production Web site. Although they have a certain level of ODBC support, and therefore PHP can in theory get data from them, they were mostly designed for ease of use rather than speed. Even worse, most users of these products refuse to avail themselves of what relational features there are, preferring to repeat text information in each entry rather than creating a separate table representing a relationship. Finally, these databases generally lack threading, locking, and other advanced features. There must be people out there trying Microsoft Access with PHP, because they post to PHP mailing lists and forums, but evidently not for public sites with significant traffic. (We do, however, know developers who use Access or Filemaker Pro as development tools on their laptops, so they can program on the airplane; and there are always porting and other projects using legacy data from these semi-relational databases.)

Finally there are object-oriented and object-relational databases, new and still developing models of data access. The object-oriented database is intended to work more smoothly with object-oriented programming languages; whereas the object-relational is a hybrid used for data types (such as astronomical and genetic data) that are not well served by ordinary relational databases. However, PHP is not itself wholly object-oriented and probably never will be, so it's hard to see why you'd select PHP as your scripting language of choice with one of these DBMSs. A good if dated overview of these types is available here:

```
http://www.cai.com/products/jasmine/analyst/idc/14821E.htm/
```

ODBC/JDBC versus native API

There are two generic standard APIs for database access: Open Database
Connectivity (ODBC), and Java Database Connectivity (JDBC). ODBC is closely
associated with Microsoft, and JDBC is even more closely associated with Sun.
Nevertheless, other companies have implemented these standards in their own
products, with the addition of specific drivers for each client program.

ODBC and JDBC are more or less mutually exclusive. Something called the "ODBC-
JDBC bridge" is used to allow Java programs to access ODBC databases, but it is
very slow. There are also proprietary drivers that do the same job more quickly.

There are also databases that clients can access through their own APIs rather than
ODBC or JDBC. This is invariably faster because there are fewer layers in the stack.
Most open source databases fall into this category. Some of these also have ODBC
or JDBC drivers. So for instance, PHP can access MySQL with a native API, whereas
a Java subsystem can use the same database via JDBC. Before you commit to any
multiple-access scheme, be very sure the drivers you need are available, affordable,
and maintainable.

Swappable databases

Although ODBC is slower than native APIs, it has the advantage of being an open
standard. Therefore, PHP code written with the ODBC commands will mostly work
with any ODBC-compliant database. This feature is very handy if you must start a
project with a database that you know will not scale, such as Microsoft Access, and
later switch to a more industrial-strength database. Although both are good products in their niches, it can be a lot of work to switch from a lightweight database
like Mini SQL (a.k.a. mSQL) to an enterprise-ready server suite like Oracle. (Again,
a good programmer who is given the time and resources can make any application
relatively easy to port while an inexperienced or rushed developer may not be able
to do so.)

Advanced Features to Look For

This section mentions specific SQL database features, with which you may not yet
be familiar. We're hoping you will instantly have a gut feeling, even from so brief a
description, if you truly need one or more of these features.

A GUI

Databases vary enormously in their user interface tools. Choices range from the
starkest command-line interactions to massive Java-powered development toolkits.

You pay for what you get, both in cash and in performance. Look for the lightest interface that meets your needs, because a GUI can add substantially to overhead costs.

One lower-cost alternative to the built-in GUI is Web interface. These are often custom developed, but there are also third-party products which may meet your needs. For instance, MySQL has several freely available Web-based interfaces which can be found by searching at Freshmeat (`www.freshmeat.net`).

Subquery

A *subquery* or *subselect* is an embedded select statement, like this:

```
SELECT * FROM table1 WHERE id IN (SELECT id FROM table2);
```

or this:

```
INSERT INTO table2[(col2, col3, col7)] SELECT lastname,
firstname, state FROM table1 WHERE col5 = NULL;
```

There are ways to work around a lack of subselects, and not everyone needs them. However, they can save some time if you consistently need to make large selects, inserts, and deletes.

Complex joins

A *join* is a way of searching for something across tables, by using shared values to match up the tables. The simplest form is:

```
SELECT textfield FROM table1,table2 WHERE table1.id=table2.id;
```

This yields the complete contents of whichever rows in the two tables share ID numbers. There are more specific and extensive types of joins, including left or right, straight or cross, inner and outer, and natural.

```
SELECT * from table1 LEFT JOIN table2 ON table1.id=table2.id
LEFT JOIN table3 ON table2.id=table3.id;
```

Joins are very handy and timesaving, sometimes well nigh essential; but in practice few need the more esoteric forms, so don't reject a database out of hand for lacking an outer cross join.

Threading and locking

Threading and *locking* are very important for multiple-tier sites and two-tier sites that have many contributors. They prevent two database calls from bumping into each other, so to speak, by giving editorial control to only a single transaction at a time.

An example that clearly illustrates the value of threading and locking is a Web site that sells tickets to popular rock concerts (assigned rather than "festival" seating). Obviously you would not want two people to be able to purchase the same seat at the same event due to a database error. The database needs some way to recognize unique requests and let only one user (or thread) make changes at any given moment.

Unless you're sure your project (a Web log, for instance) will have only one user at a time, be careful of committing to a nonthreaded database.

Transactional

This is a database design scheme that seeks to maximize data integrity.

The transactional paradigm relies on commits and rollbacks. Briefly, transactions that are concluded successfully will be committed to the database. Those that are not successfully concluded will be deleted, or the database will be "rolled back" to its previous condition. An e-commerce system might use rollbacks in situations where a customer's credit card is declined, choosing not to record anything about such purchase attempts. Rollbacks are also useful in the case of data corruption, as when a database server experiences a hardware failure.

An alternative data integrity design is called "atomic." Proponents of the atomic paradigm claim it is much faster and just as safe, but many users of transactional databases will prefer to stick to what they're comfortable with.

Procedures and triggers

Procedures are stored, precompiled queries or routines. A common procedure would be one that selects out all the e-mail addresses of customers who made purchases on a particular day. If you use the same select statements over and over, procedures can package them up in a handy way for you.

Triggers are procedures that occur when some tripwire event is registered by the database. Depending on the database, you could write a trigger to send an account statement e-mail to customers or associates of your site, and set it to go off at midnight every Sunday. Another handy use would be to send e-mail to the database administrator every time an error was registered. Relatively few databases use triggers, because they take a good deal of programmatic power and lots of extra cycles to track potential events.

Foreign keys and integrity constraints

The relational structure of a database is often implicit in the ways fields of one table refer to row IDs of another, but your database won't necessarily do anything helpful to make sure that structure is respected as changes are made. One way your database can help is via "cascading deletes" — automatically deleting rows that depend on other rows being deleted (this is sometimes implemented as a trigger). For example, if you delete a hospital patient record, you might want all the "orphaned" rows in the corresponding table of patient visits to automatically be deleted too. Alternatively, a database system can simply not permit the deletion of "parent" rows unless potential orphans are deleted first. Whether this kind of a constraint is a lifesaver or just an annoying restriction depends on how crucial it is that the relational structure be completely reliable and consistent.

Database replication

As your data store expands, you will need to think about scaling up. For a certain amount of time, one can just move the database server to faster machines with more processors and bigger disks — but sooner or later a growing database will need to be replicated on more than one server.

To do this, there must be some means of automatically keeping the different servers synched up. This usually involves a journaling system, and often a "master-slave" relationship between database servers. One database is designated the "master," and all new data is inserted into it. A journal keeps track of these changes in chronological order. All the other servers are "slaves," which serve up data rather than taking it in. They periodically read the master journal and make the same changes in themselves.

The next step up is some kind of failover mechanism, by which a "slave" can become the "master" database server if the "master" goes down. Think carefully about how bombproof your data needs to be, as this type of safety is expensive.

PHP-Supported Databases

If you've never chosen a database before, the large choice of PHP-supported products can be dizzying at first. The table below will give you a first-glance introduction to the various databases most easily available to PHP users, with notes on drivers and licensing. For more information (which we couldn't fit in this table), please see our Web site at:

```
http://www.troutworks.com/phpbook
```

Table 16-1
PHP-Supported Databases

Database	Type	Support	Platform	License	Notes
Adabas D	R	ODBC (deprecated)	U, W	C	German, distributed with SuSE Linux
DBA/DBM	FF	Abstraction layer	U	OS	Sleepycat, Gnu DBM, cdb
dBase	P	Import only	W	C	No SQL
Empress	R	ODBC	U, W	C	Enterprise, JDBC driver avail.
filepro	P	Import only	U, W	C	Not for production
IBM DB2	R	ODBC	U, W	C	Enterprise, JDBC driver avail.
Informix	R	Native	U, W	C	Enterprise
Interbase	R	Native	U, W	C	Enterprise, JDBC driver avail.
MS Access	R	ODBC	W	C	Not for production
MS SQL Server	R	Native	W	C	Enterprise?
mSQL	R	Native	U	Sh	Very small
MySQL	R	Native	U, W	C, Sh	Several licenses
Oracle	O-R	Native	U, W	C	Enterprise
Oracle8	R	Native	U, W	C	Enterprise, Java integration
PostgreSQL	O-R	Native	U	OS	Commercial support
Solid	R	ODBC (deprecated)	U, W	C	Embedded db, Finnish company
Sybase	R	Native	U, W	C	Enterprise

Our Focus: MySQL

We, like most every other team who has ever written a book about PHP, love MySQL and will use it in all the upcoming examples in Part II. MySQL is quite likely the fastest, cheapest, simplest, most reliable database that also has most of the features you'd want and—this is the real differentiator—comes in more or less equally good UNIX and Windows implementations. There's just an ineffable synergy between PHP and MySQL (especially on the Linux/Apache platform), recently recognized by the development teams, who have announced plans to move the products even closer together.

However, we run straightforward content sites and therefore don't need some of the more sophisticated features offered by PostgreSQL or Oracle. If you need an object-relational or transactional database, PHP can still accommodate you for most of your basic needs. However, PHP may not be philosophically aligned with all your high-end desires.

Because the PHP developers generally use standardized function names and MySQL supports a relatively small set of SQL constructs, it should be easy to apply our examples to other databases by searching for and changing the function names to those of your chosen database: instead of `mysql_query`, you would use `mssql_query` and so forth.

Summary

The great advantage of the Web is its ability to make large quantities of information publicly available quickly and cheaply. This functionality has been tremendously enhanced by the recent increase in availability of inexpensive, reliable databases.

Since many experienced programmers may never have had to choose a database before, we describe some of the basic points that should be taken into account in the decision-making process. These include the basic database design (flat-file, relational, or object-relational), the API or driver, and ease of future porting. Optional features, such as transactions or a graphical interface, may also figure into the choice of database. PHP supports many databases of a variety of types, so you have an excellent chance of finding exactly the feature set you need.

✦   ✦   ✦

SQL Tutorial

This chapter is a basic introduction to SQL databases in which we discuss standards, database design, data manipulation language, data definition language, and database security procedures common to all SQL databases.

However, this chapter is in no way a comprehensive guide to SQL or to any particular SQL database. To go beyond the simplest common features, you will need to consult your particular manufacturer's documentation and/or specific books. A couple of popular guides to SQL in general are:

> *SQL for Dummies* by Allen G. Taylor (IDG Books 1998)
>
> *The Practical SQL Handbook* by Judith S. Bowman, Sandra L. Emerson, and Marcy Darnovsky (Addison-Wesley 1996)

You will also want to look at documentation and books relating to your specific SQL database.

SQL Standards

According to Andrew Taylor, original inventor of SQL, SQL does not stand for "Structured Query Language" (or anything else for that matter). But for the rest of the world, it does now. As you would expect from the (non-)title, SQL represents a stricter and more general method of data storage than the previous standard of flat-file dbm-style databases.

SQL is a standard under both ANSI and ECMA. You can read the standards on payment of a fee to these organizations:

```
http://www.ansi.org
http://www.ecma.org
```

However, within the general guidelines of the standard there is very considerable difference between the products of individual companies and open source database development organizations. The past few years, for instance, have seen the rapid growth of so-called "object-relational" databases as well as SQL products specifically slanted toward the Web market.

SQL standards

Basic SQL statements

Designing SQL databases

Using SQL connections

Privileges and security

The key to choosing a database is to be selfish, or at least supremely self-centered. You will see plenty of unusually virulent postings out there opining that a certain advanced database feature (like rollbacks or cross joins) is a "must" and any SQL installation without this feature hardly deserves the name. Take this stuff with a grain of salt. It's far better to make a blind shopping list of functions you need in order of importance, and then go out looking for the product that best meets your requirements.

That said, a good deal of SQL really is pretty standardized. There are a few statements that you will be using over and over and over, no matter which specific product you choose to deploy.

The Workhorses of SQL

The basic logical structure of a SQL database is very simple. A given SQL installation can contain multiple databases — for instance, one for customer data and one for product data. (There's the problem that both the SQL server itself and the collections of tables within it are commonly referred to by the term "database" — but what can you do?) Each database contains a number of tables. Each table is made up of carefully defined columns, and every entry can be thought of as an added row.

Four so-called data manipulation statements are supported by every SQL server and will constitute an extremely high percentage of all the things you'll want to do with a relational database. These four horsemen of the database are SELECT, INSERT, UPDATE, and DELETE. These commands are your friends and helpmates; get comfy with them, and they will serve you well.

The thing to remember about these four SQL statements is that they only manipulate database *values,* not the structure of the database itself. In other words, you can use these commands to add data but not to make a database; and you can get rid of every piece of data in a database, but the shell will still be there — so, for instance, you wouldn't be able to name another database on the same server with the same name. If you want to add or get rid of columns, blow away entire databases as if they never existed, or make up new databases, you need to use other commands such as DROP, ALTER, and CREATE.

SELECT

SELECT is the main command you need to get information out of a SQL database. The basic syntax is extremely simple:

```
SELECT field1, field2, field3 FROM table WHERE condition;
```

That's no harder than asking your coworker to get you last month's sales records from the file cabinet in the hallway.

In some cases, you'll want to ask for entire rows instead of picking out individual pieces of information. This practice is deprecated for very good reasons (it may be slower than requesting just the data you need, and it can lead to problems if you redesign the table), but it is still used and therefore we need to mention it. A whole row is called for by using the star or asterisk symbol:

```
SELECT * FROM my_table WHERE my_date = 01-05-2000;
```

Joins

There's only one thing about SELECT statements that is even slightly taxing: *joins*. Because joins are one of the main useful features of SQL, we should explain them in some detail here.

A SELECT statement on a single table without joins is easily imagined as being something like a row in a spreadsheet. This is not really how the data are stored or arranged in a SQL database, but for this purpose it's a handy visualization device.

But a SQL database is by definition relational. To understand the relational database concept, you have to think back to some occasion on which you were forced to fill out a whole bunch of forms — such as applying for a loan, visiting a doctor's office for the first time, or dealing with some kind of governmental formality. (If you've never had this experience, it's because you're young enough to have lived entirely in a world of relational databases). As you were writing down your name, address, phone, and social security number for the fifteenth time, you probably thought, "Why can't I just write this stuff down once, and then they could refer to it on a need-to-know basis." That's exactly the concept behind a relational database.

Where a relational database differs from paper forms is the main identifier. Humans do well with text and prefer to categorize by textual identifiers such as names. If a dentist's office or auto body shop stored their paper files in numerical order, it would be difficult for them to lay their hands on John Johnson's forms when he next required service. Frankly, most paper file users these days ask for your social security number as a backup — it works solely to differentiate you from other people in their files with exactly the same first, last, and middle names.

Databases, on the other hand, work fastest with integers. Because integers are unique by nature, a database only needs one to identify a person, place, or thing uniquely no matter how many tables refer to that piece of information.

So instead of needing to repeat information several times, like this:

```
Name:  John Johnson
SS#:   123-45-6789

Name:  John Johnson
Fears:  Cats, Friday the 13th, Flying
```

```
Name:  Jane Jones
SS#:   987-65-4321

Name:  Jane Jones
Fears: Heights, Flying
```

with a relational database you can write down each piece of information just once and then relate it to each other piece, as shown in Tables 17-1 to 17-3.

Table 17-1 People		
PersonID	Name	SS#
1	John Johnson	123-45-6789
2	Jane Jones	987-65-4321
3	Jerry Johnston	564-73-8291

Table 17-2 Fears	
FearID	Fear
1	Black cats
2	Friday the 13th
3	Water
4	Heights
5	Flying

Table 17-3 Person_Fear		
ID	PersonID	FearID
1	1	1
2	1	2
3	1	5
4	2	4
5	2	5

This is clearly a neater and faster (for a database) way to store this information. But when you need to pull out the data into a human-readable form, there's a problem: you have to get and correlate information from more than one database. That's the job of a join.

To find out what phobias were suffered by Ms. Jones, you could first look up her personal unique ID,

```
SELECT PersonID FROM People WHERE Name = 'Jane Jones';
```

which would return the unique integer 2. Then you can define another SELECT statement using that information:

```
SELECT Fear FROM Fears WHERE Person_Fear.PersonID = 2 AND
Person_Fear.FearID = Fears.FearID;
```

This will return the values Heights and Flying.

Alternatively, you can perform a join which will return the same information in a single SELECT statement:

```
SELECT Fear FROM People, Fears WHERE Name = 'Jane Jones' AND
People.PersonID = Person_Fear.PersonID AND Person_Fear.FearID =
Fears.FearID;
```

As you can see, you need only know one single piece of information to be able to get all the data in the database about that subject using joins. In effect, a join makes two or more tables into one for purposes of searching for a particular piece of information.

Joins come in several different flavors. The one in the preceding example is called a straight join, which is the most common type. If you need to make complex and frequent joins, this will severely constrain the brand of SQL database you can use, because not all of them support every type of join.

Subselects

Before we leave the realm of SELECT statements, we should mention the *subselect*. This is a statement such as:

```
SELECT phone_number FROM table WHERE name = 'SELECT name FROM
table2 WHERE ID = 1';
```

Subselects are more of a convenience than a necessity. They can be very handy if you're working with enormous batches of data; but you can get the same result with two simpler selects (although this will be somewhat slower, even in PHP 4).

INSERT

The command you need to put new data into a database is INSERT. The basic syntax here is:

```
INSERT INTO table (col1, col2, col3) VALUES(val1, val2, val3);
```

Obviously the columns and their values need to match up; if you mix up your array items, nothing good will happen. If some of the rows will not have values for some of the fields, you will need to use an empty, null, or auto-incremented value—and, at a deeper level, you may need to have ensured beforehand that fields can be nullable or auto-incrementable. If this is not possible, you should simply leave out any columns you wish to default to an empty value in an INSERT statement.

A twist on the basic INSERT is the INSERT INTO...SELECT. This just means you can INSERT the results of a SELECT statement:

```
INSERT INTO customer(birthmonth, birthflower, birthstone)
SELECT * FROM birthday_info WHERE birthmonth = $birthmonth;
```

However, not every SQL database has this capability. Also, you need to be careful with this command because you can cause problems for yourself quite easily. In general, it's not a good idea to select from the same database you're inserting into.

UPDATE

UPDATE is used to edit information already in the database, without deleting any significant amount. In other words, you can selectively change some information without having to delete an entire old record and insert a new one. The syntax is:

```
UPDATE table SET field1='val1', field2='val2', field3='val3'
WHERE condition;
```

The conditional statement is just like a SELECT condition, such as WHERE ID=15 or WHERE gender='F'.

DELETE

DELETE is pretty self-explanatory: you use it to delete information permanently from the database. The syntax is:

```
DELETE datapoint FROM table WHERE condition;
```

The most important thing to remember is the condition—if you don't set one, you will delete every entry in the specified columns from the database, without a confirmation or a second chance in many cases.

Caution
Let us take a moment to re-emphasize: you *must* remember to use a condition every single time you update or delete. If you do not, every single row in the table will experience the same alteration or deletion. Even very experienced programmers have forgotten the condition, to their vast professional embarrassment. You should also give a good deal of thought to restricting database permissions so the minimum number of people can perform these potentially dangerous operations.

Database Design

As should be obvious from the previous section, learning to use a SQL database isn't exactly rocket science — you can get a lot done with just a few simple commands. The hard part is designing the database in the first place, and of course operating it in the real world over time.

At the most fundamental level, database design can be broken down into the following mantra cum children's jingle:

```
One to one,
One to many,
Many to many,
Many to one;
And always use a unique ID.
```

An example of one to one data for Americans is the Social Security Number (other nations probably have similar identification cards with unique numbers) — each U.S. citizen will have only one unique identifier, and it is in fact a crime to use the Social Security number of another individual. Database designers seize upon truly unique identifiers such as this, since almost every other piece of personal information is subject to change — which accounts for the large number of businesses who inappropriately use the Social Security number for identification purposes.

Many-to-one and one-to-many data are the same, differing only in how the columns are placed in a database. An example of one to many data comes from the medical realm: patients to visits. Each patient will always be a discrete individual, but may have any number of visits to the doctor. If you designed the table to represent visits to patients, it would instantly become many to one data.

Finally, many to many data is well represented by the relationship of authors to books. Not only can a given book have multiple authors; but each author may have written or co-authored many books. This is not a matrix of relationships that would be easy to represent efficiently in a spreadsheet, but it is precisely this category of data at which relational databases most excel.

Every data relationship falls into one of these categories. As a database designer, it's your job to decide which one of these represents what you need to know in the way you need to know it.

This is not as trivial as it sounds. For instance, imagine you want to develop a database of movie information. One decision you might have to make is whether "movie" and "title" are in a one-to-one relationship with each other, or whether enough films have alternate titles to merit an "alternate title" field or even a one-to-many representation. There's no right answer here — the decision depends on exactly how the information will be used, how large the database will be, if the extra resources required to maintain a more precise data structure are worth the cost, and whether there's a better-than-even chance that today's tangential trivia will become tomorrow's crucial discovery. Some people may be surprised to learn that archiving information can be as much about ruthless excluding as about careful hoarding. As historians say, history is about forgetting as much as it is about remembering.

The simplest relationship is the one-to-one, because you can group all of these fields into a single table that can be searched more quickly. For instance, a table holding customer information might contain the following fields:

```
Customer ID
Customer name
Administrative contact
Technical contact
```

The hardest thing about the one-to-one relationship is definitively deciding that you will never need to make it into a one-to-many relationship.

However, as soon as you have a one-to-many, many-to-one, or many-to-many relationship, you're looking at going from a single table to multiple tables: one each for the main variables, and one stating the relationship. Tables 17-4 through 17-6 show a common example of a many-to-many relationship.

Table 17-4 Customer	
Customer_id	*Name*
1	Acme Bread
2	Baker Construction
3	Coolee Dam

Table 17-5
Interactions

Interaction_id	Type
1	Phone support incident
2	On-site incident
3	Written complaint
4	Phone complaint
5	Kudo

Table 17-6
Customer-interaction

Customer-interaction_id	Customer_id	Interaction_id
1	1	1
2	3	5
3	2	4
4	2	3
5	1	2

Once you've decided on a database design, the mechanical details of constructing the database are minimal. The main data structure statements of SQL are CREATE, ALTER, and DROP.

CREATE is used to make a completely new database or table. Actually creating a database amounts to little more than naming it.

```
CREATE DATABASE db_name;
```

All the work is in defining the tables and their columns. First you declare the name of the table, and then you must detail the specific types of that table's columns in what is called a "create definition."

```
CREATE TABLE table (
   ->id_col INT NOT NULL AUTO_INCREMENT PRIMARY KEY,
   ->col1 TEXT NULL INDEX,
   ->col2 DATE NOT NULL
);
```

Different SQL servers have slightly different data types and definition options, so the syntax of one may not transfer exactly to another.

DROP can be used to completely delete a table or database and all its associated data. It's not the most subtle command:

```
DROP TABLE table;
DROP DATABASE db_name
```

Obviously you need to be very careful with this statement.

ALTER is the way to change a table's structure. You simply indicate which table you're changing, and redefine its specs. Again, SQL products differ in subtlety here.

```
ALTER TABLE table RENAME AS new_table;
ALTER TABLE new_table ADD COLUMN col3 VARCHAR(50);
ALTER TABLE new_table DROP COLUMN col2;
```

Using Database Connections

The main thing to remember about PHP-SQL connections is that all data must be fetched one row at a time. It's a pretty narrow pipe, so it behooves you to bring over the minimum number of rows that will give you the desired result. That means eschewing sloppy queries that return a lot of rows that you'll have to sort through later.

PHP and SQL are optimized for different tasks. For instance, arranging many rows of data by alphabetical order of one field value is very much faster and easier in SQL than in PHP. Filtering is another area in which SQL is tremendously more efficient than PHP: learning to write good conditional SELECT statements is far more meaningful than performing PHP loop-de-loops after fetching the data. SQL servers can perform far fewer tricks, but they can't be beaten on the ones they do.

For more information on optimizing PHP-SQL interactions, see Chapter 23, "PHP/Database Efficiency and Style."

Privileges and Security

As we state in Chapter 31 "Security and Cryptography," security online is analogous to security in the real world. Any cop will tell you that you cannot make your home absolutely crime-proof. A more realistic goal is to increase the difficulty and risk to a level where a large percentage of intruders will choose to go to an easier target down the block.

Using a database with PHP can be similar to using two locks on your front door, substantially enhancing the safety of your site — but only if you follow a few elementary rules of database hygiene. PHP makes many of these techniques a little easier to implement, which means you have a little less reason to skimp on security.

Setting permissions

The most fundamental rule of database use is to give each user or group only the minimum permissions necessary to do what needs to be done. You wouldn't let a stranger walk into your house and kick back in your bedroom and read your diary — so why should you give them the option to do analogous things on your site? It's a little more work to manage multiple users and make sure all the permissions are set to the right levels at all times; but if that tiny pinprick of pain can prevent a massive infection later, you'd be extremely foolish to refuse this simple but effective prophylaxis.

Besides the threat of malicious/experimental outsiders, setting the correct permissions can protect you from yourself. Insiders have been known to cause massive problems through disgruntlement, ignorance, or a combination of motives. You do not want to have to cope with the consequences of a fired employee's parting shot, or a new intern "trying out" the DROP database command just to see what happens.

A typical database permissions package might be something like:

- ✦ Web visitor: SELECT only
- ✦ Contributor: SELECT, INSERT, maybe UPDATE
- ✦ Editor: SELECT, INSERT, UPDATE, maybe DELETE, maybe GRANT
- ✦ Root: SELECT, INSERT, UPDATE, DELETE, GRANT, DROP

DROP in particular is the nuclear bomb of SQL because it allows you to blow away an entire database with a single command. Someone's got to have the ability, but heavy lies the tiara of responsibility on the head of the root database user. Use the power wisely, grasshopper.

In many databases, including MySQL, passwords are encrypted using a different algorithm from system passwords (and of course they are typically stored in entirely different locations). Even if one is cracked, the other is not necessarily vulnerable. This assumes you take the time to set permissions correctly, pick good passwords, and usually employ a special command to insert usernames and passwords correctly into the grant table (as opposed to inserting them like other data).

Tip   Database usernames and passwords should not be identical to systems usernames and passwords. Never ever *ever* set any database password to the root system user's password! If crackers should happen to get into your database via Web scripts, you don't want to offer them the key to the whole system.

Keep database passwords in a different location

It's a good idea to separate passwords from the files that use them. With PHP's INCLUDE and REQUIRE functions, it's very easy to drop in text (such as database passwords) from another file at run time. Remember that these INCLUDE files do not have to be in a PHP- or Web server-enabled directory! Whenever possible, keep them somewhere outside your Web tree, such as in your home directory.

Taking the database variables out of PHP files is also good for other reasons. If you have many PHP scripts using the same database, they can all use the same password file. When you suspect the password has been compromised, or when you change the password on a regular schedule, you need only alter one script for all the files to be updated.

The unavoidable downside of this technique is that the file must be *readable* by the Apache user. Because the Apache user and the database user are seldom the same, that means in practice the file must be world-readable. This should still be safer than keeping the database variables inside a public Web root directory.

If you have a set of database variables you use infrequently — a configuration script or the like — you can keep it in a non-Apache-readable directory and change the permissions only on the rare occasions necessary. For instance, we infrequently have to go to the trouble to delete postings from our sites' forums; so it's easier to keep this file in a non-Apache-user-owned directory and once in awhile change the permissions just long enough to delete the offending post, then immediately change everything back.

If for whatever reason you decide to put your database username, password, hostname, and database name into a PHP script in plain text, this is what you can expect. If the httpd is functioning normally, the database passwords should be as safe as any file on that server — which is to say, not extremely. But if the daemon goes down, there is some chance your raw PHP (including plain-text database variables) will be delivered in a human-readable form. You can reduce this risk by avoiding the use of the ".html" suffix for PHP files.

In PHP3, if database connectivity went down and you hadn't specified "silent mode," you would see something like the following:

```
Warning: MySQL Connection Failed: Access denied for user:
'someuser@localhost' (Using password: NO) in
/home/web/html/mysqltest.php3
on line 2
```

This constituted a security breach, because it revealed your MySQL username and whether or not you used a password. In PHP 4, MySQL error messages are no longer displayed by default. Two new functions, mysql_errno() and mysql_error(), allow you to opt for error codes or text warnings — but now you have to deliberately choose to ask for the information. Because in most cases you can opt for the more configurable die() instead, or remove error messages after debugging, it's still not a good idea to use mysql_error on a public production server.

Use a PHP form to check passwords

Belt and braces types can apply even another layer of database protection to their PHP scripts by means of another round of usernames and passwords stored in the database itself, which you can check directly from the PHP script. So you would have your systems login/password, plus database user permissions stored in a non-Web-accessible directory, plus a PHP name/passphrase testing script with values entered by hand just before the script is run.

```
<HTML>
<BODY>
<FORM METHOD=POST ACTION="<?php print("form_check.php"); ?>">
<P>Username:  <INPUT TYPE="TEXT" SIZE=20 NAME="try_user"></P>
<P>Password:  <INPUT TYPE="PASSWORD" SIZE=10
NAME="try_pass"></P>
<P>Date:  <INPUT TYPE="TEXT" SIZE=10 NAME="try_date"></P>
<P>Entry:<BR>
<TEXTAREA COLS=50 ROWS=10 NAME="try_entry"></TEXTAREA></P>
<P><INPUT TYPE="SUBMIT"></P>
</BODY>
</HTML>

form_check.php
<?php
// Check database user
include("/home/Webvars.inc");
mysql_connect($hostname, $db_user, $password);
// Check form user
mysql_select_db("Weblog");
$query = ("SELECT password FROM finalcheck WHERE
user='$try_user'");
$result = mysql_query($query);
$passcheck = mysql_fetch_array($result);
if($passcheck[0] == $try_pass)
    {
    /* Enter new entry. */
    $query = ("INSERT INTO log (ID, date, entry) VALUES(NULL,
'$try_date', '$try_entry')");
    $result = mysql_query($query);
    print("New entry result is $result.");
    }
```

```
else
    {
    mail("security@localhost", "Weblog database alert",
"Someone from $REMOTE_ADDR is trying to get into your Weblog
entry screen.");
    }
?>
```

As you can see from this example, this script will not insert anything into the
database if username and password are not provided or the user isn't logged
into the localhost. You will also get an e-mail message warning you of a possible
breach attempt.

Learn to make backups

And finally, the biggest part of security may be backing up. Take an hour to learn
the best way to back up data in your particular database (for example, via the `dump`
command in MySQL), and then schedule regular backups right away. Even better,
with a little foresight you can also set up an automatic database backup schedule.

Summary

SQL is not rocket science. The four basic data manipulation statements supported
by essentially all SQL databases are SELECT, INSERT, UPDATE, and DELETE. SELECT
gets data out of the database, INSERT puts in a new entry, UPDATE edits pieces of
the entry in place, and DELETE gets rid of a whole entry.

Designing databases is where most of the difficulty lies. The designer must think
long and hard about the best way to represent each piece of data and relationship
for the intended use. Well-designed databases are a pleasure to program with, while
poorly designed ones can leave you pulling your hair out while contemplating
numerous connections and icky joins.

SQL databases are created by so-called data structure statements. The most
important of these are CREATE, ALTER, and DROP. As one would expect, CREATE
DATABASE creates a new database and CREATE TABLE defines a new table within a
database. ALTER changes the structure of a table. DROP is the nuclear bomb of SQL
commands, since it entirely deletes whole tables or databases.

Good database design is also a security issue. By employing reasonable prophylactic
measures, a SQL database can enhance the security of your site. The best defense
against intrusion, of course, is maintaining a strict backup schedule — so every new
SQL maintainer should learn the most efficient way to make backups.

✦   ✦   ✦

PHP/MySQL Functions

Once you've designed and set up your MySQL database, you can begin to write PHP scripts that interact with it. Here we will try to explain all the basic functions that enable you to pass data back and forth from Web site to database.

Connecting to MySQL

The basic command to initiate a MySQL connection is:

```
mysql_connect($hostname, $user, $password);
```

if you're using variables, or

```
mysql_connect('localhost', 'root', 'sesame');
```

if you're using literal strings.

The password is optional, depending on whether this particular database user requires one (it's a good idea). If not, just leave that variable off. You can also specify a port and socket for the server ($hostname:*port*:*socket*), but unless you've specifically chosen a nonstandard port and socket, there's little to gain by doing so.

Next, you'll want to choose a database to work on:

```
mysql_select_db($database);
```

if you're using variables, or

```
mysql_select_db('phpbook');
```

if you're using a literal string.

You must select a database each time you make a connection, which means at least once per page, or every time you change databases. Otherwise, you'll get a "database not selected" error. Even if you've only created one database per daemon, you must do this, because MySQL also comes with default databases (called mysql and test) you might not be taking into account.

 Note You will sometimes see these two functions used with a '@' prepended, such as "@mysql_select_db($database)." This symbol denotes silent mode, meaning the function will not return any message on failure, as a security precaution.

Now that you've established a connection, you're ready to make a query.

Making MySQL Queries

A database query from PHP is basically a MySQL command wrapped up in a tiny PHP function called mysql_query(). This is where you use the basic SQL workhorses of SELECT, INSERT, UPDATE, and DELETE that we discussed in the previous chapter. The MySQL commands to CREATE or DROP a table (but *not*, thankfully, a database) can also be used with this PHP function if you do not wish to make your databases using the MySQL client.

You could write a query in the simplest possible way, like this,

```
mysql_query("SELECT Surname FROM personal_info WHERE ID<10");
```

PHP would dutifully try to execute it. However, there are very good reasons to split up this and similar commands into two lines with extra variables, like this:

```
$query = "INSERT INTO personal_info (ID, Surname, Name,
Occupation) VALUES (NULL, 'Adams', 'Sam', 'Patriot Brewer')";
$result = mysql_query($query);
```

The main rationale is that the extra variable gives you a handle on an extremely valuable piece of information. Every MySQL query gives you a receipt whether you succeed or not — sort of like a cash machine when you try to withdraw money. If things go well, you hardly need or notice the receipt — you can throw it away without a qualm. But if a problem occurs, the receipt will give you a clue as to what might have gone wrong, similar to the "is the machine not dispensing or is your account overdrawn?" type of message that might be printed on your ATM receipt.

The function `mysql_query` takes as arguments the query string (which should not have a semicolon within the double quotes) and optionally a link identifier. Unless you have multiple connections, you don't need the link identifier. It returns a TRUE (nonzero) integer value if the query was executed successfully *even if no rows were affected*. It returns a FALSE integer if the query was illegal or not properly executed for some other reason.

If your query was an INSERT, UPDATE, DELETE, CREATE TABLE, or DROP TABLE and returned TRUE, you can now use `mysql_affected_rows` to see how many rows were changed by the query. This function optionally takes a link identifier, only necessary if you are using multiple connections.

```
$affected_rows = mysql_affected_rows();
```

If your query was a SELECT statement, the integer returned will have a slightly different meaning: instead of being TRUE or FALSE, it returns an integer called a *result identifier*. This is a unique identifier for each SELECT, generally incremented from 1 beginning with the first such statement in each script. You cannot use the `mysql_affected_rows` function with a SELECT, because no rows were changed. Instead, you can use `mysql_num_rows($result)` to find out how many rows were returned by a successful SELECT.

Tip   Instead of using `mysql_select_db` and `mysql_query`, you can combine the two into one function: `mysql_db_query($db, $query)`. This function returns values similar to `mysql_query`.

Fetching Data Sets

One thing that often seems to temporarily stymie new PHP users is the whole concept of fetching data from PHP. It would be logical to assume the result of a query would be the desired data, but that is not correct. As we discussed previously, the result of a PHP query is an integer representing the success or failure or identity of the query.

What actually happens is that a `mysql_query()` or `mysql_db_query()` command pulls the data out of the database and sends a receipt back to PHP reporting on the status of the operation. At this point, the data exists in a purgatory that is immediately accessible from neither MySQL nor PHP — you can think of it as a staging area of sorts. The data is there, but it's waiting for the commanding officer to give the order to deploy. It requires one of the `mysql_fetch` functions to make the data fully available to PHP.

The fetching functions are:

   ✦ `mysql_fetch_row`: Returns row as enumerated array

   ✦ `mysql_fetch_object`: Returns row as object

✦ mysql_fetch_array: Returns row as associative array

✦ mysql_result: Returns one cell of data

Caution

In our humble opinions, the functions mysql_fetch_field and mysql_ fetch_lengths are misleadingly named. They both provide information *about* database entries rather than the entry values themselves. For instance, one might expect a function named mysql_fetch_field to be a quick way to fetch a single-field result set (the ID associated with a particular username, for instance), but that is not the case at all. The actual purpose of these functions is explained in the chart at the end of this chapter—but for the moment, the point is not to be misled into thinking these functions will return database values.

The difference between the three main fetching functions is small. The most general one is mysql_fetch_row, which can be used something like this:

```
$query = "SELECT ID, LastName, FirstName FROM users WHERE
Status = 1";
$result = mysql_query($query);
while(list($ID, $LastName, $FirstName) =
mysql_fetch_row($result))
   print("$ID $LastName $FirstName)<BR>\n");
```

This code will output the specified rows from the database, each line containing one row or the information associated with a unique ID (if any).

Tip

In an enumerated array, the integers in brackets are called *field offsets.* Remember that they always begin with the integer zero. If you start counting at 1, you will miss the value of your first column.

The function mysql_fetch_object performs much the same task, except the row is returned as an object rather than an array. Obviously this is helpful for those among the PHP brethren who utilize the object-oriented notation:

```
$query = "SELECT ID, LastName, FirstName FROM users WHERE Status
= 1";
$result = mysql_query($query);
while($row = mysql_fetch_object($result))
   echo $row->ID $row->LastName $row->FirstName;
```

The most useful fetching function, mysql_fetch_array, offers the choice of results as an associative or an enumerated array – or both, which is the default. This means you can refer to outputs by database field name rather than number:

```
$query = "SELECT ID, LastName, FirstName FROM users WHERE
Status = 1";
$result = mysql_query($query);
while($row = mysql_fetch_array($result))
   echo$row["ID"] $row["LastName"] $row["FirstName"] ."<BR>\n";
```

Remember that `mysql_fetch_array` can *also* be used exactly the same way as `mysql_fetch_row`—with numerical identifiers rather than field names. By using this function, you leave yourself the option. If you want to specify offset or field name rather than making both available, you can do it like this:

```
$offset_row = mysql_fetch_array($result, MYSQL_NUM);
or
$associative_row = mysql_fetch_array($result, MYSQL_ASSOC);
```

It's also possible to use MYSQL_BOTH as the second value, but since that's the default it's redundant.

In early versions of PHP 3, `mysql_fetch_row` was considered to be significantly faster than `mysql_fetch_object` and `mysql_fetch_array`, but this is no longer an issue, as the speed differences have become imperceptible. The PHP junta now recommends use of `mysql_fetch_array` over `mysql_fetch_row` because it offers increased functionality and choice at little cost in terms of programming difficulty, performance loss, or maintainability.

Last and least of the fetching functions is `mysql_result()`. You should only even *consider* using this function in situations where you are positive you need only one piece of data to be returned from MySQL. An example of its usage:

```
$query = "SELECT Surname FROM personal_info WHERE ID = 255";
$db_result = mysql_query($query);
$datapoint = mysql_result($db_result, 0, 0);
```

The `mysql_result` function takes three arguments: result identifier, row identifier, and (optionally) field. Field can take the value of the field offset as above, or its name as in an associative array ("Surname"), or its MySQL field-dot-table name ("Surname.personal_info"). Use the offset if at all possible, as it is substantially faster than the other two. Even better, don't use this function with any frequency.

Caution   You should never use `mysql_result()` to return information that is available to you through a predefined PHP-MySQL function. The classic no-no is inserting a row and then selecting out its ID number (extra demerits if you select on MAX(ID)!). Wicked bad style—use `mysql_insert_id()` instead.

A special MySQL function can be used with any of the fetching functions to more specifically designate the row number desired. This is `mysql_data_seek`, which takes as arguments the result identifier and a row number, and moves the internal row pointer to that row of the data set. The most common use of this function is to reiterate through a result set from the beginning by re-setting the row number to zero, similar to an array reset. This obviates another expensive database call to get data you already have sitting around on the PHP side.

```php
<?php
echo("<TABLE>\n<TR><TH>Titles</TH></TR>\n<TR>");
$query = "SELECT title, publisher FROM books";
$result = mysql_query($query);
while($book_row = mysql_fetch_array($result))
{
   echo("<TD>$book_row[0]</TD>\n");
}
echo("</TR></TABLE><BR>\n");
echo("<TABLE>\n<TR><TH>Publishers</TH></TR>\n<TR>");
mysql_data_seek($result, 0)
while($book_row = mysql_fetch_array($result)
{
   echo("<TD>$book_row[1]</TD>\n");
}
echo("</TR></TABLE><BR>\n");
?>
```

Getting Data about Data

You only need three or four PHP functions to put information into a preexisting MySQL database and get it out again: mysql_connect, mysql_db_query (or mysql_select_db plus mysql_query), and mysql_fetch_array. Most of the rest of the functions in this section are about getting information about the data you put into or took out of the database, or about the construction of the database itself. For instance, there are built-in functions to help you learn the name of the table in which your data resides, the data type handled by a particular column, or the number of the row into which you just inserted data.

Obviously you don't want J. Random Hacker to be able to find out everything about the structure and contents of your database for the asking. If you have scripts that use these functions extensively—for instance, some kind of Web database-administration tool—you need a higher level of security. Make sure only the root MySQL user can use these tools, and preferably use forms to pass in a password every time, or one of the methods to limit usage to certain IP addresses.

The MySQL metadata functions fall into two major categories:

✦ Functions that return information about the previous operation only

✦ Functions that return information about the database structure in general

A very commonly used example of the first type is mysql_insert_id(), which returns the autoincremented ID assigned to a row of data you just inserted. A commonly used example of the second type is mysql_field_type(), which reveals whether a particular database field's data must be an integer, a varchar, text, or what have you.

Most of the data-about-data functions are pretty self-explanatory. There are a couple of things to keep in mind when using them, though. First, most of these functions are only effective if used in the proper combination—don't try to use a `mysql_affected_rows` after an SELECT query and then wonder what went wrong. Second, be careful about security with the functions that return information about your database structure. Knowing the name and structure of each table is very valuable to a hacker. And finally, be aware that some of these functions are shopping baskets full of simpler functions. If you need several pieces of information about a particular result set or database, it could be faster to use `mysql_fetch_field` than all of the `mysql_field` functions one after the other.

Multiple Connections

Unless you have a specific reason to require multiple connections, you only need to make one database connection per PHP page. Even if you escape into HTML many times within the page, your connection is still good (assuming it was good in the first place). You do not want to make multiple connections if you don't have to, because that is one of the most costly and time-consuming parts of most database queries.

The main reason you would need to use different connections is if you're querying two or more completely separate databases. This is a somewhat rare usage, but one PHP can handle. You simply open connections to each database as needed, and make sure to hang on to the right result sets. PHP will help you do this, by utilizing the result identifiers discussed previously. You pass them along with each MySQL function as an optional argument. If you're completing all your queries on one connection before moving on to the next, you don't even need to do this; PHP will automatically use the last link opened.

```php
<?php
$link1 = mysql_connect('host1', 'me', 'sesame');
mysql_select_db('userdb', $link1);
$query1 = "SELECT ID FROM usertable WHERE username = '$username'";
$result1 = mysql_query($query1, $link1);
$array1 = mysql_fetch_array($result1);
$usercount = mysql_num_rows($result1);
mysql_close($link1);
$today = '2000-05-01';
$link2 = mysql_connect('host2', 'myself', 'benne');
mysql_select_db('inventorydb', $link2);
$query2 = "SELECT sku FROM widgets WHERE ship_date = '$today'";
$result2 = mysql_query($query2, $link2);
$array2 = mysql_fetch_array($result2);
$widgetcount = mysql_num_rows($result2);
mysql_close($link2);
if($usercount > 0 && $widgetcount > 0)
```

```
  {
  $link3 = mysql_connect('host3', 'I', 'seed');
  mysql_select_db('salesdb', $link3);
  $query3 = "INSERT INTO saleslog (ID, date, userID, sku)
VALUES (NULL, '$today', '$array1[0]', '$array2[0]')";
  $result3 = mysql_query($query3, $link3);
  $insertID = mysql_insert_id($result3);
mysql_close($link3);
  if($insertID >= 1)
  {
    print("Perfect entry");
  }
  else
  {
    print("Danger, danger, Will Robinson!");
  }
}
else
{
  print("Not enough information");
}
?>
```

In this example we have deliberately kept the connections as discrete as possible for clarity's sake, even going to the trouble to close each link after we use it. Without the `mysql_close()` commands, we would be running multiple concurrent connections. Just remember to pass the link value carefully from one function to the next, and you should be fine.

Building in Error-Checking

This section could have been titled "Die, die, die!" because the main error-checking function is actually called die(). There was something about that title that failed to reinforce the warm hospitable learning environment we cherish, so we went with the more prosaic subheading.

Die is not a MySQL-specific function — the PHP manual lists it in "Miscellaneous Functions." It simply terminates the script (or a delimited portion thereof) and returns a string of your choice.

```
mysql_query("SELECT * FROM mutual_funds WHERE code =
'$searchstring'")
or die("Please check your query and try again.");
```

Note the syntax: the word "or" (you could alternatively use ||, but that isn't as much fun as saying "or DIE") and only one semicolon per pair of alternatives.

Until quite recently, MySQL via PHP returned very insecure and unenlightening (except to hackers) error messages upon encountering a problem with a database query. Die was often used as a way to exert control over what the public would see on failure. Now that no error messages are returned at all, die may be even more necessary — unless you want your visitors to be left wondering what happened.

The other built-in means of error-checking is error messages. These are particularly helpful during the development and debugging phase, and they can be easily commented out in the final edit before going live on a production server. As mentioned, MySQL error messages no longer appear by default. If you want them, you have to ask for them by using the functions mysql_errno (which returns a code number for each error type), or mysql_error (which returns the text message).

```
if(!mysql_select_db($bad_db))
  print(mysql_error());
```

Creating MySQL Databases with PHP

You can, if you wish, actually create your databases with PHP rather than the MySQL client tool. This practice has potential advantages — you can use an attractive front end that may appeal to those who find the MySQL client horribly plain or finicky to use — counterbalanced by one big disadvantage, which is security.

To create a database from PHP, the user of your scripts will need to have full CREATE/ DROP privileges on MySQL. That means anyone who can get hold of your scripts can potentially blow away all your databases and their contents with the greatest of ease. This is not such a great idea from a security standpoint. Furthermore, most external Web hosts very sensibly won't let you do it on their servers anyway.

If you're even considering creating databases with PHP, do yourself a big favor and at least don't store the database username and password in a text file. Make yourself type your database username and password into a form and pass the variables to the inserting handler each and every time you use this script. This is one case where keeping the variables in an include file outside your Web tree is not sufficient precaution.

For those who like to live dangerously, the relevant functions are:

✦ mysql_create_db(): Creates a database on the designated host, with name specified in arguments

✦ mysq_drop_db(): Deletes the specified database

✦ mysql_query(): Pass table definitions and drops in here

A bare-bones database-generation script might look like this:

```
<?php
$linkID = mysql_connect('localhost', 'root', 'sesame');
mysql_create_db('new_db', $linkID);
mysql_select_db('new_db');
$query = "CREATE TABLE new_table (id INT NOT NULL
AUTO_INCREMENT PRIMARY KEY, new_col VARCHAR(25))";
$result = mysql_query($query);
$axe = mysql_drop_db('new_db');
?>
```

There are also prefab tools that do much of this for you in a pretty way. You simply fill out a Web form, and the PHP script on the back end will create the database according to your specifications. In many cases, the tool will also enable you to perform other administrative tasks, such as checking the sizes of your databases or backing them up. This is even less secure than doing it yourself insofar as you probably won't check over every line of the code with an eye to security, but apparently people do use these tools without incident.

A highly attractive and popular Web database admin tool specifically for MySQL is Tobias Ratschiller's phpMyAdmin, which you can try out and download from:

```
www.htmlwizard.net/phpMyAdmin
```

Several other tools are available that are not database-specific but will probably work with MySQL.

MySQL Functions

Table 18-1 includes a recap of all the MySQL functions to date. All arguments in brackets are optional.

Table 18-1 PHP-MySQL Functions	
Function name	*Usage*
`mysql_affected_rows([link_id])`	Use after a nonzero INSERT, UPDATE, or DELETE query to check number of rows changed.
`mysql_change_user (user, password[, database] [, link_id])`	Changes MySQL user on an open link.

Function name	*Usage*
mysql_close([*link_id*])	Closes the identified link (usually unnecessary).
mysql_connect ([*host*][:*port*][:*socket*] [, *username*][, *password*])	Opens a link on the specified host, port, socket; as specified user; with password. All arguments are optional.
mysql_create_db (*db_name*[, *link_id*])	Creates a new MySQL database on the host associated with the nearest open link.
mysql_data_seek (*result_id*, *row_num*)	Moves internal row pointer to specified row number. Use a fetching function to return data from that row.
mysql_db_query (query_string, *db_name* [, *link_id*])	Selects database and sends query in one step.
mysql_drop_db (*db_name*[, *link_id*])	Drops specified MySQL database.
mysql_errno([*link_id*])	Returns ID of error.
mysql_error([*link_id*])	Returns text error message.
mysql_fetch_array (*result_id*[, *result_type*])	Fetches result set as associative array. Result type can be MYSQL_ASSOC, MYSQL_NUM, or MYSQL_BOTH (default).
mysql_fetch_field (*result_id*[, *field_offset*])	Returns information about a field as an object.
mysql_fetch_lengths(*result_id*)	Returns length of each field in a result set.
mysql_fetch_object (*result_id*[, *result_type*])	Fetches result set as an object. See mysql_fetch_array for result types.
mysql_fetch_row(*result_id*)	Fetches result set as an enumerated array.
mysql_field_name (*result_id*, *field_index*)	Returns name of enumerated field.
mysql_field_seek (*result_id*, *field_offset*)	Moves result pointer to specified field offset. Used with mysql_fetch_field.
mysql_field_table (*result_id*, *field_offset*)	Returns name of specified field's table.
mysql_field_type (*result_id*, *field_offset*)	Returns type of offset field (e.g., TINYINT, BLOB, VARCHAR).
mysql_field_flags (*result_id*, *field_offset*)	Returns flags associated with enumerated field (e.g., NOT NULL, AUTO_INCREMENT, BINARY).

Continued

Table 18-1 *(continued)*

Function name	Usage
`mysql_field_len` `(result_id, field_offset)`	Returns length of enumerated field.
`mysql_free_result(result_id)`	Frees memory used by result set (usually unnecessary).
`mysql_insert_id([link_id])`	Returns AUTO_INCREMENTED ID of INSERT; or FALSE if insert failed or last query was not an insert.
`mysql_list_fields` `(database, table[, link_id])`	Returns result ID for use in `mysql_field` functions, without performing an actual query.
`mysql_list_dbs([link_id])`	Returns result pointer of databases on `mysqld`. Used with `mysql_tablename`.
`mysql_list_tables` `(database[, link_id])`	Returns result pointer of tables in database. Used with `mysql_tablename`.
`mysql_num_fields(result_id)`	Returns number of fields in a result set.
`mysql_num_rows(result_id)`	Returns number of rows in a result set.
`mysql_pconnect` `([host][:port][:socket]` `[, username][, password])`	Opens persistent connection to database. All arguments are optional. Be careful— `mysql_close` and script termination will not close the connection.
`mysql_query` `(query_string[, link_id])`	Sends query to database. Remember to put the semicolon outside the double-quoted query string.
`mysql_result` `(result_id, row_id,` `field_identifier)`	Returns single-field result. Field identifier can be field offset (0), field name (FirstName) or table-dot name (myfield.mytable).
`mysql_select_db` `(database[, link_id])`	Selects database for queries.
`mysql_tablename` `(result_id, table_id)`	Used with any of the `mysql_list` functions to return the value referenced by a result pointer.

Summary

PHP's MySQL functions are easy to use, if sometimes named confusingly. Each instance of a PHP-MySQL interaction must have a connection, a database select, and a query or command which returns a result identifier. The result identifier is like an ATM receipt that reports on the success or failure of an operation.

If data is returned after a SELECT statement, one of the PHP-MySQL fetching functions must also be employed. Data pulled from a MySQL database exist in a kind of limbo until one of the fetching functions is applied to the result set. If you wish to loop through the result set again, you can use `mysql_data_seek()` to reset the row pointer back to zero.

PHP also has a large number of functions that return data about the database itself, or about a particular operation. Two of the most common are `mysql_num_rows()` which returns the number of rows in a result set; and `mysql_insert_id()`, which returns the ID of the proximate INSERT operation.

PHP handles much of the MySQL connectivity for you without requiring specific link identifiers or result pointers. The exception comes when you need multiple database connections on the same Web page. In this case, you use exactly the same functions and syntax but simply pass the correct link identifier with most commands.

✦   ✦   ✦

Displaying Queries in Tables

Much of the point of PHP is to help you translate between a back-end database and its front-end presentation on the Web. Data can be viewed, added, removed, and tweaked as a result of your Web user's keystrokes and mouse clicks.

For most of this chapter, we restrict ourselves to ways to use PHP to *look* at the contents of a database without altering it, using only the SELECT statement from SQL, and displaying the results in HTML tables. We use a single database example to show different strategies, including some handy reusable functions. Finally, we look at code to create the sample data shown in the display examples, using the INSERT statement.

The two big productivity points from this chapter are:

♦ *Reuse functions* in simple cases. The problem of database table display shows up over and over in database-enabled site design, and if the display is not complicated, you should be able to throw the same simple function at the problem rather than reinventing the wheel with each PHP page you write.

♦ *Choose between techniques* in complex cases. You may find yourself wanting to pull out a complex combination of information from different tables (which of course is part of the point of using a relational database to begin with). You may not be able to map this onto a simple reusable function, but there aren't that many novel solutions either — get to know the alternatives, and you can decide how to trade off efficiency, readability, and your own effort.

Note This chapter uses the MySQL database and functions exclusively, but the display strategies should be directly transferable to almost any SQL-compliant database supported by PHP.

HTML Tables and Database Tables

First of all, some terminology — unfortunately, both relational databases and HTML scripting use the term "table," but the term means very different things in the two cases. A database table persistently stores information in columns, which have predefined names and types, so that the information can be recovered later. An HTML table is a construct that tells the browser to lay out the table's arbitrary HTML contents in a rectangular array in the browser window. We'll try to always make it clear which kind of table we are talking about.

One-to-one mapping

HTML tables are really constructed out of rows (the "<TR> </TR>" construct), and columns have no independent existence — each row has some number of table datum items (the "<TD> </TD>" construct), which will produce a nice rectangular array only if there are the same number of TDs for every TR. (There is no corresponding "<TC>" construct that lets you display by column first.) By contrast, fields (a.k.a. columns) in database tables are the more primary entity — defining a table means defining the fields, and then you can add as many rows as you like. In this chapter, we will focus on printing out tables and queries in such a way that each DB field prints in its own HTML "column," simply because there are usually more DB rows than DB fields, and people are more used to up-and-down scrolling than left-to-right scrolling. If you find yourself wanting to map DB fields to HTML rows, it is a simple inversion exercise.

The simplest case of display is where the structure of a database table or query *does* correspond to the structure of the HTML table we want to display — the database entity has m columns and n rows, and we'd like to display an m-by-n rectangular grid in the user's browser window, with all the cells filled in appropriately.

Example: a single-table displayer

So let's write a simple translator that queries the database for the contents of a single table, and displays the results on screen. Here's the top-down outline of how the code will get the job done:

✦ Establish a database connection.

✦ Construct a query to send to the database.

✦ Send the query and hold on to the result identifier that is returned.

✦ Using the result identifier, find out how many columns (fields) there are in each row.

✦ Start an HTML table.

✦ Loop through the database result rows, printing a `<TR> </TR>` pair to make a corresponding HTML table row.

✦ In each row, retrieve the successive fields, and display them wrapped in a `<TD> </TD>` pair.

✦ Close off the HTML table.

✦ Close the database connection.

Finally, we'd like to wrap all of the preceding steps up into a handy function that we can use whenever we want. Also, for reasons of efficiency, we don't want to include the first and last steps of creating and closing the database connection in the function—we may want to use such a function more than once per page, and it wouldn't make sense to open and close the connection each time. Instead, we'll assume we have a connection already and pass the connection to the function along with the table name.

Such a function is shown in Listing 19-1, embedded in a complete PHP page that uses the function to display the contents of a couple of tables.

Listing 19-1: **A table displayer**

```php
<?php
include("/home/phpbook/phpbook-vars.inc");
$global_dbh = mysql_connect($hostname, $username, $password);
mysql_select_db($db, $global_dbh);

function display_db_table($tablename, $connection)
{
  $query_string = "select * from $tablename";
  $result_id = mysql_query($query_string, $connection);
  $column_count = mysql_num_fields($result_id);

  print("<TABLE BORDER=1>\n");
  while ($row = mysql_fetch_row($result_id))
    {
      print("<TR ALIGN=LEFT VALIGN=TOP>");
      for ($column_num = 0;
           $column_num < $column_count;
           $column_num++)
        print("<TD>$row[$column_num]</TD>\n");
      print("</TR>\n");
```

Continued

Listing 19-1 *(continued)*

```
    }
    print("</TABLE>\n");
}
?>

<HTML>
<HEAD>
<TITLE>Cities and countries</TITLE>
</HEAD>
<BODY>

<TABLE><TR><TD>
<?php display_db_table("country", $global_dbh); ?>
</TD><TD>
<?php display_db_table("city", $global_dbh); ?>
</TD></TR></TABLE></BODY></HTML>
```

Some things to notice about this script:

✦ Although the script refers to specific database tables, the `display_db_table()` function itself is general. You could put the function definition in an include file and then use it anywhere on your site.

✦ The first thing the script does is load in an include file that contains variable assignments for the database name, database username, and database password. It then uses those variables to connect to MySQL and then choose the desired database. (The fact that this file is located outside the publicly available Web hierarchy makes it *slightly* more secure than just including that information in your code.)

✦ In the function itself, we chose to use a while loop for printing rows, and a for loop to print the individual items. We could as easily have used a bounded for loop for both and recovered the number of rows with `mysql_num_rows()`.

✦ The main while loop reflects a very common idiom, which exploits the fact that the value of a PHP assignment statement is the value assigned. The variable `$row` is assigned to the result of the function `mysql_fetch_row()`, which will be either an array of values from that row or a false value if there are no more rows. If we're out of rows, then `$row` is false, which means the value of the whole expression is false, which means that the while loop terminates.

✦ We put line breaks ("\n") at the end of selected lines, so that the HTML source would have a readable structure when printed or viewed as source from the browser. Notice that these breaks are not HTML line breaks (<BR>) and do not affect the look of the resulting Web page. (In fact, if you want to make it annoying for someone else to scrutinize the HTML you generate, don't put breaks in at all!)

The sample tables

To see the Listing 19-1 script in action, see Figure 19-1, which shows the displayed contents of the "country" and "city" sample tables.

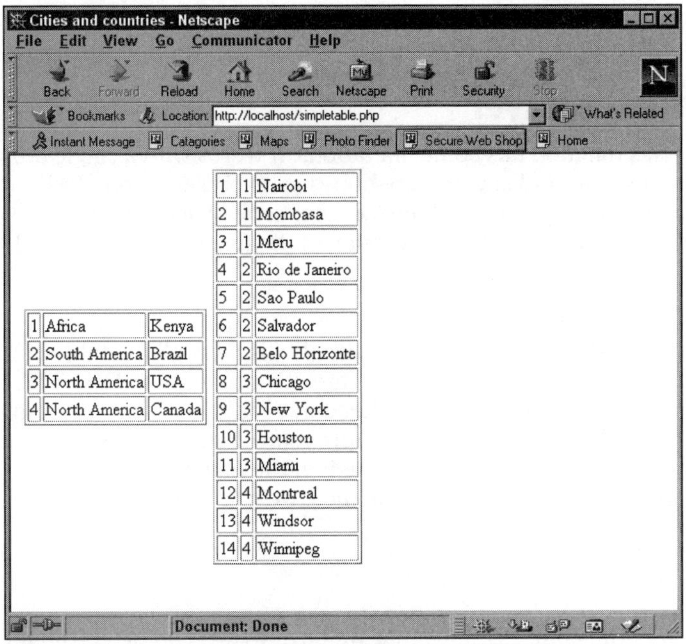

Figure 19-1: A simple database table display

These tables have the following structure:

```
Country:
    ID int (auto-incremented primary key)
    continent varchar(50)
    countryname varchar(50)
City:
    ID int (auto-incremented primary key)
    countryID int
    cityname varchar(50)
```

Think of these tables as being a rough draft of the database for an eventual online almanac. They employ our usual convention of always having one field per table called "ID," which is a primary key and has successive integers assigned to it automatically for each new row. Although you can't tell for sure from the preceding description, the tables have one "relation" embodied in their structure—the "countryID" field of the city table is matched up with the ID field of the Country table, representing which country the city belongs to. (If you were designing a real almanac database, you would want to take this one step further and break

the Country table into a relational pair of Country and Continent tables.)

Cross-Reference To see how we created these tables and populated them with sample data, see the last section of this chapter.

Improving the displayer

Our first version of this function has some limitations: it works with a single table only, does no error-checking, and is very bare-bones in its presentation. We'll address these problems one by one and then fix them in one fell revision. (If you want to look ahead, the new-and-improved version of the function is in Listing 19-2.)

Displaying column headers

Our first version of a database table displayer simply displays all the table cells, without any labeling of what the different fields are. It's conventional in HTML to use the `<TH>` element for column and/or row headers — in most browsers and styles, this displays as a bold table cell. One improvement we can make is to optionally display column headers that are based on the names of the table fields themselves. To actually retrieve those names, we can use the function `mysql_field_name()`.

Error-checking

Our original version of the code assumes that we have written it correctly, and also that our database server is up and functioning normally — if either of these is not the case, then we will run into puzzling errors. We can partially address this by appending a call to `die()` to the actual database queries — if they fail, an informative message will be printed.

Cosmetic issues

Another source of dissatisfaction with our simple table-displayer is that it always has the same look. It would be nice, at a minimum, to control whether table borders are displayed. The simple solution we will use in our new function is just to permit passing in a string of arguments that will be spliced into the HTML table definition. This is a pretty crude form of style control that style-sheet proponents would discourage, but it will permit us to directly specify some elements of the table's look without writing an entirely new function.

Displaying arbitrary queries

Finally, it would be nice to be able to exploit our relational database and display the results of complex queries rather than just single tables. Actually, our single-table displayer has an arbitrary query embedded in it — it just happens that it is hard-coded as "select * from *table*," where *table* is the supplied table name. So let us transform our simple table-displayer into a query-displayer and then recreate the table displayer as a simple wrapper around the query displayer. These two functions, complete with the cosmetic improvements and better error-checking, are in Listing 19-2.

Listing 19-2: A query displayer

```php
<?php
include("/home/phpbook/phpbook-vars.inc");
$global_dbh = mysql_connect($hostname, $username, $password);
if (!$global_dbh)
    die("No database connection");
mysql_select_db($db, $global_dbh);

function display_db_query($query_string, $connection,
                          $header_bool, $table_params)
{

  // perform the database query
  $result_id = mysql_query($query_string, $connection)
             or die("display_db_query:" . mysql_error());

  // find out the number of columns in result
  $column_count = mysql_num_fields($result_id)
                or die("display_db_query:" . mysql_error());

  // TABLE form includes optional HTML arguments passed
  //   into function
  print("<TABLE $table_params >\n");

  // optionally print a bold header at top of table
  if ($header_bool)
  {
    print("<TR>");
    for ($column_num = 0;
         $column_num < $column_count;
         $column_num++)
    {
      $field_name =
        mysql_field_name($result_id, $column_num);
      print("<TH>$field_name</TH>");
    }
```

Continued

Listing 19-2 *(continued)*

```
      print("</TR>\n");
    }
    // print the body of the table
    while ($row = mysql_fetch_row($result_id))
    {
      print("<TR ALIGN=LEFT VALIGN=TOP>");
      for ($column_num = 0;
           $column_num < $column_count;
           $column_num++)
        {
          print("<TD>$row[$column_num]</TD>\n");
        }
      print("</TR>\n");
    }
    print("</TABLE>\n");    }

function display_db_table($tablename, $connection,
                          $header_bool, $table_params)
{
  $query_string = "select * from $tablename";
  display_db_query($query_string, $connection,
                   $header_bool, $table_params);
}
?>

<HTML><HEAD><TITLE>Countries and cities</TITLE></HEAD>
<BODY>
<TABLE><TR><TD>
<?php display_db_table("country", $global_dbh,
                       TRUE, "BORDER=2"); ?>
</TD><TD>
<?php display_db_table("city", $global_dbh,
                       TRUE, "BORDER=2"); ?>
</TD></TR></TABLE></BODY></HTML>
```

The result of using this code on the same database contents is shown in Figure 19-2. The only visible difference is the column header. Also, though, splitting the functions apart means that we also have a new function in our bag of tricks — we could do the same kind of display with an arbitrary query string that joined data from different tables.

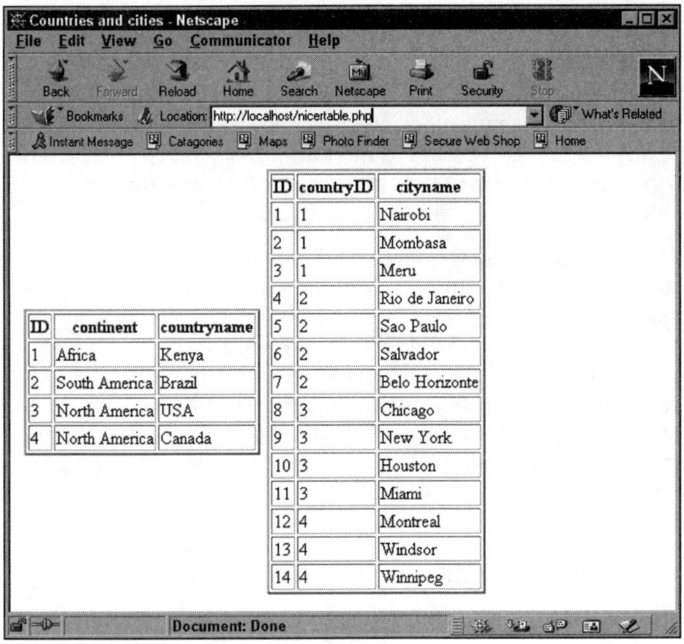

ID	continent	countryname
1	Africa	Kenya
2	South America	Brazil
3	North America	USA
4	North America	Canada

ID	countryID	cityname
1	1	Nairobi
2	1	Mombasa
3	1	Meru
4	2	Rio de Janeiro
5	2	Sao Paulo
6	2	Salvador
7	2	Belo Horizonte
8	3	Chicago
9	3	New York
10	3	Houston
11	3	Miami
12	4	Montreal
13	4	Windsor
14	4	Winnipeg

Figure 19-2: Using the query displayer

Complex Mappings

So far in this chapter we've enjoyed a very nice and simple-minded correspondence between query result sets and HTML tables — every row in the result set corresponds to a row in the table, and the structure of the code is simply two nested loops. Unfortunately, life isn't often this simple, and sometimes the structure of the HTML table we want to display has a complex relationship to the relational structure of the database tables.

Multiple queries versus complex printing

Let's say that, rather than displaying our sample "city" and "country" tables individually, we want to match them up in a tabular display.

Views and stored procedures

Our query-displayer assumes a particular division of labor between the PHP code and the database system itself—the PHP code sends off an arbitrary query string, which the database responds by setting up a result set. In particular, this means that the database system has to parse that query and then figure out the best way to go about retrieving the results. This is part of what can make querying a database a mildly expensive operation.

In cases where your code may construct novel queries on the fly, this is the best you can hope for. However, some databases offer ways to set up queries in advance, which gives the database system a chance to preoptimize how it handles the query. One such construct is called a "view" under MS SQL Server and some other RDMSs—once you have set up a query as a named view, it can be treated just like a real table. A related idea is the "stored procedure," which is like a view that also accepts run-time arguments that are spliced into the query. In general, if you realize that you are suffering from slow query performance, you may want to investigate what optimizations like this your particular database makes available.

We can easily write a SELECT statement that joins these tables appropriately:

```
select country.continent, country.countryname,
       city.cityname
from country, city
where city.countryID = country.ID
order by continent, countryname, cityname
```

Now, this would be a handy place to use our query-displayer function—all we have to do is send it the preceding statement as a string, and it will print out a table of cities matched up with their continents and countries. However, if we do this, we will see an individual HTML table row for each city, and the continent and country will print each time—for example, we'll see "North America" printed several times. Instead, what if we want one name matched with many titles? This is a case where the structure of what we print differs from the structure of the most convenient query.

If we want to do a more complex mapping, we have a choice: we can throw database queries at the problem, or we can write more complex display code. Let's look at each option in turn. (For each of these examples, we'll be moving away from the reusable generality of the functions we wrote earlier, toward functions that address a particular display problem.)

A multiple-query example

If we want to print just one HTML row per country, we can make a query for the countries, and then make another query for the relevant cities in each trip through a country row. A function written using this strategy is in Listing 19-3.

Listing 19-3: **A display with multiple queries**

```php
<?php
include("/home/phpbook/phpbook-vars.inc");
/* open database connection */
$global_dbh = mysql_connect($hostname, $username, $password);
mysql_select_db($db, $global_dbh);

function display_cities($db_connection)
{
  /* Displays table of cities and countries */
  $country_query = "select id, continent, countryname
                    from country
                    order by continent, countryname";
  $country_result =
     mysql_query($country_query, $db_connection);

  /* begin table, print hard-coded table header */
  print("<TABLE BORDER=1>\n");
  print("<TR><TH>Continent</TH><TH>Country</TH>
           <TH>Cities</TH></TR>");

  /* loop through countries */
  while ($country_row = mysql_fetch_row($country_result))
    {
      /* set up country info */
      $country_id = $country_row[0];
      $continent = $country_row[1];
      $country_name = $country_row[2];

      print("<TR ALIGN=LEFT VALIGN=TOP>");
      print("<TD>$continent</TD>");
      print("<TD>$country_name</TD>");

      /* begin table cell for city list */
      print("<TD>");
      $city_query = "select cityname from city
                     where countryID = $country_id
                     order by cityname";
      $city_result =
         mysql_query($city_query, $db_connection)
           OR die(mysql_error());
      /* loop through cities */
      while ($city_row = mysql_fetch_row($city_result))
        {
          $city_name = $city_row[0];
          print("$city_name<BR>");
        }
      /* close city cell and country row */
      print("</TD></TR>");
    }
```

Continued

Listing 19-3 *(continued)*

```
    print("</TABLE>\n");
}
?>

<HTML>
<HEAD>
<TITLE>Cities by Country</TITLE>
</HEAD>
<BODY>
<?php
    display_cities($global_dbh);
?>
</BODY>
</HTML>
```

The strategy is appealingly simple: There is an outer loop that uses one query to proceed through all of the countries, saving the country's name and the primary ID field of each country row. Then for each country, the ID field is used to look up all the cities belonging to that country. Notice the trick of embedding the $countryid variable in the inner query—the query string sent is actually different on each iteration through the country loop.

Simple? Yes. Efficient? Probably not. This code makes a *separate* city query for each country. If there are 500 countries in the database, this function will make 501 separate database queries (the extra one being the enclosing country query). Your mileage will vary according to how efficient your particular DB is in parsing queries and planning query retrieval, but the sum of these queries will certainly take more time than the simple query we started this section with.

A complex printing example

Now let's solve exactly the same problem, but using a different strategy. Instead of multiple queries, we will make a single query and print the resulting rows selectively, so that each HTML table row corresponds to more than one database row (see Listing 19-4). The resulting browser display is exactly the same as in the previous example.

Listing 19-4: **A complex display with a single query**

```php
<?php
include("/home/phpbook/phpbook-vars.inc");
/* open a single DB connection for this page */
$global_dbh = mysql_connect($hostname, $username, $password);
mysql_select_db($db, $global_dbh);

function display_cities($db_connection)
{
  /*  print table of countries and their cities,
      selectively printing only one HTML table row
      per country */
  $query = "select country.id,
                    country.continent, country.countryname,
                    city.cityname
                    from country, city
                    where country.id = city.countryID
                    order by country.continent,
                            country.countryname,
                            city.cityname";
  $result_id =
     mysql_query($query, $db_connection)
       OR die(mysql_error($query));

  /* begin table, print hard-coded table header */
  print("<TABLE BORDER=1>\n");
   print("<TH>Continent</TH><TH>Country</TH>
             <TH>Cities</TH></TR>");

  /* Initialize the ID for the "previous" country.
     We will rely on the fact that Country.ID is
     numbered beginning with 1, so a previous ID
     value of zero means that the current country
     is the first */
  $old_country_id = 0;

  /* loop through result rows (one per city) */
  while ($row_array = mysql_fetch_row($result_id))
    {
      $country_id = $row_array[0];
      /* if we have a new country */
      if ($country_id != $old_country_id)
        {
```

Continued

Listing 19-4 *(continued)*

```
            /* set up country info */
            $continent = $row_array[1];
            $country_name = $row_array[2];

            /* if there was a previous country
               close the city datum and country row */
            if ($old_country_id != 0)
              print("</TD></TR>\n");

            /* start a row for the new country,
               and begin the city table datum */
            print("<TR ALIGN=LEFT VALIGN=TOP>");
            print("<TD>$continent</TD>");
            print("<TD>$country_name</TD><TD>");

            /* the new country is no longer new */
            $old_country_id = $country_id;
          }
        /* the only thing that is printed for every result
           row is the name of a city */
        $city_name = $row_array[3];
        print("$city_name<BR>");
    }
  /* close off final country and table */
  print("</TD></TR></TABLE>");
}
?>
<HTML><HEAD><TITLE>Cities by Country</TITLE></HEAD>
<BODY>
<?php display_cities($global_dbh);
 ?>
</BODY></HTML>
```

This code is somewhat tricky—although it goes through the result rows in order, and everything it prints is grabbed from the current row, it only prints countries when their values have changed (continents are still printed redundantly). The change in a country is detected by monitoring the ID field of the country row. A country change is also a signal to print out the HTML necessary to close off a previous table row and start a new one. Finally, the code must handle printing out the HTML necessary to start the first row and end the last one.

Creating the Sample Tables

Now we will show you the PHP/MySQL code we actually used to create the sample tables. (Such data might more normally be created by interacting only with MySQL, but we decided to respect our book's title by doing it from PHP.) The code (shown in Listing 19-5) is a special-purpose one-time hack, not a model of style, but it has useful examples of using the SQL INSERT statement.

Listing 19-5: Creating the sample tables

```php
<?php
include("/home/phpbook/phpbook-vars.inc");
$global_dbh = mysql_connect($hostname, $username, $password);
mysql_select_db($db, $global_dbh);

function add_new_country($dbh, $continent, $countryname,
                         $city_array)

{
  $country_query =
    "insert into country (continent, countryname)
     values ('$continent', '$countryname')";
  $result_id =  mysql_query($country_query)
                OR die($country_query . mysql_error());
  if ($result_id)
    {
      $countryID = mysql_insert_id($dbh);
      for ($city = current($city_array);
           $city;
           $city = next($city_array))
        {
          $city_query =
            "insert into city (countryID, cityname)
                    values ($countryID, '$city')";
          mysql_query($city_query, $dbh)
             OR die($city_query . mysql_error());
        }
    }
}

function populate_cities_db($dbh)
{
  /* drop tables if they exist -- permits function to be
     tried more than once */
```

Continued

Listing 19-5 *(continued)*

```
    mysql_query("drop table city", $dbh);
    mysql_query("drop table country", $dbh);

    /* create the tables */
    mysql_query("create table country
                (ID int not null auto_increment primary key,
                 continent varchar(50),
                 countryname varchar(50))",
               $dbh)
              OR die(mysql_error());
    mysql_query("create table city
                (ID int not null auto_increment primary key,
                 countryID int not null,
                 cityname varchar(50))",
               $dbh)
              OR die(mysql_error());

    /* store data in the tables */
    add_new_country($dbh, 'Africa', 'Kenya',
            array('Nairobi','Mombasa','Meru'));
    add_new_country($dbh, 'South America', 'Brazil',
            array('Rio de Janeiro', 'Sao Paulo',
                     'Salvador', 'Belo Horizonte'));
    add_new_country($dbh, 'North America', 'USA',
            array('Chicago', 'New York', 'Houston', 'Miami'));
    add_new_country($dbh, 'North America', 'Canada',
            array('Montreal','Windsor','Winnipeg'));

    print("Sample database created<BR>");
}
?>

<HTML><HEAD><TITLE>Creating a sample database</TITLE></HEAD>
<BODY>
<?php populate_cities_db($global_dbh); ?>
</BODY></HTML>
```

You should be able to use this code to recreate the sample database on your development machine, assuming that you have PHP and MySQL configured, and an appropriately located file called phpbook-vars.inc containing username, password, and database-name strings.

Just as in the display examples, this code sends off query strings (with embedded variables), but this time the queries are INSERT statements, which create new table rows. For the most part, the data inserted is just string data passed in to the function, although we chose to pass in an arbitrary number of cities per country by using an array.

The only tricky thing in creating these sample tables is setting up the relational structure. We want each city row to have an appropriate countryID, which should be equal to the actual ID of the appropriate row from the country table. However, these country IDs are automatically assigned in sequence by MySQL and are not under our control. How can we know the right countryID to assign? The answer is in the incredibly handy function `mysql_insert_id()`, which recovers the ID associated with the last INSERT query made via the given database connection. We insert the new country, recover the ID of the newly created row, and then use that ID in our city insertion queries.

Summary

Database interaction is one of the areas where PHP really shines. One very common use for database-enabled web code is simply to display database contents attractively. One approach to this kind of display is to map the contents of database tables, or select statements, to corresponding HTML table elements.

When the mapping is simple enough you can employ reusable functions that take arbitrary table names, or select statements, and display them as a grid. When you need a more complicated combination of information from relational tables, you probably need a special-purpose function, but certain tricks recur there as well. One such trick is to craft a SQL statement that returns all the information you need, in the order you want, and selectively print only the non-redundant portions.

Near the end of this chapter, we saw a quick example of populating a set of database tables using INSERT statements. Aside from that, all the techniques in this chapter were "read-only," and do not modify the contents of databases at all. In the next chapter, we'll see how you can get a more intimate connection to your database by combining SQL queries with HTML forms.

✦   ✦   ✦

Building Forms from Queries

Form handling is one of PHP's very best features. The combination of HTML to construct a form to input data, PHP to handle the data, and a database server to store the data lies at the heart of all kinds of supremely useful Web tasks.

HTML Forms

You already know most of what you need to make good forms to be handled by PHP and a database. There are a few PHP-specific points to keep in mind.

- ✦ Always always *always* use a NAME for every data entry element (INPUT, SELECT, TEXTAREA, and so on). These NAME attributes will become PHP variable names. If your WYSIWYG editor doesn't allow you to do this, you'll need to remember to add these NAME attributes by hand.

- ✦ A form NAME does not need to be the same as the corresponding database field name, but it's often a good idea.

- ✦ You can (and often should) specify a VALUE rather than let PHP use the default value. Consider substituting a numerical value for a text value if possible, because the database is much slower at matching strings than integers.

- ✦ Remember that you can pass hidden variables from form to form (or page) using the HIDDEN data entry elements.

- ✦ Remember that you can pass multiple variables in an array but you need to message the user that this is a possibility.

Self-Submission

An HTML form is basically just a pretty face, a graphical device on top of a simple method to pass variables to the server. It can't actually do much except hand data off to a form-handling script written in some more full-featured programming language.

However, in PHP you can merge form and form-handler in one script if you wish. In fact, PHP makes the process of self-submission so spectacularly easy and useful that you may find yourself preferring it to the separate form-plus-handler method.

Self-submission is not a new form of autoeroticism. It simply refers to the process of combining one or more forms and form-handlers in a single script, using the HTML FORM standard to submit data to the script one or more times. Self-submission is accomplished by the simplest of means: specifying itself as the ACTION target in the FORM tag like this,

```
<FORM METHOD="POST" ACTION="myself.php">
```

or, using a built-in feature unique to PHP,

```
<FORM METHOD="POST" ACTION="<?php print("$PHP_SELF"); ?>">
```

 Tip   Although you always have the option to just use the file's pathname, the built-in `$PHP_SELF` variable is preferable in UNIX. Then the file will continue to be handled correctly if you rename or move it (into a PHP-enabled directory, needless to say). On the other hand, there have been reports of problems with this predefined variable on Windows.

The great advantage of self-submission is that it enables you to build more programmatic logic into your HTML forms. For instance, you might like slightly different forms to be displayed depending on where the request originated. Or we've all been frustrated on occasion by the fact that an HTML form can only have one ACTION attribute target — meaning each form can only send data to one form-handler. With PHP, you can handle forms differently according to your visitor's self-reported preferences.

 Caution   To use self-submission with controls, you will need to employ a more programmatic PHP-writing style — what in Chapter 14 we term the "Maximum" or "Medium" style. Beginners may find this somewhat more difficult than a clear division between the functions of HTML (form display) and PHP (form handling).

Figure 20-1 shows the simplest example of a branching form where self-submission could be handy.

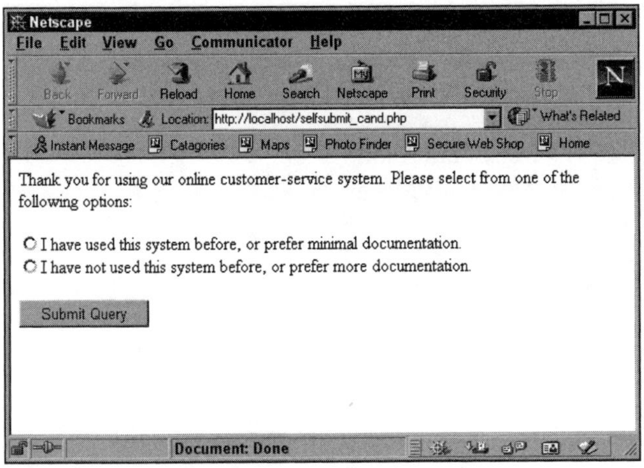

Figure 20-1: A potential self-submitted form

```
<HTML>
<BODY>
<P>Thank you for using our online customer-service system.
Please select from one of the following options:</P>
<FORM METHOD="POST" ACTION="formhandler.php">
<INPUT TYPE=RADIO NAME="userlevel" VALUE=1>I have used this
system before, or prefer minimal documentation.<BR>
<INPUT TYPE=RADIO NAME="userlevel" VALUE=2>I have not used this
system before, or prefer more documentation.<BR>
<INPUT TYPE=SUBMIT>
</FORM>
</BODY>
</HTML>
```

Obviously in this form, you would like to be able to go to either a "Beginner" or an "Expert" follow-up form depending on which of the options a particular visitor selects. Of course you could write a CGI script that would enable you to handle both options, but it might be a bit wasteful to spawn a whole new process just to pull up one of two different HTML pages. In PHP 4, a form self-submission is served up almost as fast as a plain HTML request; and when the Zend cache is available, self-submission will probably be faster than sending data to a separate PHP form handler.

Handling Form Submissions

Form submission is straightforward in PHP if form and form-handler are two discrete pages. Figure 20-2 shows a basic form and matching handler to insert data into a database.

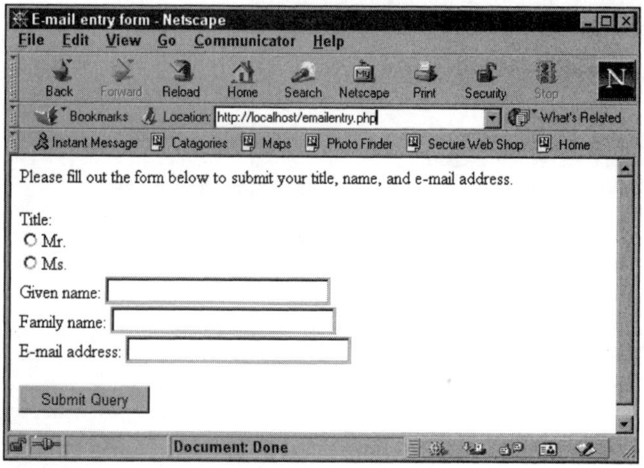

Figure 20-2: An e-mail address entry form

```
<HTML>
<HEAD>
<TITLE>E-mail entry form</TITLE>
</HEAD>
<BODY>
<P>Please fill out the form below to submit your title, name,
and e-mail address.</P>
<FORM METHOD="POST" ACTION="emailaddress.php">
Title:<BR>
<INPUT TYPE=RADIO NAME="Title" VALUE=1>Mr.<BR>
<INPUT TYPE=RADIO NAME="Title" VALUE=2>Ms.<BR>
Given name:  <INPUT TYPE=TEXT NAME="GivenName" SIZE=25><BR>
Family name:  <INPUT TYPE=TEXT NAME="FamilyName" SIZE=25><BR>
E-mail address:  <INPUT TYPE=TEXT NAME="Email" SIZE=25><BR>
<INPUT TYPE=SUBMIT>
</FORM>
</BODY>
</HTML>

<HTML>
<HEAD>
<TITLE>E-mail entry form-handler</TITLE>
```

```
</HEAD>
<BODY>
<?php
/* Open connection to the database */
mysql_connect("localhost", "phpuser", "sesame") or die("Failure
to communicate with database");
mysql_select_db("phpbook");

/* Insert values */
$query = "INSERT INTO addressbook (ID, Title, GivenName,
FamilyName, Email) VALUES('NULL', '$Title', '$GivenName',
'$FamilyName', '$Email')";
$result = mysql_query($query) or die("Unable to record your
information.  Try again later.");
print("Your information has been recorded.");
?>
</BODY>
</HTML>
```

Things get slightly trickier if you decide to use self-submission, because this allows for more power and flexibility. There are a few additional techniques you'll definitely want to learn.

A most useful technique is the hidden stage variable. This lets you keep track of how many times the form has submitted values to itself and therefore which stage of a multi-step process you have reached. You need to use a variable like this (it can be called anything and can be a string rather than an integer) to indicate whether the form and/or the form-handler parts of your script should be called.

```
<HTML>
<HEAD>
<TITLE>E-mail entry form</TITLE>
</HEAD>
<BODY>
<?php
if(!IsSet($stage))
    {
?>
<P>Please fill out the form below to submit your title, name,
and e-mail address.</P>
<FORM METHOD="POST" ACTION="<?php print("$PHP_SELF"); ?>">
Title:<BR>
<INPUT TYPE=RADIO NAME="Title" VALUE=1>Mr.<BR>
<INPUT TYPE=RADIO NAME="Title" VALUE=2>Ms.<BR>
Given name:  <INPUT TYPE=TEXT NAME="GivenName" SIZE=25><BR>
Family name:  <INPUT TYPE=TEXT NAME="FamilyName" SIZE=25><BR>
E-mail address:  <INPUT TYPE=TEXT NAME="Email" SIZE=25><BR>
<INPUT TYPE=HIDDEN NAME="stage" VALUE=1>
<INPUT TYPE=SUBMIT>
</FORM>
```

```php
<?php
    }
else
    {
    /* Open connection to the database */
    mysql_connect("localhost", "phpuser", "sesame") or
die("Failure to communicate with database");
    mysql_select_db("phpbook");

    /* Insert values */
    $query = "INSERT INTO addressbook (ID, Title, GivenName,
FamilyName, Email) VALUES('NULL', '$Title', '$GivenName',
'$FamilyName', '$Email');
    $result = mysql_query($query);
    if($result == 0)
        print("There's been a problem.");
    else
        print("Your information has been recorded.");
    }
?>
</BODY>
</HTML>
```

But be careful with those controls! In the preceding example, the form will only display once, before the variable $stage has been set by the HIDDEN input in the form. Thereafter, you should just see a printed message — so in effect site visitors won't be able to edit their entries. If you want the form to display both before and after values have been submitted, you need to use a slightly different logic.

Another issue with self-submitted forms is navigation. With the traditional HTML form, navigation is strictly one-way: form to handler to whatever navigational device (if any) the designer decrees. Self-submitted forms need not conform to this rule, however. In each individual instance, you need to decide:

✦ Whether the form can be resubmitted multiple times by the user, in whole or in part

✦ Whether the user decides when to move on, or the form moves users along automatically

✦ Whether you need to pass variables on to the next page, hidden or in plain view

✦ Whether you want to control where the user can go next, or want to give users multiple choices

The answers to these questions will determine whether you need a control, another form, a simple link, or multiple links.

Tip   Whatever you decide about navigation, remember to provide plenty of text that clearly explains what's going to happen at every step. Because PHP gives you so much flexibility with forms, new users' default expectations may be crossed up and they could end up uncertain whether they accomplished their mission with your form.

Forms That Depend on Variables

PHP is brilliant at putting variables into a database, but it really shines in forms that display variables from a database. Its HTML-embeddedness, easy variable-passing, and slick database connectivity are at their best in this kind of job. These techniques are extremely useful, because you will find a million occasions to take data from SQL, display it in an editable format, and replace the new variables back into the database.

Let's look at the various kinds of HTML FORM data elements and how they are handled.

TEXT and TEXTAREA

TEXT and TEXTAREA are the most straightforward types because they enjoy an unambiguous one-to-one relationship between identifier and content. In other words, there is only one possible VALUE per NAME. (Remember that in an HTML form integers and doubles must use the TEXT or TEXTAREA type.) You just pull the data field from the database and display it in the form by referencing the appropriate array position, as shown in Figure 20-3.

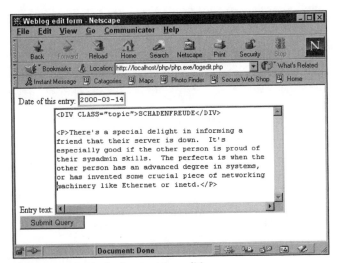

Figure 20-3: Displaying text for editing

```
<HTML>
<HEAD>
<TITLE>Weblog edit form</TITLE>
</HEAD>
<BODY>
<?php
if(!IsSet($stage))
```

```php
    {
?>
    <FORM METHOD="POST" ACTION="<?php print("$PHP_SELF"); ?>">
    Date of entry you wish to edit (YYYY-MM-DD):  <INPUT
TYPE=TEXT NAME="LogDate" SIZE=10><BR>
    <INPUT TYPE=HIDDEN NAME="stage" VALUE=1>
    <INPUT TYPE=SUBMIT>
    </FORM>
<?php
    }
elseif($stage == 1)
    {
    /* Open connection to the database */
    mysql_connect("localhost", "phpuser", "sesame") or
die("Failure to communicate with database");
    mysql_select_db("phpbook");

    /* Fetch values */
    $query = "SELECT ID, LogText FROM weblog WHERE LogDate =
'$LogDate'";
    $result = mysql_query($query);
    $LogRow = mysql_fetch_array($result);
    $LogID = $LogRow[0];
    $LogText = stripslashes($LogRow[1]);
?>
        <FORM METHOD="POST" ACTION="<?php print("$PHP_SELF");
?>">
    Date of this entry:  <INPUT TYPE=TEXT NAME="LogDate"
SIZE=10 VALUE="<?php print($LogDate); ?>"><BR>
    Entry text:  <TEXTAREA NAME="LogText" COLS=75 ROWS=10><?php
print("$LogText"); ?></TEXTAREA><BR>
    <INPUT TYPE=HIDDEN NAME="LogID" VALUE="<?php echo $LogID;
?>">
    <INPUT TYPE=HIDDEN NAME="stage" VALUE=2>
    <INPUT TYPE=SUBMIT>
    </FORM>
<?php
    }
elseif($stage == 2)
    {
    /* Open connection to the database */
    mysql_connect("localhost", "phpuser", "sesame") or
die("Failure to communicate with database");
    mysql_select_db("phpbook");

    /* Insert values */
    $query = "UPDATE weblog SET LogDate = '$LogDate', LogText =
'LogText' WHERE ID = $LogID";
    $result = mysql_query($query);
    if($result == 0)
        print("We have a problem.\n");
    else
```

```
              print("Edit complete.\n");
    ?>
          <FORM METHOD="POST" ACTION="<?php print("$PHP_SELF");
    ?>">
        Want to edit another entry? Enter the date here (YYYY-MM-
    DD):  <INPUT TYPE=TEXT NAME="LogDate" SIZE=10><BR>
          <INPUT TYPE=HIDDEN NAME="stage" VALUE=1>
          <INPUT TYPE=SUBMIT>
          </FORM>
    <?php
          }
    ?>
    </BODY>
    </HTML>
```

Tip You may need to use the `stripslashes` function when displaying TEXTAREA and TEXT if there's any chance the values might have single quotes or apostrophes. Watch out for people with apostrophed names like O'Malley or D'Nesh!

CHECKBOX

The CHECKBOX type has only one possible value per input: on (checked) or no value (unchecked). However, check boxes are often used in bunches to convey more complex aggregate meanings. Although they are rarely prepopulated from a database (checkboxes are commonly used for relatively few choices, which usually obviates the need for a database to be involved), it can be done, as shown in Figure 20-4.

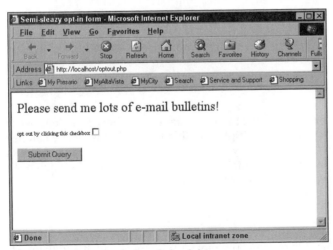

Figure 20-4: A prepopulated check box

```
<HTML>
<HEAD>
<TITLE>Semi-sleazy opt-in form</TITLE>
</HEAD>
<BODY>
<?php
if(!IsSet($stage))
{
?>
<FORM METHOD=POST ACTION="<?php print("$PHP_SELF"); ?>">
<INPUT TYPE=CHECKBOX CHECKED NAME="OptOut" VALUE="On"><FONT
SIZE=+2>Please send me lots of e-mail bulletins!</FONT><BR>
<FONT SIZE=-2>opt out by unclicking this checkbox</FONT><BR>
<INPUT TYPE=HIDDEN NAME="stage" VALUE=1>
<INPUT TYPE=SUBMIT>
</FORM>
<?php
}

elseif($stage == 1 && !IsSet($OptOut))
{
/* Open connection to the database */
mysql_connect("localhost", "phpuser", "sesame") or die("Failure
to communicate with database");
mysql_select_db("phpbook");

/* Update value, in this case from On to Null */
$query = "UPDATE checkbox SET BoxValue = NULL WHERE BoxName =
'OptOut'";
$result = mysql_query($query);
print("You have been removed from our mailing list.");
}
?>
</BODY>
</HTML>
```

RADIO

RADIO data elements allow for a one-to-many relationship between identifier and value. In other words, they have multiple possible values, but only one can be pre-displayed or selected. Otherwise, they closely resemble checkboxes in functionality. They are best for small sets of options, generally fewer than 10, which need more than a word or two of text to identify themselves.

SELECT

The SELECT data element is perhaps the most interesting of all. It can handle the largest number of options, and it also allows the user to select multiple options that can be passed back to the database using arrays.

See Chapter 27, "PHP and JavaScript," for ideas about using JavaScript to make even more interesting SELECT forms.

Cross-
Reference

In Figure 20-5, we are using the SELECT form element with multiple options. In PHP, this is done by creating an array of the multiple selected option values to pass to the form handler. You set up the array in the HTML form by declaring the MULTIPLE attribute of the SELECT element, and by naming the SELECT element something like "$val[]"—in other words, appending a set of square brackets to the variable name. This will indicate to PHP that it's dealing with an array rather than a single variable, and it will construct the array appropriately with the multiple selected values. When the array gets to the form handler, you will need to deal with the values as you would any array's values—by de-referencing, or by listing out the contents of the array.

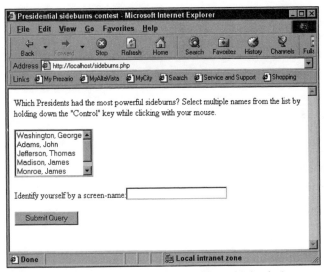

Figure 20-5: A prepopulated select with multiple choice

```
<HTML>
<HEAD>
<TITLE>Presidential sideburns contest</TITLE>
</HEAD>
<BODY>
<P>Which Presidents had the most powerful sideburns? Select
multiple names from the list by holding down the "Control",
"Alt", "Apple", or Command key while clicking with your
mouse.</P>
<FORM METHOD=POST ACTION="sideburns.php">
<SELECT NAME="PresID[]" SIZE=10 MULTIPLE>
<?php
/* Open connection to the database */
```

```
mysql_connect("localhost", "phpuser", "sesame") or
die("<OPTION>Database error!</OPTION></SELECT>");
mysql_select_db("phpbook");

/* Download list of Presidents */
$query = "SELECT ID,Name FROM presidents ORDER BY Name";
$result = mysql_query($query);
while($president = mysql_fetch_array($result))
    {
    print("<OPTION VALUE=\"$president[0]\">$president[1]\n");
    }
?>
</SELECT>
<P>Your e-mail address:<INPUT TYPE=TEXT NAME="email"
SIZE=25></P>
<INPUT TYPE=SUBMIT>
</FORM>
</BODY></HTML>

sideburns.php
<HTML>
<BODY>
<?php

while(list($key, $val) = each($PresID))
    {
    $query = "INSERT INTO votes (ID, PresID, email) VALUES
(NULL, '$val', '$email')";
    $result = mysql_query($query);
    }
print("Thanks for voting!  We'll send e-mail to the winners of
our sideburns contest on President's Day.");

?>
</BODY>
</HTML>
```

Forms That Depend on Queries

The complex-compound type of form is a self-submitting one with several divergent FORM elements, all being displayed or handled by a single script. In these cases, it's usually necessary to write slightly more involved code to cover all the possibilities.

For instance, here is one of a series of forms to input a book review. A book entry has already been completed, and now an author is being associated with the book.

```
<HTML>
<HEAD>
<TITLE>Book review: author</TITLE>
</HEAD>
<BODY>
```

```php
<?php
if($stage == 1)
{
  /* Open connection */
  mysql_connect("localhost", "phpuser", "sesame") or die("Can't
establish connection.");
  mysql_select_db("phpbook");

  /* Associate books with preexisting authors */
  $query1 = "INSERT INTO author_book (ID, authorID, bookID)
VALUES(NULL, $authorID, $bookID)";
  $result1 = mysql_query($query1);
}
elseif($stage == 2 && STRLEN($firstname) > 0)
{
  /* Open connection */
  mysql_connect("localhost", "phpuser", "sesame") or die("Can't
establish connection.");
  mysql_select_db("phpbook");

  /* New authors must first be entered in the db, then
associated with a book. */
  $query1 = "INSERT INTO author (ID, firstname, lastname)
VALUES(NULL, '$firstname', '$lastname')";
  $result1 = mysql_query($query1);
  $authorID = mysql_insert_id($result1);
  $query2 = "INSERT INTO author_book (ID, authorID, bookID)
VALUES(NULL, $authorID, $bookID)";
  $result2 = mysql_query($query2);
}
?>
<P>Is the author in this alphabetical list? If so, select
him/her and click the "Select" button. If not, fill out the
form below.</P>

<?php
/* Open connection */
mysql_connect("localhost", "phpuser", "sesame") or die("Can't
establish connection.");
mysql_select_db("phpbook");

/* Fetch previous authors */
$query = "SELECT ID, lastname, firstname FROM author ORDER BY
lastname";
$result = mysql_query($query);
?>

<FORM METHOD=POST ACTION="<?php print("$PHP_SELF"); ?>">
<SELECT SIZE=1 NAME="authorID">
/* A loop which outputs current authors to a picklist */
<?php
while($authorname = mysql_fetch_array($result))
    {
```

```
        print("<OPTION VALUE=\"$authorname[0]\">$authorname[1],
$authorname[2]\n");
        }
?>
</SELECT>
<INPUT TYPE=HIDDEN NAME="stage" VALUE=1>
<INPUT TYPE=SUBMIT VALUE="Select">
</FORM>
<HR ALIGN=CENTER WIDTH=80% SIZE=1>

<P>If you are ABSOLUTELY positive that your author isn't on the
list yet, enter his/her information below.</P>
<FORM METHOD=POST ACTION="<?php print("$PHP_SELF"); ?>">
First name:  <INPUT TYPE=TEXT NAME="firstname" SIZE=25><BR>
Last name:  <INPUT TYPE=TEXT NAME="lastname" SIZE=25><BR>
<INPUT TYPE=HIDDEN NAME="stage" VALUE=2>
<INPUT TYPE=SUBMIT VALUE="Add author">
</FORM>
</BODY>
</HTML>
```

Summary

PHP is an extremely powerful form handling tool, especially in conjunction with a database. You can use PHP to generate form values from database-stored data, and of course you can also store form-generated data in the database.

To prepare your HTML forms to work smoothly with PHP, you need to follow a few simple rules. First and foremost, remember to always name every single form element — the HTML standard itself doesn't require this, but PHP does because the element names will become variable names in the form handler. A good idea is to make the form element name the same as the corresponding database field name so they are easy to match. PHP also allows you to make clever use of hidden form inputs, and of multiple SELECT options which should be delineated with square brackets (denoting an array) after the element name.

You have the choice with PHP to have separate HTML forms and PHP form handlers; or to commingle the two in a single PHP script. The latter option is perhaps the more powerful, but it can also be more difficult to work with. You will need to set a variable within the form to indicate whether the entries have been submitted; and generally much of the PHP logic will be placed before the HTML display.

With PHP, you can even have multiple forms on one page that are handled by the same PHP script. Each form can, of course, be assembled from data pulled from a database. This allows you to enjoy the maximum flexibility in form usage, although you need to be careful with the slightly more complex structure and logic of the multiple parts.

✦   ✦   ✦

Weblogs

Small standalone PHP applications, such as polls and bulletin boards, are all very well; but complete content sites are where PHP really shines. Here we give complete instructions for developing the simplest type of stand-alone site, which is the Weblog.

Why Weblogs?

A personal Weblog is the simplest kind of dynamic site. It can be thought of as a dynamic version of the personal home page: a content site organized by chronology and whim rather than by the demands of a particular business or domain. Most Weblogs do not create all their own content in the sense of covering the news or producing a trove of artwork; they rather exist to comment on other people's content and events of the day. On the high end of the genre, public Weblogs like Slashdot can become extremely popular meeting places for online communities to chew the fat of their common interests.

If you are a newcomer to server-side scripting, we encourage you to immediately start a personal Weblog as your first major project. Nothing helps you learn faster than running an actual complete site of your own, where you can try out a range of new techniques and ideas in context. Especially because PHP and other Open Source technologies grow and change so quickly, it's well-nigh essential to have a preexisting test bed always available to doodle around on.

Weblogs are also just fun and therefore worthwhile even for those who also use PHP in more serious contexts. There's no pleasure quite like that of conducting an intellectual debate, an argument, or a romance by Weblog. Forget movies, pop music, and TV—the Weblog is the true medium of the age, baby!

The Simplest Weblog

The easiest Weblog is just a template and some included text files. It's limited to local development only — in other words, you won't be able to make entries by HTTP but only by writing text files while logged into the PHP server as a trusted user. You also won't be able to assign different levels of permissions, so this style of Weblog is most appropriate for a purely personal single-author site.

You may be asking yourself, what's the point? Our intention is to lay out the code and show how the PHP part works before adding form-based file-writing and database connectivity, which we will do in the next two sections. Seeing a file-based data store versus a database will also effectively demonstrate why the latter is such a good idea. Also, you could use this design for a purely personal diary which you want to read in a browser window on a localhost but have no intention of actually putting on the Internet.

 Caution We do not recommend putting the Simplest Weblog design on a public Web site as is, because using a GET-style URL with an included file can be a security risk. For public sites, you really want to use a database to store the data.

We decided to use the most basic type of navigation, Next and Previous text links that we'll maintain by hand. This gives you the maximum flexibility to decide how often you want to change the front page of your Weblog — we'll do it daily, but you may prefer a weekly, monthly, or irregular changeover depending on how much you have to write about. We'll also include an old reliable left-side navbar with links to stand-alone pages, such as About Me and Favorite Things information.

A finished Weblog page is shown in Figure 21-1.

It is assembled from these files:

✦ `weblog.php:` page template

✦ `20000101.txt, 20000102.txt, and so on:` Weblog entries (changed daily)

✦ `not_today.txt:` default message for days with no content

✦ `faves.php, links.php, aboutme.php:` static pages (changed infrequently)

✦ `navbar.inc:` navigation bar on every page

✦ `style.inc:` internal style sheet

You can grab the code for all these pages (shown here in Listings 21-1 through 21-6) from our Web site, `http://www.troutworks.com/php4bible/weblog/`. You must change the variable "`$first_date`" in `weblog.php` to the date of your first entry, or you may start an infinite loop that will eat up all your server memory!

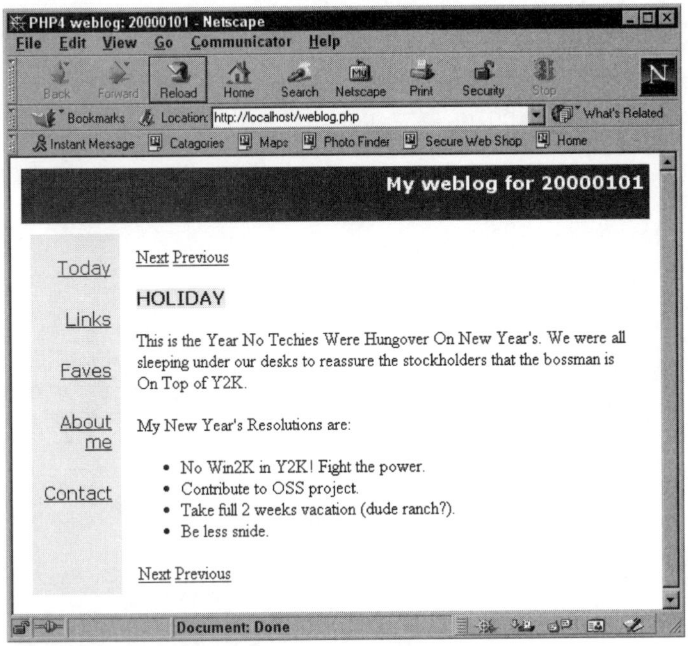

Figure 21-1: A Weblog page

Listing 21-1: **Main Weblog template (weblog.php)**

```php
<?php

/* Change this to the date of your first log entry. */
$first_date = 20000101;

/* Internal links specify via GET-style URL. If no date given
(calling page without arguments), default to today's date. */
if(!IsSet($date))
    {
    $date = date("Ymd");
    }

?>
<HTML>
<HEAD>
<TITLE>PHP4 weblog: <?php print("$date"); ?></TITLE>
<?php include("style.inc"); ?>
</HEAD>
```

Continued

Listing 21-1 *(continued)*

```
<BODY BGCOLOR=#FFFFFF>
<TABLE BORDER="0" CELLPADDING="5" WIDTH=100%>
<TR BGCOLOR=#822222>
<TD ALIGN=RIGHT><H1>My weblog for <?php print("$date"); ?></H1>
</TD></TR>
<TR><TD>
    <?php include("navbar.inc"); ?>
    <TD WIDTH=85%>

<?php
/* It's a bit risky for beginners to automatically generate
"next" and "previous" links because you can easily get into an
infinite loop. We'll do the links by hand on each dated entry.
*/

/* Include the specified dated entry, or give a default "not
today" message when there's no fresh new content. */
if(file_exists("$date.txt"))
    {
    include("$date.txt");
    }
else


    {
    include("not_today.txt");
    }
?>
    </TD></TR>
    </TABLE>
</TD></TR>
</TABLE>
</BODY>
</HTML>
```

Listing 21-2: A dated entry (20000101.txt)

```
<CENTER><P>

<A HREF="weblog.php?date=20000102">Next</A>    <A
HREF="weblog.php?date=19991231">Previous</A>
</P></CENTER>

<DIV CLASS="topic">HOLIDAY</DIV>
<P>This is the Year No Techies Were Hungover On New Year's. We
were all sleeping under our desks to reassure the stockholders
that the bossman is On Top of Y2K.</P>
```

```
<P>My New Year's Resolutions are:
<UL>
<LI>No Win2K in Y2K! Fight the power.</LI>
<LI>Contribute to OSS project.</LI>
<LI>Take full 2 weeks vacation (dude ranch?).</LI>
<LI>Be less snide.</LI>
</UL>
</P>

<CENTER><P>
<A HREF="weblog.php?date=20000102">Next</A>     <A
HREF="weblog.php?date=19991231">Previous</A>
</P></CENTER>
```

Listing 21-3: **Default message (not_today.txt)**

```
<P>Sorry, nothing new today!  Check back tomorrow..</P>
```

Listing 21-4: **A static page (faves.inc)**

```
<!-- Remember to add or delete a link on navbar.inc -->
<HTML>
<HEAD>
<TITLE>My favorite things</TITLE>
<?php include("style.inc"); ?>
</HEAD>

<BODY BGCOLOR=#FFFFFF>
<TABLE BORDER="0" CELLPADDING="10" WIDTH= 100%>
<TR BGCOLOR=#822222>
<TD ALIGN=RIGHT VALIGN=BOTTOM><H1>My favorite stuff</H1>
</TD></TR>
<TR><TD>
    <?php include("navbar.inc"); ?>
    <TD WIDTH=75%>

<P>These are a few of my favorite things.</P>

<DIV CLASS="topic">BOOKS</DIV>
<DL>
<DT>Cryptonomicon, by Neal Stephenson</DT>
<DD>The techie masterpiece -- it's our life, put in the blender
of a massive inventiveness. Be sure to also download the essay
"In the beginning was the command line" from his site,
www.crytonomicon.com .</DD>
</DL>
```

Continued

Listing 21-4 *(continued)*

```
<DIV CLASS="topic">MUSIC</DIV>
<DL>
<DT>When The Pawn..., by Fiona Apple</DT>
<DD>Just another bubblegum Latin pop entry. Merengue,
anyone?</DD>
</DL>

    </TD></TR>
    </TABLE>
</TD></TR>
</TABLE>
</BODY>
</HTML>
```

Listing 21-5: Included navigation file (navbar.inc)

```
    <TABLE WIDTH=100% CELLPADDING=10><TR>
    <TD WIDTH=15% BGCOLOR=#FFFECC VALIGN=TOP>
    <P CLASS=sidebar><A HREF="weblog.php">Today</A></P>
    <P CLASS=sidebar><A HREF="links.php">Links</A></P>
    <P CLASS=sidebar><A HREF="faves.php">Faves</A></P>
    <P CLASS=sidebar><A HREF="aboutme.php">About me</A></P>
    <P CLASS=sidebar><A
HREF=mailto:me@localhost>Contact</A></P>
    </TD>
```

Listing 21-6: Included stylesheet (style.inc)

```
<STYLE TYPE="text/css">
<!--
BODY    {font-family: verdana, arial, sans-serif; font-size:
10pt; color: #000000; text-align: left}
H1      {font-family: verdana, arial, sans-serif; font-size:
14pt; color: #FFFFFF}
.sidebar {font-family: verdana, arial, sans-serif; font-size:
12pt; color: #822222; text-align:right; margin-top:10px}
.topic    {font-family: verdana, arial, sans-serif; font-size:
12pt; font-weight: bold; color: #000000; background: #FFFECC;
text-align: left}
-->
</STYLE>
```

Entering Information via HTTP

This simple Weblog is quite adequate for many purposes, but it has one big disadvantage: you can't make entries in the journal using the Web itself. Instead, you must write up each entry in HTML using a text editor like emacs or Notepad and save it to your Web server's doc root. This can be a significant issue over time, especially if you are not allowed telnet/ssh/ftp access to your server or aren't comfortable with the process. HTTP is the next logical step for many users.

You can use PHP to make good entry screens as well as display pages. There's one big problem with this process: you need to give read/write permissions to the HTTP user (usually Nobody or Everybody). This is an inherently insecure process, and we *do not* recommend it. We'll describe the HTTP entry scripts here so that you can become comfortable with the new aspects before moving on to a better solution, which is using a database instead of separate include files for each entry. We'll try to keep the security problems to a minimum, employing a password and letting you send mail to yourself if an unauthorized person tries to log in.

The display screens are exactly the same as the locally developed version of the Weblog. In addition, you need these files, shown in Listings 21-7 through 21-10:

```
login.php
logentry.php
logentry_handler.php
password.inc
```

Put `password.inc` in a directory outside the Web tree, such as `/home/mydirectory`. The directory must be world-executable and the document must be readable by the httpd user (Nobody). If you have root access on this server, you could chown it to belong to the httpd user; if not, you may have to make the file world-readable, which is a security breach. Be sure to use a password that is not your system user password, just in case it's compromised.

Listing 21-7: **Weblog entry login screen (login.php)**

```
<HTML>
<HEAD>
<TITLE>Weblog login screen</TITLE>
</HEAD>

<P><B>Supply a username and password.</B></P>
<FORM METHOD=POST ACTION="logentry.php">
<P>USERNAME:<INPUT TYPE=TEXT NAME="test_username" SIZE=20></P>
<P>PASSWORD:<INPUT TYPE=PASSWORD NAME="test_password"
SIZE=20></P>
```

Continued

Listing 21-7 *(continued)*

```
<P><INPUT TYPE="SUBMIT" VALUE="SUBMIT">
</FORM>
</BODY>
</HTML>
```

Listing 21-8: **Included password file (password.inc)**

```php
<?php
$username = "logwriter";
$password = "logpass";
?>
```

Listing 21-9: **Weblog data entry screen (logentry.php)**

```php
<HTML>
<HEAD>
<TITLE>Weblog data entry screen</TITLE>
</HEAD>

<?php
include("/home/mydirectory/password.inc");
if($test_username == $username && $test_password == $password)
    {
?>
    <BODY>
    <FORM ACTION="logentry_handler.php" METHOD="POST">
    <P>Enter today's weblog text here:<BR><TEXTAREA
NAME="logtext" COLS=75 ROWS=20 WRAP="VIRTUAL"></TEXTAREA></P>
    <INPUT TYPE="hidden" NAME="test_username" VALUE="<?php
print("$test_username"); ?>">
    <P><INPUT TYPE="SUBMIT" NAME="SUBMIT" VALUE="Enter"></P>
    </FORM>

<?php
    }
else
    {
    mail("me@localhost", "Weblog snoop", "Someone from
$REMOTE_ADDR is trying to get into your weblog entry screen.");
    }
?>
</BODY>
</HTML>
```

Listing 21-10: Weblog form handler (logentry_handler.php)

```php
<?php
$date = date("Ymd");


/* Don't filewrite unless a username is passed from previous
page */
if($test_username)
    {
    $fp = fopen("$date.txt", "w");
    $try_entry = fwrite($fp, "$logtext");
    print("Weblog entry for $date entered with $try_entry
characters.");
    }
else
    {
    mail("me@localhost", "Weblog snoop part deux", "Someone
from $REMOTE_ADDR is trying to get into your weblog entry
handler.");
    }
?>
```

Adding Database Connectivity

Once you see how HTTP entry is effected using the PHP file writing function, it's a short step to keeping your entries in a database rather than in discrete text files. This is neater — important as your site grows — and considerably more secure. Furthermore, you can give different database permissions to different users, enabling multiple content developers to work on the site safely.

By using a database, you get two more bonuses. First, you can write a script to edit your previous journal entries using a Web form, as well as just enter them. Even better, you can now have your navigation links assembled programmatically rather than having to maintain them by hand.

Although they have similar names and functions, the files shown in Listings 21-11 through 21-17 are somewhat different from the preceding set. You also need a script to create the database (unless you'd rather do it using the MySQL command line tool); and if you want to edit previous entries, you have to add a script called db_logedit.php.

Caution   Most of these scripts will not fail gracefully if the database has no data in it, particularly usernames and passwords in the login table. Since the whole thing is designed to be nonfunctional until you enter at least one entry into these tables, and we want you to focus on the main functionality rather than error-checking, there didn't seem to be a lot of point in testing for empty tables.

Listing 21-11: **Database Weblog login screen (db_login.php)**

```
<HTML>
<HEAD>
<TITLE>Weblog login screen</TITLE>
</HEAD>

<P><B>Use this login to add a new entry.</B></P>
<FORM METHOD=POST ACTION="db_logentry.php">
<P>USERNAME:<INPUT TYPE=TEXT NAME="test_username" SIZE=20></P>
<P>PASSWORD:<INPUT TYPE=PASSWORD NAME="test_password"
SIZE=20></P>
<P><INPUT TYPE="SUBMIT" VALUE="SUBMIT">
</FORM>

<P><B>Use this login to edit a previous entry.</B></P>
<FORM METHOD=POST ACTION="db_logedit.php">
<P>USERNAME:<INPUT TYPE=TEXT NAME="test_username" SIZE=20></P>
<P>PASSWORD:<INPUT TYPE=PASSWORD NAME="test_password"
SIZE=20></P>
<P>EDIT DATE:<INPUT TYPE=TEXT NAME="edit_date" SIZE=8></P>
<P><INPUT TYPE="SUBMIT" VALUE="SUBMIT">
</FORM>
</BODY>
</HTML>
```

Listing 21-12: **Included database password file (db_password.inc)**

```
<?php
$hostname = "localhost";
$user = "dbuser";
$password = "dbpass";
?>
```

Listing 21-13: **Database Weblog data entry screen (db_logentry.php)**

```
<HTML>
<HEAD>
<TITLE>Weblog data entry screen</TITLE>
</HEAD>

<?php
/* Connect to db, check login. */
include("/home/mydirectory/password.inc");
```

```php
mysql_connect($hostname, $user, $password);
mysql_select_db("weblogs");
$query = "SELECT password FROM login WHERE username =
'$test_username'";
$result = mysql_query($query);
$password_row = mysql_fetch_array($result);
$db_password = $password_row[0];

if($test_password == $db_password)
    {
?>
    <BODY>
    <FORM ACTION="db_logentry_handler.php" METHOD="POST">
    <P>Text:<BR><TEXTAREA NAME="logtext" COLS=75 ROWS=20
WRAP="VIRTUAL"></TEXTAREA></P>
    <INPUT TYPE="hidden" NAME="test_username" VALUE="<?php
print("$test_username"); ?>">
    <P><INPUT TYPE="SUBMIT" NAME="SUBMIT" VALUE="Enter"></P>
    </FORM>

<?php
    }
else
    {
    mail("me@localhost", "Weblog snoop", "Someone from
$REMOTE_ADDR is trying to get into your weblog entry screen.");
    }
?>
</BODY>
</HTML>
```

Listing 21-14: Database Weblog data edit screen (db_logedit.php)

```php
<HTML>
<HEAD>
<TITLE>Weblog data edit screen</TITLE>
</HEAD>

<?php
/* Connect to db, check login. */
include("/home/mydirectory/password.inc");
mysql_connect($hostname, $user, $password);
mysql_select_db("weblogs");
$query = "SELECT password FROM login WHERE username =
'$test_username'";
$result = mysql_query($query);
$password_row = mysql_fetch_array($result);
$db_password = $password_row[0];
```

Continued

Listing 21-14 *(continued)*

```php
if($test_password == $db_password)
    {
    $query1 = "SELECT logtext FROM mylog WHERE date =
$edit_date";
    $result1 = mysql_query($query1);
    $entry_row = mysql_fetch_array($result1);
    /* When you get text from a SQL database, you will need to
strip backslashes from single-quotes. */
    $edit_entry = stripslashes($entry_row[0]);
?>
    <BODY>
    <FORM ACTION="db_logentry_handler.php" METHOD="POST">
    <P>Text:<BR><TEXTAREA NAME="logtext" COLS=75 ROWS=20
WRAP="VIRTUAL"><?php print("$edit_entry"); ?></TEXTAREA></P>
    <INPUT TYPE="hidden" NAME="edit_date" VALUE="<?php
print("$edit_date"); ?>">
    <INPUT TYPE="hidden" NAME="test_username" VALUE="<?php
print("$test_username"); ?>">
    <P><INPUT TYPE="SUBMIT" NAME="SUBMIT" VALUE="Enter"></P>
    </FORM>

<?php
    }
else
    {
    mail("me@localhost", "Weblog snoop", "Someone from
$REMOTE_ADDR is trying to get into your weblog edit screen.");
    }
?>
</BODY>
</HTML>
```

**Listing 21-15: Database Weblog form handler
(db_logentry_handler.php)**

```php
<?php
$date = date("Ymd");
if($test_username)
    {
    include("/home/mydirectory/password.inc");
    mysql_connect($hostname, $user, $password);
    mysql_select_db("weblogs");

/* Enter new entry or update edited entry. */
    if(!$edit_date)
        {
        $query = ("INSERT INTO mylog (ID, date, logtext)
VALUES(NULL, $date, '$logtext')");
```

```php
        $result = mysql_query($query);
        print("Result is $result.");
        }
    else
        {
        $query = ("UPDATE mylog SET logtext = '$logtext' WHERE
date = $edit_date");
        $result = mysql_query($query);
        print("Updated result is $result.");
        }
    }
else
    {
    mail("me@localhost", "Weblog snoop part deux", "Someone
from $REMOTE_ADDR is trying to get into your weblog entry
handler.");
    }
?>
```

Listing 21-16: **Main database Weblog template (db_weblog.php)**

```php
<?php

/* This page has 5 possible cases:
1.  You got to this page by following a link, so a date is
supplied.  This is neither the first nor the last entry in the
db.

2.  You got to this page by following a link, so a date is
supplied.  This is the first entry in the db.

3.  You got to this page by following a link, so a date is
supplied.  This is the last entry in the db.

4.  You're viewing this page without a supplied date (so
default to today's date), and there is a fresh entry for today.

5.  You're viewing this page without a supplied date (so
default to today's date), and there's no fresh entry.  Give a
default message with link to the last entry.
*/

/* Get today's date for Cases 4 and 5. */
if(!IsSet($date))
    {
    $date = date("Ymd");
    }
```

Continued

Listing 21-16 *(continued)*

```php
?>
<HTML>
<HEAD>
<TITLE>PHP4 weblog: <?php print("$date"); ?></TITLE>
<?php include("style.inc"); ?>
</HEAD>

<BODY BGCOLOR=#FFFFFF>
<TABLE BORDER="0" CELLPADDING="5" WIDTH=100%>
<TR BGCOLOR=#822222>
<TD ALIGN=RIGHT><H1>My weblog for <?php print("$date"); ?></H1>
</TD></TR>
<TR><TD>
    <?php include("navbar.inc"); ?>
    <TD WIDTH=85%>

<?php
/* Open database connection. */
include("/home/mydirectory/password.inc");
mysql_connect($hostname, $user, $password);
mysql_select_db("weblogs");

/* Identify the last entry for Cases 3, 4, and 5. */
$query = ("SELECT MAX(ID) FROM mylog");
$result = mysql_query($query);
$lastID_row = mysql_fetch_array($result);
$last_ID = $lastID_row[0];

/* The first branch of this test displays weblog entries in
Cases 1 - 4... */
$query1 = ("SELECT ID, logtext FROM mylog WHERE date = $date");
$result1 = mysql_query($query1);
$row_test_num = mysql_num_rows($result1);
if($row_test_num > 0)
    {
    $entry_row = mysql_fetch_array($result1);
    $entry_ID = $entry_row[0];
    $logtext = stripslashes($entry_row[2]);

    /* Gets Previous date for Cases 1, 3, and 4.  This test
assumes a database that auto-increments from 1; if this is not
the case, you need to change the integer below. */
    if($entry_ID > 1)
        {
        $prev_ID = $entry_ID - 1;
        $query2 = ("SELECT date FROM mylog WHERE ID =
$prev_ID");
        $result2 = mysql_query($query2);
        $prevdate_row = mysql_fetch_array($result2);
        $prev_date = $prevdate_row[0];
        }
```

```
        else
            {
            $prev_date = "";
            }

    /* Gets Next date for Cases 1 and 2. */
    if($entry_ID != $last_ID)
            {
            $next_ID = $entry_ID + 1;
            $query3 = ("SELECT date FROM mylog WHERE ID =
$next_ID");
            $result3 = mysql_query($query3);
            $nextdate_row = mysql_fetch_array($result3);
            $next_date = $nextdate_row[0];
            }
    else
            {
            $next_date = "";
            }
/* Output text for... */
    /* Case 1 */
    if($next_date != "" && $prev_date != "")
            {
            print("<CENTER><P><A
HREF=\"weblog.php?date=$next_date\">Next</A> <A
HREF=\"weblog.php?date=$prev_date\">Previous</A></P></CENTER>\n
$logtext\n<CENTER><P><A
HREF=\"weblog.php?date=$next_date\">Next</A> <A
HREF=\"weblog.php?date=$prev_date\">Previous</A></P></CENTER>")
;
            }
    /* Case 2 */
    elseif($next_date != "" && $prev_date == "")
            {
            print("<CENTER><P><A
HREF=\"weblog.php?date=$next_date\">Next</A></P></CENTER>\n$log
text\n<CENTER><P><A
HREF=\"weblog.php?date=$next_date\">Next</A></P></CENTER>");
            }
    /* Cases 3 and 4. */
    elseif($next_date == "" && $prev_date != "")
            {
            print("<CENTER><P><A
HREF=\"weblog.php?date=$prev_date\">Previous</A></P></CENTER>\n
$logtext\n<CENTER><P><A
HREF=\"weblog.php?date=$prev_date\">Previous</A></P></CENTER>")
;
            }
        }

/* ...while this branch covers Case 5. */
else
```

Continued

Listing 21-16 *(continued)*

```
    {
    /* Get the date of last entry. */
    $query2 = ("SELECT date FROM mylog WHERE ID = $last_ID");
    $result2 = mysql_query($query2);
    $lastdate_row = mysql_fetch_array($result2);
    $last_date = $lastdate_row[0];
    print("<P>Sorry, nothing new today!  My last entry is <A
HREF=\"weblog.php?date=$last_date\">here</A>.</P>");
    }
?>
    </TD></TR>
    </TABLE>
</TD></TR>
</TABLE>
</BODY>
</HTML>
```

Listing 21-17: Database creation script (weblog_db.php)

```
<?php
include("/home/mydirectory/password.inc");

mysql_connect($hostname, $user, $password) or die("Failure to
communicate");
$try_create = mysql_create_db("weblogs");
if($try_create > 0)
    {
    echo ("Successfully created database.");
    mysql_select_db("weblogs");
    $query = "CREATE TABLE login (ID SMALLINT NOT NULL
AUTO_INCREMENT PRIMARY KEY, username VARCHAR(20), password
VARCHAR(20))";
    $result = mysql_query($query);
    // Since we're not using the standard MySQL
    // date format, store date as an integer
    $query2 = "CREATE TABLE mylog (ID SMALLINT NOT NULL
AUTO_INCREMENT PRIMARY KEY, date SMALLINT, logtext TEXT)";
    $result2 = mysql_query($query2);
    mysql_close();
    if($result > 0 && $result2 > 0)
        {
        echo ("Successfully created tables");
        }
    else
        {
        echo ("Unable to create tables.");
        }
    }
```

```
else
    {
    echo ("Unable to create database");
    }
?>
```

Potential Additions

Things you might want to immediately change, add, or alter in this code include:

✦ Alter colors, styles, layout

✦ Change frequency of expected update (weekly, monthly)

✦ Change to calendar-based navigation rather than Next/Previous links

✦ Change to topic-based rather than date-based navigation

✦ Stop automatic entry changeover by date

✦ Allow future entries in database

✦ Allow multiple authors/editors with different permissions

Besides a personal Weblog, you could use this code for any simple, chronological note taking, such as

✦ A family-vacation journal

✦ A project log

✦ The story of your vast weight loss through heroic diet and exercise

✦ A chronicle of your pregnancy and child's development

Summary

Although it's handy for small standalone projects such as polls, PHP's most impressive use is in developing complete data-driven content sites. The easiest such site to develop is the personal Weblog. We encourage every PHP user to keep one, if only as a handy testbed for new ideas and techniques.

If you wish, you could store your data in ordinary text files, using PHP to plug these files into a template based on a criterion such as date. This wouldn't be a heck of a lot better than static HTML, but it might save a certain amount of formatting-related repetition at the cost of somewhat decreased security. Far better in every way is to keep the data in a database.

The Weblog format is very flexible. It can scale up to a major public site like Slashdot, with tons of contributors and a steady stream of new content upon which to comment. Or you can keep a little secret diary on your own laptop, reading it in a browser window on the sly. The important point is that once you've made a complete data-driven site with PHP, you'll never go back to static Web pages.

✦   ✦   ✦

A User Rating System

This chapter is a tour through some PHP code that is
much like code actually used on a popular Web site. In
addition to being a more sustained piece of programming than
we have presented so far, it shows a nontrivial interaction
with a database, some use of cookies, and a couple of other
interesting tricks and techniques.

Note   Although for most of this book we have striven for clean
and self-contained examples, in this particular chapter we
have opted instead for warts-and-all realism. Because we
can show you only an excerpt of the code that actually
runs this site, the listings in this chapter will not function
on their own.

Cross-Reference   This chapter assumes knowledge of all the content from
Part II of this book and also uses techniques from Chapter
26, "Cookies and HTTP." Readers can either jump ahead to
that chapter or read this chapter as is, taking the parts
about cookies on faith until later.

What Does It Do?

In our "spare time," your humble authors run a couple of
book-review-and-recommendation Web sites. One of these
is devoted to crime fiction (www.mysteryguide.com),
whereas the other covers works of popular science
(www.sciencebookguide.com).

We and our reviewers give opinions about the books in question, but we also offer a way for our viewers to vote on which
books they liked the best, on a 1-to-5 scale. (Although it is
hardly a scientific survey, our users seem to enjoy this quite
a bit.) This chapter covers the pieces of PHP code we use to
collect and display those user ratings.

Goals of the system

When we started adding this feature to our Web sites, we had a few goals in mind. We wanted a system that:

✦ Collected ratings for each book from its review page

✦ Displayed ongoing ratings for each book on its review page

✦ Displayed aggregated ratings on a central page

✦ Made it very, very easy to vote at least once

✦ Discouraged voting multiple times for the same book

The last two points (ease of use and discouragement of ballot stuffing) deserve a word or two. Although at the time we were unaware that the term would become part of a patent controversy, we wanted voting to be, as they say, "one-click." That is, we wanted the user to be able to simply click once to vote, rather than fill out a Web form and then press a "Submit" button.

Second, we wanted the normal use of the voting system to discourage voting multiple times for special favorites. We knew that it would be very difficult to make the system bulletproof enough that no script kiddie could work around its safeguards. So we resigned ourselves to a cookie-based scheme to enforce one vote per user per book, with a backup scheme of simply tossing out votes that were obviously part of a ballot-stuffing campaign.

Structure

Our existing Web sites devoted a single "page" to each book that was reviewed. In the earliest incarnation of our sites, each page was in fact a static HTML page. In more recent versions, each "book page" is dynamically generated from the contents of a MySQL database.

The code itself is in two parts: the code that controls both collection and display of ratings on book pages, and the code that handles the display on our central "Reader Ratings" page. We deal with each separately in the next two sections: "Collecting Votes" and "Displaying Aggregated Results."

Database support

All of the code in this chapter assumes the support of a MySQL database. Although the tables that support the whole site are many and varied, the ones involved in this particular code have the following tables and columns:

Table 'book'

```
ID int (not nullable, primary key, auto incremented)
title varchar(75)
```

```
[.. many columns not used in this code]
```

Table 'ReaderRatings'

```
ID int (not nullable, primary key, auto incremented)
bookid int (not nullable)
RatingDate timestamp
ClientIP varchar(100)
Rating tinyint
BogusBit tinyint
```

Collecting Votes

The first fragment of code is responsible for the ratings-related "boxes" on the individual book pages. It includes a box that invites "one-click" votes, and a box that displays votes to date for that book. Figure 22-1 shows the vote-inviting box itself—to see the full page, you can visit www.mysteryguide.com or www.sciencebookguide.com.

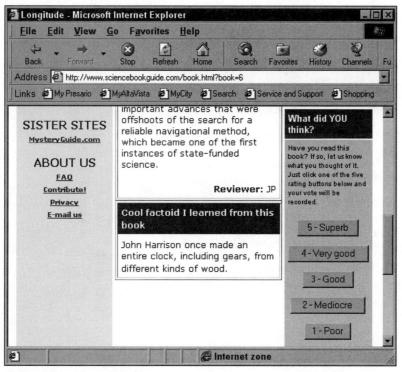

Figure 22-1: The ratings box

The actual behavior of these voting-related boxes is:

✦ If the user has never voted for this book, then both boxes are displayed: the invitation to vote and the summary of votes to date.

✦ If the user votes, the form submits to the same book-review page. This time, rather than an invitation to vote, the user sees a "Thanks for voting" message.

✦ Subsequently, if we can detect via a cookie that the user has already voted for this book, we simply display nothing instead of the invitation.

The display of these boxes, and the handling of submitted ratings, are largely taken care of by the functions in Listing 22-1, which are loaded via an include file into the "book.php" file, which handles the display of book pages.

Listing 22-1: **Book page display functions**

```
function HandleRatings()
{
global $Rating, $RatingCookieName, $$RatingCookieName, $book,
        $dbhost, $dbuser, $dbpass,
        $REMOTE_ADDR, $REMOTE_HOST;

if (IsSet($REMOTE_HOST))
    $remote = $REMOTE_HOST;
else
    $remote = $REMOTE_ADDR;

if ($Rating && !IsSet($$RatingCookieName))
  {
    SetCookie($RatingCookieName, $Rating);
    static $dbh;
    if (!IsSet($dbh))
      $dbh =
        mysql_connect($dbhost, $dbuser, $dbpass);
    mysql_select_db('scienceguide');
    $query = "insert ReaderRatings
                    (bookid, ClientIP, Rating)
              values ($book, '$remote', $Rating[0])";
    mysql_query($query);
  }
}

function DisplayRatings()
{
    global $book, $global_bar_color, $global_box_color,
            $dbhost, $dbuser, $dbpass;
```

```
        static $dbh;
        if (!IsSet($dbh))
           $dbh = mysql_connect($dbhost, $dbuser, $dbpass);
        mysql_select_db('scienceguide');
        $resultID = mysql_query(
                      "select Rating, Count(ID)
                      from ReaderRatings
                      where bookid = $book
                      and BogusBit <> 1
                      group by Rating
                      order by Rating desc");
print("<A NAME=ReaderRating>

<TABLE BORDER=0 CELLPADDING=5 WIDTH=100%>
<TR BGCOLOR=$global_bar_color COLSPAN=1>
<TD>
<FONT SIZE=-1
     FACE=\"ARIAL, GENEVA, SANS-SERIF\" COLOR=\"#FFFFFF\">");
print("<B>Reader Ratings</B></FONT>");
print("</TD></TR>
<TR ALIGN=LEFT BGCOLOR=\"$global_box_color\"><TD>
<FONT SIZE=-2 FACE=\"ARIAL, GENEVA, SANS-SERIF\">");
        if (mysql_num_rows($resultID) == 0)
          {print("No one has rated this book yet.<BR>");}
        else {
        print("Ratings so far for this book:<BR><BR>\n");
        print("<TABLE ALIGN=CENTER BORDER=1><TR><TH><FONT SIZE=-2
FACE=\"ARIAL, GENEVA, SANS-SERIF\">Rating</FONT></TH><TH><FONT
SIZE=-2 FACE=\"ARIAL, GENEVA, SANS-
SERIF\">Number</FONT></TH></TR>");
        while($row_array = mysql_fetch_row($resultID))
          {
            print("<TR ALIGN=CENTER>
                    <TD><FONT SIZE=-2
                        FACE=\"ARIAL, GENEVA, SANS-SERIF\">");
        if ($row_array[0] == 1)
          print("1 - Poor");
        else if ($row_array[0] == 2)
          print("2 - Mediocre");
        if ($row_array[0] == 3)
          print("3 - Good");
        if ($row_array[0] == 4)
          print("4 - Very good");
        if ($row_array[0] == 5)
          print("5 - Superb");
        print("</FONT></TD><TD>
         <FONT SIZE=-2
        FACE=\"ARIAL, GENEVA,
            SANS-SERIF\">$row_array[1]</FONT></TD></TR>");
      }
    print("</TABLE>");
    }
```

Continued

Listing 22-1 *(continued)*

```
print("<BR>See how other books have done at the
<A HREF=\"readerratings.html\">Reader Ratings</A> page.");
print("</TD></TR></TABLE>");
}

function GetFeedback ()
{
  global $book, $Rating,
         $global_bar_color, $global_box_color;

$target_path = "book.html";

print("<A NAME=ReaderRating><TABLE BORDER=0 CELLPADDING=5
WIDTH=100%>
<TR BGCOLOR=\"$global_bar_color\" COLSPAN=1>
<TD>
<FONT SIZE=-1 FACE=\"ARIAL, GENEVA, SANS-SERIF\"
COLOR=\"#FFFFFF\">");

print("<B>What did YOU think?</B></FONT>");

print("</TD></TR>
<TD ALIGN=LEFT BGCOLOR=\"$global_box_color\">
<FONT SIZE=-2 FACE=\"ARIAL, GENEVA, SANS-SERIF\">");
if ($Rating)
  {
    print("<B>Thanks for voting!</B>");
  }
else
  {
print("<B>Have you read this book?</B>
If so, let us know what you thought of it.
Just click one of the five rating buttons
below and your vote will be recorded.
<CENTER>
<FORM ACTION=\"$target_path\">
<INPUT TYPE=SUBMIT NAME=Rating VALUE=\"5 - Superb\"><BR><BR>
<INPUT TYPE=SUBMIT NAME=Rating VALUE=\"4 - Very good\"><BR><BR>
<INPUT TYPE=SUBMIT NAME=Rating VALUE=\"3 - Good\"><BR><BR>
<INPUT TYPE=SUBMIT NAME=Rating VALUE=\"2 - Mediocre\"><BR><BR>
<INPUT TYPE=SUBMIT NAME=Rating VALUE=\"1 - Poor\"><BR><BR>
<INPUT TYPE=HIDDEN NAME=book VALUE=$book><BR><BR>
</FORM>
</CENTER>
<B>Something on your mind</B> that doesn't fit into
a 1 through 5?  Let us all in on it, and <A HREF=\"post.php3\">
post a comment</A> to the <A
HREF=\"index.php3\">ScienceBookGuide forum</A><BR>");
```

```
  }
  print("</FONT></TD></TR></TABLE>");
  }

  function ReaderRating ()
  {
    global $book, $Rating, $RatingCookieName, $$RatingCookieName;

    if (!IsSet($$RatingCookieName))
      {
        GetFeedback();
      }
    DisplayRatings();
  }
```

The way these functions are actually invoked on a book page are:

```
(.. setting of global variables, including $book, omitted)
$RatingCookieName = sprintf("Rating%s", $book);
HandleRatings();
ReaderRating();
```

In general, these functions assume that that they are embedded in a book page that has, among other things, assigned variables $book (with the DB ID of a row in the book table); $dbhost, $dbuser, and $dbpass (for accessing the MySQL database); and $global_box_color (a poor man's color style sheet).

These are the functions (not in order):

✦ DisplayRatings() shows a box with the ratings for this book to date.

✦ GetFeedback() displays a form inviting votes for this book.

✦ HandleRatings() is invoked when someone has actually clicked a voting button, thereby submitting a vote to the very same page. It takes care of storing the vote in the database.

✦ ReaderRating() wraps up the other functions, displaying the GetFeedback() box only if we don't have a cookie stored for this browser/book.

The following sections provide more detail on some functions.

DisplayRatings()

The DisplayRatings() function provides a fairly straightforward tabular display of a SELECT statement on the ReaderRatings table, much like those described in Chapter 19.

GetFeedback()

The GetFeedback() function is mostly dedicated to a straightforward presentation of a form, which is targeted to submit back to this same book.php page, with one slightly tricky twist. If the $Rating variable is bound, it is because we are in the very process of displaying the book page in response to the submittal of a vote. In this case we display a thank-you message in place of the solicitation to vote.

HandleRatings()

Under the appropriate conditions, the HandleRatings() function will insert a new row into the ReaderRatings table, in response to a user's click. We want those appropriate conditions to be that:

1. The user just submitted such a rating.

2. The user has not submitted such a rating earlier (as detected by a cookie).

This leads to one nefariously nasty trick. We set one cookie for each book that might be voted for (see the following note on this practice), and the name of that cookie depends on the ID of the book. So in the body of this file we set $RatingCookieName to be a name that depends on this book's ID. We set a cookie by that name when the vote is processed. Finally, we check to see if the variable $$RatingCookieName is bound (note the two $$'s). This variable variable means "a variable whose name is the string that the variable $RatingCookieName is bound to." This amounts to a check that we have previously set a cookie corresponding to this book.

If all is okay, we insert a new row including this vote and including the IP address of the voter. This is not for any evil privacy-invading purpose — we have just found it easier to detect intentional abuses if some of the abusing votes are grouped together. (See "Abusability," later in this chapter.)

Note When we wrote the preceding code we were young and foolish and had not yet learned that it is a bad idea for one site to set a large number of cookies per browser. This code sets one cookie per book that a user votes on, which could legitimately add up to quite a few cookies and run into per-server limits. If we were older and wiser now, we would rewrite it to include all the voting information for our site in one cookie, or store a key that enabled its retrieval from our database.

Displaying Aggregated Results

Finally, Listing 22-2 includes, in its entirety, a PHP page that shows aggregated voting data and rankings for the books voted on. Figure 22-2 shows a representative page display.

Listing 22-2: **Ratings display page**

```php
<?php
include "globals.inc";
include("sbg-functions.txt");

$max_rating_display = 5;
$min_votes = 2;
$min_best_votes = 2;
$min_worst_votes = 2;
?>


<HTML>
<HEAD>
<TITLE>Reader Ratings</TITLE>
<META NAME="description" CONTENT="ScienceBookGuide.com Reader
Ratings page">
<META NAME="keywords" CONTENT="Reader ratings, votes, poll,
ScienceBookGuide.com">
<!-- ScienceBookGuide.com Reader Ratings page -->
</HEAD>


<BODY TEXT="#000000" LINK="#006400" VLINK="#800080">
<FONT FACE=<?php print("$fontlist");?> >
<TABLE BORDER=0 CELLPADDING=0 WIDTH=100%>
<TR>
<?php include "sbg-navbar.txt" ?>

<TD BGCOLOR="#FFFFFF" ALIGN=LEFT VALIGN=TOP WIDTH=83%>
<?php
$dbh =  mysql_connect($dbhost, $dbname, $dbpass);
mysql_select_db('scienceguide');
?>
   <TABLE>
   <TR>
   <TD ALIGN=LEFT VALIGN=MIDDLE>
   <FONT FACE=<?php print("$fontlist");?> SIZE=+2><B>Reader
Ratings</B></FONT>
   </TD></TR></TABLE>
   <BR>
   <TABLE ALIGN=CENTER VALIGN=TOP BORDER=1>
   <TR BGCOLOR="#FFFFFF">
   <TD WIDTH=400><FONT FACE=<?php print("$fontlist");?> SIZE=-
1>Every book page in the ScienceBookGuide has buttons that let
you rate the book on a 1-5 scale (5 is 'Superb', 1 is 'Poor').
Here's a summary of which books are apparently loved, hated, or
at least noticed by ScienceBookGuide readers.
   </FONT></TD></TR></TABLE>
<BR>
```

Continued

Listing 22-2 *(continued)*

```
<TABLE COLS=1 BORDER=1 CELLPADDING=15 WIDTH=100% ALIGN=CENTER
CELLSPACING=2>
<TR VALIGN=TOP ALIGN=CENTER>
<TD><H3><FONT FACE=<?php print("$fontlist");?> >Books with the
best ratings<sup>*</sup></FONT></H3>
<TABLE WIDTH=100% CELLPADDING=1>
<?php
    $resultID = mysql_query(
        "select avg(Rating) as avgrating,
                Count(ReaderRatings.ID) as countrating,
                book.id,
                book.title
         from ReaderRatings, book
         where BogusBit <> 1 and
               book.id = bookid
         group by bookid
         order by avgrating desc, countrating desc");
    print("<TR
ALIGN=LEFT><TH>Book</TH><TH>Number</TH><TH>Average</TH><FONT
FACE=$fontlist SIZE=-1>");
    $counter = 0;
    while(($row_array = mysql_fetch_row($resultID)) &&
          ($counter < $max_rating_display))
      {
        if ($row_array[1] > $min_best_votes - 1)
          {
            print("<TR ALIGN=LEFT><TD>");
            $bookid = $row_array[2];
            $booktitle = stripslashes($row_array[3]);
            $author_string = book_to_author_string($bookid);
            $bookurl = sprintf("book.html?book=%d", $bookid);
            $bookstring = sprintf("%s by %s", $booktitle,
$author_string);
            print("<A HREF=\"$bookurl\">$booktitle</A> by
$author_string</TD><TD> <FONT FACE=$fontlist SIZE=-
1>$row_array[1]</FONT> </TD><TD> <FONT FACE=$fontlist
SIZE=-1>");
            printf("%3.1f",$row_array[0]);
            print("</FONT></TD></TR>");
            $counter = $counter +  1;
          }
        }
?>
</TABLE>
* <FONT FACE=<?php print("$fontlist");?> SIZE=-2>Must have at
least <?php print("$min_best_votes"); ?> votes</FONT>
```

```php
    </TD>
  </TR>
  <TR VALIGN=TOP ALIGN=CENTER>
  <TD><H3><FONT FACE=<?php print("$fontlist");?> >Books with the
worst ratings<sup>*</sup></FONT></H3>
  <TABLE WIDTH=100% CELLPADDING=1>
  <?php
      $resultID = mysql_query("select avg(Rating) as avgrating,
  Count(ReaderRatings.ID) as countrating, book.id, book.title
  from ReaderRatings, book where BogusBit <> 1 and book.id =
  bookid group by bookid order by avgrating asc, countrating
  desc");
      print("<TR
  ALIGN=LEFT><TH>Book</TH><TH>Number</TH><TH>Average</TH><FONT
  FACE=$fontlist SIZE=-1>");
      $counter = 0;
      while(($row_array = mysql_fetch_row($resultID)) &&
            ($counter < $max_rating_display))
        {
          if (($row_array[1] > $min_worst_votes - 1) &&
              ($row_array[4] != $row_array[3]))
          {
            print("<TR ALIGN=LEFT><TD>
                    <FONT FACE=$fontlist SIZE=-1>");
            $bookid = $row_array[2];
            $booktitle = stripslashes($row_array[3]);
            $author_string = book_to_author_string($bookid);
            $bookurl = sprintf("book.html?book=%d", $bookid);
            $bookstring = sprintf("%s by %s",
                                  $booktitle, $author_string);
            print("<A HREF=\"$bookurl\">$booktitle</A> by
  $author_string</TD><TD> <FONT FACE=$fontlist SIZE=-
  1>$row_array[1]</FONT> </TD><TD> <FONT FACE=$fontlist
  SIZE=-1>");
            printf("%3.1f",$row_array[0]);
            print("</FONT></TD></TR>");
            $counter = $counter +  1;
          }
        }
  ?>
  </TABLE>
  * <FONT FACE=<?php print("$fontlist");?> SIZE=-2>Must have at
  least <?php print("$min_worst_votes"); ?> votes</FONT>

    </TD>
  </TR>
  <TR VALIGN=TOP ALIGN=CENTER>
  <TD><H3><FONT FACE=<?php print("$fontlist"); ?>>Books with the
  most ratings</FONT></H3>
```

Continued

Listing 22-2 *(continued)*

```
<TABLE WIDTH=100% CELLPADDING=1>
<?php
    $resultID = mysql_query("select avg(Rating) as avgrating,
Count(ReaderRatings.ID) as countrating, book.id, book.title
from ReaderRatings, book where BogusBit <> 1 and book.id =
bookid group by bookid order by countrating desc");
    print("<TR
ALIGN=LEFT><TH>Book</TH><TH>Number</TH><TH>Average</TH>");
    $counter = 0;
    while(($row_array = mysql_fetch_row($resultID)) &&
        ($counter < $max_rating_display))
    {
      if ($row_array[4] != $row_array[3])
      {
        print("<TR ALIGN=LEFT><TD><FONT SIZE=-1
FACE=$fontlist>");
        $bookid = $row_array[2];
        $booktitle = stripslashes($row_array[3]);
        $author_string = book_to_author_string($bookid);
        $bookurl = sprintf("book.html?book=%d", $bookid);
        $bookstring = sprintf("%s by %s", $booktitle,
$author_string);
        print("<A HREF=\"$bookurl\">$booktitle</A> by
$author_string</TD><TD> <FONT FACE=$fontlist SIZE=-
1>$row_array[1]</FONT> </TD><TD> <FONT FACE=$fontlist
SIZE=-1>");
        printf("%3.1f",$row_array[0]);
        print("</FONT></TD></TR>");
        $counter = $counter +  1;
      }
    }
?>
</TABLE>

<BR>
</TD>
</TR>
</TABLE>
<BR>
</TD></TR></TABLE>
<P ALIGN=RIGHT><FONT FACE=<?php print("$fontlist");?> SIZE=-2
>&#169 1999 Troutworks, Inc. All rights reserved. <BR>Revised
constantly</FONT></P>
</BODY></HTML>
```

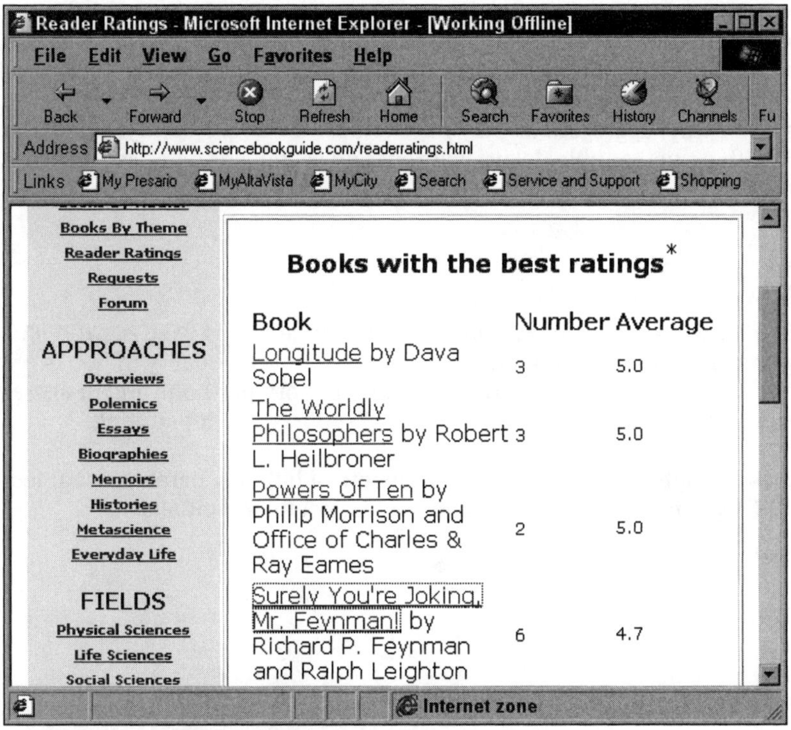

Figure 22-2: Ratings display page

This code shows three tables with "Top 10"–style lists, showing the most popular, least popular, and most-voted-on books. Stylistically, the repetition of code for each table is ugly — the right thing to do would be to have one function that took arguments specifying the type of table and sorting order. But this is cinema verité, and so we're showing it like it is.

Abusability and scale

The system sketched in this chapter does a nice job of collecting and displaying votes on our book-guide sites, and people seem to enjoy it. In addition, a cookie-based system is in place that tries to discourage "voting early and often" for the same book. Please do not mistake this discouragement for security, however — you do *not* want to elect presidents this way. There are any number of ways to go over, under, and around this system. We have found that most of our users have accepted the feature in the spirit it was offered; on occasion, we have had to throw out a number of suspicious votes that were obviously scripted or hand-spoofed, which of course proved nothing but that our time could be wasted by people we'd never met. (OK — we're not going to go off on a rant here. . . .)

In terms of scaling, only one of these sites (`www.mysteryguide.com`) has been visible for long enough to handle a perceptible number of votes, receiving nearly 10,000 to date. Although this is a trivial number of rows for an industrial-strength database, we were anecdotally pleased that our $400 refurbished K6 Web server machine was able to serve up the aggregate display page under Linux/Apache/MySQL/PHP, and display it with no perceptible delays, without any caching or database optimization.

Summary

In this chapter we saw a more extended piece of code that is used in production of a fairly popular Web site. It collects users' votes about the quality of books on the site, stores them in a database, and displays them both per-book and in aggregate. It also uses a cookie-based scheme to gently discourage ballot-stuffing.

Our next two chapters deal with general aspects of building database-enabled Web sites in PHP: writing code with style and avoiding common pitfalls.

✦   ✦   ✦

PHP/Database Efficiency and Style

✦   ✦   ✦   ✦

In This Chapter

Using database
resources efficiently

Making the database
work for you

Time-stamping
insertions and
updates

✦   ✦   ✦   ✦

This quick chapter is for people making database-enabled PHP Web sites who suspect that they are doing things awkwardly or inefficiently. Maybe you are new to databases, or maybe you know there must be a way to speed things up just because your pages are loading unacceptably slowly.

We offer some tips and tricks for making things run faster, and we show you some common ways that database systems can save you from writing unnecessary PHP code. As usual, some of our code examples will use MySQL functions, although the lessons are mostly general and independent of particular database implementations.

Cross-Reference
This chapter will do little to help you get your database-enabled code working in the first place. For a guide to common errors, gotchas, and problems with PHP/DB code, see Chapter 24.

Connections — Reduce, Reuse, Recycle

One important thing to realize is that establishing an initial connection with a database is never a cheap operation. Unless your PHP script is doing some unusually computationally-intensive work, the overall database interaction will be the most time- and resource-intensive part of your code, and it is frequently true that the establishment of a connection is the most expensive part of code that interacts with a database, even if the connection is only established once in serving the page.

You have two potentially competing goals here. On the one hand, you want to minimize the number of times your code makes the expensive and time-consuming call to open an entirely new database connection. This argues for leaving connections open during the course of page execution, rather than closing and reopening. On the other hand, there are sometimes hard limits on the number of simultaneous connections that a database program can support. This might argue for closing connections whenever possible, in hopes that less connected time per script might allow more scripts to execute simultaneously.

In our experience, though, most Web scripts are evanescent enough that it is never worth the overhead to close and reopen a database connection within one page's execution. If you want to minimize total time connected, then open the connection immediately before the first call to the database, and close it immediately after the last one.

A bad example: one connection per statement

Our first bad example seems stylistically reasonable in one sense, because it uses a function to eliminate repetitive code.

```php
<?php
function box_query ($query, $user, $pass, $db)
{
  $my_connection =
     mysql_connect('localhost', $user, $pass);
  mysql_select_db($db, $my_connection);
  $result_id = mysql_query($query, $my_connection);
  print("<H3>Results for query:  $query</H3>");
  print("<TABLE>");
  while ($row = mysql_fetch_row($result_id))
  {
    print("<TR>");
    $row_length = mysql_num_fields($result_id);
    for ($x = 0; $x < $row_length; $x++)
    {
      $entry = $row[$x];
      print("<TD>$entry</TD>");
    }
    print("</TR>\n");
  }
  print("</TABLE>");
  mysql_close($my_connection);
}
/* code that uses box_query() */
?>
```

The idea is that we take a function that packages up an arbitrary MySQL query and displays the returned data in an attractive HTML table. The main virtue of this function as defined is that it is very self-contained — it opens its own database connection for its own purposes, and then it disposes of that connection when the function is done.

The preceding code is fine if we expect to display only one such table per page. If we use this function more than once per page, however, we will find ourselves opening and closing connections every time the function is invoked, which is bound to be more inefficient than leaving the connection open. As we have said, the general rule is to leave a single connection open for as long as it is needed in the execution of a single page's script. Applying this rule to the preceding function would mean rewriting it so that it takes a connection as argument (or implicitly uses a connection opened at the beginning of the script), and then opening a single connection per page.

Multiple results don't need multiple connections

One thing that surprised us the very first time we saw Web-database scripting was that with many database programs it is possible to retain the results from more than one query at once, even though only one connection has been opened. For example, with a MySQL database you can do something like this:

```
mysql_connect('localhost', $user, $pass); //opens connection
mysql_select_db('scienceguide');
$author_result = mysql_query("select ID from author")
                 or die(mysql_error());
while ($author_row = mysql_fetch_row($author_result))
{
  $book_result =
    mysql_query("select title from book
                 where authorID = $author_row[0]");
while ($book_row = mysql_fetch_row($book_result))
  {
    $title = $book_row[0];
    print("$title<BR>");
  }
}
```

This would print out titles of books after retrieving them from the book table, using IDs from rows retrieved from the author table. Now, this is in fact an extremely inefficient way to retrieve the data (see "Make the DB work for you" below), but it illustrates that two different result sets (identified by the variables $author_result and $book_result) can be actively used at the same time, after having been retrieved over a single pipe.

Persistent connections

Finally, if you become convinced that the sheer overhead of opening new database connections is killing your performance, you might want to investigate opening *persistent* connections. Unlike regular database connections, these connections are not automatically killed when your page exits (or even when `mysql_close()` is called) but are saved in a pool for future use. The first time one of your scripts opens such a connection, it is opened in the same resource-intensive way as with a regular database connection. The next script that executes, however, might get that very same connection in response to its request, which saves the cost of reopening a fresh connection. (The previous connection will be reused only if the parameters of the new request are identical.)

The PHP function to request such a persistent connection for MySQL is `mysql_pconnect()`, which is used in exactly the same way as `mysql_connect()`. This naming convention seems to be stable across PHP functions for the different databases — if you use a particular DB "connect" function, you should consult the documentation to see if a "pconnect" version exists.

> **Note**   Persistent database connections only work in the module installation of PHP. If you ask for a persistent connection in the CGI version, you will simply get a regular connection.

> **Note**   Other than offering a particular kind of increased efficiency, persistent database connections do not provide any functionality beyond that of regular database connections. In particular, you should not expect persistent connections to have any "memory" of previous queries or of variables from previous page executions.

Make the DB Work for You

Just as when you write code in a programming language, writing code that interacts with a database is an exercise in appropriate division of labor. People who write programming languages and databases have agreed to automate, standardize, and optimize certain tasks that come up over and over again in programming, so that programmers don't have to constantly reinvent the wheel when making their individual applications. The very general rule is that, unless you're willing to spend a lot of energy in optimizing code for your special case, you are better off using a database-provided facility than trying to invent your own solution for the same task.

It's probably faster than you are

Database programs are judged partly on their speed, and so database programmers devote a large proportion of their effort toward ensuring that queries execute as quickly as possible. In particular, any searching or sorting of the contents of a database is best done within that database (if possible), rather than by your own code.

A bad example: looping, not restricting

For example, take the following code fragment (and please don't laugh—we have actually seen code like this):

```
function print_first_name_bad ($lastname, $dbconnection)
{
  $query = "select firstname, lastname from author";
  $result_id = mysql_query($query, $dbconnection);
  while ($row = mysql_fetch_array($result_id))
  {
    if ($row['lastname'] == $lastname)
        print("The first name is " . $row['firstname']);
  }
}
```

When this code is handed a last name string, and a database connection, it will print out associated first names, if any, in the "author table" of the database. For example, a call to print_first_name_bad('Sagan', $dbconnection) might produce the output

```
The first name is Carl
```

If there were multiple authors in that table with the same last name, then multiple lines would be printed.

The problem here is that we don't need to grab all the data in this table, pull it through the narrow pipe of a connection, and then pick and choose from it on our side of the pipe. Instead, we should restrict the query with a "WHERE" clause:

```
function print_first_name_better ($lastname, $dbconnection)
{
  $query = "select firstname, lastname from authors
            where lastname = $lastname";
  $result_id = mysql_query($query, $dbconnection);
  while ($row = mysql_fetch_array($result_id))
  {
      print("The first name is " . $row['firstname']);
  }
}
```

The WHERE clause ensures that only the rows we care about are selected in the first place. Not only does this cut down on the data passed over the SQL connection, but the code used to locate the correct rows on the database side is almost certainly quicker than your PHP code.

Sorting and aggregating

Exactly the same argument applies if you find yourself writing code to sort results that have been returned from your database, or to count, average, or otherwise aggregate those results. In general, the ORDER BY syntax in SQL will allow you to presort your retrieved rows by any prioritized list of columns in the query, and that sort will probably be more efficient than either homegrown code or the PHP array-sorting functions. Similarly, rather than looping through DB rows to count, sum, or average a value, investigate whether the syntax of your particular DB's flavor of SQL supports the GROUP BY construct, and in-query functions like `count()`, `sum()`, and `average`. In general, executing a query like

```
$query = "select count(ID) from author";
```

will be a radically more efficient approach to counting table rows than selecting them and iterating through them with a PHP looping construct.

Creating date and time fields

It is very common to want to associate a date and/or time with a row's worth of data. For instance, your table rows might represent requests made by your Web site users, and the associated date/time is the time that that request hit your database.

Now, one way to insert or update date fields is to include a string that represents the desired date in a format parsable by your database. For example, if you want to set the `mydate` datetime field of all rows of `mytable` to a particular date, you might set up a query like this one:

```
$query = "update mytable set mydate = 'September 4, 2001'";
```

Then send that query off for evaluation. (Unfortunately, the exact standards of readable date formats vary quite widely from one SQL database system to another.)

The preceding approach is fine, as long as you take care that the particular date string you send is in fact readable as a date by your DB. Things get more complicated if you need to construct such a string on the fly to represent a date that depends on the value of variables in your script.

The main thing to remember is that, with most database systems, there is no need to go through such contortions to set a field to the current date or time. Many have a current-date function that can be embedded directly in your query. For example, a MySQL version of the preceding query, that sets the relevant date/time field to the current instant, looks like this:

```
$query = "update mytable set mydate = now()";
```

(Note that the call to now() is not enclosed in single quotes.) The analogous query for Microsoft SQL Server looks like:

```
$query = "update mytable set mydate = getdate()";
```

Finally, even if the time you want stored is not that of the instant of execution, there may still be better alternatives than constructing readable date strings in your script. In addition to functions returning the current date, many versions of SQL offer functions for performing date arithmetic—start with a particular date/time, and then add or subtract years, months, or hours. In MySQL, these functions are:

✦ date_add(date, date-interval)

✦ date_sub(date, date-interval)

where date-interval is a string that includes a number of time units and the type of unit. A MySQL query to set all rows to a time a week from now might look like this:

```
$query = "update mytable set mydate =
    date_add(now(), '7 days')";
```

Finding the last inserted row

Another surprisingly helpful capability offered by some database systems is finding the ID of the last row inserted.

This problem arises when you are trying to create a new database entry that is distributed across several database tables, each of which has an automatically incremented primary key. As an example, take the tables created by the following MySQL statements:

```
create table author (ID int primary key auto_increment,
                lastname varchar(75),
                firstname varchar (75));
create table book (ID int primary key auto_increment,
                authorID int,
                title varchar(100));
```

One intent of these statements is that the book table is linked to the author table by joining them so that book.authorID = author.ID. Another intent is that we don't have to worry about assigning unique ID fields for either table—the database will automatically assign them. Unfortunately, the combined intent leads to a problem. How do we write code that will gracefully insert a linked book-author pair, when both the author and the book are new to the database? If we insert a new author, the ID field of the inserted row will be automatically created by the database and so will not be a part of our SQL insert statement. How can we give the correct authorID to our new book row?

One possible strategy is to do something like the following (in MySQL):

```
$author_lastname = 'Feynman';
$author_firstname = 'Richard';
$book_title = 'The Character of Physical Law';
$author_insert = "insert into author (lastname, firstname)
        values ('$author_lastname','$author_firstname')";
mysql_query($author_insert) OR die(mysql_error());
$author_id_query =
  "select ID from author
   where lastname = '$author_lastname'
   and firstname = '$author_firstname'";
$author_id_result =
   mysql_query($author_id_query) OR die(mysql_error());
if (mysql_num_rows($author_id_result) <= 0)
  die("Inserted author not found!");
else
  $author_row = mysql_fetch_row($author_id_result);
$authorID = $author_row[0];
$book_insert = "insert into book (authorID, title)
                 values ($authorID, $book_title)";
mysql_query($author_insert) OR die(mysql_error());
```

In this code we create a new author row, use the last name and first name of the author to select the row we have just created, pull out the unique ID of that newly created row, and then incorporate that ID in a statement inserting a new row into the book table. This code would probably work in this particular instance, if we assume that the author's last name and first name are sufficient for unique identification. But for many databases we will not be able to make such an assumption, which is of course why the convention of unique IDs developed in the first place.

A similar approach that is sometimes used is to insert a row (for example, into the author table) and then select the maximum ID from that table, on the theory that the highest row ID will be the one most recently inserted. If the most recently inserted row is in fact the one we just inserted, this will work like a charm. Unfortunately, this is exactly the kind of approach that appears to work when tested by a solitary user/programmer and then breaks when used with a real database server that is dealing with requests from multiple connections at the same time. The problem is that an insertion from another connection might well arrive in between our own insertion and the statement we send to retrieve the maximum ID to date, with the result that our second insertion is matched with an inappropriate ID.

The best solution, when it is available, is to have the database itself keep track of the last inserted ID in a retrievable way, and do this tracking on a *per-connection* basis, so that there are no worries about the synchronization issues in the previous paragraph. For MySQL users, PHP offers the function `mysql_insert_id()`, which takes a connection ID as argument and returns the autoincremented ID of the last inserted row. We can use it to rewrite our previous code example:

```
$author_lastname = 'Feynman';
$author_firstname = 'Richard';
$book_title = 'The Character of Physical Law';
$author_insert = "insert into author (lastname, firstname)
        values ('$author_lastname', '$author_firstname');
mysql_query($author_insert) OR die(mysql_error());
$authorID = mysql_insert_id();
$book_insert = "insert into book (authorID, title)
            values ($authorID, '$book_title')";
```

As with many PHP/MySQL functions, the connection argument to `mysql_insert_id()` is actually optional and defaults to the most recently opened connection.

In some other database systems, the ID of the most recent autoincrement is available (per-session) as a "special" variable that can be embedded in the next query. In Microsoft SQL Server, for example, the variable is '`%%identity`', which can be embedded in a query as follows to retrieve the last insert ID:

```
$query = "select @@identity";
```

Summary

Because database-related functionality is among the most resource-intensive things PHP can do, you can become a hero by giving just a little thought to efficient coding practices. Particularly if your data-driven PHP scripts are sluggish, you want to learn to work with the database instead of against it.

The basic principles of database-intensive coding are simple. It costs a lot to open a connection to a database, so don't turn the tap on and off unnecessarily. Remember the pipe is narrow — you want to transport the bare minimum of data you need for each page. And take the time to learn all the functionality your particular database can offer you. SQL is really good at sorting, filtering, restricting, numbering, and grouping — use these powers rather than doing it less well and more slowly with PHP.

In the next chapter we move from these tips and stylistic concerns to problems and gotchas that can actually break your database code or give you unintended results.

✦   ✦   ✦

PHP/Database Gotchas

T his chapter details some of the common difficulties that arise with using PHP and databases. The goal is to help you diagnose and solve problems more quickly and with less frustration. As usual, our specific code and function references are to MySQL, although the set of gotchas is fairly independent across different databases.

Cross-Reference This chapter is about diagnosing and fixing PHP/database code that is genuinely broken—that is, not successfully retrieving data, or producing error messages. If your scripts are working, but too slowly, see the previous chapter.

No Connection

If you have a database call in your PHP script and the connection can't be opened, you will see a version of one of these two warning screens (depending on how high your error reporting levels are cranked up, and, to some extent, on precisely the cause of the problem).

The first possibility is the No Connection warning, as shown in Figure 24-1.

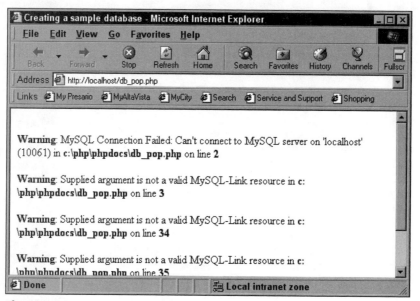

Figure 24-1: A no connection warning

This option indicates a problem either with the MySQL server itself or with the path to mysqld. In its own special way, PHP is telling you that it knows about MySQL but can't hook up to it.

Caution   The very first release version of PHP 4, version 4.0.0, had a buggy version of `mysql_connect()` that would not succeed if given any arguments at all. The persistent connection version (`mysql_pconnect()`) worked without problem. This bug was fixed as of PHP 4.0.1. If you have version 4.0.0 and need to use `mysql_connect()`, you should upgrade.

If the problem is on the PHP side, your error screen will look more like the one shown in Figure 24-2.

This means PHP doesn't know about MySQL at all.

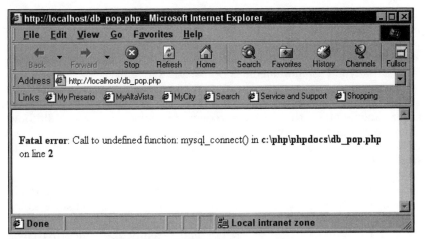

Figure 24-2: An undefined function fatal error

Of the two, the fatal error is much more straightforward to fix. Clearly if you're running into an undefined function that is supposed to be in the PHP function set, you can be pretty sure you simply forgot to build that module into your installation. So on the UNIX side, you will need to recompile with the "—with-mysql" option. On the Windows side, all the options are precompiled into the binary for you; either they should be immediately available or you will be able to turn them on and off by means of the php.ini file. In the case of MySQL (or any other supported database), you merely need to uncomment the "php_mysql.dll" line in your php.ini to be ready to go, unless you put your MySQL executable in a very, very strange place (which you shouldn't do unless you're prepared to handle the consequences, including fatal errors).

The innocuous-looking "No Connection" error is actually a little harder to diagnose because there are several possible causes. They fall into two main categories:

1. The MySQL daemon isn't running.

2. The MySQL socket isn't where PHP is looking for it.

It's easy to check whether mysqld is running, so you may as well do that first. Just use whatever method you prefer to check running processes. On Windows NT, this means it's time for the old Ctrl+Alt+Delete action to bring up the Task Manager. On UNIX, where freedom of choice is the watchword, you can check the system processes by means of ps or a graphical system monitoring utility or even by querying mysqladmin directly.

If `mysqld` is down, perhaps you have merely forgotten to (re)start it (don't laugh, it happens). If it's been running continuously for 143 days before suddenly quitting in the middle of an operation, your problem is beyond the scope of this book. We can only direct you to the MySQL Web site with our deepest sympathies and most fervent hopes that you've maintained a good backup schedule.

The socket problem usually arises the first time you fire up MySQL on a new server. It's rather uncommon for this problem to occur in a long-running site, although it does happen. For instance, we recently had a Web host move our MySQL daemon to another server on short notice, at which point all of our scripts that used the hostname "localhost" immediately crashed.

The solution to your database connection problems is generally to be found in the `php.ini` file. There's a section of MySQL variables that you must carefully check against whatever hostname, port, and socket you're specifying in your PHP scripts. You want to ensure you're not inadvertently directing PHP to look for MySQL on an odd port or at the wrong default host. On UNIX, you can also check the `/etc/services` file for a different socket address. In general, you should leave these variables open unless you have a specific reason to set them.

Problems with Privileges

Error messages caused by privilege problems look a lot like the connection errors described previously.

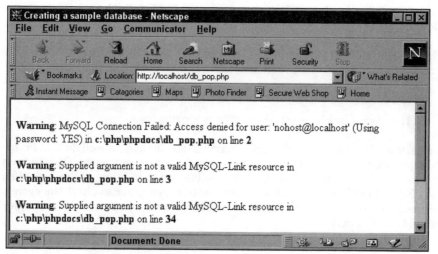

Figure 24-3: Privilege problems

The key differentiator is that little piece about the user and password.

Caution   Because of the security issues caused by these failure messages, it's best to use silent mode on a production site. You do this by putting the character "@" in front of the functions `mysql_connect` **and** `mysql_select_db`.

These errors are many in number but fall into pretty clear major types:

✦ Mistyping usernames/passwords

✦ Failing to use a necessary password

✦ Trying to use a nonexistent password

✦ Trying to use your system's username/password instead of the MySQL username/password

✦ Employing a database username that lacks the necessary permissions for the task

✦ Logging in from a location or client that the MySQL database does not allow for a particular user

✦ PHP being unable to open the database-password include file due to incorrect file permissions (must be a world-readable file in a world-executable directory)

✦ The database root user having deliberately changed permissions on you

These are not structural problems, but usually just simple slips of memory that result in miscues or misrecollections. They should be trivial to fix in the vast majority of situations.

Unescaped Quotes

Quotes can cause many small but annoying buglets between PHP and MySQL. The crux of the issue is that PHP evaluates within double quotes and largely ignores single quotes, whereas MySQL evaluates within single quotes and largely ignores double quotes. This can lead to situations where you have to think hard about the purpose of each quotation mark. An example is:

```
MYSQL_QUERY("INSERT INTO book (ID, title, year, ISBN)
VALUES('NULL', '$title', '$year', '$ISBN')");
```

In most of PHP, variables within single quotes are not expanded, whereas variables in double quotes or unquoted variables are—so this query looks a bit strange. But if you think about it, the statement is valid in both languages. The single quotes exist within double quotes, so PHP takes them as literal characters; and the variables are actually within double quotes, so PHP replaces them with their values. You can think of the division of labor this way: in a database query, PHP does its thing on the stuff between double quotes (treating single quotes literally), and MySQL later deals with the stuff left over within single quotes.

Obviously you'll need to exercise some care when writing these statements. This is one of the reasons why it's preferable to break up your MySQL queries into two parts, like so:

```
$query = "INSERT INTO book (ID, title, year, ISBN)
VALUES('NULL', '$title', '$year', '$ISBN')";
$result = mysql_query($query);
```

This style also eliminates the double parentheses that account for common PHP errors.

Even greater issues arise with strings that use single quotes and double quotes within the text. Remember that apostrophes and single quotes are the same thing for PHP and MySQL—there is no smart-quoting feature (not that most smart quotes are all that smart anyway). So this insertion query will break as follows if any of your lastname entries ever has an apostrophe in it (for example, O'Hara, D'Souza, and M'Naughten):

```
$query = "INSERT INTO employee (ID, lastname, firstname)
VALUES('NULL', '$lastname', '$firstname')";
$result = mysql_query($query);
```

Other very common problems are caused by names of businesses with apostrophes in them, such as Rosalita's Bar and Grill or Yoshi's Hair Salon; and by any string that might have a contraction or possessive in it (such as can't, what's, or Mike's).

The parallel issue on the PHP side is a string with a double quote in it. This construction will definitely not work as intended.:

```
$string = "He said, "I'm not angry," but I knew he was.";
$statement = mysql_query("INSERT INTO diary (ID, entry)
VALUES('NULL', '$string')");
```

Caution In very long text entries, a quote problem may present as a partial string being inserted; or it may appear as a complete failure; or it may seem as though only short entries are being accepted while longer entries fail.

To review the three ways of dealing with quoting issues:

1. In cases where the string is directly stated within the code, you can escape the necessary characters with a backslash.

```
$query = "INSERT INTO employee (ID, lastname, firstname)
VALUES('NULL', 'O\'Donnell', 'Sean')";

$result = mysql_query($query);
```

2. In cases where the string is represented by a variable, you can use addslashes(), which will automatically add any necessary backslashes.

```
$string =

addslashes("He said, 'I'm not angry,' but I knew he was.");
```

```
$statement = mysql_query("INSERT INTO diary (ID, entry)
VALUES('NULL', '$string')");
```

3. You can build PHP with the -with-magic-quotes option, and/or set magic-quotes at run time in the php.ini file. This will add slashes without your needing to specify addslashes() each time. If your ISP controls the php.ini file, you should still be able to set these variables by changing your own .htaccess file.

For some murky psychological reason, many PHP users seem exceedingly averse to using addslashes() and its partner, stripslashes(). People will tie themselves in knots using single quotes when they really shouldn't, just so they don't have to escape double quotes. This practice is bad style at any time but is especially dangerous when using a database.

You need to add slashes when inserting values into a database; and conversely you'll need to strip out the slashes when pulling strings from a database (unless you have magic quotes turned on).

```
$query = "SELECT passphrase FROM userinfo WHERE
username='$username'";
$result = mysql_query($query);
$query_row = mysl_fetch_array($result);
$passphrase = stripslashes($query_row[0]);
```

If you fail to do this, more and more slashes will be added each time you reenter the data into MySQL! This is an issue that is very frequently encountered with editable Web forms that redisplay values pulled from a database, as shown in Figure 24-4.

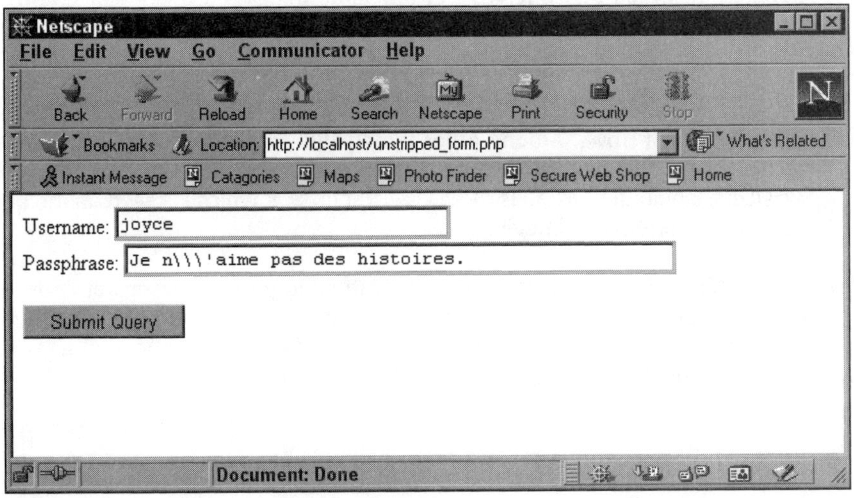

Figure 24-4: Unstripped slashes in a form

Broken SQL Statements

In addition to quoting problems, there are a number of easy ways to send a "bad" query to the database. That query might be syntactically malformed, or have the right syntax but refer to tables that do not exist, or have any of a number of problems that make the database unable to handle it properly. A typical error message is shown in Figure 24-5.

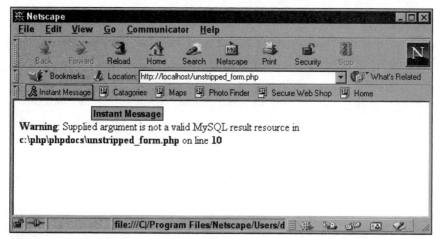

Figure 24-5: A bad SQL statement error

> **Note**
>
> A broken or invalid SQL query is not the same thing as a query that returns no rows. You can write a perfectly fine SQL query like the following:
>
> ```
> "select ID from cust where name = 'nonexistent'"
> ```
>
> You send it to your DB and get back a perfectly valid result set, which happens to contain exactly 0 rows. Among other things, this means that error-trapping that catches query failures will not help you detect the case of zero rows. For MySQLers, a helpful function is `mysql_num_rows()`, which is called on the query result ID and returns an integer.

How exactly this kind of problem will present itself in your browser depends on your PHP version, your database version, your error settings, and how much error-checking code you yourself have incorporated in your script. Just as with other kinds of malignancy, early detection of a failed query is key.

Tip

Your new best friend for making MySQL queries looks like this:

```
$result_id = mysql_query($query) or die(mysql_error());
```

Because `mysql_query()` will return a false value if it fails, the `die()` portion will be executed only if a failure occurs. The low operator precedence of `'or'` ensures that the `die()` call also plays no role in the assignment statement—if the assignment succeeds, it is as if the `die()` portion did not exist. Failure leads to the script exiting just as soon as it has printed the most informative error message that the MySQL designers could concoct. If your particular database lacks such an error variable in PHP, you might want to simply call `die($query)`. Often the problem is obvious once you see the query that is actually being sent.

If you have not incorporated error-checking into your query calls, then you will get the first bad news when you try to use the query result ID in subsequent database code. The typical pattern is

```
$my_result = $mysql($bad_query);
// ... other processing and display code
$row = mysql_fetch_row($my_result); // error shows up here
```

The typical error message for MySQL is "0 is not a mysql result identifier in [etc.]." This is because, rather than detecting the 0 value that `mysql_query()` returns when it fails, you have tried to use that value as if it were a valid identifier for a result set.

Note

Although a bad query is by far the most common way of producing the "0 is not a valid result identifier" message, it is not the only way. You would also get that message if you misspelled the name of the result identifier variable (and it was therefore unbound) or if the query statement had never actually executed (with the same result). Again, it is much easier to distinguish these problems if you trap the errors early on.

Misspelled names

The sad truth is that for every bug that plumbs the depths of programming esoterica, there are a gazillion cheap mistakes that seem obvious once you've discovered them. The former may break your brain, but afterward you feel a certain exhilaration at testing your skills against a really hard nut; the latter just leave you feeling empty and regretful at the time you wasted on something so trivial.

So let us start with the single most common error: simple misspelling of table, column, and value names. It doesn't help that PHP and MySQL are both case-sensitive. Ask for 'mytable' instead of 'MyTable', and you can expect a quick return of el número céro. No force on earth can prevent you from doing this once in awhile, and the error messages will be uninformative at best. So what can we say? Remember that even the most experienced programmers do it too.

Comma faults

Remember to put the comma outside the single quotes within a SQL statement. This will not work:

```
$query = "UPDATE book SET title='$title,' subtitle='$subtitle,'
isbn='$isbn'";
```

But this will:

```
$query = "UPDATE book SET title='$title', subtitle='$subtitle',
isbn='$isbn'";
```

Unquoted string arguments

Any values that should be treated by the database as string data values typically need to be single-quoted within a SQL statement. For example, this query has the correct syntax:

```
$query = "select * from author where firstname = 'Daniel'";
```

By contrast, if we make a mysql_query() call using the following query, we should expect an error:

```
$query = "select * from author where firstname = Daniel";
```

The actual error returned by the database may be deceiving, though — quite likely the complaint will be about an unknown column named 'Daniel'. This is because unquoted strings are assumed to name columns, as in

```
$query = "select * from author where firstname = lastname";
```

This would be a perfectly acceptable way to search our database for Humbert Humbert and Lisa Lisa.

Unbound variables

One of the sneakier ways to break a SQL statement is to interpolate an unbound variable into the middle of it.

When it works, the automatic splicing of variables into double-quoted strings is a perfect match for a SQL-based dialog with your database. Your code can determine values, for example, that are used to restrict the scope of a query made to the DB, as in this snippet:

```
$customerID = find_customer_id(); // imaginary, returns int
$result_id = // BUG
  mysql_query("select from customers where ID = $customer_ID");
$row = mysql_fetch_row($result_id);  // CRASH
```

Because this code makes no attempt to trap query errors, you will again see a complaint about the fact that 0 is not a valid MySQL result identifier. It's possible (for us anyway) to stare at code like this for quite a while without seeing anything wrong. The problem, of course, is that we assigned a variable ($customerID) and then embedded a different one ($customer_ID) in our SQL statement. The latter variable is unbound and so behaves like an empty string when interpreted by the double-quote parsing. The result is that the database sees the following query, which is not valid SQL:

```
select from customers where ID =
```

This kind of problem is one reason why it is often a good idea to construct your query and assign it to a variable in a separate statement, like this:

```
$my_query = "select from customers where ID = $customer_ID";
```

Then make a distinct subsequent call to mysql_query($my_query). If you do this, it is very easy to add printing or debugging statements that show you the actual query you are sending.

Too Little Data, Too Much Data

Finally, you may find that your PHP/database script is working apparently without error but is displaying no data from the database, or far more than you expected. As a vague and general rule, if your query function is returning successfully (and your code checks that), then your suspicions might rightly turn to the SQL itself. Recheck the logic, particularly of WHERE clauses. It is easy, for example, to write a query like

```
"select * from families where kidcount = 1 and kidcount = 2"
```

In this query, you are really intending an 'or' rather than an 'and', with the result that zero rows will be returned regardless of the contents of your database.

If your script is iterating through database rows and displaying them and you find that you have far, far too many of those rows, the problem is very often a SQL join that has too few restrictions. As a general rule, the number of restrictions in a WHERE clause should not be fewer than the number of tables joined minus one. For example, a query like the following has three tables but only one joining restriction.

```
"select book.title from book, author, country
    where author.countryID = country.ID"
```

It is likely to return every possible book/author pair, without reference to whether the author wrote the book, which is probably not what was intended.

A Sanity Check

If you are nearing your wit's end in trying to debug query-related errors and misbehavior, it can be extremely useful to actually compare the results of your PHP-embedded queries with the same queries made directly to the database. If your technical setup permits actually running a SQL interpreter directly (for example, by typing mysql at a command prompt), as well as cross-program cutting and pasting, then try this two-step process:

1. Insert a debugging statement in your PHP script that prints the query itself immediately before it is actually used in a DB query call (for example, print($query);).

2. Directly paste that query from your browser output (or the HTML source) into your SQL interpreter program.

If the query looks reasonable to you but breaks both in the SQL program and in PHP, then there is some syntax or naming error in that SQL statement itself that you are missing, and your PHP code is not to blame (unless of course your code constructed that query in the first place). Similarly, with a dearth or overabundance of rows — if the behavior is the same in both places, the query is to blame. If, on the other hand, the behavior in the SQL interpreter looks like what you wanted, then the query is fine, and your suspicion should turn to your PHP code that actually sends that query and processes the results.

One final and general tip is to study any error messages very carefully, paying attention to phrases like "link identifier" and "result identifier." In MySQL, the former means an identifier of a database connection, and the latter identifies the set of rows returned by a particular query. It is easy to confuse the two, as in the following code:

```
$my_connect = mysql_connect('localhost', $myname, $mypass);
mysql_select_db('MyDB');
$result = mysql_query($my_query, $my_connect);
while ($row = mysql_fetch_row($my_connect)) {    //WRONG
...
```

This code will probably yield an error that contains the words "not a valid result identifier." The problem is that we are using the connection ID where the result ID should be. The resulting error message is justified yet opaque.

Summary

PHP/database bugs are often not very deep or subtle but can still be difficult to diagnose. In general, the earlier in a script you can detect trouble, the easier the diagnosis will be. Especially when you are debugging, every statement that interacts with the database should have an associated `or die()` clause, containing an informative error message.

By far the most common cause of database connection problems is incorrect arguments to the connection function (hostname, username, password). The most common causes of failed queries are quote faults, unbound variables, and simple misspellings.

If you have repeated failures with database queries that seem like they should be working, have your code print out the very query that it is sending to the DB; if possible, try making that very query to the database directly. If the problem persists when PHP is out of the loop, you can safely restrict your attention to database design and your understanding of SQL queries.

✦   ✦   ✦

Advanced Techniques

✦ ✦ ✦ ✦

Sessions

In other parts of this book you will find the occasional
"New Feature" warning, which usually indicates a capability that was new as of PHP 4.0. This entire chapter needs
such a warning, because there is no built-in session tracking
in PHP 3.*x*—if you want to track user sessions, you must
either install PHP 4, or grab the popular PHPLIB code, or roll
your own solution.

What's a Session?

What do we mean by a "session"? Informally, a session of Web
browsing is a period of time during which a particular person,
while sitting at a particular machine, views a number of different Web pages in his/her browser program, and then calls it
quits, either for the night or because the person in question
actually has a life. If you run a Web site that this person visits
during that time, then for your purposes the session runs
from that person's first download of a page from your site
through the last. For example, a Caribbean hotel's Web site
might enjoy a session of five pages duration in the middle of a
real user's session that began with a travel portal and ended
with that user booking his or her vacation with a competitor.

So what's the problem?

Why is the idea of a session tricky enough that we're just talking about it now, even though PHP is at version 4 already? It's
because, as we've said in earlier chapters, the HTTP protocol
by which browsers talk to Web servers is *stateless,* with the
result that your Web server has less long-term memory than
your housecat. That is, your Web server reacts independently
to each individual request it receives and has no way to link
requests together even if it is logging requests. If I sit at my
computer in Chicago, and you sit at yours in Monterey, and
we both ask for page 1 and then page 2 of the Caribbean hote-
lier's site, the HTTP protocol offers no help toward figuring
out that two people looked at two pages each—what it sees

is four individual requests for pages, with various information attached to each request. Not only does this information not identify you personally (by name, email address, phone number or any other traceable identification), it also offers nothing reliable to identify your two page requests as being from the same person.

Why do we care?

If our Web site's only mission in life is to offer various pages to various users, then we may in fact not care at all where sessions begin and end. On the other hand, there are a number of reasons why we might in fact care. For example:

✦ We want to customize our users' experiences as they move through the site, in a way that depends on which (or how many) pages they have already seen.

✦ We want to display advertisements to the user, but we do not want to display a given ad more than once per session.

✦ We want the session to accumulate information about users' actions as they progress — as in an adventure game's tracking of points and weapons accumulated, or an e-commerce site's shopping cart.

✦ We are interested in tracking how people navigate through our site in general — when they visit that interior page, is it because they bookmarked it, or did they get there all the way from the front page?

For all of these purposes, we need to be able to match up page requests with the sessions they are part of, and for some purposes it would be nice to store some information in association with the session as it progresses. PHP sessions solve both of these problems for us.

Home-Grown Alternatives

Before we look at PHP's treatment of sessions, let's look at a few alternative ways the problem can be handled. As we'll see, the PHP treatment combines a couple of these techniques.

IP address

Web servers usually know either the Internet host name or the IP address of the client that is requesting a page. In most configurations of PHP, these show up for free as variables — $REMOTE_HOST and $REMOTE_ADDR, respectively. Now you might think that the identity of the machine at the other end is a reasonable stand-in for the person at the other end, at least over the short term. If you get two requests in quick succession from the same IP address, your code can safely conclude that the same person followed a link or form from one of your site's pages to another.

Unfortunately, the IP address your browser knows about may not belong to the machine your user is browsing from. In particular, AOL and other large operations employ proxy servers, which act as intermediaries. Your user's browser actually requests a URL from the proxy server, which in turn requests the page from your server and then forwards back the page to the user. The result is that many different AOL users might be browsing your site simultaneously, all apparently from the same address. IP addresses are not unique enough to form a basis for session tracking.

Hidden variables

Every HTTP request is dealt with independently, but each time your user moves from page to page within your site it is usually via either a link or a form submission. If the very first page a user visits can somehow generate a unique label for that visit, then every subsequent "handoff" of one page to another can pass that unique identifier along.

For example, here is a hypothetical code fragment that you might include near the top of every page on your site:

```
if (!IsSet($my_s_id))
  $my_s_id =
    generate_s_id(); // warning! hypothetical function
```

This fragment checks to see if the $my_s_id variable is bound — if it is, we assume that it has been passed in, and we are in the middle of a session. If it is not, we assume that we are the first page of a new session, and we call a hypothetical function called generate_s_id() to create a unique identifier (this is actually the hard part, and we have punted on implementing it).

Once we have included the preceding code we assume that we have a unique identifier for the session, and our only remaining responsibility is to pass it along to any page we link or submit to. Every link from our page should include the $my_s_id as a GET argument, as in

```
<A HREF="next.php?my_s_id=<?php echo $my_s_id;?>">Next</A>
```

and every form submission should have a hidden POST argument embedded in it, like this:

```
<FORM ACTION=next.php METHOD=POST>
body of form
<INPUT TYPE=HIDDEN NAME=my_s_id
      VALUE="<?php echo $my_s_id;?>" >
</FORM>
```

What's wrong with this technique? Nothing. It works just fine as a way to keep different sessions straight (as long as you can generate unique identifiers). And once we have unique labels for the sessions, we can use a variety of techniques to associate other kinds of information with each session, such as using the session ID as a key for database storage. However, this approach to sessions is a pain to maintain — you must make sure that *every* link and form submission propagates the information as described, or the session identifier will be dropped. Also, if you send the information as GET arguments, your session-tracking machinery will be visible in the Web-address box of your user's browser, and such arguments are easily edited (and spoofed) by the user.

Cookies

Another approach to session tracking is to use a unique session identifier as in the previous section, but perform the "handoff" by setting or checking a cookie.

Cookies are a special kind of file, located in the file system of your user's browsing computer, that Web servers can read from and write to. Rather than checking for a passed GET/POST variable (and assigning a new identifier if none is found), your script would check the user's machine for a previously written cookie file and store a new identifier in a new cookie file if none is found. This method has some benefits over using hidden variables: the mechanism works behind the scenes (typically not showing any trace of its activity in the browser window), and the code that checks or sets the cookie can be centralized (rather than affecting every form and link).

What's the drawback? Some very old browsers do not support cookies at all, and more recent browsers allow users to deny cookie-setting privileges to Web servers. So, although cookies make for a smooth solution, we can't assume that they are always available.

> **Note** There is a subtle difference in the "coverage" of cookie-based sessions and that of sessions based on GET/POST variables. A variable-based session will only maintain its identity as long as your user stays within your site, following intrasite links or form postings. However, there are any number of ways that a user might go away and come back again within a short period of time — by visiting a site that your site links to, which in turn links back, or by wandering away and then finding your site again with a search engine. Cookie-based approaches will treat returns from these little detours as a continuation of the same session, whereas variable-propagation approaches have to treat them as new visits.

> **Cross-Reference** Functions for setting and using cookies are covered in Chapter 26, "Cookies and HTTP." Also, see the sidebar in that chapter about the privacy implications of cookies. Finally, do not put any sensitive information in cookies before reading the discussion of cookies in Chapter 31, "Security and Cryptography."

How Sessions Work in PHP

Good session support takes care of two things: session tracking (that is, detecting when two separate script invocations are in fact part of the same user session) and storing information in association with a session. Obviously, you need the first capability before you can hope to have the second.

Note   Until session handling was added to PHP 4, the main session alternative was the PHPLIB package, which includes this capability, among many others. Treatment of sessions by PHPLIB is conceptually similar but differs in the details—there are people who feel strongly that PHPLIB sessions are preferable to PHP 4 sessions, and there are people who strongly believe the opposite. PHPLIB is available at `http://phplib.netuse.de`. (At this writing, PHPLIB is not entirely PHP 4–compatible, but that is likely to be resolved by the time this book is available.)

PHP session tracking works by a combination of the "hidden variables" method and the cookie method described in the last section. Because of the advantages of cookies, PHP will use them when the user's browser supports it, and otherwise will have recourse to GET and POST. Fortunately, though, the session functions themselves operate at a more abstract level and take care of checking for cookie support and so on all by themselves. If your version of PHP 4 has been appropriately configured for sessions, you should be able to use the session functions without worrying which method is being used.

Note   If you want PHP to transparently handle passing session variables for you when cookies are not available, you need to have configured PHP with both the `--enable-trans-sid` and `--enable-track-vars` options. If PHP is not handling this for you, you must arrange to pass a GET or POST argument in all your links and forms, of the form *session_name=session_id*. When a session is active, PHP provides a special constant, SID, that contains the right argument/value pair. Here is an example of including this constant in a link: `<A HREF="my_next_page.php?<?php echo(SID);?>">Next page</A>`

Caution   When cookies are not available, the automatic ID-passing feature (if enabled) will propagate the session ID via the GET method for links and the POST method for forms. However, it does not take care of passing this information via GET forms. In that case, you have to pass the session ID explicitly as a hidden variable. (This may well be an oversight in the beta versions that may be fixed in future releases.)

As we will see, if PHP is tracking a session for you, you can also store data by "registering" certain variables to let PHP know that their values should be saved in association with the session ID.

Making PHP aware of your session

The first step in a script that uses the session feature is to let PHP know that a session may already be in progress, so that it can hook up to it and recover any associated information. This is done by calling the function session_start(), which takes no arguments. (If you want every script invocation to look for a session without having to call this function, set the variable session.auto_start to 1 in your php.ini file [the usual default is 0]). Also, any call to session_register() will cause an implicit initial call to session_start().)

The effect of session_start() depends on whether PHP can locate a previous session identifier, as supplied either by HTTP arguments or by looking for a cookie. If one is found, then the values of any previously registered session variables are recovered, and those assigned variables are turned into regular page-level variables. For example, if a previous page in a session has registered the variable $city and assigned it the value 'Chicago', then our script can take advantage of it simply by calling session_start():

```
session_start();
print("$city, $city, that toddlin' town<BR>");
```

The lyric will be as we expect. If no such variable has been previously registered and assigned, or if we forget the call to session_start(), the variable will act as though it is unbound.

Note Pulling session bindings into a page by calling session_start() will overwrite any variable bindings with the same name that already exist at that point in the script. In particular, this means that if a given variable is passed by GET/POST and there is also a cookie-based session-level binding, the session binding will "win." (See the next chapter for more on the ordering of GET, POST, and cookie variables.)

If PHP cannot find a previous session identifier, then the call to session_start() actually does start a new session. The main effect of this is that a new unique identifier is created, which can now be used to register variables.

Registering variables in sessions

Calling session_start() takes care of "importing" any variables from the session context to our current script—now all we have to worry about is "exporting" them again, to see that they make it to later pages in the same session. This is done with the function session_register(). As it turns out, the import business is wholesale (one call to session_start() does it), but the export business is retail (we have to name each registered variable individually). Furthermore, what's imported does not automatically get exported again unless we say that it should.

Say that, as in the previous example, a previous page has set the value of $city to be 'Chicago'. Here's how we would take advantage of it, and set it up (or change it) for later pages as well:

```
session_start();
print("$city, $city, that toddlin' town<BR>");
session_register('city');
print("$city, $city, I'll show you around<BR>");
$city = 'San Mateo';
```

The `session_start()` call pulls in the binding of $city to 'Chicago' as before, so it can be used in the first print statement. From then on, $city would normally be treated just like any other global page variable. The call to `session_register()`, however, puts the session mechanism on notice that the 'city' variable is to be exported again out to session-world, and that later pages in the same session should receive whatever binding $city has at the end of this script. In the preceding excerpt, the value gets changed to 'San Mateo', so future pages should expect to do their toddlin' there.

Note   Variable names given as arguments to `session_register` should not include the leading '$'.

If we had forgotten the `session_start()` call, the first print line would have empty strings in place of the $city variable. The second print line would look good even so, because calling `session_register()` causes an implicit call to `session_start()`, if such a call has not already been made. Finally, if we had omitted the `session_register()` call, then everything on this page would look fine, but subsequent pages would not receive any session variable called 'city'.

Note   Registration of a variable is entirely independent of assigning a value to it. You can assign a value to a variable without registering it (in which case it will simply be a normal page variable that is not propagated to other pages), or you can register a variable without assigning it a value (in which case it will show up in later pages as unset).

Registered variables are super-globals

As an aside, one useful way to think of registering a session variable is as a "super-global" declaration. Variables that appear inside function definitions have scope local to that function, unless they have been declared to be global. Similarly, regular global variables have page-only scope unless they have been registered as being (super-global) session variables.

Where is the data really stored?

There are two things that the session mechanism must hang onto: the session ID itself, and any associated variable bindings.

As we have seen, either the session ID is stored as a cookie on the browser's machine, or it is incorporated into the GET/POST arguments submitted with page requests. In the latter case, there is really no storage happening — the ID is submitted as part of a request and is returned folded into HTML code for links and forms, which may generate the next request. The browser and server pass this vital information back and forth like a hot potato, and the session is effectively over if either side drops it.

By default, the contents of session variables are stored in special files on the server, one file per session ID. (It's already slightly rude to be storing the session ID as a client-side cookie — it would be even more rude to store session variable data on the client disk when it's not necessary.) Doing this kind of storage requires the session code to serialize the data, which means turning it into a linear sequence of bytes that could be written to a file and read back to recreate the data.

Caution   Although in theory you should be able to register variables that contain any PHP data whatsoever, as of PHP 4 beta versions there was still no reliable support for serializing objects. Such support may be in the final release or a later version, but at a minimum it's worth testing any code that registers object variables to make sure they are being recreated correctly.

It's possible to configure PHP to store the contents of session variables in a server-side database, rather than in files. For more on this, see the "Configuration Issues" section later in this chapter.

Session Functions

Table 25-1 lists the most important session-related functions, with descriptions of what they do. Note that in some cases the behavior of these functions depends on configuration options detailed later in this chapter.

<table>
<tr><td colspan="2" align="center">Table 25-1
Session Function Summary</td></tr>
<tr><td>*Function*</td><td>*Behavior*</td></tr>
<tr><td>session_start()</td><td>Takes no arguments and causes PHP either to notice a session ID that has been passed to it (via a cookie or GET/POST) or to create a new session ID if none is found.
If an old session ID is found, PHP will retrieve the assignments of all variables that had been registered and make those assigned variables available as regular global variables.</td></tr>
</table>

Function	Behavior
session_register()	Takes a string as argument and registers the variable named by the string—for example, session_register('username'). (Note: the variable-name string should not include the leading '$'.) It can also be passed an array of string arguments to register multiple variables at once. The effect of registering a variable is that subsequent assignments to that variable will be preserved for future sessions. (After a script completes, the registered variables and their values are serialized and propagated in such a way that later calls to session_start() can recreate the bindings.) If session_start() has not yet been called, session_register will implicitly call it before executing.
session_unregister()	Takes a string variable name as argument and unregisters the corresponding variable from the session. As a result, the variable binding will no longer be serialized and propagated to later pages. (The variable-name string should not include the leading '$'.)
session_is_registered()	Takes a variable-name string and tests whether a variable with a given variable name is registered in the current session, returning TRUE if so and FALSE if not.
session_destroy()	Calling this function gets rid of all session variable information that has been stored. (Note: a browser's session ID may still be the same after this function call.) It does not unset any variables in the current script.
session_name()	When called with no arguments, returns the current session-name string. This is usually 'PHPSESSID' by default. When called with one string argument, session_name() sets the current session name to that string. This name is used as a key to find the session ID in cookies and GET/POST arguments—for successful retrieval, the session name must be the same as it was when the values were serialized and stored. Note that there is no reason to change the session name unless you have some need to distinguish session types that are being served by the same Web server (such as in the case of multiple sites that each track sessions). The session name is reset to the default whenever a script executes, so any name change must happen in every script that uses the name, and before any other session functions are called.

Continued

Table 25-1 *(continued)*

Function	Behavior
session_module_name()	If given no arguments, returns the name of the module that is responsible for handling session data. This name currently defaults to 'files', meaning that session bindings are serialized and then written to files in the directory named by the function session_save_path(). If given a string argument, changes the module name to that string. (This could presumably be, for example, 'user' for a user-defined session database, but it should not be changed unless you know what you are doing.)
session_save_path()	Returns (or sets, if given an argument) the pathname of the directory to which session variable-binding files will be written (which typically defaults to /tmp on UNIX systems). This directory needs to exist and have appropriate permissions for PHP to write files to it.
session_id()	Takes no arguments, and returns a string which is the unique key corresponding to a particular session. If given a string argument, will set the session ID to that string.
session_encode()	Returns a string encoding of the state of the current session, suitable for use by string_decode(). This can be used for saving a session for revival at some later time, such as by writing the encoded string to a file or database.
session_decode()	Takes a string encoding as produced by session_encode() and reestablishes the session state, turning session bindings into page bindings as session_start() does.

Sample Session Code

The code shown in Listing 25-1 serves a dual purpose: it shows some session functions in action (specifically session_start(), session_register(), session_id(), and session_destroy()), and it can be downloaded for testing your own session setup. (Code listings from this book can be found at http://

www.troutworks.com/phpbook, and for this particular chapter at http://www. troutworks.com/phpbook/ch25). The script specifies a single page, which has a link to itself and a form that submits to itself.

Listing 25-1: A session test script

```php
<?php
session_start();
session_register('pagecount');
session_register('username');
if (IsSet($pagecount))
  $pagecount++;
else
  $pagecount = 1;
$pagecount_limit = 5;
?>
<HTML><HEAD><TITLE>Session testing page</TITLE>
</HEAD><BODY>
<H3>Session testing</H3>
Your session ID is <?php print(session_id());?><BR>
There might be any number of other session IDs, but
this one is yours.

<P>Don't bother writing your session ID down.<BR>
It's really a behind-the-scenes kind of thing.<BR>
PHP needs to know it but you probably don't.<BR>
<?php
  if (IsSet($posted_username))
    $username = $posted_username;
if (IsSet($username))
  {
    print("<P>We know your name! It's $username<BR>");
  }
?>
<P>You have visited <?php print($pagecount);?>
  page(s) this session.<BR>
<?php if ($pagecount == 1)
        print("You must have just arrived!<BR>"); ?>
You are only allowed <?php print($pagecount_limit);?>
  pages per session.<BR>

<P>This is a link to
<A HREF="<?php echo $PHP_SELF;?>">this very page</A>.<BR>
Following it will increase the number of pages<BR>
you have visited in your session, but won't do much else.
<P>Here is a form you can use to tell us
  your name if you feel like it.<BR>
```

Continued

Listing 25-1 *(continued)*

```
We won't sell it to anyone.<BR>
<P><FORM METHOD=POST ACTION="<?php echo $PHP_SELF;?>" >
    My name is:
    <INPUT TYPE=TEXT SIZE=20 NAME=posted_username><BR>
    <INPUT TYPE=SUBMIT NAME=SUBMIT VALUE="Remember me!">
    </FORM>
</BODY></HTML>

<?php
if ($pagecount >= $pagecount_limit)
    session_destroy();
?>
```

In order, the sample code does the following things with session function calls:

1. It calls `session_start()` to tell PHP to look for a preexisting session — if none is found, a new session ID is created. (This is actually redundant, because the immediately following call to `session_register()` would take care of starting the session if `session_start()` had been omitted.)

2. The function `session_register()` is used to let PHP know about two variables: `'username'` and `'pagecount'`. After this call, they are both registered but still unbound.

3. We increment `$pagecount` — because it was unbound, it was interpreted as 0, so it is 1 after the incrementing.

4. The function `session_id()` is used to print the unique ID for this session. (This would be unusual to do in a production site — this is not need-to-know info for the user.)

5. If this page has posted the `$posted_username` variable to itself (using the form at the bottom), that name is stored in the `$username` variable, which is registered. As a result `$username` will persist to future script invocations, even though `$posted_username` will not.

6. Finally, somewhat arbitrarily, this page has decided that people are only allowed a limited number of views of this page before the session starts over. It uses `session_destroy()` to get rid of all session-variable information, which means that we start over with both `$pagecount` and `$username`.

Figures 25-1, 25-2, and 25-3 show browser shots of what Listing 25-1 might produce as the user first arrives, then posts the username form, then follows the link. In this case we were using a browser that accepted cookies, so no session information appears in the URL.

Figure 25-1: The session test page upon arrival

Figure 25-2: The session test page after form submission

Figure 25-3: The session test page after following the self-link

Configuration Issues

The variables in Table 25-2 are settable in the php.ini file and viewable by calling phpinfo(). We offer descriptions and the "typical" default values (some defaults are platform-dependent).

Table 25-2 Session Configuration Variables		
Php.ini Variable	**Typical Value**	**Description**
session.save_path	/tmp under UNIX systems	Pathname for the server-side folder where session variable-binding files will be written.

Php.ini Variable	Typical Value	Description
session.auto_start	0	When 1, sessions will initialize automatically every time a script loads. When 0, no session code will be code unless there is an explicit call to either session_start() or session_register().
session.save_handler	'files'	String that determines underlying method for saving session variable information. Other methods are currently not very well documented — changing this is not recommended for the casual user.
session.cookie_lifetime	0	Specifies how long session cookies take to expire, and consequently the lifetime of a session. The default of 0 means that sessions last until the browser is closed — any other value indicates the number of seconds the session is allowed to live.
session.use_cookies	1	If 1, the session mechanism will attempt to propagate the session ID by setting/checking a cookie. (If the browser refuses the cookie, then GET/POST vars are used.) If this variable is 0, no attempt to use cookies is made.

Gotchas and Troubleshooting

If you are having trouble with sessions, first make sure that your session support exists and is doing what you think it is. Try downloading the sample session code from http://www.troutworks.com/phpbook/ch25, and debug from the earliest error, if any.

If sessions are not working or are giving errors, check the pathname returned by session_save_path(), and make sure that it exists and is PHP writable. If not, you should either make it be so or change the value of 'session.save_path' in php.ini.

Remember that session functions that have variable names as arguments do not expect a leading '$' in the name.

If you ever run into a complaint that refers to already having sent HTTP headers, it may be that your script is sending some text (even blank lines) before the `session_start()` or `session_register()` functions. Scrutinize any included files for blank lines, or move the session functions to the very beginning of your file.

When testing session-related code, remember to try it out both with a browser that accepts cookies and with a browser that is set up to refuse them. If you see no session name in the URL of a link (such as, `'PHPSESSID'`) with a cookie-refusing browser, then either sessions are not working or your version of PHP is not configured to transparently pass session IDs in the `GET/POST` arguments.

Summary

Sessions are useful for tracking a user's behavior over interactions that last longer than one script execution or page download. If what you present to the user depends on which previous pages they have seen or interacted with, your code will need to store or propagate that information in a way that distinguishes one user from another. Because the HTTP protocol is stateless, this inevitably entails some kind of workaround technique — usually either "hidden variables" (which impose maintenance headaches) or cookies (which are not universally supported by client browsers).

The PHP implementation of sessions encapsulates these messy issues and presents a clean layer of abstraction to the scripter. Unique session identifiers are automatically created and propagated, and a registration mechanism lets the programmer associate arbitrary PHP data with a session. Aside from one's having to connect to a session initially and register the variables that should persist beyond the current page, session use is virtually transparent to the programmer.

✦   ✦   ✦

Cookies
and HTTP

◆ ◆ ◆ ◆

In This Chapter

Setting and
reading cookies

Sending raw
HTTP headers

Redirecting
the browser
using HTTP

◆ ◆ ◆ ◆

T he HyperText Transfer Protocol (HTTP) is the "language"
that Web servers and Web clients use to talk to each other.
Whenever you visit a Web site, you are engaging in a conversation over the Internet in HTTP (or a variant, such as the secure
protocol HTTPS). Typical Web users do not have to concern
themselves with the details of HTTP, nor do most Web programmers. For most of this book, for example, we use PHP to
produce an HTML document or a client-side script that will display appropriately when displayed in the user's browser. HTTP
is just the vehicle that transmits requests to our PHP script and
then carries our HTML responses back to the user for display.

In this chapter, we look at a few techniques that depend
on other parts of this client/server interaction, such as storing client-side information in cookies on the user machine,
or explicitly using HTTP headers for purposes like user
authentication or redirection to a different Web page. The
PHP functions that implement direct HTTP interaction are
actually very simple, and there are only a couple of them —
any difficulties or pitfalls really arise from constraints
imposed by the protocol itself.

Cookies

A *cookie* is a small piece of information that is retained on the
client machine, either in the browser's application memory
or as a small file written to the user's hard disk. It contains
a name/value pair — "setting a cookie" means associating a
value with a name, and storing that pairing on the client side.
"Getting" or "reading" a cookie means using the name to
retrieve the value. (See the sidebar "Cookies and privacy"
for a summary of the controversy surrounding the use
of cookies.)

Note

As a general rule, you only want to store information in a client-side cookie when storing it on the server is not an option. This is partly simple politeness, but it is also because there are constraints that prevent server abuses of the client's hard disk (typically one Web server can store a maximum of 20 cookies per client, for example). If you need to store a lot of info, consider developing a scheme where the cookie file contains an ID that enables you to look up the rest of that information on the server.

In PHP, cookies are set using the setcookie() function, and cookies are read nearly automatically. That is, any cookies that have been set by your server will show up as page-level variables (much as GET/POST variables do).

Cross-Reference

Many uses of cookies amount to session-tracking—keeping track of some piece of information as a single user navigates through your site. If you are tempted to use cookies for a purpose like this, and you are using PHP 4, you might want to consider simply using the built-in session functions that are covered in the previous chapter. Not only do they offer a nicer level of abstraction, but they have a built-in fallback mechanism that deals with refusal of cookies by propagating the information via GET/POST arguments instead.

The setcookie() function

There is just one cookie-related function, called setcookie(). Table 26-1 shows its arguments, in order, all but the first of which are optional:

Table 26-1 Arguments to setcookie()		
Argument Name	*Expected Type*	*Meaning*
name	string	The name of your cookie (analogous to the name of a variable).
value	string	The value you want to store in the cookie (analogous to the value you would assign to a variable). If this argument is not supplied, the cookie named by the first argument is deleted.
expire	int	Specifies when this cookie should expire. A value of 0 (the default) means that it should last until the browser is closed. Any other integer is interpreted as an absolute time (as returned by the function mktime()) when the cookie should expire.

Argument Name	Expected Type	Meaning
path	string	In the default case, any page within the Web root folder would see (and be able to set) this named cookie. Setting the path to a subdirectory (for example, "/mysteryguide") allows distinguishing cookies that have the same name but are set by different "sites" or subareas of the Web server.
domain	string	In the default case, no check is made against the domain requested by the client. If this argument is nonempty, then the domain must match. For example, if the same server serves mysteryguide.com and sciencebookguide.com, then one site's code can ensure that the other site does not read (or set) its cookies by including this argument as "mysteryguide.com."
secure	int (0 or 1)	Defaults to 0. If this argument is 1, the cookie will only be sent over a secure (https) connection. Note that a secure connection must already be running for such a cookie to be set in the first place.

Cross-Reference For details about the representation of time used by the expire argument, see Chapter 13, "Filesystem and System Functions," specifically the functions time() and mktime().

Caution Calling setcookie() results in sending HTTP header information, which cannot be done after you have already sent some regular PHP output (even if that output consists of a single space or blank line!).

Examples

Some example calls follow to setcookie(), with comments:

```
setcookie('membername', 'timboy');
```

This sets a cookie called membername, with a value of timboy. Because there are no arguments except for the first two, the cookie will persist only until the current browser program is closed, and it will be read on subsequent page requests from this browser to this server, regardless of the domain name in the request, or where in the Web root file hierarchy the page is served from. The cookie will also be read regardless of whether the Web connection is secure.

```
setcookie('membername', 'troutgirl', time() + 86400,
          "", "www.troutworks.com", 1);
```

This sets the cookie to have the value `'troutgirl'` and would overwrite the previous example's value if it had been set by a previous page. The expiration time is set to 86,400 seconds (or 1 day = 60 seconds × 60 minutes × 24 hours) after the current time. The path argument is skipped by giving it an empty string (`""`), so this cookie will still be read regardless of where it is in the Web directory hierarchy. The host argument is set to `'www.troutworks.com'`, which means that subsequent page views will not cause the cookie to be read unless the user actually was making a request of that host. Finally, the last argument specifies that this cookie will only be read or written over a secure connection. (If the very connection used by this page is not secure, then presumably the cookie will not be set at all.)

Caution   Multiple calls to `setcookie()` will typically be interpreted in the opposite order that they appear in your PHP script, although not every browser version does this. The best rule is to never send two different values for the same cookie from a single page execution. (Sending more than one is pointless anyway, since one of them will always overwrite the other).

Note   If you want to specify later arguments to `setcookie()` while leaving the earlier ones with their default values, it is best to give the empty string ("") for the domain argument, a string containing a slash character ("/") for the path argument, and 0 for the expiration.

Cookies and privacy

Cookies have always been controversial from a privacy point of view, and that controversy has heated up recently. As we write this, DoubleClick (an Internet advertising agency) is being flamed for its announcement that it plans to cross-correlate cookie information with a very large database of consumer names, addresses, and buying habits (in an apparent reversal of earlier promises about such behavior). The worry is that, once a consumer reveals his or her identity on a site by filling out a form and accepting a cookie, then any other site that compares notes with the original site can know the true identity of the user (and lots of other information as well). If this practice became widespread, every e-commerce site you visit might be able to figure out not only your name, address, and buying habits, but also a list of other pages you have visited on the Web.

So, cookies are worrisome, but at the same time they are also a reasonable and benign workaround to the statelessness of the HTTP protocol. There are plenty of good reasons to want a Web client/server interaction to coherently span a few page requests in a row, rather than covering just a single request. As a Web designer, you might well decide to use cookies for such a purpose, comfortable in the knowledge that there is no substantive invasion of privacy occurring.

Your comfort is not the same as the user's comfort, however, and many users have quite reasonably set up their browsers to refuse all cookies. (Remember that what is at issue here is not only the user's privacy, but also the use of their own personal hard disks!) Any server-side code you write should gracefully handle a cookie refusal from the client side, and any Web sites you design should have easily found privacy policies, so that your users know what they are getting into.

Deleting cookies

Deleting a cookie is easy. Simply call `setcookie(cookie_name)`, with no second argument for the value. This does not set the cookie's value to an empty string — it actually removes the cookie.

Reading cookies

Cookies that have been set automatically appear as page-level global variables if they are successfully read. So, for example, setting a cookie as follows:

```
setcookie('membername', 'timboy');
```

would mean that on a *later* page access you might be able to print out the value again as easily as this:

```
print("The member name is $membername<BR>");
```

Note

> If you set a cookie in a given script, it won't be set on the client until that page (and its HTTP headers) are sent off to the client, which is too late for you to be able to take advantage of it in that very script. This means that the corresponding global variable won't be available to you until the next page request.

The following typically will not work as you might expect:

```
setcookie('membername', 'timboy');
print("I set a cookie!  Now I will grab the value<BR>");
// (WRONG - the following membername will most likely be blank)
print("The member name is $membername<BR>");
```

This is because, as the preceding note points out, the cookie will not be set until the current page's worth of HTTP headers arrives at the client. Because that has not yet happened in this example, and the variable $membername has not been otherwise set, it will probably be an empty string in the preceding print statement.

The following gets it right:

```
$cookievalue = 'timboy';
setcookie('membername', $cookievalue);
print("I set a cookie for the benefit of future pages<BR>");
// (RIGHT - only print variables that this page actually set)
print("Its name is membername, its value is $cookievalue<BR>");
```

Any subsequent scripts that are loaded into the same browser can now refer to $membername.

Cross-Reference   We have already noted some privacy risks to users of accepting cookies from servers. It's worth noting that there are risks that go the other way as well. If you write scripts that depend on the integrity of data that you include in cookies, you should remember that a clever end user can edit those cookies and install arbitrary values in them. See Chapter 31, "Security and Cryptography," for techniques for encrypting sensitive data, even inside cookies.

Get, post, and cookie variables

Your humble authors heartily endorse the decision of the PHP designers to make various kinds of information immediately accessible in the form of global variables. GET/POST arguments, cookie values, and various kinds of configuration and environmental information all just show up ready for use, without the hassle of making some kind of formal requisition. Of course, the inevitable downside of global availability is namespace clashes—at some point or other in your PHP career, you will probably run into a confusing bug arising from the fact that a particular global variable was bound when you thought it wouldn't be, or was overwritten unexpectedly. This is less of a problem with Web scripts (which typically can do what they like with their namespace, because no regular variable assignments persist downstream to any other code) than with other kinds of programming, but that will be small comfort when you are debugging.

The values of GET variables, POST variables, and cookies all show up as global page variables at the beginning of a script. If two or more of these sources have a variable with the same name, one or more of the values will be overwritten. The default overwriting order is "Get, Post, Cookie"—this means that POST arguments will overwrite any GET variables of the same name, and cookie variables will overwrite POST arguments.

Example: variable overwriting order

Listing 26-1 shows code that plays with all three sources of global variables and shows the default overwriting order in action.

Listing 26-1: Showing the overwriting order of Get, Post, Cookie

```php
<?php
  if ((!IsSet($VarSource)) ||
      ($VarSource != "a cookie"))
    setcookie("VarSource", "a cookie");
  else
    setcookie("VarSource");
?>
<HTML>
<HEAD>
  <TITLE>Displaying variable overwriting order</TITLE>
</HEAD>
<?php
if (IsSet($VarSource))
  print("VarSource: $VarSource<BR>");
else
  print("VarSource has not been set");
?>
<P>This is a self-posting form:
 <FORM METHOD=POST
   ACTION="<?php echo $PHP_SELF?>?VarSource=Get">
   <INPUT TYPE=SUBMIT VALUE=SUBMIT>
   <INPUT TYPE=HIDDEN NAME=VarSource VALUE=Post>
 </FORM>
</BODY></HTML>
```

In the code, there are three possible ways that the global variable $VarSource might be bound: from a POST variable, from a GET variable, and from a cookie. Somewhat whimsically, the very beginning of the code sets the 'VarSource' cookie if $VarSource was not set as a cookie, and deletes that cookie if it was set. Under the default ordering, this will result in an alternation of setting and unsetting the cookie if we keep reloading the page.

The only other purpose of this page is to display the value of $VarSource (if it is set), and also to present a self-posting form that has both GET and POST arguments of that same name. (Using GET and POST at the same time is unstylish, but not illegal.)

Figure 26-1 shows the result of loading the code from Listing 26-1 into the browser for the first time.

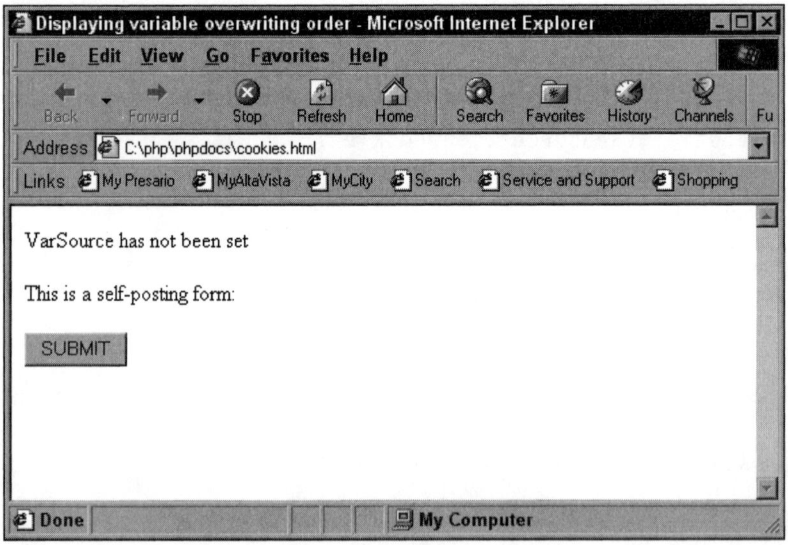

Figure 26-1: A first visit to the overwriting-order script

The first time we visit, we have supplied no GET or POST arguments, and although a cookie is probably being set this time, it is not available to this script yet. As a result, $VarSource is not yet assigned.

Figure 26-2 shows the response after we press the Submit button from our first visit. Now $VarSource is bound to "a cookie," because the cookie was set the first time. Actually, in this particular case, all three sources (GET, POST, and the cookie) supplied values for $VarSource, which was overwritten in that order.

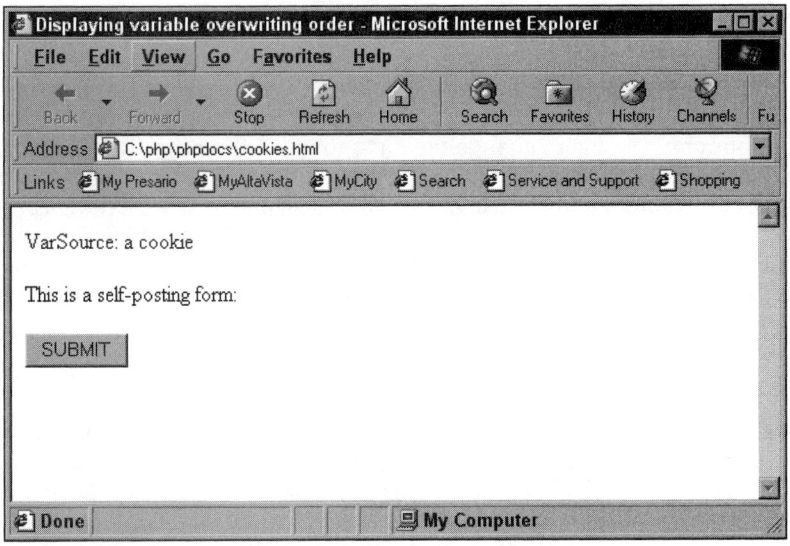

Figure 26-2: The overwriting-order script after self-posting

Finally, if the Submit button is pressed again, we will see Figure 26-3. The cookie was unset on the second visit, so the POST variable survives. Note the GET variable in the URL itself, which was overwritten.

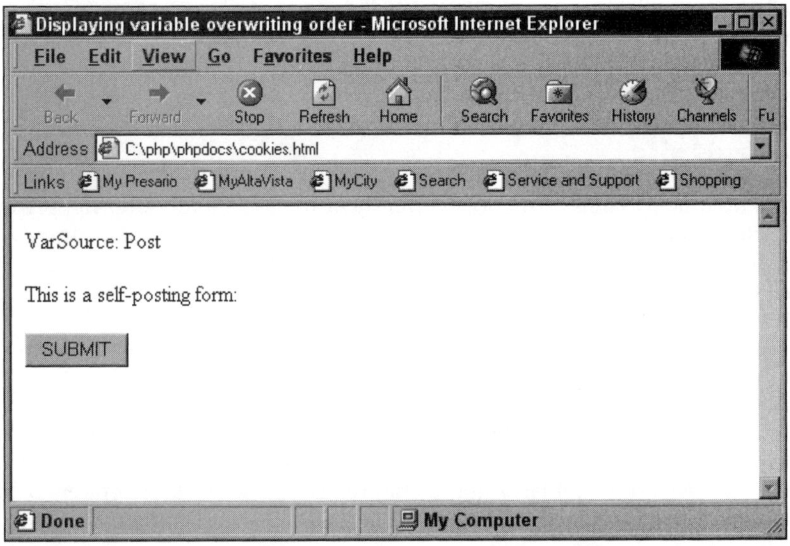

Figure 26-3: The overwriting-order script after self-posting twice

Customizing the overwriting order

The default overwriting order for producing global variables from different HTTP sources is "GPC," a shorthand for "get-post-cookie." If you are running your own PHP installation and decide that you don't like this default behavior, you can override it by editing your php.ini file to change the "gpc_order" directive from "GPC" to something else. Global variables will be set by using the HTTP information sources in the order of the letters in that string, with later assignments overwriting earlier ones. If you omit a letter, then the corresponding source will not be used in assigning to a global variable. For example, if you set the gpc_order directive to "PG", then POST variables will be overwritten by GET variables of the same name, and cookies will have no effect on global variables.

The GET, POST, and COOKIE variable arrays

Finally, if all this namespace merging seems confusing or ad hoc, it is possible to recover exactly which variables came from which source, by using the arrays HTTP_GET_VARS, HTTP_POST_VARS, and HTTP_COOKIE_VARS. Each of these is an associative array that maps names to values and holds the variable mappings from the given source, independently of later assignment to globals. For example, the script in Listing 26-1 printed the value of the global variable $var_source, with a value that depended on the overwriting order. If you knew that your desired value came from a particular HTTP source, you could choose to print the value of HTTP_GET_VARS['var_source'], HTTP_POST_VARS['var_source'], or HTTP_COOKIE_VARS['var_source'] instead.

> **Note** PHP will only keep track of the HTTP variables in these arrays if the track_vars configuration variable is set to TRUE. It will be true if you have configured PHP with --enable-track-vars, which sets the default; otherwise, you can change the configuration by editing that variable in your php.ini file.

Cookie pitfalls

It is hard to do much wrong with cookies purely at the PHP level. After all, setting a cookie involves only one function (set_cookie()), and reading cookies involves no functions at all (because cookie values automagically appear as global variables). What could be easier than that? The problems that typically arise are those imposed by the HTTP protocol itself.

Sending something else first

The single most common error in using cookies is trying to set a cookie after some regular HTML content has already been generated. (We may be repeating ourselves here, but we will also repeat it later in the chapter, because this fact applies to other direct HTTP protocol manipulations in addition to cookies and is the cause of a great deal of debugging confusion.)

The reason this doesn't work is that the HTTP protocol requires headers to be sent before the content of the HTML page itself — they can't be intermixed. As soon as any regular content is generated, PHP figures that it must already know about all headers of interest, and so it sends them off and then begins the transmission of HTML content. If it encounters a cookie (or other header information) later on, it is too late, and an error is generated.

It's surprisingly easy to write code that violates this prohibition. Consider the following:

```
 <?php /* A subtle, insidious cookie error */
setcookie('mycookie', 'myvalue');
?>
<HTML><HEAD>
<TITLE>A seemingly benign cookie-setting page</TITLE>
</HEAD><BODY>
  <H3>This page is so simple it absolutely must be right</H3>
</BODY></HTML>
```

When we load this script, we get browser output indicating "cannot add header information." The culprit is the very first character in the file: the space before '<?php'. Because PHP files start off in HTML mode by default, this file causes one space's worth of generated content to be sent to the client before PHP mode kicks in and the attempt is made to set the cookie.

A similar way to accidentally send header information too early is to load an include file that includes blank lines at the end, after the closing PHP tag. Finally, of course, you can violate the prohibition entirely in PHP mode, but only if you include something like a print or echo statement.

If you ever run into this kind of error, it is relatively easy to debug if you are methodical about it. Try moving HTTP-related code toward the beginning of the script file first — if you still get the error after that, then trace backward from the offending line toward the beginning of the file. Somewhere between the beginning and the failing statement you either have some characters that are being interpreted in HTML mode, or else you have a PHP printing construct. If you have any included PHP files before the offending statement, make sure that there are no characters at all before the start tags or after the end tags.

New Feature

Our repeated warnings about the order of HTTP header information and page contents are valid for all versions of PHP 3, and for PHP 4 versions up through beta 3. However, the PHP 4 designers have announced that the full release of version 4 will include an "output buffering" feature, which will collect certain kinds of PHP output and save it up to be sent all at once, rather than sending it to the client as soon as it is generated. This means that PHP itself will take care of holding off on regular page content until all HTTP headers have been sent, which in turn will mean that your script can interleave them at will. You should be able to test to see if this buffering is enabled in your version of PHP 4 by trying one of the violating examples in this chapter (if it works without problems, then output is being buffered). Alternatively, check the output of php_info() for mention of output buffering — if it is present, then you should be able to change the setting by editing your php.ini file.

Reverse order interpretation

As with most HTTP commands, calls to setcookie() will actually be executed in the opposite order from how they appear in your PHP script. This means that a pair of successive statements like the following will probably have the counterintutive result of leaving the "mycookie" cookie with no value, because the unsetting statement is executed second.

```
setcookie("mycookie");// get rid of the old value (WRONG)
setcookie("mycookie", "newvalue");// set the new value (WRONG)
```

 Tip

There is typically no need to remove a cookie before setting it to a different value — simply set it to the desired new value. Among other things, this means that the confusing reverse order of interpretation of setcookie() calls should not usually matter — if the effect depends on the order, it may mean that you are doing something wrong (or at least something unnecessary).

Cookie refusal

Finally, be aware that setcookie() makes no guarantees that any cookie data will in fact be accepted by the client browser — setcookie() just agrees to try, by sending off the appropriate HTTP headers. What happens after that is up to the client, and the client may be an older browser that does not accept cookies, or a browser whose user has intentionally disabled cookies.

The setcookie() function does not even return a value that indicates acceptance or refusal of the cookie. If you think about it, this is imposed by the timing of the script execution and the HTTP protocol. First the script executes (including the setcookie() call), with the result that a page complete with HTTP headers is sent to the client machine. At this point the client browser decides how to react to the cookie-setting attempt. Not until the client generates another request can the server receive the cookie's value and detect whether the cookie-setting attempt was successful. The implication of this for scripting is that you must always ensure that something reasonable happens even in cases where setcookie() is called without success. One common technique is to set a test cookie with the name "CookiesOn," and then check on a subsequent page load if the $CookiesOn variable has been set.

Sending HTTP Headers

The setcookie() call provides a wrapper around a particular usage of HTTP headers. In addition, PHP offers the header() function, which you can use to send raw, arbitrary HTTP headers. You could use this to roll your own cookie function if you liked, but you can also use it to take advantage of any other kind of header-controlled functionality.

The syntax of header() is as simple as it could be: it takes a single string argument, which is the header to be sent.

Caution

All of the cautions from earlier in this chapter about sending HTTP before any real page content apply to the header() function as well. Unless you are running PHP 4 with the output-buffering feature enabled, then all your calls to header() must precede any HTML output from your script. This is true even if the HTML output is a single space or blank line.

Example: Redirection

One useful kind of HTTP header is "Location:", which can act as a redirector. Simply put a fully qualified URL after the "Location:" string, and the browser will start over again with the new address instead. An example:

```php
<?php
  if ((IsSet($gender) && ($gender == "female"))
    {
      header(
"Location: http://www.troutworks.com/phpbook/ch26/secret.php");
      exit;
    }
?>
<HTML><HEAD><TITLE>The inclusive page</TITLE></HEAD></HTML>
<BODY>
<H3>Welcome!</H3>
We welcome anyone to this page, even men!  Talk amongst
yourselves.
</BODY></HTML>
```

If we simply enter the URL for this page (http://www.troutworks.com/phpbook/ inclusive.php), we will see the rendering of the HTML at the bottom. On the other hand, if we include the right GET argument (http://www.troutworks.com/ phpbook/inclusive.php?gender=female), we find ourselves redirected to a different page entirely. Note that this is significantly different from selectively importing contents with the "include" statement — we actually end up browsing a different URL than the one we typed in, and that new Web address is what shows up in the "Location" or "Address" bar of your browser.

This kind of redirection can be useful when you want the structure of your Web site to conditionally "branch" without having to make the user explicitly choose different links.

Example: HTTP authentication

Another useful thing you can do with HTTP is ask the browser to ask the user for a username and password, via a pop-up window. This is done with the WWW-Authenticate header, as in the following example:

```php
<?php
  $the_right_user = 'user';  // example only! not recommended
  $the_right_password = 'password';  // example only!

  if(!isset($PHP_AUTH_USER)) {
    Header("WWW-Authenticate: Basic realm=\"PHP book\"");
    Header("HTTP/1.0 401 Unauthorized");
    echo "Canceled by user\n";
    exit;
  } else {
    if (($PHP_AUTH_USER == 'user') &&
        ($PHP_AUTH_PW == 'password')) //see caution below
      print("The realm is yours<BR>");
    else
      print("We don't need your kind<BR>");
  }
?>
```

If we visit this script for the first time (and are using the appropriate browser and server versions), we will get a pop-up window. Once the user enters the information into the pop-up box, the script is automatically called again with new variables $PHP_AUTH_USER (set to the user string entered), $PHP_AUTH_PASSWD (set to the password string entered), and $PHP_AUTH_TYPE (which will be "Basic" until such time as PHP supports another type of HTTP authentication). The nice thing about this is that these variables will continue to be set by the browser on each request, and you do not need to do anything in your scripts to propagate them — one verification of identity per session should suffice.

Caution

The preceding code is the bare minimum necessary to demonstrate the HTTP authentication mechanism and is not a model for how user/password combinations should really be verified! Our code fragment simply compares the values of the variables delivered to hard-coded strings, which is a bad idea for several reasons. To make this part of a real verification system, you would probably want to compare the result of encrypting the password to a similarly encrypted version in a database or password file. See Chapter 31 for more on encryption and real security measures.

Note

The WWW-Authenticate mechanism only works under the Apache Web Server, with PHP as a module. It does not currently work in the CGI version, or under IIS/PWS.

In addition to redirection and authentication, the ability to send real HTTP headers offers finer control of many aspects of the HTTP client/server relationship, which usually are set by default. For example, you can explicitly set the expiration and caching behavior of your page, or send return status codes that tell the client whether whatever is returned should be considered a success or not. Because PHP is just acting as a channel to the underlying HTTP protocol, most of these techniques are beyond the scope of PHP documentation and this book.

Header gotchas

As we have said innumerable times by now, the header() function is subject to the same restriction as the setcookie() function: no headers may be sent after regular page content is generated, unless you are using a post-beta 3 release of PHP 4 that has output buffering enabled.

More generally, be aware that using the header capability requires not only some knowledge of the HTTP protocols, but also some knowledge of the extent to which different browser versions conform to them. Unless you are writing for a known population of users that all use the same browser, then you will probably need to do more cross-browser testing than with vanilla HTML-generating scripts.

 Tip   Most browsers can be set to warn you whenever they are about to accept a cookie. Although this can be annoying when viewing benign yet cookie-intensive sites, it can also be a great debugging tool when writing your own cookie-setting code.

Summary

PHP offers several ways to use the capabilities of the HTTP protocol, in addition to the obvious one of constructing HTML pages that are transmitted via HTTP. The setcookie() function allows you to set and delete cookies in your user's browser, the values of which show up in subsequent page views as ordinary global variables.

The header() function allows you to send arbitrary HTTP headers. Among other things, header() can be useful for authentication and page-level redirection.

The HTTP functions in PHP are very simple, and the main complexities that arise are a consequence of the HTTP protocol itself. One such complication is the fact that that HTTP requires all headers to be sent before any page content is sent. This was a very common source of errors in PHP 3 and beta versions of PHP 4. Fortunately, the release version of PHP 4 buffers HTTP output in such a way that you can now interleave headers and content at will.

✦   ✦   ✦

PHP and JavaScript

In this chapter, we try to get the best of both client-side and server-side scripting by combining PHP with JavaScript. We briefly touch upon the question of when to use which scripting language, and stylistic points that may be helpful when writing the code. Then we move on to pragmatic examples of the type you might see on a real-world PHP site.

Tip   If you've never worked with JavaScript before, you won't learn how just by reading this chapter. We will only touch on aspects of JavaScript that materially impinge upon PHP. If you're wondering what an `onBlur` event is, we recommend Danny Goodman's superlative *JavaScript Bible* (IDG Books, 1999).

Outputting JavaScript with PHP

Because PHP is server-side and JavaScript is client-side, you may expect problems using both on the same page. In actuality, it's the difference that makes them such a good match.

Although PHP offers plenty of power for creating dynamically generated Web pages, it is strictly a server-side language. There's a common category of Web site tasks that perhaps don't require all the processing power of a server and would best be done quickly—for instance, changing the look of a button on mouseover. JavaScript, a purely client-side language (there's a server-side version, but we're assuming you've already chosen PHP on that end), can be easily integrated into PHP to fill in many of these gaps.

On the other hand, client-side JavaScript (a.k.a. Javascript, JScript, ECMAScript) itself has many limitations. For example, because it can't communicate directly with a database,

JavaScript cannot update itself on the fly. Even worse, it's impossible to depend on client-side technologies, because they may not be present in a visitor's browser or may be disabled. Conscientious client-side Web developers must either decide to code probabilistically (and accept complaints from minority-browser users) or maintain several versions of a site at the same time. (Nonconscientious developers simply adapt themselves to the market-leading browser's full capabilities and damn the torpedoes . . . but that's another story.) PHP can help to mitigate the effects of client-side indeterminacy.

Dueling objects

Perhaps the biggest divergence between JavaScript and PHP is in the area of object models. The two are quite divergent conceptually, and they use different styles of notation. Some people consider this a good thing, because at least there's no chance of mixing up objects that look similar (as there is with, say, ASP and JavaScript). Probably just as many consider it a pain, an incompatibility, or a design flaw. In any case, there is no chance you can access the same object with both PHP and JavaScript — so forget it.

JavaScript is consistently object-oriented from top to bottom. Every statement requires an object and a method or function to be specified, and may also have event handlers. JavaScript uses the so-called "dot" object notation (`object.method`), which is similar to that of other common programming languages such as C, Java, and Microsoft's VBScript.

The downside is that JavaScript's document object model has been shakily standardized: although in theory ECMA and the W3C shepherd the international standard, in practice the various browser manufacturers violate/add to this core at their whim. Proficient JavaScripters spend a good deal of energy keeping track of incompatibilities and workarounds for various browsers and platforms.

As we discuss elsewhere in this book (notably Chapter 30), PHP's classes are more of an add-on, retrofit, or convenience than an essential part of the language. The notation is the "arrow" or "pointer" style that is sometimes seen in C++ code (`$this->variable`). There is no mechanism in place to use a "dot" style. Honesty compels us to admit that PHP classes probably don't ever add up to anything like a thoroughgoing object model. Not that we ever wanted one anyway — and who are you calling defensive?

PHP doesn't care what it outputs

The main thing to keep in mind is that PHP doesn't know or care what it returns. You can (and people do) use PHP to write out plain text, HTML, XHTML, DHTML, JavaScript, XML, MathML, various graphical formats, CSS, XSL, or even (for the ironic ironists among us) ASP. There's no real technical barrier to having PHP output C code, although it's probably not a usage whose popularity is going to sweep the nation. Remember, PHP does not always output PHP — its ultimate end product is usually code that will be run by another application, usually a browser.

There are a couple of ways to write out the JavaScript with PHP. The simplest is to escape from PHP whenever you get the urge to go client-side. This is accomplished in precisely the same way you would escape from HTML.

```
<?php
echo("Imagine tons of complex PHP code in this block.");
?>
<script language="JavaScript">
<!-- Hide from JavaScript disabled browsers
document.write("Strict separation of client-side and server-
side code is a good thing.")
// end hiding -->
</script>
<?php
echo("More PHP in this block.");
?>
```

Even this example doesn't show the fullest extent of PHP/JavaScript separation. A lot of JavaScript is actually defined within the <HEAD> element of an HTML page and simply called in the <BODY>, whereas PHP is generally used in the latter.

As with HTML, there are occasions when you don't want to escape from PHP — or this style may just be your personal preference. In that case, you can use PHP's echo or print statements to output JavaScript.

```
<?php
echo("This is some complex PHP code.");
echo("<script language=\"JavaScript\">\n");
echo("<!-- Hide from JavaScript disabled browsers\n");
echo("document.write(\"Strict separation of client-side and
server-side code is a good thing.\\n\")");
echo("// end hiding -->\n");
echo("</script>\n");
echo("More PHP in this block.");
?>
```

This style is not at all incorrect, but it can be considerably harder to keep everything straight. Unless you're an experienced programmer, you might want to limit this style to occasions in which you simply call predefined JavaScript functions, such as onSubmit events.

Caution You may run into trouble if you use JavaScript-style tags (for instance, <script language="PHP">) to delineate PHP chunks — the PHP parser may have a hard time figuring out which </script> tag goes with what <script> tag.

> **Tip**   Remember to escape double-quotes in JavaScript sections if using `echo`/`print` to output code. See line 3 of the preceding snippet.

Where to use JavaScript

Client-side JavaScript doesn't do heavy lifting, but it is faster at certain tasks and also allows for some effects that you can't easily duplicate with PHP. Some places you should definitely consider replacing or enhancing PHP with JavaScript include:

✦ Simple arithmetic in forms and calculators (such as shopping-cart running total, mortgage calculator).

✦ Browser sniffing

✦ Simple form validation (such as making sure e-mail addresses have "@" symbols)

✦ Site navigation (such as pull-down navigation menus)

✦ Pop-ups (alerts, search boxes)

✦ Mouseover and on-click events

PHP as a Backup for JavaScript

The flip side of our "where to use JavaScript" advice is that PHP can help caulk the cracks in JavaScript. Sometimes you can seamlessly implement both client-side and a server-side methods of doing a task. If a visitor's browser is JavaScript-enabled, fine—the visitor will be able to take advantage of the zippier method, generally without even noticing that they've had a choice. If not, at least you won't suffer the ignominy of totally locking them out of your site's functionality.

A perfect example is the double-barreled pull-down menu for site navigation. JavaScript gives you an instant redirect, whereas PHP provides the same result after a longer wait for those without JavaScript-enabled browsers. This trick takes advantage of the fact that JavaScript has event handlers (for example, `onChange`) that work off the structure of HTML forms without requiring an actual button-clicking submission. Therefore, the Submit button can be reserved for PHP's use.

```
<html>
<head>
<title>Navigation pulldown</title>
<script language="JavaScript">
<!--
function Browse(form, i){
  var site = form.elements[i].selectedIndex;
  if(site > 0){
```

```
        top.location = form.elements[i].options[site].value
    }
}
// -->
</script>
</head>

<body>
<form method="post" action="redirect.php">
<select name="category" onChange="Browse(this.form,0)">
<option selected value=0>Choose a Category</option>
<option value="desktop.php">Desktops</option>
<option value="laptop.php">Laptops</option>
<option value="monitor.php">Monitors</option>
<option value="input.php">Input devices</option>
<option value="storage.php">Storage devices</option>
</select>
<input type="submit"">
</form>
</body>
</html>
```

The file called `redirect.php` need only have one line:

```
<?php header("Location: $category/"); ?>
```

You could use a similar division of labor with form validation. If JavaScript is enabled, you can use it to make sure zip codes have 5 digits, phone numbers have 10 digits, and e-mail addresses have both an "@" and a ".". If JavaScript is not enabled, you can write a little PHP script that will do the same things when the form is submitted and return the form with warnings if the values are bad.

Caution   JavaScript form validation should be relied upon only for quick convenience reminders, never for data sanitization. See Chapter 31, "Security and Cryptography," for more information.

Another kind of form is arithmetic — a shopping cart with running totals, or a car payment calculator. Again, you can combine both JavaScript and PHP in an arithmetic form to cover all the bases.

Static versus Dynamic JavaScript

Although the static JavaScript-PHP form described in the preceding section is handy for many applications, there's one big problem with it: you have to maintain it by hand. Every time you decide to add a software page to your site, you'll have to remember to manually add it to the drop-down list. Big deal, you're thinking — but these are the little things that become time-sucking nightmares when you're running a huge and high-traffic site.

With PHP and a database, you can update some of your JavaScript automatically — or, as we might say, dynamically. You want to take this option whenever possible, as it will help you save time in the long run.

This is how you'd rewrite the preceding example for even better client/server integration:

```
<html>
<head>
<title>Navigation pulldown</title>
<script language="JavaScript">
<!--
function Browse(form, i){
  var site = form.elements[i].selectedIndex;
  if(site > 0){
    top.location = form.elements[i].options[site].value
  }
}
// -->
</script>
</head>

<body>
<form method="post" action="redirect.php">
<select name="category" onChange="Browse(this.form,0)">
<option selected value=0>Choose a Category</option>
<?php
mysql_connect("localhost", "user", "password");
mysql_select_db("site_db");
$query = "SELECT filename, my_text FROM categories WHERE
display = 1";
$result = mysql_query($query);
while(list($filename, $my_text) = mysql_fetch_array($result))
    {
    print("<option value=\"$filename\"> $my_text</option>\n");
    }
?>
</select>
<input type="submit">
</form>
</body>
</html>
```

You will doubtless have realized by now that a similar technique would be valuable even if you were making a straight JavaScript form (such as by using the onSubmit event handler rather than onChange). It would enable you to make a basic

JavaScript function more flexible by allowing PHP to change variable values within the function before it was sent to the browser. So feel free to use PHP to output straight JavaScript using variables from a data source, if you like.

Dynamically generated forms

You can usefully extend this train of programming thought even further, by setting up a series of dynamic drop-downs that change according to previous form inputs. PHP will fetch all the data from a database and load it into the HTML page; while JavaScript will decide which data set should be visible under various conditions.

In this example, we want to help users find information on specific cars. The list of the model of every car made by every manufacturer is dauntingly large, too long for even a well-designed drop-down list. Furthermore, car names tend to be eerily similar to each other, like the first names of a large family of sisters in a Swedish farming village — Integra, Sentra, Jetta, Elantra, Sephia, and so forth. So one way to narrow things down logically is to have the user pick a manufacturer from a pull-down menu, which would narrow the list to only models made by that company.

The database table we need looks like this (actually it doesn't if you're using a relational database — but here we want to focus on the JavaScript part, not the database part):

```
----------------------
| make     | model     |
----------------------
| Audi     | A4        |
| Audi     | A6        |
| Audi     | A8        |
| Audi     | Quattro   |
| Chrysler | Cirrus    |
| Chrysler | Concorde  |
| Chrysler | PT Cruiser|
| Toyota   | Camry     |
| Toyota   | Corolla   |
| Toyota   | Rav4      |
----------------------
```

Using this database and server-side PHP scripts, you would be limited to two sub-optimal choices. You could opt for one extremely large list (either drop-down or full-page) of manufacturers and models; or you could make the visitor go through two sequential forms. But once we add JavaScript to the mix, we can start a page with two drop-downs and have the contents of the second list change depending on what is selected in the first.

Our double drop-down design is based on Andrew King's very clever JavaScript code, available at www.webreference.com under the Gnu General Public License.

We used PHP simply to connect to the database and fetch data to populate the two-dimensional arrays from which the JavaScript works. All of the interesting functionality here is provided by the JavaScript portion.

```html
<HTML>
<HEAD>
<META NAME="save" CONTENT="history">
<STYLE>
  .saveHistory {behavior:url(#default#savehistory);}
</STYLE>

<SCRIPT LANGUAGE="JavaScript">
<!--
v=false;
//-->
</SCRIPT>

<SCRIPT LANGUAGE="JavaScript1.1">
<!--
if (typeof(Option)+"" != "undefined") v=true;
//-->
</SCRIPT>

<SCRIPT LANGUAGE="JavaScript">
<!--
// Universal Related Select Menus - cascading popdown menus
// by Andrew King. v1.34 19990720
// Copyright (c) 1999 internet.com LLC. All Rights Reserved.
// Modified by Joyce Park 20000703
//
// This program is free software; you can redistribute it
// and/or modify it under the terms of the GNU General Public
// License as published by the Free Software Foundation; either
// version 2 of the License, or (at your option) any later
// version.
//
// This program is distributed in the hope that it will be
// useful, but WITHOUT ANY WARRANTY; without even the implied
// warranty of MERCHANTABILITY or FITNESS FOR A PARTICULAR
// PURPOSE.  See the GNU General Public License for more
// details.
//
// You should have received a copy of the GNU General Public
// License along with this program; if not, write to the Free
// Software Foundation, Inc., 59 Temple Place, Suite 330,
// Boston, MA  02111-1307  USA
//
// Originally published and documented at www.webreference.com
// see www.webreference.com/dev/menus/intro2.html for changelog

if(v){a=new Array(22);}
```

```
function getFormNum (formName) {
  var formNum =-1;
  for (i=0;i<document.forms.length;i++){
    tempForm = document.forms[i];
    if (formName == tempForm) {
      formNum = i;
      break;
    }
  }
  return formNum;
}

function jmp(form, elt)
// The first parameter is a reference to the form.
{
  if (form != null) {
    with (form.elements[elt]) {
      if (0 <= selectedIndex)
        location = options[selectedIndex].value;
    }
  }
}

var catsIndex = -1;
var itemsIndex;

if (v) { // ns 2 fix
function newCat(){
  catsIndex++;
  a[catsIndex] = new Array();
  itemsIndex = 0;
}

// Andrew chose to name this function "O", presumably standing
// for "Option".  It's not a zero, here or in the array below!
function O(txt,url) {
  a[catsIndex][itemsIndex]=new myOptions(txt,url);
  itemsIndex++;
}

function myOptions(text,value){
  this.text = text;
  this.value = value;
}

// fill array
<?php
mysql_connect("localhost", "db_user");
mysql_select_db("auto_db");
// Get the makes
$make_query = "SELECT DISTINCT make FROM cars";
$make_result = mysql_query($make_query);
```

```
while($make_row = mysql_fetch_array($make_result)) {
   $i = 0;
   $make[$i] = $make_row[0];
   // Now fill the array with models for each make
   echo "newCat();\n";
   $model_query = "SELECT model FROM cars WHERE make =
'$make[$i]' ORDER BY model";
   $model_result = mysql_query($model_query);
   while(list($model) = mysql_fetch_array($model_result)) {
      echo "O(\"$model\", \"/$model.php\")\n";
   }
   echo "\n";
   $i++;
}
?>
} // if (v)

function relate(formName,elementNum,j) {
if(v){
var formNum = getFormNum(formName);
   if (formNum>=0) {
      formNum++; // reference next form, assume it follows in
HTML
      with (document.forms[formNum].elements[elementNum]) {
         for(i=options.length-1;i>0;i--) options[i] = null; //
null out in reverse order (bug workarnd)
         for(i=0;i<a[j].length;i++){
            options[i] = new Option(a[j][i].text,a[j][i].value);
         }
         options[0].selected = true;
      }
   }
} else {
   jmp(formName,elementNum);
}
}

// BACK BUTTON FIX for ie4+- or
// MEMORY-CACHE-STORING-ONLY-INDEX-AND-NOT-CONTENT
// see www.webreference.com for full comments
function IEsetup(){
   if(!document.all) return;
   IE5 = navigator.appVersion.indexOf("5.")!=-1;
   if(!IE5) {
      for (i=0;i<document.forms.length;i++) {
         document.forms[i].reset();
      }
   }
}

window.onload = IEsetup;
```

```
//-->
</SCRIPT>
</HEAD>
<BODY BGCOLOR="#ffffff">                                        .

<CENTER>
<TABLE BGCOLOR="#DDCCFF" BORDER="0" CELLPADDING="8"
CELLSPACING="0">
<TR VALIGN="TOP">
<TD>Choose a make:<BR>
<FORM NAME="f1" METHOD="POST" ACTION="redirect.php"
onSubmit="return false;">
<SELECT NAME="m1" ID="m1" CLASS=saveHistory
onChange="relate(this.form,0,this.selectedIndex)">
<?php
while(list($key, $val) = each($make)) {
  echo "<OPTION VALUE=\"/$val.php\">$val</OPTION>\n";
}
?>
</SELECT>
<INPUT TYPE=SUBMIT VALUE="Go" onClick="jmp(this.form,0);">
</FORM>
</TD>

<TD BGCOLOR="#FFFFFF" VALIGN=MIDDLE><B>---&gt;</B></TD>

<TD>Choose a model:<BR>
<FORM NAME="f2" METHOD="POST" ACTION="redirect.php"
onSubmit="return false;">
<SELECT NAME="m2" ID="m2" CLASS=saveHistory
onChange="jmp(this.form,0)">
// These are placeholder values for the first time the page is
// loaded.  They will not change when the form values change.
// If you delete them, the forms will still work, but the
// second select menu would come up empty until changed.
// These values could be generated dynamically, but we wanted
// to show them in place.
<OPTION VALUE="/A4.php">A4</OPTION>
<OPTION VALUE="/A6.php">A6</OPTION>
<OPTION VALUE="/A8.php">A8</OPTION>
<OPTION VALUE="/Quattro">Quattro</OPTION>
</SELECT>
<INPUT TYPE=SUBMIT VALUE="Go" onClick="jmp(this.form,0);">
<INPUT TYPE="hidden" NAME="baseurl" VALUE="http://localhost">
</FORM>
</TD>
</TR>
</TABLE></CENTER>

</BODY>
</HTML>
```

If you were to add to or change any of the data in the database, the JavaScript would change automatically. Dynamic integration of new data makes this a very powerful tool and keeps page maintenance to a minimum.

Passing data back to PHP from JavaScript

Finally, we close the data loop by passing form values back to PHP with JavaScript. This code uses JavaScript to force at least one check box to be checked at all times. In addition, it passes an array to a PHP script. We've chosen to use frames here to maximize the speed of the changes; and we wrote all values out by hand for clarity, rather than assembling them dynamically from a data source:

```
sandwich_frames.html
<HTML>
<HEAD>
<FRAMESET ROWS="50%, 50%" FRAMEBORDER="no" BORDER=0>
<FRAME SRC="main.html" NAME="main" SCROLLING="auto">
<FRAME SRC="results.php" NAME="results" SCROLLING="auto">
</FRAMESET>
</HEAD>
<BODY></BODY>
</HTML>

main.html
<HTML>
<HEAD>
<SCRIPT LANGUAGE="JavaScript">
<!--

function deselectAllOthers(boxVals) {
  for (var x = 1; x < boxVals.length; x++) {
    boxVals[x].checked=false;
  }
}

function confirmOne(boxVals) {
  var count = 0;
  for (var x = 1; x < boxVals.length; x++) {
    if (boxVals[x].checked == false) {
      count++;
    }
  }
  if (count == (boxVals.length−1)) {
    boxVals[0].checked = true;
  } else {
    boxVals[0].checked = false;
  }
}
```

```
function toArray(boxVals) {
  for (var x = 0; x < boxVals.length; x++) {
    var valArray = boxVals[x].name+"[]";
    boxVals[x].name = valArray;
  }
}

// -->
</script>
</HEAD>

<BODY BGCOLOR=#FCFCF0 onLoad="document.selector.submit();">

<TABLE CELLPADDING=20>
<TR>
<TD VALIGN="top">
<B>Order a sandwich with...</B>
<BR><BR>
<FORM NAME="selector" TARGET="results" METHOD="post"
ACTION="results.php">
<B>Fillings (check one or more)</B><BR><BR>
<INPUT TYPE="checkbox" name="filling" value="everything"
checked onClick="deselectAllOthers(document.selector.filling);
confirmOne(document.selector.filling);
toArray(document.selector.filling); submit();"> Everything
<BR>
<INPUT TYPE="checkbox" name="filling" value="turkey"
onClick="confirmOne(document.selector.filling);
toArray(document.selector.filling); submit();"> Turkey
<BR>
<INPUT TYPE="checkbox" name="filling" value="roastbeef"
onClick="confirmOne(document.selector.filling);
toArray(document.selector.filling); submit();"> Roast beef
<BR>
<INPUT TYPE="checkbox" name="filling" value="pastrami"
onClick="confirmOne(document.selector.filling);
toArray(document.selector.filling); submit();"> Pastrami
<BR>
<INPUT TYPE="checkbox" name="filling" value="eggplant"
onClick="confirmOne(document.selector.filling);
toArray(document.selector.filling); submit();"> Eggplant
<BR>
</TD>
<TD VALIGN="top"><BR><BR>
<B>Cheese</B><BR><BR>
<SELECT NAME="cheese" onChange="submit();">
<OPTION VALUE="none">None</OPTION>
<OPTION VALUE="cheddar">Cheddar</OPTION>
<OPTION VALUE="swiss">Swiss</OPTION>
<OPTION VALUE="camembert">Camembert</OPTION>
<OPTION VALUE="bleu">Blue</OPTION>
```

```
<OPTION VALUE="cottage">Cottage</OPTION>
</SELECT>
<BR><BR>
</TD>
<TD VALIGN="top"><BR><BR>
<B>Bread</B><BR><BR>
<SELECT NAME="bread" onChange="submit();">
<OPTION VALUE="white">White</OPTION>
<OPTION VALUE="wheat">Wheat</OPTION>
<OPTION VALUE="rye">Rye</OPTION>
<OPTION VALUE="kaiser">Kaiser roll</OPTION>
<OPTION VALUE="onion">Onion roll</OPTION>
<OPTION VALUE="dutch">Dutch crunch</OPTION>
</SELECT>
</FORM>
<BR><BR>
</TD>
</TR></TABLE>
</BODY>
</HTML>

results.php
<HTML>
<HEAD></HEAD>

<BODY BGCOLOR=#666680 TEXT=#ffffff>
<TABLE CELLPADDING=30><TR><TD>
<B>Da Results</B><BR><BR>
<?php
if($filling) {
  if(is_array($filling)) {
    reset($filling);
    while(list($key, $value) = each($filling)) {
      echo("$value<BR>\n");
    }
  } else {
    echo($filling);
  }
}
?>
<BR><BR></TD>
<TD VALIGN=top><BR><BR>
<B>Cheese</B><BR><BR>
<?php echo($cheese); ?>
<BR><BR></TD>
<TD VALIGN=top><BR><BR>
<B>Bread</B><BR><BR>
<?php echo($bread); ?>
</TD></TR>
</TABLE>
</BODY>
</HTML>
```

This form admittedly doesn't actually do very much yet — but the point is that it would obviate one or two trips from client to server and back. It also demonstrates another of the interesting effects PHP developers can get by experimenting with JavaScript.

Summary

JavaScript is a client-side scripting language that is highly efficient at many tasks which do not require server-side processing. Not everyone will want to use JavaScript, which has longstanding usability and security issues; but for those who do, the combination of client-side and server-side programming languages can offer an attractive combination of functionalities.

PHP and JavaScript have different object notations. JavaScript uses the so-called "dot" notation, while PHP uses the "arrow" or C++ style notation. JavaScript is thoroughly object-oriented, while PHP treats objects as an optional feature. The good news is that you'll never confuse a JavaScript object for a PHP object, or vice versa. The bad news is that you cannot access the same object from both languages.

It's often possible to implement a feature in both a client-side and a server-side way. Users with JavaScript-enabled browsers can enjoy greater speed and convenience, while those without can still get the functionality. This makes it possible to consider using JavaScript without its greatest drawback, which is unpredictability leading to alienation of segments of the userbase.

Perhaps the greatest service PHP can perform for JavaScript is to enable database connectivity — resulting in what we might call "Dynamic JavaScript." JavaScript, being purely a client-side technology, cannot query a server-side database for variable data with which to dynamically generate content. Without a server-side helper like PHP, this means that JavaScripts must be updated by hand whenever variable data is changed. PHP's ability to pass in up-to-date variables from a data store can make it considerably less labor-intensive to maintain JavaScript-enabled forms and functions.

✦   ✦   ✦

E-Mail

T his chapter is all about using PHP (and in some cases databases) to send and receive e-mail. It assumes a very basic familiarity with e-mail systems and protocols such as POP, IMAP, and SMTP.

Understanding E-Mail

E-mail is obviously one of the killer apps of the Internet, and it's been around in basically the same form for years. But to judge from postings to the PHP and other mailing lists, there are few more misunderstood or frustrating topics even now. Because recent developments, such as cheaper connectivity and free server operating systems and the explosion of corporate domains, have made it possible for everyone and their grandmas to run their own mail servers, there's a lot of frustration to go around.

We don't have the space or the expertise to explain every detail of e-mail. If you become fascinated with the topic after our necessarily short synopsis, you will want to immediately visit the Web site of the International Mail Consortium, at http://www.imc.org, which will explain in dizzying detail every abstruse jot and tittle of Internet mail that the most exacting engineer's heart could desire. In the meantime, we'll stick to the quickest and dirtiest of explanations.

A model e-mail system

To help you visualize the considerable number of moving parts involved, we're going to build a simple model mail server.

This explanation will mostly use UNIX terms, for the simple reason that the vocabulary of e-mail was perfected long before Microsoft or Lotus came along. Exchange Server is quite likely very similar underneath—it even has a daemon

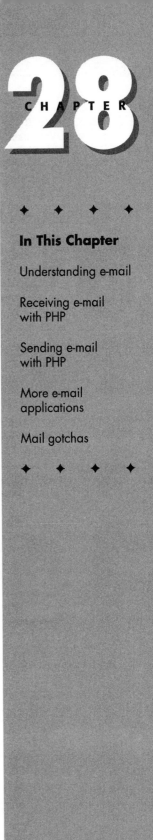

◆ ◆ ◆ ◆

In This Chapter

Understanding e-mail

Receiving e-mail with PHP

Sending e-mail with PHP

More e-mail applications

Mail gotchas

◆ ◆ ◆ ◆

called "sendmail" — but who knows for sure, because we can't lift the hood. Vendors of proprietary software also have the annoying habit of making up their own terminology for things rather than using the names everyone knows already, a practice that considerably hinders anyone trying to understand these systems in an abstract, cross-platform way. Finally, most proprietary mail systems these days are incorporated into very powerful groupware packages that confuse the issue even more. There is no question that for these reasons UNIX mail servers are easier to learn from and implement.

We are mentioning specific products so that you can contact them directly to learn more about these pieces of the puzzle. This does not constitute a recommendation. We have deliberately chosen to list only products that are available without monetary cost.

The major parts of our model e-mail system are as follows:

✦ TCP/IP server

✦ Mail Transfer Agent (MTA), a.k.a. SMTP server

✦ Mail spool

✦ Mail User Agent (MUA, a.k.a. mail client)

✦ Mail retrieval program, a.k.a. POP/IMAP server

✦ Mailing list manager (MLM)

Let's examine these in greater detail. We're going to use a cheesy but apt metaphor to help you remember who does what: Mail Server Mansion.

TCP/IP server

A good way to visualize a *TCP/IP server* is to think of it as the footman who answers every knock at the front door of Mail Server Mansion. Actually, if you think of every separate port as a door, maybe TCP/IP server is more like a security guard who sits in a cubbyhole and monitors a bank of video cameras pointed at multiple avenues of ingress and egress. In any event, it's simpler and more picturesque just to think of an old-fashioned single footman at a single door.

The footman does not actually speak to any visitors. He simply opens the door when he hears a knock, recognizes the type of interaction this will be, and calls the correct person (say a butler or a bouncer) to handle the request. This person, who has a speaking role, will take over to find out what the visitor wants.

The point is not to open the door — it is to know there is a door to be opened. A TCP/IP server maintains a list of several services for which it is responsible, and it answers each request by invoking the proper daemon — in the case of mail, either `sendmail` or a POP/IMAP authenticator. This saves resources, because a single daemon monitors all the requests and the other daemons are only invoked on an "as needed" basis.

Well-known TCP/IP servers include:

✦ GNU inetd, the TCP/IP super server usually found by default on UNIX setups (`http://www.gnu.org/software/inetutils/inetutils.html`)

✦ xinetd, a secure replacement for inetd (`http://www.synack.net/xinetd/`)

✦ Dan Bernstein's tcpserver, often used with qmail (`http://cr.yp.to/ucspi-tcp.html`)

Mail Transfer Agent a.k.a. SMTP server

The *Mail Transfer Agent (MTA)* is the heart of any mail server, and the part whose workings we are most radically simplifying.

The most important task of an MTA is to accept e-mail from another SMTP server and deliver it to the correct addressee's mail spool. There's a lot more involved in this than one might think, but we can't get into it here. Also, the MTA will collect outgoing e-mail and try to send it to other SMTP servers.

So the MTA is roughly in the position of the butler at Mail Server Mansion. It is he who is called by the footman to deal with mail, to inquire of the visitor (with the utmost politeness, of course): "Who are you, and what do you want?" If the visitor happens to be a known spammer, for instance, the butler might outright refuse delivery of any letters from that address. If the visitor is not recognized as a spammer, the butler will check the envelope to see if the intended recipient is in fact a resident of Mail Server Mansion. If not, he will write "Undeliverable as addressed" on the envelope and drop it in the outgoing mailbag. Finally, if the addressee is recognized and the message is good, the butler will put the letter on a silver platter and carry it up to the resident's sitting room and leave it there.

The actual SMTP protocol — the script by which one server asks another, "Who are you, and what do you want?" — goes something like this (sendhost and receipthost are dummy servernames):

```
220 receipthost ESMTP
HELO
250 receipthost
MAIL From:<sender@sendhost>
250 ok
RCPT To:<receiver@receipthost>
250 ok
DATA
354 Go ahead
Body of message.

.
250 Message accepted for delivery
QUIT
221 receipthost closing connection
```

Well-known MTAs — along with their corresponding URLs — include:

Sendmail	`http://www.sendmail.org`
Qmail	`http://www.qmail.org`
Zmailer	`http://www.zmailer.org`

Mail spool

The silver platter on which the butler places the letters is analogous to a *mail spool* or *mailbox*. Different mail systems use different types of mailboxes. At the level we're discussing, the main difference is whether a new message simply goes on the end of a single long spool (like a single sheet of paper with the text of all the mail you've ever received transcribed on it in order of time of receipt); or whether each message becomes its own text file inside a directory.

Some well-known mailbox formats are:

mbox	Used by many UNIX mail clients
maildir	Closely associated with qmail
mbx	Microsoft proprietary format

Mail User Agent a.k.a. local mail client

So the letter is lying on a silver platter in the recipient's sitting room, which is actually their home directory. When a resident of Mail Server Mansion decides she wants to read her mail, she sends a maid to go to the sitting room, collect the silver platter full of letters left there by the butler, return to the boudoir with them, and hold them up to the light so she can read them more stylishly. This maid is the *Mail User Agent.*

Popular MUAs and their URLs include:

Pine	`http://www.washington.edu/pine`
Elm	`http://www.instinct.org/elm`
Mutt	`http://www.mutt.org`

In many cases, the choice of MUA will be closely tied to the choice of MTA and mailbox. For instance, Mutt makes it especially easy to use Qmail's maildir format, and it seems to be the MUA of choice for the Qmail community.

Mail retrieval program a.k.a. POP/IMAP server

Sending the maid out to the sitting room to fetch the mail works fine if you happen to be at home in your local domain. But let's say the residents of Mail Server Mansion travel a lot to remote domains (remember, a remote domain can be in the same room — as long as it's not local in the sense of being one of the domains handled by this particular mail server, it's remote). How will they get their mail?

The short answer is that they will send a request to Mail Server Mansion periodically, and another butler will forward any letters that have collected on the addressee's silver platter since the last time. This butler does not accept mail at all — he only forwards mail.

This second butler needs to be very security-conscious. It's one thing for the SMTP butler to send and receive letters for people he knows to be in residence in the household; but anyone can send a request for mail to be forwarded to some distant address. Therefore, Butler Number Two has arranged a secret password with each resident of Mail Server Mansion, and no mail will be forwarded without that password.

These e-mail messages can then be read on a remote mail client — more and more of which are Web-based and/or no-cost — such as:

Microsoft Outlook Express	`http://www.microsoft.com/windows/IE`
Netscape Communicator	`http://www.netscape.com/download/index.html`
Qualcomm Eudora Light	`http://www.eudora.com`
Hotmail	`http://www.hotmail.com`
AOL mail client	`http://www.aol.com`

One of the consequences of implementing a mail retrieval program is that now clients on every platform can receive mail from a UNIX server. MUAs are limited to UNIX clients, and preferably local UNIX clients.

There are a diversity of mail retrieval protocols; and a large number of products (often of wildly varying design) implementing those protocols. The most popular are called *POP3* and *IMAP*.

A POP server (sometimes called a POP toaster) simply verifies a name, password, and mailspool location by having this little dialog with a client,

```
user peter
+OK
pass rabbit
+OK
data
```

checking the answers in a file, and looking up where this user's mailbox is located. If there are new messages there, it will forward them to the client. Some POP systems can be configured to save a copy of every message forwarded to a client, some will allow clients to delete messages remotely, but most will just forward and forget. A user can take as much time as necessary to read and respond to messages offline, and then connect to the SMTP server to send replies.

POPular POP servers include:

Qualcomm Qpopper	`http://www.eudora.com/qpopper/index.html`
qmail-pop3d	`http://www.qmail.org`

In addition, most well-known IMAP servers also implement the POP3 protocol. PHP's IMAP functions also work as POP functions.

IMAP is a newer and more powerful mail retrieval protocol. Instead of forwarding and forgetting, IMAP allows for a simulacrum of the local client/server experience. The potential downside is that, unlike for a relatively quick POP3 data dump, each client must maintain a connection to the IMAP server as long as the user is reading and responding to e-mail — so the process is quite resource-intensive. An IMAP server is also somewhat more difficult to learn, install, configure, and maintain.

The most popular IMAP servers are:

Washington IMAP	`http://www.washington.edu/imap`
Cyrus	`http://asg.web.cmu.edu/cyrus`

There is also a category of program called a *mail retrieval utility*. The most famous of these is Eric Raymond's Fetchmail (`http://www.tuxedo.org/~esr/fetchmail`), which is particularly useful with dial-up connections. It implements POP, IMAP, and other protocols.

Mailing List Manager

Finally, a mail server is hardly complete without a *mailing list manager*. This is a software package that helps send large volumes of e-mail automatically. Think of this program as the social secretary of Mail Server Mansion: her job is to send out invitations to the endless parties given by the Mansion's residents. Needless to say, she must write out copy after copy after copy of each invitation — and then drop batches of them into the outgoing mailbag. She also handles all responses according to a standard set of scripts.

Common MLMs include:

Majordomo	`http://www.greatcircle.com/majordomo`
Ezmlm	For qmail, `http://www.ezmlm.org`

So there you have our model mail server. Now, having most carefully defined our terms first, we can whip through the rest of this chapter.

Receiving E-Mail with PHP

Web-based e-mail clients — which download mail from the POP/IMAP server and relay outgoing mail through the SMTP server — are taking over a larger and larger slice of the market. PHP is one of the tools that can be used to develop these most useful applications.

However, we cannot really imagine writing this type of project totally from scratch anymore — and anyone who can do so doesn't need our advice anyway. Therefore, this discussion of e-mail clients will focus on doing things (as the immortal Tina Turner says) nice . . . and easy.

Development by denial

The single easiest way to get a great POP3 client with PHP is . . . to forget it. Unless you have a good deal of free time on your hands, think hard about whether you really need your own custom POP mail client. Free mail services all over the world will practically pay you to use their service, which you can use to connect to any POP server anywhere. Extremely secure Web mail applications, such as Hushmail, are also starting to show up on the market at no cost to the consumer. We are personally more than happy to let the hardworking engineers at a major Web portal handle our personal e-mail accounts for us.

Development by direction

If you have some unusual and pressing reason why you need to write your own POP3-only client in PHP, make it a little easier on yourself by using Manuel Lemos's e-mail classes. The author, a well-known PHP community member, offers one for POP3, one for SMTP, and one for composing MIME messages. Put some nice screens on top of these, and you're halfway home. You can find them at:

    http://phpclasses.upperdesign.com/browse.html/class/2

Even better, an amazingly full-featured, stylish, and well-supported IMAP client named IMP is available under the GPL from those fun-loving systems guys at Horde.org:

    http://www.horde.org/imp

Actually, IMP also has POP3 support via PHP's `imap-open()` function, but it's kind of an add-on to their main thing and therefore less well supported. It's hard to imagine there being much need to improve on this program. At press time, the Horde were just making the switchover to PHP 4 but still supported a PHP 3 version of IMP.

Development by decoration

Finally, remember that many open source programs (including the two mentioned previously) make it very easy to grab some code and slap a coat of makeup on, or redesign the user interface altogether. If you want to design a mail page that looks like a paper letter, a TV screen, or the command deck of the starship Enterprise — grab your copy of the GIMP and go to it. Let a thousand cosmetic changes bloom!

This is particularly helpful to those who would like to put out a branded Web mail client, as many ISPs do. But remember it's not cool to implicitly take credit for work you haven't done — a little acknowledgment, in the form of a small logo or an e-mail link, goes a long way in the open source community.

Sending E-Mail with PHP

Sending mail from all angles and for all reasons is where PHP really comes into its own with e-mail. But before you can send any mail from your server, you need to tweak the configuration file a little.

Windows configuration

You need to set two variables in the `php.ini` file:

✦ `SMTP`: a string containing the DNS name or IP address of an SMTP server that will relay for the Windows machine on which PHP is installed. If it is on the PHP server, specify "localhost."

✦ `sendmail_from`: a string containing the e-mail address of the default PHP mail sender (for example `info@exampledomain.com`).

Note   IIS4 has an SMTP server built in, which is lighter than Exchange Server if you don't need the latter.

UNIX configuration

You need to check and possibly change one variable in the `php.ini` file: `sendmail_path`: a string containing the full path to your sendmail program (`/usr/sbin/sendmail` or `/usr/lib/sendmail`), a replacement, or a wrapper (such as `/var/qmail/bin/sendmail`).

If you are not using `sendmail`, and you do not reset this configuration directive to the correct alternative daemon, your mail transfer may be very, very slow, as several alternative programs are tried and allowed to time out before the correct one is found.

Also, be aware that PHP 4 designates the root user as the default mail sender on a UNIX system. PHP 3 used the PHP user (generally "Nobody"), but apparently too many servers were rejecting mail from this account.

Caution   In some mail systems, notably qmail, there is no mail account for root. Therefore, you'll need to specify a "reply-to" and/or "bounce-to" address in each outgoing mail message.

The mail function

There is only one real mail sending function in PHP: `mail()`. This function, which is a Boolean, attempts to send one message using the data within the parentheses and returns 0 or 1. The simplest use of this function (keeping in mind that this is a dummy address and should not be used for testing purposes) is:

```php
<?php
mail("receiver@receipthost.com", "A Sample Subject Line", "Body of
e-mail\r\nwith lines separated by the newline character.");
?>
```

This is the default and minimum format: address of recipient, subject line, body. In this case, PHP will automatically add a `From: root@sendhost` line to each message header.

Caution   Even though e-mail has been around in substantially the same form for decades, there is still no universal format for messages that is guaranteed readable by all MTAs or mail clients. Some clients require a carriage return plus a newline ("\r\n") instead of just a newline character. Some will choke on multiple addresses separated by commas. Some will not deliver e-mails without a proper date. There's really not a lot one can do to ameliorate this situation, except try as hard as you can to cover all the ground.

You can also, as always, use variables instead of hard values:

```php
<?php
$address = "santa@claus.com";
$Subject = "All I want for Christmas";
$body = "Is my two front teeth.\r\nSincerely, Joey";
$mailsend = mail("$address", "$Subject", "$body.");
print("$mailsend");
?>
```

Multiple recipients all go into the address field, with commas separating them (this feature is not supported by all MTAs):

```php
<?php
$mailsend = mail("receiver@receipthost, jane@hotmail.com, john@aol.com", "A
Sample Subject Line", "Body of e-mail\r\nwith lines separated by the newline
character.");
```

```
print("$mailsend");
?>
```

However, most people would like more control over the addresses, appearance, and format of their e-mails. You can do that too, by adding an additional header *after* the three default headers.

```
<?php
$mailsend = mail("receiver@receipthost", "A Sample Subject Line", "Body of
e-mail.", "From: me@sendhost\r\nbcc: phb@sendhost\r\nContent-type:
text/plain\r\nX-mailer: PHP/" . phpversion());
print("$mailsend");
?>
```

This "additional header" field is somewhat odd because it crams in several types of information that would normally be given their own fields. Ours is not to wonder why, ours is but to explain the kinds of things you might want to put in this field:

✦ Your name

✦ Your e-mail address

✦ A reply-to or bounce-to address

✦ X-mailer and version number

✦ MIME version

✦ Content-type

✦ Charset (this uses a "=" to assign, not a ":")

✦ Content-transfer-encoding

✦ Copy and blind-copy recipients

Sending attachments with the PHP mail function is a bit more complicated at the moment. You need to grab Y. Lee's CMailFile classes (`http://renoir.vill.edu/~ylee/mailfile.html`) or use one from Manuel Lemos's PHPClasses.com, or construct something functionally equivalent for yourself.

However, there are relatively few instances in which using PHP to send mail with attachments is the optimal solution. Consider putting the attachment on the Web (with or without password protection) for people to grab themselves, and just sending them an e-mail message informing them it's available for grabbing.

Caution

The mail() function returns 1 (TRUE) *when PHP believes it has successfully sent mail.* This has no relationship to any mail actually being sent or received. There are still an endless number of things that can go wrong: bad e-mail address, SMTP daemon incorrectly designated or configured, local Internet conditions, and so on. Think of "1" as a message meaning no more than "PHP has applied the function to the inputs without a big choke."

More Fun with PHP E-Mail

Besides using PHP to construct full-blown mail clients, it's quite common to use the `mail()` function to send occasional mail when a particular event occurs on your Web site.

Sending mail from a form

Sending mail from a form is quite likely the single most popular application of PHP's `mail()` function. It's a functional alternative to HTML's `mailto` link tag, which of course results in e-mail being sent from the client machine's mail program.

Why use a server-side method rather than a client-side method of sending mail? After all, in many cases it's slower and more awkward, and it's certainly more work. Some reasons that might make you decide to choose this method:

✦ A significant proportion of your audience uses public browsers or Web mail or both.

✦ You want to impose tighter syntax on the messages you receive.

✦ You want to put the contact information into a database as well as send mail.

✦ You want to reduce unwanted messages and/or obviate the need for SMTP relaying by configuring your mail server for local-only service.

This type of form-based mail-sending page can be useful for many purposes, such as requesting quotes, reporting bugs, and getting technical support.

```
<html>
<head>
<title>ThrillerGuide: The "What Was the Name of That Thriller?" Form</title>
</head>
<body>
<center>
<table width="550">
<tr bgcolor= #FF9933><td align="center"><BR><H3>The ThrillerGuide.com<BR>"What
was the name of that thriller?"<BR> Form</H3></td></tr>
<tr><td>
Did you once read an unforgettable thriller, but now you can't remember the
name?  Fill out as many of the fields below as you can, press the button to
submit, and we'll search our sources and e-mail you back.
</td></tr></table>
</center>
<FORM METHOD=post ACTION="TitleHelp.php">
<P>First name: <input type="text" size=30 name="FirstName">
<P>Last name: <input type="text" size=30 name="LastName">
<P>Your Email Address: <input type="text" size=30 name="Email">
```

```html
<P>In approximately what year did the action of the book occur? <input
type="text" size=4 name="Year">
<P>Can you remember any settings from the book? <input type="text" size=30
name="Setting">
<P>The gender of the protagonist(s) was: <br>
<ul>
<input TYPE="radio" NAME="Gender" VALUE=1>Female<br>
<input TYPE="radio" NAME="Gender" VALUE=2>Male<br>
<input TYPE="radio" NAME="Gender" VALUE=3>One of each<br>
<input TYPE="radio" NAME="Gender" VALUE=4>Two males<br>
<input TYPE="radio" NAME="Gender" VALUE=5>Two females<br>
</ul>
<P>When the book first came out, it was: <br>
<ul>
<input TYPE="radio" NAME="Status" VALUE=1>A bestseller<br>
<input TYPE="radio" NAME="Status" VALUE=2>A critic's darling<br>
<input TYPE="radio" NAME="Status" VALUE=3>Neither<br>
<input TYPE="radio" NAME="Status" VALUE=4>I don't know<br>
</ul>
<P>Please tell us anything else you can remember about this title (plot,
characters, settings, cover, movie versions, etc.):
<br><textarea NAME="Other" ROWS=6 COLS=50></textarea>
<P><input type="submit" name="Submit">
</body>
</html>


<html>
<head>
<title>ThrillerGuide: TitleHelp.php</title>
</head>
<body>
<?php
/* If you wished, you could also save this information to a database */
$formsent = mail("help@thrillerguide.com", "What was the name of that
thriller?", "Request from: $LastName $FirstName\r\nYear: $Year\r\nSetting(s):
$Setting\r\nProtagonist gender: $Gender\r\nBook status: $Status\r\nOther
identifying characteristics: $Other", "From: $Email\r\nBounce-to:
help@thrillerguide.com");
if($formsent == 1)
    {
    print("<P>Hi, $FirstName.  We have received your request for help, and will
try to respond within 24 hours.  Thanks for visiting ThrillerGuide.com!");
    }
else
    print("I'm sorry, there's a problem with your form.  Please try again.");
?>
</body>
</html>
```

Sending mail from a database

It's probably not a very good idea to send batch mail from PHP rather than using a mailing list manager for the task. It's definitely a very bad idea if you have a large, active list to serve. However, there are programmatic people who are just more comfortable with a function than a special-purpose tool — and in the right situation, this can work equally well.

```
<html>
<head>
<title>ThrillerGuide: Site update notification</title>
</head>
<body>
<?php
mysql_connect("localhost", "root");
mysql_select_db("thriller");
$query = "SELECT email FROM mailinglist";
$result = mysql_query($query);
while ($MailArray = mysql_fetch_array($result))
    {
    $formsent = mail($MailArray[0], "2000.1.23 ThrillerGuide update", "This is
to inform you that ThrillerGuide has recently been updated.\r\n\r\nYou requested
these e-mail notifications. If you do not wish to receive them, reply to this
mail with \"Cancel\" in the subject line.", "From:
mailinglist@thrillerguide.com\r\nReply-to: help@thrillerguide.com");
print("The result is $formsent.\n");
    }

?>
</body>
</html>
```

A custom PHP mail application

Various organizations have their own special needs, for which you might be called upon to design a custom gizmo. For instance, here is a not-uncommon situation in which a custom mail application might be appropriate:

✦ The client wants to send personalized e-mail messages, each containing a password, to several hundred people.

✦ The client will enter each name and e-mail address by hand into a form. The program will insert this data into a database, along with passwords generated by PHP.

✦ PHP will compose and send a batch of e-mail using boilerplate text.

This is the code for a sample application to meet these specs. It combines the functionality of the two previous code samples and adds a couple of twists such as arrays and a random password generator (based on an example from Chapter 10).

```
address_entry.php
<HMTL>
<HEAD>
<TITLE>Name and address entry form</TITLE>
</HEAD>

<BODY>
<CENTER><TABLE WIDTH=550><TR><TD>
Enter the names and e-mail addresses of recipients on this page. You do not have
to complete all 25 entries. When you are ready to actually send the e-mails,
click the Submit button at the bottom of the page.<BR><BR>
</TD></TR></TABLE></CENTER>

<FORM METHOD=post ACTION="email_send.php">
<?php
/* To keep the page sizes and mail batches to a manageable size, we will
arbitrarily limit each batch to 25 names. If anything goes wrong -- the client
accidentally closes the browser window before submitting, the PHP module isn't
working, whatever -- the maximum number of entries that must be retyped is 25.
To alter the batch size, change the number in the while loop below; and also in
the form handling script. */


for($batch_size = 0; $batch_size <= 25; $batch_size++)
    {
    print("<P>First name: <input type=\"text\" size=30
name=\"FirstName[]\"><BR>Last name: <input type=\"text\" size=30
name=\"LastName[]\"><BR>E-mail Address: <input type=\"text\" size=30
name=\"Email[]\">");
    }
?>
<BR><BR>
<P><INPUT TYPE="Submit" NAME="SUBMIT">
</FORM>
</BODY>
</HTML>

email_send.php
<html>
<head>
<title>E-mail sending screen</title>
</head>

<body>
<?php
/* This screen enters the names, addresses, and passwords into a database and
sends the e-mails off into the wild black yonder of cyberspace. */

include("password_maker.inc");
```

```
mysql_connect("localhost", "root");
mysql_select_db("mailinglist");
$list_length = 0;
/* Includes a test to stop the loop sooner if fewer than 25 names have been
entered. */
for ($list_length = 0; $list_length <= 24 && STRLEN($FirstName[$list_length]) >
0; ++$list_length)
    {
    /* 8 is the number of characters desired in each password. */
    $Password = random_string($charset, 8);
    $query = "INSERT INTO recipient (FirstName, LastName, Email, Password)
VALUES('$FirstName[$list_length]', '$LastName[$list_length]',
'$Email[$list_length]', $Password)";
    $result = mysql_query($query);
    $formsent = mail($Email[$list_length], "Login and password info", "Your
login is: $FirstName[$list_length] $LastName[$list_length].\r\nMake sure there
is only one space between the two words when you log in.\r\nYour password is:
$Password.\nGood luck!", "From: mailinglist@sendhost\r\nReply-to:
help@sendhost");
    print("The result is $formsent for $list_length.\n");
    }

?>
</body>
</html>

password_maker.inc
<?php
/* random_string is the function you actually call, and it in turn uses
random_char */

function random_char($string)
{
$length = strlen($string);
$position = mt_rand(0, $length - 1);
return($string[$position]);
}

function random_string ($charset_string, $length)
{
$return_string = random_char($charset_string);
for ($x = 1; $x < $length; $x++)
$return_string .= random_char($charset_string);
return($return_string);
}

// magic line to seed random generator
mt_srand((double)microtime() * 1000000);

$charset = "abcdefghijklmnopqrstuvwxyz";
?>
```

Summary

E-mail is one of the most useful and attractive functions of the Internet. PHP gives you the ability to both send and receive e-mail from a Web page. However, PHP is not a specialized e-mail program and will perhaps not cope gracefully with large quantities of messages.

Unfortunately, e-mail is one of the more complicated services in most domains, with a large number of moving parts and a surprising lack of standardization for such a relatively long-established functionality. Do not blame this on PHP — it's inherent to e-mail itself.

One of the most common uses of PHP's mail function is to send an e-mail (often to yourself) with values generated from a Web form. This is more reliable than a mailto link, and allows you to impose more structure on the data. You can also use PHP to send off small batches of e-mail using data from a database. However, large batches probably require a mailing-list manager or other solution.

✦   ✦   ✦

PHP and XML

XML is one of the hottest buzzwords in the software business today; but what does it mean for Joe or Jane Average PHP Developer? Well, it could very well be the necessary precondition for a better Internet — one that is faster to develop, more interactive, less junky, and more accessible to a larger audience. With PHP, you're already in an excellent position to smoothly integrate XML into your Web development arsenal as the technology matures.

What Is XML?

XML stands for *eXtensible Markup Language*. XML is a simplified form of SGML, the Standard Generalized Markup Language, but you don't need to know anything about SGML to use XML. It defines a syntax for structured documents that both humans and machines can read.

Note   Our explanation of XML will necessarily be extremely brief (since this is a book about PHP rather than XML, don't you know). For those who want to learn more, we highly recommend Elliotte Rusty Harold's *XML Bible* (IDG Books, 1999). Although this book is neither short nor a specific guide to programming XML-based applications, it will give you a firm conceptual grasp of XML that should set you up nicely for any particular XML-based task.

Perhaps the easiest way to understand XML is to think about all the things HTML can't do. HTML is also a markup language, but HTML documents are anything but structured. HTML tags (technically known as elements) and attributes are just simple identification markers to the browser. For instance, a pair of matched <H1> and </H1> tags designate a top-level heading. Browsers interpret this to mean you want heading text to be displayed in a really big, bold, possibly italicized font. HTML does not, however, indicate whether the text between those tags is the title of the page, the name of the author, an invitation to enter the site, an apposite quotation, a promise of special sale prices, or what. It's just some text that happens to be big.

One implication of HTML's lack of structure is that search engines have little built-in guidance about what's important on each page of your site or what each chunk of text means in relation to the others. They use various methods to guess, none of which are foolproof. <META> tags are notoriously prone to abuse—porn sites often load popular but irrelevant search terms into their headers to fool unwary Web surfers—and spiders can end up giving too much weight to portions of the page that designers might think are unimportant. If XML becomes ubiquitous, it could eliminate many of these problems and lead the way to much more meaningful Web searching.

Now let's say you work for a content Web site which has just signed a major distribution deal with a top-five portal. After you wake up from the champagne hangover, you're faced with the hard question of how you plan to deliver the content. HTML isn't going to do the job: obviously the portal's page design and Web serving technology are different from your site's, and they won't be able to just plug your HTML into theirs. Just to make things really interesting, let's presume you and Big Portal Company use different programming languages, different data stores, different HTML editors, different style sheets—in short, different everything. The necessary bridge is a data-exchange format which is easy for you to output with your technical setup, clearly understood by both parties with existing software, and equally easy for the Big Portal Company to convert to its own purposes and designs. XML promises to be that data-exchange format.

Hopefully these examples begin to answer the "why XML?" question. If you forget the hype and focus on what problems XML might begin to solve, you'll be in a much better position to assess whether it can help you today or sometime in the future. In the simplest terms, XML is a flexible data-exchange format that is not dependent on any particular software or domain, can be parsed easily by both machines and humans, and allows content providers to include information about the structure of the data along with the data itself.

The next question about XML is typically, "What does XML look like anyway?" Actually, XML looks a lot like HTML. A simple XML file such as the one shown in Listing 29-1 is easy for HTML-users to understand:

Listing 29-1: A simple XML file

```
<?xml version="1.0"?>
<book>
 <publisher>IDG Books</publisher>
 <title>PHP4 Bible</title>
 <chapter title="PHP and XML">
  <section title="What is XML?">
   <paragraph>
If you know HTML, you're most of the way to understanding XML.
   </paragraph>
   <paragraph>
```

```
They are both markup languages, but XML is more structured than
HTML.
    </paragraph>
   </section>
  </chapter>
 </book>
```

As you can see, XML has tags and attributes and the hierarchical structure that you're used to seeing in HTML. In XML, each pair of tags (`<paragraph>` ... `</paragraph>`) is known as an element. Actually, this is true in HTML too but most people strongly prefer the term "tag" (the construction that marks an element) over "element" (the conceptual thing that is being marked by a tag) — we're not picky, use whatever term you want as long as you know what you mean. The biggest difference is that XML tags are self-defined; and they carry absolutely no display directive to the Web browser or other viewing application.

XML makes the following minimal demands:

✦ There must be a single root element that encloses all the other elements, similar to `<HTML>` ... `</HTML>` in HTML documents. This is also sometimes called the document element.

✦ Elements must be hierarchical. That is, `<X> <Y> </Y> </X>` is allowed, but `<X> <Y> </X> </Y>` is not. In the first example, `<X>` clearly contains all of `<Y>`. In the second example, `<X>` and `<Y>` overlap. XML does not allow overlapped tags.

✦ All elements must be deliberately closed (in contrast to HTML, which allows some unclosed elements such as `<OPTION>` or `<LI>`). This can be accomplished with a closing tag (`<title></title>`) as in HTML; or by using an XML feature with no HTML equivalent called a self-closing element (`<logo href="graphic.jpg"/>`). A self-closing element is also known as an empty element.

✦ Elements can contain elements, text, and other data. If an element encloses something that looks like it might be XML — such as `<hello>` — but isn't, or you don't want something parsed, it must be escaped.

Caution The &, <, >, ', and " characters are all restricted in XML. You can use them in your data by escaping them — using codes such as `&amp;` and `&lt;` — or by putting them in `CDATA` Sections, discussed later.

In addition to these mandatory requirements for what is called well formedness, the XML standard also suggests that XML documents should start with an identifying XML declaration. This is a processing instruction giving the MIME type and version number, such as `<?xml version="1.0"?>`. This is not required, but some parsers will complain if it isn't present.

> **Note**
>
> It's the XML declaration, and other processing instructions with the same format, that prevent you from using PHP's short-open tags with XML. Since the two tag styles are identical (`<?  ?>`), it would be unclear whether this character sequence set off a PHP block or an XML processing instruction.

XML documents are usually text. They can contain binary data, but they aren't really meant to. If you want to put binary data in your XML documents, you have to encode it first and then decode it later. Note that including binary data may break some of the platform-independence of pure XML.

Working with XML

By now you may or may not think XML is the greatest thing since cinnamon toast; but in either case you're probably asking yourself, "OK, but what can I actually *do* with it?" This is actually not such an easy question to answer. In theory, you can do three main things with XML: manipulate and store data; pass data around between software applications or between organizations; and display XML pages in a browser or other application using style sheets to apply display directives.

In practice, almost no one actually uses XML as a primary data store when SQL is so ubiquitous. It's possible although still difficult to manipulate data using XML — for instance, to edit documents by creating and manipulating XML nodes rather than straight text. Furthermore, although it's possible to (laboriously) display a simple XML document using style sheet display directives, in reality there are few (if any) Web sites that are currently outputted in XML rather than HTML. For more information about displaying XML, see the sidebar "The promises and pitfalls of displaying XML."

This leaves one main job for XML right now: exchanging data between applications and organizations. This happens to be the area in which PHP can have the most immediate impact. For instance, a C program might perform some operations on data from a data store and then output the results in XML, which PHP could transform into HTML for display in a browser or other application. This data flow actually makes sense if substantial amounts of computation need to happen behind the scenes, since you do not want to have a big program both performing complex operations and outputting HTML if you can possibly help it.

PHP can also read in data from a data store and write XML documents itself. This can be helpful when transferring content from one Web site to another, as in syndicating news stories. You can also use this functionality to help non-technical users produce well-formed XML documents with a Web-form front-end. At the moment, writing XML might well be the most common category of XML-related PHP task.

The promises and pitfalls of displaying XML

XML attempts to do something that HTML has only very imperfectly accomplished: enforce real separation between content and display. XML tags contain no display-oriented meaning whatsoever—so an element called `<header></header>` in XML does not imply anything about large bold text, and hopefully never will. All display information will be applied through style sheets. These can be either Cascading Style Sheets, which are already familiar to many HTML developers; or XSL (eXtensible Style Language), which is the next-generation style sheet.

A single XML document will in theory be displayable in any number of ways simply by applying a different style sheet. The promise is that you will be able to take an XML document and, by simply swapping in various XSL templates, be able to create a version of the page for very large screens, a version for cellular phones, a version for the visually handicapped, a version with certain lines highlighted in red, and so forth.

However, the reality of the situation right now is not that rosy. The XSL standard is still quite shaky, and no major browser has yet implemented it to any very useful extent (although Mozilla promises to do so soon). Cascading Style Sheets have been around since 1997 and browser support for them remains so problematic that most major Web sites still use font tags—indicating that XSL has quite a way to go before it gains wide acceptance. It's an perfect example of the truism that "worse is better"—people have been complaining about HTML's limitations almost since it was invented; but a technology which is better yet harder to implement, like XML, might not have so quickly acquired such a large userbase.

In the meantime, XML must be transformed into HTML on the server side. It is possible to do this using XSL itself, but so far relatively few sites have chosen this option. Among other discouraging factors, XSL transformations can only result in HTML that still meets the requirements for XML well formedness. It's far more common at this point to use some other program, such as PHP, to translate the XML into HTML.

Documents and DTDs

As we explained above, the requirements for a well-formed XML document are fairly minimal. However, XML documents have another possible level of "goodness," which is called *validity*. A valid XML document is one that conforms to certain stated rules that together are known as a *document type definition*, or DTD.

To get in the mood to understand the value of DTDs, let's imagine that you are the head of an Open Source project that exists to make books and other documents freely available in electronic form on the Internet. You're very excited about XML from the moment you learn about it, because it seems to meet your need for a data exchange format that can adapt easily to new display technologies as they evolve. Your group members vote to encode all of the project's books and documents in XML, and soon the XMLized documents start to pour in.

But when you look at the first couple of submissions, you get a rude shock. One of them is in the same format as Listing 29-1; but one of them looks like Listing 29-2 below:

Listing 29-2: **A book in XML format**

```
<?xml version="1.0"?>
<book title="PHP4 Bible">
 <publisher name="IDG Books"/>
 <chapter number="29">
  <chapter_title>PHP and XML</chapter_title>
  <p>
   <sentence>If you know HTML, you're most of the way to
understanding XML.</sentence>
   <sentence>They are both markup languages, but XML is more
structured than HTML.</sentence>
  </p>
 </chapter>
</book>
```

The two XML files express similar but not identical hierarchical structures using similar but not identical tags. This is the potential downside of the self-defined markup tags that XML enables: random variation that makes it difficult to match up similar kinds of information across files. You quickly realize that you will need to implement some rules about what kinds of information should be in a book file, and what the relationships between these elements will be. You've just realized you need a DTD.

A document type definition, or DTD, describes the structure of a class of XML documents. A DTD is a kind of formal constraint, guaranteeing that all documents of its type will conform to stated structural rules and naming conventions. A DTD enables you to specify exactly what elements are *allowed,* how elements are *related,* what *type* each element is, and a *name* for each element. DTDs also specify what attributes are required or optional, and their default values.

You could of course just write down these rules in a text file:

```
The top-level object of this document is a BOOK
A BOOK has one and only one TABLE OF CONTENTS
A BOOK has one and only one TITLE
A BOOK is composed of multiple CHAPTERS
CHAPTERS have one and only one CHAPTERTITLE
All CHAPTERTITLEs are listed in the TABLE OF CONTENTS
etc.
```

You could give a copy of the list to anyone who might need it. A DTD is just a more concise, well defined, generally agreed upon grammar in which to do the same thing. It's a useful discipline to apply to XML documents, which can be chaotic because of their entirely self-defined nature. Furthermore, if you can get a group of people to agree on a DTD, you are well on the way to having a standard format for all information of a certain type. Many professions and industries, from mathematicians to sheet-music publishers to human-resources departments, are eager to develop such domain-specific information formats.

Let's return our imaginative example above, which uses XML to store books electronically. Your group members may have to argue for months before hashing out the details of a DTD which perfectly describes the relationships between the table of contents, chapters, titles and headings, indexes, appendices, sections, paragraphs, forwards, epilogues, and so on. You can, of course, iterate on DTDs as frequently as necessary.

But once your DTD is finalized, you can enjoy another value-add of XML. It's possible to run any XML document through a so-called "validating parser" which will tell you whether it's meeting all the requirements of its DTD. So instead of a human editor having to read each electronic book submission to see whether it has the required elements and attributes in the correct relationship, you can just throw them all into a parser and let it do the formal checking. This won't tell you anything about the quality of the content in the XML document, but it will tell you whether the form meets your requirements.

Honesty compels us to admit that PHP does not (exactly) support a validating XML parser. However, you will still need to learn about the basic structure of DTDs and the XML documents they describe whether you validate or not.

The structure of a DTD

A document type definition is a set of rules which define the structure of a particular group of XML documents. A DTD can be either a part of the XML document itself (in which case it is called an `internal DTD`); or it can located externally, in another file on the same server or at a publicly available URL anywhere on the Internet (in which case it is called an `external DTD`).

Note   Although a DTD can be internal (part of the XML document itself), it is usually better to make it external (a separate file). DTDs are meant to define a class of documents; so separating it from the XML will save you from editing every XML document of that class if you have to change the DTD later on. However, because it's easier to demonstrate on an internal DTD, we will use both as examples in this chapter.

Let's start by looking at a simple XML document with an internal DTD, Listing 29-3:

Listing 29-3: An XML document with internal DTD (recipe.xml)

```
<?xml version="1.0"?>

<!DOCTYPE recipe [

<!ELEMENT recipe (ingredients, directions, servings)>
<!ATTLIST recipe name CDATA #REQUIRED>
<!ELEMENT ingredients (#PCDATA)>
<!ELEMENT directions (#PCDATA)>
<!ELEMENT servings (#PCDATA)>
]>

<recipe name ="Beef Burgundy">
 <ingredients>Beef</ingredients>
 <ingredients>Burgundy</ingredients>
 <directions>
 Add beef to burgundy. Serve.
 </directions>
 <servings>12</servings>
</recipe>
```

We've divided the XML document into three subsections for easier reading. The first section is the standard one-line XML declaration that should begin every XML document. The second section is the internal DTD, marked by lines beginning with the `<!` sequence. The third section is the XML itself, strictly speaking. For the moment we will be focusing on the second section, the DTD. In our example the stuff outside the square brackets is a document type declaration (not to be confused with "document type definition"): `<!DOCTYPE recipe [...]>`. The document type declaration gives information about the DTD this document will be using. Since this is an internal DTD, we simply give the name of the root element (`recipe`) and then include the rest of the definition within square brackets. However, if you were using an external DTD you would use the document type declaration to state the type and location of the DTD. Two example document type declarations referring to external DTDs are:

```
<!DOCTYPE recipe SYSTEM "recipe.dtd">
<!DOCTYPE HTML PUBLIC "-//W3C//DTD HTML//EN">
```

External document type declarations give a root element name, the type (`SYSTEM` meaning on the server, or `PUBLIC` meaning a standardized DTD), and the location where it can be found.

The DTD proper consists of the lines inside the square brackets. These lay out the elements, element types, and attributes contained in the XML document.

Element	A start and end tag pair, e.g., `<b>` *something* `</b>`, or an empty element (` `). Elements have types, and some times content and attributes.
Element Type	A constraint on the content and attributes of an element. A type can be used to specify what kind of data it can contain, and to specify what attributes it can have.
Attribute	A name and value pair associated with an element, in the form `<element attributename="attributevalue">`.

In the example DTD in Listing 29-3, we've declared that our root element, `recipe`, contains three child elements — `ingredients`, `directions`, and `servings` — and has one required attribute, `name`. Each child element is of the parsed character data type, and the attribute is of the character data type.

If you wanted to split up Listing 29-3 into an XML document and an external DTD, it would look much the same, except that instead of providing the definition in square brackets you would give a reference to the external DTD file. The result would look like Listings 29-4 and 29-5:

Listing 29-4: An XML document with external DTD (recipe_ext.xml)

```
<?xml version="1.0"?>
<!DOCTYPE recipe SYSTEM "recipe.dtd">

<recipe name ="Beef Burgundy">
 <ingredients>Beef</ingredients>
 <ingredients>Burgundy</ingredients>
 <directions>
 Add beef to burgundy. Serve.
 </directions>
 <servings>12</servings>
</recipe>
```

Listing 29-5: An external DTD (recipe.dtd)

```
<!ELEMENT recipe (ingredients, directions, servings)>
<!ATTLIST recipe name CDATA #REQUIRED>
<!ELEMENT ingredients (#PCDATA)>
<!ELEMENT directions (#PCDATA)>
<!ELEMENT servings (#PCDATA)>
```

Since the XML used in both examples conforms to the internal and external DTDs, both documents should be declared valid by a validating parser.

There's a lot more to know about the specifics of DTDs and XML documents, but these basics should let you understand most of PHP's XML functions.

Validating and Nonvalidating Parsers

XML parsers come in two flavors: *validating* and *nonvalidating*. Nonvalidating parsers only care that an XML document is well formed: that it obeys all the rules for closing tags, quotation marks, and so on. Validating parsers require well-formed documents as well, but they also check the XML document against a DTD. If the XML document doesn't conform to its DTD, the validating parser outputs specific error messages explaining what has gone wrong.

PHP 4's SAX parser, expat, is nonvalidating. That doesn't mean you should ignore DTDs. Going through the process of creating a DTD for each of your document types is a good design practice. It forces you to think out the document structure very carefully. Plus, if your documents ever have to go through a validating parser, you're covered. In fact, many experts recommend that you put all XML documents through a validating parser even if you never plan to use one again.

Most validating parsers are written in Java, and are a pain to set up and use. The easiest way to validate your XML is to use an online validator. A well-known one is the STG validator:

```
http://www.stg.brown.edu/service/xmlvalid
```

Actually, it's possible to use Gnome libxml to validate an XML document — but it takes some work. There are examples of validation using C on the libxml Web site (www.xmlsoft.org).

SAX versus DOM

There are two common APIs for handling XML and XML documents: the Document Object Model, and the Simple API for XML. PHP 4 has one module for each API. The SAX module is included by default (although you may need to download the Expat library if you're not using Apache); the DOMXML module is optional.

You can use either API to parse an XML document. To create or extend an XML document entirely through the PHP interface (in other words, without writing any of it by hand), you must use the DOM. Each API has advantages and disadvantages.

SAX

SAX is much more lightweight and easier to learn, but it basically treats XML like flowthrough string data. So if you want to parse a recipe, you could whip up a SAX parser in PHP, which will let you boldify the ingredient list. However, it would be very difficult to add a completely new element or attribute and laborious to even change the value of one particular ingredient. SAX is, however, very good at repetitive tasks that can be applied to all elements of a certain type—for instance, replacing a particular element tag with <P></P> tags as a step toward transforming XML into HTML for display. SAX also parses through a document once, in the order it was written—so it cannot "go back" and do things based on inputs later in the document.

DOMXML actually builds a model of the structure of an entire XML document. This allows you to pick out one particular node and change its value, or add another node to the tree. However, this process can be quite resource-intensive and therefore unsuitable for large XML documents. Also, it can be overkill for straightforward tasks like a simple transformation.

DOM

The Document Object Model is a complete API for creating, editing, and parsing XML documents. It is an object-oriented API, so some familiarity with object-oriented programming will help, but it is not necessary. DOMXML is not strictly speaking a parser, although most implementations include a parser.

The DOM reads in an XML file and creates a "walkable" object tree in memory. Starting with a document or an element of a document (both called *nodes* in the DOM), you can retrieve or set the children, parents, and text content of each part of the tree. You can save DOM objects to containers as well as write them out as text.

DOM works best if you have a complete XML document available. If your XML is streaming in very slowly or you want to treat many different XML "snippets" as sections of the same document, you want to use SAX. Since DOM builds a tree in memory, it can be quite the time and resource hog with large documents.

The parser behind the scenes in the DOM API is gnome-libxml 2.0 (a.k.a. Gnome libxml). This is available at the following site:

```
http://www.xmlsoft.org
```

The Gnome DOM implementation is supposedly less memory-intensive than others.

The Document Object Model is a recommendation of the World Wide Web Consortium. You can read all about it in the W3's inimitable prose, at:

```
http://www.w3.org/DOM/
```

The ultimate goal of DOM is to allow all HTML and XML documents to be written and edited as object trees rather than strings — so instead of typing `<H1>This is a header</H1>`, you would use a DOM application to create a new header node object in the appropriate place in your tree. Unfortunately, at the moment the standard is rather immature and PHP's interface with the DOM library even more so. At the time of writing, the PHP DOMXML extension was not usable (at least by us) or documented, so we were unable to write example code. Please see this book's companion Web site for up-to-date information:

```
http://www.troutworks.com/phpbook/
```

PHP Functions for DOM

The DOM API is object-oriented: its top-level functions create and return objects. You have the option of calling more top-level functions with these objects as parameters, or taking a more object-oriented approach and calling methods inside the objects. For example,

```
$attr = $node->attributes();
```

is the same as

```
$attr = domxml_attributes($node);
```

To call the top-level function, just prefix the method name with the word **domxml** and add a parameter, the object, to the beginning of the parameter list. You are free to mix and match styles.

Note   If it can be called from anywhere, it is a function. If it is called in the context of an object or class, it is a method. See Chapter 30 for more information on working with classes and objects.

Table 29-1 lists the top-level DOM functions, with descriptions of what they do.

Note   The DOM API in PHP 4 is in flux as this chapter is being written. By the time of release, additional classes or methods may be available.

Table 29-1
XML DOM Top-Level Function Summary

Function	Behavior
xmldoc()	Takes a string containing an XML document as an argument. This function parses the document and creates a Document object.
xmldocfile()	This convenience function takes a string as an argument and reads the file named by the string. Otherwise behaves like xmldoc().
xmltree()	Takes a string containing an XML document as an argument. Creates a tree of PHP objects and returns a DOM object.
	Note: The object tree returned by this function is read-only.
new_xmldoc()	Creates a new, empty XML document. Returns a Document object. You must add a root element by calling its add_root() method.

Table 29-2 lists the classes of the DOM API, with descriptions of how they are used.

Table 29-2
XML DOM Class Summary

Class	Behavior
Document	This class encapsulates an XML document. It contains the root element and a DTD if any.
Node	Encapsulates a node, a.k.a. an element. A node can be the root element or any element within it. Nodes can contain other nodes, character data, and attributes.
Attribute	This class encapsulates a node attribute. An attribute is a user-defined quality of the node.

Table 29-3 lists the methods of the Document class, with descriptions of what they do.

Table 29-3
Document Class Summary

Method	Behavior
root()	Takes a string containing an XML document as an argument. This function parses the document and creates a DOM object. This function, which takes no arguments, causes PHP either to notice a session ID that has been passed to it (via a cookie or GET/POST) or to create a new session ID if none is found.
	If an old session ID is found, PHP will retrieve the assignments of all variables that had been registered, and make those assigned variables available as regular global variables.
add_root()	This convenience function takes a string as an argument and reads the file named by the string. Otherwise behaves like xmldoc().
intdtd()	Takes a string containing an XML document as an argument. Creates a tree of PHP objects and returns a DOM object. Note: The object tree returned by this function is read-only.
dump_mem()	Creates a new XML document. Returns a DOM object. You must add a root element by calling its add_root() method.

Table 29-4 lists the methods of the Node class, with descriptions of what they do.

Table 29-4
Node Class Summary

Method	Behavior
attributes()	Returns an associative array of attribute names and their values.
getattr()	Returns the value of the named attribute of the node.
setattr()	Sets the value of a named attribute. This attribute will be created if it does not already exist.
children()	Returns a complete list of the node's children.
lastchild()	Returns the last child node in the child list.
parent()	Returns the node's parent node, or false if this is the root node.
node()	Creates a new node and returns it.
new_child()	Creates a new node as a child of the current node and returns it. Takes as arguments a string containing the name of the new node, and a string containing the node's character data contents.

Table 29-5 lists the methods of the Attribute class, with descriptions of what they do.

Table 29-5		
Attribute Class Summary		
Method	**Behavior**	
`attrname()`	Sets an attribute name.	

SAX

The Simple API for XML is widely used to parse XML documents. It is an event-based API, which means that the parser calls designated functions when it recognizes a certain trigger in the event stream.

SAX has an interesting history, especially in contrast to the DOM. The SAX API is not shepherded by an official standardizing body. Instead, it was hammered out by a group of programmers on the XML-DEV mailing list, many of whom had already implemented their own XML parsers without a standard API. You can learn more at the Web sites of SAX team members, such as:

```
http://www.megginson.com/SAX/index.html
```

SAX works from a number of "event hooks" supplied by you via PHP. As the parser goes through an XML document, it recognizes pieces of XML such as elements, character data, and external entities. Each of these is an event. If you have supplied the parser with a function to call for the particular kind of event, it will pause to call your function when it reaches that event. The parsed data associated with an event is made available to the called function. Once the event-handling function finishes, the SAX parser continues through the document, calling functions on events, until it reaches the end. This process is unidirectional from beginning to end of the document—the parser cannot back up or loop.

A very simple example would be an event hook that directs PHP to recognize the XML element `<paragraph></paragraph>`, and substitute the HTML tags `<P></P>` around the character data. If you wrote this event hook, you would not be able to specify a particular paragraph—instead, the function would be called for every instance of this event.

The parser behind the scenes in the PHP SAX extension is James Clark's expat, a widely used (and supposedly the world's fastest) XML parser toolkit. More information about expat can be found on Clark's Web site:

```
http://www.jclark.com/xml/
```

Expat is also distributed with the Apache server. You may have to download a copy from Clark's Web site if you use a different Web server.

> **Caution**   Unfortunately, the term "xml_parser" can refer either to a software library like expat, or to a block of XML-handling functions in PHP. Verbs like "create" and "call" indicate the latter, more specific meaning. Any PHP XML function that uses the term "parser" also refers to the latter meaning.

Using SAX

How you use the SAX will depend on your goals, but these steps are common:

1. Determine what kinds of events you want to handle.

2. Write handler functions for each event. You'll almost certainly want to write a character data handler a start element and end element handlers.

3. Create a parser with `xml_parser_create()`, then call it with `xml_parse()`.

4. Free the memory used up by the parser with `xml_parser_free()`.

The simple example in Listing 29-6 shows all the basic XML functions in use.

Listing 29-6: A simple XML parser (simpleparser.php)

```php
<?php
$file = "recipe.xml";

// Call this at the beginning of every element
function startElement($parser, $name, $attrs) {
    print "<B>$name =></B>   ";
}

// Call this at the end of every element
function endElement($parser, $name) {
    print "\n";
}

// Call this whenever there is character data
function characterData($parser, $value) {
    print "$value<BR>";
}

// Define the parser
```

```php
$simpleparser = xml_parser_create();
xml_set_element_handler($simpleparser, "startElement",
"endElement");
xml_set_character_data_handler($simpleparser, "characterData");

// Open the XML file for reading
if (!($fp = fopen($file, "r"))) {
  die("could not open XML input");
}

// Parse it
while($data = fread($fp, filesize($file))) {
if (!xml_parse($simpleparser, $data, feof($fp))) {
  die(xml_error_string(xml_get_error_code($simpleparser)));
  }
}

// Free memory
xml_parser_free($simpleparser);
?>
```

SAX Options

The XML parser in the SAX API has two configurable options, one for case folding and the other for target encoding.

Case folding is the residue of a series of past decisions, and may not be relevant any more now that XML has been definitely declared case-sensitive. Early versions of SGML and HTML were not case-sensitive and therefore employed case-folding (making all characters upper or lower case during parsing) as a means of getting a uniform result to compare. This is how your browser could tell match up a <P> tag with a </p> tag. Case folding fell out of favor due to problems with internationalization, so after much debate XML was declared case-sensitive. When case folding is enabled, node names passed to event handlers are all turned into all uppercase characters. A node named mynode would be received as MYNODE. When case folding is disabled, a <paragraph> tag will not match a </PARAGRAPH> closing tag.

Note　Case folding is enabled by default. Unless you disable it with xml_parser_set_option(), your event handlers will receive tags in UPPERCASE.

Event handlers receive text data from the XML parser. The encoding of text passed to event handlers is known as the *target encoding*. This is by default the same encoding as in the source document, known as the *source encoding*. You can change the target encoding if you need to process the text in an encoding other than the encoding it was stored in.

These options are retrieved and set with the functions `xml_parser_get_option()` and `xml_parser_set_option()`. Case folding is controlled with the constant `XML_OPTION_CASE_FOLDING`, and target encoding with the constant `XML_OPTION_TARGET_ENCODING`.

```
$new_parser = xml_parser_create('US-ASCII');
$case_folding = xml_parser_get_option(XML_OPTION_CASE_FOLDING);
$change_folding = xml_parser_set_option($new_parser,
XML_OPTION_CASE_FOLDING,1);

$target_encoding = xml_parser_get_option(XML_TARGET_ENCODING);
$change_encoding = xml_parser_set_option($new_parser,
XML_OPTION_TARGET_ENCODING, 'UTF-8');
```

PHP Functions for SAX

Table 29-6 lists the most important SAX functions, with descriptions of what they do.

Note   The table refers to two new concepts: XML entities, and processing instructions. Entities are a storage unit in XML; generally the term is used for an XML document that is written as several files but will be parsed as a single document. Every single-file XML document is also an entity. Processing instructions are instructions to the server: `<?php ?>` or `<?xml ?>`.

Table 29-6
XML SAX Function Summary

Function	Behavior
`xml_parser_create()`	This function creates a new XML parser instance. You may have several distinct parsers at any time. The return value is an XML parser or false on failure.
	Takes one optional argument, a character encoding identifier (such as UTF-8). If no encoding is supplied, ISO-8859-1 is assumed.
`xml_parser_free()`	Frees the memory associated with a parser created by `xml_parser_create()`.
`xml_parser_get_option()`	Retrieves the value of a parser option set with `xml_parser_set_option()`. The options currently available are `XML_OPTION_CASE_FOLDING` and `XML_OPTION_TARGET_ENCODING`.

Function	Behavior
xml_parser_set_option()	Sets a parser option. The options currently available are XML_OPTION_CASE_FOLDING and XML_OPTION_TARGET_ENCODING.
xml_parse()	This function starts the XML parser. Its arguments are a parser created with xml_parser_create(), a string containing XML, and an optional finality flag. The parser will not finalize its parse of a document until it is called with the finality flag set to true.
xml_get_error_code()	If the parser has encountered a problem, its parse will fail. Call this function to find out the error code.
xml_error_string()	Given an error code returned by xml_get_error_code(), it will return a string containing a description of the error suitable for logging. Example: `print xml_error_string(xml_get_error_code ( $parser ) );`
xml_get_current_line_number()	Returns the parser's current place in the XML document it is parsing. The return is either a line number or false if an invalid parser is specified.
xml_get_current_column_number()	Returns the parser's current place in the XML document it is parsing. The return is either a column number or false if an invalid parser is specified.
xml_get_current_byte_index()	Returns the parser's current place in the XML document it is parsing. The return is either a number indicating how many bytes the parser has parsed so far or false if an invalid parser is specified.
xml_set_object()	Takes a parser and a reference to an object (syntax: &$object). Once this function is called, all event handlers are assumed to be methods of the supplied object. This call can't be undone with a parser, so only call it if you mean it.

Continued

Table 29-6 *(continued)*

Function	Behavior
`xml_set_element_handler()`	This function actually sets two handlers. The first is a start-of-element handler, which has access to the name of the element and an associative array of its elements. The second is an end-of-element handler, at which time the element has been fully parsed. The contents of the element are available to called functions.
`xml_set_character_data_ handler()`	Sets the handler to call when character data is encountered. The handler function takes a string containing the character data as an argument.
`xml_set_external_entity_ ref_handler()`	Sets the handler to call when an external entity reference is encountered. Internal references are handled automatically. The handler's arguments are a parser, a string containing the name of the notation, a string containing a base URI for use in resolving the SYSTEM or PUBLIC URIs, a string containing the SYSTEM URL if supplied in the <!NOTATION declaration, and a string containing the PUBLIC string if supplied. Note: The base URL is currently always empty.
`xml_set_processing_ instruction_handler()`	Sets the processing instruction handler. The handler receives as arguments the parser, the target of the processing instruction, and the text of the processing instruction. It is the handler's job to do something with the processing instruction. If the target is familiar, e.g., PHP, then the handler might eval() the text. This is a great way to embed scripts in an XML file. Caution: Only evaluate PHP code from a trusted source. Additionally, be prepared for error messages like: "Undefined error: 0 in **Unknown** on line 0".
`xml_set_unparsed_entity_ decl_handler()`	Sets the unparsed entity handler. When the parser encounters an entity declared NDATA, it won't attempt to parse the entity but will call the unparsed entity declaration handler.

Function	Behavior
	The handler takes as arguments the parser, a string containing the entity name, a string SYSTEM or PUBLIC URIs, a string containing the SYSTEM URI if supplied in the <!NOTATION declaration, and a string containing the PUBLIC string if supplied. Note: The base URI is currently always empty.
xml_set_notation_decl_handler()	This function sets the name of the handler function that the XML parser will call when it encounters <!NOTATION declarations. Notations are names and identifiers attached to an unparsed entity. Because unparsed entities are by definition not handled by the XML parser, it is up to the application to determine what to do with it. Notations are intended to assist applications in determining the type and handling of unparsed data. The handler's arguments are a parser, a string containing the name of the notation, a string containing a base URI for use in resolving the SYSTEM or PUBLIC URIs, a string containing the SYSTEM URI if supplied in the <!NOTATION declaration, and a string containing the PUBLIC string if supplied. Note: The base URI is currently always empty.
xml_set_default_handler()	Sets the default handler. If no handler is specified for an event, the default handler is called if it is specified. Takes as arguments the parser and a string containing unhandled data, such as a notation declaration or an external entity reference.
utf8_decode()	This convenience function recodes a string from UTF-8 to ISO-8859-1. It takes a UTF-8 string as an argument and returns an ISO-8859-1 string.
utf8_encode()	This convenience function recodes a string from ISO-8859-1 to UTF-8. It takes an ISO-88590-1 string as an argument and returns a UTF-8 string.

A Custom SAX Application

This series of scripts (as shown in Listings 29-7 through 29-10) will write out XML to a file using data from a form, and then rather laboriously allow you to edit the values in that file. The editing part uses a freely-available PHP class called xml-tree written by Eric van der Vlist, which you can download from:

```
http://patches.dyomedea.com/php3/generic/xml/xmltree.inc
```

Listing 29-7: A form to collect values for an XML file (pollform.php)

```
<HTML>
<HEAD>
<TITLE>Make-a-poll</TITLE>
</HEAD>

<BODY>
<CENTER><H3>Make-a-poll</H3></CENTER>

<P>Use this form to define a poll:</P>
<FORM METHOD="post" ACTION="writepoll.php">

<P>Give this poll a <B>short</B> name, like <FONT
COLOR="red">Color Poll</FONT>.<BR>
<INPUT TYPE=TEXT NAME="PollName" SIZE=30>
</P>

<P>This poll should <B>begin</B> on this date (MM/DD/YYYY):
<INPUT TYPE=TEXT Name="Poll_Startdate" SIZE=10>
</P>

<P>This poll should <B>end</B> on this date (MM/DD/YYYY):
<INPUT TYPE=TEXT NAME="Poll_Enddate" SIZE=10>
</P>

<P>This is the poll question (<FONT COLOR="blue">e.g. Why did
the chicken cross the road?</FONT>):
<INPUT TYPE=TEXT NAME="Poll_Question", size=100>
</P>

<P>These are the potential answer choices you want to offer
(<FONT COLOR="darkgreen">e.g. Yes, No, Say what?</FONT>).   Fill
in only as many as you need.  Keep in mind that brevity is the
soul of good poll-making.<BR>
<INPUT TYPE=TEXT NAME="Raw_Poll_Option[]" SIZE=25><BR>
<INPUT TYPE=TEXT NAME="Raw_Poll_Option[]" SIZE=25><BR>
<INPUT TYPE=TEXT NAME="Raw_Poll_Option[]" SIZE=25><BR>
```

```
<INPUT TYPE=TEXT NAME="Raw_Poll_Option[]" SIZE=25><BR>
<INPUT TYPE=TEXT NAME="Raw_Poll_Option[]" SIZE=25><BR>
<INPUT TYPE=TEXT NAME="Raw_Poll_Option[]" SIZE=25><BR>
</P>

<INPUT TYPE="submit" NAME="Submit" VALUE="Add a poll">
</FORM>

</BODY>
</HTML>
```

Listing 29-8: **A script to write out an XML file (writepoll.php)**

```
<html>
<head>
<title>Write an XML file</title>
</head>

<body>
<?php

$pollfile = "poll.xml";

// Reading in the xml file as a string
$fd=fopen("$pollfile", "r") or die("Can't open file.");
$fstr = fread($fd, filesize($pollfile)) or die("Can't read
file; check permissions.");
fclose($fd);

// Format response sets.
$PollName = str_replace("\'", "", $PollName);
$PollName = str_replace(" ", "_", $PollName);

for($r=0; $r<=5; $r++) {
  if(!empty($Raw_Poll_Option[$r]))
    {
    $Poll_Option[$r] = "$PollName-".str_replace("'", "",
$Raw_Poll_Option[$r]);
    $Poll_Option[$r] = "$PollName-".str_replace(" ", "_",
$Raw_Poll_Option[$r]);
    }
  else
    {
    $Poll_Option[$r] = "";
    }
  $RespSet .= "\t<response resource=\"$Poll_Option[$r]\"/>\n";
  $Resps .= "<response
id=\"$Poll_Option[$r]\">\n\t<text>$Raw_Poll_Option[$r]</text>\n
</response>\n";
```

Continued

Listing 29-8 *(continued)*

```
//Add new poll data
$separator = "</PollList>";
$divide = explode($separator, $fstr);
$glue =
"\t<Poll name=\"$PollName\"/>
</PollList>

<Poll id=\"$PollName\">
\t<StartDate>$Poll_Startdate</StartDate>
\t<EndDate>$Poll_Enddate</EndDate>
\t<name>$PollName</name>
\t<text>$Poll_Question</text>
\t<display type=\"poll_display-Bar-Graph\"/>
\t<responseSet resource=\"$PollID-responseSet\"/>
</Poll>

<responseSet id=\"$PollName-responseSet\">
$RespSet</responseSet>

$Resps";

$newxml = implode($glue, $divide);

//Write to file
$fd = fopen($pollfile, "w") or die ("Can't open file for
writing; check file permissions");
$writestr = fwrite($fd, $newxml);

//Message
echo "Wrote $writestr to $pollfile.";
?>

</body>
</html>
```

Listing 29-9: **An XML editor (editpoll.php)**

```
<html>
<head>
<title>Poll XML editor</title>
</head>

<body>
<?php

require "xmltree.inc";
```

```php
$pollfile = "poll.xml";

// Reading in the rdf file as a string
$fd=fopen("$pollfile", "r") or die("Can't open file.");
$fstr = fread($fd, filesize($pollfile)) or die("Can't read
file; check permissions.");
fclose($fd);

//Show old values or write new values
if(!IsSet($stage)) {

  // Getting elements and attributes
  $XMLtree = new XMLtree;
  if ($err = $XMLtree->parse("$harrisfile"))
    {
    die ($err);
    }

  //Display form with old values
  echo "<FORM METHOD=\"post\" ACTION=\"editpoll.php\">";

  $pollname = $XMLtree->
getEltByPath("/rdf(1)/poll($i)/name(1)");
  echo "Poll Name:  <INPUT TYPE=\"text\" SIZE=50 NAME=\"PollName\"
VALUE=\"$pollname\"><BR>";

  $poll_startdate = $XMLtree->
getEltByPath("/rdf(1)/poll($i)/startdate(1)");
  echo "Start Date:  <INPUT TYPE=\"text\" SIZE=10
NAME=\"Poll_Startdate\" VALUE=\"$poll_startdate\"><BR>";

  $poll_enddate = $XMLtree->
getEltByPath("/rdf(1)/poll($i)/enddate(1)");
  echo "End date:  <INPUT TYPE=\"text\" SIZE=50 NAME=\"Poll_Enddate\"
VALUE=\"$poll_enddate\"><BR>";

  $poll_question = $XMLtree->
getEltByPath("/rdf(1)/poll($i)/text(1)");
  $poll_question = stripslashes($poll_question);
  echo "Poll question:  <INPUT TYPE=\"text\" SIZE=100
NAME=\"Poll_Question\" VALUE=\"$poll_question\"><BR>";

  $t=1;
  $low = (($i-1)*6)+1;
  $hi = (($i-1)*6)+6;
  for($r=$low; $r<=$hi; $r++) {
    $poll_option[$t] = $XMLtree->
getEltByPath("/rdf(1)/response($r)/text(1)");
    echo "Option:  <INPUT TYPE=\"text\" SIZE=25
NAME=\"Raw_Poll_Option[$t]\"
VALUE=\"$poll_option[$t]\n\"><BR>";
```

Continued

Listing 29-9 *(continued)*

```
    $t++;
  }

  echo "<INPUT TYPE=\"hidden\" NAME=\"i\" VALUE=$i>";
  echo "<INPUT TYPE=\"hidden\" NAME=\"stage\" VALUE=1><BR>";
  echo "<INPUT TYPE=\"submit\" VALUE=\"Presto-chango\">";
  echo "</FORM>";


} else {


//Reading in the xml file as a string
$fd=fopen("$pollfile", "r") or die("Can't open file.");
$fstr = fread($fd, filesize($pollfile)) or die("Can't read
file; check permissions.");
fclose($fd);

  // Getting elements and attributes
  $XMLtree = new XMLtree;
  if ($err = $XMLtree->parse("$harrisfile"))
    {
    die ($err);
    }
  $pollname = $XMLtree->
getEltByPath("/rdf(1)/poll($i)/name(1)");
  $poll_startdate = $XMLtree->
getEltByPath("/rdf(1)/poll($i)/startdate(1)");
  $poll_enddate = $XMLtree->
getEltByPath("/rdf(1)/poll($i)/enddate(1)");
  $poll_question = $XMLtree->
getEltByPath("/rdf(1)/poll($i)/text(1)");
  $t=1;
  $low = (($i-1)*6)+1;
  $hi = (($i-1)*6)+6;
  for($r=$low; $r<=$hi; $r++) {
    $raw_poll_option[$t] = $XMLtree->
getEltByPath("/rdf(1)/response($r)/text(1)");
    $t++;
  }

  // Format response sets.
  for($t=1; $t<=6; $t++) {
    if(!empty($raw_poll_option[$t]))
      {
      $poll_option[$t] = "$pollname-$raw_poll_option[$t]";
      }
    else
```

```
      {
      $poll_option[$t] = "";
      }
    $respSet .= "\t<response
resource=\"$poll_option[$t]\"/>\n";
    $resps .= "<response
id=\"$poll_option[$t]\">\n\t<text>$raw_poll_option[$t]</text>\n
</response>\n";
  }

//format new data
  $PollName = str_replace("\'", "", $PollName);
  $PollName = str_replace(" ", "_", $PollName);

  for($r=1; $r<=6; $r++) {
    if(!empty($Raw_Poll_Option[$r]))
      {
      $Poll_Option[$r] = "$PollName-".str_replace("\'", "",
$Raw_Poll_Option[$r]);
      $Poll_Option[$r] = "$PollName-".str_replace(" ", "_",
$Raw_Poll_Option[$r]);
      }
    else
      {
      $Poll_Option[$r] = "";
      }
    $RespSet .= "\t<response
resource=\"$Poll_Option[$r]\"/>\n";
    $Resps .= "<response
id=\"$Poll_Option[$r]\">\n\t<text>$Raw_Poll_Option[$r]</text>\n
</response>\n";
  }

  //Edit PollList entry
  $separator = "\t<Poll name=\"$pollname\"/>\n";
  $divide = explode($separator, $fstr);
  $glue = "\t<Poll name=\"$PollName\"/>\n";
  $fstr = implode($glue, $divide);

  //Edit main poll
  $separator = "<Poll id=\"$pollname\">
\t<StartDate>$poll_startdate</StartDate>
\t<EndDate>$poll_enddate</EndDate>
\t<name>$pollname</name>
\t<text>$poll_question</text>
\t<display type=\"poll_display-Bar-Graph\"/>
\t<responseSet resource=\"$pollname-responseSet\"/>
</Poll>

<responseSet id=\"$pollname-responseSet\">
$respSet</responseSet>
```

Continued

Listing 29-9 *(continued)*

```
$resps";

  $divide = explode($separator, $fstr);

  $glue = "<Poll id=\"$PollName\">
\t<StartDate>$Poll_Startdate</StartDate>
\t<EndDate>$Poll_Enddate</EndDate>
\t<name>$PollName</name>
\t<text>$Poll_Question</text>
\t<display type=\"poll_display-Bar-Graph\"/>
\t<responseSet resource=\"$PollName-responseSet\"/>
</Poll>

<responseSet id=\"$PollName-responseSet\">
$RespSet</responseSet>

$Resps";

  $newxml = implode($glue, $divide);

  //Write to file
  $fd = fopen($pollfile, "w");
  $writestr = fwrite($fd, $newxml);

  //Message
  echo "Wrote $writestr to $pollfile.";
}
?>

</body>
</html>
```

Listing 29-10: An XML file (poll.xml)

```
<PollDefs>

<PollList id="movie-PollList">
  <Poll name="Best_Summer_Film"/>
</PollList>

<Poll id="Best_Summer_Film">
  <StartDate>09/01/2000</StartDate>
  <EndDate>10/01/2000</EndDate>
  <name>Best Summer Film</name>
  <text>Which was the top summer blockbuster?</text>
  <display type="poll_display-Bar-Graph"/>
```

```
    <responseSet resource="Best_Summer_Film-responseSet"/>
</Poll>

<responseSet id="Best_Summer_Film-responseSet">
    <response resource="Best_Summer_Film-Shaft"/>
    <response resource="Best_Summer_Film-Xmen"/>
    <response resource="Best_Summer_Film-Gladiator"/>
    <response resource="Best_Summer_Film-Battlefield_Earth"/>
    <response resource="Best_Summer_Film-MI2"/>
</responseSet>

<response id="Best_Summer_Film-Shaft">
    <text>Shaft</text>
</response>
<response id="Best_Summer_Film-Xmen">
    <text>X Men</text>
</response>
<response id="Best_Summer_Film-Gladiator">
    <text>Gladiator</text>
</response>
<response id="Best_Summer_Film-Battlefield_Earth">
    <text>Battlefield Earth</text>
</response>
<response id="Best_Summer_Film-MI2">
    <text>Mission Impossible 2</text>
</response>

</PollDefs>
```

Gotchas and Troubleshooting

The DOM and SAX parsers will only parse a well-formed XML document. If the parser rejects your XML, make sure it is well formed. If it looks good to your eye, run it through a different validating parser or an online XML checker, such as the one at http://www.xml.com/xml/pub/tools/ruwf/check.html.

If you cannot read and write XML documents to disk, check that the Web server process has permission to do so.

If the DOM API returns a "fatal function not found error," the DOMXML module may not be installed. Use the phpinfo() function to check for a "domxml" entry. If it isn't there, you will have to recompile PHP 4 with the DOMXML module.

Caution At press time there was no DOMXML support for Windows. The Gnome xml libraries are available in a precompiled Windows binary for the daring C programmer, but there is no PHP dll.

The DOM API is new in PHP 4, so all the kinks may not be worked out yet. Keep this in mind and check the bug databases if you encounter problems.

```
http://bugs.php.net/
```

Remember that you're supposed to make a strenuous effort to search the mailing list archives before you search the bugs database. Please be certain your problem is really a bug and has not been resolved before filing it as a bug. If there's any doubt in your mind, read the "Dos and Don'ts" document attached to the bugs database.

Summary

XML is an application-independent data exchange format that promises to make Web development faster and easier in the future. XML and HTML are both descended from SGML, accounting for their close resemblance at first glance. Both have tags and attributes, although XML's are self-defined and structured while HTML's are defined by the HTML standard and contain no information about document structure.

XML has only a few minimal requirements for well formedness. These include closed tags, no overlapping tags, escaped special characters, and the presence of a single root element for each document. However, XML can also be valid in the sense of conforming to a formal declaration of its structure in a document type definition or DTD. DTDs can be internal or external to the XML document, and even located on another server. They contain declarations of the type, attributes, and names of the various elements within the XML file.

For the present, there are few prefabricated tools to help you write, edit, and display XML. You can use one of the two PHP XML APIs, SAX or DOM, to write your own tools. The two APIs have different tradeoffs and uses. SAX is an event-based parser while DOMXML creates an object tree in memory.

At the moment, PHP with the SAX extension can be used to write out well-formed XML from values entered into a Web form. It is also commonly employed to transform XML into HTML for less problematic display in current Web browsers. Another possible task is to pull data from a data store and write it out as XML for exchange with another organization.

✦   ✦   ✦

Object-Oriented Programming with PHP

Object-oriented programming (OOP) is a set of techniques for organizing code around the entities, or objects, that your code represents. Object-oriented programming languages provide built-in support for this kind of organization.

Traditional procedural programming languages operate by applying procedures to data. The data might be represented in strings, numbers, arrays, or any of a number of data structures; procedures are usually represented by procedure or function definitions. For example, a piece of cooking software might represent a recipe by a carefully structured array of strings; other parts of that same program might have functions for doing thing to recipes, like printing them in a pleasing way. On the one hand, there is recipe data; on the other, there are recipe functions. The only thing that links the two together in procedural code is the care the programmer takes to make sure that recipe functions are only called on recipe data.

In object-oriented programming, however, data objects like recipes have a more official existence, and package up both code and data, rather than just data. An object-oriented version of our cooking program would declare a new datatype (or *class*) for the recipe, and would not only define what data parts a recipe had, but would define what functions (or *methods*) could be called on it. That is defining a recipe class might amount to saying that it consists of ingredients (data), and steps (data), and a way that recipes should be printed (method). It's important that these methods are internal to classes — defining how a recipe prints has no effect on how anything else prints.

To write an object-oriented program, then, you must define classes and then build objects with the classes you define. Instead of relying on global functions and variables, you package related variables with functions that use or modify them.

What Is Object-Oriented Programming Good For?

OOP doesn't give you any magical powers — there is nothing you can write in an object-oriented program that you absolutely cannot duplicate in another kind of program. But OOP does force you into a certain kind of organization of your code. This kind of organization can be a very clarifying way to think about programming problems, because it leads to a very natural way to model real-world situations.

An extra benefit of OOP is *inheritance* of classes. Once you define a class, you can define new subclasses that inherit from your original class, so that your subclass has all the same datatypes and behavior, except where you specifically say that it should differ. This can turn out to be an interesting way to reuse code, whether it's your own code or classes that have been predefined in implementations of languages like Java and C++.

With that said, it's important to note that most of the benefits of OOP only become evident when programs become very large. For designers of 100,000-line programs coded by multiple programmers, the discipline and help provided by OOP are essential; for sole authors of two-page scripts, OOP is probably just a distraction.

Object-oriented terminology

Before we get specific about PHP's version of OOP, let's nail down some terms. These terms vary from one OOP language to another, so we will try to tell you both the usual variants and what the thing is called in PHP.

✦ A *class* is a blueprint that tells the programming language how to build a named object type.

✦ An *object* is an instance of a class. If a class is a blueprint, then an object is a building made from the blueprint. Classes aren't usually used alone. Instead, they are used to create one or more instance objects.

✦ A *member variable* is a named variable that belongs to a particular class. (Database programmers should think of it this way: a member variable is to a class what a field is to a table definition.) PHP happens to call member variables *attributes*.

✦ A *member function* is a function that is specific to a class. Member functions are also called methods. PHP happens to refer to *member functions* simply as functions.

✦ A *subclass* is a class that inherits from, or extends, a previously defined class.

✦ A *superclass* is a class that is inherited from or extended.

Limitations of object-oriented programming in PHP: What's missing

This sidebar is intended to bring developers used to other object-oriented languages up to speed quickly on what PHP 4 does and doesn't support. PHP is traditionally a non-object-oriented scripting language. Classes and objects were added after the first release, and there are areas where it becomes obvious to a skilled OO programmer that it was an afterthought.

PHP 4 itself is written in C, not C++, and its development continues to be primarily procedurally (that is, non-object) oriented. But with the vast growth of popularity of PHP and the expansion of its user and developer base, an increasingly object-oriented attitude is developing.

PHP 4 supports most of the basic functionality necessary to define classes and instantiate objects. Here's a brief list of what PHP 4 *doesn't fully* support, so you don't waste time looking for it:

✦ *Multiple inheritance:* PHP 4 supports only single inheritance, but it does support chained subclassing.

✦ *Interfaces:* No support.

✦ *Abstract classes:* No support.

✦ *Overloading:* No support (subsequent functions with the same name in a class definition, irrespective of arguments, completely overwrite and hide previous functions.)

✦ *Privacy:* There are no private or protected modifiers in PHP 4 classes. Everything is public.

✦ *Destructors:* No support.

✦ *Polymorphism:* Polymorphism will generally work, if only because it requires special syntax to access overridden base class functions.

Objects, classes, and types in PHP

All variables in PHP 4 have a type. A variable's type can be an integer, a double, a string, an array, or an object. If the variable is an object, then it also has a class.

If you've written some PHP code, you're probably ready to start writing with classes and objects. A simple class is easy to understand:

```
class myClass
{
  var $attribute = "my attribute.";

  function show_attribute()
    {
      echo $this->attribute . "<br>\n";
    }
}
```

Class definitions are usually straightforward. Their structure doesn't change:

```
class CLASSNAME [extends PARENT_CLASSNAME ]
{
    [attributes]
    [functions]
}
```

where the brackets indicate optional parts of the definition. Attributes and functions are not required, but a class would be useless without at least one of them. The order of attributes and functions in the class definition isn't important, but typically the attributes are put first and the functions second.

Attributes

Attributes are defined in the form:

```
var $attribute = "my attribute.";
```

Attribute definitions may not be initialized to a nonstatic value. That is, you can set a variable's initial value to a simple scalar, a string, an integer, a floating-point number, or an array, but not to an object.

An attribute may be of any PHP 4 type and any defined class type including objects. You can declare the same attribute as many times as you like, but only the last one initialized has an effect.

Attributes declared in a class can be initialized or not. If an attribute is assigned a value when it is declared in a class, it is initialized.

Note   You cannot initialize an attribute with an object.

Caution   PHP 3 allowed programmers to use non-static initialization for class variables. PHP 4 considers this an error and will stop parsing. This is an issue for people who want to port existing libraries to PHP 4, or reuse existing object-oriented code from earlier versions of PHP.

Functions

Functions are defined in a class just as they are outside a class. There are only two major differences:

✦ To access an attribute of the object, you must use the syntax $this-> attribute. Do not use the form this->$attribute, because it doesn't work. The form $this->$attribute will work only if $attribute is a string containing the name of the attribute you wish to use. This also works for functions.

```
var $attr1;
...
$attr_name = "attr1";
echo $this->$attr_name;

function function1() { ...}
...
$function_name = "function1";
$this->$function_name();
```

✦ PHP 4 functions that take callbacks, such as array_walk(), generally do not support object functions (methods). This is a known problem that may be fixed in the near future. Some APIs have a separate interface for objects, such as the new XML DOM API.

The special variable $this appears in the preceding fragment. $this is a pointer to the current object. It is automatically available in any function in a class, unless the function is called statically.

Cross-Reference   See also "Scope" in this chapter.

In OO parlance, a function defined inside a class is called a *method*.

Constructors

A *constructor* is a specialized function defined in a class. It has the same name as the class and may take arguments. Each class can have only one constructor.

Constructors are automatically called when an instance of the class — an object — is created. They are useful for initializing the attributes of an object with reasonable starting values.

Inheritance

A class in PHP 4 can be derived from another class. The derived class "inherits" all the functions and attributes of the class it is derived from, without having to declare them all again.

```
class super
{
  function super_echo()
    {
      echo "SUPERCLASS.<br> \n";
    }
}

class sub extends super
{
  function sub_echo()
    {
      echo "SUBCLASS.<br> \n";
    }
}

$object = new sub();    // instantiate an object
$object->sub_echo();    // call a subclass function
$object->super_echo();  // call an inherited superclass function
```

We call the class named "super" the superclass or base class.

We call the class named "sub" the subclass or derived class. It inherits from, or extends, one or more classes. A PHP 4 class can only inherit from one other class, but that superclass can also inherit from another super class. (Or to put it another way, PHP classes can have only one parent, but they can also have a grandparent.)

```
class grandparent
{
}
class parent extends grandparent
{
}
class child extends parent
{
}
```

Extending a class is a process of specialization. The superclass serves a general purpose, and subclasses specialize to fill narrow purposes:

```
class Shape
{
}
class Two_Dimensional_Shape extends Shape
{
}
class Circle extends Two_Dimensional_Shape
{
}
```

In this example, the class Circle inherits from Two_Dimensional_Shape and from Shape, and you would be able to call any function in either superclass on an object of type Circle.

Overriding

Subclasses automatically inherit the attributes and functions of their superclasses, but this presents an opportunity for namespace confusion. A superclass may have a function with the same name as a subclass. PHP 4 must decide which function to call when presented with this code:

```
class super
{
  function my_function()
    {
      echo "SUPERCLASS.<br> \n";
    }
}

class sub extends super
{
  function my_function()
    {
      echo "SUBCLASS.<br> \n";
    }
}

$object = new sub;

$object->my_function();
```

When a subclass has a function with the same name as the superclass, the subclass has *overridden* the superclass's function. When the overridden function is called on an instance of the subclass, the subclass's definition of the function is called, not the superclass's. The superclass's function isn't gone, but we must use a different syntax to access it. We must use a scope modifier to tell PHP 4 which function we want to use:

```
class sub extends super
{
  function my_function()
    {
      super::my_function();
    }
}
```

In this example, the subclass function calls the superclass function by using a scope modifier, the ": :" operator, to signal PHP 4 to look in the class super for the function my_function.

This syntax does not allow access to superclass attributes that have been over-ridden by subclass definitions.

Overloading

In object-oriented programming, *overloading* is when you have more than one function with a given name in a class. The interpreter or compiler differentiates between the functions by the number and types of arguments — each function is required to have a unique *argument signature*. PHP 4 does not support overloading. It is syntactically correct to define more than one function with the same name in a class; however, all but the last function with a given name will be ignored.

Scope

If you have written functions in PHP 4 before, you have already encountered scope. *Scope* is the space of available variables. Within any function, you cannot access your global variables without declaring them as global variables inside the function or accessing them through the GLOBALS[] array.

Scope in PHP 4 also determines which functions you can call. You cannot directly call a function inside a class without using a scope modifier to tell PHP 4 where to look for the function.

The following things are always in scope, and PHP 4 can find them without complaint:

✦ Built-in PHP 4 functions and functions from any loaded modules

✦ Variables handled automatically by PHP 4, that is, PHP_POST_VARS

In the "normal space" of a PHP 4 page, outside of classes or functions, these things are also in scope:

✦ Functions defined outside of a class

✦ Variables declared outside of a class or a function

Functions, variables, and class definitions are in scope even when included through the `include()` or `require()` functions.

Within a function, these things are in scope:

✦ Variables declared inside the function

✦ Variables passed as arguments to the function

Within a class definition:

✦ Functions in the same class, accessed through the `$this` variable.

Note Attributes cannot be initialized to the value of a global variable. In a class definition, global variables cannot be accessed outside a function.

✦ The only variables you can access outside of scope are global variables. Declare them global in your function before use or access them through the `$GLOBALS` array.

✦ To access a function outside the current scope, use the scope modifier, "`::`". This allows you to specify the class PHP 4 can find the function in, that is:

```
class::function_name( argument1, ...);
```

✦ If the current scope is a class function definition, the named *class* is a super-class of the current class, and the named *function* is overloaded, then the function called is the inherited superclass's function. The inherited function will have full access to the object's variables and methods.

✦ But if this syntax is used outside a class definition or names a class that is not a superclass of the current class, then this syntax calls the specified function as a static function call. The function will have no access to or knowledge of the `$this` pointer and will be unable to call other functions in the class without itself using the `::` scope modifier.

Assignment, aliasing, and references

PHP 4 uses a technique called *reference counting* to reduce unnecessary copying and memory use. It can speed up the processing of existing code without modification, but a new feature in PHP 4 — aliasing — gives us reason to examine the change.

You use assignment all the time. When you create or reuse a PHP 4 variable and give it a value, you are assigning:

```
$new_variable = $old_variable;
```

Assignment in previous versions of PHP 4 copied the value of the variable. That is, if $old_variable pointed to an object, and you assigned $new_variable to $old_variable as $new_variable = $old_variable, you then had two objects.

If you subsequently changed the value of $new_variable or $old_variable, they didn't affect each other.

New Feature   Reference counting is new in PHP 4. It shouldn't affect the processing of existing code except to speed it up.

But in PHP 4, what in fact happens when you make this assignment is that you still have only one object, with two variables pointing to it. What happens to $new_variable when you change $old_variable? Only *then* does PHP 4 make a copy of $old_variable. Making a change to $old_variable won't affect the value of $new_variable or vice versa.

But if you want $new_variable and $old_variable to continue to point to the same value, and changes to $new_variable to affect the value of $old_variable and vice versa, PHP 4 has a new mechanism to support this arrangement: aliases.

New Feature   Aliases are new in PHP 4.

An *alias* is a variable that is a reference to another variable. It has no value of its own but points to the value of the other variable. It acts like a variable for all other purposes; you can assign it a value or call its functions if it is an object.

```
$alias = &$variable;
```

Here is an example of the differences between using an alias and using a variable:

```
$variable = "Test String One"
$new_variable = "Test String One"
$alias = &$variable;
echo "<br>";
echo "Starting values:<br>";
echo "Original Variable: " . $variable . "<br>";
echo "Assigned Variable: " . $new_variable . "<br>";
echo "Alias: " . $alias . "<br>";

echo "<br>";
echo "Changing the Assigned Variable...";
```

```php
$new_variable = "Changed Test String One - Variable";
echo "<br><br>";

echo "<br>";
echo "After changing the new variable:<br>";
echo "Original Variable: " . $variable . "<br>";
echo "Assigned Variable: " . $new_variable . "<br>";
echo "Alias: " . $alias . "<br>";

echo "<br>";
echo "Changing the Alias...";
$alias = "Changed Test String One - Alias";
echo "<br><br>";

echo "<br>";
echo "After changing the alias:<br>";
echo "Original Variable: " . $variable . "<br>";
echo "Assigned Variable: " . $new_variable . "<br>";
echo "Alias: " . $alias . "<br>";
```

which produces output

```
Starting values:
Original Variable: Test String One
Assigned Variable: Test String One
Alias: Test String One

Changing the Assigned Variable...

After changing the new variable:
Original Variable: Test String One
Assigned Variable: Changed Test String One - Variable
Alias: Test String One

Changing the Alias...

After changing the alias:
Original Variable: Changed Test String One - Alias
Assigned Variable: Changed Test String One - Variable
Alias: Changed Test String One - Alias
```

Setting $variable doesn't affect $new_variable because $new_variable is a distinct copy of $variable. However, changing $alias does change $variable as well, because $alias is not a distinct copy of $variable, only a different name for it.

Aliases can also refer to specific places in an array or attributes of an object:

```php
$alias = &$object->attribute;

$alias = "New Value for the Attribute";

echo "<br>Alias: " . $alias . " is the same as ";
echo "Original: " . $object->attribute . "<br><br>";
```

You might want to use an alias for three reasons:

1. To store a pointer to a variable in multiple places, such as in object attributes, such that any change made to any alias affects every other.

2. To prevent PHP 4 from making extra copies of a large object when it is passed into a function (syntax: *function(&object)*);

3. To shorten a variable name from something unwieldy to something easy to type or read.

> **Note**   If you have very large objects, always pass them as arguments using an alias, as it will reduce execution time and memory use.

Displaying and printing objects

PHP 4 has two built-in functions that will format and print out an object: `var_dump` and `print_r`. Their output formats are slightly different, but they accomplish the same thing. They output text, not HTML, so if you want to dump them to the screen, envelope them in a ⟨pre⟩ tag:

```
echo "<pre>";
var_dump($object);
echo "</pre>";

echo "<pre>";
print_r($object);
echo "</pre>";
```

PHP 4 has other functions that will display the value of a variable: `print()`, `echo()`, and `strval()`, but they do no special handling of objects.

Later in this chapter there is an example of a custom object displayer.

Introspection

An object is a package of data and functions. PHP 4 provides a way to see the names, types, and values of all of the data in an object. Objects can be treated as arrays and "walked" to find every variable's name, type, and value.

PHP 4 has functions for looking at and even changing the types of variables and classes.

Type and Class Introspection Functions

Tables 30-1 through 30-3 list the most important type, class, and variable functions in PHP 4.

Cross-Reference See Chapter 6 for more detail on types and type-checking in general

Table 30-1
Boolean Type Check Function Summary

Function	Behavior
is_array($var)	Returns true if $var is an array.
is_int($var)	Returns true if $var is an integer. Note: PHP 4 makes no distinction between the types int, integer, and long.
is_integer($var)	Returns true if $var is an integer. Note: PHP 4 makes no distinction between the types int, integer, and long.
is_long($var)	Returns true if $var is an integer. Note: PHP 4 makes no distinction between the types int, integer, and long.
is_float($var)	Returns true if $var is a double-precision floating-point number. Note: PHP 4 makes no distinction between the types float, double, and real.
is_real($var)	Returns true if $var is a double-precision floating-point number. Note: PHP 4 makes no distinction between the types float, double, and real.
is_double($var)	Returns true if $var is a double-precision floating-point number. Note: PHP 4 makes no distinction between the types float, double, and real.
is_numeric($var)	Returns true if $var is an integer or a double-precision floating-point number or a string containing either.
is_string($var)	Returns true if $var is a string.
is_object($var)	Returns true if $var is an object.
class_exists (string)	Returns true if string is the name of a predefined or user-defined class.

Continued

Table 30-1 *(continued)*

Function	Behavior
empty($var)	Returns true if $var is a variable name that is not set and not in use *or* has a value of zero, such as 0 or "0".
Isset($var)	Returns true if $var is a variable name that is not set and not in use.

Table 30-2
Type and Class Function Summary

Function	Behavior
gettype($var)	Returns a string representing the type of $var, that is, "string," "object," "double."
settype($var)	Attempts to force the type of $var to "array," "double," "integer," "object," or "string." This function may have counter-intuitive results, so test your use before trusting it.
doubleval($var)	Returns a double determined by the value of $var; that is, "0.045" becomes 0.045, and 6 becomes 6.0. This function does not work on arrays or objects.
intval($var)	Returns an integer determined by the value of $var; that is, "45" becomes 45, and 4.0 becomes 4. Be cautious, as intval (4.0004) returns 0! This function does not work on arrays or objects.
unset($var)	Removes the specified variable. This variable is no longer available, and a call to isset($var) will return false.

Table 30-3
Type and Class I/O Function Summary

Function	Behavior
print_r($var)	Prints a string representation of a variable or object.
var_dump($var)	Prints a string representation of a variable or object. This function's output is slightly different from print_r()'s.
strval($var)	Returns a string representation of a variable. Does not spell out the details of arrays or objects. Does not print.

Function	Behavior
serialize($var)	Returns a byte stream representation of a variable including objects. This output is suitable for storage in a database or transmission between pages. This stream may need to be further encoded with base64_encode( ) for some tasks.
unserialize($var)	Returns a variable constructed from the output of a serialize( ) function.

We'll look at three of these functions in depth:

```
is_object()
gettype()
get_class()
```

We can combine our ability to dynamically find the variables of a class with the type introspection functions to write our own object display function. Listing 30-1 shows two functions, display_object(), which does most of the work, and spaceout(), a helper function that assists with formatting inner objects.

The display_object() function traverses the object it is given, displaying each variable's name, type, and value. If the variable is an object, the function calls itself with the new object. This lets us see the full depth of most objects and any objects inside them, but it opens up the possibility of infinite recursion if an object contains a reference to itself!

Listing 30-1: **Displaying Objects**

```
function spaceout($depth)
{
  for ($i = 0; $i < $depth*4; $i++)
    echo " ";
}
function display_object($obj, $depth = 0)
{
  if (!is_object($obj))
    return;

  if ($depth == 0)
    echo "<b>Printing Object Details:</b> <br><br>";

  reset($obj);
```

Continued

Listing 30-1 *(continued)*

```
  while ( list($slot) = each($obj) )
    {
      echo spaceout($depth) . "<b>$slot Details:</b> <br>";
      echo spaceout($depth) . "variable name: $slot<br>";
      echo spaceout($depth) . "variable type: ". gettype($obj-
>$slot) . " <br>";
      if ( is_object($obj->$slot) )
          echo spaceout($depth) . "variable class: " .
                    get_class($obj->$slot) . "<br>";

      echo spaceout($depth) . "slot value: ";

      if ( gettype($obj->$slot) == "string")
        echo $obj->$slot;
      else if ( gettype($obj->$slot) == "integer")
        echo $obj->$slot;
      else if ( gettype($obj->$slot) == "double")
        echo  $obj->$slot;
      else if ( gettype($obj->$slot) == "array")
        print_r($obj->$slot);
      else if ( gettype($obj->$slot) == "object")
        {
        echo spaceout($depth) . "<i>Object of class </i><b>" .
get_class($obj->$slot) . ":</b><br>";
    display_object($obj->$slot, $depth+1);
    continue;
    }
      echo "<br>";
    }
  }
```

Here is a class containing variables of each type, and an inner object:

```
class walkme
{
  var $stringOne = "String One Original Value";
  var $stringTwo = "String Two Original Value";
  var $objectOne;
  var $integerOne;
  var $doubleOne;
  var $arrayOne;

  function init()
    {
      $this->stringOne = "String One New Value"; //string
      $this->objectOne = new intro();             //object
      $this->objectOne->objectOne = new intro(); //inner object
      $this->integerOne = 6;                      //integer
```

```
      $this->doubleOne = 6.5;                      //floating-
point
      $this->arrayOne = array("a","b","c");        //array
    }
  }
```

Because we can't initialize variables with nonstatic values such as an object, we must set the value of $objectOne after the object is instantiated. Here we do this through a function call that sets other variables as well for good measure. Next we create an object and send it through the displayer:

```
$obj = new walkme();
echo "Created Object<br>\n";
$obj->init();
display_object($obj);
```

This produces the output shown in Listing 30-2.

Listing 30-2: **Displaying Objects Output**

```
Created Object
Printing Object Details:

stringOne Details:
variable name: stringOne
variable type: string
slot value: String One New Value
stringTwo Details:
variable name: stringTwo
variable type: string
slot value: String Two Original Value
objectOne Details:
variable name: objectOne
variable type: object
variable class: intro
slot value: Object of class intro:
    stringOne Details:
    variable name: stringOne
    variable type: string
    slot value: String One Original Value
    stringTwo Details:
    variable name: stringTwo
    variable type: string
    slot value: String Two Original Value
    objectOne Details:
    variable name: objectOne
    variable type: object
    variable class: intro
    slot value:     Object of class intro:
```

Continued

Listing 30-3 *(continued)*

```
            stringOne Details:
            variable name: stringOne
            variable type: string
            slot value: String One Original Value
            stringTwo Details:
            variable name: stringTwo
            variable type: string
            slot value: String Two Original Value
integerOne Details:
variable name: integerOne
variable type: integer
slot value: 6
doubleOne Details:
variable name: doubleOne
variable type: double
slot value: 6.5
arrayOne Details:
variable name: arrayOne
variable type: array
slot value: Array ( [0] => a [1] => b [2] => c )
```

Object Serialization

For several different reasons, it can be useful to be able to encode an object as a linear sequence of bytes, and then decode that sequence into an object again. With this capability, you can write out an object to disk and then read it in again, or pass it to another program over a network and have it be reconstructed at the other end. This kind of encoding and decoding of objects is called serialization.

PHP 4 provides two handy functions for accomplishing this task, serialize() and unserialize(). These functions automatically handle turning a PHP object into a savable string and then later turning a saved string back into a PHP object.

Caution   You cannot serialize an external object, such as a COM or Java object returned by COM and Java extension interfaces. Some handles and types, such as database connection handles, may not survive serialization.

You can save serialized objects into a file or database or even pass them from one page to another via a link.

```
if ( !isset($in_object) )
{
```

```
    $in_object = new walkme();
echo "Link below contains an encoded object.<br>";
echo "<a href=\"session.php4?in_object=" . base64_encode(serialize( $object ) )
. "\">Click here </a>";
}
else
{
  echo "Decoding and restoring object serialized across the URL.<br>";

  $out_object = unserialize( base64_decode(( $in_object ) ));

  echo "<pre>";
  var_dump($out_object);
  echo "</pre><br><br>";
}
```

One thing to watch out for is to make sure that the class of the serialized object is defined when it is unserialized. If it is not defined, the unserialized object's variables will be available, but you will not be able to call any of the object's functions.

Caution   Although passing serialized objects via GET and POST works in theory, be aware that length limits may truncate your object. This is especially in the case of GET methods, which are only required to hold 255 characters.

Extension Interfaces: COM, DCOM, Java, and CORBA

In theory, PHP 4 extension modules currently provide support for connecting to and manipulating COM, DCOM, and Java objects. CORBA is not supported in the 4.0.0 release, but at least one module project is underway based on the ORBit ORB.

PHP 4 supports "wrapping" of external objects as PHP 4 objects. These external objects are created by calls to modules and can be called like standard PHP 4 objects.

Note   PHP 4 objects created by modules that wrap external objects are not exactly standard PHP 4 objects. They cannot be serialized, and you may notice other differences.

The COM and DCOM interface is only available on Windows platforms. The Java interface should be available on most platforms.

Note   Although Java support is part of the PHP 4 release, we had no success in testing the Java support in beta versions of PHP 4. Please check our Web site at http: www.troutworks.com for updates on PHP 4 Java support.

COM and DCOM

The COM module supports both COM and DCOM objects that have an IDispatch interface. The COM module is part of the Win32 binary distribution of PHP 4. Table 30-4 summarizes the available COM interface functions.

PHP 4 can recognize automation constants if you specify a type library in the php.ini file. See the module's README file for the most up-to-date notes on how to do this.

DCOM is supported but is disabled by default. To enable DCOM, place a line in the php.ini file: allow_dcom = 1; The module automatically converts types between COM and PHP 4, but it will not convert PHP 4 objects or arrays.

The following is an example of using COM to communicate with a database.

```php
$db = new COM("ADODB.Connection");
$database_name = "librarians";
$table_name = "librarians";

  echo "COM object type: ";
  echo gettype($db);
  echo "<br>";
  echo "COM object class: ";
  echo get_class($db);
  echo "<br>";
  echo "<br>";

$db->Open($database_name,"","");

$result = $db->Execute("SELECT \"First Name\",\"Last
Name\",\"State\" FROM  " .$table_name . " order by state" );

  echo "New COM object type: ";
  echo gettype($result);
  echo "<br>";
  echo "New COM object class: ";
  echo get_class($result);
  echo "<br>";
  echo "<br>";


while(!$result->EOF)
{
  echo $result->Fields["First Name"]->Value;
  echo " ";
  echo $result->Fields["Last Name"]->Value;
  echo ", " ;
  echo $result->Fields["State"]->Value;
```

```
    echo "<br>";
    $result->MoveNext();
}
```

The preceding code produces this output:

```
COM object type: object
COM object class: COM

New COM object type: object
New COM object class: COM

Janet Baker, AL
Jason Nesbitt, AZ
Scott D. Croff, AZ
Valerie Vinge, AZ
Richard Lynn, CA
Robert G. Willis, CA
Peter Butler, PA
Mary Stewart, CA
Darvid Bergman, CA
Lisa Bates, CA
Mark Miller, CA
Tony Smith, NJ
```

Table 30-4
COM Interface Function Summary

Function	Behavior
com_load()	**Parameters:** (*string object name*, [*string server name*]). The server name is only required for DCOM access.
com_invoke()	**Parameters:** (*object*, *string function name*, [*argument1 . . . argumentN*])
com_propget()	**Parameters:** (*object*, *string attribute name*)
com_get()	**Same as** com_propget();
com_propput()	**Parameters:** (*object*, *string attribute name*, *variable value*). Cannot set a property to an object or array.
com_propset()	**Same as** com_proput();
com_set()	**Same as** com_propput();

Sample Object-Oriented Application Code

The comprehensive example in Listing 30-3 demonstrates attribute inheritance, function inheritance, and polymorphism.

Listing 30-3: **Database Interface Abstraction Example**

```
<?
session_start();
?>
<html>
<head></head>
<body>
<?

// ********************************************
class database
{
  var $server_name;
  var $database_name;
  var $user_name;
  var $user_password;
  var $suppress_errors = 0;

  function connect() { ; }
  function error_string() { ; }
  function error_number() { ; }
  function execute_query($query) { ; }
  function select_database() { ; }
  function commit() { ; }
  function rollback() { ; }
  function fetch_row_array() { ; }

  function check_connect()
  {
    if ( $this->connection == 0 )
      $this->connect();
  }

  function print_error($error_string)
  {
    if (!$this->suppress_errors)
      echo "Nonfatal Database Error: " . $error_string .
"<br>";
  }
}

// ********************************************
```

```php
class failover_database extends database
{
  var $backup_server_name;

  function failover_database( $server_name,
$backup_server_name,$database_name, $user_name, $user_password)
    {
      $this->server_name = $server_name;
      $this->backup_server_name = $backup_server_name;
      $this->database_name = $database_name;
      $this->user_name = $user_name;
      $this->user_password = $user_password;

      $this->suppress_errors = 1;   // turn off warning for first
attempt.
      $result = $this->connect();
      $this->suppress_errors = 0;   // turn our errors back on

      $this->connect();

  }

  function connect()
    {

      if ( ($result == 0) && isset($this->backup_server_name) )
        {
        $original = $this->server_name;
        $this->server_name = $this->backup_server_name;
        $this->backup_server_name = $original;

        // try the backup server.
    $result = database::connect();
    }
}

}

// *****************************************
class mysql_database extends failover_database
{
  var $connection;

  function mysql_database( $server_name,
$backup_servername,$database_name, $user_name, $user_password)
    {
      // call the superclass constructor
      failover_database::failover_database($server_name,
$backup_servername,$database_name, $user_name, $user_password);
    }
```

Continued

Listing 30-3 *(continued)*

```php
function connect()
{
   $this->connection = @mysql_pconnect($this->server_name,
$this->user_name, $this->user_password);
   if ($this->connection == 0)
     $this->print_error("Unable to establish a connection with
the database. Check the server, username, and password, and try
again.");

   $this->select_database($this->database_name);

   return $this->connection;
}

function error_string()
{
  return mysql_error();
}

function error_number()
{
  return mysql_errno();
}

function execute_query($query)
{
  $this->check_connect();

  $result = @mysql_query($query, $this->connection);
  if ($result == 0)
    $this->print_error("Unable to execute query (" . $query .
"). Error returned is: (" . $this->error_string() . "). Check
the syntax and the server connection and try again.");
  return ( $result );
}

function select_database($db_name)
{
  $this->check_connect();

  $result = @mysql_select_db($db_name);
  if ($result == 0)
    $this->print_error("Unable to select the database (" .
$db_name . "). Error returned is: (" . $this->error_string() .
"). Check the database name and the server connection and try
again.");
  }
```

```
    function fetch_row_array($query_result)
    {
      $this->check_connect();

      if ($query_result == 0)
        $this->print_error("Unable to fetch the result of a
query. Error returned is: (" . $this->error_string() . ").
Check the query and the server connection and try again.");

      return ( @mysql_fetch_array( $query_result, MYSQL_ASSOC )
);
    }

    function commit()  { ; } // no commit support in mysql.

    function rollback()  { ;  } // no rollback support in mysql.
}

// *******************************************
// all the classes above could be put in an include file,
database.inc
// include("database.inc");


$server = "your.server.name";
$backupserver = "your.backup.server.name";
$database = "your_database_name";
$username = "your_user_name";
$password = "your_password_name";


if ( ! isset($mydb) )
{
  $mydb = new mysql_database($server, $backupserver, $database,
$username, $password);
  echo "Creating database connection object...<br>";
}
else
{
  echo "Reusing database connection object...<br>";
}

session_register("mydb");

$query = "select name, id from people";

$result = $mydb->execute_query($query);

if ($result != 0)
{
```

Continued

Listing 30-3 *(continued)*

```
while( $row = $mydb->fetch_row_array($result) )
   {
      echo "Name: <b>" . $row["name"] . "</b><br>";
      echo " ID : <b>" . $row["id"] . "</b><br>";
      echo "<br>";
   }
}
?>
</body>
</html>
```

Summary

Object-oriented programming is programming with class. PHP 4 has the basic tools for developing object-oriented applications. Not everything you might like in an OO language is included; more is probably missing than is present. But the spirit is there, and with the tools provided you can:

✦ Make your applications smarter and more flexible.

✦ Package data and functions together so that data doesn't get corrupted or invalidated.

✦ Manage your namespace, hiding potentially thousands of functions in classes so that you don't accidentally overload functions in global scope.

✦ Write applications that interact with COM, DCOM, and Java objects.

✦ Learn the basics of object-oriented design and programming.

✦   ✦   ✦

Security and Cryptography

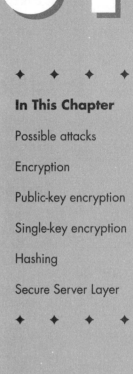

"**S**ecurity is not a joking matter," proclaim signs at airports everywhere. The same sign should be posted near your PHP server. Anyone connecting a server to the Internet must take proper security measures or risk loss of data or even money to the keystrokes of malicious crackers.

The mantra of the security-conscious site designer is "*Don't trust the network.*" If you're worried about the security of your site, chant this mantra as you code your pages. Any information transmitted to your server via the network — be it a URL, data from an HTML form, or data on some other network port — should be treated as potentially hazardous. This chapter suggests several techniques for "sanitizing" incoming information. You should apply these techniques and spend some time trying to discover other potential hazards and ways to prevent them.

The second rule of thumb for a secure site is "*Minimize the damage.*" What if the program you just wrote, which you are *sure* is secure, is actually vulnerable? Just to be on the safe side, limit the damage an intruder can cause, once he or she has taken advantage of the vulnerability.

When visitors come to your site, they trust that it contains valid information, that it is not harmful to them or to their computer, and that any information they provide to it will be handled properly. Interacting with a site, whether an e-business, recreational, or informational site, involves certain security risks for a visitor. As a site designer, it is your responsibility to protect the visitor from these risks. Besides being sure their information is safe on your server, this means you should take measures to safeguard their information while it is in transit from their computer to your server.

But all of this should not scare you away from putting your e-business online. The first section of this chapter describes some possible attacks against your server and ways to avoid

them. We then discuss cryptographic techniques for protecting your data. At the
end of this chapter, we list some Web sites that contain up-to-the-minute information
on the latest cracker techniques. By watching these sites, you may learn of possible
security vulnerabilities before an attacker does and, thereby, avoid disaster.

Possible Attacks

Connecting your server to the Internet is like setting up a storefront on a busy
street. You're likely to have quite a few visitors, but if you're not careful, some less
than desirable visitors may take advantage of you.

Site defacement

Often more embarrassing than harmful, site defacements are fairly common,
because the cracker has an opportunity to publicize his or her exploitation. Site
defacements are sometimes left as calling cards by a cracker who entered a system
by more complicated means.

It is possible to deface a badly designed Web site using only a Web browser. Take,
for instance, the following program:

```
<?php if (IsSet($visitor)) {
  $fp = fopen("database", "a");
  fwrite($fp, "<li>$visitor\n");
  fclose($fp); } ?>
<HTML>
<HEAD></HEAD>
<BODY>
<H1>Visitors to this site:</H1>
<OL>
<?php $fp = fopen("database", "r");
  print(fread($fp, filesize("/path/to/database")));
  fclose($fp) ?>
</OL>
<HR>
<FORM><INPUT TYPE="TEXT" NAME="visitor">
<INPUT TYPE="SUBMIT" NAME="submit" VALUE="Sign in!">
</FORM>
</BODY>
</HTML>
```

This program implements a very rudimentary guest book. In reading this code,
however, you should feel a bit uneasy. *Don't trust the network.* This program accepts
form data that we expect to contain the visitor's name (in the variable $visitor)
and stores it in a text file for display to subsequent visitors. For the inputs we
expect, there is no trouble.

Now put on your script-kiddie hat for a moment and imagine what would happen if the input contained HTML tags. This simple program would blindly insert those tags into the pages it generates, and other visitors' browsers would interpret them as usual. One particularly malicious tag is the `<SCRIPT>` tag. A cracker wishing to deface this Web page could duplicate the page's appearance on his or her own server (`www.badsite.com`) and then sign into the guestbook with the "name":

```
<SCRIPT LANGUAGE="JavaScript">
window.location="http://www.badsite.com/"</SCRIPT>
```

When visitors load the guest book, their browsers will receive this tag and immediately begin loading the hacked site. With a little ingenuity, the cracker could then take advantage of the visitor's trust of your site to extract personal information such as passwords or credit card numbers.

The solution to this problem is to sanitize the input data. In this case, we want any characters that have special meaning to a browser to be translated into something harmless. Luckily, PHP provides a way to perform just such a translation. The function `htmlspecialchars()` converts the characters '<', '>', '"', and '&' to their representations as HTML entities (such as `&lt;`). We change the first part of our program to use this new function as follows:

```php
<?php if (IsSet($visitor)) {
    $fp = fopen("database", "a");
    $clean_visitor = htmlspecialchars($visitor);
    fwrite($fp, "<li>$clean_visitor\n");
    fclose($fp); } ?>
```

And we have patched a very significant security hole in our site.

Crackers, script-kiddies, and other fiends

The term "hacker" is commonly used to describe individuals more correctly labeled crackers. Within the computer community, "crackers" are those who, through luck or skill, break into computer systems and cause damage. "Hackers" are those who can "hack" — read and write efficient (and often obscure) code in many languages. To a programmer, being labeled a hacker is an honor, whereas being labeled a cracker probably means he or she should start reading the help wanted section.

As if "cracker" was not sufficiently derogatory, young crackers who use tools and scripts they find on the Web are called "script-kiddies." These budding lawbreakers often have little understanding of what they are actually doing. They are usually the culprits behind low-tech attacks such as site defacement. A fairly good indicator of the work of a script-kiddie is the excessive use of misspelling and capitalization, as in "W3 R KOOL D00Dz."

Accessing source code

Even if your PHP source code isn't a trade secret, you should still protect it from exposure to the network. If an intruder can read your source code, then he or she need not experiment to find a weakness. Instead, the intruder can simply analyze the code, looking for common mistakes and other security holes. In general, the more helpful information you provide to potential intruders, the more likely an intrusion. By hiding such tidbits as source code, directory names, or user names from the network, you can reduce the likelihood of an attack.

When PHP is used as a Web server module, there is little risk of source code being released by the Web server, as any file with the proper extension will be parsed by the PHP module. However, if PHP is installed as a CGI program, things are not so simple.

If you cannot run PHP as a server module, the next most secure setup is to run it as an interpreter for CGI scripts, just as you would Perl or Python. That is, place all of your PHP programs in the `cgi-bin` directory for your server or your account and arrange for the PHP interpreter to be invoked when they are executed. On UNIX, this is done by adding a line similar to the following as the first line of every script:

```
#! /usr/local/bin/php
```

To use this setup, you must compile PHP with the `--enable-discard-path` configuration option. This setup has the disadvantage that the URLs for most of your pages will contain `/cgi-bin/`.

The next most secure setup is a bit more complicated and is actually counter to the recommendations of CERT, a respected authority on computer security: we place the PHP interpreter itself in the `cgi-bin` directory. It is usually inadvisable to put an interpreter in the `cgi-bin` directory, because the rules for invoking CGI programs would allow any file on the server to be parsed as a program.

However, PHP is written to operate safely from the `cgi-bin` directory, if configured correctly. If you intend to use this setup, first carefully read the security and configuration sections of the PHP manual, as they may contain important information not available as this book went to press.

This setup relies upon the Web server to redirect URLs of the form

```
http://your.server/program.php
```

to URLs of the form

```
http://your.server/cgi-bin/php/program.php
```

The precise directives that will cause your Web server to do this vary. For Apache they are:

```
Action php-script /cgi-bin/php
AddType php-script .php
```

If you are using Apache, be sure to compile PHP with the `--enable-force-cgi-redirect` configuration option. This option utilizes a feature specific to Apache to prevent PHP from executing when invoked by URLs of the second form. Your setup is complete.

If you are using any other server software, you must compile PHP with the `--disable-force-cgi-redirect` configuration option. PHP cannot distinguish the two types of URLs and will serve a document of either type. This allows a visitor to view files without regard for Web server–based access restrictions. For example, assume that the URL `http://www.secrets.com/top/secret/hush.php` has access restrictions placed on it. A cracker could use the URL `http://www.secrets.com/cgi-bin/php/top/secret/hush.php` to read the file anyway.

In this case, the Web server is giving PHP the pathname `/top/secret/hush.php`. PHP determines the location of the program file by prepending the configuration value `doc_root` to the given pathname. By default, this value is the same as the Web server's document root (the directory corresponding to `http://www.secrets.com/`). Setting `doc_root` to another directory will limit PHP to programs in that directory and its subdirectories, instead of the entire collection of Web server documents. However, any visitor may access any of the PHP programs by the method just described, without regard for Web server–based access controls. *Be careful!*

Reading arbitrary files

A few common PHP programming mistakes can make it easy for a hacker to read almost any file on the server. Study the following page:

```
<HTML>
<HEAD></HEAD>
<BODY>
<?php if (IsSet($poem)) {
  $fp = fopen($poem, "r");
  print (fread($fp, filesize($poem)));
  fclose($fp);
  } ?>
<HR><FORM>Pick a poem:
<SELECT NAME="poem"><OPTION VALUE="jabb.html">Jabberwocky
<OPTION VALUE="graves.html">Cat-Goddesses</SELECT>
<INPUT TYPE="SUBMIT" VALUE="Show Me"></FORM>
</BODY>
</HTML>
```

This simple program displays a number of poems, selectable from a pop-up menu given in the form near the end. Invoke the security mantra, *Don't trust the network.* Clicking "Show Me" on this page results in URLs such as ......poetry.php?poem= graves.html. A cracker might substitute the filename of some more sensitive file, such as ...poetry.php?poem=/etc/passwd. The program as given would dutifully serve up the UNIX password file, possibly enabling the cracker to break into a visitor account and do further damage.

The following is an appropriate solution to this problem:

```php
<?php if (IsSet($poem)) {
  switch ($poem) {
    case "jabb":
      $poem_file = "jabb.html";
      break;
    case "graves":
      $poem_file = "graves.html";
      break;
  }
  if (IsSet($poem_file)) {
    $fp = fopen($poem_file, "r");
    print (fread($fp, filesize($poem_file)));
    fclose($fp);
  }
} ?>
```

The advantage of this method is that it explicitly lists the acceptable inputs and gracefully handles unacceptable inputs. If there were more poems to be processed, the switch statement could be replaced with a database query, where failure of the query indicates invalid input.

This is not a good solution:

```php
<?php if (IsSet($poem)) {
  if (!strstr($poem, "/") && !strstr($poem, "\\")) {
    $fp = fopen($poem, "r");
    print (fread($fp, filesize($poem)));
    fclose($fp);
  }
} ?>
```

The second conditional in this code segment checks for pathname separators in the given filename. This program explicitly describes a set of unacceptable inputs and considers anything else acceptable. It depends on the programmer imagining and checking for every possible undesired input. In this case, the programmer has missed something by making the implicit assumption that no sensitive files are stored in the same directory as the script.

What if a file that should be private escapes your server anyway? There is a chance that some misconfiguration (perhaps by someone else) or an unnoticed security hole will render some or all of your server's files publicly accessible.

PHP allows you to explicitly specify the set of directories in which files may be opened with the configuration value open_basedir. See Chapter 32 for more information on the PHP configuration file. This configuration value can be useful to prevent access to entire directories and is a good way to *minimize the damage*.

However, many sensitive files must be opened from PHP programs as visitors access the site. A common example is a password file. Access to such a file cannot be blocked with open_basedir, but the sensitive information it contains can be encrypted to render it useless to anyone who might steal it.

A password-protected site must verify the password given by a visitor wishing to gain access. One way to do this would be to store a password for safekeeping in encrypted form and then decrypt it when you need to compare it to the user-supplied password. The problem is that if we can decrypt the password, others may be able to decrypt it too. Also, we would have to make sure that no one could see the password after we decrypted it for comparison. Instead, we can use an encryption function that only goes one way, and is easy to use for encryption but can't be decrypted. Rather than decrypt a stored password and compare the decrypted versions, we *encrypt* the *given* password and compare the encrypted passwords. UNIX uses this strategy with its own password file, /etc/passwd, and PHP allows programmers to use the same encryption function for their own password files.

The function crypt(*password*, *salt*) encrypts the given password. The salt adds an extra bit of chance and should be chosen randomly when the password is first recorded. (PHP will choose a random salt if this parameter is omitted.) The function returns the concatenation of the salt value and the encrypted version of the password. The following function will create a new password for a visitor:

```
function new_pw($given) {
  return crypt($given)
}
```

And this function will compare a password given by a visitor with a stored, encrypted password:

```
function verify_pw($given, $stored) {
  $salt = substr($stored, 0, CRYPT_SALT_LENGTH);
  $given_encrypted = crypt($given, $salt);
  return ($stored == $given_encrypted);
}
```

Human engineering

Human engineering is an often overlooked part of cracking. Sometimes it's easier for crackers to extract information (particularly passwords) from human beings than from computers:

Cracker: Hi, John, this is Gary in the IT department. When was the last time you used your company account?

John: Well, I entered a few new purchase orders about an hour ago.

Cracker: Well, John, I'm afraid your account has been compromised. Some of the information in it may have been lost. This could cost the company millions if we don't catch the intruder quickly. We need to open your account and assess the damage immediately. Can you give me your password?

John: Sure, it's . . .

Worse yet, sometimes forgetful visitors note their passwords on scraps of paper in their desks! A determined cracker can easily find a job as a night janitor and look for such notes.

Running arbitrary programs

It's every system administrator's worst nightmare. The server's running more slowly than usual. A look at the running programs on the server reveals that a program entitled `crack` is burning 98 percent of the processor's time. Most likely, this program has been placed here by a cracker who is using it to decrypt (crack) passwords. The administrator logs in to kill the offending program but finds that his password is incorrect. His server has been "root compromised," and there is no telling how much damage has been done.

In a compromise such as this, an intruder gains interactive access to the server, usually via a UNIX shell or MS-DOS command line. Clearly, this is the most difficult type of heist to pull off, but it also bears the greatest reward. Once "inside" a server, the cracker has virtually unlimited power to bring down the server, steal or modify information, or make use of the server's computational power to enable further wrongdoing. Worse yet, a truly skilled cracker can conceal his or her steps by editing log files and erasing any temporary files he or she has created.

PHP has several program execution functions: `system()`, `exec()`, `popen()`, `passthru()`, and the back-tick (`) operator. As an example of the use of one of these functions, the following page returns the UNIX finger information for a visitor specified through an HTML form:

```
<HTML>
<HEAD></HEAD>
<BODY>
```

```
<FORM>Get information on <INPUT TYPE="TEXT" NAME="username">,
<INPUT TYPE="SUBMIT" VALUE="Please"></FORM>
<?php if (IsSet($username)) { ?>
  <H1>Results for <?php echo $username; ?></H1>
  <pre><?php system("finger " . $username); ?></pre>
<?php } ?>
</BODY>
</HTML>
```

The program as given takes a user name from the HTML form and executes the UNIX program `finger` to look up information about that user. You should hear *Don't trust the network* repeating loudly in your head. UNIX commands are separated by a semicolon, so anything following a semicolon in the string passed to `system()` will be treated as a new command. This new command will be executed with all of the permissions of the user under which the Web server is running.

Under UNIX, the command "`rm -rf /`" will delete all files on the server. Imagine the damage if an ill-intentioned visitor typed "`; rm -rf /`" into the form and clicked "Please."

The best solution to this problem is to filter out everything but valid user names before invoking `finger`. This requires specific knowledge about user name formats on your server, so we will not present an example here. PHP presents a solution that is almost as good. The function `escapeshellcmd()` will sanitize a string for use in a program execution command, rendering harmless any special characters such as the semicolon. We replace the line invoking `system()` in the preceding code snippet with

```
<pre><?php
    system(escapeshellcmd("finger " . $username)); ?></pre>
```

Magically, no value the visitor may enter can result in arbitrary programs being executed. However, this does not prevent the visitor from providing unexpected input to `finger`. Although `finger` will do no harm if given incorrect input, other programs may not be so forgiving. When in doubt, err on the side of caution!

To *minimize the damage* of a compromise of this sort, most modern Web servers run as a dummy user (often called "nobody" on UNIX systems). This user has only the permissions required to run the Web server (and any PHP scripts) and read and write the necessary files. But remember, any databases or files that your scripts can modify are modifiable by this user, and thus they are vulnerable if an attacker can run arbitrary programs.

System administrators

System administrators, also called *sysadmins,* are the folks who make sure the computers we all use keep on computing and that the Internet keeps on networking. Their jobs are shrouded in mystery: they hold the keys to the mysterious "machine room" where all of the critical servers are stored. It's not unusual to see them hurrying into the office at midnight, surely to avert some crisis that could bring the company to its knees.

Sysadmins are also a very cautious lot. They tend to program their servers to report any unusual activity immediately (often to the large-screen alphanumeric pager they carry at all times) and to take swift, decisive action against anything they deem improper or unsafe.

A professor in a Computer Science department once asked his students, as homework, to break into his Linux desktop. To make things a little easier, he gave the encrypted text of his password (see the description of `crypt()` under "Reading Arbitrary Files"). In a testament to the security of the UNIX `crypt()` function, none of the students cracked his desktop. However, several of his students were denied access to their campus accounts and questioned by university officials because they were running computationally expensive programs named `crack`!

If you aren't your own system administrator, but you are concerned about the security of your site, it is probably a good idea to befriend your local sysadmin. He or she may be able to suggest ways to make your site more secure, and will also be an enormous help in recovering from an incident.

Viruses and other e-critters

Visitors trust software coming from a trusted site. If your site allows visitors to download files uploaded by other visitors, you should warn your visitors to check files for viruses before running them, and you should consider periodically scanning the files on your server for viruses as well. This is a hard problem to solve, particularly with the possibility of embedding viruses in such seemingly harmless files as word processor documents. Indeed, Microsoft was caught in this very bind when they inadvertently released a CD-ROM with a Word document containing the Melissa virus.

Cross-Reference See "Site Defacement" at the beginning of this chapter for other ways that your visitor may inadvertently receive malicious code.

E-mail safety

E-mail is the least secure of any of the Internet protocols. As it travels to its destination, it may be spooled on several intermediary servers. If security is weak on a server, then it is not difficult for a cracker to read e-mail passing through that server. Send as little critical information as possible via e-mail. That is, never e-mail credit card numbers, and try to avoid sending passwords via e-mail unless absolutely necessary. It is interesting that most existing sites do not adhere to the latter point.

Whenever your site asks for your visitor's e-mail address, it should explain exactly how the address will be used and to whom it will be released. Whenever an e-mail address is presented on a Web page, it should be modified so as not to be easily identified by automated search engines picking up e-mail addresses to produce SPAM. The easiest and most elegant way to do this is to replace the @ symbol by the word "at."

Unless absolutely necessary, avoid creating `mailto:` links. These links are excellent sources of spam addresses and are inconvenient for visitors who do not use their Web browser for sending e-mail.

Encryption

Encryption is the process of *encrypting* some message, referred to as *plaintext,* into unrecognizable *ciphertext.* Without certain information (a *key* of some sort), it is extremely hard to reconstruct the plaintext from the ciphertext. However, someone equipped with the proper key can easily *decrypt* the ciphertext, revealing the original plaintext — at least if the chosen encryption function is not one-way.

We have already seen one use of encryption in this chapter: passwords are stored in encrypted form. However, password encryption is usually one-way. There is no key to decrypt an encrypted password. Such a key is not needed, and the encryption can be made stronger if it doesn't need to be reversible. Encryption has many other uses in online business, both for storing data on the server and transmitting it across the network.

Public-key encryption

Meet Alice and Bob, professional cryptographic examples. They were chosen by the mathematical community not for their acting talent, but because their names begin with A and B. Alice and Bob want to communicate securely, but their only method of communication is via Pony Express — not particularly secure. Each of them selects a public key and a secret key. We shall call Alice's keys P_{alice} and S_{alice}, respectively, and likewise Bob's keys P_{bob} and S_{bob}. They each publish their public key in the newspaper but hide their secret key under their mattresses.

Alice has a sensitive message M for Bob. With her keys, Alice received a set of instructions for translating a message with a key. We'll write the translation like this: $P_{bob}(M)$. She translates her message with Bob's public key and hands the result to a shady looking character on a pony.

Our friends' keys were not chosen arbitrarily. They have the special property that if they translate a message with one key, then translate the result with the other, they get the original message back. That is, $S_{alice}(P_{alice}(M)) = P_{alice}(S_{alice}(M)) = M$. There's no other way to resurrect the original message. In this case, Bob translates the message he receives, which he knows to be $P_{bob}(M)$ with his secret key. $S_{bob}(P_{bob}(M)) = M$, so he can read Alice's original message.

Bob knows that nobody else could have read that message, because nobody else has his secret key. But he does not know that it came from Alice: anyone who reads the newspaper might have sent that message, signing the name "Alice" at the bottom.

Now Alice wants to send another message to Bob, and this time she wants no doubt that it was from her. First, she translates the message with her secret key and writes the result after her message, as a *signature:* $M + S_{alice}(M)$. She sends this off to Bob, who reads Alice's message, which instructs him to translate the signature with her public key: $P_{alice}(S_{alice}(M)) = M$, and he sees her message again.

Because nobody else has Alice's secret key, she is the only one who could have created this signature, so this message must have come from her. But note that this time Alice sent her message M to Bob directly. Any rogue could have waylaid the Pony Express and read it. If she had so desired, she could have first signed the message, then encrypted the message and the signature using the first method, resulting in a signed, encrypted message.

There is a hitch in this scheme. Without meeting Alice, Bob can't be sure that the public key he found in the newspaper is really Alice's key. What if someone else had his or her key printed under her name? This could become a real problem if Bob communicates with lots of people — he simply doesn't have the time to check keys with each of them face-to-face.

Assume that there is at least one person everyone trusts; call him Tom. Tom picks a set of keys and offers to sign documents with his secret key, if the owner of the document shows proof of his or her identity. Alice has her public key signed by Tom, and then publishes the signed key, called a *certificate,* in the newspaper. Bob checks the signature on the key he sees in the newspaper, using Tom's public key. He knows that Tom signed that message, and Tom must have checked Alice's identification, so the key in the newspaper must really belong to Alice.

We now leave behind the era of the information pony-trail. The preceding techniques were implemented by Ronald L. Rivest, Adi Shamir, and Leonard M. Adleman, who quickly patented them under the name RSA. The RSA system forms the backbone of almost every strong encryption scheme in use, and RSA charges a license fee for every application. This fee, in combination with restrictions on export of strong cryptographic technology from the United States, has dampened Open Source participation. However, as this book goes to print, the United States seems to be relaxing its export restrictions, and the RSA patent expires on September 20, 2000, so the situation may be different by the time you read this.

U.S. export regulations

Cryptography was, and still is, an important factor in military intelligence. During World Wars I and II, encryption and code-cracking (breaking the enemy's encryption) played very important roles. After the wars, encryption technology was classified as a munition by the U.S. State Department. This meant that, as with bombs, it was illegal to export encryption technology. At the time, civilians had no use for encryption, so this posed little problem. However, encryption is now big business, and the State Department's prohibition of its export is preventing American companies from participating in the international market.

At present there are many challenges to the State Department's position. In one, an individual has applied for permission to mail a disk containing the source code from a central text of cryptography, Bruce Schneier's *Applied Cryptography,* out of the country. The book, because it is in the public domain, may be freely exported. But the disk, containing identical information, has been tied up in legal restrictions.

Single-key encryption

In single-key encryption, the same key can encrypt and decrypt a message. In general, it runs much more quickly than other forms of encryption, but it is more difficult to use for communication, because the key must somehow be transmitted from one end to the other without any eavesdroppers picking it up. This is precisely where public-key encryption can lend a hand.

Returning briefly to our characterization, imagine Alice and Bob want to have a private conversation using single-key encryption. Alice asks Bob for his certificate, which contains his public key. She then picks a new single key and encrypts that key with Bob's public key, sending the result to Bob. Using his secret key, he decrypts the message to reveal Alice's single key and then uses it to begin a single-key encryption conversation.

Single-key encryption is not covered by the RSA patent and has many variants that are not so strong as to be export-restricted in the United States. The UNIX version of PHP provides a set of functions that implement single-key encryption, using a publicly available library called *mcrypt.* To use these functions, you will have to download and install mcrypt (there is a link to the library's source available in the PHP manual) and recompile PHP with the `--enable-mcrypt` configuration option.

Tip   As this book went to press, PHP was not compatible with the latest version of mcrypt. The latest compatible version was libmcrypt-2.2.6. Further, when compiling this version of mcrypt, you must specify the configuration option `--disable-posix-threads` during the mcrypt configuration. Missing this step will cause Apache to crash.

Mcrypt offers a choice between a number of ciphers — different single-key algorithms. Each has its relative pros and cons in terms of speed and strength. In general, DES and Blowfish are fairly well-known algorithms with a good balance of speed and strength, but if you need extreme speed or great strength, you should research the algorithms available in your implementation (listed in `mcrypt.h`) and choose the one most suited to your needs.

Mcrypt also allows you to choose four cipher modes. These are summarized in Table 31-1.

Table 31-1
Cipher Modes Provided by mcrypt

Mode	Description	Initialization vector (IV)
ECB (electronic code book)	Just translate the block of data given. Suitable for small blocks of data that aren't very predictable, such as other keys. Do not use for text: the high frequency of letters and punctuation might be used to break the encryption.	no
CBC (cipher block chaining)	This stronger mode is far better suited for use with textual data.	opt
CFB (cipher feedback)	Like ECB, CFB is well suited for short blocks of data.	yes
OFB (output feedback)	OFB is very similar to CFB but designed to be better behaved when it encounters errors in its input.	yes

The last two modes require an initialization vector (abbreviated IV), which functions as a starting state for the encryption algorithm. The differences between these modes are relevant to interactive use, where individual keystrokes are encrypted one at a time. In that case, it is crucial that the algorithm not encrypt 'a' the same way each time. However, the PHP interface to mcrypt only allows us to encrypt strings, so any of the modes except ECB are perfectly acceptable.

Depending on the cipher mode you want to use, call `mcrypt_ecb()`, `mcrypt_cbc()`, `mcrypt_cfb()`, or `mcrypt_ofb()` like this:

```
mcrypt_cbc(cipher, key, data, direction, [iv])
```

Where `cipher` is `MCRYPT_DES`, `MCRYPT_BLOWFISH`, or whichever cipher you have chosen. (See the PHP documentation for an updated list of supported ciphers.)

Pass your key and the data you wish to encrypt or decrypt in the key and data arguments, respectively. To encrypt, pass MCRYPT_ENCRYPT in the direction argument; to decrypt, pass MCRYPT_DECRYPT. Finally, for cipher modes that support initialization vectors, pass your own IV in the iv argument.

Your key must be of the correct size for your cipher. To find out what this size is, use

```
mcrypt_get_key_size(cipher)
```

where cipher is the cipher you have chosen.

To generate a random IV or key, use

```
mcrypt_create_iv(size, source)
```

Here, size is the size of the desired object and source is one of MCRYPT_RAND, MCRYPT_DEV_RANDOM, or MCRYPT_DEV_URANDOM, specifying the random number generator to use: rand(), /dev/random, or /dev/urandom, respectively. If you use rand(), be sure to call srand() to seed the random number generator first. (See Chapter 10 for more information on random numbers.) The proper sizes for IVs and keys are obtained by calling mcrypt_get_block_size(cipher) and mcrypt_get_key_size(cipher), respectively.

Note that all data handled by mcrypt is in the form of PHP strings of binary data. If you wish to display the data in some human-readable format or store it as a text string, you must apply some translation to it. PHP provides the functions base64_encode() and base64_decode() for just this purpose. Check the PHP manual for more information on these functions.

Encrypting cookies

Cookies your site sends to a visitor's browser contain information about that visitor. When the browser sends the cookie back, your site uses the information it contains to generate a new page. *Don't trust the network* — sound familiar? A cookie could be modified or forged by a malicious user, perhaps fooling your site somehow. This extremely simple program will serve as an example:

```php
<?php
  $visits = $visits + 1;
  setcookie("visits", $visits);
?>
<HTML><HEAD></HEAD>
<BODY>
<H1>You have been here <?php echo $visits ?> times</H1>
</BODY>
</HTML>
```

Cross-Reference   See Chapter 26 for more information on cookies.

Here a count of our visitors' visits to this site is kept in the cookie visits. However, a visitor could modify his or her cookie to make the visit count 10,000. Our program would have no idea that this visitor has not been to the page 10,000 times and would blindly display, "You have been here 10000 times."

But with some help from mcrypt and a few friends, we can make this impossible:

```php
<?php
  $key = base64_decode("NCiUmfiRByg=");
  if (IsSet($visits)) {
    $encrypted = base64_decode($visits);
    $visits = mcrypt_cbc(MCRYPT_DES, $key, $encrypted,
                         MCRYPT_DECRYPT); }
  $visits = $visits + 1;
  $encrypted = mcrypt_cbc(MCRYPT_DES, $key, $visits,
                          MCRYPT_ENCRYPT);
  setcookie("visits", base64_encode($encrypted));
?>
```

Mcrypt deals with strings full of binary data, so we can't easily type them in or send them to browsers without modification. In this case, we have chosen to use the PHP base64 functions to turn them into well-behaved strings. Before writing this program, we invented a DES key with the following code:

```php
<?php
  $key_size = mcrypt_get_key_size(MCRYPT_DES);
  $key = mcrypt_create_iv($key_size, MCRYPT_DEV_RANDOM);
  echo base64_encode($key);
?>
```

We copied and pasted the resulting key (in base 64 encoding) into our cookie program's first line. We store the number of visits in the cookie named visits, encrypted and in base 64 encoding. So if the visits variable is set, we first base64_decode it, then decrypt it. We then increment the counter, encrypt it, base64_encode it, and store it in a new cookie. The visitor sees cookie values such as IQ1O9yQCEgw%3D, which are not editable.

The program is not completely secure! The cookie value just given will *always* correspond to visit number 7. A cracker wishing to make your site believe he had only visited seven times could simply substitute this value for the visits cookie. However, if you know it would not benefit a visitor to return to a prior cookie (in this case, if the visitor wants a large visit count), this method is adequate: there is no way to easily invent a cookie for a state that has not been seen yet.

Cross-Reference   To maintain a more useful visitor state, you should use sessions, which are described fully in Chapter 25.

This example should bring home the need to keep your source code private: if a cracker could view this program from his or her browser, he or she would have your site's encryption key and could decrypt your cookie values with ease.

Hashing

Signing a document with your private key produces a signature that is as large as the original document. This becomes a problem when we want to sign long documents such as files. For instance, most security software (including mcrypt) is digitally signed so that downloaders know that the latest version really was written by the author. Otherwise, sysadmins worry, an eager cracker could circulate a version of a security program into which he or she has installed a "back door" and then walk into the systems running that version with no difficulty.

What we need is a digital fingerprint for a large file. What if we treat the binary data of the file as a list of integers, add them all together, then chop off all but 128 bits of the sum? We'll call the final 128-bit number the *checksum*. The author of the file then encrypts the checksum with his or her secret key and attaches the result to the file as a signature.

Assume a cracker makes modifications to the file. He or she can then calculate the sum C of the changes and put the number $-C$ at the end of the file, creating a file that he or she knows to have the same checksum as the original. The cracker then appends the same encrypted checksum to the file as its signature.

When some unsuspecting user downloads the modified file, the user calculates the new checksum, decrypts the signature to find the original author's checksum, and sees that they match. The user proceeds to use the modified file, incorrectly assuming that it was written by the stated author.

Of course, the cryptographers are right on the spot with a solution. It should be very difficult to make changes to a file to produce a certain fingerprint. To ensure this, many *hashing* algorithms have been developed. Hashing algorithms are generally modifications of single-key encryption algorithms to make them create a ciphertext of a specific length, from which it is not possible to reconstruct the original message.

As you would expect, PHP provides a set of functions for hashing. These functions depend on the publicly available mhash library. You can find the latest version of the mhash library through a link in the PHP manual.

Tip   Be sure to compile the mhash library with the `--disable-pthreads` configuration option. Without this option, Apache will fail to run.

The function `mhash(type, input)` computes the hash value of `input`, using the method specified by `type`. Common values for this argument are `MCRYPT_MD5` and `MCRYPT_SHA1`. For a complete list of possibilities, see the PHP manual.

Digitally signing files

Now let us present a PHP program to accept uploaded files only when they are correctly signed. We assume that our site is equipped with a list of usernames and Blowfish keys, where each user has a key known only to that user and our site. The function get_user_key(*username*) retrieves these keys for us. The uploader generates the signature for an upload by first hashing the upload file with the MD5 hash algorithm and then encrypting the resulting hash value with her Blowfish key.

```
<HTML><HEAD></HEAD>
<BODY>
<?php if (empty($file) || !IsSet($username) || empty($sig)) {
?>
<H1>Upload a file</H1>
<FORM ENCTYPE="multipart/form-data" METHOD="POST">
<INPUT TYPE="HIDDEN" NAME="MAX_FILE_SIZE" VALUE="2000000">
Upload the file: <INPUT NAME="file" TYPE="file"><br>
With this signature: <INPUT NAME="sig" TYPE="file"><br>
For user <INPUT NAME="username" TYPE="text"><br>
<INPUT TYPE="SUBMIT" VALUE="Go"></FORM>
<? } else {
  $fp = fopen($file, "r");
  $hash = mhash(MHASH_MD5, fread($file, $file_size));
  fclose($fp);
  $key = get_user_key($username);
  $encr_hash = mcrypt_cbc(MCRYPT_BLOWFISH, $key, $hash,
                          MCRYPT_ENCRYPT);
  $sfp = fopen($sig);
  $sig_data = fread($sig, $sig_size);
  fclose($sfp);
  if ($encr_hash != $sig_data)
    echo "<H1>Rejected -- signature did not match</H1>";
  else {
    echo "<H1>Accepted</H1>";
    // Continue handling the uploaded file
  }
} ?>
</BODY>
</HTML>
```

This program parallels the uploader's steps, first hashing the uploaded file and then encrypting the result with the user's key. If the results are the same, then the uploader must have used the same key, and we can assume they are genuine. If the results differ, then the upload is a forgery.

Secure Server Layer

The uses of cryptography presented so far protect the server's data. The single-key encryption example protects information the server stores on clients (cookies) from unwanted modification. The hashing example enables the server to detect forged files and refuse to accept them.

We now turn our attention to the security of your site's visitor. The visitor often transmits private information to your site. The visitor's password and credit card information must somehow travel from his or her machine to the server, across the untrustworthy network.

The *Secure Server Layer* (SSL) protocol provides a way to do this, making it impossible for an eavesdropper to listen in. It also provides a way for the site to prove its identity to the visitor and, optionally, for the visitor to prove its identity to the site. Although we won't delve into the cryptographic details, SSL does its work by using public-key encryption to prove the identity of the server and exchange a new key to be used to encrypt the conversation. It then switches over to single-key encryption, which is much faster, using this new key.

Open Source implementations of SSL are available, but they do not include the public-key software. Because of RSA's patent on public-key encryption, U.S. citizens currently must license one of RSA's encryption toolkits to use SSL. Non-U.S. citizens may use RSA's reference implementation, *RSAREF*, without any licensing restrictions.

Regardless of how you acquire and license the SSL software, you will have to purchase a certificate for your site from a well-known *certificate authority*. These authorities are the trusted third parties in the conversation between your server and a browser, but they do not give away their services for free.

It is beyond the scope of this book to make comparisons of competing SSL servers. In the tradition of Open Source, the authors believe that the free implementations are the best and most reliable; indeed, many of the commercial SSL servers are based on the Open Source implementations! However, if you buy a commercial implementation, you receive support from that company, and you will satisfy management's desire to pay for something.

FYI: Security Web Sites

If you are losing sleep after reading this chapter, fear not. Every administrator and site designer around the world is grappling with the same issues, and there is a strong feeling of solidarity among computer security professionals. Many Web sites are devoted to computer security, and almost all of them contain full descriptions of recent security incidents and ways to protect your system from duplicate attacks. Some are designed for security professionals, whereas others have the cracker in mind. Either way, the information they provide is useful and often very interesting.

Begin your explorations by checking out these sites:

✦ **CERT: Computer Emergency Response Team** (`http://www.cert.org/`)

CERT is one of the most popular repositories of official descriptions of security incidents. They publish advisories on all sorts of security issues, including very clear descriptions of the problem, vulnerable systems, and possible solutions.

✦ **Security-focus.com** (`http://www.securityfocus.com/`)

Security-focus.com provides a great deal of information on all aspects of computer security, from the legal and political to the technical. They also host the well-known security mailing list, BugTraq (it can be found under "Forums").

✦ **Rootshell** (`http://rootshell.com/`)

Rootshell is a well-respected site that contains fairly technical descriptions of many, many security vulnerabilities, including detailed descriptions of how to exploit the vulnerability as well as instructions on removing the vulnerability.

✦ **Insecure.Org** (`http://insecure.org/`)

Insecure.Org is a fairly well-established site that is not afraid to make cracking tools available, and to discuss the nitty-gritty details of many "exploits." This site can be extremely useful when you want to try to break into your own site.

✦ **L0pht Heavy Industries** (`http://www.l0pht.com/index.html`)

L0pht is another on-the-edge site, run by people who crack into machines for a living. They are paid to do this in the hopes that they will find a vulnerability before someone with malicious intent does, and they report what they've done on this site and others. The site also contains lots of interesting opinions on its "soapbox."

Summary

For any significant Web site, security is a crucial part of the site's implementation. You should take extreme care to secure your server from attack, and also be sure to protect your visitors' private information from prying eyes. In a time of enormous growth for online businesses, publication of a story about a major security breach can destroy visitors' confidence in your site, driving them to the competition and possibly leaving your site to evaporate as quickly as it appeared.

In this chapter, we've driven home three basic lessons:

Don't trust the network. Every byte of data that comes from the Internet should be treated as potentially hazardous. Be as restrictive as possible in defining the inputs you allow. Prefer the solution that lists the acceptable inputs to the one that lists the unacceptable inputs. Be sure that your Web server configuration does not allow clients to view your source code or to work around your access restrictions.

Minimize the damage. Where possible, make sure that the damage possible from a particular type of security breach is minimal. Encrypt sensitive data. If you run your own Web server, make sure it is running as a dummy user.

Finally, if you run your own server, spend some time breaking into it. If you're successful, then you've identified a vulnerability that you can patch before an intruder finds it. If you're unsuccessful, then you've learned something about your server, and your security precautions have weathered a good test. If you don't run your server, find out who does, and see what he or she can tell you about your site's security.

✦　　✦　　✦

Configuration and Tuning

We discuss the many configuration options available with PHP, particularly the UNIX Apache module version, in some detail. The goal is for you to better understand the tradeoffs of each capability you might enable or disable, and how they might affect each other. We'll also touch on ways you can measure and improve the performance of your PHP scripts.

Viewing Environment Variables

To see any of the settings discussed below, you have only to use the phpinfo() function in a valid PHP script. This file begins with a quick recap of the PHP version, your platform, date of build, and compile-time options; it then moves methodically through your PHP settings. The UNIX Apache version will also give you an exhaustive list of Apache settings.

This file is a potential bonanza for crackers, so you shouldn't leave it sitting around on a production server.

Understanding PHP Configuration

Like most of the best open source software packages, PHP is highly configurable. It's left up to you, the individual PHP user, to find your own balance among the competing virtues of power, flexibility, safety, and ease of use.

Configuration is difficult to describe fully because there are so many possible combinations of options — about 25 factorial combinations, as a matter of fact. In some cases, there is an obvious conflict between two configuration directives — you simply have to choose one or the other, end of story. In other cases, you can have both but may need to remember some workarounds. We'll try to point out as many of these implications as we can, but no one can honestly claim to have tested every possible combination.

PHP configuration differs substantially between platforms. Not to mince words about it, UNIX is like a gourmet meal ordered à la carte, whereas Windows is like a cheap buffet with only a few choices. The worst is an RPM build, which is like going over to someone's house for dinner — you eat what you're served, whether it's delicious or mediocre.

The Windows version of PHP offers you very little choice — especially if you also select a proprietary Web server such as Microsoft IIS. Beginning PHP users may find this lack of choice rather comforting, as it takes the responsibility off the individual's shoulders and puts it on the judgment of whoever created the binary executable. In any case, Windows users only need to worry about the variables that can be set with the `php.ini` file — not all of which are applicable to Windows versions of PHP anyway. Feel free to skip down to the `php.ini` section below.

UNIX users have a much richer and more specific palette of options. To take full advantage of this power, you need to clearly understand the various means by which you can analyze and control your PHP installation. The three most important on the UNIX side are:

✦ Compile-time options

✦ Web server configuration files

✦ The `php.ini` file

There are also a few things that can be controlled with run-time options, system settings, or the presence/absence/configuration of other software packages.

Compile-time options

During the configure/make process, PHP allows you to specify a number of specific flags. This will cause the appropriate files to be built into your custom version of the PHP module.

It's important to understand that most compile-time options are merely necessary preconditions for using a particular function set — but that this capability can still be turned on or off in the `php.ini` file. The compilation step and the configuration file work together. Think of it this way: you must compile with the flag to use the functionality; but you needn't use the functionality just because you compiled with the flag.

Tip If you fail to employ the appropriate compile-time option, you will get an undefined-function fatal error. This error is almost never seen outside of user-defined functions for any other reason, so it should be considered a red flashing light that you need to check your compilation options.

Tip Remember that all third-party servers and libraries must be downloaded and installed *before* you attempt to build PHP. This means the Web server, a database server, mail and LDAP servers, XML and encryption and bcmath libraries must all be in place before PHP.

--with-apache[=DIR]

This is the most important flag of all for most users, as it causes PHP to be built as a static Apache module. Even though the Apache module version is now by far the most popular build, the PHP developers have chosen to leave the CGI build as the default choice. If you forget this flag when trying to make a static Apache module, you will end up with the CGI version.

You almost certainly will want to set the Apache base directory parameter, as `make` will default to `/usr/local/etc/httpd`. Remember that Apache installs in different default directories in the source versus RPM builds — so if you've previously installed an httpd via RPM (perhaps as part of a Red Hat Linux installation), you probably want to uninstall the package and leave a clean background for the source build you need now.

--with-apxs

This flag specifies that the PHP module be built as a dynamic Apache module. This saves disk space for Apache, and some people claim the build is easier. For most people there's little to choose between the static and dynamic Apache modules.

--with-fhttpd[=DIR]

This flag specifies that PHP be built as a module of the fhttpd server. The default directory is `/usr/local/src/fhttpd`.

Caution The preceding three module-compilation options are mutually exclusive. You must limit yourself to one of them. In particular, don't try to specify both `-with-apache` and `-with-apxs`.

--with-database[=DIR]

All the databases supported by PHP use a similar compile-time flag. The directory need only be specified if it is not the default installation directory. For more information on choosing a database for use with PHP, see Chapter 16.

Table 32-1
Database compile-time information

Database Name	Default Directory	Flag Syntax
Adabas D*	/usr/local/adabasd	--with-adabas[=DIR]
Custom ODBC*	/usr/local	--with-custom-odbc[=DIR]
DBase	bundled	--with-dbase
Filepro	bundled	--with-filepro
iODBC*	/usr/local	--with-iodbc[=DIR]
mSql	/usr/local/Hughes	--with-msql[=DIR]
MySQL	/usr/local	--with-mysql[=DIR]
Openlink*	/usr/local/openlink	--with-openlink[=DIR]
Oracle	ORACLE_HOME	--with-oracle[=DIR]
PostgreSQL	/usr/local/pgsql	--with-pgsql[=DIR]
Solid*	/usr/local/solid	--with-solid[=DIR]
Sybase	/home/sybase	--with-sybase[=DIR]
Sybase-CT	/home/sybase	--with-sybase-ct[=DIR]
Velocis*	/usr/local/velocis	--with-velocis[=DIR]

The databases marked with an asterisk use ODBC-based interfaces. These ODBC choices are mutually exclusive — you must limit yourself to a maximum of one. An additional compile-time directive you may want to employ for these databases is --disable-unified-odbc. This will help prevent conflicts between ODBC libraries.

Each database mandates slightly different configuration options in php.ini or other configuration files. For instance, Oracle has its own environment variables that obviate PHP settings. Sybase uses a different style of escaping single quotes, which requires the magic_quotes_sybase option in php.ini. MySQL allows you to specify a default hostname, username, and password — not at all a good idea unless you understand the security implications! However, most of these options are standard and self-explanatory, and they have little impact on other parts of PHP.

If you're using a database heavily, you may very well want to also build with the --enable-magic-quotes option. However, it's not strictly necessary because magic-quoting capability is already built in — you can simply enable it by using the magic_quotes_runtime directive in php.ini instead. For the ultimate level of control, you can add and strip slashes yourself as needed instead of relying on magic quotes.

--enable-track-vars

This flag enables use of PHP's predefined `HTTP_GET_VARS`, `HTTP_POST_VARS`, and `HTTP_COOKIE_VARS` variables. This can be very helpful for development if you use multiple methods of data transfer, as it enables you to be positive where each value is coming from. You can turn off this capability with the `track_vars` directive in `php.ini`.

Tip   The new `php.ini-optimized` turns off track_vars to improve performance. If you use it, don't expect to have all your variables available through $HTTP_ POST_VARS and its brethren. More importantly, read the `php.ini-optimized` file as many times as it takes to understand the implications of its changes.

--with-ldap[=DIR]

This option allows PHP to establish a connection to an LDAP (Lightweight Directory Access Protocol) server. The default directory is `/usr/local/ldap`. You must download and install LDAP client libraries from one of these sources before building PHP:

```
http://developer.netscape.com/tech/directory/
http://www.openldap.org
```

LDAP is a database-like protocol that helps to manage user profiles and network access permissions. It can be used as a centralized, networked address book, making e-mail addresses available to you from any mail client throughout the network. It also aids security because network permissions can be set in a centralized location — so when an employee leaves the company, for instance, you can quickly revoke all their privileges at once (there are other ways to do this, of course).

We chose not to cover LDAP in this book because, for the moment at least, the protocol seems to be used mostly by large, networked organizations, such as multinational companies and government research labs, which do not represent the vast majority of PHP users. Lincoln Stein has written a nice introductory article about using LDAP in the latter context:

```
http://www.webtechniques.com/archives/1999/11/webm/
```

Now that Open Source implementations are available, LDAP is beginning to be found outside the large organizations. Rasmus Lerdorf, father of PHP, has written an informative piece about using LDAP on his home network with PHP 3.

```
http://www.webtechniques.com/archives/1999/05/junk/junk.shtml
```

--with-mcrypt[=DIR]

This flag builds in the mcrypt library, which includes many of the most popular open cipher algorithms. Mcrypt is available for download from Greece:

```
ftp://argeas.cs-net.gr/pub/unix/mcrypt/
```

There is no documented default directory, although PHP will probably find the one mentioned in the libmcrypt documentation. See Chapter 31 for more information on using PHP's cryptography capabilities.

--with-xml

This flag builds in the expat XML parser. You do not need a separate library if you're making PHP as an Apache module, because expat is included with Apache. Otherwise, you can download the package from:

```
http://www.jclark.com/xml/
```

To use XML, you must disable short-open tags (such as `<? ?>`)with the `--disable-short-tags` compile-time flag or the `short_open_tag` directive in `php.ini`. The XML parser requires this style of tag for its own purposes, so PHP must not be able to confuse the situation. As ever, the standard PHP tag (`<?php ?>`) is the best option, unless for some reason you can't use it.

 Cross-Reference To learn more about XML and PHP, see Chapter 29.

--with-dom

This flag builds with DOM XML support, using the GNOME xml library (aka `libxml`, `gnome-xml`). You can download and learn more about GNOME xml from:

```
http://www.xmlsoft.org/
```

--enable-bcmath

This option builds support for arbitrary-precision mathematics. You can set the number of decimal places in `php.ini`.

--with-config-file-path=DIR

This option allows you to specify the location of your `php.ini` file. You only need to use it if you've deliberately moved it away from the default location, `/usr/local/lib`.

--enable-url-includes

This option allows you to include or require files from remote HTTP or FTP servers, like this: `include(http://remotehost/include.inc.)`.

--disable-url-fopen-wrapper

This flag turns off the default capability to open files on remote HTTP and FTP servers, like this: `include(http://remotehost/include.inc.)`.

--enable-magic-quotes

The magic quotes option automatically escapes quotes from external data sources, such as text files and databases. If you don't use any magic quotes, you'll need to add and strip slashes yourself. You can turn magic quotes on and off by using the `magic_quotes_runtime` directive in the `php.ini` file. There are also configuration settings in `php.ini` for magic quotes in `GET`, `POST`, and `COOKIE` variables; and for Sybase-style quote-escaping.

--enable-debugger

This flag allows you to access the built-in PHP debugger. At press time, this feature was not stable and was incompatible with the Zend optimizer.

--disable-syntax-hl

This option disables syntax highlighting.

CGI compile-time options

All compile-time options just described are available for the CGI version, except for the module-specific flags (`--with-apache`, `--with-apxs`, and `--with-fttpd`).

--enable-safe-mode

Safe mode was originally designed for and is still very strongly recommended for users of the CGI version of PHP. Module users have to think through the trade-offs for themselves — you might be just as well off using the `open_basedir` and `include_path` directives in `php.ini` instead.

Safe mode basically does three things:

1. It limits PHP parsing to files in a specified directory.

2. Even within that directory, it prevents PHP from reading files that are owned by a different user than that running the PHP process.

3. It limits PHP to executing only external programs in a specified directory, such as `/usr/local/bin`.

Remember that "user" in this formulation means the PHP user rather than a systems user.

In Chapter 31 we discuss the reasons why you might want to run in safe mode. However, the increased security comes at a cost — and that cost is inconvenience. Inconvenience is probably the number-one reason that people do insecure things in the first place — which leaves us right back where we started.

For instance, CVS checkouts are generally made under a real system user's name; and of course if you are directly editing files in the Web directory, you'll have to do so under a real system UID. For PHP to use any of these files under safe mode, they will need to be chowned to nobody. If you're dealing with a large number of files and directories, it can be a time-consuming and annoying process to keep changing file ownership back and forth.

Another example is password files kept outside the www tree, for instance in /usr/local/lib. They can be owned by a particular user and need only be world-readable for PHP to usefully substitute their values into variables within scripts. But under safe mode, this little dodge won't work — leaving you to stash your database password somewhere in your Web document root.

In general, if you lack root access on the server you can forget about using safe mode (the exception is if your ISP has set you up with a CGI version of PHP running under individual UIDs with suExec or functional equivalent). It's next to impossible to switch file ownership between a real UNIX system user and nobody without becoming the superuser once in awhile.

 Caution   Apache's suExec feature, which allows CGIs to be run under user IDs different than that of the httpd, is *not* compatible with PHP safemode. You must choose one or the other, as your PHP binary will get dumped to the browser if you try to use both.

The safe mode restriction on executing programs is intended to limit access to system utilities. PHP can still connect to certain programs that are already running, regardless of their location or user — such as a database server or mail server — because it's talking to a port rather than running a program.

The main Apache configuration directive related to safe mode is document root. Remember that under safe mode you will not be able to include or require files from outside this directory, so set it at a high enough level. You can alternatively set the PHP document root in php.ini by means of the doc_root variable — you might choose to do it this way if, for instance, only part of your site is PHP-enabled. Configuration directives in php.ini related to safe mode include safe_mode=on/ off and safe_mode_exec_dir (you only need to set this if you want to change from /usr/local/bin to something else). You can also use include_path to specify particular subdirectories *within your document root directory only* for your include files.

 Tip   Safe mode cannot be enabled or disabled in Apache's per-directory .htaccess files. Changes related to safe mode must be made in the main Apache configuration file, httpd.conf.

The function set_time_limit() cannot be used in safe mode. You must depend on the global configuration directive max_execution_time in php.ini instead.

--with-exec-dir[=DIR]

Another compile-time option relating to safe mode is `--with-exec-dir`. This option sets the default safe-mode execution directory to `/usr/local/bin`, but that can be changed with the `safe_mode_exec` directive in `php.ini`. Remember you will only be able to run programs from this single directory under safe mode.

--enable-discard-path

If you'd like to place the CGI version of PHP outside the Web tree and call it as you would a Perl CGI script (such as with `#!/usr/local/bin/php` as the first line of each script), you need to specify this compile-time flag. You must also make all PHP CGI scripts executable.

--enable-force-cgi-redirect

This flag is a security must for the CGI module. It prevents browser users from calling CGI-bin files directly, thereby bypassing Apache security settings. This is an Apache-specific configuration directive; don't bother trying to enable it if you are running on a different Web server.

Apache configuration files

When PHP is used with Apache as a module or CGI, much of PHP's basic file-serving capability is determined by Apache's configuration files. The main ones from recent versions of Apache Server are the `httpd.conf` file for global settings, and the `.htaccess` file for per-directory access settings. Older versions of Apache split up `httpd.conf` into three files (`access.conf`, `httpd.conf`, and `srm.conf`), and some users still prefer this arrangement.

In PHP 3, there were specific Apache configuration directives which could substitute for almost every `php.ini` setting. For example, instead of setting "Engine = On" on the first substantive line of `php.ini`, you could put "php3_engine on" in an `.htaccess` file for a similar effect. However, as the number of PHP configuration directives increased, it was decided that so many flags were cluttering up Apache's namespace. Therefore, the naming scheme was generalized to encompass these four basic, configurable directives:

`php_value name value`	Sets value of variable
`php_flag name on|off`	Sets Boolean
`php_admin_value name value`	Sets value of variable, can only be used in main Apache conf file(s) rather than .htaccess
`php_admin_flag name on|off`	Sets Boolean, can only be used in main Apache conf file(s) rather than .htaccess

An example would be magic quotes for GET, POST, and COOKIE variables. In PHP 3, it could be set with this specific line in `httpd.conf` or `.htaccess`:

```
php3_magic_quotes_gpc Off
```

In PHP 4, you would use php_flag with the name of the variable, like this:

```
php_flag magic_quotes_gpc off
```

If this is all too confusing, don't worry: the new-style Apache configuration directive naming only applies to settings you can change in `php.ini` anyway.

Apache Server has a very powerful but slightly complex configuration system of its own. Learn more about it at the Apache Web site:

```
http://www.apache.org/
```

The following headings describe settings that affect PHP directly and cannot be set elsewhere.

Timeout

This value sets the default number of seconds before any HTTP request will time-out. In safe mode, this value will be ignored; you must use the timeout value in `php.ini` instead.

DocumentRoot

DocumentRoot designates the root directory for all HTTP processes on that server. It looks something like this on UNIX:

```
DocumentRoot    "/usr/local/apache_1.3.6/htdocs"
```

It looks like this on Windows:

```
DocumentRoot    "C:/Program Files/Apache/htdocs/"
```

The document root can be almost any directory—it needn't be in the Apache installation directory. You can specify a subdirectory of this as the PHP document root, using the `doc_root` setting in `php.ini`.

AddType

The PHP mime type needs to be set here for PHP files to be parsed. Don't reflexively uncomment the line for PHP source (`.phps`) just because it's mentioned in the installation instructions; consider whether you ever want PHP source to be down-loadable from your server.

Remember that you can associate any file extension with PHP; many administrators set the .php3 and .html types for backward compatibility—but if you wanted to, you could have files called "filename.asp" or "filename.jsp" be parsed by PHP. You can also add multiple types for different versions of PHP. These are sample AddType lines; the first one is the most common for PHP 4, but add as many of the others as you wish.

```
AddType application/x-httpd-php4 .php
AddType application/x-httpd-php3 .php3
AddType application/x-httpd-php4 .html
AddType application/x-httpd-php4 .php4
AddType application/x-httpd-php4 .phtml
```

You can also set this on a per-directory basis with .htaccess, simply by adding type lines to .htaccess files. This will make PHP files be parsed only in one directory of your site, for instance in a forum folder. Alternatively, you can set up a directory with archived versions of files that may have old extensions—so just in that directory, Apache will allow files with the .phtml extension to be parsed.

Action

You must set this line for the CGI version of PHP with Apache, generally used with Windows.

```
Action application/x-httpd-php4 "/php/php.exe"
```

ScriptAlias

You must set this line for the CGI version of PHP with Apache, generally used with Windows.

```
ScriptAlias /php/ "c:/php/"
```

The php.ini file

The PHP configuration file, php.ini, is the final and most immediate way to affect PHP's functionality. Important changes have been made in the structure of this file since even the beta versions of PHP 4; so if you haven't bothered to really look at every line recently, now might be a good time.

The php.ini file is read each time PHP is initialized—in other words, whenever httpd is restarted for the module version or with each script execution for the CGI version. If your change isn't showing up, remember to stop and restart httpd. If it still isn't showing up, use phpinfo() to check the path to php.ini (near the top of the file); if necessary, recompile with the --with-config-file-path flag or just move php.ini to wherever PHP expects to find it.

Caution

What happens if PHP can't find php.ini? Under Windows, right up until the formal release of PHP 4, you used to get an "unable to parse configuration file" fatal error. Under UNIX and now under Windows as an ISAPI module, interestingly enough, you will get no warnings or errors—PHP will carry on with default settings, which are the same as if you had not changed any settings in php.ini-dist. You only need to install php.ini if you want to change the default settings.

The configuration file is well commented and thorough. Keys are case-sensitive, keyword values are not; whitespace, and lines beginning with semicolons are ignored. Booleans can be represented by 1/0, Yes/No, On/Off, or True/False. The default values in php.ini-dist will result in a reasonable PHP installation that can be tweaked later.

What follows are notes explaining the settings in php.ini that are not completely documented in the file or the PHP manual's configuration.html page.

short_open_tag = Off

Short open tags (called short tags in PHP 3) look like this: <? ?>. At press time, they didn't work in PHP 4, thereby encouraging users to move over to standard PHP tags (<?php ?>). This option *must* be set to Off if you want to use XML functions.

safe_mode = Off

If this is set to On, you probably compiled PHP with the --enable-safe-mode flag. Safe mode is most relevant to CGI use. See the explanation under "CGI compile-time options" earlier in this chapter.

safe_mode_exec_dir = [DIR]

This option is only relevant if safe mode is on; it can also be set with the --with-exec-dir flag during the UNIX build process. PHP in safe mode will only execute external binaries out of this directory. The default is /usr/local/bin. This has nothing to do with serving up a normal PHP/HTML Web page.

safe_mode_allowed_env_vars = [PHP_]

This option sets which environment variables users are allowed to change in safe mode. The default is only those variables prepended with "PHP_." If this directive is empty, most variables will be alterable.

safe_mode_protected_env_vars = [LD_LIBRARY_PATH]

This option sets which environment variables users are not allowed to change in safe mode, even if safe_mode_allowed_env_vars is set permissively.

disable_functions = [function1, function2, function3...functionn]

A welcome addition to PHP 4 configuration is the ability to disable selected functions for security reasons. Previously, this necessitated hand-editing the C code from which PHP was made. Filesystem, system, and network functions should probably be the first to go, since being able to write files and alter the system over HTTP was never such a safe idea.

max_execution_time = 30

The function `set_time_limit()` won't work in safe mode, so this is the main way to make a script time out in safe mode. In Windows, you have to abort based on maximum memory consumed rather than time. You can also use the Apache timeout setting to timeout if you use Apache, but that will apply to non-PHP files on the site too.

error_reporting = E_ALL & ~E_NOTICE

Until recently, this was a bitfield that added up to a maximum value of 15 (and at press time, the explanatory text still referred to it that way). Due to widespread misunderstanding, this directive seems to have been changed in PHP 4 to a string type. The default value is all errors except notices, which corresponds to the old value of 7. If you don't know what this setting is all about, we highly recommend you set this value to `E_ALL`. This will give you all possible errors and warnings, which should help you debug faster and learn PHP more efficiently. Development servers should be set to at least the default; only production servers should even consider a lesser value.

error_prepend_string = ["<font color=ff0000>"]

With its bookend, `error_append_string`, this setting allows you to make error messages a different color than other text, or what have you. We recommend setting the value to "<blink>" (and `error_append_string` to "</blink>" of course) for a special treat! The default values result in a red error message. Remember to uncomment these if you want to use them—they're commented out by default.

warn_plus_overloading = Off

Issues a warning if the "+" operator is used with strings, as in a form value.

variables_order = "EGPCS"

This configuration setting supersedes "`gpc_order`". It sets the order of the different variables: Environment, GET, POST, Cookie, and Server (aka Built-in). You can change this order around. Variables will be overwritten successively in left-to-right order, with the rightmost one "winning" the hand every time. This means if you left the default setting and happened to use the same name for an environment variable, a POST variable, and a cookie variable, the cookie variable would own that name at the end of the process. In real life, this doesn't happen much.

register_globals = On

Allows you to decide whether you wish to register EGPCS variables as global. If you use `track_vars`, probably unnecessary.

gpc_order = GPC

Deprecated. Use the new and more complete "variables order" setting instead.

magic_quotes_gpc = On

This setting escapes quotes in incoming `GET/POST/COOKIE` data. If you use a lot of forms, you may need to set this directive to "On" or prepare to use `addslashes()` on string-type data. For instance, let's say you have a form with a field where people enter their last names:

```
<FORM METHOD="post" ACTION="formhandler.php">
<INPUT TYPE="text" NAME="surname" SIZE=25>
...
</FORM>
```

Your form handler has some code like this:

```
echo 'Hello, ' . $surname . 'it\'s a pleasure doing business
with you';
```

Now let's say that an individual with the fine name of "O'Donnell" comes along and fills out the form. Without magic quotes, when O'Donnell's name hits the form handler you get an instant parse error. With magic quotes, you will need to use `stripslashes()` on `$surname` before it will display correctly — but your script won't come grinding to a halt either.

magic_quotes_runtime = Off

This setting escapes quotes in incoming database and text strings. Remember that SQL adds slashes to single quotes and apostrophes when storing strings, and does not strip them off when returning them. If this setting is Off, you will need to use `stripslashes()` when outputting any type of string data from a SQL database. If `magic_quotes_sybase` is set to On, this must be Off.

magic_quotes_sybase = Off

This setting escapes single quotes in incoming database and text strings with Sybase-style single quotes rather than backslashes. If `magic_quotes_runtime` is set to On, this must be Off.

auto-prepend-file = [path/to/file]

If a path is specified here, PHP will automatically `include()` it at the beginning of every PHP file. Include path restrictions do apply. Remember that you cannot send HTTP headers twice.

auto-append-file = [path/to/file]

If a path is specified here, PHP will automatically `include()` it at the end of every PHP file — unless you escape by using the `exit()` function. Include path restrictions do apply.

include_path = [DIR]

If you set this value, you will only be allowed to include or require files from these directories. The include directory is generally under your document root; this is mandatory if you're running in safe mode. Set this to "./" to include files from the same directory your script is in.

doc_root = [DIR]

If you're using Apache, you've already set a document root for this server or virtual host in `httpd.conf`. Set this value here if you're using safe mode, or if you want to enable PHP only on a portion of your site (for example, only in one subdirectory of your Web root).

upload_tmp_dir = [DIR]

Do not uncomment this line unless you understand the implications of HTTP uploads!

session.save-handler = files

See the Sessions chapter.

ignore_user_abort = [On/Off]

This setting controls what happens if a site visitor clicks the browser's Stop button. The default is On, which means the script will continue to run to completion or timeout. If the setting is changed to Off, the script will abort. This setting only works in module mode, not CGI.

Improving PHP Performance

There are two basic schools of thought about Web performance. The first is that PHP script performance, theoretical Web server speed, chip clock speed, server RAM, and almost everything else is made irrelevant by throughput issues — so why sweat the small stuff? The other is that there's no thrill quite like that of shaving a few microseconds off your script execution time. This section is basically useless for proponents of the former view.

Before you can improve your performance, you have to measure it. The good people at Zend are working on a commercial tuning debugger, but at press time it was not available to the public. Therefore, we default back to the time-honored programming performance metric: measuring microseconds. Whip up a little function like this:

```
function exec_time()
  {
  $mtime = explode( " ", microtime());
  $msec = (double)$mtime[0];
  $sec = (double)$mtime[1];
  return $sec + $msec;
  }
```

Paste or include it at the top of the script you'd like to measure. Now divide the main body of your script into sections, and scatter calls to exec_time() at strategic points, like so:

```
<?php
$start_db_call = exec_time();
$result = mysql_db_query("test", "SELECT * FROM user WHERE
ID=1");
while($testrow = mysql_fetch_array($result))
  echo $testrow[0];
$end_db_call = exec_time();
$runtime = $end_db_call - $start_db_call;
echo "Database call and echo took $runtime seconds";
?>
```

The next time you hit the Web page, voila! A self-timing PHP script, at your service.

Caution   Using microtime() to measure PHP will only tell you what happens between the time PHP begins working on the first measured line of code and the time it finishes working on the last measured line of code. It will not tell you how long it's taking your Web server to spawn a child process or your CGI to start up, how much latency your server is suffering from, what traffic conditions at your Web farm are like, or a lot of other things that affect real-world performance at least as much if not more. To find out that kind of thing, you need measuring tools far beyond PHP. A good start for Apache on Unix is the program called "ab" (aka Apache benchmark tool) which ships with Apache.

Now that you know how long the various parts of your script are taking, you can take steps to improve performance. Actually, a little logic should tell you that functions that touch other files or call other daemons should take longer than those that are self-contained within a discrete file. So database calls, include and require statements, objects with inheritance, and XML parsing are just going to take longer than simple arithmetic or echoing a string. But because these advanced functionalities are the best part of PHP, obviously it would be pointless to get rid of them for the sake of squeezing out a few more microseconds.

What you can and should do instead is hunt and destroy gross programming errors that cause unnecessary latency. Infinite loops, you know, are never very stylish. If you can notice a script running slowly with the naked eye, especially on a localhost, it's cause for concern — whip out the microtime and find out where it's going wrong. Pay special attention to known bottlenecks such as: using regex instead of explode() in a tight loop; object-oriented programming where it's not needed; bad use of SQL; including multiple instances of the same files; and long loops.

Although it would be better to eliminate all errors in the code itself, you can also help matters by setting the Apache or PHP timeout and max-memory configuration variables as low as possible. Come on — no Web page should need a 300-second timeout and you know it. Another configuration setting that might have a good effect on extremely slow scripts is `ignore_user_abort` in `php.ini`.

Recent distributions of PHP have also offered an optimized php.ini which sets variables for maximum speed at the possible expense of other virtues. If you choose to use this file, please take the time to understand the effects of its changes — in other words, don't just slap on your server and then ask where your HTTP_*_VARS values went.

The Zend optimizer

Until recently, speed-shavers had few options but homemade metrics like the `microtime` function just described. But now, there's an intriguing new tool available without cost: the Zend optimizer. This tool makes multiple passes over a PHP script and replaces slower constructs with faster ones that have the same effect. Zend predicts 40 to 100 percent performance improvement over stock PHP 4 — evidently the more complex the script's logic, the greater the potential room for improvement.

This product is somewhat controversial. Some Free Software types are not in favor of the optimizer or any of Zend's products, because they are only free as in beer, not as in speech. More pragmatic Open Source users feel that it's fine to let corporate clients with deep pockets meet their enterprise needs by purchasing commercial add-ons. Each individual PHP user will have to make his or her own decisions about licensing issues.

You can download the Zend optimizer from the Zend Web site, `http://www.zend.com/php/optimizer.php`. At press time, the optimizer and the PHP debugger were not compatible with each other, requiring a debug build. Under UNIX, you should recompile without the `--with-debugger` flag; under Windows, you need to get a special debuggerless binary from Zend. Since few PHP users actually work with this debugger, the impact should be minimal.

Another Zend product which promises to affect performance positively is the forthcoming cache. This will compile and store a version of each page in memory, reducing disk reads and redundant compilation and thus speeding Web service. At press time, no licensing details had been released but the product was said to be intended for heavy-traffic sites. As PHP becomes more popular with bigger, mission-critical uses, we can expect to see a steady stream of optimizing tools from Zend and perhaps others.

Summary

The good thing and the bad thing about PHP configuration are the same thing: there are a whole heck of a lot of options and more than one way to set many of them. The UNIX Apache module is particularly rich in choices, but the development team has labored long and hard to make PHP as customizable as possible.

There are three main ways to configure PHP. The first is via build-time flags, which are only available to those who build from source. Many of these directives are only necessary preconditions, meaning they set default conditions that need to be confirmed or can be reversed elsewhere. The second is via Apache configuration files (httpd.conf and .htaccess), which are only available to users of Apache server. The third is via the php.ini file which comes with every PHP distribution.

The php.ini file has experienced a few significant changes with PHP 4. One of the most important is the ability to disable functions on an individual basis. Certain features of PHP 3 and PHP 2 are beginning to be deprecated in this file, such as gpc_order (superseded by variables_order). And the php.ini is no longer an absolute necessity on Windows — versions of PHP 4 now recognize default values even without the file being present in the Windows path.

Once you've run PHP for a while, you may wish to tune its performance. PHP 4 is considerably faster at the same tasks than PHP 3, and in general script execution time isn't the bottleneck to total performance — but you may want to maximize the efficiency of your PHP-enabled anyway. The main tool available to measure performance is simply echoing microtime() at intervals throughout a script. With this simple method, you can try to narrow down and improve the parts of your scripts that are taking the most time. This does not measure anything outside PHP which may affect its performance; for that, you need external tools such as ab (Apache benchmark).

Zend.com is in development of tools which will also help improve performance, for those sites with enough traffic and complex script logic to merit the boost. They have already released an optimizer; and PHP users in larger companies are eagerly awaiting the promised cache and other tools.

✦   ✦   ✦

PHP for C Programmers

In this appendix, we assume that you have more C (or C++) programming experience than PHP experience and are looking to get up to speed in PHP quickly. First we'll give a quick overview of PHP from a C perspective, then we'll break down the similarities and differences, and finally we'll point out which parts of the book you are likely to benefit from the most.

The simplest way to think of PHP is as interpreted C that you can embed in HTML documents. The language itself is a lot like C, except with untyped variables, a whole lot of Web-specific libraries built-in, and everything hooked up directly to your favorite Web server. The syntax of statements and function definitions should be familiar, except that variables are always preceded by '$', and functions do not require separate prototypes.

Similarities

In this section we offer some notes (by no means exhaustive) on ways in which PHP can be expected to be C-like.

Syntax

Broadly speaking, PHP syntax is the same as in C: code is blank-insensitive, statements are terminated with semi-colons, function calls have the same structure (`my_function (expression1, expression2)`), curly braces ('{' and '}') make statements into blocks. PHP supports C and C++-style comments (`/* */` as well as `//`), and also Perl and shell-script style (`#`).

Operators

The assignment operators (=, +=, *=, and so on), the Boolean operators (&&, ||, !), the comparison operators (<, >, <=, >=, ==, !=), and the basic arithmetic operators (+, -, *, /, %) all behave as they do in C.

Control structures

The basic control structures (`if`, `switch`, `while`, `for`) behave as they do in C, including supporting `break` and `continue`.

Many function names

As you peruse the documentation, you'll see many function names that seem identical to C functions. It's a safe bet that these functions perform the exact same task, although they may sometimes take a slightly different form in terms of arguments, or the way results are returned. Most string-modifying functions, for example, return new strings as the value of the function rather than modifying a string passed as an argument.

Differences

While PHP has quite a bit of C ancestry, it also has some other ancestors (Perl, shell scripts), as well as some unique features that are not at all C-like.

Those dollar signs

All variables are denoted with a leading '$'. Variables do not need to be declared in advance of assignment, and they have no intrinsic type—the only type a variable has is the type of the last value that was assigned to it. The PHP version of the C code

```
double my_number;
my_number = 3.14159;
```

would simply be

```
$my_number = 3.14159;
```

Types

There are only two numerical types in PHP: integer (corresponding to a long in C), and double (corresponding to a double in C).

Strings are of arbitrary length. There is no separate character type. (Functions that might take character arguments in their C analogues typically expect a one-character string in PHP (ord( ), for example). Beginning with PHP 4, there is also a genuine Boolean type (TRUE or FALSE). (See following sections for arrays and objects.)

Type conversion

Types are not checked at compile time, and type errors do not typically occur at run time either. Instead, variables and values are automatically converted across types as needed. This is somewhat analogous to the way arithmetic expressions in C will "promote" numerical arguments as needed, but it is extended to the other types as well. (See Chapter 6 for details of the conversion rules).

Arrays

Arrays have a syntax superficially similar to C's array syntax, but they are implemented completely differently. They are actually associative arrays, and the "index" can be either a number or a string. They do not need to be declared or allocated in advance.

No structure type

There is no struct in PHP, which is partly because the array and object types together make it unnecessary. (The elements of a PHP array need not be of a consistent type.)

Objects

PHP has an very basic OOP syntax, which allows definition of classes with member data items and member functions. There are no destructors (see "Memory Management," which follows).

No pointers

There are no pointers per se in PHP, although the typeless variables play a similar role. PHP does support variable references.

No prototypes

Functions do not need to be declared before their implementation is defined. The only ordering rule in PHP 3 is define-before-use (and putting a function call in another function's body does not count as use until the latter function is called itself). It suffices to define all functions before making any top-level calls to functions. In PHP 4, functions do not even need to precede their calls, as there is an automatic pre-compilation step before execution.

Memory management

The PHP engine is effectively a garbage-collected environment (reference-counted), and in small scripts there is no need to do any deallocation. You should freely allocate new structures — such as new strings and object instances — especially because they will reliably go away when your script terminates. If you need to free memory within a script's execution, call unset() on the variable that refers to it, which will release the memory for collection. External resources (such as database result sets) can also be explicitly freed within a script, but doing so is worth it only if the script would use an unacceptable amount of the resource before terminating.

Compilation and linking

There is no separate compilation step for PHP scripts — the development cycle is simply edit-reload. Errors and warnings show up in the browser output. Typically there is no dynamic loading of libraries (although such a capability exists) — you decide at PHP configuration time which function families to include in your module, and they are then available to any script.

Permissiveness

As a general matter, PHP is more forgiving than C (especially in its type system) and so will let you get away with new kinds of mistakes. Unexpected results are more common than errors. In particular, under the default error-reporting level PHP does not warn you if you use a variable that has not yet been assigned (although it does supply reasonable default values rather than garbage). If you would rather be warned, you can set the error-reporting level by evaluating error-reporting(E_ALL) (or, equivalently error-reporting(15)) early in your script, or set the error-reporting level to 15 permanently by editing the php.ini file.

Guide to the Book

In writing this book, we very intentionally did not assume that the reader had prior knowledge of C. Because PHP resembles C in many aspects, some of the chapters may cover familiar ground. This is especially true of Part I, which is essentially a language introduction.

In Table A-1, we label the chapters of Part I according to how familiar they are likely to be to C programmers. Parts III and IV are very PHP-specific and likely to be novel, but you may also find portions of Part II to be familiar if you have some experience with SQL databases.

Table A-1
Guide to Part I for C Programmers

Chapter	Chapter Title	Verdict?	Notes
1	Why PHP?	Novel	The chapter you need to justify PHP to your boss
2	Server-Side Web Scripting	Novel	Important if you have not seen Web-scripting languages before
3	Getting Started with PHP	Novel	Installation, hosting, and so on
4	Adding PHP to your HTML	Novel but easy	"Hello world" for PHP
5	Syntax, Variables, and Output	Mostly familiar	Skimmable until the section on variables (which really are different in PHP)
6	Types in PHP	Somewhat familiar	PHP performs automatic type conversions. Also see the late material on arrays and objects
7	Control	Familiar	All the PHP control structures (`if`, `while`, `switch`, `for`) work the same way as in C
8	Using and Defining Functions	Mostly familiar	Skimmable—differences include scoping rules, treatment of number of arguments, and the final section on variable function names
9	Strings and String Functions	Mostly familiar	Some identically named string functions (`sprintf`) return new strings rather than operating on a passed string. Doubly-quoted strings do automatic interpolation of variable values. Material late in the chapter on built-in functions for regular expressions, URLs
10	Math	Familiar	Similarly named functions behave the same way. Novel section on arbitrary-precision arithmetic ("bc" functions).

Continued

Table A-1 (continued)			
Chapter	**Chapter Title**	**Verdict?**	**Notes**
11	Arrays and Array Functions	Novel	Deceptively familiar — PHP arrays are syntactically like C arrays but behave totally differently
12	Passing Information between Pages	Novel	Specific to Web-scripting
13	Filesystem and System Functions	Mostly familiar	Some novel touches, including reading a remote Web page (via HTTP) exactly like a file
14	PHP Style	Mostly familiar	The same stylistic mandates as with C code — only the final sections are specific to Web site design
15	Basic PHP Gotchas	Novel	Error messages and stumbling blocks do not have much overlap with C

A Bonus: Just Look at the Code!

As a final bonus, C programmers are uniquely qualified to benefit from the open-source nature of PHP. Although the combination of this book and the online manual should answer almost all of your questions, if you have the PHP source available you may be able to gain some extra insight by poking around in it and seeing how things are implemented. Although you would need to be familiar with lexing/parsing technology to get much out of the parser code itself, many PHP functions are simple wrappers around their C counterparts, and some others that have no C counterparts are at least written in clear and simple C.

Then, once you become familiar with the source, the obvious next step is . . . to contribute!

✦   ✦   ✦

PHP for ASP Programmers

As open source software becomes more widely accepted for commercial applications and personal projects both, some ASP developers may consider adding a PHP string to their bows. This appendix is intended to help you get off to a quick start in what will doubtless turn into a wholehearted love affair with PHP (because to use it is to love it).

Although ASP is (in theory) platform-, Web server, and language-independent, in practice only a fraction of the ASP market uses anything but Microsoft NT, IIS, and VBScript. We will assume the default combination of technologies here; ASP coders who use JScript exclusively may feel more comfortable with Chapter 27, "PHP and JavaScript."

Similar Concepts

In the big picture, ASP and PHP are very similar. (And before you ask, PHP was invented before ASP, so there is no question of copying Microsoft.) They're both HTML-embedded, non-tag-based, server-side scripting preprocessors. For most purposes, they are interchangeable.

OK, we'll come right out and say it: anything ASP can do, PHP can do better (except possibly session management and application variables). PHP is, to swipe a NASA motto, "better, cheaper, faster" than ASP for most common Web development purposes.

Main Differences

The differences between the two languages are found in the areas of syntax, object model, and philosophies.

ASP is Basic, PHP is C-like

The syntax of the two languages is somewhat different because PHP inherits largely from C, whereas VBScript is a subset of Visual Basic. For example, an if statement in VBScript:

```
<% If varPreference = "coffee" Then
Response.Write "cream"
Elseif varPreference = "tea" Then
Response.Write "lemon"
End If %>
```

versus the same in PHP:

```
<?php
if($Preference == "coffee")
    echo "cream";
elseif($Preference == "tea")
    {
    print("lemon");
    }
?>
```

As you can see, C-style syntax makes greater use of symbols, indentation and bracketing, and parentheses for grouping. PHP syntax is even more flexible than C's, however. In this example, the curly brackets are optional because only one command is given per conditional; we chose to include them in the elseif branch for demonstration purposes. PHP's print and echo (which are interchangeable for most uses) don't strictly require parentheses around the string to be printed, so we used them once and left them out once..

C is perhaps more math-like, whereas Basic tries to employ a syntax closer to natural language. The difference is especially clear in loops, as in this example:

```
<% For Each Item in Request.QueryString
    For iCount = 1 to Request.QueryString(Item).Count
        Response.Write Item & " = " &
Request.QueryString(Item)(iCount) & "<br>"
    Next
Next %>
```

You can accomplish the same task in PHP with either a while loop or a for loop:

```
<?php
$i = 0;
```

```
    while($i <= count($Item))
        {
        print("$Item[$i] = $i<BR>");
        $i++;
        }
    ?>
    or
    <?php
    for($i=0; $i <= count($Item); $i++)
        {print("$Item[$i] = $i<BR>")};
    ?>
```

If you need a brush-up on C-style syntax beyond the charts at the end of this chapter, there are many free tutorials on the Web; or you can pick up a book like Patrick Henry Winston's excellent (and short) *On to C* (New York: Addison-Wesley, 1994).

Tip   Um, don't forget the semicolons.

ASP uses objects for everything; PHP does not

ASP is built around an object model. PHP is not, and it is consequently less fussy all around.

Some of the most important consequences of this design difference are:

✦ You don't need to call for form variables with `Request.Form` or `Request.QueryString`. Named variables are automatically transferred for you from form to form-handling script and are immediately available for use. See Chapter 12 for more details.

✦ You don't need to make a connection object for database connectivity. Just compile PHP with the database capability you prefer, and use the specific commands for that database or protocol.

✦ You need not instantiate an object you might not even use.

✦ You don't have to type `Response.Write` for every stinkin' echo/print.

✦ You never, ever need to think about ActiveX components in PHP.

Although PHP has some notion of objects and classes, it is not a thoroughly object-oriented language and probably never will be. Individuals and companies can choose the notation that works best for them in each situation. Since object-oriented code finds its maximum value in large-scale projects with numerous programmers, and so far most Web sites developed with PHP have been relatively small-scale, there has been little true need for objects (as opposed to personal preference). But as companies push the frontiers of PHP use, its object-oriented capabilities are becoming more common.

Tip   Remember that PHP uses the C++-like arrow style of object notation (such as, `$this->title`), unlike VBScript's "dot" notation. A dot or period in PHP is a concatenation operator.

ASP is proprietary, PHP is not

It's difficult to enumerate all the ways in which Open Source software makes life better for a Web programmer. Even for those who are left unmoved by the ideological aspects of the Open Source movement, there are plenty of pragmatic ways in which PHP's status will help you get your job done more effectively.

The most immediate consequence of PHP's Open Source character is better connectivity to a wider choice of Web servers and back-end servers. Microsoft's implementation of ASP runs only on Windows/IIS and uses a variety of schemes whose names change with bewildering frequency (pop quiz: briefly and clearly explain the relationships between OLE DB, ADO, ODBC, UDA, RDS, and ADC) to make connections to a small default number of databases. PHP supports a larger range of OSes, Web servers, databases, and other standards than any other comparable Web scripting language (with the debatable exception of Perl).

PHP was deliberately designed to be a "glue" of the Internet. It's far easier to mix and match technologies with PHP — and with the rapid pace of technological change in the Web sphere today, that is a massively good thing. So feel free to promiscuously hook up with all manner of back-end servers, knowing you can easily make a change whenever you want.

PHP is almost unique in being designed from the ground up as a Web-serving programming language. It is not an desktop application development environment with the serial numbers filed off and a whole lot of application-based baggage left in. PHP's developers make design decisions based on the real life needs of Web programmers, rather than simply because that's the way some the application-oriented version of a language did things.

Because PHP is Open Source, it adds new functionality rapidly (perhaps too rapidly for the tired authors of technical books) and without regard to the constraints of proprietorship. For instance, PHP4 introduced support for DOM XML and Gnu Gettext, COM and CORBA, CyberCash and Shockwave Flash. Microsoft's development cycles are slower, and they preferentially support only their own product line except in cases of overwhelming demand (in the case of Oracle, for example). There's nothing ethically wrong with this as a business philosophy, but for Web developers who want the widest choice of best-of-breed products it can be constraining.

If you are comfortable with C, you can lift the hood of PHP and customize the ride to an almost infinite degree. Power PHP users routinely disable functions, add custom extensions, try building PHP with different Web servers and libraries, and delve into the source code to learn about undocumented abilities. Ultimately, C programmers are able to have their new functionality built into PHP itself by contributing code to the project.

Last but not least, there's the issue of technical support. PHP offers an online manual which has been covered in accolades for its usefulness, attractiveness, and strong concept—there's even a version for PalmPilots. PHP has also long enjoyed one of the most active, helpful, friendly mailing lists in the Internet programming world. Often questions are answered on the lists or in private e-mail by the programmer who implemented the functionality in the first place. There are numerous well-designed PHP Web sites with articles, forums, and code samples for the taking. And now there is commercial support for PHP, up to and including priority development of aspects of the language itself.

Oh, and did we mention that PHP is available without cost? With the exception of commercial support and certain third-party servers (such as Oracle and SQL Server), the full functionality and glory of PHP are freely available to all without regard to ability to pay. Although there is a thriving market in ASP add-ons and Windows programming tools, it is very much commercialized to say the least.

Converting ASP to PHP

If you need to convert a large number of VBScript Active Server Pages to PHP, this just might be your secret weapon:

```
http://asp2php.naken.cc/
```

Michael Kohn, author of the program, admittedly has a leeeetle bit of attitude about ASP, and he isn't shy about expressing it on his site (just to give you the flavor, let us mention that the product's motto is "Resistance is NOT futile"). And no program will be able to convert every dot and single quote perfectly—you'll still have to edit your pages by hand. But this can help you with some of the repetitive grunt-work that stands between you and your goal. If you need to convert a biggish site on a deadline, that can be the difference between determination and despair.

Note This site also has links to two database-conversion utilities you may find helpful: one (from Oracle) converts SQL Server to Oracle, and the other (from MySQL) converts Access to MySQL.

Handy Conversion Charts

To get you off to a quick start, we offer this collection of detailed differences between ASP and PHP in handy chart form. Due to design differences between the languages, exact correlates will not always be possible to find.

Table B-1
ASP and PHP operators

ASP Operators	PHP Operators
+	+
-	-
*	*
/ or \	/
&	. .=
Eqv	No exact correlate; use bitwise operators
^	pow()
Imp	No exact correlate; use bitwise operators
Is (*obj reference*)	Not necessary in PHP
Mod	%
And	and, &&
Not	!
Or	or, ||
Xor	xor
=	==, ===
>	>
<	<

Table B-2
ASP statements and PHP functions

ASP Statements	PHP Equivalents
Call *ProcedureName*	*FunctionName*();
Dim *VarName*	No equivalent

Do While/Until *[conditions]*
  [statements]
Loop
or
Do *[statements]*
Loop While/Until *[conditions]*
	do
	  {
	    [functions];
	  }
	while(*conditions*);

ASP Statements	PHP Equivalents
Erase *ArrayName*	unset(*[array]*)
Exit *[Statement]*	*[condition]* break;

For *VarName* = *[num]* To/Downto
[conditions]
  [statements]
Next
	for ($*VarName* = *[num]*;*[conditions]*;
	*[++$VarName/$VarName++/
	--$VarName/$VarName--]*)
	  {
	  [functions];
	  }

For Each *VarName* In *GroupName*
  [statements]
Next
	for(*[conditions]*):
	  [functions];
	endfor;
	or
	while(list($*variable*) = each($*group*)
	  [functions];

Public/Private Function
FunctionName([args])
  [statements]
End Function
	function *FunctionName([args])*
	  {
	  [functions];
	  }

If *[conditions]* Then
  [statements]
Else/Else If
  [statements]
End If
	if(*[conditions]*)
	  {
	  [functions];
	  }
	else/elseif(*[conditions]*)
	  {
	  [functions];
	  }
	or
	if(*[conditions]*):
	  [functions];
	else/elseif(*[conditions]*):
	  [functions];
	endif;

On Error Resume Next	function() or function(); **or** continue;
Option Explicit	No equivalent
Private *VarName*	No equivalent

Continued

Table B-2 *(continued)*

ASP Statements	PHP Equivalents
`Public VarName`	**No equivalent**

`Randomize[num]`	`mt_srand((double)microtime()*1000000)`
	or
	`srand((double)microtime()*1000000)`

`ReDim VarName`	**No equivalent**

`Rem [Comment]`
or
`'[Comment]`
	`//[Comment]`
	or
	`/* [Comment] */`
	or
	`#[Comment]`

`Select Case [testexpression]`
`  [Case [expressionlist]`
`   [statements]]`
`  [Case Else [expressionlist]`
`   [statements-n]]`
`End Select`
	`switch ($VarName)`
	`  {`
	`    case [value]: [function];`
	`  break;`
	`  case [value]: [function];`
	`    break;`
	`  }`

`Set VarName = [expression]`	**$VarName = [expression]**

`Public/Private Sub`
`SubName([args])`
`  [statements]`
`End Sub`
	`function FunctionName([args])`
	`  {`
	`  [functions];`
	`  }`

`While [condition]`
`[statements]`
`Wend`
	`while([conditions])`
	`  {`
	`   [functions];`
	`  }`
	or
	`while([conditions]):`
	`  [functions];`
	`endwhile;`

Functions and methods and statements, oh my!

In VBScript, there are functions, methods, and properties — mostly the consequence of the ASP object model. In PHP, many of the equivalent things are simply called functions.

Instead of specifying distinct objects with the same method, there are specific functions for interacting with different back-end servers. For example, Oracle functions are not the same as SQL Server functions in PHP. The differences are pretty trivial in practice, however: `Ora_Fetch` versus `mssql_fetch_row`, for instance.

All functions have the simplest of formats:

```
FunctionName([args]);
```

User-defined functions in PHP do not make a distinction between subroutines (which do not return a value) and functions (which do). The syntax for defining a function is:

```
function FunctionName([args])
    {
    [functions];
    }
```

See Chapter 8 for more specific information.

Variable types

In PHP, you don't have to explicitly declare variable types. It's wise to do so with floating-point numbers, but otherwise the notation helps take care of it and PHP juggles types for you. See Chapter 6 for more specific information.

Constants

There is very little overlap between VBScript constants and PHP constants. PHP has only a few built-in constants, such as `PHP_VERSION` and `PHP_OS`. You may also define constants at run time, which generally only happens when you `include/require` many files and define many functions.

Classes and objects

See Chapter 30 for a detailed explanation of PHP objects and classes. The short version is that a PHP class is no more than a convenient way to bundle up frequently used combinations of variables and functions. Unless you really love object-oriented programming (in which case you would probably prefer Python anyway), make sure the time you save is worth the performance maintainability hit you're going to take. Many power PHP users (including Rasmus Lerdorf, inventor of the language) never use objects at all.

Including files

PHP's mechanism for including files is dynamic, while ASP's is not. This makes it extremely easy to include chunks of PHP or HTML from separate files, throughout the code. The syntax is:

ASP

```
<!--#include file="path"-->
```

PHP

```
include("path");
or
include_once("path");
or
require("path");
```

Variable values from an included file will be fully available to the main script, and vice versa (given that they are set in the correct order, of course).

Files can be included conditionally, simply by embedding them in conditional statements:

```
if($somecondition == 1)
   {
   include("$conditional_file");
   }
else
   {
   include("$default_file");
   }
```

See Chapters 8 and 14 for more information on include and require.

There are many more specific points of difference between ASP and PHP, but hopefully this chapter will clue you in to the major issues quickly and encourage you to begin experimenting with PHP.

✦   ✦   ✦

PHP for HTML Programmers

This appendix contains specific advice for HTML-only jocks looking to trade up to something a little more powerful on the server side. If you already know ASP, JavaScript, or almost any real programming language, this appendix is not going to help you much.

The Good News

If you're proficient at HTML, it's not a huge step to begin using PHP. Because PHP is embedded in HTML, extending the functionality of static Web pages with a programming language can be a very natural progression. So there's plenty of reason to believe you can learn PHP fairly quickly.

You already know HTML

You presumably have a lot of practice debugging HTML—which is all to the good. Many errors occur within the HTML parts of scripts or during the transitions between modes, so the ability to read and write HTML with great facility is crucial. Plus, PHP-mode error messages are much more informative than those in HTML!

Also, your stuff will probably end up looking better than ours because you know about all that layout and design stuff. So go out there and show the world that PHP sites don't have to be ugly, clunky, or at best really plain—we sure can't.

PHP is an easy first programming language to learn

Unlike many major programming languages, PHP lets you do useful stuff from the very beginning instead of playing endless games of tic-tac-toe or coding up abstruse math problems. The Web browser and markup languages, however primitive and clunky they are now, point the way to the universal I/O, windowing, and multimedia solution the world has been waiting for. PHP takes full advantage of the Web's power; plus it takes a loose, inclusive approach to issues like types, variables, and syntax. All the overhead that programmers used to have to put into these areas, you can now apply more directly to functionality.

And frankly, PHP makes it possible to just learn those parts that are useful to you and ignore the rest. So if you don't need to write some huge math function right off the bat, go ahead and skip that chapter. If and when you ever need it, the math capabilities will still be there.

Web development is increasingly prefab anyway

Finally, the Web is increasingly making development a matter of altering prefab open-source code rather than hacking it all up yourself. Much of this work is about changing what the page looks like rather than how it functions. Learn to be a smart script shopper, and you're more than halfway there.

The Bad News

Before we get too carried away, honesty compels us to admit there may be a few hurdles to jump before you become a power PHP user.

If programming were that easy, you'd already know how

PHP is a real programming language, similar to C (albeit strictly Web server-dwelling), rather than a tag-based markup concept like HTML or ColdFusion. This point introduces whole new levels of complexity. It simply takes time and practice to develop a bag of tricks, work out routines for solving problems, and just get better at development — and there's no shortcut for these things.

So here's the bottom line: most of PHP will be completely new to you. Unlike new PHP developers who are already proficient with ASP, JavaScript, or C, you can't expect to pick up any specific points here that are highly similar to things you already know how to do. Uh, sorry.

However, if you already know some JavaScript or have taken an "Intro to C" class in school—even if you wouldn't describe yourself as a JavaScript or C guru—you're ahead of the curve. Some of the logic will come back to you as you begin to work with PHP. By the time this book comes out, there are almost certain to be some sort of PHP training courses you could take if you feel comfortable learning that way.

Backend servers can add complexity

PHP is mostly useful in conjunction with backend servers such as database and mail, which have their own syntax and implementation issues to be learned. Because open source software like PHP is often used in noncorporate settings, you probably don't have the luxury of a team of database, network, and design experts doing their various things while you just worry about the middle tier.

If possible, don't try to learn everything at once. The most important task is to become comfortable with the Web server itself; Apache in particular is an extremely powerful but involved piece of software that rewards study. After that, you'll almost certainly want to learn SQL if you don't know it already; and mail service is also very rewarding. Once you've mastered those three, new servers will be easier to learn.

Concentrate On...

One of your humble authors was an experienced programmer before learning PHP, but one had basically only done HTML before—so we can dare to offer a few words of advice from our own learning experience. These steps to learning programming might make the task a bit easier.

Reading other people's code

Learning to read other people's code can be harder than it sounds. One of the best things about PHP is its loose syntax and inclusive "don't worry, be happy" design— but that can also mean different scripts can look very different, even if they return similar results. Beginners can be boggled by stylistic issues, finding it difficult to sort out which parts of a script are functionally irreducible and which are the product of one individual's programming quirks. But regardless of difficulty, the sooner you can parse other people's PHP and the more you can look at, the better off you'll be.

One potentially helpful exercise is to visit the mailing list archive or a code exchange (see Appendix D) and print out multiple examples of code that solves the same issue (preferably one you're interested in). Then lay the sheets side by side, take a big ol' red pen, and go through it all circling the common parts. Give extra brownie points to any scripters who commented their code well (which doesn't necessarily mean the most voluminous comments, but rather the most useful), and look for more code from those people.

Thinking about programming

As we've said before, this is inevitably going to take time, practice, and lots of examples to look at. There's just no way around it, and really not a whole lot more to say.

One thing that might be helpful to new developers, particularly those of a narrative rather than mathematical bent, is judicious use of pseudocode.

1. Write down the tasks you want this page to accomplish. It's more important at this stage to be complete than cogent.

   ```
   This page should display a form with any old answers already
   filled in, and then let you update your answers if you want
   to. And I want it to be password-protected, so it needs to
   handle a User ID from the login screen.
   ```

2. Break this down into steps and substeps, as in a recipe. Rearrange these if necessary.

   ```
   1. Get the User ID that was passed from the login screen; if
   none, don't display anything.

   2. Display HTML form.

   3. Make any old values from the database show up in the form.

      a. connect to the database server

      b. download data about this item

      c. put it into the HTML form's item "value=X" variables

   4. Change the values, and put them into the database too.

   5. Pass the User ID to the next page.
   ```

3. Pick one of the steps and turn it into actual PHP code. It's generally easiest to start with a core PHP task—like sending e-mail or returning something to the screen—rather than peripheral tasks like connecting to a database. Any time you might want to connect to a database, use a commented variable, array, or include file for the moment.

   ```
   1. Get the User ID that was passed from the login screen; if
   none, don't display anything.
   ```

   ```php
   // Dummy UserID pretending to be passed from login.
   // Will be superseded later.
   <?php $UserID = 1; ?>
   ```

```
2. Display HTML form.

<HTML><HEAD></HEAD>
<BODY>
<FORM>
First name: <input type="text" size=30 name="FirstName"><BR>
Last name: <input type="text" size=30 name="LastName"><BR>
E-mail: <input type="text" size=30 name="Email">

3. Make any old values from the database show up in the form.

I'm using these variables now, but later I'll get them from
the database instead
<?php
$FirstName = "Joyce";
$LastName = "Park";
$Email = "root@localhost"
?>
Oh, I think I need to put them before the form is rendered.

4. Change the values, and put them into the database too.

5. Pass the User ID to the next page.
```

4. Gradually fill in more and more of the code, fixing any new issues that arise. You might want to keep some of the pseudocode, suitably edited, as comments.

```
/* Pass the User ID to the next page. The best way is to have
it show up as a hidden input type and PHP variable in the
form; then HTML can pass it with the rest of the POST values.
*/
```

Learning SQL and other protocols

It's generally a good idea to spend some time interacting with back-end servers directly, via whatever interface is provided, before adding the complexity of PHP between you and it.

You can kill two birds with one stone by using the back-end server's own interface to construct the database (or whatever), even though there are tools for some of these tasks in PHP. For instance, even though Tobias Ratschiller's phpMyAdmin tool is a very slick and handy way to deal with the MySQL database, the newbie db admin will learn a heck of a lot more by using MySQL's deliberately primitive command-line interface.

Making cosmetic changes to prefab PHP applications

It might help motivate you client-side types to jump right into customizing a prefab application for yourself, such as Phorum or IMP. A couple hints:

◆ First try just changing the colors — that's generally pretty safe. If that goes well, try customizing the buttons. The next safest thing is spacing — table widths, columns, and so forth. You can also add graphics, add links, or play around with style sheets pretty much without worries.

◆ If there are include files (especially header.inc), the cosmetic part is often in there. Look first in headers and footers for colors, the basis of page layouts, and so forth. Remember to match header changes with corresponding footer changes, and vice versa.

Never, ever erase a line beginning with a conjunction (such as if, while, or for).

Debugging is programming

Few people truly enjoy debugging; as one of our colleagues once observed, "I'd rather implement new features than eat someone else's leftovers." However, debugging can be a useful learning experience because you can fix things at the edges of a big project rather than having to jump in to writing the whole thing from scratch.

One of the most efficient ways to debug is in pairs. Particularly when you're tired or have seen a piece of code too many times, it can be difficult to focus on every detail. At this point, it becomes very helpful to have to talk through your logic — briefly stating why you're doing each step, and checking them off very deliberately. A fresh set of eyes can often more quickly find cheap mistakes such as misspelled variable names or missing brackets. If you have an opportunity to debug with a more experienced programmer, take it.

Avoid at First

There are a few things that are extremely unfamiliar to HTML coders, and generally are not extremely necessary to writing functional PHP. Try to avoid these if you can, at least at first.

Objects

Objects can be confusing even for experienced non-object-oriented programmers, so do yourself a favor and avoid them if at all possible. Because PHP is not even a truly object-oriented language, the "object notation" can also cause problems later.

Maximal PHP style

See Chapter 14. The maximal style is deprecated by Rasmus Lerdorf himself, and only hard-core C programmers have the slightest excuse to use it except in very specific, brief instances. There are just too many single quotes, double quotes, forward slashes, backslashes, ASCII line breaks, and HTML line breaks for most coders.

Programming large applications from scratch

Why reinvent the wheel? In Opensourceland, you don't have to. It's often more efficient to be a good customizer and recycler of other people's code than the world's greatest programmer from scratch. Learn to shop for what you need.

Consider This

These are completely optional ideas that may prove helpful. You may not agree with all of them, but we offer them for what they're worth.

Reading a book on C programming

Unfortunately, we are not able to write a complete programming tutorial. Part I of this book explains these topics, but necessarily very briefly. We've tried to comment our code samples extensively, but there's only so much you can do to explain these techniques in passing.

Mailing-list regulars frequently counsel new PHP developers to buy a book on C programming — but in a snotty RTFM way that too often elicits a naturally passive-aggressive response. Nevertheless, separated from the unspoken message that you must be a clueless idiot, it's good advice and something to seriously consider if you're having trouble with the programming aspect of PHP.

A clearly written, brief tutorial book is Patrick Henry Winston's *On to C* (Addison-Wesley, 1994). It's less than 300 pages long, and a lot of the PHP-relevant material is right at the beginning. The standard reference is Brian W. Kernighan and Dennis M. Ritchie, *The C Programming Language* (Prentice Hall, 1988), which is quite definitive but more reference-oriented and therefore perhaps less appropriate for HTML-only coders.

Minimal PHP style

Of the range of PHP styles, the easiest for the HTML coder to work with at first will be the most minimal. In other words, we suggest you separate the HTML and PHP sections completely. Not only will this avoid many stylistic difficulties, but by using this method you'll avoid mixing PHP and HTML glitches on the same page, which makes diagnosing problems more than twice as hard. We discuss this topic more completely in Chapter 14.

Perhaps the easiest way to do this is to finish the HTML templates first, using whatever tool you're most enamored of. Take the time to debug this completely, and perhaps run it through a tidying utility. Then and only then tackle the PHP parts, secure and comfy in the knowledge that any difficulties you encounter are sure to be on the PHP side rather than the HTML side.

One downside of this style is that you won't be able to have pages pass their variables back to themselves. This is particularly relevant with forms; so if your site has a lot of forms, you might want to change your style a bit as your PHP skills improve.

Use the right tools for the job

Finally, you want to strongly consider using a PHP-enabled text editor for the PHP parts of your scripts (see Chapter 4 for a discussion of text editors versus WYSIWYG tools). There are people who can do wonders with just Notepad or emacs, but there are certainly a lot of frustrated beginners using those tools just because someone told them that's what the cool programmers do. As Zsa Zsa Gabor said (in a slightly different context): macho does not mean mucho. If you work more effectively with vim or Visual SlickEdit, by all means use those tools.

Caution   This advice does *not* apply to WYSIWYG editors, the use of which we deprecate. Sooner or later you'll need to fix up the HTML into a human-readable form, which no WYSIWYG editor can yet produce. If it's your choice to use one, fine — but this tool should in no way be thought of as a substitute for understanding and writing clean HTML by hand.

✦   ✦   ✦

PHP Resources

This appendix lays out some basic resources that will help you learn more about the language. We have also tried to mention specific resources and products throughout the text.

The PHP Web Site

The URL (engrave it on your heart) is:

```
http://www.php.net
```

Here you'll find the latest official news, the freshest downloads, the PHP bugtracker, and a growing list of sites that use PHP.

The manual

Most important, you'll find the PHP manual in the Documentation section. It's available in several versions for your universal reference pleasure. These include:

+ Japanese and French translations
+ Several PDF, RTF, and HTML download versions (useful when traveling; HTML versions included with PHP download)
+ A PalmPilot version
+ A plain HTML online version

But when people talk about "*the* PHP manual," they mean the big annotated online version for which PHP is famous. Users from around the world have added notes and comments to each page. These are often clarifications of points made in the main text, additional insights, and reports of PHP's behavior on various platforms.

Caution The online manual is *not* the place for you to ask questions! It's intended for meaningful comments and observations only. Send e-mail to one of the previous commentators who provide their addresses — many of them will be happy to help you. Or subscribe to the mailing list or post to a PHP forum, which will be faster anyway. Remember, a stupid question posted to the manual errata *will* go down on your (semi-)permanent record.

However, you may want to keep a couple of points in mind when using this manual:

✦ The canonical manual text is in a super-terse programmer's style.

✦ The comments only edited, weeded, and verified on an episodic (not to say extremely infrequent) basis. Proceed with extreme caution — there have been numerous instances of problems getting worse because a user uncritically followed the advice in the manual notes. You can write to the person and make sure the advice is appropriate for you, or even if the person really knows what he or she is talking about.

✦ The manual may lag behind development. Furthermore, for some period of time there will be overlap between PHP 4 and PHP 3 entries and comments.

The PHP Mailing Lists

The "official" PHP community meets and greets on the PHP mailing lists. If your question is about the technical workings of PHP and needs to be answered by one of the core developers, this is the place. With the advent of PHP 4, a decision was made to split up the lists into more specific topics — so if you're surprised that volume on the main list seems to have dropped of late, that's why.

Users' lists and developers' lists

Three lists are mostly intended for active developers and very early adopters — people who are going to get down in the C code and battle bugs to the death. These are:

php-dev	The main PHP developers' list
beta	Mostly populated by bug-squishing nonproduction early adopters
phplib-dev	The PHPLIB developers' list

These are low-to-medium volume lists, meaning approximately 100–1,000 messages a month. They are highly technical, and mostly not enlightening unless you're an active team member.

Users have their own lists, many of which are new:

php-general	The main mailing list — very heavy traffic, over 100 e-mail messages per day (see below)
php-db	The database-related issues mailing list
php-install	A specifically installation-related mailing list
php-i18n	Internationalization and localization mailing list
php-migration	Discussion of migration from earlier versions of PHP
php-windows	Specific mailing list for Windows users
phplib	The PHPLIB users' list — medium volume
php-announce	Announces new releases — very occasional

There are unofficial mailing lists in many non-English languages. For a list, see the Documentation page of the PHP Web site.

There are also lists for popular PHP-based projects such as Midgard; subscribe through their own Web sites.

If you're comfortable with Internet newsgroups (which many newer users are not), you can access the PHP mailing lists at the news gateway:

```
news.php.net
```

This option has one great advantage: you can send messages to the mailing lists without being subscribed to them. However, many new users should think in terms of searching the archives for answers to old questions before (or rather than) asking new questions anyway.

Most of these mailing lists are archived and searchable at two sites:

```
http://www.phpbuilder.com/mail/
http://www.progressive-comp.com/Lists
```

The difference between the two sites is largely cosmetic: the PCC archive is deliberately bare-bones and (as of this writing) white-on-black, whereas the PHPBuilder list is more HTML-oriented. PHPBuilder's PHP 4 archive only dates from May, 2000; earlier posts are archived separately under PHP 3 and PHP 4-beta. Geocrawler (http://www.geocrawler.com) also maintained a PHP 3 archive, but it seems to be no longer updated.

Tip It's polite to try a quick keyword search on the PHP site, mail archives, and Zend.com before contacting the mailing lists. It's actually faster for you; plus, the less time the developers have to spend answering the same questions over and over, the more time they have to implement new features in the language. Actually, searching the archives is no longer just polite—it's becoming necessary. With so many new users, so-called "RTFM" (read the effing manual) questions will not be (politely) answered on the PHP lists anymore.

Regular and digest

The main PHP user list is so high-volume that it has a twice-daily digest version. The new specialized mailing lists also typically have digest versions. The raw and digested versions each have advantages and disadvantages.

If you've never had 100+ e-mail messages a day pouring into your mailbox, you have no idea how distracting and time-consuming that can be. Just reading-and-deleting can take up a couple of hours, whereas answering can easily be a full-time job. Under no circumstance should you get the full user list if your primary mailbox is a Web-based free e-mail service.

Tip It's almost mandatory to have a separate mailbox for PHP mail if you're subscribing to the full user mailing list, unless you've set up good mail filters. Otherwise, you'll quickly start to lose mail from other sources in the flood of similarly named threads.

On the other hand, the digest version makes it more difficult to get into the flow. The few brave community members who get the full user list seem to answer all the questions on the half-volley before you even get the digest, making it difficult for the time-stressed community member to participate.

For beginners, we recommend the digest version. You can always trade up later when you're ready to stop lurking and participate actively.

Everyone should also consider using one of the PHP forums (see below) instead of or in addition to the user mailing list. These are great for those who dislike mailing lists. The downside is that PHP developers generally don't hang out here, so extremely abstruse infrastructure questions will go unanswered. The up side is that they tend to be friendlier, especially to repetitive newbie questions, because the answerers can control the amount of contact they prefer and go away if they start to become annoyed.

Signing up

To sign up for any of the PHP mailing lists, go to the PHP site's Support page. Hidden in the middle of the page is a very inconspicuous signup form. Just choose the list you want, enter your e-mail address, and click the Subscribe button. You can also unsubscribe from a list here.

The PHP mailing list manager will almost instantaneously send you an e-mail message asking you to confirm your subscription. You will not be subscribed until you reply to this e-mail. When you unsubscribe, you do not have to confirm.

Mailing list etiquette

Open source mailing lists can be intimidating places, and the PHP user list is particularly active and fast-paced. The denizens of the mailing lists are people, and it can be fun to learn about their different personalities and plans over time — but they can get annoyed and fed up, too. A little netiquette can take the user a long way.

Remember, they did this for free!

Before you complain, remind yourself of your last experience with commercial software tech support. Did they solve your problem the same day? Did it cost money? At what point did you get to talk to the developers of the program?

Give detailed descriptions

Say as much as you can about your platform, the problem, and any steps you've already tried. Don't worry about being concise; it's far better to maunder on a little than to make everyone go back and forth an extra time.

Code fragments are the very most efficient way to state your problem for debugging by the community. Many people edit their raw code to make it more anonymous and/or abstract. Remember to take out any passwords!

Be sure to use a specific subject line — the more specific the better. "Subject: PHP Help" will get you ignored by most of the mailing-list regulars. You want to say something more descriptive like, "Subject: mysql_connect arguments not being passed in 4.0.0".

PHP is international

PHP is developed and used by people literally all over the world. In fact, the active development team has only a smallish minority of native English speakers on it at any given time.

Native English speakers should feel supremely lucky that theirs is the lingua franca of the Internet in general and the PHP world specifically. They should be awed by the linguistic dexterity of all the citizens of other nations, and perhaps slightly abashed that they can't return the favor in Finnish or Russian. In other words, cut people some slack already! Don't assume someone is an idiot because his or her messages aren't perfectly grammatical and smooth. Instead, you might spend the time learning how to write "Thank you" in all the languages of the various PHP community members — it will make a nice sig file.

There are limits

The mailing list and other resources are meant to help you, but you have to be prepared to make a good-faith and even strenuous effort of your own. Help does not mean someone will come to your office and write your code — this is not a remake of the Disney version of Cinderella, with dancing, sewing, chore-doing mice! Please don't ask community members to go into your server and debug your scripts for you.

Also, every once in awhile someone will get on the mailing list and whine about how PHP doesn't have precisely the feature he or she is looking for — to which the developers will very sensibly reply, "Why don't you implement it yourself?" Or, if you're not a good C programmer yourself, you could pay someone else to develop your feature and contribute it back to the PHP community. At the very least, you can avoid doing things that may alienate others or cause developers to burn out on the whole idea of developing Open Source software!

Do it yourself

Open Source software may be free to use, but it should not be considered free of all responsibilities. You are technically a "free rider" until you give back — or pay forward — to the community at large. It's your task to figure out where and how your talents can best be deployed, and then to do that thing as you are able. This doesn't mean we all have to become C developers, but there are many other ways to contribute. Answering questions on the PHP mailing lists or Web sites is always a good thing, because it lightens the load on the core developers.

It's probably you

If there's a failure to communicate, you need to ask yourself if the problem could possibly lie with you. If you do find yourself in the middle of a flame war, which happens occasionally on any mailing list, there's nothing people enjoy more than a little public acknowledgment of what a jerk you've (unknowingly) been.

Other PHP Web Sites

Besides the "official" PHP resources mentioned above, there are some well-known community members who have put up some extraordinarily helpful Web sites. Some of these enjoy a special relationship with PHP, and are quasi-"official".

Core scripting engine and tools

Zend.com

```
http://www.zend.com
```

Zend.com is the home of the core PHP 4 scripting engine, as well as a center of PHP commercialization. Although the company sells support and custom development services to larger companies, the vast majority of PHP developers are most interested in add-on products in development at Zend world headquarters in Israel. The first of these value-added tools, the Zend optimizer, is already available and the PHP community eagerly awaits new goodies such as the Zend cache. The site also offers unique content, particularly the biographies of major figures in the PHP world.

PHP knowledgebase/FAQ-o-matic

PHP Faqts (a.k.a. E-gineer)

```
http://www.faqts.com/knowledge-base/index.phtml
```

This is a beautifully articulated archive of frequently asked questions with a nice search function. Highly recommended to new PHP users.

PHP add-ons

PHP Base Library

```
http://phplib.netuse.de/index.php3
```

This is a bunch of files, classes, and functions for better session management and authentication. They also host a major project, phpslash, which is a PHP version of the famous Slashdot Web site.

PHP forums, articles, and tips

Tutorials generally have code in them, but these are not meant to be plug and play — they take a more "teach a man to fish. . ." approach.

PHP Builder

```
http://www.phpbuilder.com/
```

One of the most comprehensive and well-run PHP sites, this one includes great tutorials and an active forum, but their codebase is basically just a link.

Devshed

```
http://www.devshed.com/Server_Side/PHP/
```

A big commercial site with good tutorials and a forum, Devshed covers all the scripting languages (ASP, JavaScript, and so on), making it the best one-stop for those still in the shopping phase.

PHP codebases

Codebases take a "give a man a fish. . ." approach, simply offering their donated wares to all takers. The code quality can vary widely, from first scripts to elegant classes. Also see the Projects page on the PHP site for major applications using PHP.

PHP Wizard

```
http://www.phpwizard.net/
```

Two European indie developers' site, which offers several nice applications, such as phpMyAdmin and phpChat.

PX

```
http://px.sklar.com/
```

An uninformative site design nonetheless leads to a large variety of scripts — mostly smaller ones rather than whole applications.

Weberdev

```
http://www.weberdev.com/
```

Most of the good stuff on this general-scripting site is "members only," but they have one really neat feature: the SmartCode section, a database of good style tricks (mostly written by Rasmus Lerdorf).

Our Web Site

We've set up a Web site for this book at:

```
http://www.troutworks.com/phpbook/
```

There, you'll find most of the larger chunks of code in this book in convenient source format, which will save you from having to retype them out for yourself.

You'll also find corrections for the few paltry errors that slipped through the eagle eyes and sharp electronic red pencils of our editors.

Last but not least, you'll also be able to contact us on the site and flame away! (Or maybe just ask us a few questions.)

✦   ✦   ✦

Glossary

Active Server Pages (ASP) Microsoft proprietary server-side execution environment. The ASP engine is built into Microsoft's proprietary Web server, Internet Information Server (IIS).

Actual parameters The arguments (or inputs) that are given to a function when it is called. (The corresponding arguments that appear in the function definition are called the formal parameters.)

Apache HTTP server The most popular open source Web server. Also called *Apache server*, *Apache httpd*, and simply *Apache*.

Apache Software Foundation Nonprofit foundation which oversees several open source software projects, notably Apache HTTP server.

API See *Application Program Interface*.

Applet A Java program that can be quickly downloaded from a Web page, which executes within the environment of the user's browser.

Application Program Interface (API) A standard specifying how a program should be coded to interact with a particular operating system or service. Usually this is in the form of a small set of specified functions that can be called from the application's code.

Argument An input to a function or operator.

Array In PHP, a basic datatype that holds values in association with indices.

ASP In the context of this book, see *Active Server Pages*, although in other contexts the acronym may also mean Application Service Provider.

Assignment A process or statement that stores a value in a variable.

Back end Loose term for the part of a computer program or service that is far away in the process from what the user actually sees. In Web programming, database servers often occupy the back end, and browsers and HTML-producing programs are the front end.

Binary Several senses are relevant to this book: 1) adjective for base two, as in *binary arithmetic*; 2) description of the on-off encoding used in computer memory; 3) a computer file which uses the full range of possible byte values, not just the values that correspond to human-readable text. For example, files that are directly executable computer programs are often called *binaries*, to distinguish them from human-readable source code. (See also *compilation, interpretation, source*.)

Boolean An adjective referring to true-or-false logic. In PHP, the datatype that has only two possible values: true or false.

Browser See *Web browser*.

C A major popular programming language used for operating system and programming-language code, as well as for general-purpose programming. Closely associated with the UNIX family of operating systems.

C++ A successor to C that includes object-oriented constructs.

Cascading Style Sheets (CSS) A standard for specifying the cosmetic attributes of a Web site in a centralized and general way, which individual browsers can then interpret and render appropriately.

Case sensitive Describes programs, names, or documents where capitalization of letters makes a difference. The opposite is case insensitive.

CGI See *Common Gateway Interface*.

Class Object-oriented programming term for the programmer-defined blueprint for object instances of a certain type.

Client-side General term for computation that happens on the client machine in a client-server relationship. In a Web programming context, it refers to computation that happens on the machine the user is browsing from, rather than on the machine the Web site is being served from. (See *Server-side*.)

ColdFusion Proprietary Allaire Corporation tag-based Web scripting product.

Co-location Special type of Web hosting where the customer provides the machine that the Webserver runs on, and takes care of its administration remotely, while the service provider offers the location, the electric power, the Internet hookup, and possibly other services such as data backups. (See *hosting*.)

Column In a database context, this refers to the fields that are prescribed by the definition of a database table. Each row entry in the table contains values for all the columns.

COM See *Component Object Model.*

Common Gateway Interface (CGI) A particular protocol for the communication between Web servers and programs that produce HTML pages on demand. Now replaced to some extent by more direct integration of Web servers and Web scripting languages.

Common Object Request Broker Architecture (CORBA) A standard for distributed object-oriented programming, sponsored by the Object Management Group, a computer industry consortium. CORBA allows communication between different pieces of software running on different machines.

Cookie A small piece of information stored by a Web server in a user's browser or on the hard disk of the user's machine.

Compilation The automated process of translating a text-file program (as written by a programmer) into an executable program that will run on a computer. Compilation typically happens all at once, so that the translation is finished before any part of the executable program is run. (See *Interpretation.*)

Component Object Model (COM) A Microsoft-sponsored standard for distributed object-oriented programs, which allows communication between different programs running on the same machine. (See *DCOM, CORBA.*)

CORBA See *Common Object Request Broker Architecture.*

Datatype A blueprint for a kind of value in a computer program. A datatype determines both a range of legitimate values and also the way that such values will be represented in computer memory. The basic datatypes in PHP are integer, double, Boolean, string, array, and object.

DCOM See *Distributed Component Object Model.*

Debugger A piece of software that helps programmers find bugs in their code.

Document Type Definition (DTD) A document that specifies the structure of a class of XML documents, in such a way that the documents can be automatically checked (or validated) to see if they conform to it.

Document Object Model (DOM) A standardized interface (or API) for programs that interact with XML parsers. Under the DOM, XML parsers read in an entire XML document and construct a parse tree, and then the application program may query or manipulate the tree. (See *SAX, API.*)

DNS See *Domain Name Service.*

DOM See *Document Object Model.*

Domain name The name of a machine or service on the Internet, such as `www.troutworks.com`. A second-level domain name is a more general grouping such as `ibm.com`, which might include many domain names.

Domain Name Service A type of Internet server program that translates domain names (for example, `www.ibm.com`) into their underlying Internet Protocol (IP) addresses. (See *IP address, Domain name.*)

Double A basic PHP datatype that represents floating-point numbers. (See *Floating-point, Integer.*)

DTD See *Document Type Definition.*

Dynamic Adjective used loosely to describe Web pages using HTML plus more sophisticated technologies. On the server side, denotes pages assembled on the fly.

Dynamic HTML (DHTML) Loose term for a set of HTML extensions and browser-side programming techniques for control of the graphic aspects of Web site presentation.

ECMAScript The new official name for JavaScript, now that the standard is controlled by ECMA.

Editor Software for editing text files, especially the text of program code.

Event General term for a kind of signal from one program to another, or from one program subsystem to another, which the receiving program is expected to notice and respond to.

Expression In PHP, a combination of basic values, language constructs, operators, and function calls that itself has a value. (See *statement.*)

fhttpd A small, fast Open Source Web server written by Alex Belits.

File pointer The value in a computer program which marks the current position of an ongoing read from a disk file.

File Transfer Protocol (FTP) Standard method for transferring files from one machine to another over the Internet.

Filesystem The combination of a computer's files and directories with the low-level operating system programs that manipulate them. Application programs typically interact with filesystem, rather than directly controlling the disk-drive hardware.

Flat-file database A database system that holds a database in a single unified table, rather than splitting it up into a multiple-table relational database. (See *Relational database*.)

Floating point Term for numbers that have a fractional portion represented as numbers to the right of the decimal point. Also refers to arithmetic on such numbers.

Form processing agent A program which handles data passed by an HTML form. PHP can be used as a form processing agent.

Formal parameters The variable names that are associated with incoming arguments in a function definition. (The arguments given to a function when it is actually called are the actual parameters.)

FreeBSD A free, open-source version of the UNIX operating system.

Front end Loose term for the parts of a program or service that are closest to the user. A pull-down menu in the browser display of a Web site is part of the front end, while the database on the server machine that records the corresponding transaction is part of the back end.

FTP See *File Transfer Protocol.*

Function A basic programming language construct that allows you to name a block of code and use it in different situations with different inputs.

General Public License (GPL) A type of software license championed by the Free Software Foundation which encourages free source distribution, and which permits distribution of modifications to GPL'ed software as long as the modified versions are themselves made freely available under the GPL.

GET A basic HTTP method for submitting information in a request for a Web page. GET methods are often what a user invokes when following a link. (See *Post.*)

Global Adjective describing information or values that are available throughout the code of a particular computer program. Opposite of Local.

GPL See *General Public License.*

Hard-code Including a literal value directly in program code, when it might be better as a variable or function argument.

Hosting Providing the parts and labor necessary to serve up a Web site that someone else may have coded and designed. Hosting services usually include the necessary hardware, the Internet connection, and the administration needed to keep the site live.

HTML HyperText Markup Language, a subset of SGML that is the standard method to mark up Web pages.

HTTP HyperText Transfer Protocol. The basic protocol by which Web browsers and Web servers communicate over the Internet.

http daemon Program that runs constantly on Web server machines, looking out for requests for Web pages

IDE See *Integrated Development Environment.*

IE See *Internet Explorer.*

IMAP Internet Message Access Protocol. A mail retrieval protocol, meant to supplement or supplant POP.

Inheritance The relationship between an object-oriented class and a more general class that it is based on.

Instantiation The process of making a particular instance of a general schema or pattern. In an object-oriented context, instantiating a class means creating an object that is an instance of the class.

Integer In mathematics, a "whole" number with no fractional part, which may be positive or negative. In PHP, a basic datatype that represents such whole numbers.

Integrated Development Environment (IDE) An IDE combines several different pieces of software that help software developers write code. At a minimum, an IDE will typically include a source code editor, a debugger, and some kind of system for managing code revisions.

Internet Explorer (IE) The Microsoft Web browser.

Internet Information Server (IIS) Microsoft proprietary Web server.

IP address See *Internet Protocol Address.*

Interpretation In the context of computer languages, the process of running a computer program by successively translating and executing individual statements from a source file. Usually opposed to compilation, which performs all of the translation before any execution.

ISP Internet Service Provider.

Java An object-oriented programming language designed and promoted by Sun Microsystems, with an unusual method of compilation that makes it highly portable. In particular, it is possible to write applets in Java that are executable within several different browser environments.

Java Database Connectivity (JDBC) Database connectivity standard promoted by Sun Microsystems, which allows Java programs to connect to disparate database systems.

Java Server Pages (JSP) Web scripting standard promoted by Sun Microsystems in which fragments of Java code can be embedded in HTML.

Javascript A client-side Web-scripting language which extends the user-interface capabilities of browsers. No real relationship to Java. (See *Client-side.*)

Java Virtual Machine (JVM) Program that executes arbitrary Java code. JVM's embedded in Web browsers allow them to run downloaded applets. (See *Java, Applet, Browser.*)

JDBC See *Java Database Connectivity.*

JScript Microsoft's proprietary implementation of JavaScript.

JSP See *Java Server Pages.*

JVM See *Java Virtual Machine.*

Linux A free, open-source version of the UNIX operating system.

Local Adjective describing variables or values in a computer program that are only accessible from a restricted part of the code, or during a limited portion of the program's execution. Opposite of Global. (See also *Scope.*)

Localhost Networking designation for the very same machine a program is running on.

Mailing list Named set of email addresses of people with a special interest. Mail sent to the list's address will be remailed to everyone on the list.

Metadata Data about data. In a Web context, this usually means tags in a document that describe that document.

MySQL A free open-source relational database system, often teamed up with Linux, PHP, and Apache for a complete Web server package.

Navbar Shorthand for *navigation bar*, meaning a visually prominent collection of links that is largely consistent across the different pages of a Web site.

Netscape Navigator Web browser produced by Netscape (now part of AOL). (See *Web browser.*)

Open Database Connectivity (ODBC) Standard promoted by Microsoft that facilitates communication between applications and disparate databases.

Object Program construct that encapsulates both data and procedural information.

ODBC See *Open Database Connectivity.*

Open source software (OSS) Software that is distributed as (or including) source code, with permission to modify that code. The term is used by contrast to closed-source software, where the distribution is of the executable or binary, which cannot in practice be modified or customized.

Operating system The main program that runs a computer, and in turn allows application programs to run and communicate with the hardware. Examples of operating systems include various flavors of UNIX (Linux, FreeBSD, Solaris), Windows (Windows NT, Windows 2000, Windows 98), and the Macintosh OS.

Operator A programming language construct with up to two inputs, found to the immediate left and/or immediate right of the operator in an expression.

Operator precedence The set of priority rules that determines which operator has first claim when there are operators on both left and right sides of an argument or input.

OS See *Operating system.*

Pathname A string of characters denoting the location of a file in a filesystem, including any necessary directory or folder names.

Perl An open-source scripting language, especially loved by UNIX sysadmins and other UNIX programmers.

PHP PHP: Hypertext Proprocessor, an open source HTML-embedded server-side scripting language and engine.

Personal Web Server (PWS) Microsoft proprietary intranet server.

Personalization In a Web programming context, the process of producing dynamic Web pages with content that varies depending on who is browsing.

Polymorphism For functions and methods, the property of having different behavior depending on the number and types of arguments.

POST A basic HTTP method for submitting information in a request for a Web page. POST methods are often what a user invokes when submitting a form. (See *GET.*)

POP In the context of this book, usually the *Post Office Protocol* for retrieving e-mail from a mail server. In other contexts, can also mean a *Point-Of-Presence* on the Internet, such as an IP address.

Precedence See *Operator precedence.*

Procedural abstraction The process of wrapping lines of code up into named procedures or functions.

Programming language A standard that defines a particular set of constructs in which computer code can be written. When there is a difference between a language's specification and an implementation of a compiler or interpreter for the specification, "programming language" refers to the specification. Examples of programming languages include C, C++, Common Lisp, Scheme, Basic, Pascal, Fortran, Perl, PHP. (Scripting languages are also programming languages.) (See *Scripting language*, *Compilation*, *Interpretation*.)

Relational database A database system with the capability of splitting data into multiple tables, which are in turn associated by relationships between the column data of the different tables.

Row In a relational database context, an entry into a database table, which includes values for the columns that are implied by the table definition.

RPM Red Hat Package Manager, a system of precompiled binaries for the Red Hat distribution of Linux and its derivatives.

Run time The time of program execution. Usually opposed to the time of program compilation. (See *Compilation*.)

SAX See *Simple API for XML*.

Scope The set of rules in a programming language that determines whether multiple occurrences of the same name refer to the same thing.

Scripting language A programming language that does not require an explicit compilation step by the programmer. Early versions of scripting languages are usually interpreted rather than compiled, and are less powerful than corresponding general-purpose languages. Usually this changes as they evolve, however, and many scripting languages (Perl, PHP 4) are both compiled (although without a separate step for the programmer) and quite powerful. (See *Interpretation*, *Compilation*.)

Server-side General term for computation that happens on the server machine in a client-server relationship. In a Web programming context, it refers to computation that happens on the Web-server machine, rather than the machine the user is browsing from. (See *Client-side*.)

SGML See *Standard Generalized Markup Language*.

Side effect Any effect of an expression in a programming language other than the main value returned by the expression.

Simple API for XML (SAX) A standardized interface (or API) for programs that interact with XML parsers. Under SAX, the parser reads in an XML document, and notifies the application program of events corresponding to tags or contents as the parse progresses. (See *DOM*, *API*.)

Solaris A proprietary version of the UNIX operating system sold by Sun Microsystems.

Source See *Source code.*

Source code The actual text of code written by the programmer, as opposed to the executable program that is produced from it. (See *Compilation* and *Binary.*)

Standard Generalized Markup Language A standard for defining markup languages, which in turn are languages that structure documents so that they can be both displayed to people and manipulated by programs. HTML is a kind of markup language, although not an SGML language because it breaks many of SGML's rules.

Statement In PHP, an expression terminated by a semicolon.

Static Adjective used to describe HTML pages that do not change rapidly or feature any visible client-side functionality.

Typecast Programming language expression that explicitly requests the conversion of a value from one datatype to another.

Type conversion Translation of a value from one datatype to another. May or may not be the result of an explicit typecast.

Universal Resource Indicator (URI) An Internet address. This term is an extension of Universal Resource Locator (URL).

UNIX A family of related operating systems that run most of the Internet, except for the bit on the desks of users. UNIX implementations include Linux, FreeBSD, and Solaris.

Valid In an XML context, a valid document is one that not only is well formed, but also follows the prescriptions of its Document Type Definition. (See *Valid, Document Type Definition.*)

Validating parser In an XML context, a validating parser is an XML parser that checks parsed documents to make sure they conform to their Document Type Definitions. Not all XML parsers validate, although they all check if a document is well formed.

VBScript Proprietary Microsoft scripting language based on Visual Basic.

Web browser The application program that a user is running on their computer when they are browsing the Web. Examples include Netscape Navigator, Microsoft Internet Explorer, and Opera.

Web Server Program responsible for replying to requests for Web pages. Examples include Apache, Microsoft IIS, and iPlanet.

Weblog A personal diary or journal published on the Web

Webmail Web-based program for reading and sending electronic mail

Well-formed In an XML context, a well-formed document is one that conforms to the minimal syntactical requirements of XML, with tags properly closed off and so on. (See *Valid.*)

Whitespace Characters in a text file or computer program which display as blanks. Whitespace includes spaces, tabs, linefeeds, and end-of-line characters.

World Wide Web Consortium (W3) International consortium that promulgates major Web protocols, such as HTTP, HTML, CSS, and XML.

WYSIWYG Shorthand for "What you see is what you get," which describes programming, word processing, and design tools with visual interfaces that closely approximate the look of the thing you are designing.

XML Short for EXtensible Markup Language. A descendant of SGML, and a more structured proposed successor to HTML, designed both for display in browsers and as a data-interchange format.

XSL Extensible Style-sheet Language. A companion standard to XML, which specifies the transformation and display of XML documents.

Zend Name for the parsing and execution engine at the core of PHP 4. Also the name of a company started by the designers of that engine (**Zeev** Suraski and **Andi** Gutmans) which markets commercial consulting services, add-ons, and tools for PHP.

✦   ✦   ✦

Index

Continued

Continued

queries
  complex printing example, 368–370
  database, 278–279, 354
  described, 357–358
  displaying in tables, 357–373
  DNS, 254–255
  example, 358–360
  forms, 386–388
  forms, building from, 375–388
  multiple queries versus complex
      printing, 365–366
  multiple query example, 366–368
  MySQL, 344–345
  one-to-one mapping, 358
  parsing, 4
  precompiled, 324
  sample, 361–365
  sample, creating, 371–373
  separate databases, 349–350
  single per statement, 422–423
  strings, generating, 234
  too much, too little, 441
queues, 220–222
quotemeta() function, 168
quotes
  commas, 440
  database, unescaped, 435–437
  escaping, 167, 288, 482, 602
  magic, 595, 598
  single versus double, 70–71, 149
  unescaped, 303

R

radians, 186
RADIO data elements, 384
rand() function, 190, 192
random-number generators, 225
randomness
  arrays, 226
  math, 190–194
range, 76
rating system
  abusability, 419–420
  described, 407–409
  results, displaying, 414–419
  scale, 419–420
  votes, collecting, 409–414
read formats
  doubles, 77–78
  integers, 75–76
readability
  comments, 268–269
  conciseness versus, 280
  style, 261, 262–271
reading
  cookies, 464, 467–468
  files, 246, 248–249
  files, arbitrary, 571–573
  filesystem functions, 243–250
  numbers, 183, 185
readlink() function, 253
receiving e-mail, 501–502
recursion, 134–136
recycling database connections,
    421–424
Red Hat Linux, 41
redirection, HTTP headers, 475
reducing database connections, 421–424
redundancy
  avoiding with databases, 318
  dynamic Web page generation, 272
reference
  counting, 550
  external, 530
  functions, calling by, 141–142
  object-oriented programming,
    549–552
refusal, cookies, 474
register_globals = On, 602
registering variables, 452–453, 455, 458
regular expressions, 170–173
regulations, 579
relational databases, 320–321, 331–332
remote files, opening, 594
removing, 227
rename() function, 254
rendering, 295–299
replacement string, 158–161
replication, database, 325
repositories, 294

Continued

Continued

my2cents.idgbooks.com

Register This Book — And Win!

Visit **http://my2cents.idgbooks.com** to register this book and we'll automatically enter you in our fantastic monthly prize giveaway. It's also your opportunity to give us feedback: let us know what you thought of this book and how you would like to see other topics covered.

Discover IDG Books Online!

The IDG Books Online Web site is your online resource for tackling technology — at home and at the office. Frequently updated, the IDG Books Online Web site features exclusive software, insider information, online books, and live events!

10 Productive & Career-Enhancing Things You Can Do at www.idgbooks.com

- Nab source code for your own programming projects.
- Download software.
- Read Web exclusives: special articles and book excerpts by IDG Books Worldwide authors.
- Take advantage of resources to help you advance your career as a Novell or Microsoft professional.
- Buy IDG Books Worldwide titles or find a convenient bookstore that carries them.
- Register your book and win a prize.
- Chat live online with authors.
- Sign up for regular e-mail updates about our latest books.
- Suggest a book you'd like to read or write.
- Give us your 2¢ about our books and about our Web site.

You say you're not on the Web yet? It's easy to get started with IDG Books' *Discover the Internet*, available at local retailers everywhere.